OXFORD READINGS IN CL

The series provides students and sch
selection of the best and most influen
author, work, or subject. No single school or style of approach is
privileged: the aim is to offer a broad overview of scholarship, to
cover a wide variety of topics, and to illustrate a diversity of critical
methods. The collections are particularly valuable for their inclusion
of many important essays which are normally difficult to obtain and
for the first-ever translations of some of the pieces. Many articles
are thoroughly revised and updated by their authors or are provided
with addenda taking account of recent work. Each volume includes
an authoritative and wide-ranging introduction by the editor survey-
ing the scholarly tradition and considering alternative approaches.
This pulls the individual articles together, setting all the pieces
included in their historical and cultural contexts and exploring significant connections between them from the perspective of contemporary scholarship. All foreign languages (including Greek and
Latin) are translated to make the texts easily accessible to those
without detailed linguistic knowledge.

OXFORD READINGS IN CLASSICAL STUDIES

Aeschylus
Edited by Michael Lloyd

Ovid
Edited by Peter E. Knox

The Attic Orators
Edited by Edwin Carawan

Lucretius
Edited by Monica R. Gale

Catullus
Edited by Julia Haig Gaisser

Seneca
Edited by John G. Fitch

Vergil's *Eclogues*
Edited by Katharina Volk

Vergil's *Georgics*
Edited by Katharina Volk

Homer's *Odyssey*
Edited by Lilliam E. Doherty

Persius and Juvenal
Edited by Maria Plaza

Livy
Edited by Jane D. Chaplin and Christina S. Kraus

Horace: *Satires* **and** *Epistles*
Edited by Kirk Freudenburg

Thucydides
Edited by Jeffrey S. Rusten

All available in paperback

Oxford Readings in Classical Studies

Horace: *Odes* and *Epodes*

Edited by
MICHÈLE LOWRIE

OXFORD
UNIVERSITY PRESS

OXFORD
UNIVERSITY PRESS

Great Clarendon Street, Oxford OX2 6DP

Oxford University Press is a department of the University of Oxford.
It furthers the University's objective of excellence in research, scholarship,
and education by publishing worldwide in

Oxford New York

Auckland Cape Town Dar es Salaam Hong Kong Karachi
Kuala Lumpur Madrid Melbourne Mexico City Nairobi
New Delhi Shanghai Taipei Toronto

With offices in

Argentina Austria Brazil Chile Czech Republic France Greece
Guatemala Hungary Italy Japan Poland Portugal Singapore
South Korea Switzerland Thailand Turkey Ukraine Vietnam

Oxford is a registered trade mark of Oxford University Press
in the UK and in certain other countries

Published in the United States
by Oxford University Press Inc., New York

British Library Cataloguing in Publication Data
Data available

Library of Congress Cataloging in Publication Data
Data available

Typeset by SPI Publisher Services, Pondicherry, India
Printed in Great Britain
on acid-free paper by
CPI Antony Rowe, Chippenham, Wiltshire

ISBN 978–0–19–920769–5 (Hbk.)
978–0–19–920770–1 (Pbk.)

1 3 5 7 9 10 8 6 4 2

Acknowledgements

All the essays in this collection (apart from the Introduction) have been previously published elsewhere, as listed at the end of the volume. The editor and Oxford University Press are grateful to the publishers of the relevant journals and books for their permission to reprint. The translations from French, German, and Italian are collaborative efforts by Maya Jessica Alapin, Ada Bronowski, Leofranc Holford-Strevens, Michèle Lowrie, Alexandre G. Mitchell, Barbara Natalie Nagel, and the original authors. I am particularly grateful to Leofranc Holford-Strevens, who supplied references to much ancient and modern literature in the Heinze. These are indicated in brackets. Translations of Latin and Greek have been added by the authors, except for the deceased or non-native speakers of English, where they are by M. Lowrie. Special thanks go to Danielle La Londe, who scanned and reformatted the articles, produced the consolidated bibliography, and has been a model assistant. The articles are listed in chronological order.

Permission to reprint the following articles is gratefully acknowledged.

Richard Heinze, 'The Horatian Ode', translated from 'Die Horazische Ode', *Neue Jahrbücher* 51 (1923), 153–68.

Steele Commager, 'The Function of Wine in Horace's Odes', *Transactions and Proceedings of the American Philological Association*, 88 (1957), 68–80.

H. J. Mette, ' "Slender Genre" and "Slender Table" in Horace', translated from ' "genus tenue" und "mensa tenuis" bei Horaz', *Museum Helveticum*, 18 (1961), 136–9.

P. H. Schrijvers, 'How to End an Ode?', translated from 'Comment terminer une ode?', *Mnemosyne*, 26 (1973), 140–59.

Mario Citroni, 'Occasion and Levels of Address in Horatian Lyric', translated from 'Occasione e piani di destinazione nella lirica di Orazio', *Materiali e discussioni della cultura classica*, 10–11 (1983), 133–214.

Matthew Santirocco, 'The Maecenas Odes', *Transactions and Proceedings of the American Philological Association*, 114 (1984), 241–53.

Peter L. Schmidt, 'Horace's Century Poem—A Processional Song?', translated from 'Horaz' Säkulargedicht—ein Prozessionslied?', *Der Altsprachliche Unterricht*, 28.4 (1985), 42–53.

William Fitzgerald, 'Power and Impotence in Horace's Epodes', *Ramus* 17 (1988), 176–91.

Ellen Oliensis, 'Canidia, Canicula, and the Decorum of Horace's Epodes', *Arethusa*, 24 (1991), 107–38.

Michael C. J. Putnam, 'The Languages of Horace *Odes* 1.24', *CJ* 88 (1992), 123–35.

Denis Feeney, 'Horace and the Greek Lyric Poets', in N. Rudd (ed.), *Horace 2000: A Celebration, Essays for the Bimillennium* (London, 1993), 41–63.

Alessandro Barchiesi, 'Final Difficulties in the Career of an Iambic Poet: Epode 17', translated from 'Ultime difficoltà nella carriera di un poeta giambico: L'epodo XVII', in *Atti dei convegni di Venosa, Napoli, Roma, novembre 1993* (Venosa, 1994), 205–220.

Don Fowler, 'Horace and the Aesthetics of Politics', in S. J. Harrison (ed.), *Homage to Horace: A Bimillenary Celebration* (Oxford, 1995), 248–66.

I. M. Le M. Du Quesnay, 'Horace, Odes 4.5: *Pro Reditu Imperatoris Caesari Divi Filii Augusti*', in S. J. Harrison (ed.), *Homage to Horace: A Bimillenary Celebration* (Oxford, 1995), 128–87.

Michèle Lowrie, 'A Parade of Lyric Predecessors: Horace C. 1.12–18', *Phoenix*, 49 (1995), 33–49.

Luigi Rossi, 'Horace, a Greek Lyrist without Music', translated from 'Orazio, un lirico greco senza musica', *Seminari Romani di cultura greca*, 1 (Università di Roma, 1998), 163–81.

R. G. M. Nisbet, 'The Word Order of the *Odes*', in J. N. Adams and R. G. Mayer (eds.), *Aspects of the Language of Latin Poetry* (Oxford 1999), 135–54.

John Henderson, 'Horace Talks Rough and Dirty: No Comment (*Epodes* 8 & 12)', *Scholia* 8 (1999), 3–16.

Alessandro Barchiesi, 'Rituals in Ink: Horace on the Greek Lyric Tradition', in M. Depew and D. Obbink (eds.) *Matrices of Genre: Authors, Canons, and Society* (Cambridge, Mass., 2000), 167–82.

Contents

relevant essays ○

viii   *Contents*

Introduction

Michèle Lowrie

The secondary literature on Horatian lyric is vast, and the last twenty
to thirty years have been particularly rich for the study of this author.
A significant number of monographs and volumes of essays on
Horace has been published, particularly around the time of the
bimillennium of his death in 1992, as well as many free-standing
articles and articles in volumes on the Augustan age. Notable collections of essays on Horace are Opperman (1972), Ludwig (1993),
Rudd (1993), Santirocco (1994), Harrison (1995), Konstan (1995),
Woodman and Feeney (2002), and Harrison (2007). Just recently the
major commentaries of Watson on the *Epodes* (2003) and Nisbet and
Rudd on *Odes* 3 (2004) have come out. My selection here means to
point students toward beginning research on Horace, and to that
end, several principles of selection (not all consistent with each
other) are operative. I include classic articles, some going back to
the early twentieth century, often in French, German, or Italian, that
have never been translated, as well as pieces that represent, in my
view, the best recent thought on Horace, even when I disagree with
the method or conclusions. I try to represent a range of approaches,
and since there are many more worthy articles than could be
included, I give preference to those not already easily accessible.
Still, the influence of several articles has overridden this principle.
Although much excellent work has consisted of the close reading of
individual poems and several such are included here—by Michael
C. J. Putnam, Alessandro Barchiesi (*Epodes*), I. M. Le M. Du Quesnay,
and John Henderson—I have inclined toward research with a more

synoptic view. Given the sheer volume of work on Horace, this collection focuses on three areas: (1) intertextuality, occasion, and genre, (2) form, (3) social concerns and politics. This introduction outlines the interrelationship of these issues and provides recommendations for further readings. Pieces included in the volume are referred to by the author's full name while other bibliography goes by author and date. Although the article by Peter L. Schmidt is the only one to address the *Carmen saeculare* (Century poem), I go over some trends in recent scholarship on it below.

Much scholarship on Horace since Richard Heinze's seminal article in 1923 has revolved around the relation of lyric form to its social context. If the Greeks handed down lyric as a poetic form with a close association to a performance occasion, does that mean that Horace's adoption of these forms necessarily entails a similar occasional basis? After detailing the rich variety of speech occasions in Horatian lyric, Richard Heinze states categorically that they are all fiction and consequently that his lyric was not performed. Debate has raged since then both about the historical performance of Horace's *Odes* and whether these poems perform the same kind of communication the equivalent utterances would entail in ordinary language. Mario Citroni emphasizes the real communication that must have occurred between Horace and his historical addressees, although he acknowledges that poetic form changes the nature of that communication. This question is bound up in the scholarship, to my mind erroneously, with historical performance. We have no external evidence for the performance of the *Epodes* or *Odes* such as we have for the *Carmen saeculare*. Still, some have used this last as a model for the performance of other Horatian odes—I. M. Le M. Du Quesnay keeps company with Bonavia-Hunt (1969) and Lefèvre (1990 and 1993) in arguing for actual performance. Others, like Luigi Rossi, take the musical references in the *Odes* as metaphorical. Denis Feeney, who offers an overview of Greek lyric from Horace's perspective, begins with an emphasis on the differences between Greek society, with its wealth of performance venues, and Horace's isolation in reinventing lyric in a society that did not already have available opportunities for the performance of this sort of poetry. These differences, however, should not be overstressed and Feeney warns against romanticizing oral culture. The Greeks also composed poetry outside occasional settings and immortality comes at the price of decontextualization.

The stakes of the two debates are similar: if the poetry was performed in actual occasions, would that not imply that the poems do offer effective utterances that convey some socially grounded message? There is an assumption that a present audience implies successful communication. My own answer (Lowrie 2009) is that writing and reading are also socially grounded occasions, and that the message poetry conveys even when performed does not necessarily correspond to the one ostensibly offered. M. C. J. Putnam's close reading of *Odes* 1.24 shows how communication can take place among contemporaries, here Virgil, within the literary sphere. Alessandro Barchiesi ('Rituals') looks at the dialectic between literature conceived as ritual performance and as writing, between engagement and distanced comment in light of the relationship Horace sets up with his inherited models. If we assume, with many, that Horace's women are fictitious as opposed to his male addressees, then we have to wonder about communication strategies for a great number of his poems. The targeted recipient would structurally have to be the broader reading public rather than any particular named person and this presupposes a more literary version of communication dependent on textual circulation rather than receipt by a present addressee.

Although formalism became a dirty word by the end of the 1990s, I have chosen several articles because they vindicate formal analysis by showing how form conveys meaning. The pieces range from the way Horace puts words together on micro- and macroscopic levels to the interrelation between meaning and structure. R. G. M. Nisbet's analysis of word order elucidates one of the major obstacles to students who first encounter Horace—he jumbles up the words not simply to make things difficult; rather careful placement creates particular poetic effects, both sonic and semantic. Some of the most important work in the 1980s and early 1990s examined how the sequential order of poems within books arranged by their authors allows meaning to accrue cumulatively over the course of a collection. This interest has had to fight against Fraenkel's (1957: 208) dictum that 'every ode is self-contained'. Porter (1987), Santirocco (1986), and Putnam (1986) set the standard for the analysis of arrangement in the *Odes* and Carruba (1969) in the *Epodes*. Arrangement is also a guiding principle for many other scholars, who have looked at individual sequences within collections, such as the opening sequence or 'parade' in *Odes* 1, or use it by the way while examining other issues, for example Denis Feeney and Lowrie (1997). My article on a second 'parade' in *Odes* 1 is selected as representative of this work. The accumulation of allusions to lyric predecessors conveys a story about literary filiation that is larger than any of the allusions taken in isolation. P. H. Schrijvers' article on poetic closure also puts formal concerns within the dynamic production of meaning. Horace imparts a sense of an aesthetic whole to the reader by a variety of techniques for closing individual odes and Esser (1976) follows up on these concerns at monograph length. Closure, however, exceeds the purview of the single poem and Alessandro Barchiesi (*Epodes* 17) addresses the ending of a collection in relation to its final poem.

But form is not just an aspect of poetry that Horace uses to good effect. It is also one of his central topics. Alessandro Barchiesi ('Rituals') comments on how poetics, often questions of form, are folded into the poetry as subject matter and several articles pursue this line of thought. H. J. Mette's short but trenchant piece shows that Horace's vocabulary about genre and morals are congruent, which suggests there is an ethical component to the choice of poetic form. Similar concerns pervade Steele Commager's discussion of wine as a locus for talking about both ethics and poetics.

One of Horace's central concerns is his own poetic self-definition, whether intertextual, generic, moral, sexual, or some combination thereof. Davis (1991) is a turning point in Horatian scholarship, since he shows that Horace uses consistent rhetorical techniques that must be taken as a systematic attempt to establish his new version of the lyric genre rather than a series of *ad hoc* reactions to contemporary situations. Self-definition in Horace is strategic rather than narcissistic: he explores the role of the poet in a changing society and makes his own place in the world exemplary for larger questions of social power—or the lack thereof. Denis Feeney points out that Horace had to be selective about how to reinvent the genre. His Greek predecessors left a vast and variegated corpus from which he could pick and choose according to his own needs. Lesbian poetry with its double models of Sappho and Alcaeus allowed for the integration of personal and political poetry—or the pull between these spheres. Pindar allowed for sublimity, Callimachus for the adoption of a poetics of the small. In Lowrie (1997), I pick up from Davis and look at how Horace's decisions about his genre and self-imposed formal constraints give him an excuse for not delving too deeply into the central narrative of the age: civil war and Augustus' accession to power. He rather prefers, or says he prefers to tell stories about typically lyric occasions, i.e., wine, women, and song. But Horace is a master of indirection: by pulling back from certain topics—civil war in *Odes* 2.1 and praise of Augustus *passim*—he not only defines lyric according to his own comfort level, but indicates why a poet might choose a smaller genre during times when it is hard to praise.

One of the perennial questions asked of Horace is his stance on Augustus or rather what stance his poetry projects. This, as one could imagine, is not easy to ascertain to begin with—he approaches the subject indirectly—and his attitude furthermore changes over time. The question of whether Horace was 'pro' or 'anti' Augustus has shifted in recent years to one of how he contributes, willy nilly, to Augustan ideology. This point is made by Kennedy (1992) and parallels a shift in scholarship generally from questions about poets as historical persons to ones about the function of literature. Santirocco (1995) exemplifies this turn for Horace. He starts from the premiss that ideology is the conjunction of discourse and power and emphasizes literature's active participation in shaping public opinion. Furthermore, Augustus as a figure serves whatever poetic purpose Horace may have each time he is mentioned. Don Fowler points out that all attempts to address the question are highly contingent and reflect nationality and historical circumstance. A notorious instance is Fraenkel's (1957) appreciation of Augustus as a great leader and of state pageantry. Don Fowler aims to show that panegyric is impossible because of the contradictions inherent in ideology to begin with and more specifically in Horace's particular discursive formulation. Where Doblhofer (1966) sees sincerity in the places where Horace's praise departs most from convention, Don Fowler emphasizes the tensions between Horace's own espousal of the simple life as a moral and poetic choice over against his ostensible praise of greatness in Augustus. Johnson (2004) attempts to cut this knot in his book on *Odes* 4 by integrating the symposium, a symbol of small-scale lyric, and praise by shifting the focus away from authorial intention to the community of engaged interpreters that were the book's original audience. The strong position of this move leaves it up to the reader: some see Horace's praise as operative, while others either see contradiction as inhibiting panegyric success or question whether poetry is capable of such overt speech acts. Edmunds (2001: 19–38) argues that poetry is not pragmatic in this sense and offers a commentary on this question for Horace in the form of a dialogue between himself, Richard Heinze, and Mario Citroni (83–94), whose works are reprinted here.

Patronage, whether by Maecenas or Augustus, is the area where readers most desire some sort of extratextual historical perspective. Suetonius' life of Horace documents several requests of Augustus for poetry, all of which were met (the *Carmen saeculare*, poems in celebration of Tiberius' and Drusus' victory of the Vindelici in *Odes* 4, the Epistle to Augustus), but interpreting this material has been as controversial as that of the poetry itself. White (1993) paints a more benign picture of patronage than, for example, Syme (1939), who basically thinks the Augustan poets served the state. Although Lyne (1995) is conscious that he is reading the author figure projected by the works, his attempted reconstruction of what Horace was thinking about the important men in his society is symptomatic of the desire to recuperate history beyond the texts. Horace's complex strategies of self-positioning are read as signals of personal feeling, such as irritation or resentment, or as subtle resistance or eventual yielding to external pressure, rather than as statements about the intersection of literary and social history. In his reading of *Odes* 4.5, I. M. Le M. Du Quesnay emphasizes the sense of mutual obligation in the Roman understanding of *amicitia*. Our 'patron' is too official and 'friend' too personal to cover the range of the Roman *amicus*. As Augustus' *amicus*, Horace was expected to show appreciation for the support proffered by his social and political superior and I. M. Le M. Du Quesnay, from his rigorously historicizing perspective, finds attempts to argue for poetic independence irrelevant. By bringing Marxist criticism to patronage, Bowditch (2001) reveals the economic realities underlying the poetic representations and warns us against taking Horace's expressions of tender feelings at face value. It is less that he is deceptive than that interests generate emotions of both gratitude and resentment.

There is an equally strong movement in scholarship to fold references to historical persons into the poetry's aesthetic or discursive aims. Matthew Santirocco shows that Horace's odes to Maecenas tell a sequential and dynamic story about their relationship, progressing from analogies between patron and artist, to advice, critique, and finally the liberation of the poet from dependence and a celebration of his achievement of immortality on the basis of his own artistic merit. Since the arrangement of the poems does not correspond to the chronology of their composition, the story is crafted rather than merely reflective. Oliensis (1998) is devoted to how Horace figures his social position throughout his career and, like Davis (1991), shows the consistency of Horatian technique. By insisting that poetry intervenes in the world, rather than merely reflecting it, Oliensis explores not just how Horace represents his already existing place in society, but both fashions it and offers a satiric critique of himself as a social-climber. By the end of his career, he is willing to stake a claim to a more central role than at the beginning.

Horace is often criticized as a lukewarm or intellectual lover, particularly by way of contrast to the vaunted spontaneity of Catullus and Propertius. What is different is less spontaneity—the latter are as artfully constructed as any poetry in the Western canon. Rather, Horace takes a position of self-commentary. He is more often the observer or adviser to another or the ironic commentator on his own passion and to that extent his strategies for representing love are consistent with his other topics. Furthermore, a subliminal violence inhabits his attempted seductions. Ancona (1994) shows how Horace intertwines his more poetic concerns about time and morality in the *Odes* with a power play over the objects of his desire. The love poetry should not be isolated therefore from the poems about his social position. He is consistent in setting his own weakness on display with a frankness that masks his underlying control.

Horace's discomfort with his and others' power or weakness goes back to his earliest output and the *Epodes* have a remarkable unity that offers a complex mix of the mock vatic with deep sexual and political distress. While the *Sermones* position themselves before the outcome of the civil wars, the *Epodes* fall at or around what John Henderson calls 'the watershed moment of paradigm-shift' at Actium. William Fitzgerald traces the unity of the thematics of impotence across the collection in sex, patronage, and politics alike and Ellen Oliensis focuses similar concerns on the threat posed by the witch Canidia, a rival poetic figure emblematic of female power. In his commentary on *Epodes* 6, Watson (2003) demonstrates how Horace uses the contemporary concern with magic to explore questions of discursive and sexual potency. Sexual violence is more overt than in the *Odes*. John Henderson takes further his earlier and famous riff (1987) on some of Horace's most virulent poetry (*Epodes* 8 and 12) and directly confronts the theoretical challenge of insult poetry. Horace's aggression against women is a performative putdown at the same time as a celebration of invective. He deftly exploits the rhetoric of inability to let us know with the most calculated obscenity that he has no self-control and implicates his reader in the process. Alessandro Barchiesi (*Epodes*) examines how at the end of the collection, Horace ties it all together by reversing the iambic and magical discourses that have so far prevailed. Dissolution, palinode, writing allusion backwards, insult through adulation, the recreation of the genre's founding myth—these are Horace's anticlosural strategies for sending the reader always back to the collection and refusing to let us go.

If the *Epodes* create one kind of readerly discomfort, the *Carmen saeculare* produces another. For a poet so closely associated with decorum, it is remarkable how much of it grates and for so many different reasons. The *CS* was performed to a chorus of 27 maidens and boys each on the third day of the *ludi saeculares* ('century games') in 17 BCE on both the Palatine and Capitoline hills. If Horace seems too marginal in his iambic, he is too much part of the system by the time he composed the *CS*. The way the poem responds to and fits into the ceremonies is made clear by the *acta* of the games, which were discovered in 1890 and first published by Mommsen (1913). All these materials with extensive analysis are now to be found in Schnegg-Köhler's (2002) comprehensive and updated edition.

In the early part of twentieth-century much criticism of Horace's choral ode was devoted either to condemning the *CS* or to making it tolerable to modern readers with an aversion to state poetry. Fraenkel

(1957: 364–82) in particular makes a case for Horace's artistic independence by arguing that the poem was not intrinsically part of the ceremonies in an attempt to combat Mommsen's (1905) condemnation of it on the basis of not conforming enough. As Farrell (2005) shows, Fraenkel is schizophrenic in his approach and this is manifest to the greatest extent in his analysis of the *CS*. On the one hand, he resists both formal and historical contextualization and thinks every poem is a free-standing aesthetic object. On the other, he is a master of thick description. More recently, scholars have confronted our discomfort with this poem straight on and largely tried to remedy it by greater literary and cultural contextualization. Peter L. Schmidt sets the poem within the Roman tradition of choral hymns, reviews the debate, and rightly points out that Fraenkel overstated the poem's independence from the ceremonies themselves. He furthermore makes a plausible reconstruction of the conditions of the poem's highly contested performance and calls for an awareness of the power of the poem's medium. Cancik (1996) also insists on the poem's embeddedness in the festival. These observations make it essential we treat the poem as art within the state, whether or not in its service. The scholarship still pulls in two directions, toward self-consciousness and toward integration. Feeney's (1998: 32–8) solution is part of his understanding of Augustan culture. Both the poem and the rites are significantly innovative and part of a creative process that is more about commentary and analysis than about belief. Habinek (2005: 150–7) understands the poem within the framework of foundational song and emphasizes the social cohesion that arises in public festivals.

Only relatively recently has serious attention been paid to the *CS* as a work of literature. Putnam (2000) provides extensive close reading and focuses on how Horace represents his poetry as having a near magical power to bring his prayers about. At the end of his piece ('Rituals'), Alessandro Barchiesi considers the strangeness of a genre given at least experientially 'just once', since the games were meant to be witnessed only once in any person's lifetime. He follows up on this observation and Barchiesi (2002) considers a paradox: the poem is both unique and traditional at the same time. It is the only poem we know that Horace composed for oral performance and previous choral songs at Rome belonged to other occasions. I (Lowrie 2009, ch. 5) attempt to answer Schmidt's call for a media-based analysis and show how the games, the inscriptions recording them, and the poem all depend on both performance and textuality for transmission and are intensely interested in their own media of representation. All are integrated into their social matrix and comment on it at the same time.

Horace is often called a 'poet laureate' and the phrase comes from his self-crowning with the triumphator's laurel at the end of *Odes* 3.30, his famous boast of poetic immortality at the end of the first collection of *Odes*. Denis Feeney picks up on Horace's own metaphorics and comments on how he asserts his way into the lyric canon and turns himself into a public monument. I hope that the articles assembled here show that Horace has won his position not by self-aggrandizement, but rather by subjecting himself, his literary tradition, and the society in which he lived to rigorous examination. His bravura for reinventing obsolete poetic forms was hard-won, all the more so for a man who presented himself as so charmingly flawed.

The bibliography in this volume is consolidated from the articles and additionally contains the references made here. I have tried to cover the most recent books on Horace that have had influence on Anglo-American scholarship, but many other worthy contributions exist in English and other languages. Since I have written reviews of some of the books mentioned here, these are also listed in the bibliography for convenience.

1

The Horatian Ode

Richard Heinze

What is a Horatian ode? 'An *Aeolium carmen*' ('Aeolian song') would
have satisfied an ancient who asked. 'A lyric poem, intended for
individual, not choral performance, in aeolic metre' would mislead
a modern, for a random modern lyrical poem in aeolic metre translated into Latin would still be far from a *carmen* of the Horatian type.
To make the nature of the Horatian ode clear to modern inquiry, let
us lay particular emphasis on the differences between it and modern
lyric. These differences reside not in the subject matter—all joy and
suffering, all stupidity and wisdom in life are as good subjects for
Horace as for modern lyric—but first and foremost in the form; here
I naturally leave aside language and metre.

I

The Horatian ode consists of speech addressed by the poet himself in
his own person to some second person. There are few exceptions: two
'role poems', Neobule's song, where the girl speaks to herself (3. 12),
and the Archytas ode, where the soul of the shipwrecked sailor
addresses first Archytas and then the skipper (1. 28); a narrative,
namely Nereus' address to Paris with a brief introduction (1. 15); a
dialogue, where the addressee answers the poet (*Donec gratus eram
tibi*, 3. 9); finally, two poems where the poet himself speaks alone, but
addresses no one: in *Iam pauca aratro* (2. 15) the wealthy, construc-

tion-crazed aristocracy and in *Parcus deorum cultor* (1. 34) the deity (Jupiter or Fortuna) are conceived as addressees, but not designated by name. That makes six exceptions out of 103 poems, oddities that do not constitute their own type. The addressees of most poems by far are definite individuals, a human being or a deity, but a plurality of persons may also be addressed: a chorus of singers (1. 21), the poet's *sodales* ('companions', 1. 37), his servants (1. 19), even the whole people ('o Roma' 4. 4, 'o plebs' 3. 14); the cycle 3. 1–6 is directed, as the proem states, to *virgines puerique* ('maidens and boys', 3. 1. 4). An indeterminate 'you' representing the general public, as in popular philosophical discourse with its lively stylization, occurs twice (*Intactis opulentior* 3. 24, *Non ebur neque aureum* 2. 18). For the rest, individuals are nearly always named: the attendant *puer* ('slave-boy') of 1. 38 apart, the name is concealed in only two cases, *O matre pulchra filia pulchrior* (1. 16), and *Nondum subacta* (2. 5), where 'you' refers to the poet himself. Throughout, the persons addressed are, or are conceived as, people from his own circle. We can identify the men for the most part as contemporaries: when this is impossible, since the individuals concerned played no part in public or literary life, in only a few cases can we suspect the name or person is fictitious (Thaliarchus 1. 9, Pyrrhus 3. 20, Ligurinus 4. 10). For the female figures, who all have Greek names, this suspicion is more probable, and certainly, for example, the peasant woman or *vilica* in 3. 23, if she really existed, was not called Phidyle. However that may be, the poet wishes to make us imagine at any rate that here too he is addressing real members of his circle. Instead of persons, however, in certain cases personified objects appear. In 1. 3 Horace addresses not the departing Virgil, but the ship carrying him away and likewise the ship of *O navis, referent* (1. 14) instead of the *res publica* ('state')—ships, since they have names, are of course easily conceived of as living beings elsewhere. 3. 21 is addressed not to Messalla, whom Horace awaits as his guest, but the *pia testa* to be used in the symposium, and addressed at that entirely in the manner of a hymn to a deity, as shown by Norden (1913: 154 ff.). In 1. 32 instead of the lyre-playing deity—a Muse or Apollo—the lyre itself is addressed, first as a companion at play, then by way of deification, *salve rite vocanti* ('to one calling out ritually "greeting"', 15–16). Lastly the tree of 2. 13 is apostrophized with terms of abuse as a treacherous servant who wished to kill his innocent master. These individual cases are thus all free variations on the constant type.

II

In what follows I will speak primarily of the main three-book collection; the additional book will concern us briefly at the end. The addressees are by no means present to the poet's imagination alone, making 'you' no more than a livelier substitute for 'he' or 'she'. On the contrary, the poems present themselves as addressed quite specifically to them, spoken or sung to them, intended to be heard by them. That is immediately clear in poem after poem from the situation described or alluded to. It is especially manifest when the poem accompanies a continuous action whose phases it permits us to divine, as in *Natis in usum laetitiae scyphis* (1. 27). The poet comes along when the atmosphere at the party has become alarmingly heated and the tankards are being brandished menacingly. He calls for calm, and is invited to join in the drinking. 'Yes,' he says, 'but in due order according to the rules, everyone give a toast to his ladylove. You there, begin.—Don't you all want to? Well, I won't join in either. Are you reluctant to utter the name? Whisper it in my ear, then.—Oh poor chap, you are in a bad way; from that bondage only a miracle will rescue you.'

Or take *Quantum distet ab Inacho* (3. 19). The meal is over, but a learned gentleman is incapable of terminating his tedious disquisitions: 'Do stop: we had much rather order a cask of good wine. You, lad, put some water by the fire for a warming drink in this barbarous winter cold. Right. Now, let's start by drinking our host's health and good luck for his new position. And now music to make the whole neighbourhood echo and annoy grumpy old Lycus; his young wife will be listening and long to be with us! You're lucky, Telephus, that you can name your Rhode; I drink to Glycera who's so hard to get.'

Or *Quid bellicosus Cantaber* (2. 11): 'Don't keep looking anxiously at the imperial frontier, Hirpinus, worrying whether the barbarians are thinking of war again; leave that to the future; life is so short, enjoy it. Set about it straight away: under the tall plane-tree or there under the pine let us drink. Quick, slave, Falernian here, mixed with water from the stream over there; and you, fetch Lyde, expert at the cithara. Tell her to hurry and play for us.' We can see the impromptu symposion being arranged in Hirpinus' grounds; the master will forget the Scythians and Cantabrians over it.

Elsewhere too, Horace alludes to the situation in which he and his interlocutor find themselves, or an action that his utterance sets in motion: a single word may suffice, even if only *hic* ('this'), as in *Eheu fugaces*: the phrase *harum quas colis arborum* ('those trees you grow', 2. 14. 22) transports us into Postumus' arboretum. There are, however, plenty of other poems where such a pointer is lacking, and therefore, if considered by themselves, would not let us conclude the interlocutor was present. But they are so to speak covered by the others; there is never an indication of the interlocutor's absence, nor does the content give us the feeling that the poet, in solitary contemplation, is thinking so deeply or so passionately about the absent one as to see him as if present; and thus the reader who reads these poems together is led without more ado to suppose actual presence throughout. I know only very few poems whose content makes such presence doubtful or improbable. In *Laudabunt alii*, the phrase *seu te fulgentia signis castra tenent* ('whether the camp, shining with standards, holds you', 1. 7. 19) shows Plancus is in the field, but we still need to consider Reitzenstein's suggestion (1913: 256) that the poem dates from the Actian campaign and Horace is staying with Plancus. *Velox amoenum* (1. 17) is usually taken as an 'invitation to the countryside', addressed to the absent Tyndaris; but it might be better to think of it as sung in welcome. The invitation poem *Tyrrhena regum progenies* (3. 29) will at first be understood so: Horace lingers in the country and Maecenas in Rome. But the poet avoids saying *veni* ('come') or the like, and thus leaves open the interpretation he is visiting Rome and urging his friend to return with him. Even if not the case, at any rate *this* poem is intended, if not to be heard, at least to be read by its addressee: the *carmen* would then quite exceptionally be a letter, the substitute for conversation, and even here 'you' would not stand for 'he' by virtue of the poet's imagination. Of the gods whom the poet addresses in praise or prayer, the same is true as of the human beings: they naturally hear the person praying or extolling them, and when at the end of *Iam satis terris* (1. 2) Caesar, who is not present in reality, is addressed, he is thought of as a god, as Mercury walking upon earth, as the poet sets it up. Finally, the rule applies even in those cases where a thing takes the place of a person: the poet holds the pot in his hand, he stands next to the fallen tree, he himself is on board the ship that battles with the billows; and thus the address to the ship that bears Virgil away is not to be understood as if the poet in Rome were imagining his departure, rather he has accompanied his friend to Brundisium or Puteoli and looks up full of concern at the vessel sailing away.

Address to a person imagined as present—this is the type not only of Horatian lyric, but of ancient lyric as a whole, that is, of monodic song. I will not discuss choral lyric, which poses particular problems here. I recall, however, that elegy too, which has nothing to do with the lyre, but which we classify under the inclusive term lyric, was originally subject to the same law. But once Solon composed elegies later generations entitled εἰς ἑαυτόν ('to himself') [Diogenes Laertius 1. 61], it freed itself in the Hellenistic era. In Tibullus and Propertius address still preponderates, but it is often absent, or clearly relates to someone absent, or changes within a poem, so that it is evidently no more than a figure of style. Elegy, despite retaining many elements of dialogue form, tends to monologue. Iambus too was certainly in its first beginnings and often later, direct address, but even Archilochus, for all he wishes his poisonous invectives to reach Lycambes' ears [fragments 172 ff. West], hardly utters them to his face. Elsewhere too, when he introduces as speakers the carpenter Charon [19] or the father scolding his daughter [122], adopted freer forms. In this Horace imitated him. But in the *Odes* the rule of the old lyric, his model, is binding on him. It holds, in fact, so far as we can judge from what remains of Sappho, Alcaeus, and Anacreon with negligibly few exceptions. Horace's song in a girl's voice, *Miserarum est* (3. 12), is modelled on Alcaeus [10B Voigt], and it may have been its very singularity that attracted him. In an invective against Pittacus [72], Alcaeus addresses his certainly absent enemy; here he avails himself of the freedom of iambus, and Sappho seems occasionally to have done likewise in her abusive poems, which acquired the name ἰαμβικά [cf. Philodemus, *De poem.* 1. 117. 10–11 Janko]. If the newly discovered fragment of Alcaeus [42], where Helen is addressed and compared with Thetis, really lacks only an initial strophe addressing Helen, the lyric poet here apostrophizes a mythological figure of whom he wishes to speak, as sometimes happens in epic. The rule would not be overturned by this exception either. Then we have Sappho's hymn to Aphrodite [1 Voigt], praying she come graciously to her as often before, and a prayer to the Nereids for her brother's safe homecoming [5]; we have remains of several poems to one Atthis; in others we can be sure of the address, though not the name; Φαίνεταί μοι κῆνος [31] must also have contained the interlocutrix's name, transmitted only in corrupt form. It is significant that in the fragmentary poem [96] complaining of a distant beloved's infidelity, not she, but a sympathetic and present companion is addressed. In Alcaeus we have all the types known to us from Horace: address to a deity, to named acquaintances (Bycchis [335], Melanippos [38], Antimenidas [350], and so on); to the slave who is to mix the wine [346], to the comrades who are to drink with him; when, far from home, he wishes to inform his fellow citizens how he has fared, he does not address them, but brings in a messenger: 'go and tell them this' [428]. We see the poet, we see the situation; it would be different if he simply told his story and apostrophized his fellow citizens from a distance. Anacreon honours Artemis [*PMG* 348] or prays to Dionysus [357] or addresses the unruly 'Thracian foal' [417], Smerdies [366], and other καλοί.

Here, if I am right, we have a basic difference between ancient and modern lyric: ancient lyric is with few exceptions, to use a term that probably cannot be misunderstood, dialogic, modern lyric overwhelmingly monologic. It is instructive to see how recent theoreticians characterize lyric. Richard Maria Werner attempts in *Lyrik und Lyriker* ('Lyric and Lyrist', 1890) to distinguish lyric from epic and drama: these latter involve poet, subject, and audience, lyric only the first two: 'the poem struggles to freedom from within the poet, and once it is free lyric has completely fulfilled its task'; it 'is sufficient unto itself', is not 'transitory' but 'static'; 'the former [epic and drama] seek to transmit what has been lived through, observed, experienced to others, the latter [lyric] merely expresses it'; 'the former are communicative, whereas the latter is retentive like a diary people write only for themselves'. Emil Ermatinger in his recent book, *Das dichterische Kunstwerk* ('The Poetic Work', 1921), says much the same: the true lyric poet creates without regard for the audience: 'how indeed could he see anything external confronting him, let alone take notice of it, when his gaze is so completely directed within himself? He surveys in deep self-absorption what swells and billows in his breast, what makes him happy or torments him, and if it wells up overpoweringly in him, it forces its way out, becomes speech . . . He does not worry whether anyone hears him; but he prefers it when no one does. For what he says has no reference to any individual, it concerns only his "I", but in such a way that at the same time he also addresses everyone.'

The ancient lyric poet, however, does not prefer it when no one hears him; rather, in such circumstances he may not sing at all. His song is thus 'transitory', and it is in this transit, and certainly not in any 'struggle for freedom from within', that its task is fulfilled. But for modern lyric, so far as I am acquainted with it, the description 'monologic poetry' is overwhelmingly apt, from its origins down to the present day. Here I ignore numerous genres that, without being epic or dramatic, are yet thoroughly 'transitory' and only fulfil their function once they reach particular persons' ears or eyes: invectives, poetic epistles, congratulatory odes such as ran wild among us in the seventeenth and eighteenth centuries, and so forth. All these poems pursue a practical purpose lying outside the poet. I consider only 'lyric' in the narrower sense, what is nowadays called 'genuine' lyric. The love-songs of the troubadours do not conceal their composition in isolation; if the lady is addressed, it is at a distance. The same is true of German *Minnesang*, and has been true ever since.

The most instructive genre for this trait in modern lyric is the folksong. There are certain kinds of song that are genuinely devised for a particular occasion, when it is to be sung and have its effect. Then the song naturally addresses the persons for whom it is intended: marriage songs, for instance, addressed to the bride, or convivial songs, where the 'brothers' or 'comrades' are challenged to sing or drink or be merry. If the singer wishes to tell a new tale, he may well announce that to the audience from the start, but the song proper then has nothing more to do with them. In addition, the folksong is not at all inclined, even if it has a central character, to treat him or her as present; that does not reflect the occasion in which the poet devised the song and first sang it to himself. In the lover, the urge to compose poetry and sing awakes when he is far from the beloved, and so it is a rare exception when the popular lovesong actually allows us to see the lovers together.

At best it is the farewell song that presents itself as a real address, although it naturally was not sung at the actual parting. The song attempts to preserve retroactively this single, unforgettably painful moment. Far more frequently, however, the parting lover or the abandoned beloved laments or seeks consolation in monologue. To be sure folksong, and all lyric approaching folksong, abounds in addresses of all kinds. That caused even Werner (1890) to distinguish between monologic and dialogic lyric. But significantly enough, he discusses this distinction in the section on 'Expression' in his chapter on 'External Form', and in actual fact it is a purely stylistic distinction, though naturally based on the poet's inclination, whether he says 'the sunlight shines into my heart' or, like Reinick, 'O sunlight, how you shine into my heart' ['O Sonnenschein, wie scheinst du mir ins Herz hinein!'; set to music by Schumann] (classified in Werner as 'pseudo-dialogue with implied answer'); whether Eichendorff speaks of the 'valleys far and heights' or to them ['Abschied', 1: 'O Täler weit, o Höhen', set to music by Mendelssohn], of the 'lovely wood so high up there' or to it ['Der Jäger Abschied', 1–2, 'Wer hat dich, du schöner Wald, | Aufgebaut so hoch da droben?']. It is no different with persons: 'If I did not love you, dear Lili' [Goethe, 'Vom Berge', 1: 'Wenn ich, liebe Lili, dich nicht liebte'] or 'The only man, Lida, whom you can love' [Goethe, 'An Lida', 1, 'Den einzigen, Lida, welchen du lieben kannst']. We should infer from the poems themselves that the poet speaks into the distance, even if we knew no alternative. There are exceptions even in modern 'art poetry', to be sure, but anyone looking for them may thumb through many a poetry book in vain.

However, where modern art lyric imitates Horace—as it has done in abundance from the Renaissance to the nineteenth century—we also find Horatian form used with greater or lesser felicity. Ronsard, for example, was masterful in his handling of it, though only in the lightest genre and in poems where he employed ancient motifs. Where he is more independent, he does without it. Let us go into the matter at greater length, to see how hard it is generally for the lyric poet to transpose himself from his so to speak native monologic type to the dialogic. I pick out a few German examples.[1]

Ramler thinks he is the Prussian Horace through and through, and as he read odes with titles like *ad Apollinem, ad Romam urbem, ad Valgium*, in his copy of Horace, he also entitles his poems 'An die Stadt Berlin' ['To the city of Berlin'], 'An Apollo bei Eröffnung des Opernhauses in Berlin' ['To Apollo on the Opening of the Opera House in Berlin'], 'An Herrn Christian Gottfried Krause'. For example, in 'An Lycidas' he imitates Horace's *Quem tu Melpomene semel* (4. 3). But in Horace the poem's contents are really thoughts about and thanks to the Muse for what she has given him, and the poet speaks in the first person of his totally individual experience, ending *quod spiro et placeo, si placeo, tuum est* ('It's your doing that I breathe and please, if I do'). Ramler speaks of the poet entirely in general, and ends—since the poem must have its address—'Endlich, o Lycidas, erwartet er, gleich eines fremden Manns Besuche, den Tod mit Gleichmut' ['Finally, O Lycidas, he awaits death with equanimity, like a stranger's visit']. How that concerns Lycidas we are never told. Or again, Ramler imitates *Ad arborem* (2. 13) in his ode 'An ein Geschütz' ['To a Gun'], to which he carefully adds the scholion 'When a cannonball was propelled by the Russian artillery from an unusual distance into the middle of the city' ['Als von der russischen Artillerie eine Kugel aus einer ungewöhnlicher Ferne bis mitten in die Stadt getrieben wurde']. The tree that nearly killed Horace is lying next to him, and we understand perfectly well why the perfidy of things brings him to a fury; the gun is stationed somewhere outside and far away and hears nothing of the anger streaming from the Prussian Horace.

In Klopstock, too, address is almost a law of the ode, not only in poems whose addressee is named in the heading—'An Gott' ['To God'], 'An Ebert, Fanny, Bodmer' *et al.*—but throughout the others. Here and there Klopstock writes genuinely dialogic lyric in the ancient spirit: in one of his richest odes 'Der Rheinwein' ['Rhine Wine'], a poem with a motif based on *O nata mecum* (3. 21), he

---

[1] In this connection we may mention K. Vietor, *Geschichte der deutschen Ode* (Munich, 1923), to which Heinze later liked to refer in his lecture-course [note by Erick Burck in Heinze (1972)].

addresses the wine, really conceived as a person, and then the friend drinking with him. The action is progressive, accompanied by the poet's words. But such poems are exceptions, and where they occur, they tend to be especially close to their ancient models in content as well. Where Klopstock is at his most independent in content, the address is either a mannerism or a figure of style. In his ode 'Der Zürcher See' (Lake Zurich) he addresses in turn Mother Nature, sweet joy, merry spring, love, and pious virtue, and finally the distant lovers; nowhere is there any living awareness of a presence. In the later poems he no longer even attempts to make us feel that the address is genuine: 'Stirb, prophetischer Greis' ['Die, prophetic old man'], he says to Young, and directs poems to La Rochefoucauld's ghost, King Friedrich, and so on.

Lastly I come to Hölderlin, who knew his Horace well. In 'Emiliens Brauttag' ['Emilie's Wedding Day'], for instance, he cites a long passage from a poem [*Epode* 16] by the 'quiet Roman' in free translation. He produced masterly imitations of Horatian metres and also took over the form of the ode as address. As a personality, however, he is in all ways Horace's exact opposite: he is lonely, brooding, consumes himself in unsatisfied longing, a shipwreck against the hard and idiosyncratic external world, over against the happily sociable Roman, who cheerfully set to and so lovingly fashioned his own happiness in life. Hölderlin's nature makes it understandable that the addressees of his poetry are rarely persons; even when he turns to Diotima, one hardly has the impression she could be present. But when we read his poems to the spring or the aether, the oak trees or the imprisoned stream, the sungod or the Fates, we feel with increasing clarity the address is here truly conceived in an ancient spirit—it is no mere stylistic form, but for Hölderlin all these parts and powers of nature really live, and he feels so close to them, so much akin, that he can talk to them as friend to friend, son to father, believer to God. But it needed just such an anachronism as this dreamer, so alien to his present, to re-create as it were the forms of ancient lyric and fill them with new content. What nevertheless makes his lyric, quite apart from all the differences in their personalities and poetic gifts, almost entirely unlike Horace's, is the lack of a factor that I will now call the third essential element of the Horatian ode. It is perhaps the most important and still least noticed.

III

The Horatian ode, as we have seen, is an address to a person thought of as present. But the purpose of the address is never mere communication: the interlocutor is not meant to learn something about the poet or serve as a vessel into which he may pour his feelings, sufferings, and joys. Either the poet wishes to prevail on the other's volition—by far the most frequent case—or, much less often, he refuses a demand the other has made on him. Very rare is a third case, where the poet positively expresses his resolve, e.g., to follow Bacchus' orders (3. 25), offer sacrifice to a spring (3. 13), or dedicate a tree to Diana (3. 22). Everywhere, however, we have before us an expression of the poet's will regarding not only himself but also— usually first and foremost—the interlocutor. The attempt to determine another's choices may take the most varied forms: admonition, as in *Aequam memento* (2. 3) or *Eheu fugaces* (2. 17); often cast negatively as a pact or a warning: *Tu ne quaesieris* (1. 11), *Albi, ne doleas* (1. 33), *Ne sit ancillae tibi amor pudori* (2. 4); also in the form of the surprised or indignant question: *Cur me querelis exanimas tuis* (2. 17), *Quid fles, Asterie* (3. 7), *Icci, beatis nunc Arabum invides | gazis* (1. 29). Exceptionally, the interlocutor is simply supported in his resolve: *Nullus argenti color est* (2. 2). Furthermore, we may have a request to the beloved for admission: *Extremum Tanain* (3. 10). This type is parodied, this time with no demand but scornful prophecy, in the inverse paraclausithyron *Parcius iunctas* (1. 25); invitation to comrades to celebrate with the poet: *Nunc est bibendum* (1. 37) or without explicit address *Et ture et fidibus* (1. 36); to the lyre, the Muse, or Mercury to vouchsafe a song; prayer to the deity, or exceptionally a hymn without an expressly attached prayer, *Mercuri, facunde nepos Atlanti* (1. 10); orders to Horace's slaves.

All that is for the most part overt and obvious and rarely fails to be recognized. At the end of the prologue, *Odes* 1. 1, Kiessling rejects the future *quodsi me lyricis vatibus inseres* ('but if you will include me among the lyric bards'), because it would convey a demand; that is precisely what Horace intends. In the ode to Asinius Pollio (2. 1) there has been a suggestion to delete the stanza exhorting him not to turn away from poetry for long, or to explain it away as a subsequent addition; but it is precisely this stanza that makes the poem a Horatian ode. Less obvious is the poet's expression of will when he refuses another's demand, since he is usually too urbane to refer explicitly to the other's request. Thus in *Scriberis Vario* (1. 6), *Nolis longa ferae* (2. 12), and *Pindarum quisquis* (4. 2), Horace rejects a request for poetry. That is also how we should understand the last poem of book 4, where Horace excuses himself as it were for not having greeted Augustus on his return with a eulogy for military success. Instead, he praises the prince of peace, in whose honour the Ara Pacis was then being erected. But the form is not restricted to this type of *recusatio*: *Otium divos* (2. 16) and *Inclusum Danaen* (3. 16) cannot be understood, in my opinion, until we suppose Grosphus and Maecenas had expected the poet to exchange his impoverished and modest existence for a richer one. Similarly we should also take *Integer vitae* (1. 22) as a rejection of his friend's concern, jokingly justified by what just befell him in the Sabine wood. The poem's popularity in modern times may be partially attributed to its apparent affinity to modern lyric as a narrative and assertion of love, with the address to Fuscus only an immaterial ornament to a monologic song. *Donec gratus eram tibi* (3. 9) likewise shares modern readers' favour with *Integer vitae* and appeals especially because of the dialogue form otherwise foreign to ancient lyric (though not epigram), but so frequent in modern folksong.

As a result, Horace's gaze as lyrist is always directed towards the future. Externally that is already evident by the frequency with which poems begin or end with the imperative, jussive subjunctive, or future; exceptionally, he portrays in *Ille et nefasto* (2. 13) a future that had been warded off. The modern lyric poet's gaze, by contrast, is mostly fixed on the present. The poem is concerned with a state of affairs, the psychological state of the poet, and if this produces wishes for the future, perhaps because his heart is filled with longing, that is merely one special case among many. Thus the modern lyric poet repeatedly describes the landscape before him or the events taking place in nature around him, then the feelings it arouses in him, or he may rely on the suggestive power of his description to generate the same mood in the reader. When Horace describes nature, it serves the purpose of justifying some demand: since it is spring, Sestius or Torquatus should open his heart to joy [1. 4, 4. 7]; since it is bitterly cold, and snow lies on the mountains and trees, Thaliarchus should make a proper fire and let flow streams of warming wine [1. 9], and so on. Such possibilities for connection seldom occur without motivation. The rarity of natural description in Horace should not suggest he was himself unresponsive to nature: describing the moods it aroused in him is not his lyric task, which excludes anything purely contemplative. When memory overpowers him, the modern lyrist can, by contrast, re-create a past mood in his poem: the poem is then not present description but narrative, and indeed not a few of our finest lyric poems belong to this type (which Ermatinger strangely sees a sign of stylistic uncertainty and lyric decomposition): 'My heart beats, quickly to horse!' [Goethe, 'Willkommen und Abschied', 1: 'Es schlug mein Herz, geschwind zu Pferde!']; 'While I lay sleeping, an hour or so before dawn' [Mörike: 'Derweil ich schlafend lag, | Ein Stündlein wohl vor Tag'; set to music by several composers]; 'The stars they shone so golden, Alone by the window I stood' [Eichendorff, 'Sehnsucht', 1–2: 'Es schienen so golden die Sterne, | Am Fenster ich einsam stand']'; 'Gone was the last swallow' [Gottfried Keller, 'Die Begegnung', 1: 'Schon war die letzte Schwalbe fort'], and a host of others. Such description of the past too is alien to ancient lyric: when Horace narrates something about himself, which happens rarely enough, he does so, as in *Integer vitae* or the childhood experience of *Odes* 3. 4, to exemplify the lesson he imparts to his interlocutor.

Our material does not allow us to say with certainty how far the volitional trait of Horatian lyric is proper to the ancient genre as a whole. In Sappho we have prayers to Aphrodite and the Nereids, besides numerous relics of others, and φαίνεταί μοι κῆνος (31) may also have ended with a prayer (unusable of course for Catullus' Latin adaptation). But this very poem shows Sappho portraying her own passionate state, and newly discovered larger fragments tell us she described the past in detail, but not, apparently, to transport herself back into previous states of mind, but to explain those of now; what that led to we do not know. Sufficient traces show she often exhorted and warned in her songs, but it would be foolhardy to conclude from that about the extent of the role played by the expression of will in her lyric. It is thinkable that she, unique in every respect, there too went her own way. For Horace, Alcaeus was far more important, and in him we really do find, as I need not rehearse in detail, all the Horatian types of exhortation and warning, wish and prayer. Not to portray his own psychological state, but to affect his hearers, is obviously his foremost poetic concern; just as in Horace.

IV

The next feature of Horatian lyric, even more than the one discussed above, takes us beyond formal characteristics to the poems' overall attitude. If in Horace and Alcaeus a second person is regularly involved—indeed for that person's own interest and not merely as ornament—we should not expect the poet's inner life to be as unreservedly and thoroughly revealed as is possible and expected in modern lyric with a modern audience. The ancient lyrist does not sing to free himself from overwhelming feelings. The psychological process leading to the poem's creation does not end when the poet has rectified things internally; rather the other is always there and must be addressed because the poet wants something of him or he of the poet. And so the poet says what is important for the other, and restricts his confessions from consideration for the latter. We might expect a total lack of reserve in prayer to a deity. There the poem is not occasioned by the other's state or conduct, only by the poet's own wish or need. But again, ancient prayer is not to be put on par with ours, which may be the believer's most secret utterance to his god, can take place in a secluded private room or simply in thought, and may serve an inward liberation. Such prayer is not known in antiquity, for the simple reason that the ancients pray aloud, and praise the deity aloud in its temple amidst their fellow citizens and companions, or in their own homes when offering a sacrifice, but even there not alone: he who prays quietly arouses the suspicion that his wishes are not fit for human ears to hear and it is enough for the god if he hears the worshipper's wishes. But public delivery—I will return to that in a moment—is the generally accepted precondition for the ode: that too restricts confidentiality of utterance. So we cannot be surprised that Horace's odes portray his personality only, so to speak, in rough outline. We encounter the finer traits in the *Epistles*, which are genuinely intended as confidential dialogues where the writer pours out his heart. It is telling that Horace's one religious confessional poem, *Parcus deorum cultor* (1. 34), takes the entirely exceptional form of a monologue. There Horace found address contrary to style and, since the former Epicurean did not wish to leave the religious attitude of so many odes unexplained, broke free of his regular type.

We cannot extend this observation to the whole of ancient lyric without further consideration. After all, Sappho's songs offer proof that the lyric form *per se* permitted expression of the soul's tenderest emotions, of deepest personal feeling. But what was fitting for a woman among women need not apply to men. If the new discoveries of Alcaeus have been in general disappointing, that is probably essentially because we expected a lyric poet in the modern sense and did not find him. He whose first task is to affect others with his song has no reason to plunge into the depths of his heart; he is rather like the orator, who would also sweep away, convince, inflame. Of Alcaeus' poems on political subjects, which Horace too prized most highly, an ancient critic judged one needed only remove their metrical form to have political rhetoric—exaggeration, to be sure, yet significant for their attitude. It seems, modern lyric traits are not to be found in them. But that did not impair his esteem, and nowhere is he deemed inferior to Sappho on that account. We can see what mattered in lyric to the ancients, or rather what did not. Anyone who felt impelled to write poetry about himself had elegy and later epigram at his disposal. Even Horace's contemporaries, Tibullus and Propertius, reveal far more about their most intimate lives to us than the lyric Horace.

V

Finally, performance. There is no doubt that Sappho, Alcaeus, and Anacreon sang their own songs and accompanied their singing on the lyre. Singing does not of itself presuppose an audience; one can sing even when alone, precisely to console oneself for being alone, in antiquity as today. That there were monologic popular ditties in ancient Greece is shown by Δέδυκε μὲν ἀ σελάνα [*PMG* 976; 168B1 Voigt] or the so-called 'nomion' of Eriphanis, the solitary huntress, addressed to distant Menalcas [*PMG* 850]. But in both these cases, as in the lament of the *pastor Corydon*, singing without a listener is expressly motivated and was probably even less the rule in antiquity than nowadays. When Achilles in defiant withdrawal sings of κλέα ἀνδρῶν, at least Patroclus is listening, and when Orpheus, driven to solitude by grief, sings to the cithara, the trees and beasts of the forest become his audience. Shepherd's song, for which one could imagine solitary singing, also always presupposes listeners in Theocritus, and his lonely Cyclops sings to the sea hoping Galatea will hear him [11].

In the Lesbians especially, address suffices to indicate listeners. Should we wish to imagine, say, that Sappho's prayer to Aphrodite was sung in solitude, this is the very case where Wilamowitz (1913: 42 ff.) neatly showed that the reason we do not learn the beloved's name is that Sappho is singing among her girls, including the un-named one whom the song is meant to affect, and she well knows it is about her. As Sappho sang among her girls or female friends, so Alcaeus and Anacreon sang in male circles, preponderantly at the symposium. If Alcaeus constantly invites his comrades to drink, constantly finds a new *causa bibendi*, summer heat [347] and winter cold [338], shared grief [335] or joy [332], we should not infer he was a particularly dreadful soak. He sings from the occasion. The same is true throughout. I believe his song of a storm and ship in danger [326], the model of Horace's *O navis referent* (1. 14), is an allegory because it would be ridiculous to imagine Alcaeus with his cithara in arm while pounding waves threaten the ship, the storm rips sail and tackle apart, and the sailors are therefore not inclined to lyric tones. And when the ancient lyric poet in his song addresses his comrades or individuals from their circle, that too must result from the occa-sion: the poet sees his friend or friends in a particular mood or hears him speak; that stimulates him to utterance yeah or nay, the song rises to his lips.

Thus the ancient song, even if it need be hardly always, let alone completely improvised, was much closer to improvisation than the modern, even by the nature and occasion of its performance. The more the song that rang from the lyre seemed born of the moment, the more stirring its effect must have been. Even in subsequent repetition this moment of origin could be re-created in the listener's imagination. Modern individual lyric poetry long ago not only freed itself from song—the more decisively the more it distanced itself from folksong. But even as book poetry it all but totally dispensed with the poet's own performance, at least with performance on the occasion from which the poem originated. The latter is true even in the earliest period of modern art lyric, when the Provençal troubadours and later the German *Minnesänger* set their own songs to music and performed them. These songs were also conceived in solitude an indefinitely long time in advance and did not even attempt to create the impression of improvisation. Certainly there are special cases in the broad range of modern poetry and song: [Carl Michael] Bellman sang his 'epistles' to the lute, while [his characters Movitz the alcoholic ex-soldier and Ulla the prostitute] danced and drank around him. There too we find address and improvisation, there too the song accompanies the action as it progresses. But we admit that Bellman, as in every respect, here too was an exception. To be sure, where the poet does not owe his effect to individual ability, nor is a specially gifted personality, but his song still lives as common property, there too, at all times and in all milieux, improvisation is something perfectly normal and natural. Otto Böckel writes most instructively in his *Psychology of Folk Poetry* (1913) on the practice of improvisation and the astonishing capacity for it still preserved in many places down even to most recent times. We must imagine Archilochus and Alcaeus were also still close to such a tradition, rooted in it and feeding off it; their genius raised them high above the community, but was nevertheless sustained by it.

And Horace? When we look to the odes themselves, the poet in this respect is fully on the same plane as Alcaeus. Horace too is a *lyricus vates* [1. 1. 35] in that he sings his own songs and accompanies them on the cithara; he is the *Romanus fidicen lyrae* ('player of the Roman lyre', 4. 3. 23), who asks his *barbitos* ('lyre') for a Latin song (1. 32. 3–4) or calls on the seven-stringed *testudo* ('tortoise') to move shy Lyde (3. 11. 1–8), who begs Apollo to allow him the cithara even in old age (1. 31. 19–20), and who hangs up his lyre in Venus' sanctuary when he would renounce singing and love (3. 26. 3–6). And if we are to think of Horace singing his songs in person, we should also think of them as improvised. This applies not only to those songs accompanying the progress of an action mentioned above, but throughout. If, say, Agrippa asked Horace to compose an epic about his exploits, it would be ridiculous to imagine that a few days later the poet, his lyre in his arm, came before him and began *Scriberis Vario* (1.6). No, the riposte must have been instantaneous. And so, if we take the poet literally, the prerequisite of his lyric is that the lyre be always at hand, at the feast, in a stroll in the park, at a tryst with his beloved, and before the deity's altar. It is as in the world of our Romantics, especially Eichendorff: 'Then Leontin, who was standing up in the prow of the boat, sang the following song to the guitar' [*Ahnung und Gegenwart*, bk. 1, ch. 8: 'Da sang Leontin, der vorn im Kahne aufrecht stand, folgendes Lied zur Gitarre']; 'Romana walked in the field by herself, a guitar in her arm... She sang' [ibid., bk. 2, ch. 17: '...ging Romana auf der Wiese für sich allein, eine Gitarre im Arm... Sie sang']; 'Then Fortunatus opened all the double doors, took hold of his guitar, and strode singing up and down through the long sequence of rooms' [*Dichter und ihre Gesellen*, bk. 2, ch. 15: 'Da öffnete Fortunat alle Flügeltüren, ergriff seine Gitarre und schritt durch die lange Reihe der Gemächer singend auf und nieder']; 'Friedrich,... instead of making any answer, took the guitar and sang to a simple old melody' [*Ahnung und Gegenwart*, bk. 3, ch. 24: 'Friedrich... nahm statt aller Antwort die Gitarre und sang nach einer alten schlichten Melodie']; 'Leontin seized the guitar Julie had brought, leaped onto his chair, and drowned out the noise of the combatants with the following song' [ibid., bk. 1, ch. 8: 'Leontin ergriff die Gitarre, die Julie mitgebracht, sprang auf seinen Stuhl hinauf und übersang die Kämpfenden mit folgendem Liede']. What they sing is sometimes 'an old ballad' [ibid., bk. 3, ch. 20 'eine alte Romanze'] or 'a song I had often heard from him before', but it is mostly something improvised there and then, composed for the occasion and arising out of it. In the Romantic world, entirely filled by poetry, by sound and rhythm, this seems something entirely natural to us, and we believe Eichendorff on his Fortunatuses and Leontins, who sing and play the guitar at every opportunity, knowing as we do that he himself was accompanied through life by his 'old faithful lute'.

Possibly something of the kind is returning among today's guitar-happy youth.

But was Horace such a Fortunatus? Naturally as a boy, like any well-brought-up Roman youth, he learned to sing. Whether he also learned to play the lyre is highly doubtful. Of a girl, even of good class, we should believe it straight away. Sallust's Sempronia sings and plays the lyre *elegantius quam necesse est probae* ('more elegantly than a modest woman should', Sall. *Cat.* 25. 1); therefore even the 'modest woman' must have been capable of it at that time to a certain degree. In Nero's day, when not only the emperor himself, but Calpurnius Piso, for instance, was famous for his string-playing, that skill will have been expected as a matter of course from a lyric poet. But from Cicero's or Horace's time, I know of no Roman male who played the cithara. Was Horace a pioneer? If we examine all those references to the *cithara*, the *barbitos*, the *lyra* once again, we must be disturbed to find that, however often the odes show us a girl playing the lyre, we never see the poet with the instrument in a concrete situation. Never does he have it handed him, or represent anyone listening as he plays or the like. When he invites Lyde for a drink enhanced by music, he indeed describes them both as going to sing, but *tu curva recines lyra Latonam* ('you will sing of Latona on your curved lyre', 3. 28. 11–12). On this point the poet's silence cannot well be an accident. And it seems to me proof positive that when Horace, in his letter to Maecenas (*Epist.* 1. 19) explains the failure of his lyric poetry in part by his reluctance to perform his poems amongst his fellow poets and critical *grammatici* ('scholars'), he represents himself as saying *spissis indigna theatris scripta pudet recitare* ('I am ashamed to read my unworthy writings aloud in a crowded theatre', 41). So there too he would have recited his odes, not sung them to the lyre. Finally, I wish just to mention in passing that certain metrical peculiarities of the poems are best accounted for by recitation, not singing. Now Horace certainly wished his songs to be sung as well, just like those of his Greek predecessors, and he asks Phyllis to learn poems he composed (4. 11). We have every reason to suppose his wish was fulfilled—for even Virgil's *Bucolics* were sung.[2] But we must decide to regard the

---

[2] [Vita Donatiana 26; Vita Donati Aucti 41; Vita Philargyriana 1, Brugnoli and Stok 181, 1–3.]

picture of Horace playing the lyre as fiction. The *barbitos* he hangs up in Venus' shrine can be understood no differently from the 'little harp' ('kleine Harfe') Hölty asks his friends to hang behind the altar when he is dead ['Vermächtnis', 1–2]. But anyone who despite all counter-arguments was unwilling to admit this would have to concede what is even more important, that the songs were not composed and sung in the occasion in which they claim to have been composed and sung. We can tell they are not improvisations from the poems themselves, and precisely from their greatest virtues, even if Horace had not, admittedly not till book 4, spoken of his *operosa carmina* ('laboured songs'), which he shapes *per laborem plurimum* ('through much work') and in this very context disowned the possibility of improvisation (4. 2. 29–32).

If this is so, then those things I emphasized in the Horatian ode by way of contrast to modern lyric and that remain characteristic of it nevertheless, rest largely on fiction: it is fiction that the poet stands opposite his addressee, fiction—except where general admonitions are concerned—that he wishes to affect his interlocutor, fiction that the listener should, from the songs, recognize the occasion in which they were composed. We must therefore be clear that Horatian lyric made greater demands of his contemporaries than his archaic metrical form: he required of their imagination nothing less than to transport themselves back to the times of an Alcaeus or Anacreon, to a sympotic practice that must have seemed unfamiliar to them, to understand the form containing the Horatian ode's thoroughly modern content. This demand was too much for his contemporaries, and that was probably not the least reason why Horace's odes were at first rejected by the public and even afterwards had hardly any successors worth mentioning.

We will also have to admit that the consistently, almost obstinately maintained fiction of Horatian lyric did not always prove a blessing. Horace lived, after all, not in Alcaeus' times but in his own, and if the temper of his times, as elegy demonstrates, tended to monologue, Horace too could not completely escape it. I have the impression that not a few odes were basically conceived as monologues with the dialogue form added on. To mention but one example, the introduction to *Sic te diva potens Cypri* (1. 3) with its address certainly arises admirably from its occasion, but after the first two stanzas we have pure monologue, independent of any address. But those are questions that go beyond my task today.

Simply let me close by remarking that Horace himself, in his fourth book, when he returned to lyric after a pause of several years, did not hold on to the former fiction in all strictness. True, he did retain address, and in other matters as well poems like *Pindarum quisquis* (4. 2) or *Diva quem proles* (4. 6) fully match the earlier type. But the address (*quid debeas o Roma Neronibus*, 'O Rome, what you owe the Nerones', 4. 4. 37) in the middle of the panegyric to Drusus really seems a mere stylistic formality. And Horace in particular no longer retains the addressee's presence: even if one may perhaps still be able to take *Divis orte bonis* (4. 5) as a cletic hymn, and likewise to justify the address to the distant Augustus in *Quae cura patrum* (4. 14) by the poem's hymnic form. *Est mihi nonum* and *Iam veris comites* present themselves without concealment as invitations to Phyllis and Vergilius (*quibus advoceris | gaudiis*, 'with what joy you are called', 4. 11. 13–14; *cum tua | velox merce veni*, 'come quickly with your contribution', 4. 12. 21–2), that is, as letters in song form. Above all, the volitional element, as I call it above, and with it future reference are often in retreat or completely disappear. The prayer of thanks to Melpomene (4. 3) expresses no wish for the future, but dwells on the beatifying present. The panegyric to Drusus (4. 4) praises the exploits accomplished by the brothers Nero and their ancestors. The poem to Censorinus (4. 8) praises the power of song and leaves unspoken the thought that in this case too the addressee will be immortalized by the ode. The poem to Lollius (4. 9) begins in fact, like several in the first collection, with a warning, but we cannot suppose Lollius has in any way been its cause, and the poem mainly serves to glorify what the addressee is and has been. The lampoon on Lyce (4. 13) stays entirely within the bounds of past and present and merely states facts, like the invective on *Uxor pauperis Ibyci* (3. 13), without warning or pointing to the future like *Parcius iunctis* (1. 25). Finally, in the Lollius poem the poet dispenses even with the fiction of lyric song when he speaks openly of his *chartae* ('papers') that are not to keep silent on the excellent man's glory. He furthermore dispenses, as stated above, with the fiction of improvisation when he speaks of the great labour his songs cost him (4. 2. 29).

The supplementary book therefore differs markedly from the main collection in these points as well as in subject, composition, metre, and language. But if it thereby appears to approach modern lyric, in essence it moves even further way. If even in the main collection the 'other' exercises an influence on the content and shape of the poem unusual in modern lyric, here he advances so far into the foreground that the poet almost disappears and becomes simply a megaphone for public opinion. If the earlier type of lyric poetry reminded us of the symbouleutic orator, here the epideictic orator comes on the scene. But that is an approximation not to modern lyric, but to another ancient genre.

2

The Function of Wine in Horace's Odes

Steele Commager

Discussions of wine in Horace's work have tended towards the convivial rather than the critical. In them, Horace is more often conspicuous as a connoisseur than as an artist. The various wines he mentions have been catalogued, with their characteristics,[1] and critics have been fond of debating the degree of his indulgence. Yet many of the Odes are less instructive as a tribute to wine than as an example of how wine becomes an attribute of a poem's imaginative structure. It remains to consider these Odes, in which wine seems to represent not so much a subject as a symbol in Horace's thought, a crystallization of attitudes otherwise too abstract to be amenable to poetic development.

Libera vina is designated as one of the four traditional subjects of lyric poetry (*A.P.* 85), and it is wine's liberating effect which seems to have struck Horace most forcibly. The names Liber and Lyaeus, 'the loosener', recommended themselves: is it not wine's function to relax? The drunken brawls of Centaurs and Lapiths (*C.* 1.18.8 ff.) prove freedom of action not invariably salubrious. Yet in the Odes wine customarily exercises a beneficent influence, and courage, eloquence, wit, and hope find a common source in Liber (*C.* 3.21; *Epp.* 1.5.16–20). Bacchus presented himself to Horace less as the traditional incarnation of violence than as a figure fostering peace and harmony, a likely companion for the Graces, Venus, and Cupid.[2] Again, Liber takes his

---

[1] Sedgwick (1947), 62.
[2] *C.* 1.18.6; 1.32.9 ff.; 3.21.21 ff. In *C.* 1.12.21–2 Liber appears between Athena and Diana in the catalogue of gods whom Horace honors.

place with the Muses, Venus, and Cupid in a group which represents peace as opposed to war (*C.* 1.32.9 ff.). A similar contrast underlies the festive scene of *Natis in usum laetitiae scyphis* ('cups born for gladness' use', *C.* 1.27), which banishes brawling as unfit to a *verecundus Bacchus* ('modest Bacchus', 3). 'Let Opuntian Megylla's brother tell with what wound he is blessed, by what arrow he perishes.' The only wounds proper to banqueters are those from Cupid (11–12), the only destruction that of Venus (18 ff.).[3] The symposium approaches an ideal of genial harmony, and in it Horace encourages us to find virtually an epitome of civilized intercourse.[4]

A drink may also function as an almost archetypal symbol of release. An obvious instance is the fabled cup of Lethe, which frees us from the totality of the past. The apotheosis of Augustus and Romulus suggests a variation of the same idea, for a drink of nectar seals their release from earthly existence and their assumption to the ranks of the immortals (*C.* 3.3.12, 34). On a mundane level a banquet most often signifies freedom from a specifically unpleasant past. *Hic dies vere mihi festus atras eximet curas* ('this festive day truly will erase black cares')—a feast celebrates the safe return of Augustus (*C.* 3.14.13–14) as it does that of Pompeius (*C.* 2.7) or Numida (*C.* 1.36). The feast marking an end to anxiety for Numida serves, probably by design, as a prelude to a grander celebration, final freedom from fear of Cleopatra (*C.* 1.37). *Nunc est bibendum* ('Now we must drink'): as long as the threat from Egypt persisted, wine remained in the Roman cellars: *antehac nefas depromere Caecubum* ('before now it was wrong to bring out the Caecuban').[5] The poem is a *Trinklied* ('drinking song') in a wider sense, and Cleopatra too is allowed a symbolic drink. Before Actium she had displayed the baser effects of intoxication, being literally drunk with power: *fortunaque dulci ebria... mentemque lymphatam Mareotico* ('drunk on

[3] A traditional conceit of the battle of love (cf. Ovid, *Am.* 1.9 for an exhaustive treatment) provides an antithesis for the actual battles of the Thracians. A guest at the feast is 'blessed' (*beatus*, 11; cf. *impium lenite clamorem*, 6–7) in his wound; ruddy blushes (15) replace bloody brawls (4). In *C.* 1.6 Horace uses a similar contrast in rejecting epic military themes to write of *proelia virginum* (17).

[4] Cf. *C.* 1.17.17 ff.; 1.20; *Sat.* 2.6.65 ff.; *Epp.* 1.5. For the symposium as a literary form see Jaeger (1943), 176 ff.

[5] Cf. *curam metumque Caesaris rerum iuvat | dulci Lyaeo solvere* (*Ep.* 9.37–8).

sweet fortune, her mind crazed with Mareotic', 11 ff.). Irresponsibility changes to a higher freedom in her final drink, for *combiberet venenum* ('to drink poison', 28) marks a splendid release as surely as do the festivities of the Romans. Embracing the sting of death she makes the grave itself a victory. Her drink to the past matches the Romans' toast to the future, and her final draught celebrates a private triumph hardly less glorious than their public one.

A banquet often salutes release from more specialized forms of the past:

> 'Quantum distet ab Inacho
>   Codrus pro patria non timidus mori
> narras et genus Aeaci
>   et pugnata sacro bella sub Ilio:
>
> quo Chium pretio cadum
>   mercemur, quis aquam temperet ignibus,
> quo praebente domum et quota
>   Paelignis caream frigoribus, taces.   (*C.* 3.19.1–8)

You go on and on about Codrus' lineage—he was not afraid to die for his country—how far he stands from Inachus and the race of Aeacus and wars fought under sacred Ilium: at what price we can buy a jar of Chian, who will warm the water on the fire, who will offer his house, and what time I may escape the Paelignian cold—all this you keep silent.

The sharp inquiries of the present (*quo...quis...quo...quota*) break in upon a mythically distant past, as Horace summons an antiquarian from his researches to a feast. Horace excludes aged Lycus (22–4), inviting as more suitable companions *tempestiva Rhode* ('timely Rhode') (the adjective is important) and Glycera, whose name is practically synonymous with ripeness. The banquet seems to stand as a rejection of the past and a celebration of the present.[6] A similar invitation, now amiable rather than impatient, calls a certain nobly pedigreed Aelius to practical preparations for a

---

[6] Cf. *C.* 3.15.13 ff. A superannuated courtesan, Chloris, is banished from the wine, flowers, and music of the banquet, which are better suited to her daughter (7 ff.). Chloris prefers her memories of the past to the realities of the present. She is in fact too old (*maturo propior funeri*, 4; cf. *senex Lycus*, *C.* 3.19.24) to be allowed a place at a banquet celebrating present life.

feast (*C.* 3.17). Domestic detail confronts the catalogue of his ancestral glories:

> dum potes, aridum
> compone lignum; cras Genium mero
>   curabis et porco bimestri
>   cum famulis operum solutis.   (*C.* 3.17.13–16)

While you can, gather dry wood; tomorrow you will celebrate your birthday with neat wine, a two-month pig, your slaves on holiday.

Only if Aelius abandons the past and commits himself to the present may he enjoy the banquet.

An invitation to Pompeius, formerly one of Horace's fellow soldiers under Brutus, places the same injunction in a political context:

> ergo obligatam redde Iovi dapem,
> longaque fessum militia latus
>   depone sub lauru mea, nec
>   parce cadis tibi destinatis.
>
> oblivioso levia Massico
> ciboria exple, funde capacibus
>   unguenta de conchis.   (*C.* 2.7.17–23)

Therefore render the feast you promised unto Jupiter and set your bones, weary from long service, under my laurel, and don't skimp on the jars meant for you. Fill the smooth bean-shaped cups with forgetful Massic, pour unguents from abundant shell-pots.

The Ode was probably written just after the amnesty of 29 BC, and the promised feast is to celebrate the former Republican's homecoming. In the reference to Jove (17) Mr Wilkinson has detected a glance at Octavian.[7] *Oblivioso* ('forgetful', 21) is then not merely a stock adjective. It hints that the time has come for Pompeius to forget, or at least forego, his doctrinaire Republicanism of the past, as Horace himself had already done.[8]

---

[7] Wilkinson (1946), 33–4.

[8] Cf. *C.* 3.14.21 ff. The banquet welcoming Augustus back to Rome signals not only an end to Horace's immediate fears, but reminds us as well of his abandonment of a more distant past. Horace bids a youth summon clear-voiced Neaera; some editors have felt such 'licentious vigor' out of place in an Ode to the ruler; see Page (1895), *ad loc.* Horace warns the youth not to persevere if Neaera's gate-keeper prove

The claims of the future may be as binding as those of the past, and wine frees us from anxiety as it does from retrospection. In recommending to Plancus the example of Teucer, Horace presents a scene of wide applicability (*C*. 1.7.21 ff.). About to flee into exile, Teucer binds his wine-flushed temples with garlands, counselling his sad friends to seize the present moment with joy: *cras ingens iterabimus aequor* ('tomorrow we will journey again over the huge sea', 32). In the less august cast of the Satires rustic philosopher replaces mythological hero, but the advice of Ofellus is Teucer's own. He smoothes anxiety from his brow with wine, luxuriating in the present happiness of a simple meal: 'let Fortune storm and stir fresh turmoils: how much will she take off from this?' (*S*. 2.2.126–7). Horace's invitations to Maecenas command an equivalent commitment to the present (*C*. 3.8; 3.29). At the time of his narrow escape from a falling tree Horace vowed an annual feast to Liber, and on the event's first anniversary he calls Maecenas from *civiles super urbe curas* ('citizen cares about the city') to join him in celebrating (*C*. 3.8.17). Death's closeness in the past, of which the occasion itself is sufficient reminder, is calculated to impress Maecenas with its unpredictable certainty in the future. To devote one's time exclusively to national plans, Horace intimates, is to take part of life for the whole, to lose the present for a hypothetical future.[9] In summoning his patron to a banquet Horace does not so much belittle civic responsibility as urge a higher one, to present life itself:

> neglegens, ne qua populus laboret,
> parce privatus nimium cavere et
> dona praesentis cape laetus horae ac
>   linque severa.   (*C*. 3.8.25–8)

Neglect if the people suffer in any way, act like a private person and stop being overly careful and happily accept the gifts of the present hour and leave off austerity.

hostile, for Horace is no longer so eager for strife as he was in the consulship of Plancus (25 ff.). Plancus was consul in 42 BC, the year of Philippi, where Horace fought under Brutus. The banquet thus conceals a playful reminiscence of something Horace wishes to seem only a youthful indiscretion, and reminds us of his removal from the past and allegiance to the present.

9 Cf. *C*. 3.29.25–48, and *C*. 2.11. In the latter the reminder of old age is explicit (5 ff.) and adds urgency to Horace's advice that Hirpinus join him in a country picnic, complete with wine, flowers, incense, music, and young ladies (13 ff.).

The ancient farmers are said to have propitiated *floribus et vino Genium memorem brevis aevi* ('a spirit mindful of life's brevity with flowers and wine', *Epp.* 2.1.144), and the banquet on Horace's anniversary of near death is not the only one with such ritualistic overtones. In a scene which approaches a paradigm Chiron charges Achilles to drink and be happy in the present, even if it be the eve of death: *illic omne malum vino cantuque levato* ('there relieve all evil with wine and song', *Ep.* 13.17). Achilles is about to set sail for Troy, from which he can never return: *te manet Assaraci tellus* (13). In a sense some corner of a foreign field awaits everyone, and that awareness imports moral urgency to many of Horace's invitations:

> huc vina et unguenta et nimium brevis
> flores amoenae ferre iube rosae,
> dum res et aetas et sororum
>   fila trium patiuntur atra.[10]   (*C.* 2.3.13–16)

Have wine and unguents brought here and the blooms of the too-brief rose, while wealth and age and the black threads of the three sister Fates allow it.

One can hardly explain the fondly elegiac tone of *nimium brevis flores* except in symbolic terms. The roses suggest life's impermanence as well as its beauty, and Horace invites us to an apprehension of both. If the fact of death separates us from the gods, the fact of our knowing it distinguishes us from the animals. The country picnic becomes almost an epitome of human possibilities, embracing both an awareness of death, and a simultaneous freedom from all delays to present living:

> verum pone moras et studium lucri
> nigrorumque memor, dum licet, ignium
> misce stultitiam consiliis brevem;
>   dulce est desipere in loco.   (*C.* 4.12.25–8)

But put away delay and desire for gain and, mindful of the black fires while you can, mix brief silliness with wisdom; it is sweet to let reason go on occasion.

The Ode which ends with this summons began as a welcome to spring: *Iam veris comites, quae mare temperant,* | *impellunt animae*

---

[10] Cf. *C.* 2.11.13 ff. and Lucr. 2.29 ff., though the principal Epicurean contrast is between wealth and simplicity rather than present life and future death.

lintea Thraciae ('Now Thracian breezes, spring's companions that
soothe the sea, fill the sails'). The universal context suggests that
Horace invites a companion not so much to a specific meal as to life
itself. Other seasonal poems advance similar invitations, for a familiar symbolism made easy the transition from nature's changes to the
cycle of human life. In both literal and figurative terms Horace's
question was the same: if spring comes, can winter be far behind?
Diffugere nives... immortalia ne speres, monet annus ('snows have
fled... the year warns not to hope for immortality', *C.* 4.7.1 ff.).
The transition here explicit remains tacit in the Ode's companion
piece, where Spring Song—*Solvitur acris hiems* ('sharp winter is
dissolving', *C.* 1.4.1)—modulates abruptly into Cautionary Verses:

> pallida Mars aequo pulsat pede pauperum tabernas
>   regumque turres. o beate Sesti,
> vitae summa brevis spem nos vetat incohare longam:
>   iam te premet nox fabulaeque Manes
>
> et domus exilis Plutonia: quo simul mearis,
>   nec regna vini sortiere talis
> nec tenerum Lycidan mirabere, quo calet iuventus
>   nunc omnis et mox virgines tepebunt.   (*C.* 1.4.13–20)

Pale Death knocks with undiscriminating foot at paupers' huts and the
towers of kings. O blessed Sestius, the sum of brief life forbids us start on
a long hope: already night presses on you and the fabled shades and the poor
house of Pluto: as soon as you've gone there, you will not allot the gover-
norship of the wine with dice, nor will you admire tender Lycidas—all the
youth is hot for him now and soon the maidens will be.

The feast (*regna vini*) has become equivalent to life. The projected
sorrow for its passing (*nec sortiere*) implicitly invites Sestius to enjoy
it while he may: elegy conceals injunction.

Without directly exploiting a cyclical metaphor, *C.* 1.9 relies upon
a tentative correspondence between seasonal progression and man's
life. *Vides ut alta stet nive candidum Soracte* ('Do you see how Soracte
stands white with deep snow?'): the snow-capped peak before us
outlines the 'hoary old age' which the Ode foresees.[11] Horace's

---

11 *Canities* (17) has the primary meaning of a whitish or greyish color; the visual
effect is emphasized by its juxtaposition with *virenti*, 'blooming' or green youth. The
contrast suggests the contrast in Mt. Soracte itself, its greenery covered with heavy

response to the winter vision seems almost instinctive: *benignius deprome quadrimum Sabina* ('more generously pour four-year [wine] from a Sabine [jar]', 6–7). To drink wine while confronting Soracte is to seize the present, though remaining aware of its briefness:

> quid sit futurum cras fuge quaerere, et
> quem fors dierum cumque dabit lucro
> adpone, nec dulcis amores
>   sperne puer neque tu choreas,
> donec virenti canities abest
> morosa.   (*C.* 1.9.13–18)

Avoid asking what tomorrow will be and count as gain whatever days chance will give, and don't spare sweet love and dancing while you're young, so long as your vitality lacks crabby gray hair.

The famous *carpe diem* Ode (*C.* 1.11) reads like an explication of the Soracte Ode, which it follows, after one intervening poem:

> seu pluris hiemes seu tribuit Iuppiter ultimam
> quae nunc oppositis debilitat pumicibus mare
> Tyrrhenum: sapias, vina liques, et spatio brevi
> spem longam reseces. dum loquimur, fugerit invida
> aetas: carpe diem, quam minimum credula postero.
>   (*C.* 1.11.4–8)

... whether Jupiter has assigned more winters or this last which now wears down the Tyrrhenian sea with its pumice set over against it: show wisdom, strain clear the wine, and prune back your long hope to a brief compass. While we speak, hateful age has fled: pluck the day, believing as little you can in the next.

Winter, now expressly significant of death, again challenges us—and again the answer is the same: 'show wisdom, strain clear the wine.' To accept death's unpredictability along with its inevitability is to free ourselves for commitment to the present, and wine becomes a token of that freedom and of that commitment.[12] Horace recognized that

---

snow, its flowing streams caking with ice (1–4). Cf. *C.* 4.13.12, where *capitis nives* is contrasted with blooming youth, *virentis* (6).

[12] *Vina liques* (6) may further suggest the clarity of allegiance to the present, as opposed to the obscure prophecies of Babylonian astrologers. The name of the addressee, Leuconoë, is perhaps manufactured from λευκός and νόος, thus serving as a kind of plaintive injunction. The etymology is accepted by Mueller (1900), *ad loc.*

life was not only a gift but a calling. His invitations command not an easy oblivion, but an apprehension of the present's urgency. The vision of a long day's dying had pushed Catullus to perhaps his most famous protestations:

> Vivamus, mea Lesbia, atque amemus
>
> .   .   .   .   .
>
> soles occidere et redire possunt:
> nobis cum semel occidit brevis lux,
> nox est perpetua una dormienda.
> da mi basia mille, deinde centum,
> dein mille altera ...   (5.1, 4–8)

Let us live, my Lesbia, and let us love ... suns can set and return: when once short light has set for us, we must sleep one long perpetual night. Give me kisses—a thousand, then a hundred, then another thousand ...

Though meditated rather than impulsive, and general rather than specific, Horace's banquet invitations similarly voice a strong *vivamus*. Wine, incense, flowers, music, and complaisant girls are often called forth, as all the senses unite in the face of the ultimate blankness of *pallida Mors* ('pale Death').

Since the banquet has such associations for Horace, we may better understand why wine locked into cellars should be a favorite symbol for the failure to fulfill oneself in the present. With three hundred thousand jars of Falernian under lock and key a miser drinks vinegar:

> filius aut etiam haec libertus ut ebibat heres,
> dis inimice senex, custodis?   (*S.* 2.3.122–3)

Old man, enemy of the gods, do you hoard this so your son or even a freedman heir may drink it?

Avarice is the most pernicious of vices (*S.* 2.3.82) in that it systematically denies man's mortality.[13] Invective becomes elegy in the Odes, but the accusation remains:

---

[13] The continual land confiscations and huge constructions of the rich drew Horace's attack (*C.* 2.18.16 ff.; 3.24.1 ff.) primarily because they evidenced an arrogant refusal to recognize death. (The usual view holds that Horace's egalitarian sympathy for the evicted tenants was all important; see Carlsson (1944), 15 ff.; Mendell (1950).) *Sepulcri immemor struis* (*C.* 2.18.18–19): the rich man's disdain of

> absumet heres Caecuba dignior
> servata centum clavibus et mero
> tinguet pavimentum superbo
> pontificum potiore cenis.   (*C.* 2.14.25–8)

A more worthy heir will drink the Caecuban, kept under a hundred keys, and will stain the floor with proud wine—better than the priests' feasts.

The heir is worthier simply because he does not guard the wine with a hundred keys. Even in wasting it he displays a non-inherited awareness that life continually flows away. The miser's self-denial is actually improvidence. He neglects the present for a never-to-be-realized future: his life is diminished, not fulfilled.[14]

A banquet might equally well invite a Maecenas from his plans (*C.* 3.8 and 3.29) and a Plancus from his fears (*C.* 1.7), an Aelius from his research (*C.* 3.17) and a Pompeius from his memories (*C.* 2.7); it summons Achilles (*Ep.* 13), Dellius (*C.* 2.3), Vergil (*C.* 4.12), Sestius (*C.* 1.4), Hirpinus (*C.* 2.11), Thaliarchus (*C.* 1.9), and Leuconoë (*C.* 1.11) from whatever delays their plucking the flower of the moment.[15] Chloris, who refuses the present for her memory of the past (*C.* 3.15), or a miser, neglecting the present for some future heir, are the only ones untouched by Horace's logic. In addressing himself to these various situations Horace appeals to the authority of no doctrinaire scheme. Unembarrassed by the definitive austerity of allegory, his poems suggest a more evocative symbolism, of which he had guaranteed the terms as early as the first Satire:

> inde fit ut raro, qui se vixisse beatum
> dicat et exacto contentus tempore vita
> cedat uti conviva satur, reperire queamus. (*S.* 1.1.117–19)

So it rarely happens that we may find someone who says he lived blessed and content with his allotted time departs from life, like a sated guest.

---

the natural boundary between land and sea (20 ff.) is an emblem of his blindness to nature's final boundary of death. Such buildings suggest the same thing as the Satires' more colloquial symbol of storing wine in cellars.

[14] Cf. *Epp.* 1.5.12 ff.; 2.2.191–2; *C.* 4.7.19–20. *Epp.* 2.2.134 uses as an example of healthy wisdom a man who does not become frantic if the seal of a flask is broken.

[15] We should preserve the horticultural metaphor in *C.* 1.11.7–8: 'prune down long hope . . . pluck the day.' The overtones of inevitable natural decay add weight to the injunction. Cf. *C.* 2.11.9.

Life itself is a banquet, which at death we leave. To the Lucretian image (*De Rer. Nat.* 3.938–9) Horace gives a characteristic emphasis. Where Lucretius found difficulty in persuading the full man to leave graciously (*cur non ut plenus vitae conviva recedis?* 'why do you not leave like a guest sated with life?' 3.938), Horace proclaims how few (*inde fit ut raro*) there are who may be called full, and the preponderance of invitations over banishments is eloquent of his real concern. The present, he saw, was for most people a luxury. The effort to persuade men of its availability dictated some of his finest verse, and in the banquet he found an image to command our imaginative allegiance.

'Did Horace Woo the Muse with Wine?'[16] Although the love affair—that with the Latin language itself—is the only one we can be sure was real, Horace seems to have neglected the poet's traditional enticement to his heavenly mistress. As confidence in a definable source of poetic genius had faded, intoxication had become an increasingly acceptable substitute for inspiration, until it was finally institutionalized by the so-called 'wine drinkers' (*oinopotai*),[17] Horace did not combat their belief professionally, as did the 'water drinkers' (*hydropotai*), who seem to have maintained that mounting the Muses' chariot was only a more august confession of being on the wagon.[18] Yet Horace's fondness for contemporary *oinopotai* is not marked, nor is his sympathy for *male sanos poetas* ('not right sane') pronounced.[19] *Adde poemata . . . quae si quis sanus fecit, sanus facis et tu* ('Include poems . . . which, if anyone makes in his right mind, even

---

[16] Such is the sub-title of an article by McKinlay (1946). See this article for an exhaustive treatment of the subject, and for references to works on specialized topics.

[17] Cratinus was apparently the first to be known for his tippling; see Aristophanes' *Pax* 700 ff.; *Anth. Pal.* 13.29. Homer, Archilochus, Alcaeus, and Aristophanes were later compelled into the same category (Athenaeus 428F, 628A), and Sophocles' puzzled admiration of Aeschylus' unaccountable genius degenerated into a belief that he composed his tragedies when drunk (Ath. 428F). Cf. Ovid, *Met.* 7.432–3; Propertius 4.6.75. Representative *oinopotai* would be poets like Antipater of Thessalonica, Nicaenetus, and Antigonus. See Lewy (1929), 46 ff.

[18] Callimachus contemptuously termed Cratinus μεθυπλήξ (fr. 544, Pfeiffer) and was attacked in turn by the *oinopotai* for his prohibitionist instincts. See *Anth. Pal.* 9.406; 11.20; 11.31; 11.322; 13.29, and Sperduti (1950), 222 ff.

[19] *Epp.* 1.19.3–4. In this Epistle Horace does not, as B. Otis (1945), 179, n. 8 seems to imply, endorse a contemporary emulation of ancient poets' fabled drinking. Cato's

do you', *S.* 2.3.321–2). Damasippus' ironic reproach reminds us of the critical stance Horace maintained. It was his triumph to banish the *demens poeta* ('crazed poet') to some other Elysium, and to establish bitten fingernails rather than a roIling eyeball as poetic credentials.[20] The two Odes professing themselves written in a Dionysiac frenzy (*C.* 2.19 and 3.25) are remarkably calculated compositions, and no one to my knowledge has seriously suggested that Horace was ever incapable of treading a perfect line on poetic feet.

It is nevertheless Horace himself who draws an analogy between poet and Bacchant, and since the relation is not the traditionally ecstatic one, his association of the two figures becomes the more important. The poet is termed a *cliens Bacchi* ('client of Bacchus', *Epp.* 2.2.78), and in the opening Ode Horace invokes the Bacchic emblems as best able to convey his private sense of the poet's calling:

> me doctarum hederae praemia frontium
> dis miscent superis, me gelidum nemus
> nympharumque leves cum Satyris chori
> secernunt populo...   (*C.* 1.1.29–32)

Ivy, the prize of learned brows, mixes me with the gods above, the cool grove and the light dances of the nymphs with Satyrs shelter me from the masses...

Bacchus was a god of fertility (*fertili Baccho, C.* 2.6.19), and by invoking him Horace conveys primarily a sense of the poet's own mysterious creativity. Yet he conceives of Bacchus in a more specialized way. What are the attributes he emphasizes? How are they realized in the work of Bacchus' client, the poet? And finally, what have they in common with the significance Horace attributes to wine?

---

virtue is not available to those who ape his costume (12 ff.), nor is poetic skill attained by imitating a probably fabulous element in the poet's social life. Compare Horace's scorn for those trying to become poets by conforming to a popular tradition of the poet's madness and uncouthness (*A.P.* 295 ff.).

[20] Though Horace accepts the traditional balance of *ars* and *ingenium*, it is the former which he goes on to emphasize (*A.P.* 408–18): the very fact that he wrote the Epistle to the Pisos indicates his conviction that poetry involved an *ars* which could and should be taught. For his insistence on conscious and careful writing see *Sat.* 1.4.9 ff.; 1.10.1; 1.10.50 ff.; *Epp.* 2.1.165–7; 2.2.122.25; *A.P.* 289–94; 379 ff. Cf. Kroll (1924), 38 ff.; Howald (1948), 83 ff.

As wine proved more often a blessing than an evil, the wine god represents a civilizing rather than a destructive force. Like Castor and Pollux, Hercules, Romulus, and Augustus himself, Bacchus is honored as divine for his services to mankind (*C.* 3.3.13). He aligns himself with the forces of order by joining in the defeat of the rebellious giants (*C.* 2.19.21 ff.). The tigers he has tamed and yoked to his chariot (*C.* 3.3.13–15) demonstrate his civilizing influence: Horace does not permit us to doubt that this is the meaning of Orpheus' similar accomplishment (*A.P.* 391 ff.). Bacchus also shows his power by mastering Cerberus (*C.* 2.19.29–32).[21] In subduing the underworld monster, the patron of poetry might almost suggest an emblem of the creative process itself, an imposing of form upon chaos, of—in the terms of Coleridge's famous definition—order upon emotion. But the scene issues a more immediate appeal. It suggests a kind of Gigantomachia in miniature, civilization's conquest of a brute world without purpose or hope.

In an invocation to the lyre, Horace attributes to it the very powers which he associates with Bacchus:

> tu potes tigris comitesque silvas
> ducere et rivos celeres morari;
> cessit inmanis tibi blandienti
>   ianitor aulae,
>
> Cerberus, quamvis furiale centum
> muniant angues caput eius atque
> spiritus taeter saniesque manet
>   ore trilingui.   (*C.* 3.11.13–20)

You can lead tigers and companionable woods and delay the swift streams; huge Cerberus, the guard of the hall, yielded to your coaxing, though a hundred snakes buttress his raving head and foul breath and gore ooze from his three-tongued mouth.

Orpheus by his poetry imposes calm upon violence. Horace imagines Sappho and Alcaeus as similarly dispensing peace upon the underworld. At their songs Prometheus and Tantalus have a respite from

---

[21] Horace may imagine Bacchus as conquering Cerberus by means of a horn of wine. This is the meaning given to *aureo cornu decorum* (*C.* 2.19.29–30) in the editions of Shorey (1898), Moore (1902), Smith (1903), and Villeneuve (1927), though see Kiessling and Heinze (1955), *ad loc.*

suffering, while Cerberus, and the snakes in the Furies' hair, are momentarily frozen into stillness (*C.* 2.13.29 ff.). The Odes breathe a conviction of the poet's ability to command harmony about him, in the manner of Bacchus himself. Where Bacchus actually fought beneath Jove's aegis (*C.* 2.19.21 ff.), Horace at least celebrates the victory, and the fourth Roman Ode records the downfall of the Giants: *vis consili expers mole ruit sua* ('force without wisdom rushes to ruin on its own weight', *C.* 3.4.65). Poetry unites with politics in a hymn to *consilium* ('wisdom'), which the Muses are thought of as bestowing upon Caesar: *vos lene consilium et datis et dato gaudetis almae* ('you, nourishing Muses, give gentle wisdom and rejoice in the gift', 41–2). The introductory stanzas (1–36), in which Horace dons the robes of a traditional *vates* ('bard') declare his right to speak in the Muses' name, and thus encourage us to realize that the poem itself embodies the *lene consilium* which the Muses recommend to Caesar.[22] Again, an important poem to Octavian, placed second in the collection, implores a return to political serenity: *Iam satis terris nivis atque dirae grandinis misit Pater* ('now enough snow and dire hail has Jupiter sent to earth', *C.* 1.2.1). Mercury (*almae filius Maiae*, 'son of nourishing Maia', 42–3) is proposed as an avatar of Octavian (41 ff.). He embodies the wise restraint which the poem urges. A patron of poetry, like the Muses of the fourth Roman Ode, he too suggests a covenant between poetry and political harmony—a belief in the possible union of the two must have been a tacit prerequisite for the very conception of such national Odes. Faunus, often associated with Dionysus, seems to endorse Horace's conviction that the poet is mediator of violence. When Faunus visits the Sabine farm, pan-pipes signal a suspension of normal nature. Kids lose their fear of snakes and wolves, while the ground bears in abundance (*C.* 1.17.5 ff.). Tyndaris, if she join Horace in playing upon the lyre and drinking Lesbian wine, need fear no harm from the incontinent Cyrus (17 ff.). In the poetic estate peacefulness merges with creativity, as it does in the figures of the *almae Musae* (*C.* 3.4.42) and the *almae filius Maiae* (*C.* 1.2.42–3).

---

[22] Wilkinson (1946), 69 ff. rightly observes the note of sympathy for the fallen *monstra* on which the Ode ends. Paean for the victor unites with elegy for the fallen. The poet acts as a mediator, and the *lene consilium* he recommends includes mercy. Most editors see a reference to Actium in the Gigantomachia.

The social harmony which wine occasioned was but a small part of its significance, and Bacchus' civilizing influence does not exhaust his meaning for the poet. As a mortal made immortal by poetry (*C.* 4.8. 33–4), Bacchus approximates the role of the poet himself, made eternal by his art.[23] The analogy need not be precise to be effective, for Horace felt that the author as well as the subject of verse was caught in its immortalizing amber: *non ego... obibo nec Stygia cohibebor unda* ('I will not die nor will I be constrained by Styx's wave', *C.* 2.20.6 ff.).[24] Bacchus' conquest of Cerberus, and the underworld he epitomizes, ends the previous poem (*C.* 2.19.29 ff.). By that act the poet's inspiring deity seems to present credentials for his immortality as well as for his civilizing influence. The frozen stillness of Hades beneath the songs of Orpheus (*C.* 3.11.15 ff.) or of Sappho and Alcaeus (*C.* 2.13.29 ff.) guarantees the eternal validity poetry bestows upon the occasional, and reminds us of the poet's own triumph over death. When Faunus crosses the bounds of Horace's farm the supernal peace testifies not merely to the poet's ability to legislate harmony, but to his ambiguous mortality as well:

> nec Martialis haediliae lupos,
> utcumque dulci, Tyndari, fistula
>   valles et Usticae cubantis
>   levia personuere saxa.
>
> di me tuentur, dis pietas mea
> et musa cordi est.   (*C.* 1.17.9–14)

nor [will] the goats [fear] Mars' wolves, Tyndaris, whenever the vales and smooth rocks of reclining Mt. Ustica resound with sweet pan-pipe. The gods protect me; my devotion and Muse are dear to the gods.

Poetry and piety unite to insure the poet's divinity. Horace's protection in this life warrants his life hereafter. *Non omnis moriar* ('I will

---

[23] We should remember that the gods were divine preeminently by virtue of their immunity to death. Thus ἀθάνατοι when used as a noun means 'gods'. See Guthrie (1950), 115 ff.

[24] The boast has no real precedent in extant Greek literature. The fragment of Theognis on which it appears to be modelled (273 ff.) treats the same flight and immortal name, but significantly assigns them to the poem's subject, Cyrnus, and not to the poet himself. Cf. *C.* 3.30.6 ff. For the more traditional idea of the poet's ability to immortalize others see *C.* 3.13; 4.8; 4.9.

not die in entirety', *C.* 3.30.6): only the poet stands immune to the threat of years, and remains invulnerably of the present. Immortality is the dimension of an eternal present. Wine represents a seizing of the present, a freedom from contingencies of past and future alike. Bacchus adumbrates the poet's hold upon an eternal moment, and his apotheosis into the ultimate freedom of immortality. Meditating the *aeternum decus* ('eternal honor') with which he will decorate Caesar (*C.* 3.25.5), Horace appeals to Bacchus and to nature itself in the effort to define his feelings:

> non secus in iugis
> exsomnis stupet Euhias,
>   Hebrum prospiciens et nive candidam
> Thracen ac pede barbaro
>   lustratam Rhodopen, ut mihi devio
> ripas et vacuum nemus
>   mirari libet.   (*C.* 3.25.8–14)

Just as the wakeful Bacchante stands in awe on the ridge, looking out over the Hebrus and Thrace, white with snow, and Mt. Rhodope, traversed with barbarian foot, so it pleases me to admire the banks and empty grove off the beaten track.

The crystal stillness of nature recalls that of the underworld, frozen by the voices of Orpheus and Alcaeus, or that of the Sabine farm, touched by the pan-pipes of Faunus. Like the Bacchant, in nature but preternaturally aware, the poet, while of this world, is yet allied to another. As the Bacchant becomes one with the god, the poet becomes identified with his poetry: 'how can we know the dancer from the dance?' A mortal, he creates *aeternum decus* ('eternal honor'), freeing his subjects, and ultimately himself, from the equivocations of existence. To describe the human state is in some sense to transcend it, and if poetry is by definition an artifice, it is yet, as Yeats has reminded us, an 'artifice of eternity'.

The relation of a critic to a poet tends to be that of some uneasy Procrustes, confronted by a Proteus. Yet if Horace's imagination defies any rigorous arrangement, we may at least define the shapes it seems to assume. Wine, a *verecundus Bacchus* ('modest Bacchus', *C.* 1.27.3), promotes harmonious interchange among men: Bacchus, as god of poetry, symbolically enacts the poet's civilizing influence.

Wine also represents a commitment to present life, a freedom from temporal delays: Bacchus suggests the poet's freedom from the temporal world itself, and his commitment to eternal life. The relations between these aspects of wine and the wine god are felt rather than formulated, obscure rather than precise. Horace appears to be seeking a vocabulary to express feelings not susceptible to ordinary discourse. Wine, the banquet, the various gods, and the country itself, seem invoked in order to conceptualize something for which there was no ready language, and which in any case is perhaps best conveyed in semi-metaphorical terms. The various notions move in the solvent of a poetic consciousness, and we need not insist that they crystallize into a hard core of doctrine.

3

'Slender Genre' and 'Slender Table' in Horace

Hans Joachim Mette

I

Ode 1.1 is a programmatic poem. After a long priamel (3–28), which includes a scene whose lifestyle corresponds to the γένος λεπτόν (19–22), Horace specifies the object of his poetry with the words: *me gelidum nemus nympharumque leves cum satyris chori secernunt populo* ('A cool grove and light-footed choruses of nymphs and satyrs separate me from the people', 30–2). The grove is the 'place' of the γένος λεπτόν. Separation from the people returns as a motif at *Ode* 2.26.39–40 (*malignum sperne volgus*, 'spurn the grudging crowd') and 3.1.1 (*odi profanum volgus et arceo*, 'I hate the profane crowd and hold it off'). It comes, as we know, from Callimachus, *Epigr.* 28 (2.86 Pfeiffer). 1–4: 'I detest the great epic ['the cyclic poem'] and take no pleasure in the broad street that leads now this way, now that; I hate the boy with crowds of lovers and do not drink from the public spring; I have an aversion to everything intended for the people.' In the prologue to the *Aitia* (fr. 1. 1–12 Pfeiffer), we find the term 'continuous poem' (ἄεισμα διηνεκές, 1.3; Horace's *carmen perpetuum*, *Ode* 1.7.6). The phrase αἱ κατὰ λεπτὸν <ῥήσιες> ('<speeches> in the canon of elegance', 1.11) may refer to Minmnermus, but expresses the spirit of Callimachus' own poetry[1] and applies

---

[1] Cf. fr. 1.24–6: ...τὴ]ν Μοῦσαν δ᾿ ὦγαθέ, λεπταλέην· | [...] καὶ τόδ᾿ ἄνωγα, τὰ μὴ πατέουσιν ἅμαξαι | τὰ στείβειν (see Reitzenstein 1931: 25–40; Wimmel 1960: *passim*).

at *Epigram* 27 to the 'little' poems of Aratus in opposition to his 'Hesiodic' *Phaenomena*. In his programmatic poem, therefore, Horace confronts a choice in a Callimachean vein between the γένος ὑψηλόν ('high style') with its connotations of epic and tragedy (Pindar has not yet entered his field of vision), and the γένος λεπτόν ('elegant style'). He devotes himself to the latter.

Ode 1.6 is built on this opposition. Horace refers to Agrippa and Varius in a 'literary letter', which was naturally preceded by a genuine letter of refusal. Agrippa has approached the poet to 'entice' him with a request to glorify his and the young Caesar's exploits in an epic represented by the *Iliad* (Achilles, 5–6; Ares, Meriones, Diomedes, 12–16), the *Odyssey* (7) and the Cycle (house of Pelops, 8). Horace declines. In line 9 *tenues grandia* are mutually exclusive keywords; in lines 17–20 there appear the essential ingredients of the 'elegant style': the symposium and eros. The typology is less fully elaborated in *Ode* 2. 12, a refusal for Maecenas, who also 'entices': the Punic Wars, the Battle of Lapiths and Centaurs, and Heracles' combat with the sons of Gaia, which are all subjects of the 'high style', conflict with eros as the theme of the 'elegant style', of *molles citharae* ('gentle lyres', 3–4). Similar again is *Ode* 4. 2: this time Horace turns down Iullus Antonius, saying he does not feel on a par with the poet of the exalted *genus* ('kind/style'), Pindar, who is uniquely master of dithyramb and hymn, of epinician and lament. He himself, being *parvus* ('small', 31), cannot compose like the swan, but only like the bee, who collects honey in the wood and on the hillslopes of Tibur, the locus of the 'elegant style'. Close to *Ode* 4.2 is 4.3: it is not the high style of the epinician celebrating victory in boxing at the Isthmian Games, in the chariot-race, nor that of an encomium for a victor in war, crowned with the 'laurel of the Delian god', that has made Horace famous, but—again—the water and the woodland of Tibur (10–12). Compare also: *ne parva Tyrrhenum per aequor vela darem* ('lest I take my small sails over the Tyrrenian sea', *Ode* 4.15.1–4), where the 'sea' implies the 'high style'; *neque parvum carmen maiestas recipit tua* (Augustus'), *nec*... ('nor can your <Augustus'> majesty receive a small poem', *Epist.* 2.1.257–8).

Ode 1.7 significantly unfolds along the same antithesis. The priamel (1–11) picks up Sappho fr. 16.1–4:

οἰ μὲν ἰππήων στρότον, οἰ δὲ νάων φαῖσ᾽ἐπὶ γᾶν μέλαιναν ἔμμεναι
κάλλιστον, ἔγω δὲ κῆνῦττω τις ἔραται

Some say the cavalry, some the infantry, some an array of ships is the most
beautiful thing on the black earth, but I say it is whoever you love.

Sappho's priamel rejects as 'supreme value', and therefore as subject
of her poetry, the 'fighters on horseback and on foot and ships', that
is, the themes of the great epics, the *Iliad* and the *Odyssey*: she
declares the most beautiful thing, and therefore the object of her
poetry, to be eros. Just so does Horace repudiate the great themes of
the *carmen perpetuum* ('continuous song', 6) that would sing the
praises of cities with an exalted mythology: Rhodes, Mytilene,
Ephesus, Corinth, Dionysus' Thebes, Apollo's Delphi and valley of
Tempe, the city of Athena who 'invented' the olive, Hera's Argos, the
cities of Mycenae and Sparta—the ruling seats of Agamemnon and
Menelaus—Larisa, Achilles' home. Here, he declares his poetry's
concern in a paradigmatic choice: Tibur, the home of his addressee
Munatius Plancus, is 'off the beaten path' in Callimachean wise. It is
introduced in lines 12–14 with the typical attractions of the *locus
amoenus* (spring, river, wood, streams), which in turn enables the
'undisturbed enjoyment of wine' at the symposium, a typical theme
of the 'elegant style'. Horace has Teucer 'flee' (22) as a life choice
appropriate to the stylistic level of this literary kind, whereas he calls
the epic Achilles *cedere nescius* ('not knowing how to yield', *Ode*
1.6.6).

In *Ode* 2.1, Horace's encomium to Asinius Pollio, he consciously
abandons the stylistic level of the 'elegant style' and approaches that
of the 'grand'. In consequence, at lines 37–40 he calls back his Muse:
let her return with him to 'the grove of Aphrodite'. Only in appearance is he concerned simply with the opposition between Simonides
of Ceos' lament-poetry and his own poetry's *ioci* ('jokes') and *levius
plectrum* ('lighter plectrum'). This trope is even more clearly present
in the middle of the Roman Odes. *Ode* 3.1.9–48, at least according to
its topic, cannot have belonged to the sequence's original conception.
Horace is manifestly conscious that with this cycle, as with the
Carmen Saeculare and other related odes, he is crossing the boundary
between the two styles. And so he uses once more, at *Ode* 3.3.69–72, a

break-off formula: he calls back his Muse, saying that the lofty subject is inappropriate for the *iocosa lyra* ('joking lyre'). It does not fit his Muse to present the subject-matter of the 'high style' in the 'elegant style', that is, 'to make great things slim with small modes' (*magna modis tenuare parvis*).

II

Ode 2.16 emerges as an immediate, nearly essential link between the 'elegant style' and the *mensa tenuis, parva, pauper* ('slender, small, restrained table') of Horace's lifestyle. This lifestyle is indicated by *vivitur parvo bene* ('we live well on little', 13), by the paradigm of the *paternum . . . in mensa tenui salinum* ('father's salt-cellar on a slender table', 13–14), by Moira's gifts to Horace, which are bundled together with the 'elegant style': these gifts are the *parva rura* ('small rustic estate') on the one hand, the *spiritus Graiae tenuis Camenae* ('slender spirit of the Greek Muse') and the capacity to 'spurn the grudging crowd' (*malignum spernere vulgus*; see above) on the other (37–40). Choice of lifestyle and choice of genre are for Horace the same thing: he is the poet of the 'elegant style', his life is confined to the *parva rura*, the *tenuis mensa*; genre and life are styled to match each other.

The theme of 'living on little' (*vivere parvo*, 1), of the moderate 'slender means' (*tenuis victus*, 50–5, 70–1), dominates *Satire* 2.2. To be sure the stylistic level of the *Satires* and in part that of the *Epistles* lies below that of the *Epodes* and *Odes*, but Horace does not deliberately parade this distinction. In the foreground of *Satire* 2.2 stands the antithesis between this 'means of living' (*victus*) and that of the 'crazed rich man' (*dives insanus*). In the same spirit, in *Ode* 1.20 Horace introduces the antithesis between 'inexpensive wine' (*vile vinum*) in 'moderate cups' (*modici canthari*) and the expensive wine from Cales. In *Ode* 1.31 olives, chicory, and mallows are opposed once again to the *vinum Calenum*. It is on this basis that *Ode* 2.18 is conceived: ivory and golden ceiling panels do not adorn Horace's house (1–8); he does not build proud villas out into the lake (cf. *Odes* 2.15, 3.1.33–7, 3.24.1–4), nor, like the ageing Faust, does he drive away 'Philemon and Baucis' (17–28); he stands in secure contrast to the wealthy and the proud man (10, 31; 36), as the poor man (10, 33, 39), whom Death overtakes no more quickly than the rich. So too in *Ode* 3.1.9–48 the poet is satisfied with his 'humble house' (22)[2] in his Sabine valley (47). In *Ode* 3.29, the poet invites the 'royal' Maecenas, whose seat is great Rome, to the 'tidy feasts of the poor under a small house god' (*mundae parvo sub lare pauperum cenae*, 9–16). Compare also *Epistles* 1.7.44–5: *parvum parca decent: mihi iam non regia Roma, sed vacuum Tibur placet...* ('sparing things befit the small: to me leisurely Tibur is pleasing, not royal Rome').

This is all thoroughly conscious, as conscious as the proud reference to his birth from a freedman father, e.g.: *Satire* 1.6.71–131 (the same motifs constantly recur); *Odes* 2.20.5–6, the closing poem of the first collection of *Odes*!; 3.30.10–14, the closing poem of the second collection!, and *Epist.* 1.20.20–2 (*me libertino natum patre et in tenui re*, 'me, born from a freedman father and in meagre circumstances'), the closing poem of the first collection of epistles!

Hence too is derived the 'golden mean' that in *Ode* 2.10 Horace expressed in his own forceful terms. 'Slender means' (*tenuis victus*), a 'slender table' (*tenuis mensa*), the limitation of desire to what is enough (*desiderare quod satis est*, *Ode* 3. 1. 25; cf. Aeschylus, *Ag.* 379 ff.) guarantee the 'middle course' between the storms of the high seas and the dangerous rocks of the shore, a life in the 'mean' between the squalor of the tumbledown shack and the envy-provoking splendour of a palace; for still it is true that, as Artabanos points out to Xerxes in Herodotus (7.10ε), tall pines are more often bowed by the winds, high towers fall more heavily, the topmost summits are struck by lightning. It is a very different mean that concerns Horace here from, say, that of high tragedy, which applies to the uncompromising greats: it does without great and admirable things, or exploits for display to the broad public (cf. *Epist.* 1. 10. 30–3, with Epicurus fr. 462 Usener), or 'long hope' (*spes longa*, *Ode* 1.4.15, 1. 11. 6–7). Its opposite is the 'brief sum of life' (*vitae summa brevis*), the 'brief span'

---

[2] Lines 21–4 are transferred from the exalted sphere of tragedy (Aeschylus, *Ag.* 773–4; there Dike, here *somnus*).

(*spatium breve*), and it obtains its surest footing in the 'small life' (*vita parva*).

For this 'small life' the appropriate vessel is the 'small style' (*genus parvum*), the γένος λεπτόν: the greatest part of Horace's poetry permits the observation that this great artist has managed to weave lifestyle and literary style into one.

4

How to End an Ode? Closure in Horace's Short Poems

P. H. Schrijvers

1. In the introduction to *Horaziche Lyrik*, V. Pöschl speaks of the Horatian ode as a whole (*ein Ganzes*) and of the closed character (*die Geschlossenheit*) of Horace's poems.[1] These qualifications correspond to terms from ancient poetics: ὅλον ('whole') and τέλειον ('complete') from Aristotle's *Poetics*, and *totum* and *unum* from Horace's own *Ars Poetica*.[2] In this study on closure in Horatian lyric, emphasis will fall on identifying how the poet enables his reader to experience the ode as a complete and finished whole. In her clear-sighted book, *Poetic Closure, A Study of How Poems End*,[3] Barbara Herrnstein Smith rightly underlines the fact that the feeling of totality, integrality, and plenitude provoked in the mind of a poem's reader is to a great degree produced by its ending. Reading a literary text can be described, from a psychological perspective, as a process of reader suspense that is constantly modified and revived by elements within the text—a process we continually desire to prolong, but that reaches its conclusion at the text's end by a state of satisfaction and assuagement.[4] Techniques for concluding a poem and making it a whole occur at various textual levels: typographic, phonic, syntactic (levels

---

[1] Pöschl (1970), Introduction 9–10.
[2] Lausberg (1960), section 1191 ff.
[3] Herrnstein Smith (1968).
[4] Herrnstein Smith (1968) borrows the notions of reader expectation and satisfaction from Gestalt psychology, see 33 ff. Analogous concepts are already in Barwick's

of form), and semantic (a level of content). Here, I leave aside the formal means of achieving closure to concentrate on the level of poetic content.

2. Before analysing the ends of Horace's *Odes*, let me first make some preliminary remarks. The study of how Horace, as poet or transmitter, ends his odes calls for an analysis of the reader's perception of the poem as hearer or receiver. It is useful, with Herrnstein Smith,[5] to define a poem's structure as the sum of principles generating the poetic discourse as published by the author and received (read) by the reader—namely, from one end to the other. A poem's structure thus depends on the principles governing the sequence of its elements. This kind of definition has the advantage of highlighting the temporal and dynamic properties poetry shares with music. In these two domains, the process of reception unfolds in a linear progression over time. This definition is entirely different from that proposed by, for example, Wellek and Warren[6] or by Jakobson,[7] for whom a poem's structure resides in an ensemble of interrelations (or, to use Jakobson's own terminology, of 'classes of equivalence') between a poetic text's constitutive elements. My definition concerns the dynamic structure of a poem that begins, sustains, and finishes an aesthetic and cognitive process in the mind of the reader.

Regarding the different semantic techniques for completing an ode, I will make a distinction, following Herrnstein Smith, between structural means, which derive from a poem's generating structure, and non-structural means. In the first case, the end is determined by what precedes it in the poem, which, so to speak, begins to end from the outset. In the second case, the last verses of a poem are characterized by certain elements (*terminal features*) that produce a final effect more or less independent of the particular poem's generating structure.

(1959: 3–4), observations, which derive in turn from Lessing's theory of epigram, namely *Erwartung—Aufschluss.* See Herrnstein Smith (1968), 198–9.

[5] Herrnstein Smith (1968), 4.

[6] Wellek and Warren (1956), *passim.*

[7] Jakobson (1968), 350–77; Jakobson and Lévi-Strauss (1962); cf. also Posner (1969).

Finally, let me signal that I discuss Horace's different methods of closure in an analytic order, even though these methods often combine in different ways in individual odes.

3. I distinguish four categories of structural closure. The feeling of completion experienced by the reader at a given poem's end may be produced by logical structure (section 3.1), temporal structure (3.2), spatial structure (3.3), or cyclical composition (3.4).

3.1. Logical structure. In a famous article,[8] R. Heinze enumerates certain characteristic and fundamental traits where the Horatian ode differs from most of the so-called lyric poems of the nineteenth and twentieth centuries. The Horatian ode most often consists of an address to one, or sometimes many personages, almost always mentioned in the poem, where the poet gives counsel or an exhortation (paraenetic ode), formulates a demand or makes a vow (invitation, hymn, prayer), composes praise or criticism of the named personage, or formulates and defends a certain decision vis-à-vis the addressee. In all these cases, the situation is what A. Kibedi Varga,[9] following Aristotle, has called the internal rhetoric between the poem's 'I' and 'you', a situation characterized by deliberation (advice), epideictic (praise/blame, hymn), or of a juridical nature (accusation, justification). When advice, prayer, decision, praise etc., are motivated within the poem, they give rise to a structure of argumentation. When the counsel, prayer etc. take shape at the end of the poem and arise from the preceding argumentation, they form a structural 'ending' that produces an impression of closure—in Aristotelian terms, τελευτή. The end of the poetic message results from what preceded it, and the reader does not wish for more and does not expect the poem to continue.[10] The counsel, prayer, or reasoned decision may occur at the end of a poem under different forms, for example:

Imperative: *desine*, 'stop', *Odes* 1. 23. 11; *desine, Odes* 2. 9. 17

Subjunctive: *redeas*, 'may you return', *Odes* 1. 2. 45; *absint*, 'let them be absent', *Odes* 2. 20. 21

Future Indicative: *amabo*, 'I will love', *Odes* 1. 22. 23; *contrahes*, 'you will pull in', *Odes* 2. 10. 23

---

[8] Heinze (1960b), 172sqq. [Chapter 1 in this volume].

[9] Kibedi Varga (1970), 85sqq.; also Lausberg (1960), sections 59–65.

[10] Lausberg (1960), sections 443, 1194.

Rhetorical Question: *cur...permutem*, 'why should I exchange?', *Odes* 3. 1. 47

Such a conclusion, in the word's most proper sense, may have a generalized character in the form of a summary (*nil Claudiae non perficiunt manus*, 'there is nothing Claudian hands don't accomplish', *Odes* 4. 4. 73) or a maxim (*carpe diem, quam minimum credula postero*, 'pluck the day, believing as little as possible in the next', 1. 11. 8). Sometimes, as in *Odes* 1. 3, a poem's logical structure ascends gradually from a personal beginning (1–8) to a generalizing and final conclusion (*nil mortalibus ardui est*, 'nothing is hard for mortals', 37). Under the category of logical closure, we should also include poems beginning with a question and ending with a reasoned response (*quid dedicatum poscit Apollinem vates? quid orat*, 'What should a bard ask Apollo at his temple's dedication? What should he pray for?', *Odes* 1. 31. 1–2; *dones et, precor*, 'may you give, I pray, and...', 17–20). This is a very effective method for creating expectation and curiosity both in the poem's recipient (within the poem's internal rhetoric) and in the general reader (within the poem's external rhetoric).[11] Let us note that the logical closure of a line of argumentation fits well with cyclical composition. At the beginning of the poem, the interlocutor presents the poem's recipient with a conclusion in the form of a *demonstrandum,* whereas the poetic message ends with the repetition of *quod erat demonstrandum*. This kind of cyclical composition in fact occurs in Horace (*Odes* 2. 10), but not too often, given its didactic tone.

3.2. Temporal structure. Narratology distinguishes between the time of narration (*Erzählzeit*) and the time narrated (*erzählte Zeit*);[12] so for a short poem, we can distinguish between the time of singing, that is, the time necessary to recite or read the poem, and the time of the song (= the time of the represented object). Regarding time, we may distinguish, with the ancient philosophers and rhetoricians, between the *tempus generale* (in Greek: χρόνος)

---

[11] Eleven odes and seven epodes begin with one or more questions! For Propertius, see J-P. Boucher's remark on the elegies 'of simple construction': 'They often begin with a dedicatory address, with a question serving to set the theme' (1965: 354).

[12] Lämmert (1970), *passim.*

and the *tempus speciale* (in Greek: καιρός, in Latin: *occasio*). General time designates the environment, indefinite and of global duration, where existence unfolds inexorably in a process of change, and events and phenomena succeed one another; this time divides into past, present, and future. By particular time, I mean a delimited portion of general time, namely, a span of time that recurs periodically (a day, a season, a year), or without regularity (a human life, a war, a voyage, a banquet, a sickness, etc.).[13] For closure according to the time of the song, I propose four hypotheses based on a reading of Horace's *Odes*:

3.2.1. A feeling of closure is produced when, in a poem's temporal structure, the time of the song encompasses the three subdivisions of general time (past, present, future) and these subdivisions correspond to three sections within the poem. At the end of the poem they provoke a feeling of totality in the reader.

Odes 1. 4. 3 *neque iam*: past; 5 *iam*: present; 15 *iam*: future
Odes 4. 6. 1–30: past; 31–40: present; 41–4: future[14]

3.2.2. A feeling of closure is produced when, in the poem's temporal structure, the time of the song encompasses two subdivisions of general time, that is, the past and the future, and these two subdivisions constitute two sections of the poem as a whole. In this case, the present is not expressed in the poem, but is implied by the text in the present of poetic discourse re-enacted each time the reader reads the poem. The present takes place here in the time of singing, a special time renewed by each reading.

Odes 2. 7. 1–16: past; 17–28: future
Odes 2. 15. 1–10: future; 11–20: past
Odes 4. 15. 1–16: past; 17–32: future[15]

3.2.3. A feeling of closure is produced when the progression of the time of singing (reading the poem) is accompanied by a progression in the particular time of the song and the end of the time of singing coincides with a natural and normal end of the particular time

[13] Lausberg (1960), sections 385–9.
[14] See also *Odes* 1. 25 (1–4 present, 5–8 past/present, 9 ff. future), 3. 26 (1–2 past, 3–8 present, 9–12 future), 3. 30 (1–5 past, 6–14 future, 14–16 present), *Epod.* 2 (5–22 past, 23–4 present, 25–8 future) and Propertius 1. 12 (7 *olim*: past, 13 *nunc*: present, 20 *Cynthia finis erit*: future).
[15] Notice the symmetry in the temporal structure of *Odes* 2. 15 and 4. 15.

represented. So, there is an ideational progression of an *ordo naturalis* ending with a *finis naturalis*.

>*Epod.* 10. 1–2: leaving; 3–20: storm, shipwreck; 21–22: death
>
>*Odes* 1. 15. 1–8: beginning of the Trojan war; 33–6: end of the Trojan war
>
>*Odes* 3. 28. 5: *inclinare meridiem*, 'noon inclines'; 16: *dicetur nox*, 'night will be celebrated'

3.2.4. A feeling of closure is produced when a poem mentions one particular time at the beginning and another at the end. In this case, the beginning and end of the time of singing coincide respectively with a beginning and an unrelated ending in the time of the song. The association impresses a sense of totality and plenitude on the mind of the reader.

>*Odes* 1. 4 beginning: Spring; ending: death
>
>*Odes* 4. 7 beginning: Spring; ending: death
>
>*Odes* 4. 12 beginning: Spring; ending: death[16]

3.3 Spatial structure. Since I have distinguished between the time of singing and the time of song (section 3.2), an analogous distinction might be made between the space of singing, designating the typographic form of the poem, i.e., a scriptural space, and the space of the song. Indeed, the poet situates the object of song in space in various ways. For the space of the song, we may also distinguish *spatium generale*, an ideal place where our perceptions are localized that consequently contains all private extents, and *spatium speciale*, a place more or less well delimited where one may situate a given object. Since I would rather not speculate on the ancient scriptural space in Horace's *Odes*, and since the practice of recitation still existed, I will take the time and space of singing together. As for the feeling of closure produced by a poem's spatial structure, I offer the following hypothesis: this kind of effect occurs when the end of the space of singing (the poem's end) coincides with the totality or the extremities reached in the space of the song.

---

[16] See also 1. 10 beginning: the first times of the world (*hominum recentum*, 2); ending: death. For similar composition in a large-scale poem, see Lucretius, *De rerum natura*: beginning: spring; ending: the plague.

> *Odes* 2. 6.   1–4: the whole world (Gadès, the Cantabrians, the Syrtes)
>   5–8: Tibur
>   9–12: the river Gelasus
>   13–16: *ille . . . angulus*, 'that corner'
>   21–4: *ille . . . locus*, 'that place'
>
> *Odes* 3. 1.   9–44: the whole world
>   47–8: *valle . . . Sabina*,[17] 'the Sabine valley'

3.4. Ring composition. Often there is confusion over ring composition. One might understand it in E. Fraenkel's sense in his commentary on Aeschylus' *Agamemnon*:[18] sung or narrated time begins at a given moment x; the interlocutor goes back in time before x to return gradually to time x.

> *Odes* 1. 37.   1–4: *nunc est bibendum*, 'now it is time to drink'
>   5: *antehac*, 'before now'; progression in Cleopatra's story up to *nunc*,[19] 'now'

Ring composition can also designate the return of certain words and ideas from the beginning of a text at its end, a device studied by my compatriot W. A. A. van Otterlo.[20] An exhaustive study of this device, which is frequent in Horace, is outside the scope of this article. Let me merely cite one of the conclusions formulated by G. Hubert at the end of his thesis on *Word Repetition in Horace's Odes*: 'it is especially remarkable that in extremely many odes, the same word occurs at the beginning and in the last verse.'[21]

Moreover, I would like to signal Horace's habit of putting at the beginning and end of an ode sections pertaining to the same space of the song.

> *Odes* 1. 7.   1–11: Greece
>   21–31: Greece

---

[17] See also 2. 7 (Philippi, 9–16; *sub lauru mea*, 19 ff.), 2. 11 (the Cantaberians, Scythia, 1–4; *cur non sub alta vel platana vel hac pinu*, 13 ff.) and Virgil, *Ecl.* 1 (*fagus*, 1–5; *villae, montes*, 82; Leeman (1971), 212–13). The study by Troxler-Keller (1964) on *Die Dichterlandschaft des Horaz* gives an inventory of the constitutive elements of space in Horace, but does not take into consideration their structural function. On this point, there is still work to be done.

[18] Fraenkel (1950), ii. 119 (*ad* v.205).

[19] See the nice example of this procedure in Propertius 1. 3 (1–30: Cynthia asleep; 40–60: Cynthia, awakened, describes how she spent the night before she fell asleep).

[20] Otterlo (1944).

[21] Huber (1970), 131; see in general: Buchheit (1962), 35sqq.

Odes 2. 9. 1–4: *mare Caspium…Armeniis in oris*, 'the Caspian
sea…on Armenian shores'
20–5: *Niphaten…Medum flumen…Gelonos*, 'Niphates
…the Persian river…the Geloni'

4. Non-structural closure (elements producing a final effect more
or less independent of the poem's generating structure).

4.1 Closural formulas. The simplest and easiest way for the poet to
end a poem consists in letting the reader know he is stopping. In this
case, the poet ends his message by saying more or less explicitly that
he will stop speaking. The last stanzas of *Odes* 2. 1 (37–40) and 3. 3
(69–72) contain a 'break-off formula', as do the *Carmen Saeculare*
(73–6) and *Epodes* 2 (67–70). W. Schadewaldt coined the term
Abbruchsformel for an identical process in Pindar.[22] A formula of
this kind does not always have to be so explicit, nor need it occupy an
entire stanza. Here we have a form of literary game that admits of
variation and refinement. The poet may limit himself, in the poem's
final verses, to a single utterance that, by referring to the poetic
discourse of which the utterance is itself a part, possesses a 'meta-
literary' status with regard to the rest of the preceding poem. The
meta-literary and retrospective character of the utterance thereby
produces, in my opinion, an effect of rounding things off.

Odes 1. 21. 16: *vestra motus aget prece*, 'he will act, moved by your
prayer'
Odes 1. 28. 33: *precibus…inultis*, 'with prayers unavenged'
Odes 1. 32. 16: *rite vocanti*,[23] 'ritually calling'

Let us note that a closural formula may extend throughout the
entirety of a poem to serve as the conclusion of the book or collection
(*Odes* 2. 20 and 3. 30).

Furthermore, similar variability is possible in Horace's opening
formulas. These can be composed of a few simple words (*te
canam*, 'I will sing of you', *Odes* 1. 10. 5), or fill an ode's first stanza

---

[22] Schadewaldt (1928), 311sqq., an article cited by Fraenkel (1957), 239.
[23] See also 2. 4. 22 *laudo…*, 4. 5. 38 *dicimus*, 4. 6. 43 *reddidi carmen*, and 1. 11. 7
where the phrase *dum loquimur* implicates the conversation that the poem itself
supposes (see Nisbet and Hubbard [1970] *ad loc.*).

(*Odes* 1. 24, 3. 1), but may extend to eight stanzas (*Odes* 4. 9), or indeed to entire poems (*Odes* 4. 8).[24]

4.2. Sphragis. It is common in ancient literature to 'seal up' a poem or collection with autobiographical information about the poet at the poem's or collection's end. Literary ownership is, so to speak, established inside the literary work in question. E. Fraenkel rightly remarks of *Epistles* 20 at the conclusion of Horace's first book of *Epistles*, that a *sphragis* should strictly speaking contain the author's name.[25] A variant of this type occurs in *Odes* 4. 6, which ends: *reddidi carmen docilis modorum vatis Horati* ('I performed the song, being taught the modes of Horace the bard', 43–4).[26] A more general *sphragis* may omit the name of the author but include autobiographical information on his origins or physical stature (φύσις, *forma*), his lifestyle or character (τρόπος, *mores*).[27] Beyond the ancient *sphragis* tradition, we should keep in mind the allocutionary character of Horatian lyric and ancient poetry in general; this is why the ode and elegy are sometimes structurally analogous to the epistle, where a more personal opening and closing often frame a centre of more general interest.[28] In this last case, ring composition is obviously also relevant.

4.3. A closural, but non-structural effect is produced when the last lines contain an element that denotes or connotes 'end'/ 'limit' at either a superficial (concrete) or deep (abstract) level of the poem in question.

[24] Nisbet and Hubbard (1970), 254 (*ad* 1. 21): '... though Horace appears to ask for a song of praise, the song of praise is nothing other than the ode itself (for the same technique cf. 1. 26, p. 302, 1. 32, p. 359)'; Kiessling and Heinze (1957–8), 113, 135. For the tradition of certain formulas for beginnings and endings in ancient and medieval poetry, see Curtius (1954), 95–101 *s.v. Exordial- et Schlusstopik*.

[25] Fraenkel (1957), 362–3.

[26] Fraenkel (1957), 407.

[27] Fraenkel (1957), 363. The most general kind of *sphragis* in ancient literature has been studied by Kranz (1967) in a posthumous article, which, as far as I know, has gone remarkably unnoticed in recent research on the structure of Horace's *Odes*. *Sphragis* is defined in these terms: 'a characteristic beginning or ending, using the first person and also the name of the author, in a poetic work of greater or lesser extent. This beginning and end can be removed from the body of the poetic work, like a head or foot.' Kranz (1967: 27sqq.) cites *Odes* 1. 1. 29 ff; 1. 5. 13–16; 1. 14. 17–18; 1. 16. 22–8; 1. 31. 15–20; 1. 33. 13–16; 2. 16. 37–40; 3. 1. 45–8; 3. 13. 13–16; 3. 14. 25–8; 3. 19. 28; 4. 1. 29–32; 4. 3. 21–4; 4. 6. 41–4; *Epod.* 16. 66. I think we should add *Odes* 1. 6. 17–20; 1. 38 in its entirety; 2. 4. 21–4; 2. 20 in its entirety; 3. 2. 26–9; 3. 30 in its entirety; 4. 11. 33–4.

[28] See Allen (1962: 124) about Propertius 2. 23: 'It is presented as an ordered analysis of common experience, formally enclosed in a frame of personal statement...' For Horace, see *Odes* 1. 1; 1. 16; 1. 20; 1. 23; 3. 1; 3. 29; 4. 1; 4. 15; *Epod.* 9 and 14.

Herrnstein Smith (1968: 17 ff. 'closural allusions') rightly observes that many poems in European literature end by mentioning or alluding to what people universally experience as the final phase of a particular time. This observation inspired our hypothesis above on Horace's *Odes*. As Heinze remarks on *Odes* 3. 4. 80: 'It is noteworthy how often Horace's *Odes* end in underworld scenes, or thoughts of death and burial, the *ultima linea rerum* ("last line of things").'[29] Over ten poems mention or allude in their last lines to the term of human life.[30] To these may be added odes speaking in their last stanzas of night (*Odes* 1. 9. 19; 3. 7. 29),[31] winter *Odes* (1. 25. 19), old age (*Odes* 3. 14. 25–8), departure (*Odes* 3. 5. 53–6), a last farewell (*Odes* 1. 32. 13–16), or the end of an affair (*Odes* 1. 5. 15; cf. 3. 10. 19–20)—that is, the end point of a particular time.

4.4. A closural effect is produced when an ode's last lines contain three subdivisions that together constitute general time: past, present, and future.

Past: *Odes* 1. 7. 30: *o fortes peioraque passi*, 'you, brave men, who have suffered worse'
Present: 31: *nunc vino pellite curas*, 'now drive off your cares with wine'
Future: 32: *cras . . . iterabimus*, 'tomorrow we will cross again'

Past: *Odes* 1. 14. 17: *nuper sollicitum quae mihi taedium*, 'who were recently a cause of fretful worry for me'
Present: 18: *nunc desiderium curaque non levis*, 'now a desire and care not light'
Future: 20: *vites aequora*,[32] 'may you avoid the seas'

4.5. Closure is also produced when a poem ends with a categorical and authoritative affirmation suggesting definitive truth with the effect of the 'last word'. For instance, these odes end with a general, gnomic truth:

[29] Kiessling and Heinze (1957–8), 281.
[30] See *Odes* 1. 10. 17–20; 1. 13. 20; 1. 37. 29; 2. 6. 22–4; 2. 13. 33–40; 2. 18. 28–40; 2. 19. 29–32; 3. 4. 75–80; 3. 2. 51–2; 4. 9. 51–2; *Epod.* 13. 15; Martial 5. 20. 12–13; 10. 47. 13.
[31] For bucolic poetry, Curtius remarks (1954: 100): 'Theocritus 1, 5, and 18, Vergil, *Ecl.* 1, 2, 6, 9, and 10, and Calpurnius 5 all end with the sunset'; for satire, see also the end of Juvenal 3: *sed iumenta vocant et sol inclinat, eundum est* (316).
[32] See *Odes* 1. 16 (*me quoque . . . temptavit . . . misit*, 22–5: past; *nunc ego . . . quaero*, 25–6: present; *dum mihi fias . . . reddas*, 26–8: future), 1. 29 (*tu coemptos . . . libros Panaeti Socraticam et domum*, 13–14: past; *mutare loricis Iberis . . . tendis*, 15–16: present; *pollicitus meliora*, 16: future), 3. 6 (*aetas parentum, peior avis, tulit*, 46: past; 47 *nos nequiores*, 47: present; *mox daturos progeniem vitiosiorem*, 47–8: future).

Odes 1. 13. 17–20: *felices et amplius,* 'even more happy are those who...'

Odes 1. 24. 19–20: *sed levius fit patientia,* 'but it becomes lighter with patience'

Odes 4. 12. 28: *dulce est desipere in loco,*[33] 'it is sweet to let wisdom go in the appropriate circumstances'

Venus' prophecy on the fate of Europe (*tua sectus orbis nomina ducet,* 'one part of the world will take your name', *Odes* 3. 27. 75–6) and Horace's prediction about Bandusia (*fies nobilium tu quoque fontium, me dicente,* 'you also will become one of the noble springs, since I speak of you', *Odes* 3. 13. 13–16) are equally, to my mind, categorical and final assertions of this type. *Odes* 3. 30, ending the compendium, is in its entirety a collection of confident 'last words'.

4.6. A feeling of closure and of totality is produced when a poem's last lines contain, at either a superficial or deeper level, elements denoting or connoting the 'universal' or 'absolute': *all, everything, always, everywhere, null, nothing, never, nowhere,* etc., hyperbolic, superlative, or polar expressions, or exhaustive enumerations.

In her discussion of non-structural closure,[34] Herrnstein Smith limits her examples too simplistically to English poems where words like *all, everything, always, never,* etc. occur in the last stanza. In a study of closural techniques, we should, I think, start from notions or abstract representations, that is, from the deep level of the poem, out of which elements connoting 'totality', 'absolute', *'nec plus ultra'* ('no further'), etc. can emerge at a concrete textual level in different ways. In addition to words like *totus, omnis, semper, numquam,* etc. ('whole', 'all', 'always', 'never'), we should also consider, for instance, polar expressions (*polare Ausdruckweise*) as defined by U. von Wilamowitz:[35] 'In their attempt at fulsomeness and clarity, they express a general idea in some disjunctive form to indicate its altogether unlimited validity, and thereby frequently surpass the bounds of the truly thinkable.' Similarly, Seibourg remarks on how much the abstract notion of 'the whole' is concretized by Horace in his

[33] See *Odes* 2. 7. 27–8; 3. 2. 29–32; 3. 16. 43–4; 3. 25. 18–20; 4. 9. 46–52.
[34] Herrnstein Smith (1968), 182–6.
[35] In his commentary on Euripides' *Heracles*, Wilamowitz (1959), *ad* v. 1106.

poems.[36] In nine of Horace's *Odes*, a final polar expression concretizes the idea of a totality.[37] We should add to this group the odes ending with an exhaustive enumeration that 'makes the whole'[38] and hyperbole—both well recognized features.[39] Horace's efforts to concretize the totality or absolute character of the object of song are also manifest in his use of the superlative, or rather in its lack. In 'The Superlative in Horace',[40] Büchner rightly notes the restrained number of superlative forms in Horatian lyric compared to other Latin poets. In his emphasis on language as 'an expression of a particular disposition or personality', he offers a more or less psychological explanation for this fact: 'It is not Horace's way to heighten or magnify things'.[41] I doubt this explanation because devices of amplification occur all over in Horace (for example, disjunctive description by means of conjunctions *aut . . . aut, sive . . . sive, vel . . . vel*, or negatively *nec . . . nec . . . nec*).[42] The superlative is, however, not one of these devices, which, as Heinze rightly notes,[43] is not very concrete or evocative. Rather, he uses the well-known turn of phrase that joins a comparative to a whole in the ablative of comparison (type: *melle dulcior*, 'sweeter than honey'). There are five such turns of phrase in final position.

Odes 1. 18. 16: *perlucidor vitro* ('more translucent than glass')
Odes 1. 36. 20: *lascivis hederis ambitiosior* ('more clingy than playful ivy')
Odes 1. 33. 15: *fretis acrior Hadriae* ('harsher than the Adriatic')
Odes 3. 1. 42: *sidere clarior* ('brighter than a star')
Odes 3. 10. 17–18: *nec . . . mollior aesculo nec . . . mitior anguibus* ('not softer than oak nor milder than snakes')

These phrases' arch tone may be sampled in the alternate chants of *Odes* 3. 9, *donec gratus tibi* ('while I was pleasing to you'): *rege beatior*

[36] Siebourg (1910), 269.
[37] *Odes* 1. 6. 19; 1. 10. 19–20; 1. 31. 17–19; 1. 34. 12–16; 2. 3. 21–4; 2. 18. 32–40; 3. 12. 7–8; 4. 1. 38–40; 4. 5. 38–40.
[38] The notion of the 'whole world' is concretized in the last verse: *Odes* 2. 3. 21–8; 2. 8. 16–24; 4. 14. 41–52; 4. 15. 25–7.
[39] *Odes* 1. 1. 36; 1. 22. 17–24; 1. 27. 21–4; 1. 29. 10–16; 2. 5. 21–4; 2. 12. 21–8; 2. 13. 33–40; 3. 11. 45–8; *Epod.* 15. 17–24.
[40] Büchner (1962b), 23–37.
[41] Büchner (1962b), 23, 36–7.
[42] See the examples in Bo (1960), 174, 184 ff.
[43] At *Odes* 1. 18. 15 (Kiessling and Heinze p. 91).

('more blessed than a king 4); *clarior Ilia*, ('more famous than Ilia 8); *sidere pulchrior, levior cortice et inprobo iracundior Hadria*, ('more beautiful than a star, lighter than cork and more angry than the perverse Adriatic', 21–3)—the three last examples in the final stanza!

4.7. Having summarized cyclical composition and the *sphragis*, I can now formulate a general hypothesis about the different closural and unifying techniques available to Horace on the level of content: a feeling of closure is achieved when the poem's generating structure results in a logical conclusion, a notion of totality or limitation in time or space, or when the last lines contain, at either at a deep or superficial level, one or more elements denoting or connoting 'totality', 'limit', in sum, '*nec plus ultra*' ('no further').

4.8. Postscript. I would like to further note two categories of odes outside the analysis above that doubtless acquire a special charm from not ending in the aforementioned ways. First are the poems ending with a concrete and evocative picture.[44] There are futhermore odes that end with a surprise effect (ἀπροσδόκητον) because the ending already made by one of the techniques discussed above is interrupted by a last postscript on the poet's part. Such a postscript, precisely because of the break in the reader's expectation that the poem will not continue, enhances the emotional character of the ode's final movement.

> *Odes* 1. 35. 29–32: the hymn ends with the prayer *serves iturum Caesarem* ('may you preserve Caesar, who is about to go'); on the deep level is the idea of geographical totality (*in ultimos orbis Britannos . . . examen Eois timendum partibus Oceanoque rubro*, 'to the Britons, last of the world . . . a throng to be feared in Eastern parts and the Red Sea').

> 33–40: the poet's postscript (*eheu cicatricum*, 'alas for the scars') forms a closed unity because of its temporal structure (the three subdivisions of general time, cf. *Odes* 3. 2. 1 and 4.4): present: *pudet* ('we are ashamed', 33); past: *refugimus, liquimus, continuit, pepercit* ('we have fled, we have left, contained, spared',

---

[44] See *Odes* 1. 9. 21–4; 1. 17. 25–8; 2. 11. 23–4; 3. 18. 15–16; 4. 2. 57–60. For poems ending with a mythological scene (*Odes* 1. 28. 23–4; 3. 20. 15–16; 4. 7. 25–8; 4. 8. 29–34), adding to the ὕψος of the poem, see Fraenkel (1961), 55. For the same device in Propertius, see Boucher (1965), 357–8.

34–8); future: a second prayer containing ideas of spatial limits: ... *diffingas retusum in Massagetas Arabasque ferrum* ('may you reforge the iron against the Massagetae and the Arabians', 39–40).

Odes 4. 1. 29–32: the poem seems to end with a categorical decision *me nec femina nec puer... iuvat...* ('neither a woman nor a boy can please me').

33–40: the poet's postscript (*sed cur, heu, Ligurine, cur*, 'but why, Ligurinus, why?') ends with a series of polar expressions: *iam captum teneo, iam volucrem sequor te per gramina Martii campi, te per aquas dure, volubilis* ('now I hold you captive, now I follow you aloft over the lawn of the Campus Martius, I follow you, hard one, slipping through the waves', 38–40; cf. night in verse 37 *nocturnis ego somniis*, 'I, in nighttime dreams' and section 4.3 above).[45]

5. Some final remarks.

5.1. I should repeat the warning formulated at the beginning (section 2), that I have discussed Horace's diverse closural techniques one after the other according to an analytic order, even though, as I emphasize in my analysis of *Odes* 1. 35. 29 ff. and 4. 1. 29 ff. (section 4.8), these methods frequently combine in individual odes. This intensifies the closural effect and the final character of Horace's endings.

5.2. Let me anticipate an objection that, without doubt, has already arisen about my analysis of non-structural methods of closure, notably the use of *universalia* or *absoluta* ('universals' or 'absolutes') at a superficial or deep level in text's final lines (section 4.6). These methods are obviously not exclusive to final lines. A Horatian ode may commence, for example, with hyperbole (*Odes* 3. 24. 1 ff.); the

---

[45] The same method occurs, in my opinion, in *Epod.* 2: the first movement (1–66) culminates in day's end (see Kiessling and Heinze at 61: 'three sharply and progressive images of evening'). The closural effect is interrupted by the further unexpected closing formula: *haec ubi locutus fenerator Alfius...* (67–70). *Epod.* 2 raises the problem of the epigrammatic ending of some Horatian odes (*Odes* 1. 5; 1. 8; 1. 30; 3. 26; 4. 10). Let me cite here Herrnstein Smith (1968), 168: 'Puns, then, are neither closural not anti-closural in themselves, but they are common terminal features, because either they enhance the effect of other closural devices (setting them up through maximized instability), or their characteristic effect, wit, is maximal when combined with strong closure.'

division of a whole into parts or of a genus into species may come at a poem's centre (*Odes* 1. 2. 25 ff.; 1. 14. 3–15); an entire ode may even consist of a similar division (*Odes* 1. 1; 1. 12). To respond to these objections, let me recall that the *inventio* of a Horatian ode is sometimes relatively simple: the poem takes its scope by what the rhetoric of *inventio* called *partitio* and *divisio*.[46] Moreover, Wimmel has drawn attention to the frequent presence of series in Horace's *Odes* (*priamel*, *cumulatio* ('accumulation'), enumeration by disjunction, etc.).[47] Serial composition poses problems for the poet having to do not only with variation in the unity of the series' order, the persistence of the series' original function in its inherent abundance, and the traditionalism of the material, but also with producing closure for the reader's expectation of the series. Within a poem, a series or succession of ideas may end with the structural or non-structural methods treated above.[48] Nevertheless, the *motus auctifici* ('drive to increase') inherent in the whole poem's logical structure is stronger than the *motus exitialis* ('ending drive') of any one part of the poem.

5.3. A study like this, about Horace's *Odes*, invites expansion in three directions. First, phonic and syntactic analysis should complement the analysis of content in Horace. Second, the observations I have presented on different semantic methods of closure in Horatian lyric may be checked against short poems by other Latin authors. I have cited various examples from Propertius, Virgil, Martial, and Juvenal.[49] Third, in longer texts composed of different

---

[46] Lausberg (1960), sections 393, 669 ff.

[47] Wimmel (1954), 199–230.

[48] At *Odes* 3. 3. 65–8, Juno's speech ends with a categorical and hyperbolic affirmation; at *Odes* 3. 7. 21–2, the first movement ends with a superlative and hyperbolic expression: *scopulis surdior Icari voces audit*; at *Odes* 4. 2. 21–4: the series ends with mention of death; at *Odes* 4. 4. 69–72, Hannibal's speech ends by mentioning the destruction of Carthage; at *Odes* 4. 9. 26–8, the first movement ends with the 'whole world' that serves as a conclusion: *omnes inlacrimabiles urguentur*; at *Odes* 4. 15. 15–16, the first part ends with geographical totality: *imperi porrecta maiestas ab Hesperio cubili*.

[49] For Propertius, see Boucher (1965), 415, 424: 'often final distiches present a pointed maxim, a thought, focus on a detail independent of the preceding group of thought . . . generalization very often ends elegy'; see Williams (1968), 775. Let us note provisionally that Catullus (poems 1–60) uses the same methods of closure as Horace: logical conclusion (10; 23), prayer (34), question-answer (40), temporal totality (past, present, future 1; 8; 50), spatial structure (4), cyclical composition (6; 7; 16; 30; 31; 36; 52; 57), mention of the end of a special time (11), a final greeting (14; 46), maxim (22), hyperbolic expression (6; 12; 13), superlative idea (9; 38; 45; 48;

strands of thought, I observe something analogous to the series in Horace's *Odes* (section 5.2): subdivisions or paragraphs end in one of the various methods of closure discussed in this study.[50]

5.4. To close, I would like to underscore that certain concepts I have proposed (rhetorical context, logical structure, argumentation, general/special time) and certain closural techniques I have identified (the distribution of the time of song, the use of *universalia* and *absoluta*) bear a relation to ancient rhetoric (*inventio, dispositio, peroratio*).[51] It is heartening to see disappear in Nisbet and Hubbard on *Odes* 1 the anachronistic and romantic aversion to the rhetorical analysis of ancient poetry.[52] Nevertheless, once this aversion is overcome, we should not constrain rhetorical analysis to the categories of *elocutio* ('diction') and recognition of the *loci communes* ('commonplaces') used by the poet, important as they are. We should rather bring all of rhetoric into the analysis: especially important are *inventio* ('invention') and *dispositio* ('arrangement'). A discussion of possible links between rhetorical and literary theory exceeds the bounds of this article. I therefore conclude with an open ending.[53]

---

49), a concrete and evocative scene (11; 17; 25). He differs from Horace in the restricted number of instances of logical structure, the greater frequency of epigrammatic endings (12; 13; 32; 33; 39; 42; 44; 49; 53; 56; 58; 59), and a closural technique I have not noted in this study of Horace, namely, the exclamation (*a! tum te miserum malique fati*, 15. 17; see also 3. 16; 9. 10–11; 26. 5; 28. 14–15; 36. 18–20; 43. 8; 60. 5; and Horace, *Odes* 1. 28. 18: *a miser*).

[50] For closure within the run of ideas in Horace's *Ars Poetica*: 31 (gnomic character), 36–7 (categorical affirmation), 83–5 (exhaustive enumeration), 118 (amplification), 152 (notion of totality), 178 (summary), 201 (notion of totality), 219 (hyperbolic ending), 293–4 (apodictic advice), 330–2 (rhetorical question that serves as conclusion), 345–6 (categorical affirmation), 406–607 (conclusion), and 453–76 (evocative and hyperbolic scene at poem end). In the last part of Lucretius 5, the following marked closings should be noted: (834–6, 923–4, 1010, 1087–90, 1135, 1238–40, 1430–5, 1457; Lucretius also has the habit of completing a thesis with an amplified image, see Schrijvers (1970), 225–6). For Seneca's *Moral Epistles*, see Maurach (1970), 12 and n. 4: 'We should also heed this peculiarity, the stylistic demarcation of related thoughts through contained groups of sentences and special closural formulas.'

[51] The closure produced by *universalia* and *absoluta* (section 4.6 above) or logical conclusion, sometimes with summary, seems related to the rhetorical peroration (*contra*: Curtius 1954: 99).

[52] Nisbet and Hubbard (1970), Introduction, pp. xxiii–xxv.

[53] Schrijvers (1973) presents a first sketch of these relations; on this question, see now Cairns (1972), 31–3.

5

Occasion and Levels of Address in Horatian Lyric

Mario Citroni

1. It is usually acknowledged that Horatian lyric breaks distinctly from Neoteric poetry in both content and values. Horace, it is claimed, does not attribute overarching value to his own individual experience: his poetry intends to communicate messages transcending contingent experience, addressing the community and all humanity. We should therefore not expect to find in his poetry a significant role for private communication.[1] And yet, even in Horace, the sphere of private relations is not reducible to a fictional frame for universalizing contents: this sphere has its own reality, though it tends to accord with broader motivations and perspectives.

Even those who claim there is continuity with Neoteric experience in Horatian lyric have not emphasized the persistence of one of its most characteristic aspects: the poem is presented as communication within the private circle of the poet's relations. Forty-six poems (odes

---

[1] According to Fraenkel (1956), 281 f., (1957), 26, and *passim*, Catullus' poems have a double orientation (the general reader and a specific person), while Horace's always address the public; we should not suppose any signification directed to a more restricted circle. For Quinn (1959), 99, the Horatian addressee is merely the recipient of a poem written without particular reference to him. Also Kroll (1924), 232. As will appear throughout the notes, Fraenkel and other interpreters actually take into account case by case the individual addressee's point of view. [On private communication in Catullus, Citroni (1995), 57 ff.]

or epodes) involve real people, i.e., more than 38 per cent.[2] The
percentage is smaller than in Catullus,[3] but still high, since I have
excluded: female characters, male characters with Greek names and
among Roman names, Ligurinus,[4] poems generically addressed to
sodales[5] ('companions') or unnamed people,[6] poems involving Augustus and other members of the imperial family (Tiberius, Drusus,
Livia, Octavia) with whom Horace establishes not personal conversation but public homage.[7] A few special cases apart,[8] all poems
involve real friends, except those with erotic themes or political
(these are generally addressed to the community or the princeps;

---

[2] *Epodes* 1; 3; 9; 10; 11; 14; *Odes* 1. 1; 1. 3; 1. 4; 1. 6; 1. 7; 1. 18; 1. 20; 1. 22; 1. 24;
1. 26; 1. 29; 1. 33; 1. 36; 2. 1; 2. 2; 2. 3; 2. 6; 2. 7; 2. 9; 2. 10; 2. 11; 2. 12; 2. 14; 2. 16; 2.
17; 2. 18; 2. 20; 3. 8; 3. 16; 3. 17; 3. 19; 3. 21; 3. 29; 4. 1; 4. 2; 4. 7; 4. 8; 4. 9; 4. 11; 4. 12.
In eight cases, the person involved is not addressed in the second person: 1. 3; 1. 26;
1. 36; 2. 18; 3. 19; 3. 21; 4. 1; 4. 11 (in 3. 19 none of the characters addressed can be
identified with Murena; in 2. 18 Nisbet and Hubbard (1978), 289 f. think the '*tu*' of
lines 17 ff. alludes to Maecenas, to whom the ode refers without name at lines 10–14.
But Horace cannot place Maecenas in such a negative light. I do not agree with
Bradshaw's (1989) attempt to deny reference to Maecenas at lines 10–14. Rarely does
the same poem involve a greater number of real people: 1. 6; 1. 36; 2. 2.

[3] The percentages cannot be compared, since the female characters in Catullus
should probably also be considered real; these I exclude from Horace's statistics.

[4] We assume that for Horace, masculine Roman names refer to real people and
Greek to fictional characters, but the criterion is not secure. Although Ligurinus' name
is Roman, Horace conventionally lets erotic objects go incognito. In the gnomic odes,
however, characters are always recognizable. Dubious cases are 2. 14 (Postumus), 1. 9
(Thaliarchus), and two gnomic odes with female characters: 1. 11 and 3. 23.

[5] 1. 37; also 1. 27 and *Epodes* 13 (Shackleton Bailey acknowledges Housman's
suggestion to take *amici* as vocative of *Amicius*).

[6] Unnamed male characters: *Epodes* 4 and 6; female: *Epodes* 8 and *Odes* 1. 16
(*Epodes* 12 contains names of presumably fictional characters). 1. 38 and parts of
other odes are addressed to the poet's slaves. The anonymous addressee of 2. 5 is most
certainly the poet himself: otherwise the name Lalage, which in 1. 22 is a woman
loved by the poet, would be needlessly misleading.

[7] I have, however, included odes for other leaders of state: independent of their
real relation with Horace, they enter the odes as addressees of a communication
presented as private: Nisbet and Hubbard (1970), p. xxi.

[8] *Epodes* 2 and 5; *Odes* 1. 15 and 28 where the poet does not speak in the first
person. *Epodes* 4 and 6 are invectives against unnamed characters; 1. 38, the closing
poem of the book, is addressed to a *puer* ('slave boy'). The closing poem of book
3 addresses the reader (and invokes Melpomene). 1. 32 to a musical instrument and
3. 13 to a spring are classified as religious poems. The real exceptions are: *Epodes* 13, a
gnomic-sympotic poem, generically addressing friends and then a single unnamed
friend; two monologues, 1. 34 and 2. 13; *Odes* 3. 23 with a theme of religious ethics
addressed to Phidyle, a fictional character or at any rate unidentifiable even for
contemporaries.

see also 2. 15 with no addressee and 3. 24 to a diatribic 'you'), or religious (addressed to the gods or participants in ritual).

Thirty-two characters are certainly real (besides Augustus and family).[9] Many are *principes civitatis* ('leaders of state'): Maecenas, Agrippa, Asinius Pollio, Messalla, Plancus, Sestius Quirinus, Sallust, Proculeius, Dellius, Licinius Murena, Iullus Antonius, Paulus Fabius Maximus, Lollius; or well-known poets and literary figures: Virgil, Varius, Tibullus, Valgius, (and perhaps the jurist Alfenus Varus[10]). There are however many lesser known persons: literary figures such as Mevius, Aristius Fuscus, Quintilius Varus (commemorated at his death, and perhaps addressee of *Odes* 1. 18, unless Alfenus Varus is meant here) and others from the upper crust: Lamia, Quinctius Hirpinus, Grosphus, Torquatus, Censorinus. Sometimes addressees are little or unknown, not recognizable by readers outside the poet's circle: Pettius, Iccius, Numida, Bassus, Septimius, Pompeius, the Virgil of 4. 12.[11]

In many cases, these characters are involved in typical Neoteric situations where poetry circulates among friends. We find a dedication to a friend with the authority to judge the book's worth: 1. 1; Catullus 1. We find praise of a poet friend (1. 6), a lover of poetry (4. 2), and particularly the celebration of a new work (2. 1, 2. 12, 2. 9; Catullus 35, 95, 96 for Calvus' elegy on Quintilia; Ticidas fr. 2 Morel). In other poems, the poet tells a friend, who expects a new composition, that his state of mind precludes writing (*Epodes* 11 and 14; Catullus 65 and 68). Other Horatian *recusationes* ('refusal poems') can be assimilated in part to this situation (1. 6, 2. 12, 4. 2). We find consolation poems to friends for the loss of someone dear (1. 24, 2. 9; Catullus 96), or to a friend unhappy in love (1. 33; Catullus 68). In 1. 33, and probably 2. 9, the consolation poem's occasion is not the grief-causing event in itself but more specifically, the friend's poetic expression thereof (1. 33. 2 f *neu miserabilis / decantes elegos*, 'do not insist on singing sad elegy'; 2. 9. 9 *flebilibus modis*, 'with weepy tones'). These poems are presented as reactions to poetic laments

[9] 33 if we include Postumus. I have also excluded Canidia, Alfius from *Epodes* 2, the tribune of *Epodes* 4.

[10] Nisbet and Hubbard (1970), 227 f., 279.

[11] The identification with the Mantuan poet has been suggested many times. I consider it improbable.

written by afflicted friends and therefore participate in something of
a literary, communicative exchange between poet friends: Catullus 96
answers with consolation the elegy Calvus sent him, where he expresses his grief.[12] In poem 68, Catullus also writes a consolatory
epistle to a friend (Mallius) in response to a letter, probably poetic,
where he expressed his grief. With poem 38, Catullus seeks poetic
consolation from his friend Cornificius. *Odes* 2. 17 also offers a
friend, Maecenas, consolation. Other situations close to those of
Neoteric poetry are: a jokingly annoyed answer to another friend's
joke (*Epodes* 3; Catullus 12 and 14), greeting a friend on his return
home (1. 36, 2. 7; Catullus 9), propempticons for a poet friend (1. 3),
a friend with a taste for philosophy (1. 29), a protector friend (*Epodes*
1): compare Cinna's *Propempticon* for Asinius Pollio and that by
Parthenius. In Horace as in Catullus, we find compliments on various occasions to a friend for his happy love (*Epodes* 14. 13 ff.; *Odes*
2. 12. 13 ff. to Maecenas; 1. 36. 17 ff. to Numida; Catullus 6, 35, 45,
68, 155 ff., 100, and also 55, 58a, and 61, an epithalamium). Praise of
Paulus Fabius Maximus in 4. 1 dedicates the book to him; this
prefatory poem was probably written on the occasion of the dedicatee's engagement to a relative of Augustus.[13]

   The following poems establish a similar kind of relation between
literature and the poet's social life, though without direct parallel in
extant Neoteric poetry: invective against the adversary (Mevius) of a
poetic friend (Virgil) (*Epodes* 10); celebration of a friend, perhaps a
poet (1. 26); the gift (*munus*) of a poem to a friend for an occasion
requiring gifts and celebration (4. 8; for the poem as *munus*, see
Catullus 68. 10, 14, 32, 149; 65; 116, and instances where the book of
poems is itself presented as a *munus*); the festive celebration of happy
events for a friend (1. 2; 3. 9; 4. 11), the poet himself (3. 8), or the
whole community (*Epodes* 9). Other poems are invitations to real
people (3. 17, 3. 21, 3. 29, and 4. 12 which adopts the playful tone of
Catullus 13). But in these cases, no reference is made to a particular
festive occasion and we need not postulate one: the banquet is the
most traditional setting for ancient lyric.

---

[12] [Citroni 1995, 65 ff.].

[13] Kiessling (1876); Bradshaw (1970); Syndikus (1973), 290 f.; Syme (1978),
145 and (1985), 403; Habinek (1986).

   The poems listed above, though numerous (around thirty or so),
do not sufficiently delineate a framework for a poetry of social
relations like that within the Neoteric circles. There is no impression
of intense rapport between friends joined by a shared ideal of life and
poetry. There is also no sense of a systematic connection between
poetic activity and the communal experience of members of a social
circle. I believe, however, that these poems do establish the partial
persistence in Horace of a certain 'Neoteric' way of setting poetry in
relation to typical moments in the poet's affective life and underscore, even for Horace, the private dimension of address in specific
occasions. These poems present themselves more or less explicitly as
interventions intended to have an impact (as consolation, congratu-
lations, etc.) on the dedicatee in a specific situation which brings
author and dedicatee together and can involve, more or less directly,
a circle of people connected by personal ties to both. When a poem
involves real people, its intervention in a situation is not generally
reducible to pure fiction. Poems of well-wishing, condolences, con-
gratulations, greetings, suggestions, or answers on literary themes,
insofar as they involve real people, establish a literary communication with them different from that established with the remaining
public. The poem does not in these cases necessarily reproduce a
situation's real features, but rather interprets what the situation
means for that particular person: it conveys to that person a message
in line with what the situation requires. If Horace writes a consolation poem to Virgil (1. 24) or Valgius (2. 9), the grievous occasion
referred to by the poet will not be in doubt.[14] Beyond its ability to
translate a situation into an idealized and partly fictional form, the
poem constitutes a literary version of the friend's grief and intervenes
at the level of literary communication in the current of expressions of
condolence and consolation addressed to the mourner. The same
pertains, in hardly different terms, to the consolations to Maecenas
(2. 17) and Tibullus (1. 33). Clearly fictional are the banquets Horace

---

[14] In 2. 9 Nisbet and Hubbard (1978), 136, take Mystes as Valgius' literary
invention or a characteristic figure Horace attributes to him, as Glycera is attributed
to Tibullus in 1. 33. This hypothesis leads to reading the ode essentially as a poetic
statement. The same question has been asked of 1. 33 (see below). I am not convinced
by Quinn's (1963), 158 ff., claim, taken up often by others, that Mystes is not dead,
but snatched away (*ademptus*) from Valgius by a rich rival.

celebrates so often at anniversaries: the fiction depends on real customs, but is adopted every time for expressive reasons in conformity with well-known literary formulae. Since the occasions and anniversaries celebrated are not fictional, the poems still 'celebrate' the events in literary form and contribute to the festivity on the literary level. We could say the same of other poems written to honour, celebrate, or compliment someone. The *recusationes* presented as (negative) answers to requests for poetry (*Epodes* 11, 14; *Odes* 1. 6, 2. 12, 4. 2) are obviously not to be taken as actual exchanges of views; they are rather the interpretation and sanction, on the more general and elevated level of literary form, of a relation really existing between poet and dedicatee. These poems, insofar as they are communicated to the dedicatee, intervene in turn on this relation, marking a new stage in it by raising to a literary level a certain interpretation of that relation. Furthermore, the *recusationes* do satisfy to some degree the demands of the dedicatee in that they are *poetic* responses: they substitute in a way for the denied poem (and contain for the most part traces of the poem they refuse to provide) and for this reason participate in a real relation of exchange. They are in themselves a poetic *munus*, while denying a poetic *munus*.

Those who shared directly or indirectly with the person at issue the experience alluded to in the poem and knowledge of the people and facts, surely read the poem in view of that experience and appreciated both the degree and the manner of literary idealization. The majority of situations identified above as occasions for Horace's odes—festivities, grief, celebration, praise, poetics, and dedication—typically have a 'social' nature in that they involve, together with the poet and the dedicatee, a circle of friends. The possibility of measuring the ways the poet has transfigured and interpreted the basis of real experience underlying these poems results in a difference in condition between the readers who participate in these circles and those outside. There are two or three levels of address: the person (or persons) to whom a direct message is conveyed regarding a situation directly involving them, the circle of people who recognize the facts and people the poem refers to, and the exterior readers. This difference in conditions of receipt concerns not only the poem's reception and use post composition, but its very creation. For when Horace, like Catullus, involves in his poems real people who are part of his social circle, he is well aware that he establishes with them, through the literary work, a communicative relation different, in part, from the relation established with the anonymous public. He naturally articulates and grounds his composition with a view to all its communicative functions.

2. The entire development of poems set in particular communicative situations is conditioned mostly by these circumstances, and each expressive element depends strictly on them. However, the importance in these poems of the individual addressee's point of view does not usually conflict with the needs of address to a general reader: the two perspectives blend for the most part perfectly together. This harmony emerges particularly well when illustrious people are involved, whose private life concerns to some extent the whole community, or more generally when the presupposed situation addresses questions of broad interest: poetry, politics, morality. For instance, *Epodes* 1 to Maecenas, who is preparing to sail to war in 31 BC, is a message wholly tailored to the circumstances in which the dedicatee and the poet find themselves. It also serves, in that position, as a personal dedication of the book. But the epode also directly involves all other readers: for one, it contains an interpretation of the feelings the Romans, at least some of them, shared at that moment of their history; but also because the sense of friendship and devotion linking the poet to one of the leading figures of political life finds expression; or, finally, because in this expression Horace advances his own moral portrait, which represents him to the reader. At the same time, Horace gives Maecenas and the readers a definition and a sanction, at the literary level, of the ethical sense he attributes to his relation with him. The elements of encomium to Maecenas for his devotion to Octavian are both personal tribute and public praise of both men.

Asinius Pollio dominates the proem of book 2: Horace sings his praises and announces his work on the civil wars. But personal tribute to the great man via the book's dedication merges with the public praise of his many qualities, with the public announcement of his work, and with an intense meditation on civil war that directly involves the interest of all readers. True, from line 25 on, mournful recollection of the wars develops in a direction apparently independent of the poem's function as tribute to and literary conversation with Pollio. But it is also clear that Horace here means to anticipate and attempt to interpret the contents and spirit of Pollio's work as well as the impressions the latter will bring about in his readers. It therefore addresses both the readers and Pollio to the same degree.[15]

The impression of increasing detachment from the ode's occasion from line 25 on is confirmed by the final stanza. The poet, turning to his Muse, refuses to continue retailing political grievances and plans more light-hearted themes (2. 1. 37–40):

> sed ne relictis, Musa procax, iocis
> Ceae retractes munera neniae,
>   mecum Dionaeo sub antro
>   quaere modos leviore plectro.

But you, bold Muse, abandon not your games nor bring back Cean lament; with me, in Dione's cave, seek out rhythms with a lighter plectrum.

This stanza is clearly addressed particularly to the public, as a proemial programmatic statement. It even seems to diminish the solemnity of the celebration of Pollio. The break this stanza marks with the rest of the ode could suggest it signals a break between its function as tribute to Pollio and the more general address to the reader. For Horace does not want to betray his image as a 'minor' poet. He does not wish to give, with a constantly sustained proem, a false impression about the book's stylistic level and dominant thematics. For this reason, the hypothesis has been advanced that the last stanza was added only when the ode was placed in the collection in proemial position.[16] But this hypothesis is unnecessary: the *recusatio* interrupting the

---

[15] It is assumed Horace knew already parts of Pollio's works and some have thought it possible to identify allusions to it in the ode. Particularly bold are the reconstructions attempted by Nisbet and Hubbard (1978), 8 ff. André (1949), 44 ff. is more prudent. See Gabba (1956), 240 ff. Against such reconstructions, Sallman (1987). I think the only information the ode presupposes about Pollio's work is the choice of beginning 'from the consulship of Metellus'.

[16] Nisbet and Hubbard (1978), 10. But the ode may have been conceived from the beginning as a proem dedicating the book. According to Sallmann (1987), the last stanza would be an appeal to abandon politics (and historiography) and seek tranquillity of spirit. Similar is Poiss (1992), for whom the last stanza establishes a parallel between poet and dedicatee: both must follow their own vocation and not trespass on history. If they must, they should interpret it according to the categories of art (as tragedy does). But Horace's wish that Pollio not neglect tragedy for long is a compliment to his poetic quality, not an invitation to abandon historiography.

course of the celebration can be understood as a subtle and allusive
way of underscoring the ode's solemnity, given that it recalls
recognizable Pindaric formulae.[17] It in particular reminds the
dedicatee and the reader that in this ode the author has raised
the tone above his usual manner. The clearly elevated style is due
not only to its panegyric function—it is also required by the
theme. It is the style of Horatian political lyric. Nisbet and Hubbard have observed that in this ode, exceptionally, Horace treats
the political theme not as a panegyrist but with the authority and
prudence of an historian. This must be due to the fact that the
political theme was treated here in the same way it was handled by
Pollio. For indeed the ode's subject is not simply civil war, but
Pollio's history of it. This circumstantial fact is an essential part of
the poem's subject and necessarily conditions its articulation. Despite this, the reader does not feel at all extraneous to the poem's
creation and its significance.

The *recusatio*'s characteristic function structures *Odes* 1. 6 to
Agrippa: to lend poetic sanction to the position taken by the poet
vis-à-vis the addressee and to grant the latter concomitantly a substitute literary *munus*. Praise of Agrippa, the compliment to Varius as
the poet most suitable to celebrate Agrippa's merits in epic,[18] and the
affirmation of Horace's own poetic programme are simultaneously
interventions in the private relations between the poet and these
figures, a public celebration of public figures, and an affirmation to
the reader of the poet's artistic intentions. In *Odes* 4. 2, the *recusatio*
to Iullus Antonius, private and public moments also substantially
coincide. The communicative functions of *recusatio* and of tribute to
both Iullus, a public figure closely linked to Augustus, and Augustus
himself directly involve the whole community and all readers
through the development of themes both literary and political.
Furthermore, in book 4, the public dimension of Horace's poetic
discourse becomes manifest. He had already been recognized as the
greatest living poet and felt he had been accorded the role of speaker

[17] Nisbet and Hubbard (1978), at line 37. The last stanza of *Odes* 3. 3 is an
analogous example in Horace.
[18] Allusions to Agrippa's accomplishments and to Varius' *Thyestes* are nicely
identified in Heinze's commentary.

for the community. If already in the *Epodes* and *Odes* 1–3, the political poems generally presuppose the whole community as audience, in book 4, Horace shoulders more openly the role of official panegyrist (4. 4, 4. 5, 4. 14, 4. 15: odes for Augustus, Drusus, and Tiberius). This self-conscious adoption of a 'general' voice for the community is noticeable also in the panegyric slant of odes for other figures (4. 1, 4. 2, 4. 9) and where Horace speaks solemnly of the duties and merits of his own poetry (in the first collection, 3. 30 is comparable, as are in part 2. 20 and 3. 25).

Not only in poems with a 'public' nature (proems, eulogies, poetics), but also in poems set in more private or intimate contexts, a perfect balance usually obtains between the various levels of address, whether the addressee is known widely or only within the poet's circle. In *Epodes* 11, Pettius had asked Horace for new poems; there is a vivid sense of private confidentiality born from a typically Neoteric occasion, though the erotic experience is represented here in markedly conventional terms.[19] The reasons Horace gives for his refusal represent his spiritual condition and reinterpret a romantic experience of his, both directly involving his friend (11–19). But the reader can take the poem as an accomplished page of erotic lyric without feeling excluded because he knows nothing of Pettius and does not share the experiences recounted in the poem. *Epodes* 14 also offers a set of elements that all mean something particular to the addressee: Horace refuses Maecenas' request to complete the book of iambs, he pays a compliment to his love, and expresses his own afflicted state of mind. In this way, Horace establishes a communicative link with him, but these elements are all fully available to the reader's enjoyment. He finds there a convincing piece of erotic lyric, and also feels he has access to psychological and sentimental conflicts and to the private network of friendships within which the book of epodes arose.

Odes 1. 20 and 3. 8, invitation poems to Maecenas, offer clear examples of the complete integration of messages across distinct

---

[19] On Hellenistic themes in *Epodes* 11: Leo (1900), 9 ff.; Grassmann (1966), 34 ff. and 90 ff.; Luck (1976). Grassmann (1966), 120 f., appropriately refutes Olivier's (1963b:112, n. 2) claim, taken up by W. Wili (1965), 61 and others, that the epode dismisses aggressive and announces erotic poetry.

levels of address. Here the traditional formulation of the invitation poem is completely remodelled according to the specific link between poet and addressee. The reader can appreciate the elegant and personal variation on a conventional poetic type and the literary celebration of situations involving a public figure as well as the poet himself. A traditional moral message naturally arises, but one strictly relevant to the precise situation.

Odes 2. 7 celebrates the return of Horace's friend Varus: he participated with Horace in the battle of Philippi, subsequently continued to fight against the triumvirs, and only now, thanks probably to an amnesty, can return to Italy. The ode, while conveying the poet's feelings on his friend's return, uses the occasion to offer the reader an intense meditation on the poet's own military experience at a crucial moment of Roman history. Some have emphasized Horace's tact in addressing a friend less fortunate than himself:[20] Horace refashions his memories to his friend's state of mind, so that first and second persons are equally formative.[21] But in this case, the particular occasion and the specific relation between Horace and the dedicatee result in a poem unique in content and tone: nowhere else does he speak so directly and intensely of the everyday aspects and the intimate impressions of his military experience. Friendship for the comrade in arms is expressed with an immediate youthful friendliness quite exceptional in Horace:[22] we will see that in few other cases do communicative circumstances lead Horace to alter his usual tone and language.

3. In the consolation odes for Virgil, Valgius, Tibullus, and Maecenas, private consolation of well-known personages encounters the great and more general themes of death, love, friendship, and poetry's consolatory power.

---

[20] Meister (1952); Fraenkel (1957), 12; Commager (1962), 136 and 171; Syndikus (1972), 386. On the other hand, Nisbet and Hubbard (1978), 108 f. and then Moles (1987) emphasize Horace's tactfulness towards Octavian; they find blameable opportunism in this ode, which usually is rightly considered proof of Horace's freedom toward the princeps. [Citroni (2000)]

[21] Burck (1966), 161 remarks that, unlike Horace, Catullus essentially expresses his *own* joy in his welcome poem to Veranius (9), almost neglecting his friend's.

[22] La Penna (1969), 290.

Odes 1. 24 to Virgil on the occasion of Quintilius' death opens with two stanzas whose connection with the rest of the poem is disputed:

> Quis desiderio sit pudor aut modus
> tam cari capitis? praecipe lugubris
> cantus, Melpomene, cui liquidam pater
>   vocem cum cithara dedit.
>
> Ergo Quintilium perpetuus sopor   5
> urget, cui Pudor et Iustitiae soror
> incorrupta Fides nudaque Veritas
>   quando ullum inveniet parem?

What restraint or limit could there be to desire for such a beloved person? Teach doleful songs, Melpomene, to whom your father gave, with the cithara, a limpid voice. So, perpetual slumber weighs down Quintilius? When will Restraint and uncorrupted Loyalty, sister of Justice, and naked Truth find his equal?

The first stanza, invoking the Muse, has appeared a cold and conventional preamble; its monologic character enhances its detachment from the rest of the poem.[23] The second stanza has received similar condemnation.[24] Others have argued that the poem's opening should be considered already part of the *consolatio*, given that *consolationes* usually began by justifying the friend's grief and revealing the author's participation in it.[25] The ode's unity would thus depend on a solid tradition going back to Archilochus, whose elegy to Pericles (13 West) contains an analogous connection between grief and consolation. We can, however, ascertain a certain difference in orientation between the ode's first and second parts in that the first lines concern primarily Horace himself.[26] In addition, the slightly formal character of the first two stanzas contradicts the idea that, in

---

[23] Kiessling (1881), 86 thinks Horace added the stanza later, after Peerlkamp, who would delete it.

[24] Nisbet (1962), 195.

[25] Reitzenstein (1908), 81 ff. On the link between grief and consolation, see Esteve-Forriol (1962) and Kiessling and Heinze (1957–8) and Nisbet and Hubbard (1970) on this ode.

[26] Pasquali (1920), 249 f. argued against Reitzenstein that Horace invokes the Muse only in his own name, therefore, the poet speaks to himself until line 9 and not Virgil.

these stanzas, the poet speaks to himself and gives freer expression to his own grief.

Actually, the choice is not between words spoken by Horace himself and words addressing Virgil. The formal tone of high pathos and solemnity marking the poem's beginning gives a sense of wide-spread grief, of a θρῆνος ('lament') surpassing the poet and individual addressee to express communal feeling.[27] The first stanza owes its character as a prologue for lamentation to this function—it seeks out and justifies before the audience a modality appropriate to the mourning that follows. Mourning proper begins at line 5 with the 'public' announcement of Quintilius' death (though *ergo* suggests the inner repercussions of this announcement for the poet). The particular form chosen in praise of the deceased, i.e., the current state of abandonment of the most venerated virtues, suggests a grief shared by all sensitive to these virtues. The beginning of the third stanza makes explicit the idea of grief shared among all those who knew Quintilius:

> Multis ille bonis flebilis occidit...
>
> He is dead, a cause of sorrow for many...

Only at this point, within a framework of universal grief, is Virgil's particular perspective introduced:

> nulli flebilior quam tibi, Virgili.
> Tu frustra pius, heu, non ita creditum
>   poscis Quintilium deos
>
> A greater sorrow for none besides you, Virgil. You, alas, pious in vain, ask back from the gods Quintilius, entrusted not on these terms.

Virgil fully participates in the message of the two first stanzas, but only as one among many. The following stanzas detach him from the others. The joint presence of private and public dimensions of grief was traditional in funerary poetry and is already in Archilochus, 13 West.[28] The difference is that for Archilochus, the two points of view

---

[27] Gigante (1993) thinks the ode reflects the relations between members of the Epicurean circle; Herculaneum papyri attest Virgil's and Quintilius' participation.

[28] See also Bion *Ad. epitaph.* 5 f., 18 ff., 32 ff. and *passim*; ps-Mosch. *Bion. epitaph.* 1 ff. and *passim*; *Cons. Liv.* On this ode's relation to the tradition of funerary poetry, see Esteve-Forriol (1962), 27 ff.

are constantly present, but for Horace, they articulate a peculiar form of composition.[29] This ode rehearses a grief that united a circle of friends who found their feelings reflected within that circle; it therefore represents 'public' and 'ritual' mourning. But at the same time, it played a consolatory role for a particular member of the circle more closely tied to the deceased. The poet himself participates in the community of mourners and expresses his own personal grief and his need to react to it. This ode signals in its very articulation two levels of address: the one mourning friend and the larger circle partaking of the experience. But this situation, precisely because it is so overt, does not limit in any way full understanding for readers outside.[30] Rather, it gives the external reader at the third and broadest level of address the vivid impression of an immediate experience of grief and of the friendship at the poem's origin.

In *Odes* 2. 9 to Valgius, some have recognized precise references to Valgius' purported elegy at Mystes' death, to which the ode apparently responds. Some have even attempted to reconstruct the Valgius elegy on the basis of Horace: mere hypothesis, but in at least one case, with some merit. In the fourth stanza, Horace adduces Nestor and Priam as *exempla* of those who did not continually grieve over lost sons. Given that in the poetic tradition from at least Callimachus on, Nestor and Priam are often examples of the equation between long life and long suffering, it seems strange that Horace chose them here as examples for limiting grief. Some have therefore supposed Valgius himself compared his own continuous grief with that of these mythic

---

[29] In this fortunate case, where we can compare an ode by Horace with a Greek archaic poem—one he certainly knew and is possibly complete—the speaker's role appears more important in the Latin poet, where it determines a particular compositional structure and tonality. With the Greek poet, Pericles' grief is not differentiated from that of other citizens or the poet himself. Archilochus thus often moves from the second person singular to Pericles, to the generic first person plural, to the generic second person plural without creating an impression of detachment. See Syndikus (1972), 90 on 1. 6, compared to Ibycus frag. S 152 Davies (already Sisti [1967], 77 ff.), and 202 on 1. 18.

[30] When at lines 13 ff., Horace tells Virgil that not even a song more seductive than Orpheus' will bring his friend back to life, he probably alludes, as has been noted, to Virgil's own evocation of Orpheus. Horace opposes his own disillusioned vision to Virgil's dream of rebirth. Such an allusion would not have escaped a cultivated reader. For Khan (1967), the ode is Horace's response to Virgil's funerary poem for Quintilius, where the latter showed excessive sorrow.

figures; Horace then retorted that not even in those cases was grief interminable.[31] The relation of Valgius' text to Horace's would on this view particularly resemble the relation of Calvus' epicedium for Quintilia to Catullus 96: Horace too would take up his friend's motif and turn it instead to consolation. To admit that Horace here refers so precisely to Valgius' text entails acknowledging that a full understanding of the poem was reserved to those with direct knowledge of Valgius' elegy. But let us leave such uncertain territory. The poem as it stands is a consolation where the poet sets against his friend's—certainly poetic—lamentation a firmer attitude toward pain and advises him to devote himself instead to celebratory poetry. The general contents—pain, death, poetry's consolatory function— naturally accord with circumstances the reader has no difficulty grasping.

Scholars tend these days to privilege a further general aspect of this ode, though one intrinsically connected with Valgius: the poem argues against elegy's excessively soft and plaintive character.[32] Comparison with the implicit criticism of elegy in Virgil, *Eclogues* 10 naturally comes to mind. But it somehow strains interpretation to read an appeal to a grieving friend to have fortitude as a polemic against a whole literary genre. Indeed Horace opposes to Valgius' lament a sense of measure in grief deriving from his ethics' most authentic core and inseparable from the very roots of his own poetics. However, at the level of poetics in the strict sense, in the last lines, Horace indicates a different path to Valgius: celebratory poetry:

> desine mollium
> tandem querellarum et potius nova
> cantemus Augusti tropaea
> Caesaris et rigidum Niphaten   20
>
> Medumque flumen gentibus additum
> victis

---

[31] Kiessling and Heinze (1957–8), *ad loc.*; Esteve-Forriol (1962), 32 ff., thinks the third stanza's sentimental hyperbole, over against the sober virility of the other stanzas, results from Horace's imitation of Valgius. An indication in favour is that lines 10–12 echo Cinna fragment 6 Morel; Valgius fragment 2 Morel shows he admired Cinna, Nisbet and Hubbard (1978), 136.

[32] Commager (1962), 239 ff.; Syndikus (1972), 393 ff.; Nisbet and Hubbard (1978), 138; for those who consider Mystes a boy kidnapped by a rich rival, see above n.14.

Away with soft sorrows: let us rather sing the new trophies of Augustus
Caesar, the rigid Niphates, and the Persian river added to conquered peoples

If Horace gives him this advice, it is not because he deems this path
the absolutely right road, but because he knows this is a path
Valgius—an elegiac poet with a propensity to political poetry and
panegyric[33]—can take. In this last part of the ode, Horace organizes
his consolatory arguments more in line with the addressee's poetic
orientation (which he could consider known to most readers) than
with his own personal convictions. It is also noteworthy that, to give
his final entreaty the affectionate warmth required of consolation,
Horace, with the plural *cantemus* ('let us sing'), joins with his friend
in a celebratory project. The occasion and his addressee's poetic
vocation lead Horace, if only in an affectionate gesture, to adopt a
different attitude toward celebratory poetry from usual.[34] In the last
two stanzas, circumstantial reasons prevail on the more general
rationale of affirming Horace's own poetic programme. They give
the poem an unusual course: they create a singular contiguity, entirely dependent on the dedicatee, of funerary-consolatory motifs
with those of Augustan celebration.

When he invites Albius (most probably Tibullus) to leave the
overly sorrowful tones of elegy in *Odes* 1. 33, Horace opposes to his
friend's affliction a more detached conception of love based on the
certainty one cannot find in it the complete joy of mutual fulfilment.
In this case as well, interpretation has been forced by taking the
poem as a polemical attack on elegy[35] and discounting the personal,
consolatory rationale—this, on the contrary, gives the poem its
fundamental stamp. The tone and progress of the ode correspond
to Horace's own vision of love as an odd game, pleasant and
subtly bitter. However, the ambiguous balance between irony and

---

[33] The *Panegyricus Messallae* (179 f.) indicates Valgius as the poet who will
worthily undertake the celebration of Messalla's future glory. Pliny *N.H.* 25. 4 tells
us Valgius dedicated with enthusiasm an incomplete treatise to Augustus on medi-
cinal herbs.

[34] Syndikus (1972), 396. I disagree (also given the plural *cantemus*, 'let us sing')
with the ironic interpretation of the advice to Valgius, supported by Quinn (1963),
161; Nisbet and Hubbard (1978), 137; Jones (1986), 375 ff.

[35] Quinn (1963), 154 ff.; Nisbet and Hubbard (1970) *ad loc.* Also Commager
(1962), 240; and Syndikus (1972), 293 ff. More balanced, Putnam (1972).

melancholy characteristic of the poem probably reflects the atmosphere of the two friends' relations. The same tone of irony and
affection, the same shift from irony to self-irony at the poem's end,
the same melancholy streak occurs in *Epistles* 1. 4, likewise to 'Albius':
this cannot be coincidence. The reader intuits that the ambiguous
tone derives from the addressee's character and Horace's take on it,
and may get the impression that for the circle of those who knew the
dedicatee and the friendship between them, this tone had greater
significance.[36]

   Horace also invites the reader to enter the sphere of private
relations in *Odes* 2. 17: he cheers Maecenas in the face of his an-
guished fear of death. The ode is entirely structured around its
function as consolation.[37] The coincidence of Horace's and Maecenas' destinies, expressed through astrological doctrine, is essential to
consolation and affirmed. Since elsewhere (1. 11 and 3. 29 also to
Maecenas), Horace apparently does not believe in astrology, and we
perceive a certain ironic distance toward it even here, we might think
Horace follows this vein because Maecenas was a believer—he would
thus adapt his consolation to his dedicatee's mentality.[38] Irony is
hard in an ode charged with so much pathos, and indeed, defining
the tone in the astrological section has divided interpreters:[39] perhaps
correct interpretation was possible only for a reader who knew what
impressions and associations reference to astrology held for the poet
and dedicatee. For us, the ode is interesting especially because, in
adapting himself to his addressee's anxiety, the poet uses exceptional
language. Never in the *Odes* do we find such openly excited pathos,

[36] In other poems expressing light irony toward friends, e.g., 1. 29 and 3. 17,
Horace perhaps counted on particular effects destined for the circle of those who
knew the butt of the joke.
[37] Syndikus (1972), 455 ff. subtly traces the ode's development; on the consolatory
function, Mörland (1965).
[38] Kiessling and Heinze (1957–8) *ad loc.*; Boll (1917) and, e.g., Fraenkel (1957),
218. Doubts about the ode's taking Maecenas' utter trust in astrology for granted in
La Penna (1968), 147 f.; Syndikus (1972), 460; Nisbet and Hubbard (1978), 273.
[39] Horace is usually thought to admit, with irony, ignorance even of his own
horoscope: Boll (1917); Dicks (1963). Fraenkel (1957), 217 f. denies the astrological
lines are ironic but thinks, like others, the mythological lines are (13–16). McDermott
(1982) considers the whole ode ironic. Joined pathos and literary pleasure need not
surprise in a relation of intense friendship couched in a refined atmosphere where the
cult of literature was fundamental: West (1991).

marked by interjection, repetition, and dense enjambment probably without analogue elsewhere in Horace.[40] The anxious and passionate tone cannot be fully understood if we neglect Maecenas' anxious character, known from Seneca and the elder Pliny.

4. As seen above, in some cases, a more complete understanding of the significance of a Horatian poem depends on knowledge of facts the reader must reconstruct from elements external to the poem. Another example is *Epodes* 10, an invective against Mevius in the form of a propempticon. Given the rareness of the name Mevius and the contrast, hardly accidental, between the ill-wishing propempticon to Mevius and the well-wishing one to Virgil (*Odes* 1. 3), we may be fairly certain this Mevius is identifiable with the pettifogging poet, rival of Virgil, mentioned disdainfully along with Bavius, another minor poet, in the *Bucolics* (3. 90 f.). Horace would therefore have written this attack to please Virgil, other friends of his circle, and generally all Virgil's admirers. But the epode bears traces of no such motive: Mevius is not even identified as a poet. According to Fraenkel, given the text's silence, we should not assume understanding the poem depends in any way on knowing Mevius was a poet.[41] Fraenkel acknowledges that Virgil and his admirers could have been pleased with the choice of name, but he believes the possible implications for friends to whom the poet first recited his epode are distinctly separate from the significance of the published poem, which should not depend on external information. Fraenkel's reader should rest content with considering this epode an exercise in invective in the manner of Archilochus. I admit the poem is somewhat 'academic' in its imitation of the Strasburg epode, but why we should force ourselves to try and forget what we know about Mevius, as if that information or grounding conjecture on the poem's conditions of creation could jeopardize correct interpretation? Fraenkel himself remarks that the allusion to Mevius dates the epode, as it would be 'stale' if written much later than the *Bucolics*' publication. With this, Fraenkel concedes the epode had a fuller and more convincing life in

---

[40] Fraenkel (1957), 217; Syndikus (1972), 456.

[41] Fraenkel (1957), 24 ff.; Commager (1962), 124 f.; and others. Schetter (1971), 255, by contrast, locates the epode's rationale in literary hostility toward Mevius. Schmidt (1977), 40 ff., Harrison (1989), and Cavarzere (1992), 183 f. take the epode as invective against a *libidinosus* ('man full of libido').

contemporary literary polemic and publicly supported Virgil in an
act of friendship. Why renounce our appreciation of the poem's
originally fuller life? If Horace does not refer to Mevius' poetic
activity and therefore to the very reason for his polemic, it is probably because he had no doubt that any cultivated reader, present or
future, would understand the invective's motives, even only on the
basis of the *Bucolics*.[42] Suppressing such motivation, reducing
the attack to the mere insult of *olens* ('stinky') half-seriously exalts
the attack's force, which thus becomes absolute condemnation, the
rival's complete exclusion from all respectable humanity.

Odes 2. 12 offers another case where the reader may have the
impression of not mastering all the occasional givens that determine
a poem's content and structure. The poet denies to Maecenas that
epic themes (historical or mythological) suit lyric and claims his
Muse requires themes of love. The poem, as a *recusatio* and poetic
declaration, obviously addresses all readers. However, the particular
way the refusing argument is arranged shows that the relation with
the dedicatee conditions the poem's whole conception. In *recusationes* the poet sometimes indicates another who could more worthily fulfil the required task.[43] In 4. 2 Horace suggests the one who
commissioned the poem take on the task: the refusal becomes a
compliment to the addressee's literary talent. He does something
similar here, but more concealed and allusive. Horace could not
suggest that Maecenas write epic; Maecenas was a known dilettante
who, at most, took pleasure in composing refined little poems in the
Neoteric style. Horace refers to Maecenas' ostensible intention of
writing a historical work on contemporary events and suggests it
would be worthy celebration of Augustus. With the emphasis on *nolis*
at the beginning, Horace, who knows Maecenas' literary tastes, draws
him into his reasons for refusal. He deduces his argument from
Maecenas' own behaviour—he will choose to write Caesar's history
in prose. Horace thus insinuates Maecenas does not really believe

[42] Marsus' epigram against Bavius also does not refer to the latter's poetic activity,
which, however, would have motivated the attack. Marsus fragment 5 Morel, where a
'stinking' character like Horace's Mevius is mentioned, could refer to the same.

[43] Hor. *Odes* 1. 6; Prop. 2. 34; *Paneg. Mess.* 177 ff.; also Verg. *Ecl.* 6. 6 f.; Val. Fl. I.
12 ff.

that he, as lyrist, could properly write the political-historical celebratory poetry he nevertheless solicited. But this subtly malicious touch only adds charm to the *recusatio* and to the tribute Horace pays Maecenas by publicly announcing his intention or at least proclaiming his ability to write an arduous historical work (the announcement should perhaps be taken as encouragement). In this way, Horace also inserts within the *recusatio* a touch of encomium to Augustus in placing his accomplishments, mentioned briefly, but with incisiveness, on par with the greatest mythic and historical events.[44] It is the *recusatio*'s way to concede at least a taste of what is refused.

This ode has well-known and remarkable affinities in content and structure to Propertius 2. 1, also a *recusatio* to Maecenas.[45] Its relation to another Propertian *recusatio*, 3. 9, has attracted little attention.[46] There the poet tells Maecenas he is determined not to betray his Callimachean vocation on Maecenas' own example, who prefers to remain an *eques* ('knight') and does not covet more important positions he could easily attain. I believe the affinity of *Odes* 2. 12 with Propertius 2. 1 is due not so much to one poet's influence over the other or to the topical motifs of the *recusatio*, but more to the close affinity of the conflict both poets perceive as constraining them in their vocation. The affinity with Propertius 3. 9 lies in the surprising formulation of a refusal to an illustrious patron by affirming he himself gives authoritative example of behaviour against his recommendations. This is due not so much to one poet's dependence on the other. Rather, Maecenas' somewhat contradictory position toward the poets of his circle could indeed support such an argument. These poets certainly felt tied to Maecenas by friendship and out of affinity to his private tastes: love of luxury,

---

[44] Kiessling and Heinze (1957–8), at line 9.

[45] The affinity is often exaggerated and taken as one poem's direct dependence on the other: Wimmel (1960), 43 ff.; Nisbet and Hubbard (1978), 183 and 186. Against too mechanical an understanding of dependence on Propertius, see rightly Syndikus (1972), 412 f. Among those who think Propertius took his inspiration from Horace, see Kühn (1961), 104 f.

[46] The relation is not indicated by the main commentaries on either author. Only Wimmel (1960), 49, 250 ff.; Santirocco (1980), 233 ff.; mention in Wilkinson (1951), 82 f.; Commager (1962), 34, n. 72.

pleasure of the most modern and refined culture. An important element of this attitude is his remaining within the limits of the equestrian class, which enables his availability to *otium* ('leisure'). However, as Augustus' close collaborator, Maecenas requested of his poets what they probably perceived as a deviation from the basis of their personal rapport with him. It is thus primarily their relation with the addressee that enables Horace and Propertius to share an argument of such singular form—with the difference that Horace sustains a light and pleasant tone, while Propertius conducts a more demanding argument.[47]

In the first part of the ode, the discourse is closely linked with Maecenas, but also targets the general reader: it is a poetic statement, an announcement of a new work by Maecenas, and testimony to their friendship. In what follows, Horace pauses on his vocation as love poet: my task is to celebrate Licymnia, he says. Four stanzas are dedicated to a splendid portrait of this woman. Her eyes, voice, ability in ritual dance, absolute *fides* ('fidelity'), and restrained co-quetry in love are praised. According to the usual schema of a *recusatio*, we should expect the poet, having denied the celebratory poem, to affirm his true vocation as poet of his *own* love stories: as Horace does at the end of 1. 6, Propertius in 1. 7, and Ovid in *Amores* 2. 18 (Nisbet and Hubbard also quote *Anacreontea* 23, 26A). Every reader, at first sight, will think Licymnia is a woman—real or imaginary—loved by the poet. Some ancient interpreters (ps-Acro, note at line 13) and some modern have understood the passage so. But at *Satires* 1. 2. 64 ps-Acro tells us *Licymnia* is a pseudonym of Maecenas' wife, Terentia. However untrustworthy this source,[48] the identification has been generally accepted, given that certain passages from the second part of the ode seem more pertinent when referred not to a hetaera loved by the poet, but to a woman of high rank loved by Maecenas. And *Licymnia* is metrically equivalent to *Terentia*,

---

[47] Kumaniecki (1935), 144 ff. underscores the affinity with *Epodes* 14, to Maecenas, where Horace justifies slow progress in his iambic book by being in love and appeals to Maecenas' own erotic experience. Kumaniecki interprets both poems as playful—impossible at least for 2. 12: Horace could not joke about celebrating Augustus.

[48] On *Odes* 2. 12, ps-Acro suggests the identification as possible; at *Satires* 1. 2. 64 as certain.

following the norm in Roman poetry for pseudonyms for the beloved.[49] But we must admit the textual indications point both ways.[50]

There is a more general reason why I believe it more probable
Licymnia is Maecenas' wife. Self-congratulation on Horace's part for
his own condition as a happy lover contrasts too heavily with the
ironic distance and subtle melancholy characteristic of all his erotic
lyric. The full accomplishment of a mutual exchange of affection
guaranteed by *fides*, as portrayed in the second part of this ode, is
never presented as an experience of the poet's 'I'—neither in Horace
nor elegy: it is at most a frustrated aspiration. The celebration of the
friend's happy love rather follows naturally on the tribute to his
ability as a writer. The peculiar turn Horace thus gives the *recusatio*'s
natural progression would contribute to the subtle and almost mischievous game whereby, as in the ode's first part, Horace folds
Maecenas into the reasons for his refusal. If Horace exemplifies his
own poetic vein, not with verse about his *own* romantic experiences
but by setting the refined and gallant world Maecenas inhabits in a
resplendent, almost celebratory frame, he at the same time affirms
the basic compatibility of his own poetic style with Maecenas' lifestyle. So, the celebratory poetry Maecenas asks of Horace contradicts
not only the poet's vocation but also the patron's own aesthetic and
moral taste. The movement of the ode's last section makes this
perspective explicit: Maecenas himself 'would not wish' (*num velis*
recalls the initial *nolis*)[51] that love and sophisticated grace—what he
values in his own life and Horace's lyric celebrates—be sacrificed to
qualities more showy, but common and vulgar.[52]

If Licymnia is the woman Maecenas loves, we must also admit that
without ps-Acro's indication, it would be difficult to reach the right
interpretation. It would also be difficult for any ancient reader

[49] Bentley formulates this principle precisely in a footnote to *Odes* 2. 12, about
Licymnia.

[50] [Detailed argumentation for this view can be found in the original publication
and Citroni (1995), 316 f.] For arguments for and against the identification with
Terentia, see Williams (1962), 35–8; Morris and Williams (1963); Davis (1975);
Nisbet and Hubbard (1978), 180 ff.

[51] Davis (1975), 80.

[52] On the analogy between the ode's two parts in the transfer to Maecenas of the
rationale for his own poetic choice, see Wimmel (1960), 47 f. and Syndikus (1972).
La Penna (1963), 126 f. covers the traces of sophisticated Roman life in the ode.

outside the personal network in which these verses were created. On the basis of the arguable presupposition that a poem's meaning should not depend on external information, it has been argued that Licymnia must represent Horace's loves.[53] According to Nisbet and Hubbard, Horace built his poem on two levels: one literal for the common reader for whom Licymnia is a woman whom the poet loves, and one allusive for the initiated who could suspect that the poet speaks of Maecenas' wife.[54] I do not believe in the intentional creation of different levels of signification for different readers. I believe Horace wrote this ode thinking first of Maecenas, for whom the text was unambiguous, and of a circle of people aware of the poem's network of relations. But if the external reader could not recognize Terentia for sure, it would not derive from heedlessness for the requirements of the public. To make Terentia an exemplary character in his own poetic world, as the *recusatio* required, Horace gave her a Greek pseudonym (all Horace's lyric women have Greek names) and, to some extent, conventional features. Only by abstaining from explicit identification could Horace introduce her in the game of refined sensuality marking the odes' end.[55] Horace then consciously removed her character from general recognition: not to create ambiguity but rather from the logic of the *recusatio* and from courtly decorum. He happily submitted to these needs without concern for an external reader's difficulties.

For Fraenkel, this ode is not successful in that the tribute paid Licymnia is heterogeneous to the *recusatio*: it would please Maecenas but has created disharmony.[56] I have shown how the second section accords with the *recusatio*'s progress and reproduces its particular courtly allusivity. We may, however, agree with Fraenkel that the final tribute makes this ode more composite thematically than is usual in the first collection of *Odes*. Horace deviates here from his more normal compositional method according to the occasion, namely tribute and compliment. Fraenkel starts from an ideal of lyric unbound to occasion, so a poem bearing signs of occasionality

[53] Morris and Williams (1963); Davis (1975).

[54] Nisbet and Hubbard (1978), 181, 183; in the notes, they privilege the identification with Terentia.

[55] Williams (1962), 38.

[56] Fraenkel (1957), 219. Similarly, Morris and Williams (1963) and Davis (1975).

consequently seems defective. According to the criterion usually applied to Catullus, such heterogeneity adds charm, because it conveys the immediacy of a real communicative rapport. I think this measure also applies to Horace. The poem is unified because the second part shares in the initial theme of choice of poetic subject and playfully refers poetic choices to the addressee, but also because the single function of *munus*, offered as 'compensation' for the negative response, sustains in a coherent structure the poem's multiple motivations. The allusive and almost teasing tone with which Horace insinuates Maecenas does not believe in his own suggestions, accords with the courtly tone, tinged with mischievous gallantry, with which he pays tribute to his friend's love. The subtle sensuality, the slightly ironic light-heartedness, the satisfying equilibrium in verbal play,[57] create a tone close to Catullus' graceful compliments to his enamoured friends;[58] in this ode we also find (*negat [oscula] quae poscente magis gaudeat eripi*, 'she denies kisses she more gladly than their seeker would have him snatch', 27 f.) an elegantly concise and implicit version of the 'competition for who loves more' characteristic of tribute poems for couples.[59] The ode's thematic progress and the tone are unified by its function as a *munus* within a private relation in an atmosphere of courtly amiability. The reader can feel and appreciate this atmosphere but it is presented, as in many Catullan poems, as particular to the relations of the poet with a circle of people with their own lifestyle.

   5. Catullus' book, with its composite and 'experimental' nature, admits a wide scale of modes and stylistic levels. In poems serving as *munus* within his social circle, his style is more openly elegant, more self-consciously literary, sometimes subtly ironic.[60] It is likewise

---

[57] Suffice it to mention the complex word order of lines 13–14 and 15 f. (Nisbet and Hubbard [1978], *ad loc.*), and the final stanza's brilliant oxymorons.

[58] [Citroni (1995), 119 ff.] The affinity of this part of the ode with Catullus 45 is underscored by Williams (1968), 303; see Nisbet and Hubbard (1978) at lines 15 and 25.

[59] [Citroni (1995), 157 ff.] As at Catullus 61. 169 ff., here too, failure to recognize a conventional motif has elicited inappropriate interpretations: some have understood *poscente magis*, instead of 'more than he who asks', as an absolute ablative ('when he makes himself more insistent') or as 'more than a girl who asks'; Nisbet and Hubbard (1978), *ad loc.*

[60] [Citroni (1995), 65 ff.].

tempting to link the elegant presentation of Horace, *Odes* 2. 12 with the poem's function as a gift. In fact, Horace has a clear idea of the lyric level, dignity, and coherence needed in a work addressing a noble public coherently over time; he therefore maintains a unitary formal framework. Controlled elegance, measured equilibrium in expression, special effects in word placement, these are constants in his style—it would be otiose to derive these from the contents or functions of particular poems. In the only cases where deviation from his usual style is apparent so far, because of the relation with a particular addressee, the marker has not been a showier elegance of literary presentation but rather greater immediate expressivity and direct emotional abandon (*Odes* 2. 7 and 17).

In one case, however, the need to please the dedicatee with poetic tribute leads Horace to an exceptionally showy elegance of expression: the ode to Plancus (1. 7). Since antiquity, its bipartite structure has attracted attention: praise of Tivoli (1–14) and a moral message serving as consolation.[61] The occasion of its composition is unknown to us.[62] With greater knowledge, we could probably better judge the impact of the consolatory moment and the significance of the praise of Tivoli (we do not know whether Plancus expected to return there soon and, if so, if it would be sweet or bitter to him); the connection between the ode's two parts would perhaps be clearer. I do not think the ode refers strictly to a particular situation: *tristitia* ('sadness') and *vitae labores* ('life's labours') are probably sorrows common to all. But this moral message, however general, had to be understood by Horace, by Plancus, and by all aware of the circumstances of the ode's composition, as an interpretation of Plancus' tempestuous personal experience at that point of his career. The connotations, the import of the consolation would differ depending on the date of composition: before or after Plancus' sensational passage to Octavian in 32 BCE; just before or just after Actium; or after Plancus was already out of dark waters—mere tedious traces of some adversary's hostility lingered—and could now enjoy a quiet prestige.

---

[61] Porphyrio already opposed anyone holding that line 15 began a new poem.

[62] For the various hypotheses, see Vaio (1966). Bliss (1960) analyses the historical information useful for interpreting the ode; he, however, reaches improbable conclusions.

For many, connection between the two parts seems lacking. Some have even observed a certain contradiction between them in that the first celebrates Tivoli's beauty and the second maintains that happiness should not depend on external places and circumstances.[63] The incongruity is negligible because the preference for Tivoli is presented as a preference for a simple and familiar place as opposed to more splendid and celebrated settings, and this already presupposes that a place's excellence is not decisive.[64] But a certain incongruity cannot be denied, for if one intends to say that being absent from a welcome place should not compromise one's tranquillity of soul, insisting on the place's beauty rather suggests the setting's importance and intensifies regret at our absence from it. Clearly, this incongruity serves the desire to please the addressee by celebrating his city.[65] More than the logical, it is the stylistic incongruity that seems noteworthy to me, for the same reason. The second part is a beautiful example of sobriety and expressive concentration in Horace's lyric style. It reaches a peak of emotional intensity with Teucer's final speech, which, with a few touches, gives the ode an epic scope, setting individual experience against a grandiose and solemn background. The first part, however, is a mannerist celebratory piece, openly conventional in a way not found elsewhere in Horatian lyric. The priamel's grand progression, the elaborate selection and regular cadence of the epithets,[66] the ostentatious order of composition, all converge to give an impression of openly celebratory solemnity precisely when Horace affirms, in terms recalling a *recusatio* and valorizing the poetics of the 'small', that he wishes to escape excessive celebrations of cities (a traditional Hellenistic motif), preferring

[63] Syndikus (1972), 95 ff.

[64] Reitzenstein (1963), 7; Pöschl (1963), 20 f. and (1959), 23 ff. and especially Syndikus (1972), 95 ff. I do not agree that the first part does not celebrate Tivoli as an ideal setting, but affirms the irrelevance of place, as does the second: Horace presents his preference for Tivoli, as others prefer other places, to demonstrate the subjectivity and irrelevance of the question. Silk (1952), 148 f.; Elder (1953); see Vaio (1966), 168 and 171; Bliss (1960), 32.

[65] This has been identified as the reason for praise of Tivoli several times (a place dear to Horace himself, see *Odes* 2. 6): already Porphyrio at line 15, and e.g. Stroux (1935), 318 f.; Nisbet and Hubbard (1970), 92; La Penna (1969), 198, who sees the desire to please Plancus with praise of Tivoli as the origin of the ode's partial incongruity.

[66] Nisbet and Hubbard (1970), 94 ff.

Tivoli's simplicity. To Tivoli he devotes only a few sober touches of limpid evocation, in his most authentic manner, but the preceding priamel exalts Tivoli most richly. Pasquali thought the first part cold and scholastic:[67] indeed, in offering Plancus a worthy celebration of Tivoli, Horace has somewhat violated the limits of moderation he usually imposes on himself and has chosen a more openly literary manner of expression appropriate precisely for a celebratory *munus*. I would not say this should be considered a fault. For Horace brilliantly combines the attitude of a panegyrist with its own negation, with an appeal for sober simplicity. He gives magnificent proof of this in the lines on Tivoli and in the ode's finale, which contrast greatly with the formal grandiloquence of the first part. This contrast accompanies and underscores the passage from the evocation of the most splendid of settings to the affirmation of a setting's irrelevance.[68]

6. We have seen that the occasion supposed of many poems has a 'social' character, i.e., they involve a circle of people connected by personal relations to the poet and the particular dedicatee (*Epodes* 10; *Odes* 1. 6; 1. 24; 1. 26;[69] 1. 29; 2. 1; 2. 7; 2. 9; 2. 12; 2. 17). In the ode on Quintilius' death (1. 24) the presence of a circle of friends, the 'privileged' recipients of the lament together with Virgil, is evident in the poem's articulation; usually the reference to a circle of people including the dedicatee is not explicit. Unlike Catullus, Horace rarely names more than one real person in the same ode.[70] The few references to a wider circle of *amici* ('friends') and *sodales* ('companions') occur in poems where no identifiable character is named. Horace tends to detach his conversation with the friend from a network of relations within a circle, to convey more directly the general address beyond the single addressee.

A relevant exception is 1. 36. The poet invites friends to celebrate a sacrifice thanking the gods for Numida's safekeeping and organizes preparations for the banquet following the sacrifice. A lively scene of conviviality is sketched where real people participate along with the

---

67 Pasquali (1920), 728 f.
68 Also Syndikus (1972), 95 ff.
69 [Citroni (1995), 308 ff.]
70 See n. 2 above, end.

poet and the celebrand. The ode expresses vivid joy at the friend's return, but the joy is not primarily the poet's who seems not to have a close relation with Numida—he says hardly anything about him and he remains evanescent. The ode rather expresses the joy of an entire group of friends and especially of one who seems Horace's main object of concern: Lamia, Numida's dearest friend, will enjoy the festivities most. The terms introducing Lamia's participation are similar to those introducing Virgil's participation in the grief over Quintilius in 1. 24, a friend over whom the gods should have kept guard (*non ita creditum*, 'entrusted not so', 1. 24) contrary to Numida (*custodes Numidae deos*, 'the gods, Numida's guardians', 1. 36. 3):

> caris multa sodalibus,
>   nulli plura tamen dividet oscula
> quam dulci Lamiae ...   (1. 36. 5–7)

many kisses will he share with dear friends, but with none more than his sweet Lamia ...

> multis ille bonis flebilis occidit,
> nulli flebilior quam tibi, Vergili.   (1. 24. 9–10)

He is dead, a cause of lament for many good men, but a greater sorrow for none besides you, Virgil.

The analogy of formulation corresponds to an analogy of functions:[71] both odes arise from requirements imposed by Horace's affectionate and courtly relations with a friend and his circle. These odes express the feelings of the friend and his circle on a particular occasion and thus become literary celebrations of the event.[72] In both odes, Horace communicates to the reader a vivid sense of participation in the respective sorrow or joy. The grief for Quintilius, however, elicits general moral considerations and refers to people known to the reader, while the joy expressed in 1. 36 is confined to Numida's circle of friends. The reader is called to appreciate the scene's liveliness, the tact of the literary game; he enters in this way the circle's

---

[71] See Fraenkel (1957), 112 for other parallels between analogous syntax and thematics.

[72] Nisbet and Hubbard (1970), 401 and Murray (1985), 43 and 47, think Lamia may have 'commissioned' the ode of Horace. For prosopographic hypotheses about the friendship between them, see Nisbet and Hubbard.

rites and participates in the game of pleasant literary tribute to the friendships and romances of its members. The compliment to Lamia and Numida for their reunited friendship, the final compliment to Numida for the beautiful hetaera cheering his return, the compliment to the hetaera herself, all have the ostentatious and brilliantly playful elegance characteristic of Catullus, when he celebrates his friends' romances *lepido versu* ('in elegant verse'). Another character appears in the poem: Bassus must be real because his name is Roman and he is introduced in relation to two other real characters. This appearance of such an evanescent, ill-defined character with a Roman name is unique in Horatian lyric. His role is to convey the impression of a plurality of participants and make the festivity more vivid. Mentioning him however must have been more significant for the friends concerned.[73]

This ode has been set against Catullus 9: there, a friend's return is the occasion for a passionate, emotional poem. In Horace, it is the occasion for an 'objective' setting of festive conviviality.[74] And yet, this ode is perhaps Horace's most 'Catullan': it immerses the reader directly into the rituals of a circle of friends without providing additional moral, political, or literary messages of more general validity, as is usual in odes involving real people. It simply asks the reader to appreciate the brilliant transfer to the literature of a moment in the poet's and his friend's life. It is 'Catullan' not like poem 9—one of Catullus' more vivid and emotional poems—but like the more light-hearted and playful poems inspired by everyday moments in the circle's life.

7. In odes involving real people without an identifiable occasion, the relation with the addressee generally appears irrelevant. It is mainly regarding odes of this kind (fifteen altogether[75]) that it has been claimed that Horace's lyric addressees are only a superficial and

---

[73] The identification with Propertius' poet friend Bassus (also in Ovid) is hypothetical.

[74] Syndikus (1972), 325 ff.; see Burck (1966), 163 f.

[75] 1. 4; 1. 22; 2. 2; 2. 3; 2. 6; 2. 10; 2. 11; 2. 14 (the setting intimated at line 22); 2. 16; 3. 16 (but with proemial function); 4. 7. See also the invitation poems without specific occasion: 3. 17; 3. 21; 3. 29; 4. 12. In 2. 3 and 2. 11, conviviality is a secondary motif. 2. 3 and 2. 10 are perhaps consolatory. In 1. 18, the first two lines suggest a specific communicative context.

formal device. However, in certain cases where nothing suggests an organic tie between dedicatee and subject matter, we happen to know from external sources that such ties existed. *Odes* 2. 10 to Licinius (generally identified with Murena, Maecenas' brother-in-law[76]) contains a general moral message, with no apparent connection to a particular occasion. Nisbet and Hubbard have pointed out that Murena was the friend of the Peripatetic Athenaeus of Seleucia: the Aristotelian morality professed in the ode is therefore likely due to Murena's philosophical preferences. In *Odes* 3. 21 to Messalla, a generic invitation seems merely a pretext for the hymn to the amphora, a brilliant variation on a conventional motif, not without a subtle moral intimation. But in Servius (Auct.) *ad Aen.* 8. 310, we read that in Maecenas' *Symposium* (a dialogue where Horace and Virgil were also characters) Messalla proffered a celebration of wine. If the information is true, as is generally thought, the connection between praise of wine and Messalla must have had for Maecenas' circle a precise sense of witty play that might escape an external reader.

We are also probably unaware in other cases of the existence of connections between subject matter and dedicatee known to some contemporary readers, especially among those closest to the poet who could recognize references to experiences and personal relations.[77] But we feel no need to know about these connections. The generic presupposition is sufficient: the person addressed is as interested in the subject as any other reader. Horace however almost always seeks to convey the impression that an ode's moral content has a precise relation to its addressee. In 1. 4, the reflection that,

[76] The identification is uncertain: Nisbet and Hubbard (1978), 151 ff.; Griffin (1980), 183; Watkins (1985). Syme (1985), 391 f. rejects it.

[77] This general probability does not justify deducing from an ode's contents information on the addressee's character and ideas without external corroboration or against external testimony. Nisbet and Hubbard (1978) do the former in the introductions to 2. 14, 2. 16, and partially 2. 11, and the latter for 2. 2, where they claim that Sallust, known for his luxurious life, must have had sympathies for Stoicism and the austerity of Roman moral tradition because the poem contains Stoic material. To explain the Epicurean stamp of 2. 16, it is not necessary to postulate Grosphus was Epicurean. Macleod (1979) attributes Epicurean sympathies to the dedicatee from the moral message of 2. 3. On this interpretation, Horace's personality dissolves into his addressees'.

in the face of death, there is no difference between rich and poor, addresses Sestius qua rich man (*beate*, 'blessed', 14).[78] In 4. 7, thoughts about the transience of human affairs address Torquatus whose many gifts—nobility, eloquence, *pietas* ('respect for duty'), wealth—might bring him to 'hope for immortality' (*inmortalia sperare*). In 2. 2 the gnomic argument on the limitation of desires addresses Sallust as someone who knows the right use of riches.[79] In 2. 11 the Epicurean invitation to pleasure addresses Quinctius as a man involved in Roman politics.[80] In 2. 16 the Epicurean message about *otium* ('leisure') addresses Grosphus as a landowner.[81] Few doubt that mention of *aequa mens* ('level head') in 2. 3 targets Dellius' turbulent political affairs. Among poems with real dedicatees, perhaps only 1. 22 to Fuscus[82] and 2. 10 to Licinius utterly lack reference to the dedicatee's experience—the latter, as we have seen, had anything but a marginal relation with him.

[78] The subtle references to Sestius hypothesized by Will (1982) are improbable.

[79] Despite its gnomic generality, the ode definitely compliments Sallust and perhaps defends him against the criticism of profligacy (Hor. *Sat.* 1. 2. 48 f.; Tac. *Ann.* 3. 30), here interpreted as non-dependence on riches and the refusal of vain and miserly accumulation. Besides Sallust, Horace cites Proculeius as an example of liberality: the unusual inclusion of two real people in the same ode meant more to those who knew about the relations between Sallust (friend and collaborator of Augustus), Proculeius (brother-in-law of Maecenas), and Horace. Since both Sallust and Proculeius are known as protectors of poets (Crinagoras, *AP* 16. 40; Iuv. 7. 94), the ode has been taken as thanks for help received or hoped for by Horace: Kiessling and Heinze (1957–8), n. to line 5 and Nisbet and Hubbard (1978), 32 ff. Horace's formulation of Sallust's just liberality (silver does not shine under ground and Sallust cannot bear treasures which do not shine with use) could allude to his investments in mining: all the more so since at 3. 3. 49, Horace deploys the diatribe *topos* that gold is better left under ground.

[80] Possible confirmation in *Epist.* 1. 16: the dedicatee is probably the same and is presented as a man enjoying great renown.

[81] Lines 33–6. This element is confirmed by *Epist.* 1. 12. 22–3 and various indications collected by Nisbet and Hubbard (1978), 252 f., who however go too far in identifying allusions to Grosphus.

[82] Since in *Epist.* 1. 10 Horace contrasts himself with Fuscus as lovers of the country and the city respectively, Gantar (1983), 129–34 thinks that in *Odes* 1. 22, Horace means to tease his friend playfully with the security of the country. On the contrary, the theme of 1. 22 is the poet's security due to his own purity *even* when the countryside offers danger. Harrison (1992) thinks the ironic allusions to the presumed self-sufficiency of the Stoic sage here and in *Epist.* 1. 10 allude to Fuscus' Stoic faith.

8. In Horace's lyric, address to an interlocutor is, as Heinze lucidly shows,[83] a formal and almost constant attitude deriving from the archaic lyric tradition. But this attitude is no useless anachronistic heritage, as Heinze judges it. According to Heinze, Horace's lyric form of address, the artificial heritage of what in Greek lyric has a real function, hinders the tendency towards the free subjective-autobiographical expression characteristic of Roman poetry of the time. But it is enough to compare any of the gnomic odes with addressees to one of the few without (2. 15; 3. 1–6; 3. 24) to see the difference between a cold and impersonal moral rhetoric and the warmth of morality presented as an intimate meditation born from concrete social experience. Dialogue involving a friend responds to an authentically Horatian expressive need, which finds further original development in the *Epistles*, with their different form, and is already apparent in the *Satires*.

Reitzenstein already had objected against Heinze that, in ancient poetry, we cannot distinctly differentiate self-expression from communication with others.[84] Klingner interpreted the *Odes'* dialogic form as ideal for an ethical poet communicating moral truths.[85] Actually, address in itself implies neither limitations on subjective expression nor a tendency to moralize, as Catullus shows. Admittedly, it provides Horace with a means of expression convenient for his own moral interests, which lead naturally to recommendation, suggestion, and advice. But it corresponds more profoundly to other characteristics of his personality: reserve in direct self-expression and the desire, more properly 'artistic', to lend his poetry a concrete dimension by systematically offering specific motivations. Thus, his poetry does not appear an 'arbitrary' manifestation of his inner world and moral outlook. In this sense, Horace achieves an effect similar to that of address by presenting his poetic discourse as a

---

[83] Heinze (1923) [Chapter 1 in this volume; Citroni (1995), 271 ff.].

[84] Reitzenstein (1963), 81.

[85] For Klingner (1930), 65 ff., Horace's ethical concerns require address; they lead him away from the irresponsible subjectivism of the Neoterics and encourage a self-expression directed toward the external. Similarly Waszink (1959). For Solmsen (1932), the dialogue form in Horace derives from a desire to speak to the community as an interpreter of the ethico-political values of the Augustan state.

prayer to divinity or as thoughts born of an event, true or fictional, which seems to 'demand' poetic development.[86]

Horace fully answers this demand by frequently including people known to all readers in the poems, often in connection with facts and episodes they recognize as real. As we have seen, the non-accidental relation of a poem with the person in it is an explicit presupposition of all poems concerning real people. Devoting such a great part of one's poetry to real people to meet these requirements entails setting the poems concomitantly within a network of real relations of literary communication. The 'form of the you', when it involves recognizable people is no mere 'form' anymore. In Greek lyric, the 'form of the you' originally corresponded to a real mode of communication addressed to a present public; similarly Horace also adopts this form because it corresponds to a real situation of communication which this poetry, as a literary text, establishes with a real reception environment. The 'form of the you' enables Horace to introduce a privileged dedicatee naturally in the text as an addressee who really is one of the recipients of the literary communication the text conveys. In his systematic appropriation of the 'form of the you' and the frequency of reference to real people, Horace is influenced by literary tradition (archaic lyric but also Catullus and elegy), by the need—artistic and ethical—to set the screen of occasion before the manifestation of his own inner world, and by the real presence of a circle of people offering natural reference points for literary communication. Each of these dimensions constitutes a condition essential to the form of the Horatian ode.

To acknowledge that Horace's poetry may originate from daily circumstances and had a communicative function tied to occasion does not mean, as with Catullus, limiting its extent. Rather, it means recognizing what Horace himself wanted to display, namely the experiential environment in which his poetry circulated and was received. This environment of relations helped establish the system of formal address in his lyric and is a lively and effective component of his poetry, suggesting topics, specific forms of compositional

---

[86] Thus a particular episode (lightning in a calm sky, the tree's fall) justifies the monologues in 1. 34 and 2. 13, where Horace also veils this 'self-exhibition' with subtle self-irony. See also Fraenkel (1957), 253 ff. on 1. 24.

structure, and sometimes particular stylistic inflections. In a few cases, the reader may feel that the private occasional dimension of the communication reserves special aspects of the poetic message solely for the dedicatee and a restricted circle of readers. These situations convey to the reader a concrete and vivid impression of the circumstantial occasion out of which the message addressed to him originates.

As early as his first lyric collection, Horace counts on his poetry having an inexhaustible public over time. The condition for poetic eternity is the work's participation in the artistic programme he and the audience he constructs for himself believe in. The elitist dimension, the disdain for common opinion and taste, is the condition for the search for excellence which alone gives his poetry a universal dimension, which alone enables it to address a public, presumably always elite, but unbounded by space or time. By book 4, Horace recognizes that the Roman community sees in him their poet. But in both lyric collections, though he does not restrict his outlook to the elite closely surrounding him, he constantly refers to it. For this elite is the dimension in which he really operates, in which his poetry is born and circulates, and which at the same time constitutes for him the only tangible, verifiable incarnation of that ideal public to whom he means to address his message.

6

The Maecenas Odes

Matthew S. Santirocco

The relationship between Horace and Maecenas has long fascinated scholars because of its unusually copious documentation and its intrinsic human and literary interest.[1] Although it is generally agreed that the personal element outweighed the professional in their friendship, interpretation of Horace's poems to Maecenas must nonetheless take some account of the realities of patronage in the Augustan age.

The old view of Maecenas as 'Minister of Propaganda' and of the poets around him as paid agents of the regime was put to rest long ago.[2] Among literary critics, biographical reconstruction has given way to an appreciation of the formal, possibly even fictive, nature of the texts. Thus, *recusationes* are now explained not only as refusals of actual patronal requests for epic but also, and primarily, as manifestos of Callimachean aesthetics.[3] Similarly, there is increasing recognition that a patron's external role (if any) in occasioning a poem is far less important than his literary role within the larger poetic design.[4] On the historical level, too, there has been a significant

---

[1] Different versions of this paper were presented at the Columbia University Symposium on Roman Patronage in April 1981 and at the APA meeting later that year. I wish to thank Professors S. Commager and M. Putnam and the editor and referees of *TAPA* for helpful criticism and suggestions.

[2] See Dalzell (1956); Reckford (1959).

[3] See Wimmel (1960); Clausen (1964); Smith (1968); and, for a different view of the reality behind *recusationes*, see Griffin (1976), 104 with note 243.

[4] See Zetzel (1982), 87–102; Bright (1978), 38–65.

revaluation. It is well known that as *equites*, most of the poets did not need regular financial support.[5] Recent study has further clarified their material and social position by showing that literary patronage was but one aspect of a much larger institution, *amicitia*, by which Roman society at all levels was organized into a network of reciprocal exchanges.[6]

These various approaches agree in deemphasizing the uniqueness and completeness of the poet's dependence on his patron. Although questions of personal, political, and artistic integrity were bound to arise, given the expectations of both sides, the poets were able to cope by devising ingenious strategies of independence. These ranged from Tibullus' habitation of an insulated pastoral-erotic landscape to Propertius' outright refusal to celebrate the new regime.[7] Horace had other, more subtle, ways of reconciling his need and affection for Maecenas with his own autonomy. Critics have generally focussed on the most obviously relevant works, the *recusationes*, and poems like *Sat.* 2.6 and *Epist.* 1.7 which can be labelled declarations of independence. But Horace's most comprehensive attempt to define his relationship with Maecenas is represented by the eight poems addressed to him in the first collection of *Odes*. Although they have been studied individually, the group as a whole has not received sufficient critical attention. And yet it can be demonstrated that here, as so often in Augustan poetry, the whole is more than the sum of its parts.

The arrangement of these poems is usually explained in terms of static patterning.[8] The compliment Horace elsewhere bestows on Maecenas—*Prima dicte mihi, summa dicende Camena* (*Epist.* 1.1.1)—can almost serve as a statement of this principle, for when the epilogue is excluded, the first and last odes are addressed to the patron (*C.* 1.1, 3.29). Also, the center of each book is occupied by a rededication to him (*C.* 1.20, 2.12, 3.16). Finally, Maecenas closes Book 2 (*C.* 2.20): and opens Book 3 at the first practical opportunity

---

[5] See Taylor (1925); Taylor (1968); Nicolet (1966), 441–56.

[6] See White (1978); and, more generally, see Brunt (1965), 1–20; Saller (1981), 7–39 on the language and ideology of patronage.

[7] See Santirocco (1982).

[8] On arrangement generally see Santirocco (1980a) with full bibliography.

after the Roman odes (*C.* 3.8).[9] But this symmetry at beginnings, middles, and ends is not exact. *C.* 2.17, for instance, is addressed to Maecenas but stands outside the scheme, and it ought also to be noted that while Maecenas occurs at the midpoint of each book, that position is calculated roughly by line totals in Book 2 (*C.* 2.1–11 = 288; 12–20 = 284),[10] but in Books 1 and 3 by the total number of poems. In any case, static symmetry is not the only or the most important principle of arrangement. The Maecenas odes are also dynamically disposed to chart the poet's gradual movement toward greater independence.

C. 1.1 dedicates the entire collection. 'The worst in the book, excepting the second,' was Landor's savage judgment.[11] Landor objected to the fulsome praise of Maecenas, as others have complained that its insertion only at the beginning and the end of the ode is mechanical and gratuitous.[12] But these objections ignore the patron's function in the larger structure of the poem. On one level, this is a poetic testament, retrospective in affirming moral continuity with the *Satires*, and programmatic in establishing new generic expectations.[13] The patron's role in this process may perhaps be clarified by comparison with Catullus' first poem. Catullus proclaims his Alexandrianism not to distinguish himself from Nepos but, rather, to exploit some striking resemblances between himself and his friend. Both men, as writers, are innovative (*novum*, 1 = *ausus . . . unus*, 5); the works of both are refined (*pumice expolitum*, 2 = *doctis . . . et laboriosis*, 7); and, finally, both compose on the small scale (*libellum*, 1, and *nugas*, 4 = *tribus . . . cartis*, 6). In other words, Catullus sets up

[9] The only position closer to the beginning of the book was reserved for a poem marking both a break and a transition from the Roman Odes: see Mutschler (1978), 125–6.

[10] This is reinforced by the arrangement of the poems: see Ludwig (1957); Eisenberger (1980).

[11] Messalla at the end of 'Tibullus and Messalla' in the first series of *Imaginary Conversations*.

[12] See, e.g., Collinge (1961), 108: 'The first and last couplets certainly look to be outside the general scheme; they might be read continuously, were it not for the *quodsi*, which takes account of what intervenes.'

[13] See Shey (1971) for the continuity with satire; and Fraenkel (1957), 230 for verbal anticipation of subsequent odes.

an analogy between himself and Nepos by implying that they share an allegiance to Callimachean literary standards.[14]

Although Horace does not compare himself with his patron, his poetic programme is also inseparable from, and indeed accomplished by, the personal dedication. Deferential and dependent, it is framed by effusive compliments for Maecenas. The opening address extols the nobility of his Etruscan lineage in grandiloquent language, and the flattery is enhanced by the likelihood that it stretches the truth:[15]

> Maecenas atavis edite regibus,
> o et praesidium et dulce decus meum.   (1–2)
>
> Maecenas, sprung from royal ancestors, o my
> protection and sweet glory...

The priamel that follows enumerates a number of the occupations in which men glory. (*palma...* | *evehit ad deos*, 5–6; *honoribus*, 8) or take delight (*iuvat*, 4; *gaudentem*, 11; *iuvant*, 23). But Horace has already indicated that his glory and delight (*dulce decus*, 2) is Maecenas, and so we are prepared for the end of the ode where the proclamation of the poet's superiority prompts the patron's reappearance:

> quodsi me lyricis vatibus inseres,
> sublimi feriam sidera vertice.   (35–6)

But if you enroll me among the lyric bards, I shall strike the stars with my uplifted head.

At the end of his first poem, Catullus had prayed that the Muse allow his poetry to survive 'for a century or two' (*plus uno maneat perenne saeclo*, 10). While Horace's hope for immortality in the canon of lyric poets is surely more audacious, it is also qualified by being contingent upon the approval not only of the Muses (32–4) but also of the patron, who is the recipient of his prayer and the agent of his apotheosis.

Maecenas next appears in *C.* 1.20 where Horace invites him for a drink. The poet's tone has already become less formal and more

---

[14] See Cairns (1969); Levine (1969); Singleton (1972); Wiseman (1979), 167–74. For a different view, however, see Elder (1966).
[15] On Maecenas' dubious ancestry see MacKay (1942), 79–80.

familiar. The encomium, for instance, is no longer direct as in *C.* 1.1, but oblique. Thus, Maecenas' Etruscan heritage is only hinted at as the Tiber, whose source is in Etruria, is dubbed his 'paternal river' (*paterni* | *fluminis*, 5–6). Similarly, the title *eques* (5) becomes, in context, an oblique compliment, for it alludes to the privileged seating enjoyed by the knights at the theatre. Even the wine which Maecenas is offered is invested with indirect encomiastic significance. Its modesty (1–2) sets up an honorific contrast with the luxurious vintages to which the wealthy Maecenas is accustomed (9–12). Its bottling by the poet when Maecenas' recovery from illness was applauded in the theatre attests to the public and private devotion the great man inspires. And that the wine is Sabine (2) implies the poet's gratitude as well, for it alludes to the gift of the Sabine farm. Finally, the very image of Italian wine in a Greek jar (*Graeca . . . testa*, 2) calls to mind Horace's descriptions of his poetic achievement as a synthesis of Greek and Roman elements (e.g. *C.* 3.30.13–14; *Epist.* 1.19.21–34), and the vocabulary (e.g. *conditum*, 3) and motifs here are often calculated ambiguities, applying to poetry as well as to wine.[16] The drink is ultimately suggestive of Horace's own poetry which Maecenas, as it guarantor, is invited to imbibe.

It is not, however, just in the oblique and sometimes symbolic quality of its encomium that *C.* 1.20 differs from the first ode. It also introduces a number of motifs and themes that will recur in undeniably self-assertive odes farther along in the sequence. These include the patron's recovery from illness (cf. *C.* 2.17), his equestrian status (cf. *C.* 3.16), the invitation to drink (cf. *C.* 3.8, 29), the Etruscan river (cf. *C.* 3.29), and the social and material disparity between the rich man and the poet (cf. *C.* 2.17; 3.16, 29). When they recur in subsequent poems, these elements will be exploited to establish the poet's independence from his patron. As yet, however, they have only the honorific function that has been observed. The Maecenas odes are an ordered sequence, and while *C.* 1.20 facilitates the distancing process, we can read too much into the poem by reading too far ahead.[17]

Basically, then, the first book of *Odes* acknowledges, directly in *C.*1.1 and obliquely in *C.* 1.20, Horace's respect for and dependence

---

[16] See Commager (1962), 325–6; Putnam (1969); Race (1978).
[17] But for the other view, see Race (1978).

on Maecenas. In Book 2, however, this deferential and dependent stance is much qualified. It is significant that Maecenas does not open the volume (*C.* 2.1 is for Pollio), and that his first appearance is in a *recusatio*, *C.* 2.12. Horace's strategy here is to coopt his patron to his own position. This is accomplished by the very first word, *nolis*: Horace refuses to write heroics not because he is unable to do so (the usual gambit, as in *C.* 1.6), but because Maecenas is unwilling. Other details contribute to the cooptation of the patron. For example, when Maecenas is urged to take on the literary task himself—an unlikely eventuality in light of his neoteric tastes—he is portrayed as writing not in poetry but in prose (*pedestribus* | ... *historiis*, 9–10). Similarly, the rest of the poem (13–28) celebrates Maecenas' love for a certain Licymnia who may be a cover for his wife, Terentia, but who, in any case, has a symbolic function. Her name is a Greek translation, from *ligys* and *hymnos*, of a phrase in the poem, *dulces... cantus* (13–14). Licymnia, then, incarnates an alternative to politics and political poetry—for Maecenas love, and for Horace love poetry.[18]

This analogy between poet and patron which Horace exploits to assert his independence is further developed, and then broken down, in the sequence of four poems with which Book 2 closes.[19] In *C.* 2.17 Horace calms Maecenas' fears of death. As evidence that their stars are linked (*consentit astrum*, 22) two biographical details are adduced: Maecenas' recovery from illness (22–6) and the poet's own miraculous escape from death when a tree nearly fell on his head (27–30). These salvations were introduced independently at *C.* 1.20 and 2.13 respectively, but their conjunction here in the same poem expresses the closeness of the association between the two men. And yet, there are already some discrepancies. Although Maecenas is called, in words that recall the opening of *C.* 1.1, the glory and prop of the poet's existence (*mearum* | *grande decus columenque rerum*, 3–4), his anxiety and constant requests for reassurance which prompt this ode (*cur me querelis exanimas tuis*, 1)

---

[18] For full discussion of these points see Santirocco (1980b).

[19] Connections have been seen, not just between the last two odes (e.g. Silk 1956, who views them as prelude to the Roman Odes), but also among the last four: see Wili (1948), 233 ff., on the poet's triumph over death, and Commager (1962), 311–12 who notes briefly their movement away from Maecenas but does not pursue it beyond these four odes.

belie the compliment and anticipate the role reversals we shall observe in Book 3 in which the patron becomes dependent on his client
for support. Even more interesting are the details of salvation. It was
great Jupiter who rescued Maecenas from illness (22–5), whereas
Horace was protected from the falling tree by the minor woodland
deity Faunus (28–30). Similarly, Maecenas is advised to build a votive
shrine in thanksgiving (30–1), but Horace can only sacrifice a humble lamb (*humilem... agnam*, 32). Though appropriate to the rustic
context here, Faunus elsewhere in Horace is suggestive also of the
poet's literary inspiration,[20] and the 'humble' lamb is transparently
Callimachean, a conflation of the *Aetia* prologue's fat sacrifice and
slender Muse (fr. 1.23–4 Pf.), and so represents (as elsewhere in
Horace) the poem itself.[21] At the end of an ode ostensibly comparing
poet and patron, these contrasts are also a subtle indication of where
the resemblance ultimately breaks down.

This is made explicit in the very next ode. *C*. 2.18 is not strictly a
Maecenas ode since the patron is not addressed by name and *tu* (17)
is ostensibly an unspecified second person. Nevertheless, Nisbet and
Hubbard argue very strongly for the ambiguity of *tu*, noting a
striking number of possible covert allusions to Maecenas in the
poem. Thus, the mention of the heir of Attalus (5–6) conjures up
not only Maecenas' wealth but also his Etruscan heritage (since
Attalus' Lydian realm was the alleged origin of the Etruscans), the
rich man's clients trail Etruscan-style garments (7–8), the luxurious
architecture (17–28) calls to mind the *turris Maecenatiana* (which
will be mentioned openly in *C*. 3.29), and the emphasis on death and
the underworld (18–19, 29–40) is appropriate to Maecenas' own
morbid preoccupations.[22] It might be added that the change in
addressee from Maecenas in *C*. 2.17 to *tu* in *C*. 2.18 is paralleled by
the internal structure of several individual poems (e.g. *C*. 1.1; *S*. 1.1,

[20] See Commager (1962), 348–52; Troxler-Keller (1964), 108–18.

[21] e.g. *C*. 1.19.13–16 where the *hostia* parallels the poem in that both are offered to
Venus; *C*. 4.2.53–60 where the contrast between the two sacrifices recapitulates the
earlier contrast between Horatian and Pindaric lyric.

[22] For other indirect references to Maecenas in this and other poems, see Nisbet
and Hubbard (1978), 289–90. For discussion of second person pronouns generally
and of the function of addressees as a metaphor for the reader, see Johnson (1982),
passim, esp. 1–23 and, on Horace, 127.

Epist. 1.1) which move from Maecenas to an unspecified second person who suggests both the general reader and the patron.

Finally, whatever view we take of the second person, there are unmistakable third-person allusions to Maecenas in one passage. Having rejected wealth, Horace proclaims that his riches are invested elsewhere:

> at fides et ingeni
>   benigna vena est pauperemque dives
> me petit: nihil supra
>   deos lacesso nec potentem amicum
> largiora flagito,
>   satis beatus unicis Sabinis.   (9–14)

But I have loyalty and a rich vein of talent, and the wealthy man seeks me out, a poor man. I ask nothing more of the gods nor do I request more of my powerful friend, since I am sufficiently blessed in my singular Sabine farm.

In so personal a passage, references to a rich man who pursues Horace, to a powerful friend who grants his request, and, finally, to the Sabine farm can only point to Maecenas. Here, as in the preceding poem, there is a hint of role reversal, as the rich man seeks out the poor client: *pauperemque dives | me petit.*[23] Similarly, the contrast between poet and patron which was symbolized in *C.* 2.17 by their different tutelary deities and thank-offerings is now made explicit, specified as the difference between material wealth and the spiritual and poetic riches that infinitely surpass it.

And so, the next ode, *C.* 2.19, is a hymn to Bacchus which attempts to convey through Dionysiac imagery the essence of this poetic experience, its isolation, excitement, and mystical power. But this excludes Maecenas who is not a poet and who is neither addressed nor mentioned here. He does, however, receive the final ode in the book, *C.* 2.20. The poet has moved from inspiration to immortality, from cause to effect. Although the imagery of a bird metamorphosis is humorous, the conception behind it is basically serious and striking:

---

[23] In patronage contexts *peto* usually signifies the client's role: to the references in Nisbet and Hubbard (1978), 299, add Cat. 28.13 (*pete nobiles amicos*); *Laus Pis.* 218–19 (*dignare tuos aperire Penates, | hoc solum petimus*); Hor. *C.* 3.16.22–3 (*nil cupientium | nudus castra peto*), on which see further below.

the poet, soaring aloft on newly sprouted wings, leaves his patron grounded far below:

> non ego, pauperum
> sanguis parentum, non ego, quem vocas,
> dilecte Maecenas, obibo
> nec Stygia cohibebor unda. (5–8)

The offspring of poor parents, I shall not die, I, whom you call upon, beloved Maecenas, nor shall I be held in by the waters of the Styx.

In *C.* 2.17, we recall, Horace had announced that he and Maecenas would die together. By *C.* 2.20 the analogy between the two men has broken down completely, and Horace boasts that, as a poet, he will not die at all: *non ego | ... obibo* (6–7).

After such a bold assertion, Book 3 fully develops a role reversal in its portrayal of the patron-client relationship, as Maecenas becomes spiritually dependent on Horace.[24] This had been anticipated, as we have seen, in Book 2 where a role reversal is implicit in the context of several poems, in the patron's requests for reassurance at *C.* 2.17.1, and in the rich man's active pursuit of the poet at *C.* 2.18.10–11. Now, however, role reversal is accomplished by the poem's content, as Horace extends the paraenetic function of ancient lyric by venturing not only advice but also explicit criticism, and by setting himself up as a model for Maecenas.

C. 3.8 is a drinking song like *C.* 1.20. But whereas that poem was honorific, this is playful. Horace teases his patron in the opening address for his useless learning (1–5), and even the language may parody Maecenas' precious literary style:[25]

> Martiis caelebs quid agam kalendis,
> quid velint flores et acerra turis
> plena miraris positusque carbo in
>   caespite vivo,
>
> docte sermones utriusque linguae:
> voveram dulcis epulas et album

---

[24] Reckford (1959) observes a role reversal in the relationship, but he sees it only in biographical terms and not also as an artistic principle organizing a sequence of poems.

[25] See Bradshaw (1970).

> Libero caprum prope funeratus
> arboris ictu. (1–8)

What I, a bachelor, am doing on March first, what the flowers mean and the box full of incense, and the coal placed on living turf—do you wonder at this, who are learned in the lore of both languages? I had vowed sweet banquets and a white kid to Liber when I was nearly killed by the falling tree.

In *C.* 1.20 Maecenas had been invited to drink in celebration of his own escape from death, but now in *C.* 3.8 he is to toast his client's health. In a similar reversal, the wine which was honorific in *C.* 1.20 now takes on a hortatory significance,[26] for Horace advises Maecenas to enjoy life and to cease worrying about the state:

> mitte civilis super urbe curas
>
> .   .   .   .   .
>
> neglegens, ne qua populus laboret,
> parce privatus nimium cavere et
> dona praesentis cape laetus horae:
> linque severa. (17, 25–8)

Put aside political worries about the city. ...Unconcerned about whether the people are anywhere in trouble, as a private citizen stop worrying too much and happily take the gifts of the present hour. Leave serious matters behind.

In light of this injunction, the setting and mode of address are not only humorous but also programmatic. *Docte sermones utriusque linguae* (5): though 'learned in the lore of both tongues' (i.e. Greek and Latin), Maecenas is at a loss to explain why his friend, a bachelor, should be celebrating March first, the Matronalia. But Horace informs him that he is not observing that public holiday but rather a private anniversary that just happens to coincide with it, his deliverance from the falling tree. And this is precisely what Maecenas must learn to do, to put aside public matters (*civilis...curas*, 17) and become a private citizen (*privatus*, 26). Horace functions, then, as a model for his patron to emulate.[27]

The middle poem of the book, *C.* 3.16, goes further, taking as its subject not the cares of state but rather the cares which are engen-

---

[26] As often: see Commager (1957).

[27] But *C.* 3.8 functions also in another group of poems: see Santirocco (1985).

dered by wealth and which are equally burdensome. Drawing from myth (Danae, 1–11), heroic legend (Amphiaraus, 11–13), Greek history (Philip, 13–15), and recent Roman history (if *navium* | ... *duces*, 15–16, alludes to Menas who was twice enticed by money to desert from Sextus Pompeius to Octavian), Horace illustrates not just the destructive power of wealth but also its capacity to produce anxiety and greed, and then he dissociates himself from this way of life:

> crescentem sequitur cura pecuniam
> maiorumque fames: iure perhorrui
> late conspicuum tollere verticem,
> > Maecenas, equitum decus.   (17–20)

Care follows upon increasing wealth, as does hunger for greater riches. With good reason I have shrunk from raising my head conspicuously, Maecenas, glory of the knights.

Here too the mode of address is functional: alluding to Maecenas' equestrian status, Horace implies that his own preference for the simple life resembles his patron's lack of worldly ambition. This looks at first like the old strategy of cooptation. But what follows is problematic:

> quanto quisque sibi plura negaverit,
> ab dis plura feret: nil cupientium
> nudus castra peto et transfuga divitum
> > partis linquere gestio,
>
> contemptae dominus splendidior rei. ...   (21–5)

The more each man denies himself, the more he will receive from the gods. Naked I seek the camps of those who desire nothing, and as an exile I long to desert the quarters of the rich, a more splendid master of the wealth I despise.

As the 'glory of the knights,' *equitum decus* (20), Maecenas would presumably qualify for inclusion among the rather vaguely expressed *nil cupientium* (22) whom Horace seeks out. And yet, as a very rich man, he is at least a potential member of the camp from which Horace deserts. R. J. Shork has demonstrated, for instance, that the examples of flawed wealth with which the poem opens are all at least marginally relevant to Maecenas. All are cases of fraternal, dynastic rivalry and involve the use of money for political bribery. Maecenas' wealth must have recommended itself to Augustus for similar reasons in the years of his contested ascent to power. Thus, the address to Maecenas follows as almost the last item in the catalogue, '... the fifth exemplum, by no means parallel to the previous four, but a personal and contemporary reminder to Horace of the dangers inherent in wealth.'[28] And so, Horace ends by rejecting more help from his patron:

> inportuna tamen pauperies abest
> nec, si plura velim, tu dare deneges.
>
> .   .   .   .   .   .
>
>   multa petentibus
> desunt multa: bene est cui deus obtulit
> parca quod satis est manu.   (37–8, 42–4)

But troublesome poverty is absent, nor would you refuse to give me more if I wanted it. ... To those seeking much, much is wanting. He fares well to whom the god with a sparing hand has given what is enough.

This is more than a polite acknowledgment of gratitude made necessary by the awkward circumstance of dedicating a poem on poverty to one's benefactor. Horace's attitude throughout has been ambiguous, his gratitude tempered with wariness, and while he compliments Maecenas for his willingness to provide further assistance, he also precludes the acceptance of any such offer.[29]

The final Maecenas ode, *C.* 3.29, recapitulates themes and motifs from throughout the collection, especially from the other Maecenas odes. But now advice gives way to a critique more thoroughgoing than that contained in any of the preceding poems. Maecenas is yet again invited for a drink, but the poet's tone betrays impatience. That the wine is untouched (*non ante verso*, 2) and has long been awaiting Maecenas (*iamdudum*, 5) implies that previous invitations have gone unheeded—not just the literal summonses of *C.* 1.20 and 3.8, but also the larger philosophical messages contained therein. This is confirmed by the picture of the unreconstructed Maecenas that

---

[28] Schork (1971), esp. 531, from which I have drawn in the preceding discussion.

[29] So effectively does Horace decline further aid, that the poem has been read as his refusal of an imperial secretaryship: see Frank (1925).

follows. Gazing wistfully from his tower at the Campagna (9–12), he nevertheless delays his arrival there, still subject to the same distractions:

> fastidiosam desere copiam et
> molem propinquam nubibus arduis:
>   omitte mirari beatae
>   fumum et opes strepitumque Romae.
>
>   .   .   .   .   .
>
> tu civitatem quis deceat status
> curas et urbi sollicitus times,
>   quid Seres et regnata Cyro
>   Bactra parent Tanaisque discors.   (9–12, 25–8)

Abandon cloying abundance and the pile that reaches to the lofty clouds. Stop marveling at the fumes, riches, and noise of blessed Rome. . . . You are concerned about the state's proper condition and, anxious for the city, you fear what the Chinese are planning and Bactria ruled by Cyrus and the quarrelsome Scythians.

Just as the patron's cloying wealth (*fastidiosam . . . copiam*, 9) recalls the theme of *C.* 3.16, so his political anxieties here are familiar from *C.* 3.8. It is, of course, honorific to show Maecenas concerned with affairs of state. But in *C.* 3.8 his anxiety was shown to be groundless (18–24), and now in *C.* 3.29 Horace states explicitly that it is impious as well, for it runs counter to the intent of the god who has shrouded the future in darkness:

> prudens futuri temporis exitum
> caliginosa nocte premit deus
>   ridetque, si mortalis ultra
>   fas trepidat.   (29–32)

Prudently god hides the outcome of the future in dark night and laughs if mortals fear more than is right.

This leads to an almost perfunctory injunction to enjoy life, which is tailored to Maecenas by means of one striking and strategic image:

> quod adest memento
> conponere aequos: cetera fluminis
>   ritu feruntur, nunc medio alveo
>   cum pace delabentis Etruscum

in mare, nunc lapides adesos

stirpisque raptas et pecus et domos
volventis una, non sine montium
    clamore vicinaeque silvae,
    cum fera diluvies quietos

inritat amnis.   (32–41)

Remember calmly to set in order what is at hand. The rest is carried away like a river which now flows peacefully in mid channel down into the Etruscan Sea, but now catches up in its rush worn stones, uprooted tree trunks, and the flock and houses all together, making noise in the mountains and the neighboring woods when the wild flood enrages quiet rivers.

To convey the changeability to which Maecenas should be immune, Horace evokes the erratic course of the Tiber, identified as the river 'flowing into the Etruscan sea' (35–6). The rare hypermetron whereby the word *Etruscum* does indeed flow into the next line's *in mare* is not just a neat mimetic trick but also alerts us to the significance of the description.[30] In the opening address Maecenas had been reminded of his Etruscan lineage (*Tyrrhena regum progenies*, 1), and in *C.* 1.20 the Tiber was, for this reason, called his 'paternal river' (5–6). The river image in *C.* 3.29, then, gives point to the opening address and personalizes the injunction by implying that Maecenas should learn from his heritage. And perhaps not only the Etruscan but also the regal aspect of that heritage is exploited in the very next words:

ille potens sui
laetusque deget, cui licet in diem
    dixisse 'vixi.'   (41–3)

That man will live happily as master of himself who can say each day 'I have lived.'

In *C.* 2.18 Horace thanked, but set himself apart from, his *potentem amicum* (12), and in *C.* 3.16 wealth's destructive power (*potentius*, 10) is rejected by Horace who has thereby become its master (*dominus*, 25). Liberated from materialistic associations, the word *potens* takes on new, more spiritual meaning in *C.* 3.29. Maecenas claims

---

[30] See Mørland (1980).

regal descent, but true power is not that wielded by kings over their subjects, but that exercised over oneself, *potens sui* (41).

At this point the patron disappears from the poem, the rest of which consists of a long monologue by one who has achieved this mastery of himself. His impassioned advocacy of a life of simplicity and acquiescence to Fortune is not consistent with the previous negative picture of Maecenas. But it is a familiar Horatian theme, and the first person narrator is inevitably identified by the reader as Horace himself.[31] The poem then concludes with one final, charming image:

> tunc me biremis praesidio scaphae
> tutum per Aegaeos tumultus
> aura feret geminusque Pollux. (62–4)

Then the breeze and Castor and Pollux will bear me safely through Aegean waves protected in my two-oared skiff.

This subtle modulation from patron to poet imitates the movement of the entire collection. In the very first ode, Maecenas had been characterized as the poet's support, *praesidium* (*C.* 1.1.2). Now, in the last poem addressed to him, Maecenas gradually fades away and the word *praesidio* (62) describes the poet's own small skiff which enjoys divine protection. A transition to the epilogue is thus accomplished. *Potens sui* (41) leads up to *ex humili potens* in *C.* 3.30.12, just as *vixi* (48) is taken one step further by *non omnis moriar* in *C.* 3.30.6. The poet has moved from the satisfaction of having lived fully in this world to the assurance of life beyond it in his poetry. This was the prayer for immortality which Horace had addressed to Maecenas in the first ode (*C.* 1.1.35–6). Now it is finally answered, but it is not Maecenas who grants it, but the Muse, Melpomene, an emblem of the poet's *own* creative power.[32]

In conclusion, this brief survey of the Maecenas odes has necessarily been schematic, focussing on only one aspect of the poems. But though the complexity of the individual odes has thereby been

---

[31] The point is unaffected by punctuation, whether *vixi* alone or the entire passage, 43–fin., is enclosed by quotation marks.

[32] For other points of contact between the epilogue and *C.* 1.1 see Zetzel (1982), 95–7; on the epilogue's relationship to *C.* 3.29 and the other poems in the second half of Book 3, see Santirocco (1984).

simplified, their dramatic progress as a group is now apparent. In Book 1 Horace is deferential and dependent, emphasizing the material differences between himself and his patron. In Book 2 these acquire a spiritual dimension as Horace's poverty becomes symbolic of the artistic riches which set him apart from others, including Maecenas. Finally, in Book 3 the distinction between the two men is mainly philosophical, the superiority of Horace's very way of life to his patron's anxiety-ridden existence. Their roles are reversed as Horace becomes, in a sense, the spiritual patron of Maecenas. Since this order of publication does not seem to coincide with that of composition, it is not possible to trace in this sequence of poems the history of the relationship. Their clear movement toward independence may be based on an historical or psychological development, but is ultimately an aesthetic effect. While consistently affirming Horace's sincere affection for Maecenas, these odes, by their dynamic disposition, also create a certain distance and enable their author to maintain a high degree of personal and artistic freedom.

Author's note: This article was incorporated with modifications and translations in my book, *Unity and Design in Horace's Odes* (Chapel Hill, 1986), 153–68. The translations here come from that volume.

7

Horace's Century Poem:
A Processional Song?

Peter L. Schmidt

With Horace, who was so conscious of his art, there is a danger, such as hardly exists with any other Roman author, of trivializing the function of poetry in its historical context—or to explain it away as 'Augustan'. By contrast, this contribution on the *Carmen Saeculare* emphasizes the tradition of the Roman processional hymn and its concrete performance conditions, which bring to mind a specific form of oral literature in Roman society.

I

At the beginning of 207 BC the Roman authorities had to deal a second time with the prodigy (*prodigium*) of a hermaphrodite birth, that caused further worry to minds already disturbed by the confusions of war; Hannibal was still in Italy, his brother Hasdrubal was already on his way with another Carthaginian army from Spain. As the expiation (*piacula*) of 209 BC (Livy 27.11.4 ff.: sacrifices, prayers, games) had obviously not endured in the long run, the decision was taken this time to reinforce the elimination of the abnormal birth with a solemn processional rogation (Livy 27.37.5 ff.). Its course ran from the temple of Apollo Medicus (downriver from the Capitol by the Tiber) to that of Juno on the Aventine, but made a detour along the way to the Forum, the city's sacral as well as political heart. Two white cows, the intended sacrificial victims, led the procession; two images of gods in cypress wood (*xoana*) were borne along, and a choir of thrice nine unmarried girls in long dresses followed, who accompanied the parade (*pompa*) with a processional hymn; the rear was brought up by the *decemviri sacris faciundis*, a college of ten priests qualified to make sacrifices, in festal garb and laurel wreaths. Having crossed the city limits (*pomerium*) at the Porta Carmentalis, the procession reached the Forum along the Vicus Iugarius and stopped there, to give the girls the scope for a rope dance (*per manus reste data*, 'with a rope passed through their hands') without interrupting the hymn (*sonum vocis pulsu pedum modulantes*, 'accompanying the sound of their voice with the beat of their feet'). It then returned by way of the Vicus Tuscus, Velabrum, and Forum Boarium to the processional route proper along the Clivus Publicius over to the Aventine. There sacrifice was made to the goddess, and the carven images then deposited in the temple.

Livy's description is concise, precise, and saturated with visual detail. It evokes the analogy of comparable social rituals: the funeral procession (*pompa funebris*), the parade (*pompa*) before perform-ances at the theatre or Circus, processions in honour of the gods, the laying out of couches (*lectisternia*) and seats (*sellisternia*) for the gods, and the triumph. It is of capital importance for the literary historian on account of the texts that authorize, accompany, and record it. First there comes the 'Sibylline Oracle', that is the instruc-tion delivered by the college of ten in Greek hexameters on the basis of the Sibylline Books,[1] that governed the important elements of the ritual and promised success if it was followed exactly.

Whereas with texts of that kind we can only speculate how the prescriptions of the ritual books were adapted by the Roman magis-trates to the particular circumstances,[2] we are on firmer ground with the processional hymn rehearsed beforehand in the temple of Jupiter Stator (*id cum in Iovis Statoris aede discerent conditum ab Livio poeta carmen*, 'when they learned this poem, composed by Livius the poet,

---

[1] On the Sibylline Books in general see Radke (1979), 39 ff.; for an introduction to Roman literature on *prodigia*, see Schmidt (1968), 3 ff.

[2] Cf. e.g. Radke (1979), 47 ff.

in the temple of Jupiter Stator', Livy 23.37.7): it was written by the first poet at Rome to be known by name, the Greek Livius Andronicus. The disparaging assessment by his Augustan namesake, who (or whose source) may have known the text from antiquarian tradition, also explains the next stage in literary history: *carmen... illa tempestate forsitan laudabile rudibus ingeniis, nunc abhorrens et inconditum si referatur* ('the poem, laudable perhaps for the rude spirits of that time, would now seem shaggy and uncouth if it were repeated', 27.37.13); at any rate, when seven years later the gods intimated their displeasure in double strength through the birth of two hermaphrodites (31.12.8 ff.), the programme of 207 was repeated, except that the Tarentine's hymn, now a generation old and no longer satisfactory, was replaced by a more modern production: *carmen, sicut patrum memoria Livius, ita tum condidit P. Licinius Tegula* ('Just as Livius composed a poem in the memory of our fathers, so then did P. Licinius Tegula').

Cichorius[3] argued with both his usual acuteness and a very high degree of plausibility—at any rate he has not yet been conclusively refuted—that Livius' poem 'composed in the memory of our fathers' was identical with the hymn prescribed by the Sibylline books for the first repetition of the 'games at the Tarentum' (*ludi Tarentini*), which after 348 became the 'century games' (*ludi saeculares*) in 249, i.e., in the First Punic War, and were to remain so thereafter.[4]

A 'Century song' and sacrifice were established during the First Punic War to take place every hundred years for Dis and Proserpina according to the response of the college of ten. When they were ordered to examine the Sibylline books, they responded that the war with the Carthaginians could be waged to our advantage, if games were celebrated for Dis and Proserpina

---

[3] Cichorius (1922), 1 ff., 47–8; accepted by e.g. Altheim (1931), 1 ff.; Gagé (1934), 58, 114 with Weinstock (1936), 661–2; Mattingly (1957), 161–2; against e.g. Fraenkel, *RE* Suppl. v (1931), 600 s.v. Livius 10a; Carratello (1979), 19–20, who however in my opinion have all but insuperable difficulties in taking *patrum memoria* (Livy 31. 12. 10) as equivalent to *proxime* (§§8–9). Unlike Cichorius I relate the notice for 207 to a revival of Livius' *carmen saeculare*, while Barwick (1933), 203 ff. rejects it outright as a doublet of Livy 31. 12. 8 ff. (200); against see e.g. Flores (1973), 7 ff. The testimonia are also in Pighi (1965), 197 ff.

[4] Gagé (1955), 228 ff. and on the *ludi saeculares* in general M. P. Nilsson, *RE²* iA (1920), 1696 ff.; Radke (1978); testimonia in Pighi.

and a song were sung among the sacrifices. The books ordered that the children of nobles sing this song on the Capitoline.[5]

Traces of this chorus for Proserpina are preserved in Varro, *LL* 6.94, and we may add that the first time the hymn appears to have been used outside its original context was for a similar *prodigium* ten years before the occasion we began by describing, at the onset of the Second Punic War. In 249, 217, 207, and 200, so many gods of the 'Greek rite' were involved that the original text, which is likely to have been wide-ranging (as we shall see for Horace in due course),[6] could be effortlessly adapted.

After the Sibylline oracle and the *carmen*, the third kind of text concerned with these liturgical high points of the *Graecus ritus* is the *acta*, the records of the priestly colleges (the *pontifices*—who may have been responsible for the *annales maximi*—and the *decemviri*), and their reflections in the historical or antiquarian tradition, which in some cases preserved the only memory of the processional hymn or even its text; only in this light can Livy's comment and Varro's citation from the old *carmen saeculare* be understood. After the first wave of hermaphrodite *prodigia* in the wars of the late second century, one could read in these in and after the Gracchan period (133 to at least 92 BCE) of similar indicators, no longer of an external but an internal crisis, hermaphrodites or other sinister *prodigia*, celestial apparitions or subterranean rumblings (Julius Obsequens 43, 46), which were usually to be expiated by processions in honour of Ceres/Proserpina, Juno Regina, or both together.[7] One would dearly like to know how long Licinius Tegula's hymn remained in use.

II

Whether at the repetition of the *ludi saeculares* in 146 BCE a *pompa* with *carmen* was again put on escapes our knowledge, owing to the

---

[5] Ps.-Acro on Horace, *Carmen Saeculare* 8; text in Pighi (1965), 214.

[6] For a possible change of sex cf. Macrobius, *Sat.* 1. 6. 14 (*virginibus patrimis matrimisque pronuntiantibus carmen*)=Livy 22. 1. 13 ff., where there is no corresponding statement.

[7] Cf. Diels (1890), 37 ff.; Wissowa (1912), 426–7.

scanty and contradictory accounts of this celebration in particular.
Even though *prodigia* continued to occur and be recorded by
the annalistic tradition (known by way of Livy through Obsequens),
the cessation of the sequence of hermaphrodite *prodigium* and expi-
atory procession after 92 must presumably be explained by supposing the deployment of this special *piaculum* seemed dispensable after
the Civil War. When Augustus decided, on the basis of a festal
chronology invented *ad hoc*, to celebrate his *ludi saeculares* as the
quintessence of the new aeon, he at any rate did not need to deal with
a living continuity of such ceremonies (that of 49 had fallen victim to
the Civil War) or processional practice. Varro's *Antiquitates divinae*
made the necessary information available.[8] The preservation of historic ritual, on the basis of a new religious policy, embraced the
overall programme of the celebrations as well as the oracle from
the Sibylline books on which they were based. These had been
destroyed by fire in 83 BCE along with the temple of Jupiter Capitolinus, recompiled in 76, and preserved there until they were transferred to the care of Apollo Palatinus some time before 17.[9] Their
preservation finally furthered hymnic practice, which became a fresh
tradition in the *ludi saeculares* of the continuing principate, at least
under Domitian in AD 88 and Septimius Severus in 204.[10]
    In the new ritual system of the Augustan festival,[11] it was less
important than in comparable expiation ceremonies of the past to
take note of other gods. Jupiter, for example, had been provided with
a sacrifice of thrice nine oxen as early as the Sibylline oracle of 125 BC,
and the *carmen saeculare* of 249 had been sung according to Verrius
in Capitolio, in front of his temple. Diana is actually the only new god
to share in her brother Apollo's cult. Rather, the whole ceremony was
so to speak brightened up by the elimination of the underworld gods

    [8] See the fragments collected with commentary by Cardauns (1976), a preliminary structure of fragments attested by name; the Sibylline books were in book 4 (*De quindecimviris sacrorum* i. 42 ff.; ii. 165 ff.), the games themselves in books 9–10, having already been treated in *De scenicis originibus*, cf. Pighi (1965), 37–8.
    [9] Cf. Wissowa (1912), 75–6, 536–7; Radke (1959), 225 ff.; J. Gagé (1934), 29 (first publ. 1931 = Gagé 1972).
    [10] Domitian: cf. Pighi (1965), 87; Septimius Severus: text, as far as it can be reconstructed, ibid. 222.
    [11] Wissowa (1912), 75; Latte (1960), 298 ff.; for the *Sibyllinum* of 123 see Diels (1890), 37 ff., 111 ff.

Dis Pater and Proserpina, by the interpretation of the chthonic deities who govern time in the sense of continued human life, as δαίμονες μειλίχιοι (Sibylline oracle, v. 29), as *dei milichei* (*acta* 11), and by the dedication of three daytime festivals to the Olympian gods Jupiter, Juno, and Apollo. Indeed, overall attention is to be directed not so much towards a gloomy past as towards a bright future.

Scripta quidem eius usque adeo probavit mansuraque perpetua opinatus est, ut...saeculare carmen componendum ei iniunxerit. (Suetonius, *Vita Horatii* 17)

Indeed, [Augustus] approved of his writings to such an extent and thought that they would endure for all time, that he enjoined on him to compose a Century song.

The Princeps knew precisely why he was entrusting this demanding task to a poet who a few years earlier had placed just this proud claim (*non omnis moriar*, 'I will not entirely die', *Ode* 3.30.6) programmatically at the end of his collection of odes. But the corollary was that there was no place for the poem's text in the festival *acta*: that would have meant burial in the archives or a one-copy edition, even in so prestigious a publication as the inscription erected and discovered at the Tarentum.[12] The former had befallen the hymns of Livius and Tegula, the latter the unknown poet of the Severan *carmen*, whereas in Horace's case only the fact is recorded, but the text is lacking:

Sacrificioque perfecto pueri XXVII, quibus denuntiatum erat, patrimi et matrimi et puellae totidem carmen cecinerunt. Eodemque modo in Capitolio. Carmen composuit Q. Horatius Flaccus. (*acta* 147–9)

And when the sacrifice was completed, twenty-seven boys, to whom it was officially announced, with father and mother still alive, and as many girls sang a song. And [it was performed] in the same way on the Capitoline. Q. Horatius Flaccus composed the song.

This fact accords with the self-image of the poet, who had the poem published as a separate work in preference to simply including it in his fourth book of odes. *Odes* 4.3 and 4.6 rather present his private view of this thoroughly official event. This separate

---

[12] On the connection between transmission history (i.e. in books) and the expectation of lasting fame cf. Rösler (1980), 78 ff.

publication history gives the poem more than an ephemeral, transitory significance. Instead of incorporating it arbitrarily in another book, it also indicates that the work of art was a social success. It is enough to cast doubt on the adequacy of understanding the *carmen saeculare* as 'a typical Horatian ode'.[13] Separate publication implies the poet wished his achievement to be judged in its own right. What at *Ode* 1.1.35–6 had still been hypothetical (*quodsi me lyricis vatibus inseres | sublimi feriam sidera vertice*, 'But if you include me in the canon of lyric bards, I will strike the stars with my head') had now, thanks to the Muse, become reality: *quod monstror digito praetereuntium | Romanae fidicen lyrae | quod spiro et placeo, si placeo, tuum est* ('That I am pointed at by passers-by as the lyrist of the Roman lyre, that I breathe and please, if I do please—all this is yours', *Ode* 4.3.22 ff.). An adequate attempt at understanding the *Carmen Saeculare* will therefore need to have as its goal the explanation of the aesthetic success as a social one (or vice versa), and therefore to avoid classifying the poet either as an executive assistant of Augustan religious policies or as a free artist according to Romantic notions of poetry.

   If today this still, or again, needs emphasizing, it is because ever since the discovery and publication of the Augustan *acta saecularia* in 1890–1—the starting-point for modern interpretation of the *carmen*—as if in parallel to the developing paradigm-shift towards the interpretation of works as immanent artefacts, there is an unmistakable tendency to avoid the consequences of the *acta*'s discovery for the understanding of the historical situation that contributed to the making of the poem. Mommsen's succinct criticism, uttered almost in passing, of its want of unity and of clarity beyond its immediate audience provoked the powerful counterblast of Johannes Vahlen.[14] The reaction was necessary and legitimate ('However, I take the

[13] Fraenkel (1957), 382.

[14] Mommsen (1905), 357 ff. (orig. publ. 1891); for the traditional nature of the criticism cf. e.g. Obbatius (1848), 321. Vahlen (1923), 369 ff. (orig. publ. 1892). Besides Fraenkel (1957), 364 ff. (to be read against the background of Kiessling and Heinze's commentary 1957–8: vol. i, cf. Fraenkel 1957: 370 n. 2) profit is to be derived from Numberger's school commentary (1972: 414 ff.). More recent scholarship in Kissel (1981), 1514 f.; Radke (1978), 1108 ff. Ancient commentaries are conveniently quoted in Pighi (1965), 208 ff.

opposite route, not from the document to the poem but from the analysis of the poem to the new information afforded by the document', 379); the results of his careful structural analysis, which pursues the 'connection of ideas' (376) that Mommsen missed, remain fundamental even today: 'A double prayer develops in both parts in a closed sequence of thought [stanzas 3–8, 10–18], but is separated by the interposed appeal to Apollo and Diana.... They... together with the first two and the final stanzas, which enclose the poem, confer on both parts a framework for their sense' (380–1); in stanzas 14–18 'the poet takes what has been achieved so far as his basis... for his wish for and confidence in further prosperity' (379). 'Both prayers derived their shared content from the festival and the prophecies, both desired the same thing: the longevity and well-being of the city and the Roman state.... The first desired... the physical conditions of the common weal, afforded by the population and the fertility of the soil, the second more the ethical and political elements.... Both are brought into relation with the efforts of the ruler, to whose ordinances the first refers and who in the second... predominates in person' (381).

Such pronouncements bring the historical data into relation with the course of the poem and stand in welcome contrast to Friedrich Leo's apodeictic warning signal: 'The historical record is good for illuminating details; if it is necessary for the understanding of the whole, then it is not a poem.'[15] This is quoted by Fraenkel as 'wisdom' (1957: 370), as if the kinds of text uniquely preserved in this case, Sibylline oracle,[16] *acta*, and *carmen*, did not illuminate each other as instruction, process, and interpretation.

This line of his teacher Leo was continued by Fraenkel in the relevant chapter of his important and influential, but also selective and often subjective book on Horace—a book to which the perplexed reader will still always turn first. Fraenkel is obviously concerned to distance the *Carmen Saeculare* as far as he possibly can from the historical situation, as a typical Horatian poem: 'These new lyrics

[15] Leo in Fraenkel (1960), ii. 13, (orig. publ. 1903).
[16] Text of the oracle in Diels (1890), 133 ff., Pighi (1965), 56 ff., of the *acta* in Mommsen (1913), 467 ff., Pighi (1965), 107 ff., the public announcement not preserved in them at Zosimus 2. 5, cf. Diels (1890), 131 ff., Pighi (1965), 53 ff. and Paschoud's edition (1971: i. 74 ff.).

were self-contained. Their complete emancipation was essential.'[17]
We may for the moment serenely set aside the question whether a
poem that so obviously presupposes a particular political situation
(Augustus' efforts at reform, 17 ff.; the Julian family mythology,
41 ff.) and a religious festival prepared in such detail (the Sibylline
oracle, 5 ff., 21 ff.; a ritual programme, 13 ff.), and thus refers to a
subject historically predetermined many times over with such clarity
both for the contemporary audience and the modern scholar, can
really be interpreted as 'a piece of pure poetry', as Carl Becker
summed up Fraenkel's position.[18] Of course, Fraenkel himself is
not entirely consistent, as when he defends the allusion to the
previous year's *lex Iulia de maritandis ordinibus* against the romantic reproach of being insufficiently poetic (1957: 373 ff.)—he
really does!

Fraenkel allowed himself to uncouple the poem from its concrete
occasion, that is from the context of the festival, by plainly misunderstanding the words *sacrificio perfecto* ('when the sacrifice was completed') with which the *acta* introduce the passage concerning the
Carmen Saeculare: in contrast to the earlier processional hymns, 'the
carmen is deliberately placed outside them [sc. the ceremonies]... it
was sung when the elaborate ceremonies had *all* been completed.[19]
Therefore it keeps at a distance... after the completion of the ceremonies *proper*... ornamental... a mere appendix or epilogue' (1957:
378; my italics).

In reality the mention of the festal hymn is so inseparably incorporated in the overall structure of the *acta* that such an isolating
approach is invalid from the start: immediately after 'Q. Horatius
Flaccus' the text continues by listing the names of the *quindecimuiri*
in order with Augustus and Agrippa at their head, and thus emphasizes the significance of conducting the ceremonies on the Palatine
and the Capitol; next, as on the previous days, there are more games

[17] Fraenkel (1957), 381, cf. also 389: 'Horace's song had its being solely in the sphere
of poetry, and the only links which connected it with the cult were links of thought.'
[18] Becker (1959), 607–8 (critical); cf. also Becker (1963), 113 ff.
[19] Heinze *ad loc.* had already drawn a misleading inference from a prematurely
curtailed text of the *acta*'s ('solemn conclusion to the three-day religious festival').
The actual conclusion of the festival was of course, as is clear from its origin, the
games at the Tarentum, 'ad ludos saeculares consummandos', as the Severan *acta* put
it, IV (Va). 77.

(*ludi*), this time circus games (*circenses*) as opposed to the preceding theatrical spectacles (*ludi Latini*) (*acta* 108–9, 133). The three central days of the festival, 1–3 June, are for their part the climax of an event that, after the preparatory reports, resolutions, and edicts (1–75), begins on 29 May and ends on 12 June (76–89, 155–65). The ceremonial each time follows the order sacrifice, prayers, games, that is to say, the procession with our *Carmen* is parallel, as a *supplicatio*, to the *sellisternia* (laying out of seats for the gods) of the three nocturnal observances and that of the first daytime (109), but especially to the great prayer of the 110 matrons led by Agrippa on the second day (123 ff.). Within this point-for-point continuity,[20] *sacrificio perfecto* denotes no more than the temporal sequence. Comparable are the games and *sellisternia* after the sacrifice at line 100 and *deinde*, 'thereupon', at lines 108, 123.

Anyone who finds justification in the *acta* for considering that the hymn really is anchored in a specific phase of the festivities[21] will start from the fact that, as in 207, its performance begins in front of a temple dedicated to Apollo, now the Palatine, and ends in front of one dedicated to Juno, now the temple of the Capitoline Triad. Although primarily dedicated to the two Delian deities, the poem replicates this trajectory from the opening invocation (*Phoebe silvarumque potens Diana*, 'Phoebus and Diana, power of the woods', 1) to the final stanza (*haec Iovem sentire deosque cunctos*, 'that Jupiter and all the gods hear these things', 73). But what this movement meant in actual practice, as against the earlier processional hymns, is disputed. Is the term 'processional hymn' legitimate at all, as Mommsen had succinctly asserted ('Without question the poem was a processional hymn')[22] and his authority induced subsequent discussion for some

---

[20] Cf. the synopsis of the festival programme in Pighi (1965), 358 ff. On the connection between *sellisternia, supplicationes*, and rogational processions see Wissowa (1912), 423 ff. In ll. 18–25 of the Sibylline oracle too the requirements for hymn and matrons' prayer follow one another, cf. also Friedrich (1894), 98 ff.

[21] But cf. Fraenkel (1957), 378: 'The sense of Horace's poem is completely lost as soon as we attempt to tie it down to any particular stage in the course of the ceremonies…'.

[22] Mommsen (1905), 358, cf. Mommsen (1913), 601–2, accepted e.g. by Wissowa (1904), 206 and Wissowa (1912), 35; against e.g. Friedrich (1894), 96 ff. and in detail Dennison (1904), 49 ff. The original procession must have led from the Tarentum to the Capitol.

time to accept? Undoubtedly yes, if we define the concept as Fraenkel
does (379): 'The choir would move from one shrine to another, halt
in front of it, and there sing either the whole προσόδιον... or an
appropriate section of it';[23] in this case one may also speculate
whether the procession halted at the Forum, as it had in 207.
Undoubtedly not, if simultaneous singing and proceeding are intended, as at Livy 27.37.13: *septem et viginti virgines, longum indutae
vestem, carmen in Iunonem reginam canentes ibant* ('twenty-seven
maidens, wearing a long dress, went singing a song for queen Juno').
The second open question regarding performance concerns the rope
dance, which Livy describes at 27.37.14 and Augustus' letter provided
for (*pueros virginesque patrimos matrimosque ad carmen canendum
chorosque habendos frequentes ut adsint*, 'that boys and maidens with
both parents living be present to sing the song and dance the
choruses in number', *acta* 20). The Severan report is more detailed
in this matter and also in describing the procession by way of the
Forum: *pueri praetextati... et puellae palliolatae cum discriminalibus,
manibus conexis carmen cecinerunt... concinentibus tibicinibus...*
('boys with bordered toga and girls wearing mantles and hair orna-
ments sang the song with hands joined and the reed players accompanying them').[24] Finally, one may also ponder how the musical
component of the performance—the singing and the instrumental
accompaniment[25]—may have appeared, but that remains secondary
to the text itself.

III

By contrast, another problem leads us directly into textual analysis.
A pressing question that has been almost completely suppressed by

---

[23] I do not understand how this definition fails to cover our *Carmen Saeculare* (but
cf. Fraenkel 1957: 378).
[24] IV (Va), 59–60 (Pighi 1965: 165); on the procession ll. 75 ff (Pighi 1965: 166);
on the repetition l. 75: *ante cuius* [sc. *Iovis O. M.*] *pronaum, sicut in Palatio, carmen
conexis manibus pueri puellaque dixerunt chorosque habuerunt*, cf. Gagé (1934), 56 ff.
and Pighi (1965), 202 ff.
[25] On this, see e.g. Wille (1961), 169 ff. at 174–5, 178–9.

recent scholarship is: what was the significance of the addition of twenty-seven boys to the twenty-seven girls of the original *Carmen Saeculare* and its revivals or imitations?[26] The Sibylline oracle envisaged at least partially that the two groups should dance and sing separately, at least part of the time (χωρὶς δὲ κόραι χορὸν αὐταὶ ἔχοιεν | καὶ χωρὶς παίδων ἄρσην στάχυς, 'let the girls hold the dance apart and apart the male progeny of boys', 20–1); it finds its analogy in Catullus' long poems for double choir, the marriage-songs 61[27] and 62. How our poem ought to be divided between the two halves of the chorus constantly preoccupied nineteenth-century scholars, without eliciting an answer that met with an even partial consensus. Attributions were made stanza by stanza or triad by triad, and the only thing agreed on to any extent was that stanzas 1–2 and 19 belong to the whole choir and stanza 9 must be divided.[28] Then, owing to the authority of Heinze, who gave stanzas 1–9 to the girls, stanzas 10–18 to the boys, and stanza 19 to both,[29] and Fraenkel, who ignored it altogether, the problem has slipped from scholarly collective memory.

In the search for plausible arguments and criteria for allocating this or that portion of the text, it must dawn on one first of all that the chorus sings communally when it speaks of itself in the first person (*precamur*, 'we pray', 3; taken up in 6; 74 *reporto*, 'I bring back', 74). Stanzas 1–2, 19 had already been separated as a frame by Vahlen. This criterion has a counterpart, that whenever the text speaks about boys or girls, it is always the others who are singing, just as in Catullus 61.36 ff., 121 the boys yield to the maidens and the

[26] Cf. Fraenkel (1957), 480 n. 3 on this putative Augustan innovation, but also Gagé (1955), 388–9, 634 and the brief hymn to Diana, Catullus 34.

[27] But cf. Fedeli (1983), 5, 42–3, who apparently regards Greek influence as paramount. But then our Horatian poem too—in sapphic stanzas!—would have to count 'as a purely literary creation'. In fact we should reckon with the wide-ranging Hellenization of Roman social rituals, which naturally had to be kept up as such.

[28] Earlier positions e.g. in Obbarius (1848), 320–1, Kühn (1877), 1 ff., more recent ones in the last pronouncement known to me, Landmann (1961), 173 ff., cf. e.g. Friedrich (1894), 92 f., Frank (1921), 324 ff. (metrical arguments). On Redslob see below, n. 36. In addition, Loewe set the poem to music for two choirs, cf. Hirschberg (1915), 190 ff. at 202, 205 ff. (musical appendix); Draheim and Wille (1985), 10, 117 ff.

[29] e.g. Kiessling and Heinze (⁷1930), 470–1; cf. also n. 30.

latter again to the boys (cf. 231). In Catullus 62 this system is complicated somewhat by the soliloquies in lines 1 (not recognized as such
until line 6), 6, and 11; if we exclude them, lines 6 (*Cernitis... iuvenes,*
'youths, you see') and 12 (*aspicite, innuptae secum ut meditata requir-
unt,* 'look how the maidens recall what they have memorized') match
the complementary structure surmised for Horace's poem. This
means that in the 'centrepiece', as Vahlen calls it, lines 33–4 belong
to the *puellae,* lines 35–6 to the *pueri.*[30]

The comparison of the specific literarity of the poem with Catullus
61 and 62 is insightful in another regard as well. While in poem 62
the referential code pertains consistently to an object conceived as
literary from the beginning, so as to alert the well-informed reader of
variations in the literary competition that follows, no such explicit
rules are brought in at the start in 61, which is a historically based
epithalamium for Iunia Aurunculeia (16, 86 ff.) and Manlius Torquatus (16, 216, 222). This is similar to Horace's *Carmen Saeculare.*
At the original performance, after all, the succession of speakers was
obvious to the listener or spectactor without more ado.

As a further criterion it may be taken that the *pueri* pray to Apollo
(33–4) and the *puellae* to Diana (35–6). The respective sections of the
festal community are allocated to 'their' deity; on the previous day
the matrons had prayed to Juno. Accordingly, the stanzas concerned
with Apollo fall to the boys, those with Diana to the girls.[31]

Guided by these criteria, let us look more closely. After the introductory full-chorus stanzas invoking both deities together, the petitionary part (stanzas 3–13) begins with an address to Apollo as Sol,
thus referring both back to *lucidum caeli decus, o colendi* ('shining
honour of the sky, O you to be worshipped', 2) and ahead to Diana's
representation as Luna in line 36.[32] Thematic prayers are offered for

[30] So e.g. A. Kiessling in his commentary, i (1884), 282–3 (²1890), 315; otherwise
Heinze (³1898), 316–17.
[31] Cf. Ode 21. 1–2 *Dianam tenerae dicite virgines, intonsum pueri dicite Cynthium,*
where the poet addresses the chorus. Cf. too F. Altheim, 'Almus sol', in id., *Römische
Religionsgeschichte* (Baden-Baden, 1953), vol. 2, 239–53 (1st edn. 1932).
[32] Cf. the Sibylline oracle (16–17) Φοῖβος Ἀπόλλων, | ὅστε καί Ἥλιος κικλήσκεται,
Fraenkel (1931), 371 ff., and on the problem of religious history Altheim (1953);
unconvincing is Galinsky (1967), 619 ff. On the solar-chariot acroterion crowning the
Palatine temple of Apollo see now Zanker (1983), 32: 'In Augustan art and literature
the sun-god is identified even more closely than ever with Apollo.'

Rome's (political and military) greatness, a wish later fulfilled in
stanza 17 (*alme Sol...|...possis nihil urbe Roma* | *visere maius*,
'nourishing Sun, may you come to look on nothing greater than
the city of Rome'; *si...* [Apollo] *videt...remque Romanam Latium-
que felix*, 'if [Apollo] looks on the Roman state and Latium with good
fortune'). That the *pueri* are singing here thus seems plausible. If in
the ensuing stanzas Horace rearranges the plan of the festival by
next addressing, in the singular, the birth-goddess Ilithyia, honoured on the second night, he does so in order to set up a latent
parallel with Apollo's sister:[33] following on the address to Sol, he
uses the cult-names for Diana (*sive tu Lucina probas vocari* | *seu
Genetyllis*, 'whether you approve our calling you Lucina or Genetyllis', 15–16). The ensuing prayers for lawful marriage, painless births,
and in general fertility in human beings (stanza 5), cattle and crops
(stanza 8) seem appropriate for the *puellae*; the Parcae are brought in
as guarantors of a happily prophesied future (stanza 7), as suits this
line of thought. Furthermore, these stanzas (4–8) evoke the ancient
nocturnal ceremonies, namely the core of the original *ludi saeculares*
in their Augustan reinterpretation. In 249 BCE only maidens had
featured.

At lines 33–4 the *puellae* look back at stanza 3 and anticipate
stanzas 10–11. They pass the song over, as it were, to the boys
(*supplices audi pueros, Apollo*, 'Apollo, listen to suppliant boys') and
the boys echo them (*audi, Luna, puellas*, 'Luna, hear the girls'),
thereby reinforcing the sequence of stanzas just concluded. There
should be no doubt that after this transitional stanza it is the boys
who make the new start: the subject-matter is political and historical
and calls to mind the daytime festival for Jupiter and Juno. Furthermore, the principal reference of *si vestrum est opus* ('if it is your work',
37) is to Apollo as Rome's protector. Anyone who argues over a full
stop or colon after line 44 overlooks the simple fact of the initial
performance and reception, in which the conditional clause could, in

[33] Cf. *Carm.* 3. 22; Catullus 34. 13–16 (*Tu Lucina dolentibus* | *Iuno dicta puerperis* |
tu...notho es | *dicta lumine Luna*); on the parallels between the two poems see
especially Brakman (1921), 209 ff. Cf. further Virgil, *Buc.* 4. 10 (*Casta fave Lucina:
tuus iam regnat Apollo*).

the linear sequence of hearing, be referred only backwards.[34] The
conditional clauses at lines 15–16 and 65 likewise refer backwards.
The decisive fact is that Horace himself emphasizes the link between
Apollo and Aeneas' achievement at *Ode* 4.6.21 ff., a poem occasioned
by the same cause as the *Carmen Saeculare*. The Aeneas section of the
Carmen Saeculare alludes to the new epic of his great contemporary,
with lines 41–4 corresponding to *Aeneid* 4.345–6 and lines 51–2 to
6.853.

Equally unambiguous for an audience that had witnessed the
previous days' sacrifices to Jupiter and Juno was the decisive reference
in the next two stanzas: *quaeque vos bobus veneratur albis* | *clarus
Anchisae Venerisque sanguis* | *impetret* ('May the famous blood of
Anchises and Venus achieve what he asks of you when he worships
with white cattle', 49–51). Therewith the central prayer is brought to
an end in a climax of precise but indirect expression that links the
Capitoline deities as representatives of the entire divine cosmos (73)
with their earthly analogue Augustus.

The next stanza too remains with the boys. It sums up the preceding four and takes them as at once fulfilled: the change from sub-
junctive/imperative to indicative is decisive. Just so in stanza 15 do
the girls fulfil 'their' earlier stanzas, 4–8. The anaphoric responsion
iam . . . iam ('now . . . now') answers the divided repetition in stanza 9
(*audi . . . audi*, 'hear . . . hear'), as the military successes respond to the
moral rearmament. The pair of deities is to be regarded as present
and joins in celebrating Augustus' achievements. Again, as in stanzas
3 and 10–14, the salute to Roman history in stanzas 16–17, which
culminate in Augustus, belongs to the boys, the corresponding stanza
about Diana (18) to the girls, and the first-person stanza 19 ends in
tones full of hope.

Function and distribution are thus, in our reconstruction, as
shown in the Table.

---

[34] The clause was firmly related to the following *di* in stanza 12 by Vahlen (1923),
384–5 and Fraenkel (1957), 370. Mommsen's assertion cannot stand (1905: 367–8),
(1913: 602). Fraenkel takes Mommsen as an authority. Cf. too Heinze's punctuation:
a dash after line 36, a colon after line 44. For the correct view, albeit without reference
to the argument from aural reception, see Deubner (1933), 469 ff., and following him
Radke (1978), 1101–2.

Stanza	Function	Performers
1–2	Exposition	Full chorus
3	First Prayer	Boys
4–8		Girls
9	Transition	33 f. Girls
		35 f. Boys
10–13	Second Prayer	Boys
14	Prayers' Fulfilment	Boys
15		Girls
16–17	Reaction of Addressees	Boys
18		Girls
19	Recessional	Full chorus

In a poem like ours, intended for a listening audience, any structural analysis has to face the consequences of its initial context of reception. Mommsen did this, when in accordance with his understanding of the processional song he supposed that stanzas 1–9 were performed on the Palatine, 10–15 on the Capitol, and 16–19 back on the Palatine, but at the same time complained that the poet, in a festival poem 'also intended from the start for a wider and not too well-informed readership' (!), thereby led his public astray.[35] However, in the face of the unambiguous wording of the *acta*, which speak of a repetition on the Capitol, this over-hasty assertion could not stand, and with it fell the criticism of Horace. By contrast, Vahlen's analysis of the structure boils down to a series of speakers thus: 'we—thou—we—thou—he—we', and remains quite compatible with the reconstruction of the concrete performance conditions attempted here.

Despite his appeal to Vahlen, Fraenkel alone has maintained a rigorously triadic structure with the exception of the concluding stanza.[36] He has subscribed to a principle of articulation that presumes an immanent work of art, based on the aesthetics of production, which often cuts across the obvious movement of thought that

[35] See n. 34.
[36] Fraenkel (1957), 370–1, citing Menozzi (1905), 67 ff.; so too Heinze *ad loc.*, citing Redslob (1912), 65–6, who also distributes the chorus accordingly. In contrast to our poem, the triadic articulation of *Ode* 1. 12, also in sapphics, seems intertextually justified, cf. Schmidt (1984), 139 ff.

the listener must have been aware of. Therefore he does not mark
the break between stanzas 2 and 3; transitional stanza 9 has to be
attached to those preceding it, and the end of the strictly petitionary
part (stanza 13) to those following.

It would take us too far afield here to show how Horace keeps
himself free of any schematism precisely in the *Carmen Saeculare*,
whether in the structure and the allocation to the two parts of the
chorus, or in the freedom with which he treats concrete details of
the ritual or stereotyped formulae of the hymn tradition.[37] He
moreover maintains a distance from panegyric clichés—this for
those anxious of any contact with history, for whom an at least
relative poetical autonomy is dear to the heart. And as for the unity
of the poetic theme, Vahlen had already pointed to the balance of
the two prayer-halves, which resolves into the centrality of the
divine pair repeatedly made present for us (stanzas 1–2, 3 ff.,
10 ff., 16 ff.) and thus denotes the special protection of Augustan
rule itself (stanzas 3, 5, 10–11, 13–15, 17). Gagé[38] has shown how
lines are spun from one deity to another by way of their functions
and names, and blend into a harmonious circle of divinities of
welfare—this for those who, like Mommsen, despite all ritual
details demand a 'connection of ideas'.

IV

In our age, the new media—which are simply the old in augmented
quantity—promise paradise on earth: a hitherto lacking political
balance, cheerfulness instead of pedagogical gloom, a multiplicity
of suppliers, i.e., freedom of opinion, at least for those with the
power of capital. In this context, sensitivity to the problems of
media communication and the status of our own and previous
cultures may increase. For this reason it seemed justifiable to cast a
somewhat one-sided illumination on a central text of Roman poetry,

[37] Cf. Buchholz (1912), 36 ff.; Weinstock (1936), 659–60.
[38] Gagé (1934), 40 ff., cf. too Altheim (1953), 247 ff.

which ought still to have its place in teaching Latin, and to set aright scholarly positions based on the unassailability of book culture.

Beyond that, however, it ought in general to be rewarding to reconsider the relation between orality and writing in Latin literary history. Livius Andronicus was not of course the first poet in Rome, but the first whose productions, beyond serving their original purpose, were published as literary books for later reading and indeed read. Texts by him and others that were orally reproduced before 240 or even 249 BCE are lost for ever along with his undatable *Odusia*. The plays performed on the Roman stage from 364 onwards as a religious obligation are, like those old processional hymns, a mere antiquarian memory. For an age in which the book-roll denoted secrecy and government knowledge (for example Sibylline oracles or official registers), oral literature secured the public nature of social rituals, of communal existence at high points and in times of crisis. Its forms are perhaps banquet songs, certainly marriage-songs, the *nenia* ('lullaby' or 'dirge') and *laudatio funebris* ('funeral oration'), songs at triumphal or rogational processions, the great speech in the Forum or the Curia, the improvised theatre of the *fescennini* ('ritual marriage abuse') and *Atellanae* ('farce'). It is essential to bear in mind such ephemeral and occasional literature, not meant for written perpetuation, in order to reconstruct the overall picture and to understand texts at the point of transition to written literarity.

Strictly speaking, it was not until the Augustan age that the combination of the development of institutions presupposing and advancing literacy—advanced school education, professional editing and text fixation, publisher-booksellers, libraries[39]—and the demise of republican forms of politics and social rituals led to a fully developed literary culture. At that point, however, a new, secondary orality of recitation and declamation began as it were to sweep up the remains of the older traditions: speech, drama, and occasional poetry. While there remain on the syllabus works of characteristically republican literature—a speech by Cicero, a comedy, or indeed

---

[39] A useful overview, though it does not differentiate between historical processes, in Kenney (1982), 3 ff.

poems by Catullus—with a claim on the public matching that of the *Carmen Saeculare*, it may thus be rewarding to achieve a more nuanced historical picture, to train for the scrutiny of texts, and to highlight the multiplicity of literary options by analysing them as texts first spoken and addressed to an audience.

8

Power and Impotence in Horace's *Epodes*

William Fitzgerald

Horace's *Epodes* are seldom considered as a whole.[1] On the face of it, there would seem to be good reason for this fact. It is generally agreed that the poems were written over a period of ten years (from after Philippi to after Actium),[2] during which time there was a great deal of change in the Roman world and in Horace's circumstances. Furthermore, the collection contains a considerable diversity of themes, genres and what, for lack of a better expression, one must call levels of reality. The Archilochean persona maintained in several of the poems is a unifying factor, of course, but it has not seemed pervasive enough to have allowed a systematic interpretation of the whole collection, and even within the Archilochean group scholars have tended to separate the political poems from the invective poems.[3] Attempts to find some principle of arrangement for the

---

[1] See the survey of scholarship by Aldo Setaioli (1981). Most of the general studies he cites stress the varied nature of the *Epodes*, and many regard them as experimental, the usual fate of a poet's early work, which is too often treated as a sign of things to come.

[2] There is a convenient table of the dating of these poems by various scholars in Carrubba (1969), 16.

[3] The best treatment of the Archilochean aspect of the *Epodes* is that of Nisbet (1984). Nisbet sees Horace's adoption of the Archilochean persona as 'a declaration of his own alienation' after Philippi, and argues that after he was drawn into Maecenas' circle the persona is softened and the engagement with politics is muted; Nisbet cites *Epode* 4 as an instance of the trivialization of the poet's earlier treatment of war and politics (9). I will argue that a study of poems like *Epode* 4 in the context of the collection, rather than in terms of chronology, makes this kind of judgment inappropriate. For a table of the ways scholars have grouped the poems, see Carrubba (1969), 34 f.

collection have not been very enlightening, since they have rarely
amounted to more than classifying each of the poems by type or
theme (usually a completely unsystematic mixture of both), and then
putting them into groups, which reveals structural patterns that have
a no more than decorative function, or else simply displays Horace's
penchant for *variatio*.[4]

In what follows, I will show the interrelation between the political,
invective and erotic poems in the *Epodes*. All of these types are found
in the Archilochean corpus, and I will take Horace's adoption of the
Archilochean persona as relevant, directly or more obliquely, to all of
the poems. Adopting the Archilochean persona in the troubled
period during which the *Epodes* were written allowed Horace to
question the nature of the poet's role and position in a time of
political upheaval. As we shall see, Archilochus' confident spokes-
manship for his community is undermined in Horace's assumption
of this role by the more complex relation of the poet to political
figures and events in late republican Rome, and also by the problematic nature of human relations in general during a protracted civil
war. Archilochus projected confidence in the efficacy of his poetry
(126W), whether it was used to exhort his fellow citizens (3W) or to
avenge himself on his personal enemies (*Epode* 6.11–14); poetry for
him was power. Horace's attitude to his calling is much less secure, he
is not so much concerned with striking a pose as with questioning
this pose, and this questioning is effected primarily through the
interrelation between poems in the collection. I will be examining
recurrent themes and metaphors in the *Epodes* in order to show how
a basic set of concerns is refracted through poems of different types
and how connections between poems are used to unsettle the Archilochean persona. My focus will be on the discrepancy between the
language of masculinity and sexual potency adopted by the poet in
his Archilochean persona and the persistent concern with impotence
and helplessness that upsets this pose. I will be considering how this

---

[4] Setaioli (1981), 1689, states that 'i più equilibrati interpreti' of the *Epodes* agree
that in ordering the poems Horace was guided by criteria of metre or his taste for
variatio. His criticisms of Carrubba's elaborate symmetries (1689 f.) seem to me
justified, but I would add that the assumption, which Carrubba shares with the
more 'balanced' interpreters, that questions of organization are to do merely with
the disposition, rather than the interaction, of poems does not do Horace justice.

discrepancy reflects Horace's complex relation to Maecenas and, more broadly, the breakdown of distinctions and oppositions in a period of civil war that seemed to have entered an inextricable spiral. The reader should be warned that the extreme interwovenness of the strands that I will be examining makes a linear approach inappropriate, and I will be shuttling back and forth between poems and themes in order to be true to the texture of the collection.

The penultimate poem in the collection is the most Archilochean, at least in its pretensions to the kind of public role we associate with Archilochus' political poems. Here Horace harangues the citizens of Rome, urging them to break off the cycle of civil war by leaving Rome and emigrating to the Isles of the Blest.[5] Horace arrogates to himself the title of *vates* ('bard', 16.66) and appeals to the *virtus* of the better part of the citizenry to abandon their womanish grieving and take decisive action under his leadership (39 f.). The arrogance of this stance is remarkable and extremely unusual in the self-deprecating, ironic Horace. Fraenkel's careful analysis of the language of political procedure in this poem has shown that Horace is at pains to remove his speech from any real constitutional conditions by mingling formulas from various political systems.[6] Nevertheless, this is the most forceful claim of an effective role for the poet in a collection that is predominantly concerned with the problem of the poet's efficacy. Horace may have protected himself from the appearance of making a concrete political proposal, but he clearly claims leadership in relation to the community he addresses.

We may start by considering the effect of this poem's position in the book, always an important factor in the interpretation of a Horatian lyric. In the previous poem, Horace asserts his resolve to break off a relationship with a woman who has broken her oath of eternal love and taken up with another man. The situation challenges his manhood:

> o dolitura mea multum virtute Neaera!
>   nam si quid in Flacco viri est,
> non feret adsiduas potiori te dare noctes,

---

[5] Horace models the projected emigration from Rome on that of the Phocaeans, under pressure from the Persians, and there are similarities with the account of that event by Herodotus (Hdt.1.165; see Setaioli 1981: 1749 f.).

[6] Fraenkel (1957), 43–6.

> et quaeret iratus parem,
>   nec semel offensae cedet constantia formae,
>   si certus intrarit dolor.   (15.11–16)

O Neaera, you will suffer much from my manhood!
  For if there is any man in Flaccus
He won't endure your giving nights to a favored rival
  And will angrily seek a mate/equal,
Nor will his firmness yield to beauty now odious to him
  Once indignation has entered his mind to stay.

Horace will prove that he is not *Flaccus* (limp), but *constans*,[7] and
Neaera will feel the sting of his *vir-tus*, both his manly strength to
break off their relationship and the literary quality (*virtus, OLD*, 5b) of
his iambics. The analogies with the situation in 16 become striking
once we make the translation from the political to the erotic mode: in
both cases the issue is the need to break with a degenerate condition,
and in both cases the attempt to do so is seen as an exercise of
manhood and brings into play the power of the Archilochean poet.
In *Epode* 16, Horace berates those who do not possess the resolve to
leave Rome with the words *mollis et exspes | inominata perprimat
cubilia!* ('Let the soft and hopeless | Press their ill-fated couches',
37 f.), and turns to the better part of the citizens, urging them to
reject the womanish weakness implied by *mollis: vos quibus est virtus,
muliebrem tollite luctum* ('You who have manhood, remove your
womanish grief', 39). The juxtaposition of these two poems is, as we
shall see, only one example of the link between two elements of the
Archilochean persona: erotic invective and political harangue. What
connects them is Horace's framing of the problem of breaking off in
terms of maleness, explicitly sexual in 15 and implicitly so in 16;[8] it is
this framework that allows Horace to connect poems of apparently

[7] As I will illustrate, Horace repeatedly puns on his name, a fact that has been
noted by several commentators. The sexual pun is here continued by *constantia*, cf.
constantior... nervus in *Epode* 12.19. The precise meaning of lines 15 f. is disputed,
and some have read *offensi* instead of *offensae*. My observations, however, do not
depend on anything controversial in the interpretation of these lines. For a discussion
of these lines, see Grassmann (1966), 155–7.

[8] *Mollis* (37) connotes effeminacy, and is used of the pathic (*OLD*, 15). *Perprimat*
(38), especially in connection with *cubilia*, may have sexual connotations. For the

diverse theme and genre: the bard's urging that the Romans display fortitude in breaking off the cycle of civil war in 16 corresponds to the determination of the lover in 15 to break off an amatory relationship. I will later show that there are other themes, such as Horace's relation to Maecenas, that are cast in the same terms, terms which dominate Horace's relation to the political situation at Rome.

The juxtaposition of *Epodes* 15 and 16 not only provides the sense of a common framework for widely diverse experiences, it also connects the end of the former to the beginning of the latter in a single arc of experience. *Epode* 15 ends with an intimation of cyclicality:

> heu heu translatos alio maerebis amores:
>   ast ego vicissim risero.   (15.23 f.)

>   Alas, alas, you will mourn her love that will have gone to another,
>   But I in turn will laugh.

The successful rival will fall victim to the persistent transference of love from one object to another, which will give Horace his turn on top. *Epode* 16 begins with *another* age worn down by civil war and with a Rome that falls victim to the very strength by which it had risen:[9]

> altera iam teritur bellis civilibus aetas,
>   suis et ipsa Roma viribus ruit.   (16.1 f.)

>   Already another age is worn down by civil war,
>   And Rome collapses under its own strength.

Though Horace ends 15 with a statement that he will prevail, the fact that he begins 16 with *altera* brings out the instability implied by *vicissim* (15.24). In a world where nations fall by their own strength, the vaunts of the invective poet are bound to be unstable. Furthermore, the cyclical movement of events makes the determination to break off and make a fresh start, expressed in both 15 and 16, unlikely to result in success.

---

sexual meaning of *premo* and its compounds, see Adams (1982), 182 f. *Perprimo* itself is used in a sexual sense by Ovid, *Ars Am.* 1.394.

[9] Nisbet (1984), 3, sees a pun on the Greek transliteration of *Roma* (*Rhōmē*, 'strength') in the juxtaposition of *Roma* and *viribus*.

Epode 16 bears an interesting relation to *Epode* 2, another Archilochean poem (cf. 19W), in which the usurer Alfius praises the rustic life at
great length and then, *iam iam futurus rusticus* ('on the point of becoming a rustic', 68), calls in his capital on the Ides to loan it out again on the
Kalends. Both poems concern the action of breaking off. In view of the
fact that both poems also contain an extensive passage of *laudes ruris*
('praise of the country') intended to make a fresh start inviting (2.1–66;
16.41–62), we may be intended to see them as related. If this is so, then
the final backsliding of Alfius into the sequence of usury casts an ironic
light on the poet's claim at the end of 16 that he will help the Romans
escape the degenerating sequence of ages, from gold to bronze and then
to iron (16.63–6). It is true that the poems are distant from each other in
the collection, but it is more important that they are in symmetrical
positions, being the second and the penultimate poems of the book.

The *Epodes* begin, appropriately, with a poem addressed to Maecenas, and I will now consider the problematic relation of Horace to
his patron. Here we find a more explicit statement of the poet's sense
of his own inadequacy to meet the demands of the times, and again we
will find this inadequacy expressed in relation to a standard of masculinity. But, first of all, it is important to notice the sequence of the
epodes that specifically concern the political and military events of
the period. *Epode* 1 is a propempticon for Maecenas as he leaves to
join Octavian at Actium, the battle that will end the civil wars, and the
mood is one of danger. *Epode* 9, anticipating the triumphant return
of Octavian to Rome, is the central poem of the book and probably
the last to have been written; it is an optimistic poem. At the end of the
book, however, the mood is dark, with *Epode* 16 spoken from the
desperate midst of civil war. This reversal of chronological sequence,
and of what followers of Octavian would have seen as the rising
fortunes of Rome, probably indicates that the return of the victorious
Octavian to Rome is awaited with some trepidation. Will he be
another Sulla? Will the bloodshed start again? What can poetry do
in this situation? The latter question is one that the *Epodes* share with
Vergil's *Eclogues*, whose influence on the *Epodes* extends beyond
individual references to the whole conception of the ensemble, with
its use of a Greek poetic genre to provide a series of oblique reflections
of Roman political realities, and its playing of a group of connected
themes across poems of varied character. Above all, though, it is the

concern with the role of the poet in a time of political upheaval that
makes the *Epodes* a successor to the *Eclogues*. But where Vergil had
begun his *Eclogues* with Tityrus praising the 'god' who had given him
the *otium* to pursue his pastoral/poetic calling (*Ecl.* 1.6–10), Horace
suggests that the times require a more strenuous response:

> utrumne iussi persequemur otium,
>   non dulce, ni tecum simul,
> an hunc laborem mente laturi decet
>   qua ferre non mollis viros?   (1.7–10)[10]

> Shall we pursue our leisure as commanded
>   A leisure that is not sweet without you,
> Or shall we bear this toil with a mind
>   That befits men who are not soft?

Maecenas is about to link his own danger with that of his superior,
Octavian (*paratus omne Caesaris periculum | subire, Maecenas, tuo*,
'Prepared to undergo all Caesar's danger | Maecenas, at your own',
4 f.), and Horace feels that he should do the same for Maecenas, but
there is a worrying lack of symmetry between the relationships:

> roges, tuum labore quid iuvem meo,
>   imbellis ac firmus parum?   (1.15 f.)

> You ask how I would help your labor with my own,
>   I who am unwarlike and none too sturdy.

The terms in which Horace casts his inadequacy should now be
familiar. With *imbellis ac firmus parum* (contrast *non mollis viros*,
10), Horace is again punning on his name Flaccus. The same pun is
made in the context of his relation to Octavian in the first satire of
book two, where Horace's interlocutor asks him why he does not
write panegyric of Octavian. Horace replies that this is a ticklish
operation in view of Octavian's sensitive nature:

> nisi dextro tempore, Flacci
> verba per attentam non ibunt Caesaris aurem
> cui male si palpere recalcitrat undique tutus.
>   (*Serm.* 2.1.18–20)

---

[10] For another revision of Vergil, see Nisbet's remarks (1984), 2 f.; on the relation
between *Epode* 16 and *Eclogue* 4, the relative dating of which has been much
discussed, see Setaioli (1981), 1753–61.

> Except at the right time, Flaccus,
> Words will not penetrate Caesar's pricked ear,
> For if you rub him the wrong way he kicks free in all directions.

Clearly Horace is casting his own feelings of inadequacy or of confusion about his role in sexual terms.[11] In the first epode, Horace sees
himself as *firmus parum* in relation to the demands made by the
moment on his relation with Maecenas; he tells Maecenas that he will
accompany him, not because he can offer him any support, but
simply because his fear will be greater if he does not, adducing the
first of many animal comparisons in the book:

> ut adsidens implumibus pullis avis
>   serpentium allapsus timet
> magis relictis, non, ut adsit, auxili
>   latura plus praesentibus.   (1.19–22)

> As a brooding bird with unfledged young
>   Fears the gliding approach of snakes
> More when she has left her young, although
>   She would not afford more help to them if she were there.

The comparison, which feminizes Horace, is in sharp contrast to
those that will mark his adoption of the Archilochean persona later
in the book, most notably that of the iambic poet to the fierce dog
that protects the flocks (*amica vis pastoribus*, 'Violence friendly to
shepherds', 6.6). The writing of iambic poetry, as Babcock suggests,
may be Horace's only way of fulfilling his commitment to being
involved in the war (*libenter hoc et omne militabitur | bellum*, 'Gladly
will I fight in this and every other | War', 1.23 f.),[12] but the effect of
the positioning of this poem is to cast an ironic light on the iambic
persona adopted later in the book, as well as to connect the iambic

---

[11] Comparisons of young girls to skittish fillies that have to be handled with care
are common in the ancient world; Anacreon's is one of the first (335 Page), and
Horace himself has one that is close to this at C.3.11.9 f., where the recalcitrant Lyde is
described as a young filly who *metuit tangi* 'fears to be touched'. For *palpo* in a sexual
sense, see Juvenal 10.206. In view of these parallels, I do not think it fanciful to see
sexual connotations in the statement that the words of Flaccus will not go through
the ear of Octavian except at the right moment.

[12] This is the argument of Babcock (1974).

poems, with their claims to effective power, to the problematic issue of what sort of a role the poet can play in the political upheaval.

After the opening poem to Maecenas, we have the futile gesture of the usurer Alfius to change his life in *Epode* 2, and Horace returns to his relationship with Maecenas in *Epode* 3. Here he complains of a fearsome stomach ache caused by a dish too liberally flavored with garlic, and warns Maecenas against ever serving such a dish to him (19 f.). The poem sustains a mock epic tone until the end, where Maecenas is warned against trying this again under pain of having his partner avoid his kisses and sleep on the edge of the bed. I am being no more facetious than Horace in saying that this *jeu d'esprit* is about various kinds of intestinal war; the Romans also used this metaphor.[13] The crime described in the opening lines as being appropriately punished with the garlic that Horace has eaten is parricide:[14]

> parentis olim si quis impia manu
>   senile guttur fregerit
> edit cicutis alium nocentius.   (3.1–3)

> If someone once with impious hand
>   Snapped the aged neck of his father
> Let him eat garlic more harmful than hemlock.

In the middle of the poem there are two mythical parallels to Horace's suffering, both of which involve a disastrous relation between a hero and his partner, another 'intestinal' problem. The garlic is first compared to the substance with which Medea anointed Jason in order to help him yoke the monstrous oxen,[15] and then this same substance is identified with that with which Medea smeared the gift she sent to Creusa in order to take her revenge on Jason; the garlic is

---

[13] *OLD*, *intestinum*, 1. Compare also Catullus 77, where Rufus, the friend who played Catullus false, is described as *intestina perurens* (77.3). The Catullan usage strengthens my suspicion that in this poem Horace is ambivalent about his relationship with Maecenas.

[14] Horace seems to be parodying the Twelve Tables. Compare *Si quis occentavisset sive carmen condidisset*... as quoted by Cicero, *de Rep.*, 4.12. The archaic subjunctive, *edit* also suggests parody. For a later version of the *si quis* construction specifying a crime, see Livy 29.21.5.

[15] The sequel to Jason's yoking of the oxen is the sowing of the dragon's teeth, from which the armed men spring up and whom Jason sets fighting among themselves by throwing a stone in their midst; this battle is one of the mythical prototypes of civil war (Lucan, *BC* 10.549–69).

also compared to the substance with which Deianeira, mistakenly
believing it to be a love charm, smeared the robe she sent to Herakles
and thereby killed him. The two women stand in a double relationship, of lover and killer, to the men. As I will argue, Horace had good
reason to be ambivalent about the results of his relations with
Maecenas, which did not make him universally popular. That he
should choose to build this intimate epode around an incidence of
intestinal disturbance is no coincidence, nor is the choice of mythic
parallels, whose parodic nature does not preclude their being the
vehicle of serious matters as well.

The above observations on Horace's relations to Maecenas can be
supported if we turn to the first of the properly iambic, or invective,
poems of the collection, *Epode* 4, addressed to one of the opportun-
ists who had used the confusion of the civil wars to advance himself.
It begins by claiming a natural enmity between speaker and addressee, who are distinguished as different species of animals:

> lupis et agnis quanta sortito obtigit
> tecum mihi discordia est.   (4.1 f.)

> There is as much discord between you and me
> As has fallen to the lot of wolves and lambs.

The wolf is associated with iambic poetry,[16] but the point of the
animal comparison is not primarily to identify a literary genre, but
to establish a generic difference and an unbridgeable gulf between the
two agents. We are surprised, then, to learn that the addressee has
much in common with Horace: he is a freedman, like Horace's father,
and a military tribune, as Horace himself had been.[17] The *liberrima
indignatio* ('most outspoken resentment', 10) of the crowd of by-
standers who mock the upstart was something with which Horace
was thoroughly familiar: at *Serm.* 1.6.45 ff. he cites the jealousy to
which he was exposed as a result of becoming a friend (*convictor*, 47)
of Maecenas in spite of his birth (*libertino patre natum*, 'born of a
freedman father', 45, 46). In that passage, he contrasts his elevation to
the position of *tribunus militum*, which might justly have been a cause
of spite or envy, with his friendship with Maecenas, which should

---

[16] Nagy (1979), 242.
[17] Setaioli (1981), 1703.

not, since Maecenas is careful to adopt worthy friends, untainted by ambition (49–52). *Epodes* 3 and 4, then, are related through the passage in the *Satires*, for they juxtapose the upstart military tribune with the intimate of Maecenas. In *Epode* 3, the garlic that puts Horace and Maecenas on the same level, as the sharers of a joke, causes an intestinal war in Horace himself: the mythical parallels in lines 9–14 both elevate Horace to heroic status (Jason, Hercules) and hint at the negative effects of his elevation; Maecenas is like Medea and Deianeira in that he both exalts his friend and exposes him to suffering: the envy of others and his own self-doubt. In *Epode* 4, Horace attacks the image of himself as an ambitious opportunist that is both provoked and, he hopes, dispelled by his friendship with Maecenas. Of course, the poem purports to be an attack on someone who is generically different from, and opposite to, Horace, though in fact the *discordia* that it describes has arisen between two aspects of the same person and might be more accurately identified as the poison that *saevit in praecordiis* ('rages in the vitals') in *Epode* 3. This whole confusion between self and other, friend and enemy, is framed by the larger context of civil war, for *Epode* 3 begins with a reference to parricide, and *Epode* 4 ends with the abusive crowd that surrounds the upstart asking what is the point of fighting a war against robbers and slaves (the army of Sextus Pompeius) when this man is military tribune.

The fracturing of the passage in *Serm.* 1.6 about the results of Horace's relationship with Maecenas, and its distribution across two epodes of very different character, is far more adequate to sound the complexities of Horace's situation than the linear treatment in the satire. It shows that this collection cannot be divided into distinct groups according to literary types, or still less into poems concerned with reality on the one hand and literary exercises on the other. The collection is not simply miscellaneous: its discontinuities of tone, genre and levels of reality arise from the complexities of Horace's own intestinal strife and its relation, through his patron Maecenas, to the civil war at Rome.

The *Epodes* contain a great deal of animal imagery, and this is hardly surprising in a collection for which Archilochus is the major literary source.[18] Horace uses this imagery to refer to a natural order

---

[18] See Burnett (1983), 60–5.

that underlies the dramas of love and hate in the *Epodes*, but he does
so in ways that suggest a confusion of order on the human level, a
confusion that reflects the disruption of the civil wars. As we have
already seen, the first animal image in the *Epodes* compares Horace,
as the ineffectual but devoted follower of Maecenas, to a mother bird
(1.19–22). This image of the affection that draws Horace to war
contrasts with the very different kinds of animal imagery that describe Horace the invective poet (4.1 f.; 6.5–8) fighting his own wars.
This ambivalence in the animal comparisons is concentrated into a
paradox in the strange choice of language made by Neaera when she
swears eternal love:

> dum pecori lupus et nautis infestus Orion . . .
> fore hunc amorem mutuum.   (15.7–10)

> While the wolf is enemy of the flock and Orion of sailors . . .
> This love will be shared.

Neaera guarantees her love by an appeal to the natural order of
hatred, and with the reference to animals she anticipates the invective
that she will provoke from Horace when she breaks her oath
(cf. 4.1 f.). The whole cycle of their relationship is condensed into
this moment, so that love and hate are simultaneous.

We may compare Neaera's oath to the oath that the Romans are
urged to swear in *Epode* 16, an oath that they will not return to Rome
before certain *adynata* occur:

> in mare seu celsus procurrerit Appenninus,
>   novaque monstra iunxerit libidine
> mirus amor, iuvet ut tigris subsidere cervis,
>   adulteretur et columba miluo,
> credula nec ravos timeant armenta leones,
>   ametque salsa levis hircus aequora.   (16.29–34)

> Whether the high Appennines dive into the sea,
>   Or a strange love creates prodigies joined in a new kind of desire,
> So that the tiger should be happy to mate with the deer,
>   And the dove should commit adultery with the hawk,
> And the credulous herds should not fear tawny lions,
>   And the smooth goat should take to the salty deep.

As we know from *Epodes* 8 and 12, a *mirus amor* has already joined strange bedfellows in a *nova libido*: Horace and the *vetula* make love, though without pleasure on his part and without satisfaction on hers. The animals in the oath put us in mind of the various animals to whom Horace's partner is compared; more particularly, the smooth goat that will never be found in the sea (16.34) has already appeared as the goat that lies in the sweaty and hairy armpits of the old woman in heat (12.5): *salsa aequora* indeed! In *Epode* 12 the *vetula* complains that Horace flees her as the lamb flees the wolf and the she-goat the lion (25 f.), but from his point of view it would seem that the *adynata* cited in 16.31 f. have already occurred, insofar as he finds himself in the same bed as she.

The appeals to the natural order of the animal kingdom made by Neaera and the *vates* of *Epode* 16 both point, when taken in their wider context, to a disruption of order on the human level. The conflation of love and hate in Neaera's oath, the realization of the *adynaton* cited in a hopeful context in 16 by the perverse union of *Epodes* 8 and 12, and also the surprising affinity between Horace and the opportunist of *Epode* 4, originally distinguished as different species of animals, all this is quite appropriate to a human order disrupted by civil war.

The extreme interwovenness of the collection makes the decision of how to group the poems for critical purposes somewhat arbitrary; starting from any poem and following up its ramifications throughout the collection one would come up with the same set of concerns but with a different emphasis each time. I will turn now to the area where the amatory poems are grouped, the second half of the collection, and consider the implications of their context for the very literal poems about impotence (*Epodes* 8 and 12). *Epode* 8 is the first of the two poems of invective against an old woman with whom Horace, for some unspecified reason, is making love, in spite of the fact that he finds her repulsive and himself impotent in her presence:[19]

> rogare longo putidam te saeculo
> viris quid enervat meas,

---

[19] The ancient tradition of *vetulaskoptik* that lies behind *Epodes* 8 and 12 is dealt with in Grassmann (1966) and the Latin tradition before and after Horace by Richlin (1983), 105–16.

cum sit tibi dens ater et rugis vetus
frontem senectus exaret. (8.1–4)

That stinking you should ask endlessly
What slacks my strength
When you've a black tooth and old age
Ploughs up your brow with wrinkles.

The *dens ater*, which is here a mark of the physically repulsive, has
appeared at the end of *Epode* 6 with a quite different significance.
There Horace asks the enemy he is attacking:

an si quis atro dente me petiverit
inultus ut flebo puer? (6.15 f.)

If someone should attack me with a black tooth
Will I weep like a boy unavenged?

In *Epode* 6, the *dens ater* ('black tooth') symbolizes the aggressiveness of
a potential assailant against whom Horace is confident of victory,
thanks to the power of his words. In *Epode* 8, the *dens ater* of the old
woman who 'seeks' Horace in a different sense unmans him and
provokes invective as a substitute for the sexual *vires* that he cannot
summon up. So the *dens ater* that in both cases is connected with
Horace's iambic stance uncovers an uneasiness about the masculinity
that is supposedly manifested by his iambic *vis* ('strength'). In *Epode* 6,
Horace contrasts this *vis* with the weeping of the insufficiently masculine boy; if the *inultus puer* ('unavenged boy') of 6.16 reminds us of the
boy in *Epode* 5, helplessly awaiting his death at the hands of Canidia,
who will use his heart as a love potion, then the boy and Horace, the
impotent and reluctant lover of the *vetula* in *Epode* 8, are also related by
the similarity of the figure against whom their impotent rage is directed.[20] The end of *Epode* 6, which confidently announces the power of
the iambic poet, is thereby thrown into question.

Before continuing the amatory theme, I would like to point out
another connection between the boy of *Epode* 5 and Horace, the
iambic poet, who will resign from invective in the face of Canidia's
superior power in the final poem (17.1–7). In *Epode* 7, the speaker is
also, like the boy, a helpless individual confronting a crowd. Horace's

[20] Another link between the *vetula* and Canidia is the phrase *dente livido* used of
Canidia at 5.47.

address to the citizens rushing into civil conflict distinctly recalls the
boy's words to the crowd of witches; compare

> quo, quo scelesti ruitis? aut cur dexteris
>   aptantur enses conditi?   (7.1 f.)

> Where, where do you rush, you criminals, and why
>   Are your sheathed swords clasped by your right hands?

to

> at, o deorum quidquid in caelo regit
>   terras et humanum genus,
> quid iste fert tumultus? aut quid omnium
>   vultus in unum me truces?   (5.1–4)

> But, by whatever gods in the sky
>   Rule the earth and human race,
> What does this tumult portend? Or why do all
>   Gaze with ferocity at me alone?

The boy, who finally recognizes the futility of trying to dissuade the
witches from their murderous intentions, ends by threatening to
haunt them as a *nocturnus ... Furor* ('nocturnal fury', 5.92); in
Epode 7, the speaker who fails to get a response from the guilty
crowd he is haranguing ends by claiming that Rome is haunted by
the fratricide that attended its foundation, the blood of Remus, *sacer
nepotibus* ('cursed for his descendants', 20). In both cases, the impotence of the speaker is connected with a curse, one projected into the
future as the only means of exerting power, and the other traced from
the past to explain the speaker's inefficacy; either way, the present is
not susceptible to the power of the speaker's words.

I have been arguing that in the *Epodes* there is a connection
between the amatory and the political themes, and, more specifically, between the impotence that is the theme of the *vetula* poems
and the helplessness of the poet trying to engage with a turbulent
political situation through his friend Maecenas. *Epode* 14 confirms
this connection. At the beginning of that poem, Maecenas belabors
Horace with accusations *of mollitia* ('softness') and *inertia* ('sloth')
just as the *vetula* had done (8.1 f.; 12.14–17):

> mollis inertia cur tantam diffuderit imis
>   oblivionem sensibus,
> pocula Lethaeos ut si ducentia somnos
>   arente fauce traxerim,
> candide Maecenas, occidis saepe rogando.   (14.1–5)

Why soft inertia has spread such forgetfulness
  To the depths of my senses
As though I had drawn off two hundred cups,
  Bringing Lethean slumbers, into my thirsty gullet;
This you ask me continually, frank Maecenas, and it kills me.

In the first poem of the collection, Horace had referred to himself as *firmus parum* ('not firm enough', 1.16), but here it is Maecenas who accuses him, the occasion being Horace's failure to bring his *Epodes* to a conclusion (6–8). It is in the first epode that Horace sets up the context that allows us to connect *Epodes* 8 and 14, for there Horace's relationship with Maecenas, who is about to go to war, makes him aware of his own impotence and, I would argue, determines him to adopt the Archilochean persona as a response to this awareness (in the fictional chronology of the book, that is). We are certainly not meant to draw a complete analogy between Maecenas and the *vetula*, but we are intended to see a structural analogy in the relationships; the *vetula* poems are very much part of the imaginative exploration of Horace's situation as poet and citizen in the period of the civil wars that is the main concern of the *Epodes*.

The relation between love and invective in 8 and 14 is particularly interesting in that the situation in 14 is the reverse of that in 8: the *vetula* castigates Horace for failing in his amatory duties and he responds with invective, whereas Maecenas reproves his sluggish progress with the iambics and Horace pleads that he is in love. This reversal, and the hopeless circularity it implies, is typical of the book. If *Epode* 14 posits an opposition between love and invective, the next poem brings them together. Neaera's oath of eternal love, *dum pecori lupus infestus* ('while the wolf is enemy to the flock', 15.7), cites the natural law that accounts for invective (cf. *Epode* 4.1 ff.), and the poem ends with Horace addressing his rival, who will himself soon be the object of his mockery. The love that prevents iambic in 14 gives way to the disappointed love that causes it in 15, and this in turn provokes a rallying of the *vir-tus* (15.11 f.) that Maecenas had questioned in the previous poem. Furthermore, Horace's broken promise to Maecenas of a poem (*olim promissum carmen*, 14.7) and Neaera's broken oath to Horace produce another vantage point from which we can observe the revolving relations between love and invective. As I have been arguing, both the breakdown of distinctions and the cyclicality of relations are manifestations of the spiritual atmosphere of the last years of the Republic in which a confused Horace is attempting to orient himself.

I will end by considering *Epodes* 9–13, a varied group, but framed by two sympotic poems that raise the question of return. Once again, my isolation of this group is a somewhat arbitrary critical device because the group contains many strands that can be traced to other poems in the collection; nevertheless, it shows a striking degree of contrast and balance within itself. *Epode* 9 anticipates Octavian's return to Rome, but the poem ends with a call for more wine to drown present anxieties:[21]

> curam metumque Caesaris rerum iuvat
> > dulci Lyaeo solvere.   (9.37 f.)

> I rejoice to dissolve care and fear for Caesar's affairs
> > With pleasant wine.

The beginning of the next poem takes up the word *solvere* and surrounds it with danger:

> mala soluta navis exit alite,
> > ferens olentem Maevium.   (10.1 f.)

> The ship departs loosed by an evil omen,
> > Bearing the stinking Maevius.

---

[21] The question of the fictional (or, for some, real) time and place of this poem is one of the canonical 'problems' of the *Epodes*. For a summary of the relevant scholarship, see Setaioli (1981), 1716–30; who concludes that Horace speaks from a point when Actium has been won, and that it is to be thought of as having been composed at the site of the battle on board ship. Nisbet's careful analysis of the poem (1984), 11–17, bears this out, although he sees the poem as a running commentary on the battle, ending with the victory celebration in the evening. My only objection to Nisbet's interpretation is that he takes the symposiastic motif of the final two lines as symbolic: the release from cares that wine provides is understood by him as a *parallel* to the release from cares (and foreign bondage) provided by Octavian's victory. I would rather take the lines in a more conventional sense: Horace is still in a state of anxiety about Octavian and needs to drown it in wine; as Setaioli observes (1981), 1724, it was not immediately apparent that Actium was a decisive victory.

The poem is a reverse propempticon, invoking shipwreck on Maevius the poet. Having awaited helplessly the outcome of Actium (compare *Epode* 1), Horace now indulges in his own war of invective, giving Maevius a send-off that is intended to be final. If the anxiety for Octavian released in the symposium implies the poet's helplessness, the loosing (*soluta*, 10.1) of Maevius' ship under the curse of the iambist displays a confidence in the efficacy of words. The ill-omened bird that attends Maevius' ship is the winged word that the poet lets loose in the poem, the barrage of language that takes on the bad poet and overwhelms him.[22] In the next poem of invective, *Epode* 12, Horace lambastes the *vetula*, but of course his position is not quite so dominant here as in *Epode* 10; in fact, he describes himself as the victim of a storm of sexual rapacity in which his flaccid member (*pene soluto*, 12.8) recalls the luckless ship of Maevius, launched (*soluta*) under Horace's curse.[23] Whatever its efficacy, invective more often than not derives from a sense of inadequacy or weakness that it compensates, and this is clearly implied by the relation between *Epodes* 10 and 12.[24] But, as I have been arguing, the sexual inadequacy described in 12 is a metaphor for the inadequacy the poet feels in the political context.

In the last poem of our group, which is not situated either temporally or locally, Horace addresses some unspecified *amici*, urging them to forget the storm raging outside, drink deep, and remember the words the centaur addressed to his ward Achilles as the latter set out for Troy. The poem ends with the centaur's speech, reminding Achilles that he is fated not to return from Troy and inviting him to lighten his sorrow with wine and song. This poem is the dark shadow of *Epode* 9, for the symposium is no longer anticipating a joyful return but rather providing the opportunity to dull the knowledge

[22] Maevius is the poet attacked by Vergil at *Eclogue* 3.90. This reference allows us to glimpse a continuing literary war that runs parallel to the civil war, and one about which Horace could feel more confident.
[23] The storm that Horace calls down on Maevius' ship will break mountain oaks (*insurgat Aquilo, quantus altis montibus | frangit trementis ilices*, 10.7 f.), and this is recalled in *Epode* 12, when the member of Amyntas, compared favorably to Horace's, is described as *constantior... quam nova collibus arbor* ('firmer... than a young tree in the hills', 12.19 f.).
[24] Richlin (1983), 113, suggests that 'invective against *vetulae* constitutes a sort of apotropaic satire that attempts to belittle and control the power of old women'.

that there will be no return. Achilles, like Maevius, sets out never to return, but here poetry can only serve to mitigate sorrow (13.17 f.), it is not the efficacious weapon of the curse in *Epode* 10.

In the four poems that follow *Epode* 9, Horace is setting up a hall of mirrors that variously reflect its concerns. The central poem of the group is an erotic poem in which Horace confesses that love prevents him from writing *versiculi*, and then looks back on a previous amour that made him the talk of the town and the concern of his friends; describing his repeated and failed attempts to break it off, he declares that he is now involved in a new passion from which nothing can save him but another love for a new girl or boy. I began by arguing that the juxtaposition of *Epodes* 15 and 16 foregrounded the problem of breaking off, posed by the two poems in a political and an erotic context respectively, and that the cyclicality of the erotic world in 15 casts an ironic light on Horace's summons to his fellow citizens to break with the past. In *Epode* 11, there is an even greater emphasis on the cyclicality of Horace's love life, and, in the light of the prominence given to the question of return in the group of poems to which it provides the centerpiece, it must surely reflect the general concern as to whether Octavian's return will be the beginning of a new era or the continuation of a cycle of civil war; as I hope will be clear by now, the erotic poems are intimately related to the political poems.

If we do not restrict the presence of politics in the *Epodes* to the reference to specific events and personages, we can see the collection as a whole in its relationship to the times in which it is written. What emerges is not a miscellaneous series of exercises by a fledgling poet but a complex anatomy of the poet's position, as noncombatant, as ex-Republican, as beneficiary of Maecenas' patronage and friend of Maecenas, as social climber, as the representative of a literary tradition asserting the power of the poet and as a helpless citizen of Rome in the troubled period between Philippi and Actium. It is the conflict between the last two positions that lies at the heart of the complex relation between poems and themes in this book. Horace's adoption of the Archilochean persona is a way of questioning his status and the nature of his involvement with the political scene; it also allows him to project a basic set of relationships and narrative patterns onto a variety of different generic screens, and in this sense the *Epodes* are truly experimental rather than merely tentative.

9

Canidia, Canicula, and the Decorum of Horace's *Epodes*

Ellen Oliensis

The concept of decorum is never innocent. Decorum is always an expression of power. In any sphere—aesthetic, sexual, political, moral—decorum enforces subordination: of parts to whole, woman to man, slave to master, desire to reason, individual to state. As Michel Foucault reminds us, these hierarchical relations are analogous and mutually descriptive: 'Just as in the household it was the man who ruled, and in the city it was right that only men should exercise power, and not slaves, children, or women, so each man was supposed to make his manly qualities prevail within himself. Self-mastery was a way of being a man with respect to oneself' (1985: 82). The man who cannot master himself is no better than a woman or a slave. Consider the implicit equation in the Ciceronian caveat, *ne quid indecore effeminateve faciat* ('to avoid behaving in an improper or unmanly fashion', *Off.* 1.4.14). Manliness depends on decorum, and decorum depends on manliness.

This interdependence is exemplified by the opening of Horace's *Ars Poetica* (1–5):[1]

> Humano capiti cervicem pictor equinam
> iungere si velit et varias inducere plumas
> undique conlatis membris, ut turpiter atrum
> desinat in piscem mulier formosa superne,
> spectatum admissi risum teneatis, amici?

---

[1] Unless otherwise noted, the text used is Klingner (1959).

Suppose a painter joined a horse's neck to a human head and applied all
kinds of feathers to limbs gathered from all over, so that a woman beautifully
formed on top ended foully in a black fish; if you were granted a viewing,
could you check a laugh, friends?

'Inevitably,' according to C. O. Brink, 'the painting resembles the
hybrid monsters of Classical art ... —scyllas, sirens, centaurs, goat-
stags, etc' (1971: 85). The resemblance is there, but it is neither
inevitable nor fortuitous. Horace might easily have inverted the
elements to produce something truly alien—a horse's head atop a
man's shoulders, a woman's shapely legs culminating in a fish head.
The familiar monsters who frame this passage, the centaur and
Scylla,[2] exemplify unbridled lust, the triumph of the 'lower' body
over the superior; their deformities bring to the surface an essential
bestiality. Not until the picture resolves itself into a portrait of Scylla,
however, do we hear the tone of disgust. In line 1 the centaur is
merely polymorphous; Scylla calls forth more qualifiers, and
Horace's description thickens as it closes. *Turpiter atrum*: Scylla
embodies the morally and aesthetically deformed; she is the antithesis of decorum as 'turpitude' is its antonym.[3]

It is not by chance that Scylla, more than the centaur, best exemplifies the indecorous. The female body in itself violates Horatian
notions of order and unity. 'Make whatever you like, so long as it is of
a piece and one' (*simplex ... et unum, Ars* 23): this is a prescription
which female physiology (or better, physical illogicality) necessarily
defies (Irigaray 1985: 23–33). Although the rage for decorum has
imposed closure on Scylla, sealing her up in a fishtail, her genital
doubleness resurfaces as duplicity; Scylla automatically produces—in
the indecorous mismatch of 'above' and 'below', human and in-
human—another gap. This visible rift, emblematic of the rift between
surface and depth, outside and inside, appearance and essence, makes

---

[2] The identification of the monsters as a centaur and Scylla, while not essential to
my argument, is supported by the frequency with which the two are paired (cf. Lucr.
4.732, 5.890 ff.; Virg. *A.* 6.286: *Centauri ... Scyllaeque biformes*). Cf. Lear's misogyn-
istic outburst (*King Lear* IV vi.124–9): 'Down from the waist they are Centaurs, |
Though women all above; | But to the girdle do the gods inherit, | Beneath is all the
fiends': there's hell, there's darkness, | There is the sulphurous pit, burning, scalding, |
Stench, consumption. Fie, fie, fie! pah, pah!' On female monsters, see Vermeule
(1979) (esp. chs. 5 and 6), Barina (1980).
[3] Cf. *Carm.* 3.27.53–4: *antequam* turpis *macies* decentis | *occupet malas....*

Scylla a version of Pandora, the primordial woman whose beautifully
adorned surface or 'box' holds hidden all the ills of mankind.

Our response to this spectacle is dictated by Horace's rhetorical
question, which implicitly distinguishes insiders from outsiders,
friends from enemies, and man from woman. The solidarity of
Horace's *amici*, a product of their joint participation in an escapade
which is at once aesthetic and erotic (*admittere* bears a sexual sense),
is confirmed by the shared guffaw with which they prove their
sameness against Scylla's difference. The laugh is irrepressible: like
the lustful centaur, the spectators cannot control themselves. But this
particular failure of control is also a sign of power. The laugh
banishes Scylla from the community, which in fact forms itself
through this gesture of exclusion. Case temporarily closed, the *Ars*
proceeds on its more or less decorous way.

If Horace navigates his way past this Scylla without sacrificing any
of his manpower, in his early works the indecorous female, in the
shape of the witch Canidia, is less easily bypassed. Canidia returns
with an uncanny persistence in Horace's early poetry. In *Satires* 1.8 a
wooden Priapus narrates her intrusion into his garden, a converted
graveyard in which shades of the past still lurk, waiting to be conjured
up by her spells; in Epode 5 Canidia concocts a love-potion to lure a
wandering lover back home, while the little boy whose liver and
marrow are to furnish her secret ingredients pleads and threatens
in vain; in the dialogue of Epode 17 Horace himself pleads for mercy
and Canidia, enraged by his earlier poems, refuses to grant it.[4]
Elsewhere (*S.* 2.1, *S.* 2.8, *Epod.* 3), Horace alludes to Canidia *en
passant* as if to establish her as a fixture in his poetic world, like the
killer-tree of the *Odes*. Most astonishing (although the critics have
generally refused to be astonished)[5] is Canidia's assumption of the
place of honor at the end of Horace's early collections. Her name
breaks into the last line of Horace's last satire (*S.* 2.8.95) as suddenly

---

[4] For detailed commentary on the magical practices described in these poems, see
Ingallina (1974).

[5] Williams (1972), 7 n. 1, 20 simply describes the repetition of Canidia's name as a
'unifying element'. Likewise Fraenkel (1957), 148: 'the real purpose of the reference to
her [in *S.* 2.1.48] is to remind the reader of her role in Book I, and it is for the same
reason that her name reappears in the very last line of Book II.' Carrubba (1969), 43
offers a similar tautology: 'the result [of Horace's repeated references to Canidia] is
that the last note of the *Satires* and the last note of the *Epodes* is by design one and the
same—Canidia.'

as the banquet described in that poem breaks up, and Canidia actually speaks the closing lines of the book of *Epodes*. Canidia is thus a structural counterpart to Maecenas, who is invoked at the beginnings of both collections.

Canidia's character is implicit in her name. The old age written there (cf. *canities*) insists that she is no longer fit—if still, like other Horatian hags (Chloris in *Carm.* 3.15, Lyce in *Carm.* 4.13), indecorously hungry—for the arms of a lover. This hunger is also legible: like 'Scylla' (traditionally derived from σκύλαξ, 'puppy'), 'Canidia', who often appears in the company of dogs, herself resembles a ravenous canine. And yet by making his hag not just a hag but a witch, a producer of incantations not unlike his own, Horace activates, however grudgingly, the musical suggestion of the name (*canere*).[6] Not only the target but the producer of poetry, Canidia embodies an indecorous poetics against which Horace tries to define his own practice, particularly in the *Epodes*. Further, old age, female desire, dogs, and poetry—seemingly unlikely bedfellows—intersect elsewhere in the classical tradition in the sphere of the Dog Star, and I will argue that Canidia takes over the role of the celestial Dog known in Greek as Sirius, in Latin as Canicula. In the light of the Dog Star, moreover, the misogyny of Horace's early poetry is revealed as a gesture of self-defense, a cover story veiling an inadmissible subtext. If the opening of the *Ars* stages the interdependence of manliness and decorum, the book of *Epodes* enacts, in defiance of the author, their simultaneous collapse. One privileged form of the indecorous here is sexual, but the upheaval is general and encompasses all spheres of life.

CANIS

Canidia is associated with dogs because, throughout the classical tradition, dogs form part of a misogynistic depiction of female

[6] Varro proposes an etymological link between *canis* and *canere* (*L.* 7.32). On the multiple suggestions of *can-*, see Ahl (1985), 31–3. The association of Canidia with *canities* is the most generally accepted because of the quantity of the *a*, but there is no need to rule out other possibilities simply on this basis. Horace was a poet, not a linguist. As Ahl comments (1985: 56), 'wordplay across vowel quantities abounds in Latin literature.'

powers and desires.[7] In *Satires* 1.8 Canidia hits a bestial low as, accompanied by her fellow worker Sagana, she scrabbles in the graveyard earth and tears at a lamb with her teeth (*scalpere terram* | *unguibus et pullam divellere mordicus agnam* | *coeperunt* 26–8). Invoking Hecate and the Fury Tisiphone (both deities linked and often identified with dogs) the witches succeed in conjuring up 'snakes and hell-bitches' (*serpentes atque...* | *infernas... canes* 34–5; such joint appearances of dogs and snakes are commonplace, as we will see).[8] By the end of the satire, the witches themselves are described as 'two Furies' (*furiarum... duarum* 45), a description extended in Epode 5, where Canidia wears her hair in the style of the Furies, with short snakes woven into her tresses (*brevibus inplicata viperis* | *crinis et incomptum caput* 15–16). In the ritual cuisine of Epode 5, bones snatched from the jaws of a ravenous bitch (*ossa ab ore rapta ieiunae canis* 23) top off the list of the ingredients to be added to Canidia's magic fire, and the she-dogs who bark at 'old man' Varus as he roams the Subura (*senem... adulterum* | *latrant Suburanae canes* 57–8)[9] are Canidia's representatives *in absentia*. Canidia thus belongs in the line of vindictive hags epitomized by Hecuba, the aged 'bitch' who ends her life as a dog.[10]

But Canidia's rage, unlike Hecuba's, is always mixed with desire. The proximity of these emotions, brilliantly analyzed by John Winkler (1990: 71–98), is clearly visible in Canidia's magical practices. In the ritual puppet show of *Satires* 1.8 Canidia stages her vindictive triumph over a recalcitrant lover (30–3): 'There was one puppet of wax, another, larger one of wool to crush the smaller with punishments (*quae poenis conpesceret inferiorem*); the wax one stood suppliant (*suppliciter*), as if doomed to a slave's death'—soon (43–4) to be consigned to the fire. The slow starvation of the little boy in Epode 5 is not only a prelude to but a figure of Varus's erotic torments; the

---

[7] The evidence on dogs in ancient Greek poetry is collected and discussed by Lilja (1976).

[8] The scene is modelled on Jason's supplication of Hecate in Ap. Rh. *Arg.* 3.1214–17, where Hecate herself appears, crowned with δράκοντες and escorted by χθόνιοι κύνες.

[9] Bain (1986) makes excellent sense of the fiction underlying this poem; following his argument, I read *latrant* at *Epod.* 5.58.

[10] Cf. the comically 'rationalized' Hecuba of Pl. *Men.* 717–18: *omnia mala ingerebat, quemquem aspexerat.* | *itaque adeo iure coepta appellari est canes.*

boy's 'dried-up liver' (*aridum iecur* 37) foretells the parching of Varus in Canidia's fire (... *amore sic meo flagres uti* | *bitumen atris ignibus* 81–2).[11] In Epode 17 Canidia's puppets come to life as Horace, consumed by flames (*o mare et terra, ardeo* 30), supplicates (*supplex... oro* 2) his torturer, begging her to relinquish possession of his body. The wording of his pleading exemplum—*unxere matres Iliae additum feris* | *alitibus atque canibus homicidam Hectorem* ('man-slaying Hector, once consigned to ravening birds and dogs, was anointed for burial by the Trojan matrons', 11–12)—marks the coincidence of eros and wrath, insinuating that Canidia has as much in common with the ravenous scavengers as with the angry Achilles. In the archaic traditions analyzed by Emily Vermeule (1979: 104–9), scavenging dogs are an alternative to the funeral pyre, and both methods of corpse-cleaning have an erotic dimension.[12] They are the misogynistic counterpart, as it were, to the conventional imagery of 'consuming' love.

Misogynistic blame tends to be coupled with erotic praise, and dogs, connoting brazen shamelessness about the use of those parts which are particularly associated with shame, often appear as the other or underside of female beauty. Let us return for a moment to Scylla, a literal 'man-eater', for an illustration. Here is Virgil's hybrid version, familiarly fair above and foul below (*A.* 3.426–8):

> prima hominis facies et pulchro pectore virgo
> pube tenus, postrema immani corpore pistrix
> delphinum caudas utero commissa luporum.

She begins by looking human, a fair-breasted virgin down to her groin, but she ends as a hideous sea-monster, joining dolphin-tails to a womb of wolves.

A little later the wolves reappear as dogs, as the sailors are advised, hendiadystically, to navigate around Scylla and her dog-infested lair (*Scyllam et caeruleis canibus resonantia saxa* 3.432; note the Varronian

---

[11] The liver is commonly the seat of sexual desire; cf. *Carm.* 1.25.15, 4.1.12, *Ep.* 1.18.72. Hahn (1939) who details the interrelations of *Epod.* 5 and 17, identifying the *puer* with Horace, gives an illuminating (though literal-minded), account of Horace's 'affair' with Canidia.

[12] Cf. Putnam (1970) on the dangerous eroticism of the aptly named 'Pyrrha' of *Carm.* 1.5.

play in *canibus resonantia*). In the Ovidian account, Scylla's metamorphosis turns into a parable of the fall into sexuality. When
Glaucus asks Circe to help him arouse the virginal Scylla's dormant
desire, Circe, aflame herself for Glaucus and enraged by his indiffer-
ence, complies with his request—with a vengeance. Scylla's desire
wakes up barking (*Met.* 14.64–5): 'looking for a body made of thighs
and calves and feet, she finds in their place Cerberean snarls' (*Cerber-
eos rictus*).[13] In both accounts, Scylla's double nature may be read as
the emblematic condensation of a narrative, a tale of before and after,
innocence and experience, wherein Virgil's *prima* and *postrema*
would mark not spatial but temporal differences: all women, however
fair, are destined to end up dogs.

Ovid's *Cerberei rictus* find a natural home in the female 'underworld.' Consider Horace's 'Hypermnestra' ode, where Horace prays
to the lyre for assistance in the seduction of Lyde (*Carm.* 3.11.1–4,
13–20):[14]

> Mercuri—nam te docilis magistro
> movit Amphion lapides canendo—
> tuque testudo resonare septem
>   callida nervis....
> tu potes tigris comitesque silvas
> ducere et rivos celeres morari;
> cessit immanis tibi blandienti
>   ianitor aulae
> Cerberus, quamvis furiale centum
> muniant angues caput eius atque
> spiritus taeter saniesque manet
>   ore trilingui.

Mercury—since it was from you that Amphion learned to move stones by
singing—and you, lyre, skilled at resounding with your seven strings.... You
can draw tigers and forests in your train, you can slow swift rivers; you
wheedled the doorkeeper of the ghastly realm into yielding, Cerberus himself, though a hundred snakes guard his furious head, and foul vapor and
gore drip from his three-tongued mouth.

---

[13] With the rare adjective *Cerbereus* Ovid acknowledges Lucretius's deflation of the
myth at 4.732 ff. (Lucretius uses the adjective one line after naming Scylla). Ovid
decorously transfers the snaky tail to Glaucus, himself recently transformed: Scylla
marvels at the monster, *ultima...excipiat quod tortilis inguina piscis* (13.915).

[14] Following the arguments presented by Williams (1969), I do not bracket 17–20.

Amphion and Orpheus, paired again at *Ars* 391 ff. as paradigmatic civilizers, are initially invoked as models of erotic success, seducers who triumph over the opposition of stony girls and grim door-keepers. Orpheus (unnamed but represented by his lyre) wheedled his way past elegy's hardhearted *ianitor*, here played by Cerberus, and led Eurydice up out of the house of Hades. In a sense forced on us by the elaborate description of Cerberus, however, Eurydice is hell herself. With its fastened gate and irate guardian, the house repre-sents by synecdoche the body of the woman enclosed within it.[15] The widespread desire to excise lines 17–20 is based perhaps as much on a sense of decorum as on technical complaints; a poet meditating seduction would do better not to imagine such a beast. The overly elaborate description summons up a dreadful kind of femininity and reminds us of the later history of Orpheus. Maddened Maenads will dismember the reluctant poet, as the Danaids of this ode (although for different reasons) kill their husbands, like wild beasts savaging their prey (*quae velut nactae vitulos leaenae* | *singulos eheu lacerant* 41–2). No wonder then that the model woman of the ode plans to save her husband by refusing either to kill him or to sleep with him; the two actions seemingly amount to the same thing. It is as if Eurydice and the Maenads were the beautiful 'above' and monstrous 'below' of a single woman.[16]

When the scholiast Porphyrio identifies an estranged mistress named 'Gratidia' behind the poetic alias 'Canidia,' he renders the tension in the doubleness of the female, who should by rights bear two separate names indicative of her fair and foul selves. But Gratidia does not figure in our poems, nor is there any trace of her attractions left in Canidia. If she exists anywhere, it is in the Catullan past; the Canidia of the Horatian present is a debased version of Catullus's Lesbia.[17] The relation between the two is evident in Epode 17, where

[15] On 'doors' representing 'the external female pudenda', see Adams (1982), 89.

[16] Cf. Tib. 1.5, where 'fair' and 'foul' are parcelled out between two women, innocent Delia and the hag who has corrupted her—thus salvaging something from the wreck of the poet's illusions. The juxtaposition of dogs and genitals in the curse on the *lena* (*currat et inguinibus nudis ululetque per urbes,* | *post agat e triviis aspera turba canum* 1.5.55–6) creates the impression of an arrested, Scylla-style metamorphosis.

[17] The bawd in *Epod.* 12 is not named 'Lesbia' for nothing, Hierche (1974), 162.

Horace's allusions give an ugly turn to Catullus's *nugae*. Having fallen under Canidia's devastating spell, Horace confesses the witch's power and pleads for a release. But the plea lapses easily into mockery (19–20): 'I have paid penalties enough and to spare to you, much loved by sailors and salesmen' (*dedi satis superque poenarum tibi, | amata nautis multum et institoribus*). *Amata nautis* shockingly echoes the earlier poet's *amata nobis* (8.5)[18] while offering a bitter answer to Catullus's only initially rhetorical questions (8.16–17): 'Who will think you're beautiful? whom will you love now? whose girl will you be called?' Given that the punishment imposed by Canidia takes the form of lovemaking, the phrase *satis superque* may recall the Catullan *basia* poem which it frames (Catull. 7.1–2, cf. 9–10): 'You ask how many of your kissings, Lesbia, are enough and more than enough (*satis superque*) for me?' In Horace's version of the scene, however, it is the man who asks what would be enough to satisfy the woman's sexual demand: the desirable mistress has turned into a desiring bitch.[19]

Horace's heavy-handed allusion to Catullus 42, an invective over-laid with the thinnest veneer of praise, adds insult to injury. Catullus's hendecasyllabic attack on a brazen-faced bitch (*catuli ore Gallicani* 9; *ferreo canis... ore* 17) for refusing to return his tablets culminated in the flagrantly ironic address 'virtuous and honorable woman', *pudica et proba* (24); cited within Epode 17 to the accompaniment of a 'mendacious lyre', the phrase preserves its Catullan barb (37–44):

> ... iussas cum fide poenas luam,
> paratus expiare, seu poposceris
> centum iuvencos, sive mendaci lyra
> voles sonare: 'tu pudica, tu proba
> perambulabis astra sidus aureum.'
> infamis Helenae Castor offensus vice

---

[18] Two other readers have overheard this echo (among others) of Catullus: Fedeli (1979), 134 and Bushala (1968), 8.

[19] The transformation is foreshadowed at Catull. 60.1–2: *Num te leaena montibus Libystinis | aut Scylla latrans infima inguinum parte...* The description of Scylla, elaborated beyond the requirements of the *topos*, implies a female addressee and adds a slight iambic twist to the poem; like the suppliant Horace of *Epod.* 17, this speaker hovers between prayer and attack. Cf. Wiseman (1985), 157.

fraterque magni Castoris victi prece
adempta vati reddidere lumina.

I will faithfully pay the penalty you fix and am ready to atone, whether you
demand a hecatomb or would like me to sing, to my lying lyre, 'virtuous and
honorable woman, a golden constellation you will stroll among the stars.'
Though angry over the plight of ill-reputed Helen, Castor and great Castor's
brother were conquered by prayer and restored the blinded bard's sight.

The laudatory comparison of Canidia to Helen (made through an
optimistic reference to Stesichorus's successful palinode) is modified
by the ambiguous adjective *infamis*: is Helen a maligned matron
or rather the scheming bitch she calls herself in the *Iliad* (κυνὸς
κακομηχάνου ὀκρυοέσσης 6.344)? In this context, neighboring on
Catullus's bitch and infamous Helen, Canidia's *sidus aureum* may
be none other than the Dog Star.[20]

Before turning to Canicula, let us acknowledge that not all dogs in
Horace's early poetry are blameworthy. The dog is a figure for the
invective poet himself. By contrast with Canidia's infernal hounds,
the vigilant sheepdog who challenges a cowardly cur in Epode 6 and
the keen-scented hunter who sniffs out the ugly truth of a woman's
body in Epode 12 seem paradigms of canine virtue. Whereas Canidia
uses her magic to enflame and enfeeble her rebellious lovers, Horace's
aggressive iambs aim at protecting the integrity of the community
by driving out those who are guilty of disorderly conduct.[21] A good
example is Epode 10, where Horace uses his barbed lines to punish
'smelly Mevius' for some unspecified (but probably sexual, cf. Harrison 1989) wrongdoing. In Epode 4, an invective against an upstart
ex-slave, Horace's tongue-lashing retraces old furrows, exposing the
scars which are at once duplicated and concealed by the plowed fields
of the *nouveau riche* (11–13):

[20] The identification, never explicit, is closest to the surface in the symmetrical
structure of *Epod.* 3, where Canidia (8) corresponds to the Dog Star, unnamed (as
usual) but latent in *siderum vapor* (15). Cf. also Persius's insulting characterization of
Rex in *Satires* 1.7 (24–6): *solem Asiae Brutum appellat stellasque salubris | appellat
comites excepto Rege; Canem illum, | invisum agricolis sidus, venisse.* The parallels
between Rex (defeated by Persius) and Canidia (routed by Priapus in *S.* 1.8) are
discussed by Anderson (1972), 9–11.
[21] Cf. Nagy's characterization (1979), 251; see further 243–52 of 'Archilochean
iamboi' as 'an affirmation of *philótēs* in the community'.

> sectus flagellis hic triumviralibus
> praeconis ad fastidium
> arat Falerni mille fundi iugera....

Once lashed by the triumvir's whip until the crier got tired, now he plows a thousand acres of Falernian property.

Horace as community watchdog, keeping undesirables at bay: this is the claim in which the dialogue between Horace and the jurist Trebatius in *Satires* 2.1 culminates. Although in the middle of the satire Horace cites Canidia's poisons as an analogue for his own practice, at the end he is at pains to distinguish between the two. When Trebatius warns that there is a law against *mala carmina*, the poet replies (83–5): 'Granted, in the case of *mala carmina*; but what if one were to compose *bona carmina*, deserving praise in Caesar's judgment? What if one were to bark at a blameworthy man, being oneself blameless?' (*siquis | opprobriis dignum latraverit, integer ipse?*). While the play on *mala carmina*—slanderous invective, black magic, or just (as Horace understands it) bad poetry—suggests that his work is distinguished only by its artistic polish, Horace is quick to qualify his definition of *bona carmina*. There is another, moral condition to be met before Horace can be acquitted. The irreproachable hound with the well-aimed bark is defined by implicit contrast with those malignant biters, like Canidia with her *dente livido* (*Epod.* 5.47) and the cur with his *atro dente* (*Epod.* 6.15), who, motivated by *invidia*, attack the undeserving.[22] Two kinds of dogs, two kinds of poetry: Canidia's venomous music provides a foil for Horace's socially useful art.

But there are difficulties with this, the 'authorized' version of the story. The excoriated 'other' tends to bear an uncanny resemblance to Horace himself. Consider the final charge levelled against the upstart of Epode 4 by the outraged community (17–20): 'What point is there to launching so many heavy-prowed ships against brigands and slave gangs, if this man here is military tribune?' (*hoc hoc tribuno militum?*). As we learn in *Satires* 1.6, the world likewise resented (or

---

[22] Cf. Dickie (1981), who distinguishes between two views of archaic *iambos* and argues persuasively that in *Epod.* 6 Horace is playing the noble iambic poet off against the 'ignoble dog' motivated by *invidia* and distinguished by the *dens ater* of blame.

'enviously carped at', *rodunt*, 46, as Horace defensively phrases it) the promotion of Horace, a freedman's son (*libertino patre natum*, 46), to the military tribunate (*quod mihi pareret legio Romana tribuno*, 48). Although Horace invokes the *liberrima indignatio* of the community to back up and repeat his charges in Epode 4, their force is still blunted by the confusion between accuser and accused. Horace may well end up playing the lamb rather than the wolf in this charade.[23]

One dog's bark sounds, moreover, much like another's. The term 'epode', which can designate not only the epodic verse form but also the incantation (ἐπῳδή) of the magician/healer, is avoided by Horace, who prefers to call his invectives *iambi* (*Epod.* 14.7, *Ep.* 1.19.23, *Ep.* 2.2.59). But in Epode 17 the technical common ground of magic and rhetoric is put on display as the poet pits his *exempla* against the witch's: 'Achilles forgave Telephus,' pleads Horace, and Canidia answers, 'Tantalus suffers eternally for his sins against the gods.' An *exemplum* is a collapsed analogy ('as Achilles forgave Telephus, so ought you to forgive me', etc.); and analogy, which not only describes but decrees a relation, is a central strategy of both magic and rhetoric.[24] The main difference between the speeches of Epode 17 is, of course, that Horace is ironic at Canidia's expense whereas Canidia is straightforwardly vindictive. In this regard, the dialogue recalls the confrontation in *Satires* 1.9 between Horace and the aspiring chum who, blandly insistent on sticking to his miserable victim, either overlooks or dismisses his interlocutor's more or less politely veiled insults. But Horace is miraculously rescued from this creature—not from Canidia. In the contest of Epode 17 the witch triumphs over the poet. Canidia's vengeful grip does not relax as the book of *Epodes*

---

[23] In line with his general interpretation of the poet of the *Epodes* as 'the weak defending the weak', Schmidt (1977), 403 assumes that Horace is from the start identified with the lamb, the upstart with the wolf. But lambs don't usually sound so ferocious. Schmidt's assumption that 'weakness' is part of a programmatic stance, rather than a problematic irony underlying the aggression of the book, does not account for the tone of the *Epodes*. I would argue, with Henderson (1987), 111, that the poem is an instance of 'the poison [of invective] rebounding on the only "name" we have for the poems, their author's'.

[24] Cf. the seamless transition at Virg. *Ecl.* 8.80–9, from magical analogy (*ut ... sic*) to 'poetic' simile (*talis ... qualis*)—a brilliant demonstration of their homogeneity. The future tenses (27–8) and hortatory subjunctives (52 ff.) of Damon's song also verge on magical analogy.

closes (17.81): 'am I, with all my powers (cf. *possim ... possim* 78–9), to lament that my arts have no efficacy against you?' (*plorem artis in te nil agentis exitus?*).

Although Horace, the ironic author of Canidia's self-indicting speech, may intend us to take this rhetorical question literally, thus turning it against the speaker (this is effectively Canidia's last appearance in Horace's poetry; it is her own *exitus* which she unwittingly announces), the silence which it ushers in is hard to fathom. If Canidia's vaunt came at the beginning of the book, the effect would be quite different. It would be easier to agree with Edmund Silk, who has suggested that Canidia is condemning Horace 'to the perpetual—albeit futile—practice of literary composition' (1969: 212). As a kind of anti-Muse, the relentless inspiration or instigation of Horace's verse, Canidia is a dark double of the goddess who refuses to let Horace alone in the proem to the fourth book of *Odes* (*Carm.* 4.1.1–4):

> Intermissa, Venus, diu
>   rursus bella moves? parce precor, precor.
> non sum qualis eram bonae
>   sub regno Cinarae. ...

After so long an intermission, Venus, are you for war again? Spare me, I beg you, I beg you! I'm not the man I was under the reign of good Cinara. ...

Compare Horace's plea to Canidia (*Epod.* 17.2, 6–7): 'On my knees I pray, ... leave off (*parce*) casting spells, and loose, loose the magic wheel (*solve, solve turbinem*) so it may run backward.' In both poems, Horace pleads unfitness for love—decorously formulated in the late ode (*non sum qualis eram ...*), but spelled out in ugly detail in the epode (21–2): 'My youth has fled, the modest blush has abandoned my bones in their wrapper of sallow hide ...' (*fugit iuventas et verecundus color | reliquit ossa pelle amicta lurida ...*). If Venus is 'looking for a suitable liver to scorch' (*si torrere iecur quaeris idoneum* 12), Canidia already has Horace on the coals (30, 33–5): 'O sea and earth, I'm on fire. ... Are you going to keep up the heat, you workshop of Colchian drugs, until I'm nothing but arid ashes scattered by the injurious winds?' But Canidia's heat, unlike the rekindled eros of *Odes* 4.1, is not used to fuel more poems. No fiery invectives follow to give the lie to Horace's self-proclaimed exhaustion.

CANICULA

The companion portraits of Canidia and Horace in Epode 17—
unflaggingly energetic witch and spent poet—suggest that the old
age written in Canidia's name is only a screen for Horace's own
debility. It is Horace, after all, and not Canidia, who is distinguished
by *canities* (*tuis capillus albus est odoribus* 17.23). This reversal brings
us to Hesiod's famous description of the season dominated by the
Dog Star in the *Works and Days* (582–8):

> ἦμος δὲ σκόλυμός τ' ἀνθεῖ καὶ ἠχέτα τέττιξ
> δενδρέῳ ἐφεζόμενος λιγυρὴν καταχεύετ' ἀοιδὴν
> πυκνὸν ὑπὸ πτερύγων, θέρεος καματώδεος ὥρῃ,
> τῆμος πιόταταί τ' αἶγες καὶ οἶνος ἄριστος,
> μαχλόταται δὲ γυναῖκες, ἀφαυρότατοι δέ τοι ἄνδρες
> εἰσίν, ἐπεὶ κεφαλὴν καὶ γούνατα Σείριος ἄζει,
> αὐαλέος δέ τε χρὼς ὑπὸ καύματος.

When the golden thistle flowers and the chirping cicada sitting on the tree
pours out its shrill song continually from under its wings in the season of
hot summer, then goats are fattest and wine at its best, women are most
lustful, and men are weakest, since Sirius dries out their heads and knees,
and their skin is parched by the heat.

In this season of maximal sexual discrepancy, female desire peaks
just as male potency hits its all-year low. The parataxis of the
clauses describing this discrepancy conceals, moreover, a causal
connection: it is the woman's heat that saps the man's strength.[25]
The preeminence of the Dog Star signals an indecorous reversal of
the sexual hierarchy, a resurgence of female heat at the expense of
male potency. It is significant that the passage opens with the music
of the cicada (τέττιξ), mythical consort of the dawn-goddess,
withered counterpart of her eternally renascent desire. Eos herself

---

[25] Cf. Detienne (1977), 121–2: 'Such is the disturbing image of woman devouring
man of which the canicular period each year is a reminder impelled by her lascivi-
ousness which is fuelled by the burning heat of Sirius, the wife bids fair to transform
her husband from "green" to "desiccated".' On the significance of the head and knees
here, see Onians (1951), 110–11, 177–8.

appears in a triple anaphora in the lines just preceding (578–80). Eos and Tithonus, youthful goddess and debilitated male, provide the paradigm for human sexual relations during this season.[26] If, as Canidia boasts in Epode 17 (62–73), Horace's efforts to escape her control through suicide are destined to fail, it must be because Canidia has granted him the dubious distinction of corporeal immortality; like Tithonus, Horace is doomed to endure the heat of his mistress for all eternity.

Female heat, male debility: in Latin, these canicular extremes may be expressed by a single word, *impotentia*, which means both lack of power, or weakness, and lack of self-control, or violence. The twinned meanings of *impotentia* are played out in the three poems dominated by Canidia. In all three, an overheated Canidia is viewed through the eyes of an impotent male. In Epode 17, as we have seen, Horace is reduced to desiccated skin and bones by her relentless heat. In *Satires* 1.8 the jutting post of Priapus's *palus* (Horace's rendition of the Greek φαλλός) notably fails to do its apotropaic job, remaining, as W. S. Anderson has commented, 'quite literally *inutile lignum* throughout the poem' (1972: 6–7). Although Priapus does finally succeed in scaring the witches out of his garden, it is through no gesture of potency. Instead, like the viewers of Scylla in the opening of the *Ars*, Priapus temporarily loses control of his body: it is his terrified fart that startles the witches into flight. Rather than raping the intruders, as he customarily threatens to do, Priapus is himself split in two (his 'buttock riven', *diffissa nate* 47; cf. Hallett 1981) by his unintended self-assertion. In Epode 5, where Canidia's invidious glare (cf. *quid ut noverca me intueris* 9) initiates the process of canicular desiccation, neither the helpless little boy onstage nor the *senex* Varus offstage offers a type of virile manhood. It is as if Archilochus and Catullus—potent poets who, like Canidia, inflict

---

[26] I note in passing that the same paradigm informs the cicada simile in *Iliad* 3, where the Trojan elders murmur τεττίγεσσιν ἐοικότες, οἵ τε καθ᾽ ὕλην | δενδρέῳ ἐφεζόμενοι ὄπα λειριόεσσαν ἱεῖσι: (3.151–2). Commentators identify the tenor of the simile as the garrulousness or eloquence of the elders without remarking Helen's presence on the scene. It is the fiery beauty of Helen—an avatar of Eos—that, as it were, transforms the elders into Tithonuses. My argument presupposes an early date for the story of Tithonus's transformation, on which see King (1986).

impotence on their detractors—had disinherited Horace in favor of the witch.[27]

But canicular heat is not, of course, the exclusive property of Canidia. In each confrontation, male helplessness is shored up by the violence of invective. The withering ironies of Epode 17, the gas bomb launched by Priapus in *Satires* 1.8, the 'Thyestean curses' (86) to which the little boy resorts at the end of Epode 5, threatening his murderers with a grisly posthumous revenge: in each case, invective originates as a compensation for impotence.[28] But impotence remains a part of the story. What distinguishes the *Epodes* is precisely this failure to erase the origins of invective in impotence.[29] The failure is luridly obvious in Epodes 8 and 12, two invectives against unidentified oversexed women. It is the blending of weakness and rage that makes these poems, which are as uncontrolled as their victims, so hard to read. The veneer of metrical and rhetorical form, valiantly demonstrated by Carrubba (1969: 44–51), does not contain Horace's violence, any more than the woman's cosmetic surface withstands the heat of her lust (*Epod.* 12.9–11). His sarcasms—'But what *excites* me is your chest with those collapsing breasts...' (*Epod.* 8.7)—are as coarse a disguise for his intentions as her pretensions to Stoicism are for hers (15–16). If Horace wants to criticize not only sexual but literary excesses—if, as D. L. Clayman

---

[27] Cf. Catull. 16; the punishment of Archilochus's detractors is described in the Mnesiepes Inscription (Archilochus T4 Tarditi, E_1 col.III 35 ff.; I am grateful to G. Nagy for pointing out the relevance of this material). Horace's repeated confessions of impotence indicate a malfunction in the system—the 'cultural habit on the part of men to deal with threats of *erôs* by fictitious denial and transfer'—analyzed by Winkler (1990), 90.

[28] As Fitzgerald remarks, 'invective more often than not derives from a sense of inadequacy or weakness that it compensates' (1988: 189). Fitzgerald's illuminating study, which sets out to demonstrate 'the interrelation between the political, invective, and erotic poems in the *Epodes*' (1988: 176), appeared after this study was accepted for publication. Our main points of convergence and divergence are noted as they occur. [In this volume, Ch. 8.]

[29] *Pace* Henderson, whose suggestive reading of *Epod.* 8 elucidates the implications of the 'gender-organized coding' (1987), 112 of the epodes but nonetheless leaves Horace safely on top: he is 'playing disgust as a game' (110); *Epod.* 8 is 'a "soft" joke from within the competence of the Roman plebeian repertoire and safely defused as such' (113). Although Henderson sets out to 'try to make this poem's transgressive power come alive' (106) the transgressive possibilities of the discourses which govern his interpretation—rock lyrics and graffiti—are limited.

argues, the female body is a vehicle for a literary tenor—the Horatian critique has not managed to stay above the mud of its metaphors.[30]

While impotence is often a topic in invective, the implication being that the woman in question is too hideous to arouse a man (Richlin 1983: 118), these poems betray the temporal and logical priority of impotence. Epode 8 begins by responding to what was probably an insultingly rhetorical question (this woman sports the *dens ater* of blame) about the reasons for Horace's sexual inadequacy (1–6):

> Rogare longo putidam te saeculo,
>   viris quid enervet meas,
> cum sit tibi dens ater et rugis vetus
>   frontem senectus exaret
> hietque turpis inter aridas natis
>   podex velut crudae bovis?

You ask, do you, rotted as you are by long age, what unstrings my virile force, when you have a black tooth and old age plows your forehead with wrinkles and between your shrivelled buttocks your filthy asshole gapes like a sick cow's?

Although the phrase modifying 'you' already suggests the form of his insulting answer, the poem nevertheless begins as a defense of the poet's 'enervation'. The dynamic of Epode 12 is similar (1–3):

> Quid tibi vis, mulier nigris dignissima barris?
>   munera quid mihi quidve tabellas
> mittis nec firmo iuveni nec naris obesae?

What do you want, woman most fit for black elephants? Why do you keep sending presents and messages to me, I who am no firm youth and whose sense of smell is not coarse?

Horace's opening question recalls the annoyance expressed by the personified penis of *Satires* 1.2 (69–71): *Quid vis tibi?* 'What do you

---

[30] See Clayman (1975); (1980), 78–80. Clayman's discussion of the overlap between physical and rhetorical qualities (e.g., *turpis, tumens*) is suggestive, and the association of female body with literary text is convincing. But I doubt that the relation is allegorical here. Both woman and text are subject to the larger concerns of decorum. On the tradition of invective against old women, see Richlin (1984).

want? I don't demand a consular cunt cloaked in a nice dress from you, do I, when my passion is heated up?' But the speaker of the epode is not only more fussy than this but less capable. The black elephants may be well enough endowed for any female, however voracious; not so Horace. Although later in the poem Horace offers indirect proof of his sexual prowess by quoting the woman's complaint—a complaint which is really a backhanded compliment: 'you can do it with Inachia three times a night; with me you're always soft at the first go' (*ad unum* | *mollis opus* 15–16)—this boast should not make us forget that Horace originally blamed his impotence on himself first and on the woman second: 'Why do you keep trying to get me into bed, I who am *no firm youth* and whose sense of smell is not coarse?' Impotence, not disgust, is the premise of both poems. In a defensive reversal, the hideousness of the woman is manufactured to excuse the incapacity of the man.

The same dynamic informs the milder-mannered *impotentia* of Epode 15, where Horace threatens to punish his fickle mistress by abandoning her (11–14): 'O Neaera, you will suffer much from my manliness (*virtute*); for if there's any manhood in Flaccus (*nam siquid in Flacco viri est*), he won't endure your giving one night after another to a rival (*potiori*), and in his anger he'll seek out a mate.' The comical juxtaposition of *Flaccus* and *vir*, which proposes an etymological source for Horatian impotence, undermines Horace's tough pose (Babcock 1966: 413–14). If Neaera has left Horace for a man who is *potior*, she is unlikely to be greatly disturbed by his decision (if we believe that he has actually made the decision) to seek love elsewhere.

The poem highlights a paradox implicit in the conventions of love poetry—a paradox with important implications, moreover, for Horace's weightier political epodes. The traditional opposition of the erotic lifestyle to military heroism sets up an opposition of 'soft' to 'hard', feminine to masculine, disarmed to armored, amorous complaint to aggressive invective, and in the context of this opposition we often encounter the figure of the languishing lover. But how, we might ask, does this soft, effeminate lover-boy manage to penetrate his partner? Impotence seems to be the norm even *within* the erotic relation. To regain his potency the lover must either borrow the attributes of the soldier—hence the pervasive motif

of the 'soldier-lover,' especially in Roman elegy[31]—or else he must
assert his masculine independence from his mistress, adopting the
tough stance of invective. In the latter case, potency coincides with
the rejection of the erotic relation. Lovelorn Catullus's famous
self-exhortation (Catull. 8), with its emphasis on 'staying hard'
(*obdura* 11, *obdurat* 12, *obdura* 19) as a way of escaping the *domina*,
exemplifies the paradox. To desire Lesbia is to be, precisely, *impotens*
(9): 'Now she doesn't want it; so you too, madman/weakling (*impotens*), stop wanting it!'[32]

The misogyny of the *Epodes* may be understood as a variation on a
traditional theme which attributes the decline of Rome to the sexual
misconduct of Roman women. This is the story told, for example, in
the Roman odes (*Carm.* 3.6.17–20): 'Our age, fertile in crime, stained
first marriage and the family line and the home (*nuptias* | ... *et genus
et domos*); derived from this source, destruction flooded fatherland
and people.' To the urbane depravity of today's girls and their pimp-
ing husbands (21–33) Horace contrasts the rustic moral fiber of an
old-time Sabellian mother and son (37–41).[33] In the *Epodes* this
idealized womanhood exists only in the daydreams of the money-
lender Alfius, who is always thinking—from a distance—about the
pleasures of country living (*Epod.* 2.39–41): 'and if I had a virtuous
wife (*pudica mulier*) to do her part helping with the house and the
children—one of those Sabine-type women...' When Horace insinuates in Epodes 5 (5–6) and 17 (50–2) that Canidia's purported
children are not her legitimate offspring, he raises an issue which is
not only sexual (Canidia is too busy having fun to have children), but
social (Canidia's tricks threaten the integrity of the family). But the

[31] Cf. the famous reversal effected by Prop. 1.6, where *mollis... Ionia* (31) welcomes the military man while the lover heroically endures a life led under a *duro
sidere* (36); Tib. 1.1, where the adjective *iners* modifies first Tibullus's unheroic, rural
life (4) then the poet as Delia's contented, unheroic lover (58), and finally old age
(71), viewed as putting an end to lovemaking (I am indebted to R. J. Tarrant for this
observation)—after this reversal Tibullus can describe himself as *dux milesque bonus*
in the sphere of love.
[32] The restoration *impote<ns noli>* is as close to certain as any can be.
[33] Cf. Carm. 4.5, where the chaste but still passionate desire of the motherland for
her son Augustus—*sic desideriis icta fidelibus* | *quaerit patria Caesarem* (15–16)—sets
the stage for a scene of rural harmony (17–24) from which corrupt desires are
banished.

figure in whom sexual and political anxieties most explicitly converge within the *Epodes* is Cleopatra, whose debilitating influence on Roman manhood is described in Epode 9 (11–14): 'Roman soldiers, slaves to a woman—you men of the future will deny it!—carry stakes and weapons and have the strength (*potest*) to serve wrinkled eunuchs.' These associations persist, somewhat muted, in the ode on Cleopatra, where Horace recalls that celebration was out of place 'so long as the queen had mad ruin in store for the Capitol, destruction for the empire, with her tainted herd of men filthy with disease, a woman wild enough (*inpotens*) to hope for anything' (*Carm.* 1.37.6–11; cf. Watson 1987: 127–8). Civil war and the war between the sexes are inextricably linked. It is because Antony—conspicuously absent from these scenes—has fallen victim to Cleopatra's charms that Rome has fallen into the chaos of civil war.

But it would be a mistake to reduce the sexual epodes to allegories or moralizing diagnoses of the contemporary political scene.[34] The author of the *Epodes* is no more omnipotent than his various perso-nae; Horace is not a detached analyst of current events but a com-promised participant—sharing, let us recall, the bed of the lustful woman of Epode 8 and the social stigma of the upstart of Epode 4. The dynamics of Horatian misogyny are better understood in terms of what Neil Hertz (1983) has called, in an exemplary analysis of the interplay of erotics and politics, 'male hysteria under political pres-sure' (as the essay is subtitled). In the *Epodes*, sexual *impotentia* and civil war are related not only as cause and effect or vehicle and tenor, but also as intertwining instances of the canicular scenario.

Consider the relation between Maecenas and Canidia—an odd couple but, structurally, a couple nonetheless. Where Canidia rules the ends of Horace's early collections, Maecenas, the honored ad-dressee of *Satires* 1.1 and Epode 1, rules beginnings—a correspond-ence underscored in the *Epodes* by the use of appropriate forms of the

---

[34] For this strategy—not incorrect but inadequate—cf. Manning (1970) (Horace is attacking the vicious practices of actual witches); Nisbet (1984), 9 ('Canidia' alludes to Canidius Crassus, 'a long-standing opponent of Octavian'); Fitzgerald (1988), 189 ('The sexual inadequacy described in 12 is a metaphor for the inadequacy the poet feels in the political context'). The claim of authorial omnipotence is often a retro-jected justification for our own interpretations. But why should we believe that Horace has absolute control over all the recoverable meanings of his text—any more than we believe that his intentions are irrelevant to those meanings?

verb *ire* (*ibis* 1.1; *exitus* 17.81) to frame the collection. The two often cross paths as well: Maecenas's gardens are invaded by Canidia in *Satires* 1.8; Maecenas is among the guests fleeing the banquet 'as if Canidia had breathed upon it' at the end of *Satires* 2; and patron and witch are implicitly compared in Epode 3. Maecenas has already established his claims to a 'parental' role in *Satires* 1.6, where Horace juxtaposes 'Maecenas who recognized and accepted him for what he was, and his father who made him what he was' (Rudd 1966: 44). The nine months following Horace's first reception by Maecenas end with the poet's 'rebirth' into a new kind of family. Horace has, by contrast, absolutely nothing to say on the subject of his biological mother anywhere in his work. Something will always arise to fill such a gap, however, and in Horace's early works the lack of the mother is supplied by Canidia. The patron makes a good surrogate father, but the witch demonstrates her unfitness for her assigned role in Epode 5, where, in a monstrous perversion of mothering, she plants a child in Mother Earth to die. The opposition is underscored by the recurrence of the phrase *satis superque* in the first and last poems of the collection: 'your generosity has enriched me enough and to spare' (1.31–2) vs. 'I have paid you penalties enough and to spare' (17.19). While Maecenas enriches his protégé, Canidia drains her victim dry.

If Horace's subjection to Canidia perverts the proper order of things, his amicable subordination to Maecenas is an instance of the kind of coupling which holds Roman society together. Hierarchy is implicit in the very form of the epode, which requires the subordination of one line to another. The first epode, addressed to Maecenas on the eve of Actium, makes form part of its theme as it subordinates not only second line to first, but Maecenas to Caesar and Horace to Maecenas (1–6):

> Ibis Liburnis inter alta navium,
>   amice, propugnacula
> paratus omne Caesaris periculum
>   subire, Maecenas, tuo:
> quid nos, quibus te vita si superstite
>   iucunda, si contra, gravis?

You will go, my friend, on Liburnian vessels among the tall bulwarks of ships, prepared to undergo every risk of Caesar's at your own risk; what about me, to whom life is pleasant if you survive, otherwise heavy?

As Horace's *amicus* Maecenas is set to 'go' (*ibis*); as Caesar's subordinate he is prepared to 'undergo', *subire*, like the line in which the verb appears. Horace likewise depends on his superior's superior presence, *te ... superstite*. *Super-* appears twice more in the poem, both times in the upper line (29, 31). Failure to maintain proper subordination of 'below' to 'above' may lead, as in the case of Scylla in the *Ars*, to a failure of decorum. Canidia's *adynaton* in Epode 5 enacts the inversion it describes (79–82):

> priusque caelum sidet *inferius* mari
>   tellure porrecta *super*,
> quam non amore sic meo flagres uti
>   bitumen atris ignibus.

Sooner will the sky sink below the sea, with the earth stretched out above, than you will escape burning with my love like bitumen in black flames.

Although Canidia invokes the permanence of the cosmic order to guarantee the efficacy of her magic, cosmic inversion is a more accurate frame for her activities, which aim at giving the female power over the male, Gaia power over Ouranos. In Epode 17, the only epode to eschew the distich, doubleness resurfaces in the form of a discordant dialogue—Horace speaking the first part, Canidia the second—wherein the lower female half does not succumb to, but rather triumphs over, the man who struggles for control.

But the opposition between Maecenas and Canidia is tempered by a certain resemblance. In Epode 17 Horace longs for a respite from his amorous labor (*nullum a labore me reclinat otium* 17.24); in Epode 1, as yet uncommitted, he is pondering similar options, choosing between *otium* (7) and the *labor* (9) of a military campaign befitting 'men who are not soft' (*non mollis viros* 10). Although he makes up his mind to embark, he remains unsure of his qualifications (15–16): 'you might ask (*roges*) how I, unwarlike and infirm as I am (*inbellis ac firmus parum*), could assist your labor with my own?' As in Epodes 8 and 12, a question is raised about the poet's capabilities, and once again Horace seems not to be the man, or man enough, for the job. The question does not go away when Horace compares himself to a mother bird standing guard over her young (*adsidens inplumibus pullis avis* 19), echoing Achilles's aggrieved self-depiction in the

embassy scene of the *Iliad* (ὡς δ' ὄρνις ἀπτῆσι νεοσσοῖσι 9.323):
whereas Achilles feeds his 'chicks' while himself going hungry, Horace
is fed and fostered by Maecenas, his purported 'chick'.[35] Gifts—the
gift of the Sabine farm as well as the *munera* of the importunate
woman of Epode 12—can compromise the recipient. Horace must
differentiate between the *gratia* he hopes to win from Maecenas and
the more tangible goods others might suspect him of pursuing (23–
6): 'Gladly will I fight this and every war in the hope of winning your
favor—not so that I may have more oxen to yoke to the plow....' It is
as if Maecenas's generosity put as great a strain on Horace's resources
as Canidia's malignant demands.

Relations between men seem little better, then, than relations
between the sexes. In Epode 14 Horace responds to a familiar accusation, levelled now by Maecenas himself (1–2, 5):

> Mollis inertia cur tantam diffuderit imis
>   oblivionem sensibus...
> candide Maecenas, occidis saepe rogando.

You kill me, Maecenas, with your constant questions about why soft inertia
has poured such a profound forgetfulness over my senses....

The woman of Epode 12 also finds Horace too 'soft' (*mollis* 16) and
'inert' (*inertem* 17) to satisfy her needs. Although Horace hastens to
blame his weakness—his inability, in this case, to complete the book
of *Epodes*—on 'the god' (presumably the god of love), there may be a
relation between the *inertia* at the beginning of this first sentence and
the 'constant questions' at the end. *Rogare* can mean not only a
question but a demand, often a sexual demand. Compare the opening of Epode 8, where the woman's 'question' (*rogare...*) about
Horace's inadequacy tropes her sexual solicitation (cf. Grassmann
1966: 48). In Epode 14 the comparison between Horace's passion and
Anacreon's (*non aliter Samio dicunt arsisse Bathyllo* | *Anacreonta
Teium* 9–10) conjures up the specter of Maecenas's infatuation (assuming it dates from this period) with his freedman Bathyllus, the

---

[35] The Homeric echo is noted by Hierche (1974), 163–4. Schmidt (1977), 402–3,
remarking the incongruity of the simile, reads it as a programmatic claim appropriate
to the *Epodes* as a whole.

famous actor.[36] The outlines of the poem Horace could not write (but also could not help writing) begin to emerge: Horace as Bathyllus, the entertainer, answerable to the wishes of his master.... The erotics of the poet–patron relation would be the subject of another paper. Suffice it to say that, although Horace closes by sorting the two out into separate, contrasting couples (*gaude sorte tua: me libertina nec uno | contenta Phryne macerat* 15–16), the poem is still discolored by the shadow of pathic *mollitia*. Horace's relation to Maecenas is not the solution to *impotentia*, but part of the problem.[37]

The intercontamination of sexual and political *impotentia* is disturbingly clear in the juxtaposition of Epodes 16 and 17—two versions, in different registers, of the same canicular story. If the success of the *vates* Stesichorus (17.44) gives Horace hope that he too may escape the wrath of his angry goddess, the only other *vates* of the *Epodes* (16.66) is also planning an escape—this time from Rome itself. In both poems, potency may be regained only through flight. Hence Horace's strange proposal, in Epode 16, that the entire virile population of Rome simply flee to the mythical isles of the blest, leaving the violence of the civil wars behind them. The city will be populated only by *mollis* men (37); the real Archilochean he-men, those possessing *virtus* (39), will assert their manliness by escaping to a better world.[38] In this scenario, Rome herself plays the role of the indomitable mistress. Although the very name of Rome makes a claim for virile power, ῥώμη (Latin *virtus* or *vis*), in the despairing pun which opens Epode 16 Rome has devolved into the violence of

---

[36] Cf. Sen. *Con.* 10 pr. 8: *Bathyllo Maecenatis*; Tac. *Ann.* 1.54: *Maecenati . . . effuso in amore Bathylli.*

[37] The language of *mollitia* in *Epod.* 1 and 14 was remarked by Büchner (1970a), 74. Fitzgerald, who likewise connects the poems to Maecenas with *Epod.* 8 and 12, points out that Horace 'had good reason to be ambivalent about the results of his relations with Maecenas, which did not make him universally popular' (1988), 182.

[38] Büchner, who notes the echo of Archilochus at line 39, comments (1970a), 80: '*Desidia* und *virtus*, weibisches Verhalten und *virtus* stehen sich hier wie sonst in den Epoden programmatisch gegenüber.' While I am in agreement with Büchner on the importance of the opposition and on many of its ramifications, I do not share his optimistic reading of Horace's 'redefinition' of manliness. Cf. his peculiar discussion, which both acknowledges and passes over Horatian unmanliness, of *virtus* as a 'leitwort' of the collection (73–4). My comparison of *Epod.* 16 and 17 is complemented by Fitzgerald's discussion (1988), 177–9 of *Epod.* 15 and 16, in both of which 'the issue is the need to break with a degenerate condition'.

ruere, 'rushing' (1–2).[39] 'Another generation is being worn down by civil wars, and Rome herself is rushing to ruin through her own power' (*suis et ipsa Roma viribus ruit*). Like Horace fighting the spell of Canidia, like Catullus struggling against the fascination of Lesbia, the Romans must reject the indecorous disorder which saps their strength at home.

The relation between the two poems is underscored by the reappearance in Epode 17 of several characters from Epode 16. Horace's idyllic retreat is untouched even by the voyagers of myth (16.57–60):

> non huc Argoo contendit remige pinus
>   neque inpudica Colchis intulit pedem;
> non huc Sidonii torserunt cornua nautae,
>   laboriosa nec cohors Ulixei.

Not here arrived the ship of pine rowed by the Argo's crew, nor did the shameless Colchian set foot here; not here did the Sidonian sailors turn their prow, nor Ulysses's hard-working company.

When the adjective 'Colchian' recurs in Epode 17 (*cales venenis officina Colchicis?* 35), we remember that Medea is not only a great traveler but a model, as the forceful adjective *inpudica* suggests, for the shamelessly lustful Canidia, ironically termed *pudica* at Epode 17.40 (contrast the *pudica mulier* of Epode 2.39). The Sidonian sailors are demoted to form part of Canidia's coterie of lovers (*amata nautis multum et institoribus* 17.20). And, as Eugene Bushala (1968) has shown, when Horace invokes Ulysses's encounter with Circe as a paradigm of his own sufferings (*saetosa duris exuere pellibus* | *laboriosi remiges Ulixei* | *volente Circe membra* 15–17), the heroic epithet πολύτλας ('much enduring', *laboriosus*) is deflated and reinflected, reminding us that the Homeric hero, like Horace, 'labored' in the service of a lustful, unmanning witch.

---

[39] Citing the language of a Sibylline oracle (καὶ ῾Ρώμη ῥύμη *Or. Sib.* 3.364), Macleod (1979), 221 argues that '*ruit* echoes both the sound and sense of ῥύμη.' Cf. *Carm.* 1.37.7 ff. (*inpotens* Cleopatra prepares *ruinas* for the Capitol) and the gnomic formula at *Carm.* 3.4.65 (vis *consili expers mole* ruit *sua*).

One particularly ominous echo associates Canidia with the barbarian invader who (like Canidia in Epode 5 and *Satires* 1.8) threatens the burial grounds of Rome in Epode 16 (11–14):

> barbarus heu cineres insistet victor et urbem
>   eques sonante verberabit ungula;
> quaeque carent ventis et solibus ossa Quirini,
>   —nefas videre—dissipabit insolens.

The barbarian conqueror will trample our ashes, alas, and on horseback batter the city with resonant hoof; he will scatter in his insolence (sight not to be seen) those Roman bones which are sheltered from wind and sun.

Canidia's apocalyptic vaunt paints the same picture (17.74–5): *vectabor umeris tunc ego inimicis eques | meaeque terra cedet insolentiae* ('I'll ride horseback one day on enemy shoulders, and earth will yield before my unfamiliar insolence').[40] These insolent riders ride roughshod over the decorous hierarchies of Roman sovereignty (Roman over barbarian, man atop woman) and over the virginal Roman earth. By contrast, in the paradise to which Horace urges his countrymen to flee in Epode 16, Mother Earth bears fruit without ever feeling the stroke of the plow, and female sexuality is safely under control (43–6):

> reddit...cererem tellus inarata quotannis
>   et inputata floret usque vinea,
> germinat et numquam fallentis termes olivae
>   suamque pulla ficus ornat arborem....

Earth unplowed renders grain each year and the vine always flourishes unpruned, the olive which never cheats breeds and the dark fig adorns its own tree....

No plowing, no pruning, no grafting: the moral excellence of these plants mirrors the original virtue and integrity of the human race before the corruption of desire. It should not surprise us, then, that the purity of Horace's *arva beata* is guaranteed by the absence of the Dog Star: in the promised land, Horace insists, 'no star's blazing *impotentia* consumes the flock' (*nullius astri | gregem aestuosa torret*

---

[40] The iconographic tradition relates the whore of Babylon to classical monsters like Echidna and Scylla (Barina (1980), 12 ff., with illustrations).

inpotentia 16.53–4). Occurring only here in Horace's poetry, *impo-tentia* is rightly associated with the Dog Star,[41] the source of all the varieties of impotence that Horace hopes to leave behind. In the here-and-now to which Epode 17 returns us, however, the dream of escaping Canicula is no more than a fantasy.

In the only poem which escapes Canidia's baneful influence almost entirely, the finely tuned Epode 13, Horace rewrites the canicular scenario so as to exclude female desire altogether. The party that Horace here recommends to his disconsolate friends is for men only—and for men, moreover, whose 'knees are strong' (*dumque virent genua* 4), not parched like the knees of Hesiod's heat-parched men. Unlike the drug-laced perfumes manufactured by Canidia (*Epod.* 5.59, 17.23) and the disgusting secretions of the woman of Epode 12 (7–8), the nard in which the drinkers are drenched (*nunc et Achaemenio | perfundi nardo iuvat* 8–9) is a true restorative.[42] It is no accident that Horace chooses Chiron as his spokesman—Chiron the 'good' centaur, the famous healer, the antithesis of the centaur Nessus, whose gore (consuming Hercules in the literalized flames of Deianeira's desire) is featured in two epodes, in both instances parallel to Canidia's drugs (*Epod.* 3.17–18, 17.31–2). It is with Chir-on's wise words to Achilles, on the eve of his departure for Troy, that the poem concludes (17–18):

> illic omne malum vino cantuque levato
>   deformis aegrimoniae dulcibus adloquiis.

There lighten every ill with wine and song, misshapen grief's sweet com-forters.

The alliterative interweaving of the final line aims at healing the rift—Achilles will not return home from Troy—figured in the

[41] The identification is supported by the scholia here and at *Epod.* 1.27, where Horace is not interested in being rich enough to move his cattle to summer pastures *ante sidus fervidum* (Ps.-Acro glosses *ante caniculares dies*). More interesting evidence is afforded by a comparison of the idyllic landscape of *Epod.* 16, complete with ilex and down-leaping waters (47–8), to that of *Carm.* 3.13, Horace's great sublim-ation of canicular *impotentia* into Callimachean refinement (*te flagrantis atrox hora Caniculae | nescit tangere*...9–10).

[42] On the significance of unguents, see Onians (1951), 209–12; on the odors of the *Epodes*, Henderson (1987), 115–16; on the various interrelated 'poisons' (garlic, drugs, blood), Porter (1987), 255–9.

divisive diaeresis. But Chiron's beneficent *adloquia* (a loose translation of ἐπῳδαί) offer only temporary relief, and *aegrimonia* recurs
soon enough (*fastidiosa tristis aegrimonia* 17.73). The exceptional
Epode 13 only proves the general rule of Canidia.

Although the prescription of the *Ars Poetica* would have us maintain decorum by subordinating female to male and erotics to politics,
we are closer to the matter of the *Epodes* when we recognize the
breakdown of such hierarchies. *Impotentia*, in its double aspect of
violence and weakness, infects all spheres of life—including the
sphere in which the poet composes his poems. While this manifold
impotentia is often hard to take, it is good to be reminded of the
monstrous and discordant elements within the Horatian corpus.
These elements may be brought under tighter control in later
works, but they do not disappear.

Author's note: Though we have drifted apart over the years, I retain a
quasi-parental affection for this my first article. For this reissue,
I have made superficial corrections only. Readers interested in my
second thoughts on the *Epodes* are invited to consult Chapter 2 of
Horace and the Rhetoric of Authority (Cambridge 1998), where I offer
a more comprehensive account of the collection in the context of
Horace's career.

10

The Languages of Horace *Odes* 1.24

Michael C. J. Putnam

To Vergil, for VARUS (...de?)

Quis desiderio sit pudor aut modus
tam cari capitis? praecipe lugubris
cantus, Melpomene, cui liquidam pater
    vocem cum cithara dedit.

ergo Quintilium perpetuus sopor
urget; cui Pudor et Iustitiae soror
incorrupta Fides nudaque Veritas
    quando ullum inveniet parem?

multis ille bonis flebilis occidit,
nulli flebilior quam tibi, Vergili.
tu frustra pius, heu, non ita creditum
    poscis Quintilium deos.

quid? si Threicio blandius Orpheo
auditam moderere arboribus fidem,
num vanae redeat sanguis imagini,
    quam virga semel horrida

non lenis precibus fata recludere
nigro conpulerit Mercurius gregi?
durum: sed levius fit patientia
    quidquid corrigere est nefas.

What restraint and limit can there be to our yearning for so dear a being?
Teach songs of grief, Melpomene, to whom the father gave a clear voice in

This essay was written in June 1992, at the American Academy in Rome. I dedicate it
to Lucilla Marino, retiring as Librarian of the Academy, in gratitude for her unstint-
ing help to all those who have made use of the library during her tenure of office.

company with the lyre. And so does everlasting sleep weigh heavy upon Quintilius? When will Modesty and untainted Faith, sister of Justice, and naked truth find any his equal? His death was mourned by many good people, mourned by no one more than you, Vergilius. Pious in vain, you demand of the gods Quintilius, alas, not entrusted in this way. What? Were you to master more seductively than Thracian Orpheus the lyre heard by the trees, would blood return to the empty image, which once Mercury, not prone to undo the fates by prayer, with his dread wand has herded in the black flock? Hard, but whatever is wrong to correct becomes easier by patience.

C. 1.24, Horace's second ode to be addressed to Virgil, is at once *epicedium* and *consolatio,* a lamentation for the death of Quintilius Varus, Horace's critic and friend, and an offering of condolence to the great poet who was likewise Varus's intimate.[1] It is carefully positioned between two poems concerned with time. The first is *c.* 1.23, addressed to Chloe, who will not yet accept the arousal of spring in her life. The second, *c.* 1.25, locates the courtesan Lydia on the threshold of an ugly old age which she cannot face. The intervening, pivotal ode deals with the event which 'centers' us all, from which Chloe is still distant but which Lydia draws near, namely death, the ultimate temporal finale. The poem offers a double warning to Virgil that death's pressures are insurmountable and that survivors, however grief-stricken, must properly put limits on their mourning.[2]

This implicit dialogue between poets has a history in Latin letters which will help us initially capture the nuanced intonation of Horace's apostrophe to Virgil. Horace is thinking back to poem 96 of Catullus, addressed to his fellow-poet Calvus on the occasion of the death of his wife:

> Si quicquam mutis gratum acceptumve sepulcris
>   accidere a nostro, Calve, dolore potest,
> quo desiderio veteres renovamus amores
>   atque olim missas flemus amicitias,
> certe non tanto mors immatura dolori est
>   Quintiliae, quantum gaudet amore tuo.[3]

---

[1] For a general survey of the intellectual background to Horace's *consolatio* see Kassel (1958) and, with particular reference to *C.* 1.24, Pasquali (1920), 249–57.

[2] To place *c.* 1.24 in its setting in the first book of odes is the principal goal of Pascal (1969). See also Minadeo (1982), 35–6 and, most recently, Santirocco (1986), 57–60.

[3] E. Fraenkel (1956) has examined Catullus 96 in detail. Other reminiscences of Catullus dot *c.*1.24. The phrase *tam cari capitis* (2), for instance, as commentators

If anything pleasant or agreeable can befall silent tombs, Calvus, from grief, by which yearning we refresh old loves and mourn friendships once lost, be sure that the untimely death of Quintilia is not so much a cause for her to sorrow as for rejoicing in your love.

The phrase *quo desiderio* which initiates Catullus's third line becomes *Quis desiderio*, Horace's opening words, and the name of Calvus's departed consort, Quintilia, slides easily into Quintilius. We happen also to possess two fragments of Calvus's poetry which appear likely to have come from an elegiac *epicedium*, probably his own poetic expression of the loss of Quintilia,[4] but it is the testimony of Propertius which brings Calvus's grief most vividly before us.[5] Propertius's verses (2.34.89–90) place Calvus carefully between Catullus and Gallus while linking Lesbia, Quintilia and Lycoris. It is the *epicedium* for Quintilia that the later elegist singles out:

> haec [carmina amoris] etiam docti confessa est pagina Calvi,
>   cum caneret miserae funera Quintiliae.

The page of Calvus also gave vent to these [songs of love] when he sang of the death of pitiable Quintilia.

But we can also judge the power of Calvus's verses by the enormous compliment which Catullus gives them. Instead of addressing a mute tomb, as the poem's opening line intimates, Calvus through his words will elicit rejoicing from Quintilia, even after her death. If we are correct in assuming that fr. 16—

> Forsitan hoc etiam gaudeat ipsa cinis—

Perhaps her ash might also rejoice in this.

comes from Calvus's *epicedium*, perhaps even bringing it to an end, then Catullus's conclusion—

> certe non tanto mors immatura dolori est
>   Quintiliae, quantum gaudet amore tuo.—

note, comes from Cat. 68.119–20 as part of an analogy suggesting how life circumvents death. Likewise the vocabulary of Cat. 5, a poem whose main hypothesis is that the flagrant passion of the moment can obliterate any thoughts of mortality, is scattered throughout Horace's ode (e.g. *perpetuus, occidit, semel*).

4   Fr. 15–16 (*FPL* Morel).

5   That Calvus himself was in turn influenced by the *Arete* of Parthenius is the plausible thesis of Pfeiffer (1960), see especially 145–7.

is doubly in dialogue with the verse of his poet-friend. It exchanges possibility for certainty and transmutes the metonymic ash of our human remnant back into the being itself, the wife who rejoices in poetry's manifestation of love. In marvelling on Calvus's potential ability to communicate emotion to his dead wife, Catullus turns his colleague's wish into actual experience. In so doing he wills away a major force of death by proclaiming that emotion can be received by the dead as well as offered by the living. There can be linkage between our sublunar world and the hereafter, says Catullus, if that conversation is initiated by poets with the imaginative power to replace the evanescent with the immortal.

Allusion to this poetic interchange on Horace's part underscores the remarkable difference between it and the dialectic of his relationship with Virgil in *c.* 1.24. As Catullus builds on Calvus, there is an intensification of emotion with a parallel heightening of poetry's presumed power to challenge death. Throughout all his verse the need for communication, regularly between speaker and addressee but taking other guises as well, is a crucial element, with the connection between survivor and departed being his most challenging project. The Augustan poet suggests something quite opposite. Horace, through the agency of Melpomene, mourns for Quintilius as does Virgil, no one more so. But the later poet, unlike Catullus, bounds rather than expands emotionality by suggesting, as the gist of his ode, that there must be demarcations to Virgil's song of mourning, either as an expression of sorrow or as an attempt to exert its magic potential. On one level, Horace seems to say, he will not play Catullus to Virgil's Calvus nor will he claim from song anything beyond its circumscribed role as manifestation of suitable grief. His exhortation to Virgil seems directed toward restraint, not towards any vain reliance on piety or pious song to bring back the dead. On another, however, by his very act of allusion to Catullus, he exemplifies poetry's power to vivify and revivify, to keep the past, here in particular the accomplishment of poets and poetry, ever fresh for his and future readers.

But Virgil's presence in *c.* 1.24 is more complex than that of mere receptacle for an Horatian lecture on stringent emotional control. To illustrate this point we must turn back to the poem itself and trace one of its major structuring principles, namely word-repetition and the etymological play that here lends it support. Most immediately striking is the reiteration of *pudor* (1) in *Pudor* (6). The first abstraction forms part of the poem's opening interrogation which seems to question what restrictions there could be when the dead Quintilius is the object of our grief. But any hint at boundless mourning is immediately undercut by the sudden reappearance of Restraint, now personified, as part of Quintilius's ethical baggage. This characteristic trait, the first to be named followed by *Fides* and *Veritas*, implies that seemliness and propriety were much a part of Quintilius's moral outlook. This in turn urges us to reevaluate the opening sentence so that an equally cogent reading of Horace's interrogation would be to ask—through the medium of the deceased himself— what limitations should, rather than could, be set to expressions of sorrow for any individual's yielding to mortality.

The second repetition takes us deeper into the poem as Horace reechoes *modus* (1) from his initial question in *moderere* (14), applied to Orpheus strumming his seductive lyre. We attend carefully to the verb for two reasons. It appears only here in Horace's lyric corpus.[6] This is also the only preserved instance in Latin letters where it is associated with performance on a musical instrument. Orpheus's genius at mastering music's modes and in the manipulation of their presentation is therefore given special prominence through the uniqueness of Horace's word choice, but the etymological link with the earlier use of *modus* brilliantly complicates the reference. Orpheus may once have mesmerized the powers of the Underworld, if we follow Virgil, in order nearly to bring back his wife from below to the realm of the living. Horace's Virgil, however, though himself the grandest of singers, must practise not music's outgoing, charming modes but the delimitation of restraint on whatever poetic manifestation of grief he may choose to voice.

There is also the striking resonance of *Fides* (7) in *fidem* (14). That the Romans made a connection between the virtue of Faith and the genius of the lyre is clear from the etymologizing of Paulus-Festus: *fides genus citharae dicta, quod tantum inter se cordae eius, quantum inter homines fides concordet* ('*Fides* is said to be a type of lyre because its strings (*cordae*) have as great consonance among themselves as

---

[6] His only other use is at *epi.* 1.2.59.

faith (*fides*) does (*concordet*) among men').⁷ Horace's intimation is that *Fides*, the fidelity of Quintilius, cannot be reconstituted, any more than he himself can be, by recourse to the concordance of the lyre. To trust in the lyre, especially when the feat expected of it is to overcome death's invulnerability, is to evaluate foolishly the very virtues for which Quintilius had so clearly stood.

Finally we have the etymological connection between *Vergili* (10) and *virga* (16). There is little doubt that the proper spelling of Virgil's name in antiquity was Vergilius,⁸ but already during his lifetime there was a punning coupling between his name and *virgo* or *virga*. For the first, both the Suetonian life (11) and Servius (*ad Aen. praef.*) tell us that his nickname in antiquity was *Parthenias*, i.e. *virgo*, and it is not coincidental that the only occasion in his works that Virgil directly names himself, *geo.* 4.563, precedes mention of Parthenope, Naples as siren-muse, by only one line.⁹ As for *virga*, both Suetonius's life (5) and the *vita Focae* (36) mention a *virga populea* which, planted at the time of the poet's birth, grew with such astonishing speed that it was taken as augury for the poet's greatness and, according to Suetonius, received his name.¹⁰ We should also note that here at line 10, as at *c.* 1.3.6, the greatest manuscript authority rests with the spelling *Virgili /Virgilium.*¹¹

The etymological conjunction between *Virgili* and *virga* reenforces what the linkage of *modus* with *moderere* and of *Fides* with *fidem* has

⁷ P.-F. 89M. Cf. also Isid. *Orig.* 3.22.4: 'Veteres autem citharam fidiculam vel fidicem nominaverunt, quia tam concinunt inter se chordae eius, quam bene conveniet inter quos fides sit.'

⁸ See Schanz and Hosius (1935), 34; K. Büchner, *RE* 2.15.1037; Jackson Knight (1945), 36–7.

⁹ For further details see Hornstein (1957); Brown (1963), 103 and 106 n. 1; Thomas (1988), 139 (on *geo.* 1.427–37 and the link between the poet's name and the word *virgineum* [430]). For the possible connection between Parthenias-Virgil and his influential Greek poetic predecessor Parthenius see Brown (1963), *passim*, especially 127–32 and Nisbet and Hubbard (1970), 280.

¹⁰ The connection *virga-Vergilius* is common in the later *vitae*. For a complete listing see Bayer (1977), 758 and for further details on the etymology Gordon (1934), in particular 5 and n. 5.

¹¹ I follow here, and throughout this essay, the text of Klingner (1959). With the exception of Q, the *tituli* of *c.* 1.24 universally have the spelling *Virgilius*, as do those of *c.* 1.3 (but cf. Servius on *Aen.* 2.260, quoting *c.* 1.3.5–7, and Porphyrio on *c.* 1.24.11, also quoting *c.* 1.3.5–6). In Horace's hexameter work, the spelling is universally *Vergilius*.

already intimated. In these latter instances Horace proposes that the implied parallel that Virgil might draw between himself and Orpheus is both hubristic and overweening, an example of misplaced pride which is bound to fail. The union of *Virgili* and *virga* intimates a still greater impiety. It suggests not only that Virgil could adopt the role of Mercury as *psycopompus*, with his wand leading the souls of the dead into the underworld,[12] but also that he might contemplate implementing the process in reverse and, assuming the prerogative of god instead of poet-hero, bring life back from death.

If Horace's word-play makes Virgil's thinking very much part of the ode's development, his allusions to Virgil's poetry further emphasize this centrality. If we look to the *Eclogues*, for instance, we find that the phrase *conpulerit... gregi* (18), unique in pre-Horatian Latin literature except for its appearances in Virgil, occurs twice: at 2.30 (*gregem... compellere*) and 7.2 (*compulerant... greges*). Horace's allusion thus performs a variation on a pastoral theme of his friend, by turning ordinary shepherd and flock into the god who exchanges life for death and is possessed of a herd of souls, not white, like favored sheep in the world above, but black, like the hell in which they are now penned.

Perhaps the clearest link between *c.* 1.24 and the works of Virgil is that forged by Orpheus as common figure between the ode and the *Georgics*. Virgil offers his stunning version of the Orpheus myth at a climactic moment as the fourth *georgic* nears its end. In the didactic poet's hands it is the tale of a magical bard who has the superhuman power through music to lure his wife back to earth from her place in Hades but who loses her on the threshold of the world above because, succumbing to his human emotionality, he looks at her in disobedience to Death's demand. This potent mixture of spiritual and physical is varied in the remainder of Orpheus's career. As culture hero he is shown 'soothing tigers and leading oaks with his song' (*mulcentem tigris et agentem carmine quercus, geo.* 4.510), but by abjuring sex he draws the wrath of the Ciconian mothers who dismember his body.

Horace's bow to his friend's central masterpiece would seem, then, to have two purposes. By alluding to some of Virgil's most beautiful

[12] With *virga horrida* cf. Mercury's *virga aurea* at *c.* 1.10.18–19 (Horace's only other use of the word) and the detailed description of the *virga* at *Aen.* 4.242–6.

lines Horace offers him a form of *consolatio*, a reminder that much in his life, as Rome's premier writer of pastoral and didactic verse, has had the Orphic ability to civilize, to tame the wild and soften the hard.[13] But there is another side to the Orpheus legend, allusion to which here I take as a warning by Horace to Virgil. You have been deeply involved with Quintilius, I presume Horace to be saying to his friend, and would like to bring him back to life, imitating Orpheus's desire for Eurydice.[14] But, as the myth of Orpheus also teaches us, passion, even passion fostered by piety, can be destructive as well as creative. If it is not reined in, if the mourning which is its manifestation, is not controlled, then it becomes negatively charged, as capable of ruining present reality as it is incapable of restoring the dead to life.

But there is reason to believe that Horace was drawing not only on *georgic* 4 for his allusion to Orpheus but still more specifically on a later mention of the bard in *Aeneid* 6.[15] Aeneas has landed at Cumae, bent on visiting his father in the Underworld and in need of the Sibyl as guide. Among the analogies he offers her, in his plea, for those who have entered Hades while still alive and have returned unscathed are Pollux, Theseus and Hercules. But the Thracian bard is first and foremost (*Aen.* 6.119–20):

---

[13] This is the nub of the reading of the ode by Lee (1969), 86–9. Cf. also Commager (1962), 289–90 and n. 44.

[14] Note that the *titulus* in class Ψ of manuscripts reads *ad Virgilium amantem*, a phrase obelized by Klingner. The title is varied in Parisinus 7975 (Klingner's γ but not quoted by him): 'trenos [sic] in Quintilium a Virgilio amatum.'

[15] According to Eusebius-Jerome (Helm (1956), 165), Quintilius died in 23 BC, the year in which Horace's first three books of odes were presumably published. The quality of the *Aeneid* was already much mooted in 25 (cf. Prop. 2.34.65–6) and, if we may trust the Suetonian life (32), Virgil read books 2, 4 and 6 of his epic to Augustus and Octavia soon after the death of the latter's son, Marcellus, also in 23. There seem no reasons for skepticism that Horace would have known the work in progress as well as anyone, as he goes about the task of interconnecting Orpheus and Aeneas with Quintilius and, by allusion, Marcellus himself. (For a detailed discussion of Horace's 'reading' of the *Aeneid* in progress, see Basto (1982), especially 36–7, with accompanying notes.)

My essay concentrates primarily on the relationship between *Aen.* 6 and *c.* 1.24, but Father Lee (1969), 85–6 observes how *Fides* and *Pudor* figure in the story of Dido as well as how important *patientia* is for Aeneas from the epic's earliest episodes (cf. *c.* 1.24.19). We should also observe that Anna urges Dido to ask pardon of the gods (*posce deos veniam*, *Aen.* 4.50) in language similar to the words with which Horace addresses Virgil: *poscis Quintilium deos* (12).

> si potuit manis arcessere coniugis Orpheus
> Threicia fretus cithara fidibusque canoris...

If Orpheus, relying on Thracian lyre and sounding strings, was able to summon the shade of his wife...

These lines have more striking parallels with *c.* 1.24.3–4—

> quid? si Threicio blandius Orpheo
> auditam moderere arboribus fidem...—

than with any in *georgic* 4, not least because this is Virgil's unique use of the word *fides* and because the adjective *Threicius* appears in Virgil only here and once again later in *Aeneid* 6 (645), each time as epithet of Orpheus.[16]

If Horace is reminding his friend of *Aeneid* 6, he is recalling for him much else besides Orpheus. Aeneas himself, as we noted, draws the analogy between himself and the Thracian bard. He is also throughout the book, perhaps more directly than anywhere else in the poem, the image of piety, in his own eyes, as he craves the Sibyl's aid for his unorthodox endeavor (106–17), and in those of his father, whose first words, when they finally meet, are (687–8):

> venisti tandem, tuaque exspectata parenti
> vicit iter durum pietas?...

'Have you arrived at last, and has your piety, expected by your father, surmounted the difficulty of the journey?'

But, for all the specialness of Aeneas's journey, and in spite of the reference to Orpheus, he is not attempting to bring the dead back to life but only himself to enter, alive, the realm of the dead and return back unharmed. There are limitations to what the piety of Aeneas should or even can accomplish.

But, as the book draws to a close, we turn from the limited force of piety, as figured in Aeneas, to its utter ineffectuality, in the tale of Marcellus. *Pietas* may allow Aeneas to visit the underworld and learn of the future of Roman greatness from the lips of his father. Yet as that vision becomes a reality, and as the book draws to its sad, climactic conclusion it is on the funeral of Marcellus, the first Julian

---

[16] *Thracius* is applied to Orpheus at *ecl.* 4.55.

to be buried in Augustus's recently completed mausoleum, that we attend, on the death of the young heir, not on any greatness to come. And as Anchises begins his *elogium* of the youth's character it is with piety that he starts (878–9):

> Heu pietas, heu prisca fides invictaque bello
> dextera! . . .

'Alas the piety, alas the ancient faith, and right hand supreme in battle! . . .'

When, at the center of his ode, Horace addresses Virgil, it is with help, then, from the latter's own words that he forms the apostrophe—*tu frustra pius, heu*. . . Quintilius and Marcellus are parallel. Marcellus can no more be brought back to life, his piety revived, than Virgil, with his own vain piety, can restore Quintilius and his *Fides* to their earthly state. However brilliantly he may have imagined the mythic worlds of Orpheus and Aeneas, he cannot himself experientially possess their heroic powers. Horace would have him realize that his *pietas* toward Quintilius is as useless as that of Marcellus. He may also be offering a veiled reminder of the limitations of poetry itself, especially of its artificiality in the face of life's harsh realities.[17]

Horace therefore uses Virgil's own language, especially from the *Aeneid*, to offer a warning to his friend not to grieve too deeply and, above all, not to expect any charm, which might resist the force of death, to result from poetic expressions of that sorrow. But he also adopts for like purposes language that he had put earlier before the reader to describe Virgil in *c.* 1.3. The most striking parallel, long noted by commentators, is the double use of *creditum*, the only two

---

[17] In this context of rich reflection between Horace's ode and *Aeneid* 6 we should also remark on the difference between Mercury's *horrida virga* and that other *virga* (*Aen.* 6.144, 409), the golden bough, gift to Persephone which serves as Aeneas's passport into and nearly through the Underworld. This magic talisman, itself paradoxically both living and dead, is fit emblem for a living hero allowed to approach death and to recede from it. It assures him success in his unique mission. Virgil, poet of this wondrous staff, lends the power of his name, and the strength of his imagination, to his hero as he goes his miraculous way. Horace, by contrast, attaches his friend's name to a more universal symbol, the wand of Mercury that herds us all into Death's clutches and from which there is no recourse. Against Mercury's final trading of death for life ordinary humans have no possibility of bargaining. Quintilius is no Aeneas, and no amount of pious mourning on Virgil's part will allow him to pit the golden bough's singular force against the universality of the god's pastoral crook.

instances of the participle in the poet's work.[18] At *c.* 1.3.5 Horace
applies the participle to Virgil and his value, on deposit to the ship
which owes the safety of its precious cargo to the shores of Attica, and
at *c.* 1.24.11 to Quintilius, entrusted now permanently to the gods in
death, not in such a way that Virgil's piety can 'demand' him back, as
if he were a temporary debt.

But, details aside, the thematic thrust of each poem covers much
common ground. The first ode, which begins with Virgil preparing to
embark on his Grecian itinerary, turns quickly, first, into speculation
on what it must have meant to be the initial sailor and thence into a
diatribe against the arrogance of man. Because of the deceit of
Prometheus humankind is now haunted with disease and death's
ever more imminent inexorability. Daedalus may win his way
through the air, Hercules (whom we remember from Aeneas's list
to the Sibyl) may triumph over the rigors of death, but the result of
man's criminal folly in seeking heaven itself is to bring down on him
Jupiter's angry thunderbolts.

We may only speculate on whether or not there is a figurative side
to Virgil's enterprise that sparked his friend's impressive lyric out-
burst. Perhaps Horace is alluding to the problematics of writing the
Aeneid that parallel the details of his more explicit warning to Pollio,
engaged in telling the story of the civil wars (*c.* 2.1).[19] (The allegorical
hazards of the journey itself, as terrestrial man takes to an element

---

[18] See, for instance, Mueller (1900), on *c.* 1.3.6; Kiessling and Heinze (1958), *ad.
loc.* The conjunction is also made by Reckford (1969), 89 as part of an insightful
discussion of 'Virgil's heroism of mind'.

The economic language of *c.* 1.3.5–8 has been well discussed by Buttrey (1972), in
particular 47–8 with notes. For the use of *posco* in contexts of economic supply and
demand, see *TLL s.v.* 72.1–14, 73.34–9, 78.12–14. Virgil (*Aen.* 6.121, following
immediately on the mention of Orpheus) has Aeneas apply the word *redemit* to the
process whereby Pollux yearly elicits his brother from the Underworld.

Continuance of allusion to money in *c.* 4.12 (especially the mention of *studium
lucri* at 25) is one reason to consider its addressee to be the poet. There, too, the
stronger manuscript authority rests with the spelling *Virgilius* (13).

[19] That Horace is imagining Virgil already at work on the *Aeneid* and pondering
'the full significance for mankind of *pietas* and *impietas*' is the thesis of J. P. Elder in
his powerful reading of the ode (1952: 158). The many layers of *audacia* in the poem,
be it man's adventuresomeness, Virgil's daring and, most forward of all, Horace's
boldness in dealing with the whole have been finely explored by Pucci (1991),
especially 271–3. I am grateful to Professor Pucci for his helpful reading of the
present essay.

not his own, were surely of themselves scarcely sufficient to serve as
sole catalyst for his thoughts on man's *audacia* and *stultitia* in an ode
so deeply concerned with poetry and poets.) Whatever the case, when
we turn from the first Virgil apostrophe to the second, we move from
an ode where one special occasion melds with generalized meditation
to another poem with a careful focus on Virgil himself and his
personal reaction to a particular event.

   Given these differences, there are strong similarities between the
two odes which can be brought directly into focus if we compare
Horace's apothegmatic lines contrasting god's prudence and man's
sacrilege (*c.* 1.3.21–4)—

> nequiquam deus abscidit
>   prudens oceano dissociabili
> terras, si tamen inpiae
>   non tangenda rates transiliunt vada—

In vain did the god in his foresight cut off lands by a separating ocean, if,
nevertheless, impious ships leap across seas not to be touched.

with Horace's double-edged consolation-admonition to his friend
which reenforces the notion of barter crucial to each poem
(*c.* 1.24.11–12):

> tu frustra pius, heu, non ita creditum
>   poscis Quintilium deos.

The vanity of divine providence in the face of man's ships violating
waters that should remain virginal becomes, in the later ode, the folly
of Virgil's piety demanding back from the gods something that must
ever be theirs. In each case, whether indirectly or openly, it is Virgil's
ambiguous piety, ambiguous because it is twice allied with hubristic
attempts on a human's part to play at being god, that is in question.
The first centers on seafaring as an effort, worthy of Hercules, to
circumvent death. The second offers Orpheus as analogy for a poet
who would vainly attempt to subvert death's universality. In both
instances *nefas* is involved. In the propempticon to Virgil we ponder
the *vetitum nefas* (26) which energizes man's destructive boldness. In
the *epicedium* of Quintilius it is Virgil's *nefas* (20, the poem's last
word) in attempting to modify death's ineluctability that draws
Horace's final attention. In both instances it is the creator of *pius*

Aeneas who is subjected to scrutiny for impious adherence to the very
virtue that, for much of his epic, would seem to characterize the
endeavors of Rome's founding hero.

Finally, after looking at Virgil in Horace and then Horace's Virgil,
we may trace the language of Quintilius Varus himself. In the *Ars
Poetica*, as commentators regularly remind us,[20] Quintilius is praised
as the paragon of critics, careful, demanding, judicious, someone, in
other words, for whom Restraint, Justice, Trustworthiness and Naked
Truth[21] would be fit companions (438–44):

> Quintilio siquid recitares, 'corrige sodes
> hoc' aiebat 'et hoc'. melius te posse negares
> bis terque expertum frustra: delere iubebat
> et male tornatos incudi reddere versus.
> si defendere delictum quam vertere malles,
> nullum ultra verbum aut operam insumebat inanem,
> quin sine rivali teque et tua solus amares.

If you were to recite anything to Quintilius, he kept saying: 'Please emend
this—and this.' Were you to say that you could not do better, though you
had vainly tried three and four times, he would order you to delete, and to
return badly polished verses to the anvil. If you were to prefer to defend your
mistake rather than change it, he spent no further word or useless effort, to
prevent you from loving yourself and your works alone, without a rival.

But we are dealing in *c.* 1.24 with something more than mere
appropriateness, two poets offering acts of mourning to someone
who had helped to assure them of their vocation and impressed upon
them the constant necessity of refinement. It is striking, especially
given its prominence in the last line of the ode (*quidquid corrigere est
nefas*), that the first word which Horace puts into Quintilius's mouth,
in the lines from the *Ars Poetica*, is *corrige*. Since this is the only use of
the verb in the lyric corpus, it specifically brings the critic's own word
of admonishment to bear on a poem of which he himself is subject.[22]

---

[20] Most recently, Nisbet and Hubbard (1970), 279.

[21] The appropriateness of *nuda Veritas* to stand witness to a true critic's candor is
noted by Rudd (1989), on *A.P.* 438.

[22] The only other appearance of *corrigo* in Horace's hexameter poetry is the
allusion to *correctus Bestia* at *epi.* 1.15.37. Cf. the poet as *asperitatis et invidiae
corrector et irae* at *epi.* 2.1.129.

In place of Quintilius exercising his talents chastising poets at their work, we now have him reappearing, through the medium of Horace, to criticize his friend Virgil not for infelicities of writing but for the greater *faux pas* of mourning his death too extensively. This is his greater, final act of correction.

Yet Horace has a larger purpose in mind. Already with the initial command to Melpomene, *praecipe*, a word which also stands out as a unique usage on the poet's part,[23] Horace takes the role of pedagogue, commanding the muse as teacher does poet or philosophical master his disciple. He therefore himself becomes a reincarnation of Varus, the true and honest critic, bringing him back to life in a way that Virgil, in the high-serious intensity of his grief, cannot do. By verbal sleight of hand Horace achieves what Orpheus-Virgil, with his uncreative, misplaced piety must necessarily find impossible.

In his own way, then, Horace accomplishes something of the miracle of Catullus 96, a poem which his ode carefully restores to our attention. On the surface, following his own accustomed honesty in approaching nature's unalterable truths about time, life and death, he seems to be telling Virgil that communication with the dead is impossible. But, through lexical usage from *praecipe* to *corrigere* and through tone of presentation, he in fact revives Quintilius. In a truer way than Virgil, he keeps the *praecepta* and therefore the presence of their mutual mentor continuously before us.[24] He thus, paradoxically but brilliantly, follows the example of Catullus. Horatian poetry, less dramatically perhaps than Catullus, because accomplished so deftly through allusion, yet nonetheless compellingly, likewise after all works the magic of poetry's redemption. Like Catullus 96, it, too, celebrates the glories and power of language by reforging bonds of affection between living and dead which in turn enable the constant renewal of the deceased's voice. Perhaps this is the most extraordinary *consolatio* that Horace could offer Virgil for his loss.

---

[23] As in the case of *moderor* as well as *corrigo*, this is the only use of *praecipio* in the lyric poems. In the hexameter poetry, with the exception of *praecipies* (*A.P.* 335) and *praecepit* (*sat.* 2.2.2), the word only appears in the form of the past participle *praecepta*.

[24] This final projection of Quintilius before the reader is supported by the reflection of *pudor* (1) in *Pudor* (6) which I discussed above. *Pudor* was part of the ethical entourage of Quintilius and is now part of the speaker's. In still another way, then, he lives on in the *persona* of Horace as he addresses Virgil.

11

Horace and the Greek Lyric Poets[1]

Denis Feeney

There were nine lyric poets in the canon: Alcman, Alcaeus, Sappho, Stesichorus, Pindar, Bacchylides, Ibycus, Anacreon, Simonides. The list had been established in the Library of Alexandria some hundred and fifty years before Horace began writing his *Odes* in the late 30s BC, for these were the nine selected out of the herd by the great scholar Aristophanes of Byzantium for editing and systematic organisation in book form.[2] The list was closed, fixed for ever, as proclaimed in an epigram which was probably written around 100 BC, where the nine are named in nine lines and hailed as the ones who constitute 'the beginning and final boundary (πέρας) of the whole of lyric' (*AP* 9. 184. 9–10).

How extraordinary, then, that this list should ever be thought capable of extension, with the addition of a tenth name. And yet this is what happened, years after Horace's death, when the poetess Corinna was inserted to become number ten.[3] How much more extraordinary that Horace, without even this precedent, and a Roman, writing in Latin, could have voiced the hope, at the end of his first ode, that the reader of his collection would insert him into the canon of the Greek lyric bards. Using the lyric form of priamel

---

[1] My main debts are to Niall Rudd and Charles Martindale, to Terry McKiernan, for his thoughts on Horace and on Bacchylides, to Zetzel (1983) and, above all, to the students in my class on Horace in Madison, Fall 1988 (S. Anderson, V. Burns, D. Curley, A. Johnson, J. Manthey, T. McKiernan, P. O'Loughlin, M. Peterson, P. Roney).

[2] Pfeiffer (1968), 203–6.

[3] Färber (1936), I.26.

('some might like this, some might like that, but as for *me*…'), he surveys other life-styles for almost thirty lines before finally reaching his own poetic ambitions with the postponed *me*… *me* (29–30); line 34 appears to round off the poem with the closural device of an adjective and noun bracketing the line (*Lesboum refugit tendere barbiton*). But with *quodsi*, 'but if', we move to another, and unexpected, climax (with a repetition, this time final, of the closural pattern):

> quodsi me lyricis uatibus inseres
> sublimi feriam sidera uertice.

But if you insert me among the lyric bards, I shall strike the stars with the exalted crown of my head.

The audacity is marvellous. Greek works and Latin works may be catalogued separately in every library in the Roman world, but Horace will vault across that divide to become number ten in a Greek list of poets organised by the criteria of Greek scholarship: that Greek word *lyrici* (sitting beside the Latin *uates*) is very specifically the term used 'in references to editions of texts', almost certainly made canonical for that use by the arch-editor, Aristophanes, in preference to the older word *melici*.[4] Horace will achieve this in the teeth of the invincible chauvinism of the Greeks, virtually every one of whom had a practically pathological inability to appreciate the other literary culture. He will do it despite the sheer technical intractability of the manifold lyric metres of a foreign tongue, which were difficult even for post-classical speakers of Greek, so that the learned Alexandrian poets themselves 'were no longer perfectly at ease with [their] complexities':[5] when he speaks from hindsight of his achievement in the *Odes*, his pride focuses on his triumph in this formidable artistic challenge (*Carm.* 3.30.13–14).[6] If he succeeds in his ambition to become one of the ἐγκριθέντες, one of those included in the canon, he will be commented upon and studied;

---

[4] Pfeiffer (1968), 182–3.
[5] Bing (1988), 23.
[6] Wilkinson (1945), 11; Woodman (1974), 126. Non-poets may find it difficult to intuit how intoxicating technique is to them. Catullus wrote a poem about it, describing the quasi-sexual charge he derived from metrical experimentation with his friend Calvus (50); but this was no shared experience for Horace, he was on his own.

should he fail to make the cut, then the fate of the ἐκκριθέντες, the unselected, awaits him, neglected in the ignominious company of Eumelus, Terpander, Xanthus, Apollodorus, Lasus, Tynnichus, Pratinas, Cydias . . . [7]

What was involved in such an ambition? We must note, first of all, the monumental scale of the body of work he had to contend with. We have lost Greek lyric almost in its entirety, with only four Pindaric books preserved in the manuscript tradition, and everything else surviving only in papyrus finds or in quotations from other ancient writers. But Horace had it all, roll upon roll of it, catalogued— commentaries and all—in Pollio's library in the temple of Libertas, or, after 28 BC, in the porticoes of Augustus' Apollo Palatinus. The four rolls of Pindaric epinicians (*Olympians, Pythians, Nemeans, Isthmians*), which are the only Greek lyric books to have survived in the manuscript tradition, make up 180 pages in the Oxford Classical Text, a fair-sized volume. Horace would also have had encomia, hymns, paeans, dirges (one roll each, say another OCT); dithyrambs, hyporchemata, prosodia (two rolls each, at least one more OCT); and three rolls of partheneia (yet another).[8] At the very roughest calcula- tion, then, Horace had four times as much Pindar as we have got, and Pindar is the author for whom, by a very long way, we are best placed. Of Ibycus, we have something like 100 lines plus scraps and testimo- nia; Horace would have had seven books (two OCTs). Horace would have had at least ten books of Alcaeus, of which one was over 1,000 lines long, and another at least 800 lines long (three OCTs minimum overall); we have perhaps 2 or 3 percent of this original total in the form of 350 (often mutilated) lines, of which many are single lines or doublets, plus scraps and testimonia.

Not only bulk, but variety: maiden songs, victory songs for the athletic festivals, hymns, love songs, drinking songs, funeral dirges, narratives of myth—a mass of poems which ranged in size from just a snatch of song to the 1,500 lines (at least) of Stesichorus' *Geryoneis*. There were songs sung by individuals and songs sung by choruses—

---

[7] Only the first eight of Page's thirty-five *poetae melici minores*: Page (1962), 360. Of course, a Latin poet could never join the Greek canon in the strict sense. This is a desperately serious joke.

[8] All these figures on the lyric poets' books come from the appendices to Volume I of *CHCL*.

and Horace acknowledges both types (1.1.32–4) when he refers to the Lesbian lyre (that is, the lyre of Alcaeus and Sappho), the *barbitos*, which accompanied solo song, *and* to the *tibia*, the pipe, which accompanied the chorus[9] (note the characteristic Horatian chiasmus of thought by which the *solo* performer's instrument is to be tuned by the Muse *Poly*hymnia). A basic kind of order had been imposed upon this protean mass by Aristophanes' book arrangements, building upon the cataloguing of Callimachus; but the criteria of arrangement were bewilderingly multiple, of necessity, since the manifestations of song in archaic and classical culture were too various for any pattern of grouping to be inherent: 'the whole classification of lyric poems was determined by the needs of the editor, not by any older traditions of poetical theory or artistic practice'.[10] We find, then, books of lyric arranged by metre, addressee (human or divine), performer (maidens), by occasion (wedding, funeral), by location of athletic victory, as with Pindar (Olympia or Delphi), or by type of athletic victory, as with Bacchylides and Simonides (foot-race or chariot-race)—and this is far from being an exhaustive list.

What was Horace to make of this large and variegated corpus, and how was he to make it mean something for his own poetry? How was he to find his way into it, and how may we best follow him? To organise the enquiry, some might choose to use the category of which poets are used as models, looking at the places where Horace exploits Alcaeus, or Sappho, or Pindar, or Simonides. Some might use the category of which forms or genres are on display, exploiting the very useful book of Färber (1936), with examples of hymn, encomium, or symposiastic poem. Some might deploy the category of the various stylistic features of lyric which Horace takes over, or the range of metres he uses, or the lyric themes which he makes his own—love, death, transience. But my approach will be to organise discussion around the relationship which Horace establishes between himself and Greek lyric as he develops his own vision of what being a lyric poet means in the place and time in which he found himself—in a self-consciously modern age, in the metropolis of a Roman world empire. I speak of a 'relationship' out of dissatisfaction with the

---

[9] West (1967), 80; the metre of this poem is one used by Alcaeus (e.g., 34b, 112).
[10] Pfeiffer (1968), 183; cf. Johnson (1982), 87.

language of 'influence' and 'imitation' which we classicists are prone to employ. 'Influence' makes Horace into a passive object who is moulded, while 'imitation' preserves this passivity but foists it upon the Greek poets instead. The question is not just how we read Horace but how we read the Greeks, and how Horace makes us read the Greeks as he involves us in reading him. Any judgement of Horace's lyric is, as we shall see, inevitably bound up with a judgement of Greek lyric.

If we think of Horace, then, in his self-consciously modern age, in the metropolis of a Roman world empire, we must at the outset be struck, as he no doubt was, by a sense of the tremendous gulf which divided him from his Greek lyric exemplars. When he began writing lyric poetry in the 30s BC, after all, there was a gap of over 600 years between himself and the earliest of the Greek lyricists, Alcman—the same gap as there is between us and Chaucer. The Greek lyricist who was closest to him in time, Pindar, had still died over 400 years earlier (438 BC)—as far from Horace as Sidney or Marlowe are from us. To capture the disparity in culture which was superimposed upon the disparity in time, we should perhaps recast these comparisons and say that Horace was as far removed from Alcman as we are from Petrarch, and as far removed from Pindar as we are from Tasso.

The disparity in culture is particularly striking, for, as Fraenkel says, the source of Pindar's music 'is something established in the customs and the cults of a society to which both the poet and those for whom he wrote belonged', while 'for Horace, there exist no singers, no festival ceremonies, no tradition which he can follow'.[11] We will need to express some reservations later on about the more general ways of reading Greek lyric which are implied here, but the basic point is well taken: the forms of Greek lyric had, at least initially, a purchase in the institutions of their society (cult, athletic festival, the symposium), and Horace cannot have been ignorant of the contrast with his own modern and Roman world, which offered no niche for the performance of the lyric singer.

Our initial apprehension of this tremendous gulf needs to be followed by the recognition that between Horace and this remote

---

[11] Fraenkel (1957), 283–4, discussing Pindar's first *Pythian* and *C* 3. 4; cf. Syndikus (1972), 3–4.

world was interposed yet another culture, that of Hellenistic Greece, of Alexandria—at first sight another barrier, but also a corridor, for Hellenistic Greece was, as we have seen, the only medium through which he had access to the earlier archaic and classical culture. The Alexandrians' sense of distance from their own cultural past was also very profound, and Horace was therefore heir to an intellectual culture which had itself struggled with the problems of living as epigoni, without the social status of earlier poets.[12] From Alexandria he had inherited artistic patterns of response to this social displacement, in particular the 'interbreeding of genres' (the blending of one kind of poetry with another—a most distinctive feature of Horace's verse).[13] The very act of composing in books is a feature of Hellenistic culture, for pre-Hellenistic poets composed poems, not books; Horace, like Callimachus, both composes poems and organises his own editorial format for them. In particular, the avant-garde poets of Horace's own generation and of the generation before had responded enthusiastically to the dry and challenging aesthetics of this master-poet, Callimachus, who had laid it down that the modern poet must not show bad faith by fudging the issue of belatedness. Anyone who wished to pretend that the old certainties still obtained would not be able to claim a hearing in the circles which mattered to Horace.[14]

Horace's twin inheritance has often been polarised, so that he finds himself painted into an archaic or a Callimachean corner.[15] This was going on even in Horace's day, when the issues were already clichés, and it irritated the poet intensely, as he reveals in *Epist.* 2.2.91–101, where the labels 'Alcaeus' and 'Callimachus' are bandied about between himself and an unidentified elegist.[16] The polarisation between the 'Alcaeus' and 'Callimachus' of this little exchange, and between the traditions those straw men represent, is one which we should treat with great caution, for a number of reasons. It can, for a start, blur important continuities, of which one particularly striking example is the powerful presence of Pindar in Callimachean literary criticism and aesthetics;[17] for Horace, at a stylistic level at least, homage to

[12] Bing (1988).
[13] Kroll (1924), 202–44, on the 'Kreuzung der Gattungen'; Zetzel (1983), 100–1.
[14] Reitzenstein (1963); Newman (1967b); Syndikus (1972), 8–10.
[15] A history of the debate in McDermott (1981).
[16] Brink (1982), 325: 'H. is ridiculing a convention.'
[17] Newman (1967b), 45–8; Richardson (1985), 391–8.

Callimachus may look oddly like homage to Pindar. Again, if we set up these two traditions as polar antitheses, we run the risk of overlooking the (by now familiar) fact that Horace could not know the culture of archaic Greece through any medium other than that provided by the culture of Hellenistic Greece. At this level, at any rate, there can be no question of 'either/or'. It is not just that Horace's tastes and reading practices were inevitably those of a post-Alexandrian man. More fundamentally, it was the Alexandrian scholarship of Aristophanes of Byzantium and his fellows which made the Greek lyricists readable to Horace. Horace's use of 'mottoes' at the head of some of his poems is only one example of his double allegiance. When he begins a poem by giving a near-translation of an opening line of Greek lyric, before veering away, this is a mark of homage both to his poetic models and to the scholars who had catalogued them under the *incipit*.[18] And it is a self-referential anticipation of how he himself will one day be cited, once his own *carmina* have been catalogued in the world's libraries (and so he still is often cited by the *incipit*, despite the introduction of a new numbering system of citation).

The real threat in this polarised way of representing Horace's traditions nowadays, however, comes from those who would push the Alexandrian allegiance to dominate centre-stage, since the urge to construct an essentially Alexandrian Horace 'misses', as Don Fowler well puts it, 'the classicism of Augustan poetry, and its "postmodern" attempt to move beyond Hellenistic modernism'.[19] Speaking of Horace's classicism is not a matter of glossing over discontinuities in Horace's past or present, or of committing ourselves to the absurdity of claiming that any of his odes could be translated into Greek and passed off as a pre-Hellenistic document.[20] Horace's modernism was very precious to him, and he could be scathing in his contempt for those who underrated it in their hankering after

[18] Callimachus introduced this cataloguing principle in his *Pinakes*: Pfeiffer (1968), 129.

[19] Fowler (1989b), 236, reviewing Thomas (1988); cf. Zetzel (1983), 83. Already in 1920 Pasquali had stressed how important it is to see Horace as part of a classicising epoch: Pasquali (1920), 137–40.

[20] Here I may refer to the picture given by Zanker (1988) of the larger Augustan classicising movement of which the *Odes* are a part, and to the difficulties of periodisation within this large picture, picked out by Wallace-Hadrill (1989b) in his review of Zanker; generally, on periodisation, Martindale (1992), 9–10.

older models (*Epist.* 2.1). What is at issue is the significance of Horace's attempt to join long-dead master-poets in a list which had been definitively *closed*. The very urge to reach back five and six hundred years for inspiration and a standard of judgement is itself a classicising urge. Like all successful classicising initiatives, it looks wholly natural after the event, but it cannot have seemed so at the time. For someone of Horace's background and training, the search for the classical was not something tame and predictable, but something fraught with hazard.

Horace needed to undertake this search because the legacy of Callimachus was now only a necessary, not a sufficient, condition for poetic excellence. Alexandrianism had been liberating and enabling for the generation of Catullus, but for the next generation it threatened to become disabling and cramping. Horace wanted, as the dichotomy of the day had it, both *ingenium* and *ars* (naturally inspired genius *and* perfection of technique). For Horace (as for Virgil), this was most emphatically not a problem of aesthetics *tout court*, as it is often represented. Horace had huge ambitions in his *Odes*, of which many could be accommodated to the aesthetics of Alexandria, but among his ambitions were—to be blunt—sublimity and the right to speak to his contemporaries about their public lives. This he could not get from Callimachus.[21] The poetry (especially the sympotic poetry) of archaic and classical Greece, however, had ranged over a medley of experience, subsuming the 'serious–political' and the 'convivial–erotic', in Giangrande's terms.[22] During the Hellenistic period the 'serious–political' had been displaced from personal poetry,[23] but archaic lyric offered Horace a way of recapturing it. To achieve this he would not follow the Alexandrian path of inflating a minor form, but he would tackle the major form directly. Somewhere in the various world of Greek lyric Horace might find the voice, or voices, he needed, a voice that might be ironic but would not be perpetually hamstrung by irony, that might astonish, not just startle, a voice that would live as theirs had.

---

[21] On Callimachus' generically arch responses to the need to encompass his monarchs in his poetry, see Zetzel (1983), 100.

[22] Giangrande (1968), 119.

[23] Giangrande, loc. cit.; Murray (1985), 44–5.

Given Horace's elusiveness, and his stated aim of responding to the protean nature of the lyric corpus, any way in to these large issues is going to be selective, at best. Our main focus is Horace's rewriting of lyric tradition with himself as number ten, so let us begin by seeing how he tracks down the Lesbian tradition, the only one he explicitly names as his model in his first ode (1.1.34); in the process, we will see an increasingly clear concentration on his own posthumous fate, for his claim to immortality depends upon joining that tradition; and we will note Horace's concern not to enlist in the camp of the *stulti* ('dolts') by sullying his Callimachean source. Our progress in this initial stage will be sequential, following what strikes me as being a process of revelation.

After the introductory ode, the first time that Horace refers openly again to his literary tradition is in 1.26, where he tells his Muse that it is appropriate for her and her sisters to 'hallow [Lamia] with the Lesbian plectrum' (*hunc Lesbio sacrare plectro*, 11); the unique metrical movement of this line throws the epithet *Lesbio* into very high relief.[24] What will Horace's Muses actually do to Lamia? *sacrare*, 'hallow', is 'vague and grandiose', say Nisbet and Hubbard (1970: *ad loc.*), 'and may include the notion of conferring immortality by song'. This vagueness is very studied, and recalls the studied vagueness in the language Horace had used at the end of the introductory ode ('strike the stars with the exalted crown of my head'). Increasing precision on the topic of immortality in song will only come as Horace explicates his place in the lyric tradition.

The next odes to engage with these topics come as a pair, 1.31 and 32, poems which are linked by prayer, by Apollo and his lyre, and by references to the future of Horace and his poetry. And in the second of these odes we meet for the first time Alcaeus, as yet anonymous. 1.31 introduces a degree of slippage between Horace's public and private masks. Although the bard (*uates*, 2) is praying to the newly dedicated Apollo Palatinus, home of the new Greek and Latin libraries, he is not present on the public day of celebration which attended the dedication itself (9th October 28 BC), but is alone, two days later, on the day of the Meditrinalia, with a libation as modest as the

---

[24] This line 'is unique in the 317 lines of this type in Horace in having a break after the fourth syllable when this is not a monosyllable', Wilkinson (1945), 11 n.1.

lifestyle he advocates.[25] The preoccupation with public and private is picked up in the next poem, 1.32, where the first explicit reflection upon his lyric prototypes enables him to open up some new areas of possibility:

> Poscimus, si quid uacui sub umbra
> lusimus tecum, quod et hunc in annum
> uiuat et pluris, age dic Latinum,
>   barbite, carmen,
>
> Lesbio primum modulate ciui,
> qui ferox bello, tamen inter arma
> siue iactatam religarat udo
>   litore nauim,
>
> Liberum et Musas Veneremque et illi
> semper haerentem puerum canebat
> et Lycum nigris oculis nigroque
>   crine decorum.
>
> o decus Phoebi et dapibus supremi
> grata testudo Iouis, o laborum
> dulce lenimen medicumque, salue
>   rite uocanti.

I pray—if I have, at leisure under the shade, produced with you any idle composition which may live for this year, and for more—come, pronounce a Latin ode, lyre, first tuned by the citizen of Lesbos, who, though brave in war, still, in intervals between fighting, or if he had tied up his ship on the wet shore, would sing of Dionysus and the Muses and Venus and the boy always clinging to her, and Lycus, handsome with his black eyes and black hair. O glory of Phoebus, tortoise-shell lyre welcome at the feasts of Jupiter on high, o sweet and healing solace of toils, accept the greeting of one who invokes you with due rite.[26]

At the end of his introductory ode, Horace had expressed the hope that Polyhymnia would tune for him the *barbitos*, the lyre, of the Lesbian poets, Sappho and Alcaeus (1.1.32–4). Now the *barbitos* is his, and he may address it, commanding it to produce a Latin poem, a poem which centres on the first person to play the instrument in

---

[25] Nisbet and Hubbard (1970), on 3: 'The prayer with libation is a simple one, not involving a complicated or expensive *uotum*'.

[26] Following Nisbet and Hubbard (1970), *ad loc.*, for text and interpretation of *medicumque salue rite uocanti*.

regulated and harmonious fashion: the splendid oxymoronic effect of
Latinum, barbite, carmen has been often noted. The line in which
Alcaeus is introduced (but not named) begins with the same epithet
Lesbio which we saw carrying such weight in 1.26.11, but the epithet
is not here a collective one in which the other poet of Lesbos, Sappho,
may have a share, for emphatically at the end of the line is *ciui*,
'citizen'. This is a function which Sappho could not discharge, and it
is also, very importantly, a function which Callimachus and his
fellows could not discharge;[27] Horace is here glancing at an emerging
preference in the possibilities for his own lyric, allowing an alignment
which will empower his voice as a citizen.

It is only a glance. The disposition of Alcaeus' range in stanzas two
and three should not be overlooked. His public and his private poetry
receive a stanza each, but not with equal weight, for most of the
stanza occupied by his public poetry (citizen, warrior, sailor stand for
poetry of those respective roles) is formally in parenthesis, while his
private poetry (wine, Muses, erotica) takes up a self-sufficient and
climactic stanza. This ranking will not stay stable, however, for the
formally self-sufficient third stanza of love and wine is itself paren-
thetical 'biographically', retailing the subjects which engaged Alcaeus
in the intervals between his public activities (and compositions).
This elegant reluctance to assign clear priority to one sphere or the
other catches at the equivocations which must always accompany
attempts to bracket Horace in one sphere or the other, as he follows
the model of a life in poetry which his master offered him.

At the end of the first of these paired odes, Horace for the first time
in the collection looks ahead, not to the end of his life as such, but to
the old age which will precede that end (1.31.19); in the first stanza of
the second of the pair, he alludes for the first time to the future fate
of his poetry ('which may live for this year, and for more', 1.32.2–3).
Both these passages will have come to the contemporary reader with
a particularly Callimachean aura, as befits the relative modesty of
both poems.[28] The studied vagueness about the fate of his poetry

---

[27] Hubbard (1973), 12.
[28] Nisbet and Hubbard (1970), *ad loc.*, referring to *Aetia* fr. 1.7–8 (old age); fr. 7.14
('that [my elegies] may live for many a year'), and Catul. 1.10 ('may last for more than
one generation').

which we remarked in 1.26 and 1.1 is now coming into sharper focus, but the diffidence of the claim in the first stanza of 1.32 needs to be registered. 'This year, and more' is far more tentative even than Callimachus' 'many a year' or Catullus' 'more than one generation'.

The sixth ode of the next book shows us Horace for the first time looking to his own death. May Tibur, he says, be the fixed abode for my old age, the limit for me, fagged out from sea and land voyages and military service (*Tibur...| sit meae sedes utinam senectae, | sit modus lasso maris et uiarum | militiaeque*, 2.6.5–8). The language here looks back to Alcaeus the warrior and seaman of 1.32, and may even be based on some Alcaean prototype; we will see such language being used of Alcaeus himself again, in the next poem we look at. At the end of the poem (with Tarentum now the proposed joint retirement home for himself and his addressee), he tells Septimius *ibi tu calentem | debita sparges lacrima fauillam | uatis amici* ('there you will sprinkle with the due tear the warm ash of your bard friend', 2.6.22–4).

The first intimation that he will not simply die and have a funeral like Septimius comes seven poems further on, in 2.13, when he alludes to the posthumous fate of his Lesbian models, Sappho and Alcaeus, naming them for the first time. The progression we have been tracing so far makes sense of the fact that, as soon as he touches for the first time upon his own fate after death, his Lesbian tradition immediately becomes the topic. The ode begins with hilarious invective against the unknown man who almost provided Horace with his passport to the underworld by planting the tree which narrowly missed falling on his head (2.13.1–12). As Horace reflects upon how close he came to seeing the realm of the Queen of the dead, we are introduced to the underworld topic of judgement (*iudicantem... Aeacum*, 22), a topic which veers in an unexpected direction, as we see the two Lesbian poets singing to their ghostly audience, and submitting to another form of judgement, a literary σύγκρισις.[29] Here is the second half of the poem (2.13.21–40):

> quam paene furuae regna Proserpinae
> et iudicantem uidimus Aeacum
>   sedesque descriptas piorum et
>   Aeoliis fidibus querentem

[29] La Penna (1972).

> Sappho puellis de popularibus,
> et te sonantem plenius aureo,
>   Alcaee, plectro dura nauis,
>   dura fugae mala, dura belli!
>
> utrumque sacro digna silentio
> mirantur umbrae dicere; sed magis
>   pugnas et exactos tyrannos
>   densum umeris bibit aure uulgus.
>
> quid mirum, ubi illis carminibus stupens
> demittit atras belua centiceps
>   auris et intorti capillis
>   Eumenidum recreantur angues?
>
> quin et Prometheus et Pelopis parens
> dulci laborem decipitur sono,
>   nec curat Orion leones
>   aut timidos agitare lyncas.

How close I came to seeing the realms of dusky Proserpina, and Aeacus sitting in judgement, and the assigned abodes of the blessed, and Sappho, complaining on her Aeolian lyre about the girls of her city, and you, Alcaeus, making a more resonant sound with your golden plectrum, your subject the harsh evils of ship-board, the harsh evils of exile, and of war. The shades are enthralled that each of them says things worthy of holy silence; but battles and ejected tyrants are what the mob drinks in more with its ear, packed in thick, shoulder to shoulder. What wonder, when under the influence of those songs the hundred-headed beast is dumbstruck and lets his black ears droop, and the snakes entwined in the hair of the Eumenides are revived? Indeed, even Prometheus and the father of Pelops are beguiled of their toil by the sweet sound, nor does Orion care to harry the lions or the timid lynxes.

Sappho had been displaced from the collective epithet *Lesbio* in 1.32 (*Lesbio primum modulate ciui*, 5); she here appears for the first time, but as the victim of another displacement, for she is now saddled with the persona of a wholly private poet, while Alcaeus is left as the grander exponent of martial and political themes, his own erotic and private verses (which had taken up a stanza in 1.32) now eclipsed.[30] Sappho is laden with the shortcomings of the slighter form of neoteric attainment[31] (very unfairly, it need hardly be said,

---

[30] For an interpretation which harmonises the opposition, see Davis (1991), 85–6.
[31] La Penna (1972), 209–10.

but poets have no obligation to be fair in matters so important to them). This stark polarisation of the Lesbian tradition is, partly, Horace's way of continuing from 1.32 his process of homing in on Alcaeus as the model for the more engaged and resonant voice he wants to be able to claim—such is the point of redeploying the language of hardships at sea and in war which he had earlier used of Alcaeus and of himself. But the polarisation is also a recognition of the reductive way in which reception of a tradition works amongst posterity. For we must remember that this scene shows the judgement of the audience of the underworld. Their humorously described preference for the mightier work of this (deliberately unrepresentative) Alcaeus is Horace's way of organising his anxieties about grander poetry, and of anticipating the anxieties about that poetry which will be felt by the ironic and cultivated reader. A man who had grown up with Callimachean attachments, and who had proclaimed in his first ode that his poetic allegiances isolate him from the people (*secernunt populo*, 1.1.32)—such a man cannot, without causing some fluster in his audience, speak approvingly about how the packed mob prefers more resonant poems about battles and tyrants. 'The danger', as Ross puts it (speaking not of this poem, but of the Roman Odes), 'was clearly that the acceptance of important themes ... might appear to be a betrayal or disavowal of Callimachean poetics ...'.[32] One of Horace's aims here is to ensure that any readers of the Roman Odes who wish to raise such objections may be reminded that Horace had warned them (and himself) of the risks well in advance. The last two stanzas of 2.13 represent a very decided escalation even from battles and tyrants, for Alcaeus' mighty poetry, so we are told, may charm the barbarous and soothe the afflicted. The power of poetry to soothe looks back to the minor statement of this theme in the last stanza of 1.32, where Alcaeus' and Horace's lyre is hailed as *o laborum | dulce lenimen medicumque* ('o sweet and healing solace of toils', 14–15). Now Alcaeus' poetry is being associated openly with the more Orphic tradition which Horace had referred to in his Pindarising 1.12, where the voice of Orpheus moves and enthrals the world of nature (7–12).

After what we have seen in the Lesbian poems so far, it is important to acknowledge the ellipses in Horace's approach to the topic of

---

[32] Ross (1975), 141.

immortality in 2.13. Nisbet and Hubbard are certainly right in sensing 'an unspoken thought' here: 'if he escapes the meaningless accidents of fortune (cf. Milton, *Lycidas* 73 ff.), perhaps he himself may have the same capacity to enthral, to console, and to survive'.[33] The thought is, strictly, unspoken: as Commager puts it, 'Horace was not yet prepared to celebrate the poet's immortality explicitly, or not, at least, in his own name'.[34] Horace's alignment of himself and Alcaeus as veterans of voyaging and warfare comes into play here. In 2.6 he had said that Tibur would provide a limit for his sea and land voyages and military service (7–8); in the underworld we see that there is no limit for Alcaeus' songs on these subjects (2.13.27–8), for they still go on. The wry humour of that earlier identification is replayed here as well, for the event that so nearly placed Horace amongst the audience of shades was no shipwreck or arrow wound, but the absurd collapse of a rotten tree. This ludicrous event, and its ludicrous elaboration in Horace's poetry, will (so goes the unspoken thought) endure alongside the dramatic vicissitudes of Alcaeus. The immortality of poetry is linked to the quirky, freakish individuality of one man's quotidian life.[35]

Horace's own immortality will only be announced at the end of this book, when he will soar aloft on a wing of un-Callimachean grandeur: *non usitata nec tenui ferar | penna* ('I shall be borne aloft on no familiar or slender wing', 2.20.1–2).[36] That poem will be a culmination of the process by which his penetration to the heart of the redefined Lesbian tradition entitles him to be inscribed within that tradition, and it will provide a (decidedly bizarre) point of departure for his onslaught on his new grand style in the opening poems of the next book. Before that, many of the disparate themes of 2.13 need to be addressed again, and Horace moves into them via Bacchus, in the penultimate ode of the book, for it is the two-formed, mediating power of Bacchus which will transform Horace into the *biformis uates*, the two-formed bard, of the last poem.

[33] Nisbet and Hubbard (1978), 205.
[34] Commager (1962), 316 (for him, a question of date of composition).
[35] Cf. *Carm.* 3.4.26–8.
[36] On the programmatic force of *tenuis*, see Ross (1975), index *s.v.* When Callimachus had prayed to be a winged creature, it had been a 'dainty' one, a cicada (*Aetia* fr. 1.32).

There is no space here for an analysis of 2.19 that will do any kind of justice to this remarkable poem.[37] Let us concentrate ruthlessly on the themes which presented themselves in 2.13, and look at the second half of the poem, when Horace begins his hymn to the god (2.19.17–32):

> tu flectis amnis, tu mare barbarum,
> tu separatis uuidus in iugis
>   nodo coerces uiperino
>   Bistonidum sine fraude crinis:
>
> tu, cum parentis regna per arduum
> cohors Gigantum scanderet impia,
>   Rhoetum retorsisti leonis
>   unguibus horribilisque mala,
>
> quamquam choreis aptior et iocis
> ludoque dictus non sat idoneus
>   pugnae ferebaris: sed idem
>   pacis eras mediusque belli.
>
> te uidit insons Cerberus aureo
> cornu decorum leniter atterens
>   caudam et recedentis trilingui
>   ore pedes tetigitque crura.

You deflect rivers, you deflect the barbarous sea, you, drenched on the ridges held apart, confine the hair of the Bistonides in a knot of vipers without their suffering hurt. You, when the impious cohort of Giants was scaling your father's realm through the steep sky, flung back Rhoetus, dreadful with the claws and jaw of a lion, although (being said to be more suited to dances and fun and games) you were reported to be not properly fit for war: but you, one and the same personality, were a mediator of peace and in the middle of the fight. You, handsome with your golden horn, Cerberus saw without causing harm, gently rubbing his tail against you, and, as you departed, touched your feet with his triple tongue, and your legs.[38]

The last stanza shows the beast of hell being tamed by Bacchus, as it had been tamed by Alcaeus' song in 2.13.33–5. The beginning of the

[37] For discussion of the metaphorical power of Bacchus, see Commager (1962), 337–41; Griffin (1985), 72–8. To provide a context for 2.19 one would need to begin by looking, with the help of Lissarrague (1987), at how Horace follows, e.g., Alcaeus (346), and Anacreon (356, 409, fr. eleg. 2), in using the mixture and limiting of wine (and in his case, types of wine), as metaphors for behaviour in poetry and society (*Epod.* 9, 13; *Carm.* 1. 7, 17, 18, 20, 27, 36; 3. 8, 19, 21, 28).
[38] Following Nisbet and Hubbard (1978) on the main difficulties of interpretation.

hymn section catches his same taming power over barbarous nature
(*tu flectis amnis, tu mare barbarum,* 17); Horace then concentrates
on the radical ambivalence in Bacchus' nature which is the source of
that power, focusing on 'the god's double aspect' in the weird plays
on the binding power of the loosening god in 18 and 19.[39] The god's
double aspect comes most dramatically into its own in the next two
stanzas, where we learn that the normally unbellicose deity was able
to transform himself in order to take part in the Gigantomachy,
becoming a beast in order to fight monsters: the same personality
mediated between the polar realms of war and peace. Commager well
observes that 'the balance struck' here 'approximates that in Horace's
praise of Alcaeus (*Carm.* 1.32.6 ff.). Both passages suggest the double
capacity in which Horace himself served, poet both of convivial
themes and of such gigantic historical dramas as the fourth Roman
Ode.'[40] Although we have had some preparation for this elevation in
the images of Alcaeus in the underworld in 2.13, the surprise with
which we apprehend Bacchus at his Gigantomachic heights is a genuine
one, reinforced by the penultimate stanza's reminder that such loftiness
is not normally associated with this personality.[41] The surprise we feel
at Bacchus' leap out of the sphere normally assigned to him is parallel to
our surprise at Horace's own leap from the realm of dances and fun and
games.[42]

It is the discovery of twin-formed Bacchus as *idem pacis... mediusque belli* ('one and the same personality... a mediator of peace and
in the middle of the fight'), prepared for by the hunt for Alcaeus, that
sets up the metamorphosis into an immortal swan of song, a *biformis
uates,* which crowns the second book; the mediating god, so much
involved with transgression of boundaries, helps to set up both the
end of the second book and the beginning of the third, for Bacchus'
ode is the first of a series of eight Alcaics which bridge the book

[39] Nisbet and Hubbard (1978), 316; see their commentary on 18 for the oxymoron
of *separatis... iugis.*

[40] Commager (1962), 339.

[41] 'A surprising feat for this particular god', Fraenkel (1957), 200. *proeliis audax* in
Carm. 1.12.21 refers to Pallas, not Bacchus.

[42] On Horace's use of Bacchus for his self-consciousness about the perils of grand
composition, with reference also to *Carm.* 3.25, see Williams (1968), 70–1; Rudd
(1984), 401; Griffin (1985), 72–3.

divisions.[43] At the beginning of 2.20 Horace declines confinement to the Callimachean realm of 'slightness' in the first line with *nec tenui*, but the ever self-conscious bard remains *biformis*, and disarms criticism of hysterical afflatus with the breathtaking third stanza, in which the details of his allegorical transformation are remorselessly and hilariously actualised (2.20.9–12):

> iam iam residunt cruribus asperae
> pelles, et album mutor in alitem
>   superne, nascunturque leues
>   per digitos umerosque plumae.

Now, now my skin is going rough and shrinking on my legs, I am changing into a white swan in my top part, and light feathers are sprouting over my fingers and shoulders.

These lines have evoked revulsion and derision, but it may be that they owe their imagistic zest to an unexpected source. The Bacchus ode is an account of inspiration, and 2.20 narrates its effects. The first philosopher to talk about inspiration at length was Plato, and there may be more Plato lurking here than one at first expects. Plato's kindest account of poetic inspiration comes in his discussion of the blessings of madness in the *Phaedrus*, a discourse which is introduced as if it were that of Stesichorus, the lyric poet (*Phdr.* 244a). Here poetic madness, which comes from the Muses, is linked with prophetic madness (from Apollo), mystic madness (from Dionysus), and erotic madness, the best sort (from Aphrodite and Eros; 244a–245a; 265b). Plato is concerned to show that devotees of erotic madness are best placed to escape the cycle of reincarnation. Every soul is immortal, and winged, but souls lose their wings in cyclical failures to follow after god (248c–d), and fall back into the corporeal realm, to be incarnated in a better or worse category of human according to the degree of truth which they have glimpsed in their ascent; it is tempting to see Horace identifying with the first category, that of the lover of wisdom and beauty, the musical and erotic man, rather than with the sixth, the poetic or otherwise mimetic man (248d–e). This category of person, 'since he separates himself from human interests and turns his attention toward the divine . . . is rebuked by the vulgar,

---

[43] Silk (1956), 258–62.

who consider him mad and do not know that he is inspired' (249d, Loeb translation); and when he comes under the impulse of the beautiful, the wings of his soul may grow again (251a–c).

There may be enough here to set us thinking, but what strikes me as particularly relevant to Horace's metamorphosis is Plato's bizarre concentration on the physical detail of the business (*Phdr.* 251b, Loeb trans.):

The effluence [of beauty] moistens the germ of the feathers, and as he grows warm, the parts from which the feathers grow, which were before hard and choked, and prevented the feathers from sprouting, become soft, and as the nourishment streams upon him, the quills of the feathers swell and begin to grow from the roots over all the form of the soul; for it was once all feathered. Now in this process the whole soul throbs and palpitates...

This is precisely the kind of passage which the author of *On the Sublime* had in mind when he discussed Plato's use of metaphors, reporting criticisms which are uncannily akin to the modern criticisms of Horace's imagery in 2.20. He first quotes with approval a lengthy Platonic section on the body (one with more than a passing stylistic resemblance to our feathers passage; *Laws* 773c–d), and then remarks (32.6–7, trans. Russell (1972)):

The passage contains countless similar examples; but these are enough to make my point, namely that tropes are naturally grand, that metaphors conduce to sublimity, and that passages involving emotion and description are the most suitable field for them. At the same time, it is plain without my saying it that the use of tropes, like all good things in literature, always tempts one to go too far. This is what people ridicule most in Plato, who is often carried away by a sort of literary madness into crude, harsh metaphors or allegorical fustian.

It remains only to observe that Horace appears to have taken over the larger stylistic trope which C. J. Rowe has described in the *Phaedrus* as a whole, whereby 'something which is otherwise treated as deadly serious is now simultaneously located on a different and less serious plane'.[44]

This ode at the end of the second book marks the culmination of the strange redefinition of Alcaeus, but Alcaeus himself becomes a

---

[44] Rowe (1987), 95.

stepping-stone, as we find when we reach the Roman Odes of Book 3. Here Horace's Pindar, after two early forays (1.2 and 12), comes into his own as the prototype for inspired social song; we remember that the first ode in the collection closed with Horace hoping to play the Lesbian lyre *and* the choral pipe (i.e., Pindar's).[45] The complexity of this process has been variously analysed by Fraenkel and Ross, and I may direct the reader to them.[46]

Fraenkel in particular, as we have seen, concentrates on the profound cultural gap between Horace and Pindar.[47] The abiding distinction is that between, on the one hand, the publicly sanctioned speech offered to kings and aristocrats by Pindar, and, on the other, the speech of the freedman's son, without any recognised social tradition of public poetry. Horace is acutely aware of this distinction. One sign of his self-awareness may be seen in the fact that he can assert his own immortality by the end of the second book, in a manner characteristic of Roman poets but very rare in extant Greek lyric, while only coming late, in Book 4, ten years later, to a status from which he may claim to immortalise others in the way so commonly claimed by his Greek predecessors.[48] The same dilemmas are at least partly responsible for the remarkable fact that, although Horace claims the right to speak *about* Augustus, he never speaks *to* him in the first three books, but only in the fourth. Given the literary and social norms of the day, the problem of how to address Augustus is a problem of how to praise him, and in the first three books Horace walks around this problem but never lays both hands on it.[49]

[45] West (1967), 80.

[46] Fraenkel (1957), 273–85; Ross (1975), 139–52.

[47] Even the most fundamental categories are not the same for the two. When Pindar begins *Olympian* 2, he asks 'What god, what hero, what man shall I celebrate?', and answers 'Zeus, Heracles, and Theron' in three lines, but when Horace asks the 'same' question at the beginning of *Carm.* 1.12, the compartments prove to be far less watertight: in particular, by the end of the poem it is by no means certain in which category Augustus belongs.

[48] Fraenkel (1957), 423; Nisbet and Hubbard (1978), 336. On Greek claims to bestow immortality, see Campbell (1983), 262. On their claims for their own immortality, see *CHCL* 1.185. This seems to be a special theme of Sappho's (65, 147, 193). Horace and Sappho are the only lyric bards in the canon who are not Greek males; is it their self-consciousness about this marginalisation which makes them concentrate on their power to immortalise themselves, rather than others?

[49] On the difficulties for both parties in these negotiations, see Griffin (1984), 200–6, especially 203–4, with reference to *Epist.* 2.1.

He comes deceptively close early on. In the very last line of the second ode of Book 1, Horace's address to Mercury swerves obliquely into a near-address to Octavian/Mercury: *te duce, Caesar* ('with you as commander, Caesar'). The mighty phrase *te duce* recurs in ode 1.6, four lines in, introducing a further obliquity, for the 'commander' addressed here turns out in the next line to be not Octavian, but his right-hand man Agrippa. This is a double shock, for in the first line, when we still do not know who the addressee is, we are told that he will be written up by Varius, and Varius was the author of a *Panegyricus Augusti*.[50] The refusal (*recusatio*) to write in lofty praise of Agrippa masks a more urgent refusal to write in praise of Octavian. One of the reasons for the refusal emerges as the ode goes on and Horace botches one epic topic after another, speaking of Achilles' 'belly-aching' (*stomachum*) instead of his 'wrath', and of 'tricky' (*duplicis*), instead of 'resourceful', Ulysses (5–6); Agrippa (and Octavian) should not wish to be praised by a poet so ill-fitted for the higher genres.[51] In this connection, it certainly looks as if Horace had read a very puzzling poem by Ibycus (282a) in a helpful way. Ibycus retails mighty epic themes which he will not treat, trailing on for stanza after stanza, and many modern readers have been repelled by what strikes them as his garrulousness and incompetence.[52] Horace's tricks in 1.6 make it difficult not to read Ibycus as his imagined forerunner in this droll technique.

Augustus is not in fact addressed in Horace's lyric until the fifth ode of Book 4. Even there, he is absent from Rome, and the way this is put by Horace becomes a self-referential comment upon Augustus' absence from the list of addressees of his poetry until this point: *abes iam nimium diu*, he says, 'you have been absent now for far too long' (4.5.2). The book is almost at an end before Augustus is spoken to once more, actually addressed as present, with his proper title: *Auguste* (4.14.3; note *praesens*, 43). And even this poem veers into a celebration of the young Tiberius, a Pindarising epinicion to match the Pindarising epinicion offered to his brother Drusus in 4. 4. The difficulties in praising the *princeps* are persistent, even when Horace

---

[50] Nisbet and Hubbard (1970), 81. The effect is reinforced by the stuttering addition of *et tuas* ('and yours as well') after *laudes egregii Caesaris* ('praises of excellent Caesar') in line 11.

[51] Commager (1962), 71 n.25; now, in detail, Ahern (1991).

[52] Full account of the debate over this poem in Woodbury (1985).

might be thought to have done more than enough to claim the right
to don Pindar's mantle. An extraordinary resolution for the *biformis
uates* is sought in the *recusatio* of the last poem, when Callimachus'
famous opening of the *Aetia* is used as an exit from Horace's dilemmas and book. Apollo stops Horace singing of warlike themes
(4.15.1–2), as he had stopped Callimachus (*Aetia* fr. 1.21–4),[53] with
the twist that it is now not just poetically, but politically, inappropriate to sing of war, for peace reigns. As in the lofty 3.25, Horace
ends up promising song (*canemus*, 'we shall sing', is the last word
here; compare *dicam, loquar*, 'I shall speak', 3.25.7, 18). The gap
between himself and Pindar persists, testimony to the sweet peril of
attempting the sublime in a weary and ironic culture.[54] Margaret
Hubbard describes Pindar as setting Horace a standard: 'that was
how a poet of conscious power had been able to talk to the world and
particularly to the great'.[55] Horace had magnificently succeeded in
talking to the world and to the great; talking to the greatest remained
at the very limits of the tractable until the end.

The peril at the extreme bounds of his attempts should not blind
us to the boldness with which Horace so often does close the gaps
between himself and the Greek lyric tradition in the pursuit of his
classicising ambition. Here his difference from the Alexandrians is
most noteworthy. In a fascinating study of the Hellenistic reception
of earlier poetry, Bing describes the 'sense of rift' under which they
laboured, a symptom of 'a perceived epigonality and artistic disjunction'.[56] Callimachus, for example, brought Hipponax back to life in
his first *Iambos*, but Hipponax's revival is a 'conditional revival, one
qualified by a strong awareness of difference in tastes and aims, of
fracture in time and space'.[57] The Hellenistic poets repeatedly remind
their audience that their works are written, not performed; their
Muse has become bookish. It might seem entirely natural for Horace
to exploit such stances, using the Hellenistic poets as a paradigm
for his own belatedness, but his classicism is actually in dramatic

[53] And Virgil (*Ecl.* 6.3–5). Horace's ode moves from the *Eclogues* here at the
beginning, via the *Georgics* (5), to the *Aeneid* at the end (31–2).
[54] Williams (1968), 70–1, on the *dulce periculum* of *Carm.* 3.25.18. I end up quite
close to Newman (1967a), 50, though not wishing to say that 'in the last analysis
Horace is on [Callimachus'] side'.
[55] Hubbard (1973), 23.   [56] Bing (1988), 74–5.   [57] Bing (1988), 66–7.

contrast to this sensibility; the very fact that Greek culture is not his culture may remove him from the oedipal mesh of anxiety which necessarily entangled Callimachus and his peers. Sappho and Alcaeus in Horace's underworld are not an evocation of a past from which Horace is irredeemably cut off, but an image of a past-in-present which he may join. In contrast to his persistent habit elsewhere in his poetry, in the first three books of his *Odes* he never refers to his lyric poetry as written, but maintains the archaic and classical aura. He refers to books of philosophy (1.29.13–14); his iambs are written objects to be burnt (1.16.1–3); he mentions written inscriptions on tombs (3.11.51–2) and statues (3.24.27–8); epics may be composed in writing (*scriberis, scripserit,* 1.6.1, 14). But his own work is song (*cantamus* in that same ode, line 19), even into the future: the *fons Bandusiae* will live in Horace's speech, not book (*me dicente,* 3.13.14). Only in the fourth book does Horace speak of his own written texts (8.21, 9.30–1, pointedly inserting his written *chartae* ('sheets') into the oral terminology of his Pindaric model, *Nem.* 7.11–16); this is not an adoption of the Hellenistic trope, but a recognition of the fact that he has turned himself into a public monument and will be catalogued in the library of Apollo Palatinus.

If Horace invites his readers to read him as one of the lyric bards, most of them clearly find it quite easy to decline the invitation, for the reading practices brought to bear on the Greek lyric poets tend to be very different from those brought to bear on Horace. Horace suffers here by being compared on grounds which are even more disadvantageous to him than the grounds on which he is compared to Propertius or Catullus. Horace has been crippled by being set off against the 'sincerity' and 'spontaneity' of these two; when it comes to the Greek lyricists, the dice are even more loaded against our poet, for the Greeks have not only spontaneity and sincerity on their side, but a phalanx of yet more formidable allies—an organic social setting for their poetry, and the perennial allure of the original, the natural, and (perhaps most formidable of all) the oral.

It is striking that the most robustly anti-Romantic readers of Horace are remarkably Romantic in their reading of Greek lyric: the two reading techniques construct and reinforce each other. Nisbet and Hubbard observe (with a telling qualification) that 'Alcaeus's verses, even if less spontaneous than they pretend, at least reflect the loves and hates of a forthright aristocrat; they were capable of being sung on social occasions, whether a symposium or a religious festival...'; they go on to contrast Horace's 'imaginary, or at any rate stylized' situations, setting his 'literary sophistication' against the 'simplicities of archaic Greek lyric.'[58] Such Romantic readings of Greek lyric are very powerful and widespread, not just among readers of Horace.[59] By the Romantic account, Greek lyric, or at any rate monody, presents us with direct access to the 'I' of the man or woman singing, while the immediacy of that access, and the authenticity of the experience, are further guaranteed by the organic social setting for the spontaneous song. I may refer the reader to Burnett's *Three Archaic Poets* for a history of such interpretations, and for a trenchant exposure of their inadequacies (how, for example, were such poems preserved if they were never repeated, and what does repetition imply for the integrity of the speaking 'I' and its authenticating original setting?).[60]

Most modern readers of Greek lyric are more cautious about using the language of 'sincerity'.[61] The search continues, however, for a validating social occasion for speech. Thus Gentili seeks to explain the 'unusual features of the prayer' in Sappho's ode to Aphrodite (1) by saying that 'they are not simply derived from real episodes in the life of the *thiasos* [religious guild of Sappho's companions]', but 'must also mirror a precise ceremonial'.[62] Yet even Romantic readers have long been sceptical about whether Sappho and Alcaeus composed their hymns for a cult occasion. Page's remark on the Lesbian hymns might be taken to be a comment on Horace's hymns: 'they appear rather to be literary exercises... than devotional cult-songs'.[63] And even those who might dissent from Burnett's questioning of the

---

[58] Nisbet and Hubbard (1970), p. xii.

[59] See Genette (1992), 38–44, for the Romantic evolution of 'subjective' lyric.

[60] Burnett (1983), esp. 1–7; cf. Bowie (1986) on occasionalist readings of early Greek elegy.

[61] Even if they might not all join me in agreeing with Burnett's formulation: 'the archaic poets, like poets everywhere, invented both ego and occasion when they composed their songs', Burnett (1983), 6; cf. Emily Dickinson, quoted in Johnson (1982), 83: 'When I state myself as the Representative of the Verse—it does not mean—me—but a supposed person'.

[62] Gentili (1988), 79–80; contrast Burnett (1983), 229.

[63] Page (1955), 244; cf. Nisbet and Hubbard (1970), 343–4, on Sappho 2: 'Sappho has already broken away from the old-world piety of the cult-hymn'.

social authentication of Lesbian song may still push back into the sixth century the moment when 'the devices of poetry' were freed 'from their organic contexts in society and its institutions'.[64]

As we have seen throughout this essay, any polarised account is going to be reductive. The last thing I am aiming to do is to turn the Greek lyricists into proto-Alexandrians, or (by implication) strip Horace of his cherished literarity and turn him into some dashing improviser of the sort which he so loathed. The point is that a polarised account of some kind is inevitable, since we need to say (or even imply) *something* about Greek lyric in order to address Horace.[65] My remarks here are only a plea that we should try saying things about Greek lyric which will be enabling for Horace, rather than emasculating. We might begin by joining Burnett in seeing Greek lyric as 'more artful and less passionate, more conventional and less individual' than many readers do;[66] the Hellenistic filter has been particularly distorting here, since a lot of the talk about the Hellenistic poets' craftmanship and attention to minute detail can end up making a Stesichorus or a Bacchylides look like some kind of *idiot savant*. We might begin by reading the Greek lyricists through Horace's eyes. Although we cannot read the whole of them and of their commentaries, as he could, we must remember that Alcaeus, for example, represented to Horace the ancient equivalent of at least three volumes of Oxford Classical Text, and that he was, for non-epic poetry, the father of that most 'unnatural' and 'unspontaneous' form of speech, allegory. Such a perspective might help us see how Horace regarded these voluminous poets as being, like himself, accomplished exponents of the most demanding metrical forms, as imitators and adapters of each other in a tradition which he is continuing (*Epist.* 1.19.23–31), as self-conscious and versatile literary artists.

If we may use Horace to bring the two parties closer together, the pendulum must always be allowed to swing, and I will finish by focusing once more on the differences between Horace and the other nine of the canon. This time, instead of finding the differences to be hurdles which Horace has to surmount more or less success-fully, we shall see him turning the centuries-long and miles-wide rift

---

[64] Woodbury (1985), 206, on Ibycus 282a.
[65] For the issues, see Martindale (1992), esp. 73–4.
[66] Burnett (1983), 2.

into the source of his most potent and characteristic lyric strengths. Let us consider, briefly, place and time.

Horace loves to celebrate places which have no resonance in his tradition because they have no presence there. The names of Horace's girls may slip in and out of the memory, but no one who has read the *Odes* ever forgets Tibur, Lucretilis, Soracte, Bandusia; these names are often set off against famous Greek places, nowhere more memorably than in 1.7 (*Laudabunt alii*). He may well have found an aid in Sappho for the kind of evocation of place he achieves in 1.17 (*Velox amoenum*),[67] but the urge to do it does not come from her or from anyone else; it must have been the very absence of all these locales from Greek tradition which especially impelled him to fix them in his poetry and in our memories, and to introduce 'a new way of thinking to European literature'.[68] His confidence in his utterly unsupported efforts is so secure that he claims to immortalise a place before he ever claims to immortalise a person (Fons Bandusiae, 3.13.13–14).[69] His boldest endeavour of all is his elevation of Tibur into a self-sufficient metaphor for a frame of mind and a mode of poetry;[70] from the start, he speaks of the place as if it were numinous, as if we ought to know what it stands for, as if it had been part of a poetic tradition for centuries before him.

The centuries between himself and his models were intimidating in many ways, but it must have been partly the very sense of that great distance which made Horace such a great poet of time. Time, of course, is a perennial lyric preoccupation, and the Greek poets were well stocked for virtually anything Horace wanted to say on transience, ageing, or memory. And he wanted to say a lot: his poems on the passing of time are among his most cherished (1.4, 4.7); especially in the fourth book, when many of the people who meant most to him are dead, and when he is addressing a generation of epigoni, he creates an unforgettable atmosphere of nostalgia and loss. But Horace had ways of apprehending time which simply had not been

[67] Jenkyns (1982), 38, on Sappho's description of a temple in fr. 2, and its capturing of 'the "sentiment of place"'.
[68] Nisbet and Hubbard (1970), p. xxi, on the Sabine farm.
[69] Fraenkel (1957), 203.
[70] Davis (1991), 193–4, on 1.7, 3.4.23, 4.2.29–32, 4.3.10–13 (this last poem answering to 1.7).

available to his Greek models, and he is able to turn them to remarkable effect. Here is the beginning of 3.30 (1–5):

> Exegi monumentum aere perennius
> regalique situ pyramidum altius,
> quod non imber edax, non Aquilo impotens
> possit diruere aut innumerabilis
> annorum series et fuga temporum.

I have completed a monument more enduring than bronze and higher than the royal pile of the pyramids, which neither gnawing rain nor the wild north wind could destroy, nor the uncountable sequence of years and the flight of ages.

Fraenkel remarks: 'The magnificent opening period ... revives thoughts familiar from Greek poetry, especially choral lyrics; in it there is nothing that might not have been said by a Greek poet.'[71] We need to qualify this observation by concentrating on the phrase *innumerabilis annorum series* ('uncountable sequence of years', 4–5). Horace is able to conceive of future time as a continuous linked sequence of years (the hyperbole consists in the claim that his immortality will be so protracted that it will escape any attempt to number that series). No Greek lyric poet could have thought in terms remotely like this. To our way of thinking (which is fundamentally a Roman, specifically Julian, way of thinking), the Greeks' apprehension of the year was extraordinarily plastic, without agreed fixed points, each state having 'its own mode of time reckoning as it had its own month names and numerals'.[72] No Greek could have thought in terms even close to Horace's until the time of Hippias, the first Greek to publish a list of Olympic victors (late fifth century, after the death of Pindar), providing 'a method of dating which would be understandable everywhere'.[73] Roman literature found the patterning of time a rich theme from early on (one thinks immediately of Ennius' *Annales*, and of annalistic history itself, the distinctive Roman contribution to historiography). But a decisive shift occurs in Horace's own lifetime, with Caesar's transformation of the Roman calendar. Julian and natural time are now one,[74] and this is the mode

71 Fraenkel (1957), 302.
72 Bickerman (1980), 33.
73 Bickerman (1980), 75.
74 Wallace-Hadrill (1987), 224; cf. Bickerman (1980), 47.

of thought which we still inhabit—with the spectacular addition of a fixed point around which the numbered years go back into BC and forward into AD.

In Horace's case we are talking about more than just a sense of history (though no Greek lyric poet could have had anything remotely like the sense of history which we recognise in Horace and his contemporaries). We are dealing with a mode of apprehending time as an organised grid through which natural time flows, or flies; he articulates this mode of apprehension for us in Book 4, in words of tremendous resonance (4.13.13–16):

> nec Coae referunt iam tibi purpurae
> nec cari lapides tempora quae semel
>   notis condita fastis
>   inclusit uolucris dies.

Neither your Coan purples nor your precious stones now bring back to you time, which winged day has locked up once and for all, preserved in the public record of the calendar.

No Greek lyric poet could have thought or written in such a manner. Everything hangs on that *semel*:[75] it focuses the clash between the impersonal grid of the state's time and the uncatchable winged unit of Lyce's natural time (a winged unit which performs, not suffers, the locking up); it organises the collision between the marble of the abiding *Fasti* and the perishable pebbles of Lyce's jewellery (not to mention her garments).

This Roman mentality provides him with quite novel possibilities for his lyric. The elapse of time is marked by a dating system which carries with it great historical or sentimental charge: *ex Metello consule*, the formation of the 'first triumvirate' and origin of the civil war (2.1.1); *consule Planco*, the year Horace fought at Philippi (3.14.28); *consule Manlio*, the year of Horace's birth (3.21.1); *consule Tullo*, the year of Maecenas' birth?[76] (3.8.12); *Bibuli consulis*, the year of Julius Caesar's first consulship—and Bibulus' (3.29.8); *Martiis*

[75] From Catullus 5.5, *cum semel occidit breuis lux* ('when once our brief light has set'); cf. *Carm.* 4.7.21 (looking to *simul* in line 10).

[76] Nisbet and Hubbard (1978), 202. Or else Maecenas was born, like Horace, *consule Manlio*: Nisbet (1987), 186.

Kalendis, the day Horace almost went to join his lyric ancestors in the underworld (3.8.1); *pleno... anno |... cum tibi Nonae redeunt Decembres,* the Faunalia (3.18.5, 10); *dedicatum Apollinem,* Apollo Palatinus' birthday (1.31.1); the Ides of April, Maecenas' birthday (4.11.14–16).

The birthday in particular shows up his new power and his distance from his models. In the time of the Greek lyric poets people did not observe birthdays, and we do not know any of the poets' birthdays.[77] Horace is able to use birthdays to create new ways of organising the ancient lyric pathos about the fugitive nature of our life. Here is his description of the date of Maecenas' birthday (*Carm.* 4.11.14–20):

> Idus tibi sunt agendae,
> qui dies mensem Veneris marinae
>   findit Aprilem,
>
> iure sollemnis mihi sanctiorque
> paene natali proprio, quod ex hac
> luce Maecenas meus adfluentis
>   ordinat annos.

You must observe the Ides, the day which splits April, the month of Venus of the sea, a day rightly celebrated by me, almost more sacred to me than my own birthday, because from this light of day my Maecenas arranges in order the flow of his years.

The title of the Roman demarcation, *Idus,* is a redescription of *lux,* 'light of day', the original unit of time as given in nature. The precision of the Roman calendar, which sets up the years in an order, and which splits the month *just here,* is in tension with the watery immeasurability of the natural flow of years, *adfluentis.*[78] T. S. Eliot catches something rather akin to this sensibility in *The Dry Salvages:*

---

[77] Fraenkel (1957), 23. Pindar comes closest (fr. 193), when he says that he was born on the first day of the Pythian festival; but this is not a birthday proper, because Pindar cannot tell us the year.

[78] There is a nod towards the Etruscan ancestry of Maecenas in the use of *findit,* 'splits', for by one account the Ides derived their name from *iduare,* the Etruscan word for *diuidere,* 'divide' (Macr. *Sat.* 1.15.17). *adfluentis* ('flowing') seems to look back to the incomparable image of the flow of time in the last ode addressed to Maecenas, *fluminis ritu...* ('in the manner of a river', 3.29.33 ff.).

The tolling bell [on the buoy]
Measures time not our time, rung by the unhurried
Ground swell, a time
Older than the time of chronometers...
And the ground swell, that is and was from the beginning,
Clangs
The bell.

Again, in 3.17, the wide sweeping panorama of remote mythical periods is interrupted by the intense *cras*, 'tomorrow' (9), fixed as the day of the birthday (*cras Genium*, 14); there is a very similar movement two poems further on, in 3.19, where the question of the difference in time between remote kings is set against the increasing precision of mid-winter, new moon, and, finally, midnight, the (implied) eve of Murena's new tenure of the office of augur.

   Horace knew all about the power of anniversaries. If we went to the underworld, and interrupted the joint singing of Sappho, Alcaeus, and Horace to inform them that we were observing the bimillennium of Horace's arrival in that place, Sappho and Alcaeus would have no conception of what we were talking about. Horace would understand at once.

12

Final Difficulties in an Iambic
Poet's Career: Epode 17

Alessandro Barchiesi

Poetry was then divided in two, according to the individual character of the writers. The more elevated minds imitated noble actions, and the actions of good men. The baser minds imitated the actions of smaller persons, at first composing invectives, as the others did hymns and praises . . . thus the measure is still called the iambic measure, which people used to mock one another.

Aristotle, Poetics 1448b25 ff.

1. MAGICAL ALLUSIONS

A brief preliminary is needed. Epode 17 is the final poem of a 'post-Callimachean' poetry book, which almost all critics consider a carefully thought-out structure rich in effects. Its last words, *artis . . . exitus* ('end of art', 81), nearly compel us to take the concluding function of this text in the book seriously. Yet current interpretations tend to represent 17 as a one-off joke, easily explained: Horace, threatened by Canidia for having slandered her name, feigns to retract his words, all the better to expose her vices.[1] Few scholars are concerned by the salient position Horace gives this 'ironic

---

[1] Cairns (1978), 549: 'In this way she provides retrospective confirmation that the Epodes were truly Archilochean iambic poetry attacking vice justifiably.' He draws

palinode', and fewer still ask why Canidia is important to Horace.[2] The result is a reading focused on putting up defensive barriers. 'The epode cannot be defined in any other way than a literary *divertisse-ment* (as argued by La Penna) in which the poet enjoys contaminat-ing and parodying ... It is impossible to cull any other meaning from this epode where the dimension of the horrific and the grotesque of *Epode* 5 are reduced to playful sarcasm.'[3] 'Cannot be defined in any other way than', 'impossible to cull any other meaning', 'a *divertisse-ment* in which the poet has fun', and 'playful sarcasm' are definitions that I intend to examine a little closer.

A fundamental theme of 17 is reversibility. The scene is set when Horace requests a magical ritual in reverse. The repetition *solve, solve* ('loosen, loosen'), hardly random, sounds like an inversion of the most famous magical refrain in Latin poetry, *necte ... necte ... necto* ('bind ... bind ... I bind', Virg. *Ecl.* 8.77–8); a rhombus that turns backwards, a cured Telephus, Hector honoured with proper funerary rituals,[4] Odysseus' companions brought back to their natural state of

---

the only consequences that are possible to deduce from his own assumption, accord-ing to which one can reconstruct a 'genre' by the name of 'palinode'.

[2] The exceptions are: Oliensis (1991), a magnificent article [Chapter 9 in this volume]; since then Gowers (1993), 299–310; Cavarzere (1992), 35. Von Albrecht (1988), 373–6, makes some valuable points, born from an interpretation of Proper-tius 4.1 (thus difficult to find for specialists of Horace). On the unity of the book, see Henderson (1987), 111.

[3] Romano (1991), 1011 f. (see however Pöschl 1956b: 120).

[4] The close interaction of the three examples Telephus/ Hector/ Odysseus' sailors (three cases of a return to an original status of being, the first two examples associated with Achilles' role, and diversified by the different treatment of Telephus and Hector; three cases of a human body being healed: the rust of a lance, a body anointed, Circe's ointment to undo the poison, cf. Hom. *Od.*10.392–6, with 393 echoed with precision at 17.15) finds an almost amoebean answer in the three negative examples used by Canidia, 65–9, the unforgivable Tantalus, Prometheus, Sisyphus. As I have implied previously, I prefer to read at line 11 *unxere* to *luxere*. Cavarzere (1992), 236 (see also his bibliography; Brink 1982b: 44–7; Broccia 1982: 83; Romano 1991: 1013) finds *unxere* trivializing and notes that (i) the funerary lamentation is a more important action than anointing a body; (ii) in the *Iliad* the Trojan women lament ritually Hector's death, but the body is cleaned by Achilles' slaves (24.587). I will answer: (i) the reference to a way to restore someone to their original state of being (in this case, the care due to a corpse versus leaving it to the dogs and birds of prey) is expected if one focuses on the following example of Circe (see above) and on Canidia's actions in general, cf. 5.69 *unctis*; 3.12–13 (Medea) *perunxit ... delibutis*; 17.31 *delibutus*; 17.23 *odoribus* (with the remark by Kiessling and Heinze 1957–8). *Unxere*, then, gives the

being—and here again the same Virgilian model is inverted, *carminibus Circe socios mutavit Ulixi* ('Circe transformed Ulysses' companions with songs', *Ecl.* 8.70): the backwards rotation is applied to the treatment of literary models.

We know from the first verses (*libros carminum*, 'books of songs', 17.4; cf. *nihil hic nisi carmina desunt*, 'nothing here is lacking, except for songs', *Ecl.* 8.67) that the power of the *carmina* ('songs') is in play. *Supplex oro* ('I beg, a suppliant')—at the very beginning of an iambic *carmen*!—is the most powerful among all these palindromic signals. The homage paid to the 'magical code' is strong from the first lines. Antithesis, alliteration, assonance and repetition, the promise of undoing: these are all specific traits of magical discourse, 'words' that should be able to 'undo' the order of events. Horace's surrender could not be more total.[5] The use of persuasive *exempla* is not rare in poetry, but magical discourse is familiar with the specific tradition of *historiolae*, small incantations that contained brief mythological narrations, where suffering was brought to an end through magical sympathy.[6] To invite Canidia to reverse the flow of her magic, not only does Horace welcome magical words in his iambic poetry, but he actually makes his iambic verse turn backwards.

2. MAGIC AND LITERARY GENRE

> Bewitchment is always the effect of a *representation*, pictorial or scriptural, capturing, captivating the form of the other...
>
> J. Derrida, 'Plato's Pharmacy', in *Dissemination*, trans. Barbara Johnson (Chicago: 1981), 140.

Homeric example more pertinence; (ii) the discrepancy with the Homeric model is not worse than in Circe's case: Homer specifies that the transformation into pigs does not include the victims' minds, which are intact (*Od.* 10.240); Horace however talks of a *mens* (17. 17) that reverts fully, after the cancellation of the metamorphosis. The suggestion of Kiessling and Heinze (1957–8) that Horace worked on a moralizing exegesis he superimposed on the Homeric text, is worth mentioning, and could be confirmed by the Homeric scholia we still have access to.

[5] For all these specific traits that fluctuate between the magical and the poetic discourses, see a recent analysis of Sappho's fragment 1, Petropoulos (1993), 45–53; otherwise, Faraone (1992), 323–4.

[6] See Kotansky (1991), 112–14.

From the beginning it should be clear that Epode 17 deals with the principles of iambic poetry and its effects. Horace attacked Canidia in his iambic verse. He was a victim of her magical art and now asks for forgiveness. After only a few lines we see him compared to Telephus, a warrior, who prior to begging Achilles to cure him, had confronted him in battle: *in quem tela acuta torserat* ('into whom he had hurled his sharp weapons', 10). The iamb is usually compared to a throwing-weapon[7] (although we will soon witness other representations and other etymologies). Canidia accuses the poet of having 'filled the city with her name' (59), which is the typical function of iambic poetry as blame poetry. In this way, indirectly, the final text of the Iambs fulfils the classical function of a *finale*: to attest that this poetic venture will fulfill its ambitions through the fame produced by its publication.[8] Slander (διαβολή), on the other hand, is a speciality of iambic poetry, but is also an important function of magical discourse.[9]

Still, Horace comes very close to forswearing his own iambic poetry. He offers Canidia a palinode:

> Sive mendaci lyra
> voles sonari: 'tu pudica, tu proba
> perambulabis astra sidus aureum'.
> infamis Helenae Castor offensus vicem
> fraterque magni Castoris victi prece
> adempta vati reddidere lumina...
>
> *Epodes* 17.39–44

Or if you wish to be sung on a mendacious lyre: 'you chaste, you honest woman, you will wander the heavens, yourself a golden star'. Castor and Castor's great brother, offended at defamed Helen's lot, were won over by prayer and gave back to the bard the light they had taken away.

[7] Either in metaphoric expressions ('to throw an iamb', 'piercing iambs', see for example Catull. 116.4 and 7; Ov. *Ib.* 2, 10, 51, 54, 642) or in supporting etymologies based on ἵημι (cf. West 1974: 23 f. and n. 4). [After I published this paper in Italian, Telephus' military attack on Achilles has resurfaced in a papyrus of Archilochean elegy: Obbink (2005).]

[8] See for example the endings of Books 1–3 of Horace's *Odes*, and of Ovid's *Metamorphoses*. Lucan's *Bellum Civile* ends with a random scene, but the last words concern a centurion who deserves eternal fame—thanks to none other than Lucan, who celebrates this character in a previous book of this work (about the possibility that the *Bellum Civile* is less incomplete that it seems, see Masters 1992: 247–59).

[9] Eitrem (1924); Winkler (1991), 227–8.

The catasterism has inspired reactions of pure delight: 'Like Ariadne! Like Berenice!'[10] Even if these two candidates do not exhaust the options, it is not futile to wonder what type of star Canidia is supposed to become. If we need a precedent, we may think not so much of the lock of Berenice, but of Arsinoe in her entirety. A text called Ἐκθέωσις Ἀρσινόης is placed almost at the end (the penultimate) of Callimachus' *Iambs*—a book in seventeen poems which seems to have drawn Horace to collect seventeen epodes in his new book.[11] The fragments let us imagine an astral cavalcade (228.4–5) and we know that Arsinoe was snatched to the skies by the Dioscuri (*Dieg.* 10.10, p. 218), the same divinities Horace names in the context: it is amusing to think that Horace, asked to offer a lyric piece (*mendaci lyra...*) presents, in the pure[12] and refractory iambic mode of Epode 17, a sample of court lyric previously hosted in Callimachus' *Iambs*.

The piece that precedes the *Ektheosis*, the *Pannychis*, contained, according to the Diegesis (10.6: p. 217 Pf.), a real and proper hymn to the Dioscuri (and to Helen, but we return to her in a moment): among the scant remains there is in fact an invocation to the Dioscuri, ὦ Κάστορ... καὶ σὺ Πωλύδευκες (fr. 227.8 Pf.). (However, there is also a persistence of the tone of magical hymns, like those addressed typically to Selene: 'prayer to Selene, for every type of incantation', 'you... who in the guise of the three Graces dance *komazousa* among the stars', *PGM* 4: 2794–5; 'you have brought a man against his will to join you in your bed in the midst of your astral dancing', *PGM* 4: 2924. Canidia, after all, is always a sorceress.)

Yet, the context is tighter if we think of Helen.[13] On the one hand, Canidia will become a star, that is, a goddess, just as Helen did, though she was vilified in her lifetime. On the other hand, Stesichorus was punished for his poetic attacks by the twins Castor and Pollux—two bright stars in the sky (*fratres Helenae, lucida sidera*, 'the

---

[10] Ussani (1900), 48.

[11] This hypothesis is still being debated (Clayman 1980: 4–7) but see Cameron (1994), in favour of joining 14–17 to the books of Iambs [and the *mise au point* by Acosta-Hughes (2003)].

[12] Important observations in Questa (1984), 219.

[13] The fragment of Stesichorus recently rediscovered (Haslam, *POxy* 3876 fr. 35; Luppe 1993: 53–8) describes a woman being addressed as 'similar to the gods', and at the same time accused of polyandry.

brothers of Helen, bright stars', Hor. *Carm.* 1. 3. 2), just like the star Canidia will become.[14] In addition, *lyra* is much more appropriate to Stesichorus (Ov. *Ars.* 3.50) than to a poet of iambs and epodes. This link should be described more precisely: Canidia will become a star like Helen (except in Laconia, she is represented as a star rather than a goddess), while Horace will readapt to being a lyric poet.

Already Arsinoe had modelled her fate on Helen's—a rare precedent of a lady called to heaven: it is not a random compliment when Theocritus (15.110) defines Arsinoe as 'similar to Helen'.[15] This double analogy leads the passage from Canidia's catasterism to the palinode recalling Stesichorus': 'you want to become a golden star (like Helen, who was infamous)? Already one poet was punished for vilifying her, but the Dioscuri (her astral brothers) cured his woes after he recanted.' But what does it mean, exactly, to become a star like Helen? Helen became a protective and rescuing star: 'She's to have her throne by Castor and Polydeukes | in the heavens, and bring salvation to sailors' (Euripides, *Orestes* 1636–7, trans. Peck and Nisetich 1995: 87); 'There, by Hera and Hebe, | the wife of Herakles, | she will be seated as a goddess, | and men will forever pour | their offerings | to her and the Tyndaridai, | as she watches over | those who go down to the seas' (Euripides, *Orestes* 1684–90, trans. Peck and Nisetich 1995: 89; compare *Iph. Aul.* 1608 ff.).

But the context also requires that everything be reversible. Everything must be able to spin in both directions like Canidia's rhombus (17.7). A 'palinode' is a double-edged term: the action of reversal lends itself to new reversals. 'Prim and proper' is the shameless praise offered by Catullus in his loud and obsessive iambic aggression:

> 'moecha putida, redde codicillos,
> redde, putida moecha, codicillos!'…
> quod si non aliud potest, ruborem
> ferreo canis exprimamus ore:
> conclamate iterum altiore voce
> 'moecha putida, redde codicillos,
> redde, putida moecha, codicillos!'

[14] A hint in this direction is already found in Lindo (1969), 177 who sees a stellar connection: 'it would seem that the poet is assigning to her the privileged position formerly occupied by Castor and Pollux'.
[15] Basta Donzelli (1984).

> sed nil proficimus, nihil movetur.
> mutanda est ratio modusque vobis,
> siquid proficere amplius potestis,
> 'pudica et proba, redde codicillos!'
>   Catullus 42. 11–12, 16–24

'Stinking whore, give back my tablets, give them back you stinking whore!'. . .
But if nothing else does it, let's growl out her shame with a dog's iron voice:
yell again with louder voice, 'Stinking whore, give back my tablets, give them
back you stinking whore!' To no avail. She's not moved. You should change
your plan and rationale, if you can get any effect: 'Chaste and honest woman,
give back my tablets!'

It is significant that Horace's iambic recantation meets on its path—
over against Stesichorus' and Callimachus' lyric verse—Catullus'
most typically iambic poetry. Lyric and iambic define each other in
turn as praise poetry and slander.

3. REVERSIBILITY (I)

From the Hellenistic age on (Sosibius, *FGrHist* 595 F 20), but realis-
tically from even earlier,[16] Helen the salvific star is represented as an
ill-omened apparition and a harbinger of death hated by sailors.[17]

---

[16] Jacoby (1950), 655 explains that Sosibius develops a view which is more ancient
and deep-rooted than the evidence we possess and brings to our attention (as Moriz
Haupt already did; less clearly Wilamowitz 1921: 219 n.1) the character of Helen/
Helenaus in Aesch. *Ag.* 689—thus bringing us back to the constellation between
Canidia and the persecution of the sailors. On the basis of Haupt's point, Otto
Skutsch (1987), 192 well re-examined this question and put forward two important
points: (i) Euripides' choice of the 'good' star can be linked to occasional, contextual
motivation: Euripides would be the exception, not the rule; (ii) Aesch. *Ag.* 689–90
'Helenaus, Helandros, Heleptolis' could be a development of a popular idea and/or
etymology based on Helen, the 'evil light' of sailors. It seems to me that once it is
explained as a reference to the disastrous returns of the Greeks, the position of the
epithet in the tricolon ('destroys ships', 'destroys-man', 'destroys city') is a good clue
in this direction: Aeschylus starts from a generic suggestion, re-motivates it in
relation to the Trojan war, and on this basis constructs his own overwhelming verbal
inventions, that triple the concept of destruction.

[17] Stat. *Silv.* 3.2.8 ff.: *Theb.* 7.792–3; above all, Plin. *Nat.* 2.101 *diram illam ac
minacem appellatamque Helenam*; probably an allusion also in Hor. *Odes* 1.3.2, see
Nisbet-Hubbard *ad loc.*

Canidia will be an evil star.[18] She will be a star, but an exceptional one that brings evil on its observer. Whore and star, redeeming star and evil light (Helenaus!), goddess and witch (compare *desiderique temperare pocula*, 'temper the draughts of desire', 17.80, with the Helen of the *Odyssey*), Helen suggests Canidia's reversibility.[19] She is a beautiful woman who may also be called *kynopis* ('dog-faced', cf. *catuli ore Gallicani*, 'with the mouth of a Gallican pup', Catull. 42.9; *ferreo canis... ore*, 'with a dog's iron voice', 23). Already in the *Odyssey*, she is once and again a double agent, an elusive voice: a faithful ally of the Greeks who betrays them (4.238 ff.).[20] A strong contradiction also structures another important woman in this poetry book: the iambic Cleopatra, a royal goddess and polluted Egyptian both. The woman who calls down the stars from the sky (*refixa caelo devocare sidera*, 'to loosen the stars, call them down from the sky', 17.5; *sidera excantata*, 'stars sung down', 5.45) will become a star, but a good one or threatening? Canidia likens Horace's words to the futile prayers sailors address the rocks in a stormy sea (17.53–5). The sailors are naked, clearly shipwrecked, probably about to drown; we can wonder in how many ironical ways Canidia is *amata nautis multum* ('much beloved by sailors', 17.20); Helen, the 'star of sailors', promises desolation. The reader is free (according to the reverse logic of palinodes, *recantationes*) to read the text 'backwards'.

[18] Cf., through a different lead, Oliensis (1991) on Canidia and 'Canicula'.

[19] Helen is inseparable from her bad reputation. Ovid plays with this theme in the letters of Helen and Paris, when he shows them intending half-consciously to produce the celebrated fame/infamy that is forever bound to their names: *magna quidem de te rumor praeconia fecit* (*Her.* 16.141); *tu quoque... nomen ab aeterna posteritate feres* (16.376); *fama tamen clara est* (17.19); *ne quando nomen non sit in ore meum* (17.36); *aut ego perpetuo famam sine labe tenebo* (17.71); *sensi mala murmura vulgi* (151); *fama quoque est oneri* (169); *eadem mihi gloria damno est | et melius famae verba dedisse fuit* (172–3); *non ita contemno volucris praeconia famae | ut probris terras impleat illa meis* (209).

[20] See the interpretations of Goldhill (1991), 61–4; Dupont-Roc and Le Boulluet (1976); Downing (1990), 1–16. It seems to me quite probable that the two visions of Helen in the *Odyssey*, one of Helen as a Greek secret agent and the other as a Trojan *agent provocateur*, amid the doped atmosphere of Sparta, were all powerful stimuli for Stesichorus to invent two alternative 'Helens'. Not only could Stesichorus set his new version against the monolithic 'truth' vouched for by Homer (Helen went to Troy...) but also tie it to the forking and equivocal tradition initiated by Homer (who in truth is this woman?).

Horace, just like his enemy, seems to be in control of *libros carmi-num valentium* | *refixa caelo devocare sidera* ('books of songs strong enough to loosen the stars, call them down from the sky', 17.4–5).[21]

4. REVERSIBILITY (II)

But we too may need to recant our reading. Stesichorus' palinode, called up by Horace, was probably a text rich in irony. 'This/that discourse is not true' (Stesichorus, *PMG* 192)—and this new one is? The Muse is called upon to recant and to make the new version more realistic: it's hard to avoid thinking that the new version, any new version (after the old one has been discredited) is plastic and nego-tiable (add to this the disquieting trace left by the existence of two distinct palinodes, or of a unique text with two separate prologues).[22] If Helen is an *eidolon* ('image'), she is a poetic creation. To insist too much on the possibility of changing a story's course is not the most efficient way to lend credence to some dubious version as the 'pri-mary' level of truth.

One should not try to nail Horace's text down to one definitive meaning: the praise a palinode affords is discredited by its aggressive subtext; but can we be sure that iambic aggression operates at a level of absolute truth in comparison to the praise of the *mendax lyra*? Both produce poetic effects, and one of the fundamental themes of the *Epodes* is the idea that this poetic genre deforms its own object, constructing it by defacement. (Hipponax made his name as an iambic author by destroying Bupalus—*a sculptor* who had disfigured his image.) The poetic voice that disfigures Canidia, recomposes her in catasterism, and defaces her again as an evil star, cannot make a claim to a level of superior reality—only that in which Canidia is

---

[21] The more usual definition is 'pulling the moon down', see Virg. *Ecl.* 8. 69; Ov. *Am.* 2.1.23; Smith on Tib. 1.2.43; Bömer on Ov. *Met.* 7.207–8.

[22] Add to this Bowie's hypothesis (1993), 26–7: Stesichorus needed Helen's appar-ition in a dream (her *eidolon*?) to set in motion the new version, and Stesichorus plays knowingly with the Homeric-Hesiodic tradition of divine inspiration which legitim-izes and validates a narrative. See also the observation made by Griffith (1990), 199, according to whom the blinding—see for example the case of Teiresias—suggests a punishment for having told the naked truth, rather than a retribution for vilifying.

made and undone by iambic aggression. Emphasis falls on the inherent limitation of this genre-world, where praise necessarily steps the slander up a notch.[23]

The process of contestation and reversal that infuses Canidia's words—her *libri carminum* ('books of songs', 4), her *voces sacrae* ('sacred voices', 6), her *carmina* ('songs', 28), her *ars* ('art', 81), her *epodai* ('spells')—is inseparable from Horace's poetic crisis, the crisis of his *epodoi* ('epodes').[24]

Poetry and magic have a tendency to implicate themselves in each other (Luck 1985: 77 'poetry is a kind of magic in itself');[25] and we have already seen how evil charm and iambic poetry can constellate. In particular, iambic poetry is, like magic, a type of performative discourse.[26] The last torture among those inflicted by Canidia on Horace (72 *frustraque vincla gutturi nectes tuo*, 'and you would bind chains to your neck in vain') is an extreme version of the most spectacular success any iambic poet ever obtained—the suicide by hanging of the Lycambids. Through Canidia, the iambic word has developed auto-destructive effects.

This reading is confirmed by the symptoms Horace confesses at the beginning of the poem. (This is an opportunity to call up again our Derridean *motto*: even an evil charm, like poetry, presupposes representations are constructed and lends a certain shape to its

[23] See below, note 37.

[24] *Epodos* means 'short verse' as well as (seldom, for example Aesch. *Ag.* 1418) 'incantation', *epode* 'magical formula' and 'cure, remedy'. In this work, epodic poetry, poetry as a remedy and poetry as a magical charm are all intertwined: the ambiguity was noticeable to whoever read the title as it is transmitted in our manuscripts, LIBER EPODON. This point is sensed, although with some linguistic stretch, by Luck (1985), 73 '*Epodes* (the title can be translated as "incantations")', by Oliensis (1991), 118 ('the term "epode" which can designate not only the epodic verse-form but also the incantation, *epode*, of the magician/healer...') and by Gowers (1993), 281 '"Epode" comes from the Greek word *epode*, meaning a spell or incantation.'

[25] For meta-literary relationships between poetry and magic, see the examples in Lucan (Masters 1992: 205–15), e.g. 6.577–8 *incognita verba* | *temptabat carmenque novos fingebat in usus*; O'Higgins (1988), 208–26; Ov. *Am.* 2.1.23 ff. and *Trist.* 2.5 ff. (on which Wimmel 1960: 304 and n. 2); especially, Manil. 1. 1–6, well analysed by Wilson (1985), 289 ff.

[26] Virgil's *Eclogue* 8 well shows the paradoxical relationship between poetry and magic. Virgil tells how Alphesiboeus sings having asked the Muses to sing what a lady sings in her magical ritual—but these four different concentric voices repeat together the refrain *ducite ab urbe domum, mea carmina* ... and in this repetition, the magical charm and the poetic song become one and the same, and the 'safety distance' vanishes.

victim). The poet has turned white because of Canidia's philtres (23): and Canidia's name contains the root of *canities* ('whiteness'). But other symptoms lend themselves to a metapoetic reading. Horace has become similar to his own work: he is bony, yellowish, obsessive, unnerved, an insomniac possessed by dementia. The aggression of the iambic poets is traditionally explained in terms of *rabies* ('rage') and *cholos* ('bile'), melancholy and obsessive anger.[27] To become an iambic poet in antiquity meant to become a danger—to others and possibly to oneself. Canidia's oral *epodai* do to the poet what iambic poetry aspires to, but only in written form. Like a poet, Canidia is competitive, only preoccupied with improving her *ars*.[28] She enters the scene with vipers (5.15), a poisonous accessory well adapted to Archilochus' Muse ('the wrath of a viper', *A.P.* 7.71.2). Her venom befits an intoxicating poetry—the iamb, from *ion bazein*, 'to speak poison'.[29]

This is why Canidia's doubt about her own *ars* (*artis... exitus*, 'the end of art') and the checkmate between *epodoi* and *epodai* set the scene for the conclusion of the book. The poet and his evil creature resemble each other too much and iambic poetry can only be called off by placing oneself outside (as Horace will do in the *Odes*).

5. POETRY, MAGIC AND 'HORS-TEXTE'

'MY EYES GLOW WITH THE EERIE LIGHT OF VAMPIRE POWER. Battery included.'[30]
Ancient poetry about witches, beginning with Theocritus 2, both presupposes and engenders a strong sense of superiority. The poet's

[27] For the yellowish colour as a sign of splenetic complexion, see Plaut. *Capt.* 595–6 *viden tu illi maculari corpus maculis luridis?* | *Atra bilis agitat hominem.* For the tradition of *cholos*, see Call. Fr. 380 Pf. with Pfeiffer *ad loc.*; *AP* 7.69 and 71; 7.70. 1 *agrion phlegma*, the melancholic complexion (connected to gauntness and insomnia?); note also *dementia* (45), cf. rabies (Hor. *AP* 79 on Archilochus; cf. *Anth. Pal.* 6. 74); *in celeres iambos* | *misit furentem* (*Odes* 1.16.24–5); add to this that the anguish in lines 25–6 is being described in Archilochean terms (Broccia 1982–3: 85–6).
[28] Eitrem (1933), 34: 'es geht um ihren Ruf, die erste *maga* Roms zu sein; sie will die *antitechnos* besiegen und die Uberlegenheit ihrer *scientia* (17, 1), ihrer *ars* (17, 81, *techne*) dartun.'
[29] For this etymology, see Callimachus, *fr.* 380 Pf., with the note by Pfeiffer.
[30] From the advertisement of the toy 'Little Dracula', 1993.

(male) voice invites the reader to overcome the superstition and gullible hope that the light cast by magic rituals encircles and encloses.

But this superiority cannot exist without complicity. As readers we rush on what we despise with morbid curiosity. The poet takes some distance from what he narrates, but where does he derive his unique knowledge? Naive critics tend to ask biographical questions ('Did Theocritus frequent magicians? How did Horace compile his notes?') that are not pertinent—though hardly useless. What to say of the relationship between Horace and Canidia? We all laugh today at the tendency to write biographical fictions ('Maybe she was one of Horace's old lovers?'), but our ridicule exorcizes the serious discomfort created by texts like Epodes 5 and 17. Because of the way they are constructed, these texts do not offer enough information for us to define the narrator's relationship to events. They are written to a certain extent to elicit questions that are 'not pertinent', to open up blank spaces for the reader's fantasies, even the most morbid and arbitrary.[31]

---

[31] Recent literary critics refuse to ask themselves 'with candour' what happened between Horace and Canidia; and an isolated critic (Bushala 1968) attracted much sarcasm for having suggested that Horace was under the influence of a love potion. Are we sure that fantasies of this kind—fantasies deriving from the act of reading—are not pertinent to the interpretation of Epode 17? The language Horace uses to describe his torture (21–35) resembles in an astonishing way that of erotic curse tablets: 'enter his heart and burn his insides, his chest, his liver, his breathing, the marrow of his bones—until he comes to me, loves me, and does everything I desire' (*PGM* 4.1496); *non dormiat Sextilius, Dionysiae filius, uratur furens, non dormiat neque sedeat neque loquatur sed in mentem habeat me ... uratur furens amore et desiderio meo ... huius spiritum et cor comburatur, omnia membra totius corporis* (270 Audollent). Horace recuperates the symptoms *a parte obiecti* and eliminates any mention of Canidia's intentions: this *lacuna* justifies the reader's fantasies, since we cannot control our own morbidity. Even the poetic vocabulary is consistent with this underlying eroticization: note *ardeo* (30), *cinis* (33: 'ashes' is a typical metaphor for Meleager's ideology of passion), *cales* (35), *satis superque* (10: against Catull. 7.1–2, on sexual satisfaction) and the comparison with Etna (32–3) which recalls a sexual comparison by Catullus (68.53: in this context we find the mention of Hercules on Oeta, as in Horace: a hero who was killed by a love potion); the mythical torments listed by Canidia in 65–9 (Tantalus, Prometheus, Sisyphus) are all traditional allegories of insatiable love (see also Pöschl 1956b: 103, n. 1). It is not necessary to think that 'revenge' and 'desire' are separate magical functions: to inspire desire is *per se* a punishment (see Winkler 1991: 232 'I bind you with great suffering ... you will love me with a divine love'). Besides, what else did Canidia do with the love potion which was intended to scorch Varus 'like bitumen, from a black furnace' (5.81–2)?

What do we know of magic outside literature? Filling in an incredible gap in poetic research (thanks to Jack Winkler 1991: 227–8) scholars of magical texts have become aware of a simple statistical piece of information: the majority of curse tablets we possess attest to *male* desires. Exactly the opposite of what happens in poetry,[32] where so many abandoned women seek in magic a remedy to their naivety and powerlessness ('Take me to Daphnis' house . . . make Varus return to me'). In short, to say Canidia is Horace's creation is not so much a statement about the relationship between poetry and biography, as a statement about the relationship between fantasy and sexual difference.

When battling naive biography, the most recent critics tend to prefer this type of solution: 'Canidia is not a real person, but she is at least representative, a product of real experience.' Some appeal to the young Horace's unfortunate love stories, which thereafter would have been schematized and distorted into caricature; others, less crudely, appeal to the political climate at Rome in the 30s; some hypothesize a campaign of law and order initiated by Octavian, who had won new power in the difficult and murky years of Naulochus. Canidia then represents an image of the enemy, constructed, but corresponding to real interests.

There is something perceptive in this latter idea, because I think it is not possible to read the *Epodes* without perceiving the intertwining of the external enemy—Antony and Cleopatra, or better still Cleopatra and Antony—with the enemy 'within the walls'. As is typical of the Roman tradition and happens elsewhere in times of crisis and civil war, she is a woman. But this idea, if carried further, becomes grotesque. To imagine that Horace was interested in a kind of police campaign to hunt down the Esquiline witches is worse a theory than 'Canidia was Horace's lover'—a theory, as we have seen, that has at least the merit of showing the text is not self-contained and projects around itself a ripple of conjectural thoughts.

To claim Canidia is a synthesis of real experiences confuses historical reconstruction with the pervasive machismo of the Romans; it is

---

[32] The compromise solution 'Canidia does not exist as an individual but is representative and a product of real experiences' is thus as false as the fantasies discussed in the preceding footnote, and conceivably even more.

to historicize the text at the cost of historical evidence and to take the *tabellae defixionum* ('curse tablets') and the use of magic as typical expressions of a presumed female mentality.

We have almost forgotten that we are reading an iambic poem, the last in Horace's iambic book, and metrically the most iambic of all. It is perhaps not by chance that the Greek origins of iambos have to do with grotesque female figures, sometimes amazing creatures, a source of childish fear and liberating laughter: they have well-known names, and others less so, like Iambe,[33] Baubo, Mormo, Empousa, Mormolyke, Lamia, and most famous of all, the Gorgon—her head bristling with snakes like Canidia (5.15–16), her reincarnation in the mean streets. Ezio Pellizer has devoted a fascinating study[34] to the relationship between the terror of the monstrous and ridicule of the grotesque, a nexus that is basic to iambic poetry, and has demonstrated why archaic Greek iambic needs its female 'freaks'.

We can combine his reading of the origins of iambic poetry with our meta-literary reading of Horace: Epode 17 will then appear as a recreation of origins and Canidia can be read as a retrospective foundation myth of the literary genre Horace is appropriating.[35] I think this operation contains even a dose of ironical awareness and scepticism. When, at last, Horace's misdeed is revealed (17.56), it comes to our knowledge that he has ridiculed the Cotytian rites, even though this ritual was not considered respectable by Horace's public. (Iambic, by nature, projects around itself the complicity of a closed male community.) We would have expected the Cotytia to have been a typical female institution, to be looked upon with superiority and suspicion. But, there is a problem: our sources

---

[33] A third etymology for the iamb, after the 'throwing-weapon' (see above, p. 235) and 'venomous talk' (see above, p. 242). Note Degani (1993), 12–13; and for the possibility that the abusive old Iambe had a leading, foundational role in Hipponactean invective, Rosen (1988); Brown (1988).

[34] Pellizer (1981) (well developed in Cavarzere 1992: 35); Arans (1998) is useful too. The image of the simulated childbirth with which Horace ends his allocution (17.50–2: *puerpera* is the final word *ex persona poetae* of the entire book) brings about much curiosity in this domain. On Baubo as an 'old woman in labour', see Arans (1988), 138–47. Rohde 1989 (1893–4): 413, n. 2, explores the link between Hecate and childbirth, and discusses Baubo, Mormo, Lamia, Empusa, Gorgo as multiple manifestations of Hecate (744–9).

[35] [On the relationship between literary genre and recreation of the origins, see some other observations in Barchiesi (2001b), 123–7 (with regard to Augustan elegy).]

denounce the Cotytia as scandalous, but they do so because it
consists in a festival of male cross-dressing.[36] Probably the discrepancy is Canidia's doing, since Canidia is incompetent. Or, maybe, the
insinuation here is that Canidia is also in drag—the counterfeit voice
of her iambic censor?

The woman who sets wax figurines in motion (*movere cereas
imagines,* | *ut ipse nosti curiosus…*, 'to move wax figures, as you
know, yourself curious', 76 f.) is controlled by the poet's iambic
voice—but is also capable of bringing into crisis his poetics.[37]

The limit of her art coincides with the last words of the poet—that
is to say, this black Muse of iambic is to the *Epodes* what the elegiac
mistress is to Propertius (*eventum formae disce timere tuae,* 'learn to
fear the outcome of your beauty' are the last words of Book 3). To
understand the rhetorical figure of negation that binds Canidia to the
model of Lesbia, Lycoris, and Cynthia, means the better to understand the poetics of the *Epodes.*[38]

---

[36] *Catalepton* 13, 19; Iuv. 2.89–92 (with Courtney *ad loc.*). See Hinds (1987), 46 on
Sulpicia's friend and the impersonation of women.

[37] If she could escape the *Epodes* Canidia could finally say 'I am not as you have
made me famous', which is what the Lycambides retaliate against Archilochus in
Dioscorides, *A.P.* 7.351; Meleager (?) *A.P.* 7.352; Adesp. *Supplementum Hellenisticum*
997.

[38] The text is based on a paper I gave in November 1993, and I have not been able
to take into account later publications, except for Spina (1993) (a valuable interpretation, of which I had had an anticipation); I have inserted a couple of 2007 updates in
square brackets. There is a rich new assessment of magical discourse in the *Epodes*
in Lindsay Watson's recent commentary (Watson 2003), especially on poems 5 and
17. I thank Michèle Lowrie for her advice on the English version.]

13

Horace and the Aesthetics of Politics

Don Fowler

The attitude of Horace to the Augustan regime—'Horaz und Augustus'—is one of the perennial themes of Horatian criticism. As E. Doblhofer commented in his book *Die Augustuspanegyrik des Horaz in formalhistorischer Sicht*, critics have often divided on national lines:

> The German subject with his respect for the authorities and state power, the individualistic, Anglo-saxon democrat, and the Italian of the new Republic who wanted to let Augustus atone for the fact that fascism compared its Duce to the princeps—they have all left their traces in the interpretation of Horace and tinged the image we make ourselves of Horace's relation to Augustus.[1]

As often in the rhetoric of *Rezeptionsästhetik*, these attitudes are set against Doblhofer's own methodology, which is depicted as more

Rather than the usual acknowledgements, which in this case would be extensive, I should like to offer a memory of my first supervision with Robin Nisbet. I came into his room in Corpus, with that vast desk covered with books and papers, the radical youth prepared to have my brilliancies tempered by a dusty philologist of the old school. But we sat not at the desk, but in those high-backed chairs either side of the fire: and after we had been talking for ten minutes or so, I found that I was the one who was saying things like 'I've never thought of that' and thinking 'Isn't that going a bit far?' What I learnt from Robin (as earlier from Colin Macleod) was above all precisely always to take one's ideas further than one thought one could: as soon as one got something straight, to widen the focus and complicate it all again, looking beyond Latin to Greek, beyond the classical world to other periods, and beyond the discipline of classics to other approaches. All that, and the prose rhythm of Cicero too: riches I shall never forget.

[1] Doblhofer (1966), 13.

Don Fowler

historical and scientific than its rivals. He examines the Greek
panegyrical tradition in relation to Horace's praise of Augustus,
and argues that where the commonplaces are found in bald and
unoriginal form we have no reason to see personal engagement,
but where Horace is clever, he must be sincere: 'The further he
distances and detaches himself at any point from the tradition, or
the more independently he remodels it, the more "sincerely" does
he praise the leader—so we would like to conclude'; 'next to the
conventional, familiar topoi are other forms of expressing a ruler's
praise. Therefore we will need to grant the poet his own search
for his own expression, and with that, his own conviction.'[2] So,
for example, when Horace makes fun in *Satires* 1. 7 of Persius'
praise of Brutus, the hackneyed topoi reveal the absurdity of the
panegyric:

> laudat Brutum laudatque cohortem:
> solem Asiae Brutum appellat stellasque salubris
> appellat comites excepto Rege; canem illum
> invisum agricolis sidus venisse. (23–6)

He praises Brutus and praises the cohort: he calls Brutus the sole star of Asia,
and calls his companions saving stars—with the exception of Rex; that dog
has come as a star hateful to farmers.

When, however, Horace compares Augustus to the sun in *Odes* 4.
5, this is much more *geschmacksvoll* ('tasteful'), and therefore
sincere:

> lucem redde tuae, dux bone, patriae:
> instar veris enim vultus ubi tuus
> adfulsit populo, gratior it dies
> et soles melius nitent. (5–8)

Good leader, bring light back to your fatherland: for when your face, the
image of spring shines on your people, the day goes more pleasing and stars
shine better.

[2] Doblhofer (1966), 16, 84.

Others, of course, have found this stress on Augustus' meteorological control more of a *reductio ad absurdum*: and it is hard to see how it could be defended against this except by appealing to the accepted topoi of panegyric—in which case our criterion for sincerity disappears. The argument here is absurd,[3] but my purpose is not to criticize Doblhofer's particular thesis: his book is extremely valuable for its detailed treatment of the panegyric tradition. Rather, it shows how any concern for 'sincerity' or even 'authenticity'[4] is a blind alley. Here, for instance is a Horatian passage in praise of a later Duce, from E. Balbo's *Augusto e Mussolini* (Rome, 1937—or should we say 'Anno XV'?):

From the fertile breast of the Revolution itself, which resounds and extends into the future, an epic Singer will arise to sing of Fascism and the Duce for eternity.

He will say that fertile fields, rich pasturelands have emerged, an improvised miracle, from the indomitable and death-bringing waters of lands without limits. In their abundance, they look herds in their green-grey eyes and at the new cities: Littoria, Sabaudia, Pontinia, Aprilia and so many others.

He will say that the land, restored to its natural function, redeemed from wholesale land reclamation, removed from the hateful egotism of special interests, by taking on a social function, was a powerful font of national wealth, an oasis of physical and moral wholeness, and that the country people were in first place among the ranks and dignity of men.

He will sing the epic and the restoration of the Italian people, the victorious legions that carried the ensigns of the coast to the far and barbarous lands of oriental Africa and will say that, once they lay down their arms, they cultivated and civilized them.

Myth will tell all peoples and ages to come of an energetic youth, with humane face and signs of genius, driven by an internal force and lit by a celestial light, a tool of divine volition, protected by an occult force, who left his father's workshop to fulfil an omen.

With the labors of fortune and thought, of suffering and privation, he freed Italy from small men and raised her to a power never before assembled.

Did Mr Balbo really mean this? It is not that we could not spin a yarn about whether this was sincere or not, but that to examine this language in those terms looks like a wasted opportunity. What surely

---

[3] See Nisbet (1969).   [4] Cf. La Penna (1963).

matters here is what is said, not why it was said: the discourse of
Fascism, not the beliefs of Fascists.

This move from questions like 'Did Horace or Ovid like Augustus?' to 'What is the relation that we construct between Horatian or
Ovidian discourse and that of other contemporary systems?' is a
familiar one in contemporary criticism. What comes next tends to
take two forms. Either, in the manner of the so-called New Historicism, it is shown how the dominant 'official' discourse encompasses
and dominates all other systems, or, in the manner[5] of deconstruction, it is shown how the inevitable contradictions in those systems
prevent any stable dominance.[6] What I want to do in this piece is
firmly in the older and more conservative second tradition: I want to
show that the contradictions in the traditions which are drawn on in
Horace's works make panegyric of Augustus an impossibility. (This is
actually a milder version of the wider claim that panegyric is always
in a sense 'impossible', which I endorse but for the moment shall not
defend.) My presentation of the choice between historicism and
oppositionalist criticism as a sort of whim might look like cynicism,
and there is a sense in which I believe that which tactic you take is a
matter of personal preference. The ideological climate is also, however, a factor: if everybody else is heading for the one pole, one has a
duty to go the other way. But anyone who opts to take apart Horatian
panegyric rather than putting it back together has to resist all the
more strongly the seductions of essentialism. If we find that the
Horatian attempt to accommodate Callimacheanism and Epicureanism to praise of the great is unsuccessfully self-contradictory (as we
shall), we must beware of contrasting that with an ideology of our
own which without contradiction plainly reflects the reality of the
matter: because there is no such 'master narrative' to tell of Augustus
or anyone else. There is no escaping contradiction for any observer
historically situated in a society with as complex an inheritance
as our own (or the Romans'). The *best* we can hope for is some

---

[5] Cf. Woodman and Powell (1992), 258 n. 14.

[6] For the contrast cf. Dunn [1997], 92: 'whereas post-structuralists, in rejecting the
aesthetic unity of new Criticism, celebrated various subversions of unity, authority,
and ideology, cultural criticism tends to find a new, overriding order in the cultural
system that shapes and determines literary production'.

'energizing contradictions' in the phrase of Charles Martindale, writing of Virgil:

Virgil's myth potently mediates, or massages, a necessary 'contradiction' within the spiritual ideal of Rome, which is simultaneously the *caput rerum*, the metropolis which Augustus found brick and left marble, and an idyll of primitivism and rural simplicity, sweet especial rural scene. On this reading there is not so much conflict as the (attempted) *erasure* of conflict, in the interests of Roman identity and Augustan ideology. Rome is both an empire of unsurpassed might and yet, at heart, a simple country community. (Compare some myths of modern America, at once super-power and land of the lone cowboy.) Ideologies, in other words, may hammer together energising 'contradictions', which are not then felt as contradictions.[7]

But the recognition that if we want to set ourselves up as rebellious iconoclasts against the myths of power we are in the grip of an enlightenment myth ourselves whose foundations are no more secure need not lead to the abandonment of the oppositionalist tradition. Even Martindale cannot quite bring himself to leave out the 1960s flashback of that little '(attempted)' qualification. It is still as valuable an occupation to take apart what others have hammered together as to forge new chains.[8]

My title, 'Horace and the Aesthetics of Politics', is of course a nod in the direction of Walter Benjamin's famous dictum that Fascism renders politics aesthetic while Communism responds by politicizing art.[9] The tag is meant partly just to make the general point that Horatian politics is bound up with Horatian poetics: it is in that union that I shall seek my deconstructive opening. But I also want to take seriously the Fascist view of the ruler as artist. This has many ramifications in ancient culture: one thinks, for instance, of Richard Gordon's identification of public sacrifice as the ultimate aesthetic act under the Empire.[10] I want to stress the importance of this for panegyric. Recent studies of the Renaissance have laid great stress on the property of 'magnificence' in the ruler's display, and its roots in

---

[7] Martindale (1992), 51. Cf. Fowler [2007].

[8] There are some suggestive reflections on non-positivist oppositional reading in Sharrock [1994].

[9] Benjamin (1968), 244.

[10] Beard and North (1990), 193 (and *passim*).

Aristotle's doctrine of μεγαλοπρέπεια ('magnificence')[11] and many aspects of this topic have of course received treatment in Paul Veyne's *Bread and Circuses.*[12] Essential to Aristotle's account in the *Nicomachean Ethics* is the point that μεγαλοπρέπεια differs from simple liberality in size: it is *big* spending, a sublime act, particularly on public matters, though Aristotle allows that it may also apply to semi-private events like weddings:

> Those for whom we regard it as right and proper to make such donations are people with suitable incomes derived from property acquired by their own exertions or inherited from their ancestors or relations; or they may be persons of good family or high distinction or otherwise specially qualified. For all these are important advantages and take a high place in the estimation of the public. Now to these requirements the magnificent man answers perfectly, and it is in just such displays of magnificence that this virtue finds scope, as we have noted, these being the grandest and most highly esteemed forms it can take. But magnificence may be displayed also on unique private occasions, such as a marriage or something of that sort which may happen to excite public interest or attract people of importance, or parties to celebrate the arrival or departure of friends from abroad, or the exchange of complimentary presents. For the magnificent man reveals his character in spending not upon himself but on public objects; his gifts are a sort of dedication. It is also like him to furnish his house in a way suitable to his means, for that gives him a kind of distinction. And it is his way to spend more on things that are made to last than on things that are not, for it is the lasting things that are most beautiful and noble . . . [13]

But magnificence has to be appropriately controlled: ὁ δὲ μεγαλοπρεπὴς ἐπιστήμονι ἔοικεν· τὸ πρέπον γὰρ δύναται θεωρῆσαι καὶ δαπανῆσαι μεγάλα ἐμμελῶς, 'the magnificent man is like someone with knowledge, because he can observe what is appropriate and spend large sums with care' (4. 2, 1122ᵃ34–5). ἐπιστήμων here is variously translated by modern interpreters as 'connoisseur' or 'artist': Aspasius in his commentary glosses it τεχνίτης and compares a

---

[11] See esp. Fraser Jenkins (1970); further bibliography in Green (1990) at 98 n. 2. On the related concept of greatness as μεγαλοψυχία see Held (1993), esp. 102–7; much of interest is promised in a forthcoming book by Carlin Barton on honour in the Roman world [2001].

[12] Veyne (1990), esp. ch. 1 (7–8, 14–18) and ch. 4 (347–8).

[13] *NE* 4. 2, 1122ᵇ29 ff., trans. J. A. K. Thomson.

cobbler and a painter.[14] Stewart (1892) develops the picture in his note on 1122^{b}14: 'The result produced by the liberal man is merely a κτῆμα—something that is materially useful to the recipient, and has its market value, whereas the result produced by a magnificent man is of the nature of a work of art. It is θαυμαστόν-"displays genius and imagination". Now I am not concerned with how much of this can be read back into Aristotle's *en passant* comparison, merely to note that praise of the sublime acts of the great inevitably involves an aesthetic attitude towards them, and leads easily to the view of the great as men of 'genius and imagination', Balbo's Mussolini leaving his father's workshop 'to fulfil an omen'.

One further aspect of this fetishism of wealth and power is the central trope of all *Herrscherpanegyrik*, the ruler as superhuman, the ruler as divine.[15] God too is an artist, of peculiar sublimity: his works are wonderful, and worthy of praise. God as king—as in the pseudo-Aristotelian *On the Cosmos*[16]—or the king as god—as in Pythagorean writings[17]—alike produce Great Works. How could any mortal artist hope to compete with such perfection? The way I pose that question immediately brings to mind the *recusatio*. The poet cannot compete with regal and divine artists: it is not his to thunder, but theirs. So, at the end of the *Georgics*, Virgil contrasts his lowly achievement with that of Augustus:

> haec super arvorum cultu pecorumque canebam
> et super arboribus, Caesar dum magnus ad altum
> fulminat Euphraten bello victorque volentis
> per populos dat iura viamque adfectat Olympo.   (4. 559–62)

I was singing these things about the cultivation of field and flock and about trees, while great Caesar thundered in warfare at the deep Euphrates and victorious laid down the law for willing peoples and set out for Olympus.

And similarly Tibullus contrasts himself as a love poet with Messalla:

---

[14] Aspasius, *CAG* xix/1. 105. 2 (cf. also Heliodorus, *CAG* xix/2. 69. 22).

[15] For an excellent recent discussion of some aspects of this see Feeney (1991), especially the chapter on Ovid.

[16] See esp. 5, 396^{a}33 ff.; 6, 399^{a}15 ff.

[17] e.g. ps.-Ecphantus *On Kings* ed. Thesleff (1965), 79 ff. (cf. Delatte 1942; Thesleff 1961: 65–71). On the caution necessary in relation to the use of this material cf. Murray (1968), 676–7; Stevenson (1992), 435.

te bellare decet terra, Messalla, marique,
    ut domus hostiles praeferat exuvias:
me retinent vinctum[18] formosae vincla puellae,
    et sedeo duras ianitor ante fores.   (1. 1. 53–6)

It is fitting for you to wage war, Messalla, on land and at sea, so your house
may boast of enemy spoils: the bonds of a pretty girl hold me captive, and
I sit at guard before her hard door.

The direction of my argument will I hope be plain. If we start to think
of the deeds of the Great and the Good in aesthetic terms, as rival
artists, then poetics have a potentially political import. Caesar thun-
ders on the Euphrates: but isn't that bad art, combining thunderous
bombast with the tumid Assyrian river?[19] Isn't Greatness itself suspect? The polite tones of the *recusatio*, it is a cliché to say, conceal a
poetic manifesto in which the small-scale genres are actually *preferred*
to sublimity on aesthetic grounds: where does that leave the artistic
achievement of the Great Leader?

I take the task of panegyric for a writer like Horace to be to keep
us from asking those questions, to keep the aesthetic preference for a
particular type of poetry separate from the political endorsement of
a particular ruler. And I take it to be an impossible task, if we face
Horace not with a reader eager to co-operate in this process but
with one prepared to accept linkages 'across the grain'. In the end,
such an 'alert' reader cannot in good faith escape making the
connections we are told to avoid. In the rest of this paper I want
to look at exactly how the attempt is made to direct and control our
aesthetic judgement of Augustus, and at why it fails. The first
argument might simply be that I have manufactured this connection
between poetics and politics by my notion of the ruler as artist, and
that there is no reason to foist this on Horace. In fact, however, it
has often been observed that one of the most distinctive features of
Horace's work is a union of Callimachean poetics with Epicurean
stress on the simple life: the union, as Mette put it in one of the best

---

[18] I should prefer the *victum* of Voss and Mueller, which does not duplicate *vincla*
and which suits the contrast with Messalla's conquests. Either way, the poet is always a
loser, the great man always a victor.
[19] I accept the link with Callimachus' *Hymn to Apollo* noticed by Thomas and
Scodel (1984); cf. Clauss (1988).

treatments of the topic,[20] of *genus tenue* and *mensa tenuis* encapsulated in *Odes* 2. 16:

> vivitur parvo bene, cui paternum
> splendet in mensa *tenui* salinum
> nec levis somnos timor aut cupido
>   sordidus aufert.   (13–16)
>
> te greges centum Siculaeque circum
> mugiunt vaccae, tibi tollit hinnitum
> apta quadrigis equa, te bis Afro
>   murice tinctae
>
> vestiunt lanae: mihi parva rura et
> spiritum Graiae *tenuem* Camenae
> Parca non mendax dedit et malignum
>   spernere vulgus.   (33–40)

You can live well on little, if your father's salt-cellar shines on a modest table and fear does not carry off skittish sleep—or desire. A hundred flocks, Sicilian cows moo around you, for you a mare, good for the chariot, raises a whinny, wool dyed in African purple clothes you: a small country estate and the Fate who does not lie have given me the slender spirit of the Greek Muse and the capacity to spurn the grudging crowd.

The simple life that is represented by Horace's table is mirrored in the simplicity of his poetics, the refusal of sublime inspiration represented by his *spiritum . . . tenuem*. The *locus classicus* for this union of Callimacheanism and Epicureanism is Satires 1. 1:

> vel dic quid referat intra
> naturae finis viventi, iugera centum an
> mille aret? 'at suave est ex magno tollere acervo.'
> dum ex parvo nobis tantundem haurire relinquas,
> cur tua plus laudes cumeris granaria nostris?
> ut tibi si sit opus liquidi non amplius urna
> vel cyatho et dicas 'magno de flumine mallem
> quam ex hoc fonticulo tantundem sumere.' eo fit,
> plenior ut siquos delectet copia iusto,
> cum ripa simul avolsos ferat Aufidus acer.

---

[20] Mette (1961a) [Chapter 3 in this volume]. Cf. Syndikus (1972–3), i. 454; Bramble (1974), 156–73 ('Grandeur and Humility'); Nisbet and Hubbard (1978) on *Odes* 2. 16. 38.

> at qui tantuli eget quanto est opus, is neque limo
> turbatam haurit aquam neque vitam amittit in undis.   (49–60)

Or say what it matters to a man who lives within nature's limits, whether he plows a hundred or a thousand acres? 'But it's pleasant to take from a large heap.' So long as you allow me to take the same from a small amount, why should you praise your own silos more than my canisters? It's as if you needed no more than a jar or a mug of water and you said, 'I prefer to take the same amount from a great river than from this little fountain.' So it happens to those an abundance pleases, fuller than necessary—the fierce river Aufidus carries them off, with the bank ripped off with them. But he who wants only necessities never drinks muddied water. Nor does he lose his life in the waves.

The person who refuses to risk drowning in the great swollen river of sublimity is making a decision which is at once poetic and philosophical: and thereby political too.[21] As John Bramble put it in another of the standard treatments of this alliance of art and life: 'As we might expect given the principle of correspondence between style and character, letters and Bios, the exponent of the lower forms correlates his attitude of scorn for physical enormity with abhorrence from the grandiose and inflated in literature. Anything *grande, magnum, pingue* or *tumidum* is automatically shunned.'[22] Then again, in *Odes* 1. 35, Horace prays to Fortune to keep Augustus safe for future conquests:

> serves iturum Caesarem in ultimos
> orbis Britannos et iuvenum recens
> examen, Eois timendum
>   partibus Oceanoque rubro.   (29–32)

May you preserve Caesar, who is going to the Britons at the end of the world, and the new swarm of youth, to be feared in Eastern parts and the Red Sea.

But how does this act of imperialism sit with the urge to live *intra naturae finis* ('within the limits of nature')? More consistent are the calls to retirement Horace makes to Quinctius in *Odes* 2. 11:

> quid bellicosus Cantaber et Scythes,
> Hirpine Quincti, cogitet Hadria

---

[21] On the Callimachean elements here see conveniently Freudenburg (1993), 187–90.
[22] Bramble (1974), 158. Cf. Gowers (1993), esp. 40–6.

> divisus obiecto, remittas
>   quaerere nec trepides in usum
>
> poscentis aevi pauca,   (1–5)

Stop asking what the warring Cantabrian is thinking up and the Scythian on the other side of the Adriatic, and don't be anxious over the needs of a life span requiring little.

or to Maecenas in 3. 29:

> tu civitatem quis deceat status
> curas et urbi sollicitus times,
>   quid Seres et regnata Cyro
>   Bactra parent Tanaisque discors.
>
> prudens futuri temporis exitum
> caliginosa nocte premit deus
>   ridetque, si mortalis ultra
>   fas trepidat.   (25–32)

You are concerned with what condition befits the state and, worried for the city, fear what the Chinese and Bactrian regions, ruled by Cyrus, are up to, and unharmonious Tanais. God has in his wisdom cloaked the end of the future in foggy night and smiles if a man, subject to death, trembles beyond divine right.

If it is good to be a Callimachean Epicurean, to honour small things and respect the boundaries of the simple life, how can it also be good to hitch one's wagon to the star of sublimity and greatness?

Now, the very examples I have chosen will, I hope, suggest a number of objections. I am not making the proper distinctions here: I am reading anachronistically, because I have not tried to see the perceptual filters which would have enabled the ancient audience to distinguish between, for instance, a merchant's crossing the sea for gain and the legitimate expansion of the Roman empire. Is that not the point of Juno's injunction in *Odes* 3. 3, that if Rome avoids the greed that Troy represents, it will conquer the world?

> horrenda late nomen in ultimas
> extendat oras, qua medius liquor
>   secernit Europen ab Afro,
>   qua tumidus rigat arva Nilus,
>
> aurum inrepertum et sic melius situm,
> cum terra celat, spernere fortior

> quam cogere humanos in usus
>   omne sacrum rapiente dextra.   (45–52)

Let her spread her name, fearsome, far and wide to the ultimate shores, where the sea in the middle separates Europe from Africa, where the swollen Nile irrigates the fields; while the earth hides gold, unfound and therefore better sited, may she be strong enough to spurn it, rather than forcing it to human use—right hand snatching all that is sacred.

And that *tumidus* ('swollen') of the Nile[23] suggests another point: should not we see the Roman expansion as a civilizing and *taming* action, which restores boundaries rather than removing them, which defeats arrogance and bombast like Operation Desert Storm? Compare, for instance, Horace's injunction to Valgius in *Odes* 2. 9:

> desine mollium
> tandem querellarum et potius nova
> cantemus Augusti tropaea
>   Caesaris et rigidum Niphaten,
>
> Medumque flumen gentibus additum
> victis *minores* volvere vertices
>   *intraque praescriptum* Gelonos
>   *exiguis* equitare campis.   (17–24)

Stop those soft complaints, damn it, and rather let us sing the new trophies of Augustus Caesar and the frozen Niphates, and how the river of the Medes, added to conquered peoples, rolls lesser waves and the Geloni ride their horses within limits on slight fields.

Augustus will make good Callimacheans of the Geloni if it kills them.[24]

Moreover, if one looks to the philosophical side of Horace's ideology, one can see this as a special case of a more important objection. It is not just that the Epicurean good life for Horace is compatible with the epic achievements of the Boss, the latter ensures the former. As Matthew Santirocco remarks of *Odes* 3. 14, public and private are

[23] Cf. 4. 3. 8 'regum tumidas contuderit minas' etc.

[24] Similarly, when Augustus defeats the Euphrates at the end of *Aeneid* 8, is that not a victory for style *and* civilization over the inappropriate thunder of anarchy? If Callimacheanism is about control rather than wild inspiration, may it not go rather well with Fascism and its neo-classical rejection of *entartete Kunst* ('degenerate art')?

'not so much juxtaposed as interrelated. The day can be festive for Horace precisely because Caesar rules the earth.'[25] The topos is implicit in *Odes* 3. 29, where the reference to Maecenas' *curae* is a tribute to his power (and that of his master), and explicit of Augustus more than once: so most baldly in the last of the *Odes*:

> custode rerum Caesare non furor
> civilis aut vis exiget otium,
>   non ira, quae procudit ensis
>   et miseras inimicat urbis.   (4. 15. 17–20)

With Caesar as guardian of affairs, civil fury or force won't drive out peace, nor anger, which hammers out swords and makes enemies of unfortunate cities.

Moreover, if we stress Horace's Epicureanism, is not this perfectly Epicurean? The Epicureans favoured monarchy as a political system precisely because it enabled the ordinary citizen to stop worrying about politics and get on with life.[26] Let Caesar run the country, and have another drink:

> quis Parthium paveat, quis gelidum Scythen,
> quis Germania quos horrida parturit
> fetus, incolumi Caesare? quis ferae
>   bellum curet Hiberiae?
>   (*Odes* 4. 5. 25–8)

Who could fear the Parthian with Caesar safe, who the freezing Scythian, who those offspring shaggy Germany has borne? Who cares about the war with wild Hiberia?

Is it not reasonable for Horace to join in the prayer at the end of this, the most Fascist of his *Odes*?

> longas o utinam, dux bone, *ferias*
> praestes Hesperiae.   (37–8)

Good leader, o may you offer a long holiday to Hesperia.

---

[25] Santirocco (1985), 130.

[26] Cf. e.g. Kleve and Longo Auricchio (1992), 226: 'The Epicureans emphasised private life as an ideal: *bene vixit qui bene latuit*. One lost one's peace of mind if one meddled in the dispositions of the mighty. Epicurean rhetoric was meant for peaceful learning and panegyric. There was no need for the despot to expect flaming speeches for freedom from that part...' For a different emphasis in relation to Epicurean politics see Fowler (1989b).

Infinite power flows down, infinite responsibility flows up:[27] the consequences are well drawn by Syndikus,[28] but an Epicurean does not have to view them with distaste:

Previously, every Roman felt himself responsible for the state and its well-being; in our poem and even more so at the beginning of Epistle 2.1, this responsibility is entirely left to Caesar. The citizen enjoys still only the fruits of a prosperous rule; in fact, he is no longer a self-conscious 'Roman citizen', but a satisfied, thankful subject. The state has begun to become something alien to the Roman, no longer the 'public affair', but Caesar's affair,[29] who has drawn governing all to himself.

Being on holiday all the while sounds rather nice.[30]

Now I do not at all deny that these mechanisms exist to keep separate what I have tried to confuse, nor that my attempt to break these barriers is in a sense unhistorical. My claim is that from a different point of view such readings involve bad faith, that they necessarily entail turning a blind eye to obvious analogies. I am inclined to believe in fact that these analogies were more present to the ancient consciousness than is often supposed, but that is not part of my claim here. The problem with the Epicurean defence of kingship is that it enables government, but not panegyric. The Epicurean will be happy(-ish) in a moderate dictatorship, but she will not want to be boss, nor will she admire the king: and in this, of course, Epicureanism and Stoicism can come together:

[27] The Leadership Principle: 'unquestioned authority of the leader, combined with fullest responsibility'—Hitler (1937), 137 (and often quoted unconsciously in modern textbooks of management): but cf. 117 against the 'passive obedience and childlike faith' typical of monarchy.

[28] Syndikus (1972–3), ii. 345.

[29] On the 'privatization' of the public sphere under Augustus cf. Feeney (1992).

[30] The epistemological consequences of this Augustan abandonment of responsibility have been brilliantly sketched by Alessandro Schiesaro in respect of the move away from an aspiration to independent knowledge (as seen in the *De rerum natura*) to the scepticism and abandonment to authority represented in his view by the *Georgics*: cf. similarly Schiesaro [1997: 87] on the *Eclogues*: 'It is not the analogical science praised by Lucretius that can help Tityrus, but a form of knowledge which depends on mutually reinforcing bonds between social and religious powers, a form of knowledge, in sum, that ultimately recognizes its subordination and learns how to "know the gods"...' There are, naturally, other ways to read the *Georgics* and *Eclogues*.

nil admirari prope res est una, Numici,
solaque, quae possit facere et servare beatum.
hunc solem et stellas et decedentia certis
tempora momentis sunt qui formidine nulla
inbuti spectent: quid censes munera terrae,
quid maris extremos Arabas ditantis et Indos
ludicra, quid plausus et amici dona Quiritis,
quo spectanda modo, quo sensu credis et ore?

(*Ep*. 1. 6. 1–8)

Numicius, not to marvel at anything is just about the one and only thing
which can make and keep a man blessed. There are those who can look on
this sun, and the stars, and the seasons shifting at sure times steeped in no
fear; how do you think the gifts of the land should be looked on, and those of
the sea that enriches the Arabs far-away and the Indians, with what attitude
and expression do you believe the games should be watched, the applause,
and the donations of a citizen friend?

In a familiar tactic, Horace's use of *plausus et amici dona Quiritis* is
meant to point the reader away from the Boss to the Great and Good
of the Roman Republican tradition, but it doesn't work. One can of
course stress that the Great Man is resistant to this sort of thing: I
have no doubt that many would have seen Augustus in the opening
of *Odes* 3. 3, for instance (as the recall of *Sat*. 2. 1 suggests):[31]

iustum et tenacem propositi virum
non civium ardor prava iubentium,
   non vultus instantis tyranni
      mente quatit solida neque Auster,

dux inquieti turbidus Hadriae,
nec fulminantis magna manus Iovis:
   si fractus inlabatur orbis,
      inpavidum ferient ruinae.   (1–8)

A man who is just and keeps to his aim will not be shaken from his
determination by the excitement of citizens ordering baseness, by the face
of a threatening tyrant, or the South wind, turbulent leader of the restless
Adriatic, nor the great hand of lightning Jove: if the world falls to pieces
around him, the fragments will strike him unafraid.

---

[31] *Sat*. 2. 1. 16–20 'attamen et iustum poteras et scribere fortem...'

Another familiar tactic of monarchs is to depict themselves not as
men of power but as men still struggling, standing up to a hostile
world rather than bossing others about: a Regulus figure.[32] But when
the line-up on the other side is a *tyrannus*, a *dux*, and the great hand
of thundering Zeus, it is very difficult not to reverse the comparison.
Syndikus notes this, and argues that the reference in line 3 makes it
impossible to refer the lines to Augustus:[33] but when he goes on to
deny any 'political meaning' to the lines at all because of their Greek
content, he may be doing what Horace wanted him to do, but he is
whistling in the dark.[34]

   The traces of the Lucretian deconstruction of the terminology
of political honour and power[35] are everywhere in Horace, and
they are too powerful to be kept away from the *Capo dei Capi*. The
cover is easily blown, as Propertius made clear when he dealt with the
topics of foreign adventure and trade that Horace tried to keep
separate:

> Arma deus Caesar dites meditatur ad Indos,
>   et freta gemmiferi findere classe maris.
> magna, viri, merces[36]...   (3. 4. 1–3)

Caesar, divine and rich, thinks of waging war on the Indians and to
cleave the waves of the gem-bearing sea with his fleet. A great merchandize,
men...

A great deal of traditional classical scholarship is about building
fences between apparently continuous concepts: the rhetoric is full
of 'we should not think here of...' or 'there is no reference here
to...'. There are good reasons for this in a laudable desire to be
historical, but it produces the danger of an oppressive arbitrariness.
When Horace says to Sallustius Crispus in *Odes* 2. 2:

---

[32] For the identification of Regulus in *Odes* 3. 5 with Augustus see Doblhofer
(1966).

[33] Syndikus (1972–3), ii. 38 n. 22: 'Die verbreitete Ansicht, die beiden ersten
Strophen zielten bereits allein auf Augustus, widerlegt sich durch v. 3 von selbst.'

[34] The Greek tradition of resistance to tyranny was of course anything but inert in
Rome: cf. Berve (1967), ii. 737–8; Philostr. *Vita Apoll.* 7, esp. 7. 2.

[35] Cf. Fowler (1989b), 134–45.

[36] Attempts to defuse the force of *merces* founder on Lucan 2. 255 'castra petunt
magna victi mercede': see the whole context.

> latius regnes avidum domando
> spiritum quam si Libyam remotis
> Gadibus iungas et uterque Poenus
>   serviat uni.   (9–12)

You may rule more widely by controlling your desirous spirit than if you join Libya to remote Gades and the two Phoenician peoples serve you alone.

Nisbet and Hubbard on line 10 give us a long list of things not to think about:

As in several of the above parallels, the large land-owner is here seen as a kind of king (cf. 12 *serviat*); thus Horace can draw a contrast with the true kingship of the wise man. L. Müller thought that he meant a literal kingdom, but the target is Roman plutocracy rather than people like Juba (who in 25 B.C. was given a new domain in Mauretania). On the other hand Horace is unlikely to be alluding to African properties that Sallustius might have inherited from his great-uncle (*procos.* Africa Nova, 46–5); so hyperbolical a reminder of the historian's malversations would be unnecessarily indiscreet.

That anyone could connect *regnes* and *serviat* with Augustus' dictatorship is so unthinkable that it is not even worth arguing with. But Nisbet and Hubbard want this to have a contemporary meaning, and so point us away from real kings to Roman plutocrats. Horace of course at the end of the poem makes clear the reference to kingship:

> redditum Cyri solio Phraaten
> dissidens plebi numero beatorum
> eximit Virtus populumque falsis
>   dedocet uti
>
> vocibus, regnum et diadema tutum
> deferens uni propriamque laurum,
> quisquis ingentis oculo inretorto
>   spectat acervos.   (17–24)

Virtue disagrees with the common people and removes Phraates, who regained Cyrus' throne, from the ranks of the blessed and teaches the people not to use false voices any more; it grants a secure reign and crown, and a rightful triumph, to the one who alone can look on treasure heaped high without eyes of longing.

But if we keep rulers in mind, and respect the need for contemporary reference that Nisbet and Hubbard acknowledge, how can we avoid

looking to Augustus? I would not deny that Horace is trying to keep
us off that tack, but it is not necessarily the critic's job to reproduce
bad faith: sometimes we should expose it.

I want to look at one more example before summing up, and
answering a final objection. The example I take is Tony Woodman's
discussion[37] of *Odes* 3. 1, and in particular stanzas 2–6:

> regum timendorum in proprios greges,
> reges in ipsos imperium est Iovis,
>   clari Giganteo triumpho,
>   cuncta supercilio moventis.
>
> est ut viro vir latius ordinet
> arbusta sulcis, hic generosior
>   descendat in campum petitor,
>   moribus hic meliorque fama
>
> contendat, illi turba clientium
> sit maior: aequa lege Necessitas
>   sortitur insignis et imos,
>   omne capax movet urna nomen.
>
> destrictus ensis cui super impia
> cervice pendet, non Siculae dapes
>   dulcem elaborabunt saporem,
>   non avium citharaeque cantus
>
> somnum reducent: somnus agrestium
> lenis virorum non humilis domos
>   fastidit umbrosamque ripam,
>   non Zephyris agitata Tempe.   (5–24)

Fearsome kings have rule over their own flocks, but over them Jupiter rules,
renowned for his triumph over the Giants, moving all with his brow.... One
man may plant his shrubs in their furrows more widely than another, this
candidate descends to the polls with better lineage, while one surpasses
another in morals and fame, that one in the extent of his clientele: Necessity
sorts high and low with equal justice, the capacious urn rolls every name. If a
drawn sword hangs over a man's impious neck, Sicilian feasts will not work
their sweet flavor, the song of birds and the lyre will not bring back his sleep:
the gentle sleep of farmers does not disdain humble homes and the shady
bank, nor Tempe wafted by Zephyrs.

---

[37] Woodman (1984).

I do not want to get embroiled in the problems of the structure of the poem, but to use Woodman's interpretation as another example of this line-drawing that I have criticized. He is concerned to show that *Odes* 3. 1 is 'both a response to, and an advertisement for, the views of Augustus himself' (94) and accordingly sees no hint of criticism in the figures of stanzas 3–4 *est ut viro vir*... etc: they are rather to be contrasted with the impious man of stanza 5 and the later figures of the merchant and property speculator. They represent an idyll of Republican society as restored by Augustus after 27, an encourage-ment to the landowning classes to believe the words of the Lord. The problem again with this is that the tools of moral philosophy that Horace is wielding are too powerful to allow a conscientious reader with any degree of imagination to stop where Woodman wants her to. For Woodman, it is axiomatic that the man who *latius ordinet arbusta sulcis* is a 'blameless landowner', and indeed his blamelessness is used to reassure us that the politicians of the third stanza are equally free of criticism: he has therefore to deny any link with 2. 18. 24–36, well compared by Syndikus:

> revellis agri terminos et *ultra*
>   *limites* clientium
> salis avarus? pellitur paternos
>   in sinu ferens deos
> et uxor et vir sordidosque natos.
>   nulla certior tamen
> rapacis Orci fine destinata
>   aula divitem manet
> erum. quid *ultra* tendis? *aequa* tellus
>   pauperi recluditur
> regumque pueris, nec satelles Orci
>   callidum Promethea
> revexit auro captus.

You pull up the boundary stones and in your desire jump your clients' borders? Man and wife are turned out, bearing their paternal gods and dirty children in their arms. Still, no court awaits the rich owner more surely than the sure end of greedy Death. Why do you strive further? The same amount of land is dug for the poor man and the children of kings, nor does Orcus' attendant bring clever Prometheus back, despite the bribe.

Although the thought in *Odes* 2. 18 is expressed much more strongly, the philosophically evocative stress on respect for boundaries is at least superficially very similar—similar enough for commentators to cross-refer us to each passage. How does Woodman stop this? Then again, he is emphatic that 'the impius is in no sense to be identified with any of the four powerful men mentioned in stanzas 3–4'[38] in contrast to judgements like Syndikus's, which stress the criticism latent in Horace's descriptions of 'ordinary' life:

In Horace's eyes, excessive dominion has a special affinity not only with an irrational, but with a bad life: it lures you to cross over the boundaries set for mankind, within which alone is a good life possible. But provided no distinct wickedness is present, Horace would be of the opinion that human life is filled all the more with cares, the higher one is stationed and the more exposed one is to the blows of chance.[39]

But attached to the last word of each of Syndikus's statements is a footnote directing us to the relevant passages of the Odes:[40] what forbids us following up these footnotes? Finally, what of the really dark secret of these lines, the thing we must not at all costs be allowed to think? Isn't the king of stanza 2 like the Big Boss Man? Woodman notes that calling peoples *greges* is not like calling the ruler a shepherd,[41] but takes refuge in an appeal to the oracular style against Syndikus's point that 'Despots, who rule over men as over cattle, cannot from a Roman point of view be members of a healthy social order' and that *timendorum* makes it difficult to see a reference to the Good Shepherd.[42] But of course for Syndikus *there is no question of* referring this to Augustus: *it would not occur* to anyone at Rome to see him as a king, after all, though Hellenistic kingship theory occasionally comes in handy for footnotes. Jupiter who is over all kings in the second stanza *clearly has nothing to do* with death who affects everyone in the fourth stanza and the sword which hangs over the unfortunate in stanza 5. And it is vital that we appreciate that the reference there is *only* to a rich man like the property speculator we

[38] Woodman (1984), 91.
[39] Syndikus (1972–3), ii. 18–19.
[40] 2. 18. 23; 3. 3. 49–52; 3. 16. 11 ff.; 3. 24. 35–40; 3. 16. 17–18; 2. 10. 9–12.
[41] Woodman (1984), 185.
[42] Syndikus (1972–3), ii. 16 n. 59.

shall meet a little later on: *Siculae dapes must not be allowed* to bring to mind that the story involves the Sicilian tyrant Dionysius. It would be *quite inappropriate* for a commentator to quote here Cic. *Tusc.* 5. 62, where the story is told to illustrate the miseries of dictatorship:

Satisne videtur declarasse Dionysius nihil esse ei beatum, cui semper aliquis terror impendeat? Atque ei ne integrum quidem erat, ut ad iustitiam remigraret, civibus libertatem et iura redderet: iis enim se adolescens improvida aetate irretierat erratis eaque commiserat, ut salvus esse non posset si sanus esse coepisset.[43]

Does Dionysius not seem to declare that nothing is blessed to the man over whom some fear always hangs? And it was not even feasible for him to return to justice, to give freedom and rights back to the citizens: for as a youth without foresight, he had entangled himself in and committed such things that he could not be safe if he had begun to be sane.

That does not sound much like Augustus, does it?

Let me now sum up, and deal with that promised objection. My main point is that the inheritance of Epicurean and Stoic moral philosophy on which Horace draws throughout his work, particularly when conjoined with Callimachean poetics to produce a Callimachean ethics, makes it impossible to produce successful panegyric. Whatever attempts are made to control the force of the tradition, they flounder on its power. It is possible to collect any number of passages praising the Augustan state, as Doblhofer does: it is possible to show how subtly Horace tries to conceal analogies from us, how clever he is at supergluing over the cracks. But to take the edifice apart does not require a crowbar: it shatters at the first touch—if one chooses to let it. A poet like Horace, in his historical situation, cannot successfully praise a dictator like Augustus. But there is a more interesting objection to what I have been saying than merely to argue back in turn for an integrative, 'historical' reading in which the contradictions and tensions are subsumed again in a totalizing ideology. I have been treating Horace as if he were a Callimachean in aesthetics and an Epicurean in politics, to parody Eliot's famous self-definition. But he cannot be simply either of these. In his essay

[43] Cf. *RE* s.v. *Damokles*; Boeth. *Cons.* 3. 5. 6 with Gruber (1978) ad loc.

'Horaz und Kallimachos', which has tended to be overshadowed by the later more detailed treatments of Horatian Callimacheanism, F. Wehrli had pointed to passages like *Ep.* 2. 2. 120–1 as evidence that Horace went beyond the restrictions of Callimacheanism:

> vehemens et liquidus puroque simillimus amni
> fundet opes Latiumque beabit divite lingua.

Powerful and clear and very similar to a pure river will a man pour out his wealth and bless Latium with rich diction.

The Callimachean alternative is here surpassed with the explicit assertion that overpowering force and purity, that is, perfect form, are not mutually exclusive: Horace embraces monumental poetry as the highest kind.[44]

If Pasquali usefully reminded us of Horace's Hellenistic intertexts, recent criticism has stressed that he is also a classicist.[45] Horace imitates Pindar as well as Sappho and Anacreon: his model is the *engagé* Alcaeus. He drinks wine as well as water; and if we are stressing the Lucretian background and its emphasis on *vivere parce* ('live sparingly'), we might also note the way in which Lucretius had inserted into his Callimachean manifesto the insistence that he deserves the crown *quod magnis doceo de rebus* ('because I teach about great things', 1. 930). Rather than using Horace's moralized poetics to deconstruct his politics, maybe we could use the politics to uncover a different Horace hiding beneath this pose of exquisite modesty. There was always a potential for disagreement in the alliance of Callimacheanism and Epicureanism: *frui paratis* ('enjoy what is at hand') is not a slogan that Callimachus would have taken to, and while Lucretius was able to appropriate the trackless paths to Epicureanism, the essence of the message Epicurus brings back from his journey through the universe is one about fixed and certain *termini* ('boundaries') (albeit with its own intimations of sublimity). Maybe Horace is more of a Marinetti than he pretends, with a secret longing for sublime excess and Greatness with a capital 'G': maybe he is a better Fascist than I have allowed. *Odes* 2. 20, for instance, clearly offers us a very different picture from the *simplici myrto nihil alla-bores | sedulus curo* ('I would really rather you add nothing to the simple myrtle') of the last poem of *Odes* 1:

[44] Wehrli (1944), 74.
[45] Cf. Feeney (1993), esp. 45. [Chapter 11 in this volume].

Non usitata nec tenui ferar
penna biformis per liquidum aethera
  vates neque in terris morabor
    longius invidiaque maior

urbis relinquam.   (1–5)

I will be borne on a wing neither usual nor slender through the liquid aether, a double bard, nor will I delay longer on the earth and I will leave the cities, greater than envy.

iam Daedaleo notior Icaro
visam gementis litora Bosphori
  Syrtisque Gaetulas canorus
    ales Hyperboreosque campos;

me Colchus et qui dissimulat metum
Marsae cohortis Dacus et ultimi
  noscent Geloni, me peritus
    discet Hiber Rhodanique potor.   (13–20)

Now, more famous than Daedalus' Icarus will I visit the shores of the groaning Bosphorus as a tuneful bird and the Gaetulian sand shoals and the Hyperborean fields; the Colchian will come to know me, and the Dacian who hides his fear of the Marsian division; the learned Spaniard and drinker of the Rhone will learn me.

If *non usitata* might be seen as Callimachean in its rejection of Epicureanism, *nec tenui* turns on both: this is no 'middle flight' but an 'advent'rous soaring', an act of that *superbiam quaesitam meritis* ('pride earned by merit') to which he will return in *Odes* 3. 30.

Now it would be a mistake to read either 2. 20 or 3. 30 as simply here prophesying a Great Future for Horace. Even in the midst of his sublime rapture, Horace in that much-discussed phrase *Daedaleo notior Icaro* (if it is right) has, as Nisbet and Hubbard note, drawn back from 'the hazard of his ambition': his great and glorious fame in *Odes* 3. 30 will spread—all over Puglia and Basilicata. But such irony can always be read collusively.[46] For all this apparent restraint, it is possible if one chooses to trace in Horace, as in other Augustans, what Alessandro Schiesaro has termed a 'Bacchic Poetics' in which sublimity and inspired excess transfigure the tropes of Callimacheanism and

---

[46] Cf. Martindale (1993), 14–15.

the *furor* of the inspired poet is a guilty will to power. The pieces can be arranged very differently from the pattern I first constructed. Rather than doing a Wilkinson and taking the ethicized poetics as central, we could with Fraenkel give pride of place to the politics, and see the respect for greatness there as exposing the tensions within the poetics, rather than the other way round. We do not have to jump either way, of course: we can stay with both as themselves held in tension. But that looks a dull and cowardly way out. To jump with the sublime Horace is—with self-reflexive appropriateness—the more heroic act: more of the traditional picture of the unpretentious, ironic Horace has to go, more of the English Horace has to be jettisoned. That is too bold for me, and I would rather go with the Horace of 1. 38 (taken straight). Safe in what a recent study[47] has called 'a private space, secluded, a Horatian self-protective corner', Horace can look not up to, but down on, the Great and the Bad.

[47] Ferri (1993), 12.

14

Horace, *Odes* 4.5: *Pro Reditu Imperatoris Caesaris Divi Filii Augusti* ('For the Return of Imperator Caesar Augustus, Son of the Divine')

I. M. Le M. Du Quesnay

I. HORACE AND AUGUSTUS

In the late summer of 15 BC Augustus wrote to Horace from Gaul and requested a poem to commemorate the magnificent victory which his stepsons, Tiberius and Drusus, had won over the Vindelici.[1] The care that was being taken over the representation of this victory and its significance is revealed by the choice of 1 August as the day of victory, the fifteenth anniversary of the fall of Alexandria in 30 BC.[2] The Gallic campaign also provided a focal point for a further refinement and redefinition of the role of Augustus. The war had been conducted under the *auspicia* of Augustus by Tiberius and Drusus acting as the *legati*.[3] Since Augustus had secured through his *pietas* and his special relationship with the gods the divine support without

[1] Suet. *Hor*. 20. 5 Klingner.
[2] For the date see Hor. *Odes* 4. 14. 34–40. A land battle which involved no surrender of a city presumably left some scope for deciding on which day the victory fell. It was the *dies natalis* of the temples of Victoria and Victoria Virgo on the Palatine and the day on which the Ara Romae et Augusti was dedicated at Lyons in 12 BC: see Degrassi (1963), 489–90; Fishwick (1987), 97–9, 118; Rich (1990), 211–12.
[3] For *ductu auspiciisque* see Plin. *NH* 3. 136–7; *CIL* v. 7817 = Ehrenberg and Jones (1976), 62 No. 40: cf. Aug. *RG* 4. 2 and Hor. *Odes* 4. 14. 33–4.

which there would have been no victory, it was Augustus, not
Tiberius or Drusus, who was acclaimed as *imperator* for the victory.[4]
The importance attached to communicating effectively this carefully
nuanced relationship between Augustus and his *legati* is reflected in
the coinage of this period. For the first time the acclamation of
Augustus as *imperator* is advertised on the coinage, and there is a
famous series which shows either one or two figures in military dress
(Drusus and/or Tiberius) presenting Augustus with the laurel-
branch of victory.[5] A conscious decision had been taken about
what the message was to be, and Horace was, very clearly, not the
only person enlisted to communicate it. Horace discharged the
commission with tact and skill in two magnificent Pindaricizing
odes (4. 4 and 4. 14), each partnered in the final collection by a
shorter piece for Augustus himself (4. 5 and 4. 15).[6]

As an *amicus* of Augustus,[7] Horace will not have needed the
message to be spelt out in detail. The Latin term *amicitia* covers
not only friendship, in something like the modern sense of a relationship based on common interests, shared values and outlook, but also
includes many features more naturally covered by the modern sense
of patronage.[8] *Amicitia* was often, as in the case of Augustus and
Horace, an asymmetric relationship between individuals of unequal
status which imposed obligations and was cemented by an exchange
of gifts and services. Augustus was an extremely wealthy and powerful
man, and his gifts were made on a very generous scale. Suetonius
records simply that he enriched Horace by one or two acts of generosity (19–20 Klingner *unaque et altera liberalitate locupletavit*). Details are not known but can be inferred. L. Varius Rufus wrote the
Thyestes for performance on the occasion of the triple triumph in 29
BC, and in a single act of generosity Augustus gave him 1 m. sesterces.

---

[4] Fears (1981b), 746–9; Rosenstein (1990), 54–91.

[5] For the acclamation as *imperator* see Barnes (1974), 22; for the coins see Kraft
(1978), 321–6; Sutherland (1984), 52 Nos. 162–5; Trillmich (1988), 489, 523.

[6] See Zanker (1988), 223–7. Contrast White (1993), 127–32.

[7] For discussion of what this means see Horsfall (1981); White (1978, 1993). There
is no satisfactory way of translating *amicus*: 'friend' underplays the obligations;
'patron' or 'client' overstates them. But it is excessively pedantic always to insist on
the Latin word.

[8] See Brunt (1988), 351–81; Saller (1982), 1–40; (1989).

Virgil had died leaving 10 m. sesterces acquired *ex liberalitatibus amicorum* ('from the acts of generosity of his friends'), including, of course, Augustus.[9] The significance of generosity on this scale can be judged from the fact that when Augustus reviewed the senate and introduced a census-rating for eligibility which was eventually set at 1 m. sesterces (probably in 18 BC), the purpose was to enhance and define the *dignitas* of the *ordo senatorius*.[10] There was nothing for either party to be ashamed about concerning such gifts: they advertised the generosity of the donor and expressed his judgement of the worthiness of the recipients. The obligation of the recipient was to show himself worthy of the gift.[11] The poet could reciprocate with gifts of his own in the form of poems which would be expected to immortalize the memory of the recipient, his benefactor, and so had a value beyond price.[12] But the obligations of *amicitia* were not met by a simple exchange of poems for gifts or gifts for poems. The *potens amicus* could be expected to provide a wide range of other supportive services appropriate to his own position in society and to the needs of the poet. Like any other friend, the poet was also bound to reciprocate by providing his support in whatever way he could and in a form appropriate to the needs of his *potens amicus*. When Augustus requested a poem for the victory of his stepsons, he demonstrated his high estimation of Horace's poems.[13] It was Horace's obligation and, we must suppose, his pleasure to respond positively. To have done otherwise would have been a disgraceful display of ingratitude. For he incurred the obligation as a friend and discharged it as a friend.

---

[9] He casually bestowed 100,000 sesterces on a Greek poet he hardly knew: Macr. *Sat.* 2. 4. 31. For Varius and Virgil see Brink (1982), 252; White (1993), 276 n. 22.

[10] See Nicolet (1976); (1984), 91–3, 118–19.

[11] See Hor. *Ep.* 2. 1. 245–7 'at neque dedecorant tua de se iudicia atque | munera quae multa dantis cum laude tulerunt | dilecti tibi Vergilius Variusque poetae.' He does not explicitly state that he too had received gifts, but it can be safely inferred that he was one of those whose wishes had been granted: compare *Ep.* 2. 2. 49–52 with *Ep.* 2. 1. 226–8: and see Brink (1982), 295.

[12] See White (1978), 84.

[13] Suet. *Hor.* 20–3 Klingner 'scripta quidem eius usque adeo probavit mansuraque perpetuo opinatus est, ut non modo saeculare carmen conponendum iniunxerit sed et Vindelicam victoriam Tiberii Drusique privignorum suorum.'

Augustus and Horace had known each other for more than twenty years, and in their private communications adopted an intimate and teasing banter.[14] There is no justification for supposing that their friendship was not as genuine as their relative positions in society allowed, which is not to deny that Augustus was immeasurably Horace's social superior in terms of birth, wealth, power, and prestige.[15] Some fifteen years previously Horace had told an anecdote which shows how people assumed that he knew what was going on at the very centre of power (*Sat.* 2. 6. 51–8). They were right. *Odes* 4 shows Horace intimately connected with men close to the Princeps: Paullus Fabius Maximus (4. 1), married to a cousin of Augustus, consul in 11 BC, proconsul of Asia (without the usual interval) in 10 BC; Iullus Antonius (4. 2), a son of the triumvir but brought up by Octavia, whose daughter Marcella he had married in 21 BC, aedile in 16 BC, praetor in 13 BC, consul in 10 BC—not to mention Maecenas (4. 11), Tiberius, or Drusus.[16] It should not therefore be surprising if Horace shows in the poems of book 4 an advance knowledge of what was to be put into effect only after the return of Augustus from Gaul and Spain.

2. THE DATES OF 4. 5 AND *ODES* 4

The Suetonian *Life of Horace*, drawing on the correspondence of Augustus, provides exceptionally good evidence for the genesis and 'publication' of *Odes* 4.[17] However, the relevant passage is not without its problems. The statement 'eumque coegerit propter hoc [i.e. the request for a poem on the victory over the Vindelici] tribus carminum libris ex longo intervallo quartum addere' ('and he

[14] Suet. *Hor.* 17–19 Klingner 'praeterea saepe eum inter alios iocos "purissimum penem" et "homuncionem lepidissimum" appellat.'

[15] On the difficulties presented by a *potens amicus* see Hor. *Ep.* 1. 7, 17, 18; cf. White (1978), 81–2.

[16] For these men see White (1993), 224–39; Syme (1986), 396–420.

[17] The book is conventionally and rightly dated to 13 BC: see Fraenkel (1957), 364–5, 410, 449; Becker (1963), 190; Putnam (1986), 23. Williams (1972), 44–9 argues unconvincingly for a date as late as 8 BC.

"compelled" [i.e. he made a request that Horace could not refuse] him on account of this to add a fourth after a long interval to the three books of odes') is marked as Suetonius' own inference by the words *propter hoc*.[18] It is certainly misleading if it encourages the view that Horace was forced against his will and better judgement to return to lyric.[19] To understand *Odes* 4 it is necessary to acknowledge the significance of being asked to write for an *amicus* as important as Augustus and to recognize that the question of Horace's personal feelings as distinct from those he chose to represent in the poems is simply beside the point. Those who claim to detect lack of sincerity or enthusiasm in the odes of book 4 are well-intentioned but mis-guided in their attempts to assert the independence of the poet, for Horace makes plain his communicative intention to praise Augustus, and to accuse him of failing to convince his readers of his enthusiasm or sincerity is to impugn his skill.

Suetonius cannot be correct in suggesting that Horace did not start on book 4 until after he had received the request to celebrate the victory of Tiberius and Drusus over the Vindelici on 1 August 15 BC. *Odes* 4. 6. 29–44 and, probably, 4. 3. 22–3 refer to the *Carmen Saeculare* which had been commissioned by Augustus for perform-ance on 3 June 17 BC, on the last day of the Ludi Saeculares. The most natural inference is that both poems are more or less contemporary with the composition of the *Carmen Saeculare*, and that it was Augustus' request for that poem which provided the opportunity, at least, for Horace to return to lyric. *Odes* 4. 2 confirms that Horace was engaged continuously with the writing of lyric after 17 BC. Some time in the summer of 16 BC news had reached Rome that the Sugambri had crossed the Rhine and invaded Gaul, inflicting a defeat on the proconsul M. Lollius and capturing a Roman legionary standard.[20] Augustus left Rome some time after 29 June, when he

[18] Contrast White (1993), 43, 115, 127–32, who believes that *coegerit* also derives from the correspondence and whose understanding of the nature and significance of the formal request is different from mine: on *cogere* see Brink (1982), 243.

[19] This view has dogged criticism of *Odes* 4 in a most unhelpful way: see Brink (1982), 546–52.

[20] On the date of Lollius' defeat see Timpe (1975), 140; Christ (1977), 185–6; Halfmann (1986), 161 against Syme (1933), 17–19; Syme (1989), 115–16 with n. 14. For sources and further bibliography see Halfmann (1986), 158; Rich (1990), 198–9.

dedicated the rebuilt temple of Quirinus.[21] According to Dio (54. 20.
6), as soon as the Sugambri heard that Augustus himself had taken
the field they withdrew to their own territory and sued for peace. No
fighting actually took place. Even allowing for exaggeration, it is clear
that the threat from the Sugambri quickly evaporated. In *Odes* 4, 2
Horace is still looking forward to the return of Augustus and the
triumph he will celebrate over the Sugambri.[22] The vows for Augustus' safe return, mentioned by Dio and confirmed by contemporary
coins, have already been made.[23] The dramatic date of the poem is
thus the moment of Augustus' departure or shortly after. The actual
date of composition may be identical and must anyway be before the
news of the surrender of the Sugambri reached Rome.[24] The second
poem in the collection is, as often, one of the earliest pieces.[25]

   The latest datable reference is in *Odes* 4. 4 and 4. 14: the defeat of
the Vindelici, which is assigned to August 15 BC, the anniversary of
Augustus' conquest of Alexandria in 30 BC. If time is allowed for
Augustus to communicate with Horace and for Horace to set to

---

[21] For the dedication of the temple of Quirinus see Dio 54. 19 with Rich (1990),
196; Ov. *Fasti* 6. 795–6; Degrassi (1963), 475. Augustus may even have remained in
Rome for the celebration of the Quinquennial Games, which, as they celebrated the
victory at Actium, were presumably held on or around 2 Sept.: see Dio 51. 19. 2 with
Reinhold (1988), 146–8; 53. 1. 4 with Rich (1990), 133; Weinstock (1971), 310–17;
Kienast (1982), 67–8.

[22] The *Fasti triumphales* were inscribed on the Arcus Augusti, which had been
decreed in 19 BC and is best known from coins struck between 18 and 16 BC: see
Sutherland (1984), 50 Nos. 131–45, 68 No. 359; Nedergaard (1988). They began with
the three triumphs of Romulus. Augustus' refusal to celebrate any further triumphs
after 29 BC has been attributed to *imitatio Romuli* (see Binder 1971: 166). Perhaps the
policy was not formulated until the *Fasti* were inscribed, which would help to explain
why Horace still anticipates a triumph for Augustus in 16 BC but does not suggest one
for the victory over the Vindelici. That there was a change in attitude to claiming
triumphs around this time is also suggested by Dio 54. 11. 6, 12.1–2, 24. 7–8 with
Rich (1990), 188–9, 202.

[23] *Odes*. 4. 2. 42–3: *publicum ludum super impetrato . . . reditu*; cf. Dio 54. 19. 7 with
Rich (1990), 197; and Sutherland (1984), 57–8 n. 57, 50 No. 146, 68 Nos. 351–8 (e.g.
353, *senatus populusque Romanus vota publica suscepta pro salute et reditu Augusti*).

[24] Prop. 4. 6, which is probably also connected to the Quinquennial Games of 16
BC, belongs to exactly the same time: see 4. 6. 77. Cairns (1984), 151–4 argues that the
occasion is rather the *dies natalis* of the temple of Apollo on the Palatine (9 Oct.).

[25] That it was not revised in the light of events is clear from *Odes* 4. 14. 51–2: 'te
caede gaudentes Sugambri | compositis venerantur armis', which exactly matches
Dio's account.

work, then 14 BC is perhaps the most probable date of composition. In that year Augustus was in Spain, and the prominent references to Spain, in both *Odes* 4. 14 and *Odes* 4. 5, will have had a topical significance.[26] The view that some of the poems were written after the return of Augustus to Rome utterly fails to convince for want of tangible evidence or compelling grounds. There is nothing in the rest of the book which requires us to think of any later date.[27]

The Suetonian evidence implies that after the victory over the Vindelici Augustus' thoughts started to move towards his return. Tiberius went back ahead of him to hold the consulship in 13 BC, and in part, no doubt, to make preparations. Drusus would not return until the end of that year or the beginning of 12 BC.[28] It seems that Augustus wanted the poems written to celebrate the victory for which he had received his tenth acclamation as *imperator* and which had been achieved under his *ductu auspiciisque.* Although *Odes* 4 and 14, together with their companion pieces 5 and 15, may have been written in 14 BC, they were written with a view to being performed and published in the context of the celebrations that would mark Augustus' quasi-triumphal return.

This conclusion is hardly surprising. *Odes* 4 conforms to a generally observable pattern according to which the publication of a book of poems coincides with a significant date or event in the career of the patron-friend who is the dedicatee. So the triumphal return of Asinius Pollio in 39 BC is marked by Virgil's *Eclogues*; Octavian's ovation for the defeat of Sextus Pompey in 36 BC by Horace's *Satires* 1; Augustus' triumphal return after Actium by Virgil's *Georgics*, Horace's *Satires* 2 and *Epodes*, Varius Rufus' *Thyestes*; the departure of Volcacius Tullus to Asia by Propertius 1; the triumphal return of M. Valerius Messalla Corvinus on 26 September 27 BC by Tibullus 1; Augustus' departure for the east in 22 BC by Propertius 3; the election

[26] See *Odes* 4. 14. 41 (Cantaber), and 4. 14. 50 and 4. 5. 28 (Hiberia).

[27] Williams (1972), 44–9 argues for a later date for 4. 4, 14, and, particularly, 15. He is effectively refuted by Brink (1982), 553 and Putnam (1986), 23. Bowersock (1990), 389 is inclined to think 4. 14 later than 6 Mar. 12 BC, although Augustus' election as Pontifex Maximus was guaranteed after the death of Lepidus, which Bowersock (1990), 383 places in 13 BC.

[28] See Dio 54. 25. 1 and 33. 1 with Rich (1990), 211–12; and Bowersock (1990), 392. I am inclined to accept Bowersock's suggestion, although Dio does not mention his return before the winter of 12/11.

of Valerius Messalla's son as a *XVvir sacris faciundis* by Tibullus 2 (?);
the Ludi Saeculares in 17 BC by Horace's *Carmen Saeculare* and
Virgil's *Aeneid*;[29] the Quinquennial Games and the departure of
Augustus for Gaul in 16 BC by Propertius 4.[30]

The important thing for the reader of *Odes* 4. 5 to realize is that the
dramatic date and setting are different from the date and setting of
its intended first performance. The poem purports to be a pressing
and urgent invitation to Augustus to return to Italy. In fact all the
indications are that it was written to be performed amid the celebrations of his return. This is a variation on the familiar tactic of the
encomiast, which is neatly caught by Ovid (*Tristia* 5. 14. 45–6):[31]

> qui monet ut facias, quod iam facis, ille monendo
> laudat et hortatu comprobat acta suo.

He who warns you to do what you're already doing praises with his warning
and approves the deeds with his exhortation.

Horace guarantees the sincerity of the speaker's feelings of joy at
Augustus' return by depicting the longing for his return that had

[29] See esp. *Aen.* 6. 789–97. I assume that the *triennium* which Virgil is said (Donat.
Vit. Verg. 126–19 Hardie) to have intended to spend finishing the *Aeneid* was the
triennium which lay between the departure of Virgil from Italy in the summer of 20
BC (i.e. Virgil's 50th, not 52nd, year) and the 'publication' of the *Aeneid* in the
summer of 17 BC.

[30] It is tempting to add 'Horace's *Odes* 1–3 for Augustus' return from Spain in 24
BC'. Prof. Woodman reminds me that the same thought had occurred to Murray
(1985), 50=(1993), 103. *Odes* 1–3 shows a steady sequence of datable references from
at least 29 through 24 BC. There is then an awkward gap until the period July–Aug. 23
(from the time Sestius entered his suffect consulship until the death of Marcellus), in
which the publication of the *Odes* is generally placed: see Nisbet and Hubbard (1970),
pp. xxvii–xxxvii. Perhaps Jerome was wrong to place the death of Quintilius Varus in
23/22 BC. Sestius' suffect consulship in 23 BC is not referred to explicitly in *Odes* 1. 4,
and he may be at most *designatus* at the time of publication, or perhaps he is just
being commended by the dedication as a suitable replacement for Augustus. On the
election of *suffecti* see Talbert (1984a), 202–7, 242–3. One might compare the way in
which *Odes* 4 honours one of the consuls in each of years 13 (Tiberius), 11 (Paullus
Fabius Maximus), 10 (Iullus Antonius), 9 (Drusus), and 8 BC (Marcius Censorinus).

[31] Compare Arist. *Rhet.* 1. 9, 1367ᵇ36; Cic. *De or.* 2. 333; Quint. *Inst.* 3. 7. 28. After
a long absence it could be safely assumed that Augustus was eager to return: cf. Cic.
Pro leg. Man. 22 'noster autem exercitus, tametsi urbem ex Tigrani regno ceperat et
proeliis usus erat secundis, tamen nimia longinquitate locorum ac desiderio suorum
commovebatur, hic iam plura non dicam; fuit enim illud extremum ut ex eis locis a
militibus nostris reditus magis maturus quam progressio longior quaereretur.'

been felt during his absence and the intensity of the speaker's desire for his return. By adopting this strategy, Horace shapes and guides the audience's 'recollection' of its feelings during the absence of Augustus (regardless, of course, of whether the individual members of the audience had ever consciously experienced such feelings before) and so suggests an appropriate response to his return. The poem is aimed as much at the audience as it is at Augustus himself.

3. *REDITUS* IMPERATORIS CAESARIS DIVI FILII AUGUSTI

Augustus returned to Rome, after an absence of three years, on 4 July 13 BC.[32] The only narrative account that we have is provided by Cassius Dio (54. 25. 2–26. 1). Unfortunately, Dio's account is demonstrably lacunose, confused, self-contradictory, and in error in some particulars. As Dio implies, rumours and announcements of Augustus' approach to the city along the Via Flaminia from the north will have come in over several weeks in advance of his actual arrival.[33] Progress will have been slow and stately and attended by much pomp and ceremony: places along the route will have turned out to welcome the returning Princeps, to demonstrate their loyalty, and, no doubt, to petition on matters of local concern.[34]

Just as it had done previously on the occasion of Augustus' return from Egypt in 29, from Spain in 24, and from the east in 19, the senate met to decide on honours suitable to the occasion. Each *reditus* recapitulates earlier ones and revives memories associated with them. So the honours proposed by Cornelius Balbus on this occasion clearly recall the honours voted by the senate for Augustus'

---

[32] See Halfmann (1986), 159.

[33] It took Augustus at least three or four weeks to progress from Brundisium to Rome in 19 BC: see Halfmann (1986), 158.

[34] The practice of *adventus* was well established in the Greek world and in the Roman Republic: see Peterson (1930); Alföldi (1970), 79–118; Pearce (1970), 313–16; Versnel (1970), 387–8; Weinstock (1971), 289–90, 296, 300, 330; MacCormack (1972); Millar (1977), 28–40; Woodman (1977), 130–6; MacCormack (1981), 17–89; Woodman (1983b), 118–21; Halfmann (1986), esp. 15–29, 111–29, 143–8.

earlier *reditus*.[35] The proposal of an altar to Fortuna Redux in
the Curia is a variation on the Ara Fortunae Reducis decreed for
the Porta Capena in 19 BC;[36] while the proposal of the power to
provide asylum to supplicants sounds like an extension of the powers
of *auxilium* and appellate *cognitio* voted to Augustus in 29 BC.[37] The
final honour which Dio says Balbus proposed in 13 BC is an
ἀπάντησις, a formal welcome by representatives of the SPQR. In 29
BC it had been suggested that the whole population of the city should
go out to meet him whenever he entered the city. Augustus expressly
declined this honour.[38] Nevertheless, he seems to have accepted the
proposal that the anniversary of the day on which he had entered
the city in 29 BC should be honoured with sacrifices by the whole
population and be held sacred for ever.[39] On his return in 19 BC an
ἀπάντησις was voted by the senate.[40] Dio is simply wrong when he
claims that Augustus gave the magistrates and others who had come
to honour him the slip and entered the city at night. The reason for
his misrepresentation can easily be guessed, for Dio is known to have
suffered from the demands made in connection with the imperial
adventus,[41] and he could not have his model emperor providing
precedent and sanction for such behaviour. But the fact that Augustus recorded the honour in detail and with evident pride in the *Res
Gestae* makes it quite clear that it was accepted.[42]

[35] Dio is clearly following a source hostile to Balbus, who had celebrated a triumph
ex Africa in 19 BC, the last person to do so who was not a member of the imperial
house. He must have been among those to whom Augustus in 17 BC made the
suggestion that those who held triumphs should undertake some public work out
of their spoils to commemorate their achievements (Dio 54. 18. 2).

[36] See Dio 54. 10. 3 with Rich (1990), 186.

[37] See Torelli (1982), 32–3; Reinhold (1988), 149–51.

[38] See Dio 51. 19. 2, 51. 20. 4.

[39] See Dio 51. 20. 3 and Torelli (1982), 30. This was the formal beginning of the
imperial ceremony of *adventus*: see esp. Halfmann (1986), 143–8.

[40] For the return in 24 Hor. *Odes* 3. 14 is suggestive; note especially 13 *hic dies vere
mihi festus* together with Dio 51. 20. 3 τήν τε ἡμέραν ἐν ᾗ ἂν ἐς τὴν πόλιν ἐσέλθῃ
θυσίαις τε πανδημεὶ ἀγαλθῆναι καὶ ἱερὰν ἀεὶ ἄγεσθαι.

[41] See Dio 77. 9. 5–7 (on Caracalla); Millar (1964), 152, 216; (1977), 33.

[42] *RG* 12. 1 'Ex senatus auctoritate pars praetorum et tribunorum plebi cum
consule Q. Lucretio et principibus viris obviam mihi missa est in Campaniam, qui
honos ad hoc tempus nemini praeter me est decretus.' Cf. Dio 54. 8. 3. It should be
noted that in 29 the proposal was for all the people to go out (σύμπαντας . . .

A similar ἀπάντησις was proposed in 13 BC, perhaps including the suggestion that Balbus should lead the welcoming party as Q. Lucretius had done on the earlier occasion.[43] Dio says that the honour was again declined, and this time there is no evidence to contradict.[44] But once again he must be wrong when he says that Augustus slipped into the city under cover of night.[45] This time Dio supports his assertion by reference to a general practice.[46] Suetonius also records this practice, which he includes, instructively, among those which illustrated the *civilitas* of Augustus and distinguished his behaviour from that of more tyrannical emperors (*Augustus* 53. 2): 'non temere urbe oppidove ullo egressus aut quoquam ingressus est nisi vespera aut noctu, ne quem officii causa inquietaret' ('Not without cause did he leave the city or any town or arrive at any other than in the evening or at night so that he would not disturb anyone because of their obligations.') It is clear that, unlike Dio, Suetonius does not present this as an inviolable rule. He is thinking only of routine comings and goings during times when Augustus is resident in Italy.[47] People may well have been delighted to be relieved of this burden in connection with routine journeys.[48] But the very fact that Augustus had to go to such lengths even on those occasions to avoid the populace turning out to see him off or to welcome him shows how deeply ingrained this behaviour was.[49] It is quite another thing to suppose that

τοὺς ἐν τῇ πόλει), while in the *Res Gestae* it is some of them (*pars*). That is sufficient consistency for a politician in a changing world.

[43] It is difficult to think what else might lie behind Dio's obscure comment Κορνήλιος Βάλβος τὸ θέατρον .   . .καθιερώσας θέας ἐπετέλει ἐπί τε τούτῳ ὡς καὶ αὐτὸς τὸν Αὔγουστον ἐπανάξων ἐσέμνυνετο (54. 25. 2).

[44] Unless it could be shown beyond all reasonable doubt that the scenes on the Ara Pacis do represent the events of the day of its *constitutio*, as argued by Welin (1939). For a bibliography see Settis (1988), 424–5. Add now Bowersock (1990), 390–4, who argues that it represents 'the procession of the imperial family on the day that Augustus became *pontifex maximus* [i.e. 6 Mar. 12 BC]'; Billows (1993), who argues that the scene represents a *supplicatio* on 4 July 13 BC.

[45] The possibility of Dio's being wrong on this point, whether innocently or not, seems not to have occurred to those concerned with the Ara Pacis, who frequently find themselves forced into the most tortuous arguments in order to accommodate Dio.

[46] Dio 54. 25. 4; cf 56. 41. 5.

[47] Cf. Carter (1982), 176.

[48] Cf. Tac. *Agr.* 40. 3; *Ann.* 3. 33. 4; Wallace-Hadrill (1982), 40.

[49] See Pearce (1970), 316.

Augustus could have slipped into Rome under cover of darkness after a three-year absence without causing the greatest offence, when everybody had been eagerly preparing for his return for weeks, if not longer.[50] Suetonius (*Augustus* 57. 1–2), in fact, makes it quite plain that it was not his practice on occasions of major significance. For he goes on to talk about how the people showed their genuine affection for Augustus precisely because of his *civilitas*,[51] by the elaborate and spontaneous welcome they gave him when he returned from a province. It would be completely out of character for Augustus to have shown himself contemptuous of such a spontaneous display of affection and loyalty.

The date 4 July 13 BC was the *constitutio* of the Ara Pacis, and this enables us to reconstruct the events of that day with some certainty.[52] Augustus approached Rome from the north, along the Via Flaminia. Exactly one Roman mile from the *pomerium*, where generals returning from war exchanged their military garb for the civilian toga, he was met formally by the SPQR. Here the magistrates, the priests, and the Vestal Virgins performed a sacrifice, in thanksgiving for his safe return, to Pax Augusta.[53] This was the first occasion on which the goddess had been honoured with the new cognomen which gave her a special link with Augustus, one which honours him as much as the goddess: for it suggests that it is through him alone and through his actions that the goddess Pax manifests herself.[54] The sacrifice on this occasion no doubt set the pattern for the *anniversarium sacrificium* decreed by the senate.[55] It will have been performed at a temporary altar constructed within a *templum* duly marked out for the

[50] Cf. esp. Cic. *In Pis.* 53–5.

[51] See Wallace-Hadrill (1982), 40—but the entire article is pertinent. Compare the popularity of Germanicus: Versnel (1980), 542–8.

[52] For the nature of *constitutio arae* see Welin (1939), esp. 510, 512 (whose arguments are misrepresented by Torelli 1982: 30, 42); Fishwick (1987), 203–13.

[53] *RG* 12. 2. On the day of the *dedicatio* of the Ara Fortunae Reducis the *supplicatio* was made to Fortuna Redux; on that of the Ara Pacis Augustae it was made to the Imperium Augusti: see Degrassi (1963), 404–5, 538.

[54] On deifications such as Pax Augusta see Wallace-Hadrill (1981); Fears (1981a); Fishwick (1991), 446–74.

[55] This also seems to be the first time in Rome that a god is given the cognomen of *Augustus*.

purpose.[56] This temporary structure would later determine the orientation, size, and shape of the final altar.[57]

The choice of the site was not haphazard. For the Ara Pacis Augustae was to form part of the Horologium Solare Augusti, a monumental horizontal sundial-cum-calendar marked out and inscribed on a large paved area of the Campus Martius. The dimensions and design of the entire monument were precisely dependent on the dimensions of the massive obelisk which was to be imported from Heliopolis in Egypt only a year or more later (12 or 11 BC) on a ship to be especially constructed for the purpose.[58] Moreover, both the obelisk and the Ara Pacis Augustae would be related, with powerful astrological symbolism and with some degree of precision, to the Mausoleum which had been started long before, in 28 BC, and perhaps also to the Ustrinum.[59] The planning of the Ara Pacis and of the Horologium must have been well advanced by 4 July 13 BC, since the size and orientation of the Ara would be determined by the religious proceedings which took place on that day; and, once the site of the Ara Pacis had been fixed, there would be only one place

---

[56] See Welin (1939), 509–10; Torelli (1982), 35.

[57] Cf. Vitruv. 4. 8. 7–9. 1, where *constitutio arae* denotes the layout or design of an altar and where the importance of advance planning to achieve the required results is emphasized.

[58] For the Ara Pacis and the Horologium see Buchner (1982; 1988); Rakob (1987). For the transportation of the obelisk see Buchner (1982), 48–9. Buchner calculates that the original overall height of the gnomon (the sundial's pointer) was 100 Roman feet. The pavement area on which the sundial was marked out and on which the Ara Pacis stood covered some 12,000 square metres.

[59] It is not clear when the Ustrinum was marked out. On the site of the Ustrinum see Strabo 5. 3. 8; Jolivet (1989), 94–6; Patterson (1992), 199. For the Mausoleum see Kraft (1967); von Hesberg (1988). Schütz (1990) raises some doubts about the precision of Buchner's calculations. Schutz wrongly dismisses Buchner's interpretation of Augustus' horoscope (446–9): see Brind'amour (1983), 62–76. Buchner's main arguments seem to stand, and the excavations seem to have confirmed the all-important point that the Ara Pacis was designed and constructed as a part of the Horologium complex: see Buchner (1982), 73–4. What will have determined the symbolic value of the complex is not just mathematical precision but the means used to guide the viewer's sight-lines. For example, it would be helpful to know if the obelisks near the Mausoleum, first mentioned by Ammianus Marcellinus (17. 4. 16), were part of the original design (so Zanker 1988: 76) or added at the time the Horologium was constructed (so von Hesberg 1988: 246) or later additions (so Buchner 1982: 66). I am grateful to Prof. Snodgrass for discussing these matters with me.

that the obelisk could go.[60] The offer of alternative honours, which Dio (54. 25. 3) tells us were solicited from Cornelius Balbus by Tiberius, can only have been part of a carefully orchestrated ritual of refusal such as regularly accompanied the granting of honours.[61] Yet it is clear from the way that Augustus records the Ara Pacis in the *Res Gestae* (12. 2) that it was important to him that the honour should be seen as coming from the senate. Moreover, since there is no sign that Balbus was colluding with Tiberius, it must be supposed that the plans were known only to the very close friends of Augustus.[62] For, whoever proposed the Ara Pacis Augustae in the senate, the proposal must have come directly or indirectly from Augustus.[63] At all events, it is quite impossible to believe that the senate designed the Ara Pacis or the Horologium complex.[64] The entire episode brilliantly illuminates the degree of careful planning and the massive effort of coordination that could, at least on some occasions, go into the construction of the image of Augustus. It has long been noticed that *Odes* 4 reflects the imagery and ideology of the Ara Pacis Augustae and of public inscriptions.[65] The image of Augustus presented by both the Horologium complex and *Odes* 4 is significantly different in emphasis from that familiar in the 20s BC. Given Horace's position within the circle of the *amici Caesaris* and the chronology of *Odes* 4, this cannot be considered a matter of chance or coincidence. Both Horace and the designer of the Horologium are,

[60] So, tentatively, Buchner (1982), 48, but rightly emphasized by Bowersock (1990), 383–4.

[61] See Wallace-Hadrill (1982), 36–7.

[62] On the role of the senate see Brunt (1984), 437–8.

[63] The names of Iullus Antonius (praetor 13 BC) or Paullus Fabius Maximus (cos. 11 BC) suggest themselves: the latter was responsible for the suggestion, in language that would suit a proposal for the Ara Pacis and the Horologium, that the cities of Asia should start their new year from Augustus' birthday: see Ehrenberg and Jones (1976), 81–4 Nos. 98, 98a.

[64] Contrast Zanker (1988), 123: 'The sacrificial procession on the ara Pacis is a carefully planned reflection of the renewed Republic, designed not by order of Augustus himself, it is important to remember, but of the Senate, to honour itself and the state.' See also Zanker (1988), 3, 107, 283, 291, 338, quoted with approval by Wallace-Hadrill (1989b), 159–60, who argues that Zanker's model is applicable to poetry.

[65] For the Ara Pacis see e.g. Benario (1960); Putnam (1986), 327–9. For the inscriptions see Kiessling and Heinze (1914–30), *Odes* and *Epodes* volume (1), 416; Pasquali (1966), 178–81.

in their very different media, consciously promoting a carefully considered new image.

Augustus had accepted his tenth salutation as *imperator* for the victories won by Tiberius and Drusus over the Vindelici.[66] His return retained something of a triumphal quality, and Dio informs us that the *depositio lauri* in the temple of Jupiter Capitolinus was part of the ceremonial.[67] Among his many honours, Augustus records only the total number of *supplicationes*,[68] but the sheer number of *supplicationes* to be accounted for make it quite certain that one was voted in 13 BC.[69] The length of the *supplicatio* on this occasion is not known, but the celebrations probably went on over a couple of weeks and so must have overlapped with the Ludi Apollinares, which ran from 6 to 13 July, and perhaps even the Ludi Victoriae Caesaris (20–30 July).[70] The whole of the summer would be dominated by the celebration of major events in Augustus' career, culminating in the celebration of his birthday on 23 September.[71] Iullus Antonius, honoured in *Odes* 4.2 and consul in 10 BC, was praetor in 13 BC and organized the celebration of this birthday on an especially lavish scale in this year.[72] This was a special year for Augustus, as he then reached his fiftieth birthday.[73] No less importantly, it was the thirtieth anniversary of his *dies imperii* (7 January 43 BC, 'qua die primum imperium orbis auspicatus est' ['on which day he first inaugurated his rule of the world']: *CIL* xii. 4333 = 100.25 Ehrenberg and Jones), of his first

[66] See Barnes (1974), 22; and for the significance of the fact that the *acclamatio* as *imperator x* is the first *acclamatio* to appear on coins see Kraft (1978), 323–6.

[67] Dio 54. 25. 4 with *RG* 4. 1. Dio's account is plausible enough on this point, but the address to the people on the Palatium may be misplaced, if it took place at all and is not just part of Dio's fantasy about Augustus dashing home to his bed.

[68] *RG* 4. 2. On the *supplicatio* see Freyburger (1978); Billows (1993).

[69] Note also that the phrase *ob res ... prospere gestas* is precisely echoed in his own account of his return from Gaul (*RG* 12. 2).

[70] See Degrassi (1963), 477–9, 485–6.

[71] See Degrassi (1963), 489, 493–4, 496, 497, 499, 504, 505, 505–6, 512.

[72] See Dio 54. 26. 1 with Rich (1990), 204 and, for Iullus Antonius, Plut. *Ant.* 37. Celebrations for Augustus' birthday had been voted as an honour in 29 BC (Dio 51. 19. 2; *ILS* 112), but this is the first time there is mention of a public banquet which was decreed *senatus consulto* and therefore presumably not part of the honour voted earlier: compare and contrast Weinstock (1971), 209.

[73] See Buchner (1988), 72 n. 7. Horace emphasizes his own fiftieth birthday at *Odes* 4. 1. 6.

acclamatio as *imperator* (16 April 43 BC), and of his first consulship (19 August 43 BC).[74]

Certain themes, which can easily be seen in the Ara Pacis and the Horologium, were no doubt reiterated with subtle variations throughout the celebrations that dominated the summer of his return in 13 BC. Although the whole complex was in one sense a substitute for a triumphal monument, the emphasis was on *pax victoriis parta* rather than simply upon *victoriae*.[75] And there was an equal emphasis on Augustus as a man of destiny whose deeds had already guaranteed his apotheosis.[76] On the autumnal equinox, Augustus' birthday, the obelisk, which commemorated the conquest of Alexandria on 1 August 30 BC,[77] cast its shadow along the equinoctial line towards the centre of the Ara Pacis Augustae, voted to commemorate Augustus' safe return from the conquest of the Vindelici on 1 August 15 BC.[78] In one of the poems requested by Augustus before his return (*Odes* 4. 14. 35–40) Horace emphasizes the link between the two events, and so provides important confirmation that trouble had been taken to link them before Augustus had returned to Rome: whoever decided that 1 August 15 BC constituted the day of victory over the Vindelici did so to create the parallel.

After entering the city, Augustus attended the senate. His throat was sore, presumably from days and weeks of exchanging welcomes and greetings, as it had been in 29 BC when he rested at Atella before entering the city. In 13 BC the account of his achievements and his

---

[74] See Degrassi (1963), 392, 442, 499.

[75] See Torelli (1982), 28–9, 32–3; Settis (1988), 416–24. For the parallelism between the Ara Pacis and the Ara Fortunae Reducis see *RG* 11–12 with Welin (1939), 504–10; Torelli (1982), 27–33. For *Pax* see esp. Weinstock (1960), 44–50.

[76] There is an interesting parallel in Tib. 1. 7, where Messalla's triumph is seen as the fulfilment of his personal destiny and the emphasis is upon the peaceful consequences of victory.

[77] *CIL* v. 701–2 = *ILS* 91. 'Imp. Caesar Divi f. Augustus . . . Aegupto in potestatem populi Romani redacta Soli donum dedit.' Cf. Macr. *Sat.* 1. 12. 35 (quoting the *senatus consultum*) 'cum Aegyptus hoc mense in potestatem populi Romani redacta sit finisque hoc mense bellis civilibus impositus sit . . .'; *Fast. Praen.* 'Feriae ex s.c, quod eo die Imp. Caesar Augustus rem publicam tristissimo periculo liberavit'; Degrassi (1963), 489. Ovid (*Fasti* 1. 711–14) makes the link with Actium rather than the fall of Alexandria: 'frondibus Actiacis comptos redimita capillos, | Pax, ades et toto mitis in orbe mane . . .'

[78] See Buchner (1982), 36, 72; (1988), 242.

proposals for reforming the terms of service in the army had to be read out by a quaestor.[79] The celebrations of Augustus' return seem to have culminated in the theatre.[80] This was a standard feature of the *adventus,* as it gave the people the best opportunity of seeing their leader.[81] It is likely, in spite of the order of Dio's narrative, that the games held in honour of Augustus' return by the consuls, Tiberius and P. Quinctilius Varus, followed quite closely on the *depositio lauri* in the temple of Jupiter Optimus Maximus on the Capitol.[82] The dominant theme, the interdependence of the *salus* of the *res publica* and the *salus* of Augustus, is reflected in the coin legends of 16 BC.[83] One bears on the obverse a bust of Augustus with the abbreviated inscription reflecting the language of a senatorial decree—'Senatus consulto ob rempublicam cum salute imperatoris Caesaris Augusti conservatam' ('By senatorial decree for having preserved the state along with the personal safety of Imperator Caesar Augustus')—and on the reverse an image of Mars with the inscription 'senatus populusque Romanus vota publica suscepta pro salute et reditu Augusti' ('SPQR decree public thanks for the secure return of Augustus'). Another has on the obverse an oak wreath, symbolizing his role as saviour of citizens, and the inscription 'Iovi Optimo Maximo senatus populusque Romanus vota publica suscepta pro salute imperatoris Caesaris quod per eum res publica in ampliore atque tranquilliore

[79] See Dio 54. 25. 5–6; Donat. *Vit. Verg.* 95 Hardie; cf. Suet. *Aug.* 84.

[80] Whether the *Lusus Troiae* was also staged to mark this return, as it had been in 29 BC for the dedication of the temple of Divus Iulius (Dio 51. 22. 4), is unfortunately unclear, since Dio (54. 26. 1) associates it with the dedication of the theatre of Marcellus, which is dated more authoritatively by Pliny (*NH* 8. 65) to 7 May 11 BC. The *Lusus* may have taken place as stated, even if Dio is indeed wrong about the dedication. It is a matter of controversy whether the children in eastern dress depicted on the Ara Pacis are Gaius and Lucius dressed for the *Lusus Troiae* or Parthian hostages: see Torelli (1982), 48; Syme (1989), 119–20; Rose (1990).

[81] See Schuberth (1968), 22–5; MacCormack (1972), 723–4; Halfmann (1986), 118–20.

[82] See *ILS* 88: 'P. Quinctilius Sex f. Varus ⌈pontifex?⌉ cos. ludos votivos pro reditu imp. Caesaris divi f. Augusti Iovi optimo maximo fecit cum Ti. Claudio Nerone conlega ex s.c.'

[83] For the coins see Sutherland (1984), 68 Nos. 351–3, 356–8; Trillmich (1988), 519–20. Wallace-Hadrill (1986), 78 n. 73 makes the attractive suggestion that COMM CONS, inscribed within a *cippus* on the reverse of 357 and 358 (Sutherland) should be read as *communi conservatori* rather than *communi consensu.* This seems to suit the imagery on the obverse of both coins: contrast Trillmich (1988), 488, 519.

statu est' ('to Jupiter Optimus Maximus the SPQR decrees the thanksgivings at public expense which had been promised for the personal safety of Imperator Caesar because through him the state is in an expanded and more peaceful condition'), a significant modification of the traditional prayer for the *salus* of the *res publica* (Valerius Maximus 4. 1. 10): 'di immortales ut populi Romani res meliores amplioresque facerent rogabantur' ('the immortal gods were asked to make the state of the Roman people better and greater.')[84]

Enough has been said to indicate the festive and ceremonial nature of the welcome which had been so carefully prepared for Augustus' return. Everything possible was done to stimulate a feeling of well-being and rejoicing. The whole focus was on Augustus as the saviour of the *res publica*, as the leader whose *pietas* guaranteed victories in wars fought under his *auspicia*, whose victories brought the blessings and bounty of Pax Augusta for the benefit of all, and on whose *salus* their continuation depended.

4. *MODULATA CARMINA* AND CHORAL PERFORMANCE

Odes 4 was intended to be performed as part of the celebrations of Augustus' return. When he had returned from the east in 29 BC, Maecenas and Virgil had met him at Atella near Naples and together read the *Georgics* to him. This was clearly a private occasion.[85] L. Varius Rufus' *Thyestes* was performed as a part of the triumphal celebrations.[86] Although there is no direct evidence about the way in which *Odes* 4 was presented or the nature of the occasion, there is no

[84] There is a similar set of concerns evident in the dedication of statues in 10 BC to Concordia, Salus Publica, and Pax: Ov. *Fasti* 3. 881–2; Dio 54. 35. 2; Weinstock (1960), 49; Degrassi (1963), 433; Rich (1990), 215.

[85] Donat. *Vit. Verg.* 93–7 Hardie. In this way the *Georgics* were presented as a joint gift from the poet and his patron.

[86] See White (1993), 276 n. 22. The appropriateness of relaxing after the rigours of a military campaign was so well established that Horace could represent it figuratively in *Odes* 3. 4. 37–40; cf. Tib. 2. 5. 1–10.

doubt that music and song played an important part in the ceremonial of *adventus*.[87]

Suetonius is quite explicit about the nature of the welcome received by Augustus: 'omnes ordines [Augustum] revertentem ex provincia non solum faustis ominibus, sed et modulatis carminibus prosequebantur' ('all the orders accompanied him as he returned from abroad not only with propitious omens but also the playing of songs', *Augustus* 57. 2). What Suetonius means by *omina fausta* is revealed by the incident he relates at *Augustus* 98. 2:[88] 'As he sailed by the gulf of Puteoli, it happened that passengers and crew from a ship arrived from Alexandria, all dressed in white togas, wearing garlands and carrying incense, lavished on him words of good omen and high praise (saying that) it was through him they lived, through him they sailed and through him they enjoyed freedom and fortune. Thoroughly delighted at this, he distributed four hundred gold pieces to each of his companions [etc.]'. Such *omina fausta* are the impromptu reaction of ordinary people but could on occasion involve improvised chanting.[89] It is clear that the *modulata carmina* are much more elaborate and well prepared and that they constitute a significant and notable honour, apparently modelled on those given to earlier *triumphatores*.[90] They are at least accompanied by music, presumably played on *tibiae*.[91] But the best clue to what might have been involved is Suetonius' account of the honours devised for Caligula by the senate, which obviously had an eye on those previously paid to Julius Caesar and to Augustus: 'quas ob res inter reliquos honores decretus

---

[87] See Peterson (1930), 683–98; Alföldi (1970), 79–84; Wille (1967), 139; Schuberth (1968), 18–39; Wille (1977), 123–4; Fishwick (1991), 568–71.

[88] For comment and bibliography see Fishwick (1987), 92 n. 56; (1991), 481, 532, 569.

[89] As when the people prematurely celebrated what they thought was the recovery of Germanicus: Suet. *Cal.* 6. 1 *undique concinentium:* '*salva Roma, salva patria, salvus est Germanicus*'. Cf. Sen. *Apocol.* 13 (a parodic *adventus*), and see further Alföldi (1970), 84–8; Roueché (1984), 181–90.

[90] For the distinction cf. Livy 7. 2. 6–7. For a similar triumphal honour granted to Camillus see Dio fr. 23 = Zonar. 7. 21. 11; and for one to Duilius see *CIL* vi. 31611; Cic. *Cato* 13. 44; Florus 1. 18. 10. [2. 2]; [Aur. Vict.] *Viri ill.* 38. 4; Val. Max. 3. 6. 4; Schuberth (1968), 26–7; Wille (1967), 139; (1977), 75; Versnel (1970), 95–6.

[91] For the use of the *tibia* in the *ovatio* rather than the *tuba* see Plut. *Marc.* 22. 6–7. The same reasoning would hold good for the procession accompanying the *depositio lauri*.

est ei clipeus aureus, quem quotannis certo die collegia sacerdotum in Capitolium ferrent, senatu prosequente nobilibusque pueris ac puellis carmine modulato laudes virtutum eius canentibus. decretum autem ut dies, quo cepisset imperium, Parilia vocaretur, velut argumentum rursus conditae urbis' ('On account of these acts, among other honours a golden shield was decreed for him, which the colleges of priests were to carry every year on the appointed day to the Capitol, with senate as escort and with boys and girls of noble birth singing the praises of his virtues in a *carmen modulatum* (a choral hymn?). It was also decreed that the day on which he began his rule should be called the Parilia, as a sign that the city had been founded anew', *Caligula* 16. 4).[92]

At the very least it seems inescapable that *Odes* 4. 5 and others in the same book are intended to evoke the *carmina* that formed a part of such ceremonies. If it is assumed, with the majority of Horatian scholars, that Horace's poems were written to be read or recited and not to be sung either by a solo performer or by a chorus, then it could be argued that this is just part of the dramatic fiction of the poem. But it is difficult to see why one should proceed from this assumption.[93] The ancient view was that lyric poetry was always written with musical accompaniment and choral performance in mind, even if it was sometimes read by lamplight by the scholar/poet or declaimed at a *recitatio*.[94] So Pliny, in justifying the recitation of genres not intended for recitation, declares: 'Why should they concede (if they do) that history should be recited, which is not composed for show but for credibility and for truth? Why should tragedy, which calls not for an auditorium but for a stage and actors? Why should lyric, which calls not for someone to read it out but for a chorus and a lyre? But the recitation of all these has now become accepted as standard practice', *Ep.* 7. 17. 3.[95]

---

[92] Cf. Dio 59. 7. 1; Apul. *Met.* 11. 9.

[93] Murray (1985), 43 = (1993), 94: 'We must not of course enquire how far the poetry of Horace was actually performed within the symposium.' Why not?

[94] See Wille (1967), 234–53 (bibliography: 235 n. 271); (1977), 129–31 (bibliography: 10, 44). Wille collects the evidence, which he hopes will speak for itself, but his presentation of the case is not discriminating. See also Cairns (1984), 149–54; Wiseman (1985), 98–9, 198–206, who have also argued for choral performance.

[95] See also Quint. *Inst.* 1. 10. 20; Cic. *Or.* 55. 183, who says of the language of lyric poetry that *cantu spoliaveris, nuda paene remanet oratio.* The language of Horace is

The only poem of Horace for which we do have unequivocal evidence concerning the nature of the performance is the *Carmen Saeculare*:

When the sacrifice has been completed, 27 boys duly appointed to the task and the same number of girls, with both parents alive, sang the song [on the Palatine] and in the same way on the Capitoline. Q. Horatius Flaccus composed the song. (*ILS* 5050. 147–9)

There is no reason to assume that this is exceptional.[96] The evidence of the *Odes* themselves is explicit enough as long as we do not dismiss it all as figurative. It is perhaps time to take Horace, e.g. at *Odes* 4. 15. 25–32, as meaning what he says:

> nosque et profestis lucibus et sacris
> inter iocosi munera Liberi
>   cum prole matronisque nostris
>   rite deos prius adprecati
>
> virtute functos more patrum duces
> Lydis remixto carmine tibiis
>   Troiamque et Anchisen et almae
>   progeniem Veneris canemus.

And we, on work days and holidays, among the gifts of playful Liber with our offspring and wives, after duly praying to the gods, shall sing in song accompanied by the Lydian reed-pipes, in the manner of our ancestors, of leaders who had lived like real men, of Troy and Anchises and the offspring of nurturing Venus.

This would, after all, only be another case of the Augustans reviving and modernizing what they believed to be an ancient custom: '(sic aderant etiam) in conviviis pueri modesti ut cantarent carmina antiqua, in quibus laudes erant maiorum et assa voce et cum tibicine' ('There were even at parties modest boys to sing ancient songs, in

notoriously prosaic: see Axelson (1945), 98–113 and, for *Odes* 4. 5, Radke (1964), 74–5. Although not all of their analyses are valid, it is worth noting that the language of lyric was thought to be characteristically 'prosaic' and could afford to be because it was intended to be accompanied by music.

[96] It is sometimes said that the metrical qualities of Horace's verse preclude the possibility of actual performance: e.g. Murray (1985), 43 = (1993), 94. But the metre of the *Carmen Saeculare* is not distinguishable from that of other poems in the Sapphic stanza, and it was undeniably set to music and performed by a chorus.

which there were praises of ancestors, both with unaccompanied voice and accompanied by the player of a reed-pipe. Varro, *De vita populi Romani* fr. 84 Riposati).[97]

One feature which distinguishes *Odes* 4 from *Odes* 1–3 is the prominence of Pindar as a model, particularly for the more elevated poems.[98] Although there is a lively current debate about the nature of Pindaric lyric and whether it is in fact to be conceived of as choral poetry, there is no doubt that Hellenistic commentators generally assume that the speaker of a Pindaric poem is a chorus.[99] It is therefore reasonable to infer that Horace shared this view of the nature of Pindaric poetry and that when he is writing a Pindaric poem we are supposed to think of the speaker as a chorus. In the *Carmen Saeculare* the choric identity of the speaker is indicated in the text itself and confirmed by the inscriptional evidence cited above.[100] But Horace will have been well aware that many poems which were supposed to be performed by a chorus and in which the speaker was understood to be a chorus do not have the speaker explicitly identified as such in the text.[101]

If *Odes* 4. 5 does not seem as obviously Pindaric as 4. 4 or 4. 14, that is because the chance survival of the *Epinicians* gives us an excessively limited sense of what Pindaric poetry was like.[102] Pindar wrote poems in many genres, including paeans and prosodia or processionals which were performed as part of the Greek counterpart to the *adventus*. These genres continued long after

[97] See also Cic. *Brut.* 75; *Tusc. Disp.* 4. 2; Val. Max. 2. 1. 9; Quint. *Inst.* 1. 10. 20. See Dahlmann (1958), 353–5; Murray (1985), 40–4 = (1993), 91–5; Wiseman (1989), 134. For discussion of Murray (1985), 40–4 = (1993), 91–5; for discussion of *carmina convivalia* see Zorzetti (1990), with bibliography.

[98] See Highbarger (1935).

[99] Those contesting the general view that Pindaric poems are written for choric performance are Davies (1988); Lekowitz (1988); Heath (1988); Heath and Lekowitz (1991). The conventional position is staunchly defended by Bremer (1990); Burnett (1989); and Carey (1989; 1991). See also Cairns (1992), 10–16. For the Hellenistic view see Carey (1989), 558–9.

[100] *Carm. Saec.* 74–6 'spem bonam certamque domum reporto, | doctus et Phoebi chorus et Dianae | dicere laudes.'

[101] A very good case can be made for identifying the speaker in some of Horace's earliest Pindaricizing odes as a chorus: see Cairns (1971a, b).

[102] Bergson (1970), 359–62 recognizes the Hellenistic and rhetorical background but argues for direct influence of Pind. *Pyth.* 8. 96–7 on 4. 5. 7–8.

Pindar, although he no doubt remained the model for later writers.[103]

Choral performances also played an important part in the cultural life of Augustan Rome. In particular, the pantomime, in which a solo mime was accompanied by instrumental music and a chorus, reached new heights of sophistication during the Augustan period.[104] On appropriate occasions these performances would reflect current interests and concerns, as is revealed in an anecdote told by Phaedrus concerning a *tibicen* called Princeps who regularly accompanied Bathyllus. Phaedrus refers to a performance which was intended as an *honos divinae domus* in which

> tunc chorus ignotum [sc. Principi] modo reducto canticum
> insonuit, cuius haec fuit sententia:
> 'laetare, incolumis Roma, salvo principe!'
> in plausus consurrectum est.   (5. 7. 25–8)

Then the chorus struck up a song unknown to the recently returned (i.e. the *tibicen* Princeps), the theme of which was: 'Rejoice, Rome safe and sound, because your princeps (i.e. the emperor) is safe!' They rose to their feet in applause.

It is hardly necessary to emphasize the similarity of the *sententia* of this *canticum* and that of *Odes* 4. 5. Although Pliny claims to have disapproved, he makes it clear in his panegyric for Trajan that songs and performances of this type became frequent and ever more elaborate in the first century AD.[105] One of the main occasions when such performances will have been commonplace is the *reditus* or *adventus* of the emperor. There were many opportunities for the performance of poems from *Odes* 4 on the return of Augustus, both private and public. There is no good reason to think that they were not taken.[106]

---

[103] There is a particularly interesting account of the performance of these types of poem in the context of an *adventus* of Demetrius Poliorcetes in Athen. 6. 62 Kaibel. It is undistinguished verse, but for the potential of the genre see Bacch. *Paeans* fr. 4. 61–80 and compare Melinno's *Hymn to Rome* and the *Paean* to Flaminius.

[104] One of those credited with these developments is Bathyllus of Alexandria, a protégé of Maecenas. See Luc. *Salt*. 34; Athen. 1. 20 D-F.

[105] Plin. *Pan*. 54. 1–2; Suet. *Dom*. 4.

[106] Private occasions: Suet. *Aug*. 74, 89. 3. Public occasions: *Ludi votivi*—Dio 54. 27. 1; *ILS* 88; theatre of Marcellus—Dio 54. 26. 1; Ludi Apollinares (6–13 July)—Degrassi (1963), 477–9.

5. THE POEM[107]

The opening stanza provides a clear indication of the addressee, the
speaker, genre, and dramatic setting. The most difficult to identify for
the modern reader is the speaker. There is a deep-seated assumption
that the speaker of a lyric poem is the author himself. As we have
seen, this is at odds with the general assumption in antiquity that a
lyric poem is intended to be sung by a chorus. The question therefore
needs careful consideration. In his prescription for the kletic speech
Menander Rhetor emphasizes the need for the speaker to identify
himself and say why he has been chosen by the polis to represent it.[108]
Nothing so crude is to be expected in a Horatian poem. But the
reader surely expects to be able to infer the answers to these natural
questions, however minimal and oblique the clues may be. Of course,
Q. Horatius Flaccus is the author of the poem and we are entitled to
ask what he intended to communicate by writing it. But he does not
speak here as the *amicus Caesaris* that he was.[109] Nothing could be
further from the tones of this poem than the tones appropriate to
that relationship, which are so evident in the snippets of correspondence preserved by Suetonius in his *Life of Horace*. Nor is it adequate
to say that Horace is simply playing a role as a representative of the
state, as he does, for example, in *Epode* 16 or *Odes* 3.14, in both of
which the individuality of the speaker is marked.[110] The contrast
with the latter poem is especially striking in view of the similarity of
theme and situation.[111]

In *Odes* 4. 5, although everything underlines the representative
nature of the speaker, nothing identifies the speaker with the poet.

---

[107] For the detailed analysis that follows the reader may find it helpful to read the
conclusion of the article in advance.

[108] Men. Rhet. 424. 4–6.

[109] Contrast Fraenkel (1957), 440: 'While he [Augustus] was still absent, Horace
wrote the ode (and in all probability sent a copy of it to Augustus) . . . He, like many
others, felt deep anxiety for the safe return of the Princeps, and . . . he now, unasked
and unprompted, endeavoured to express his own feelings and those of his fellow
citizens.' Cf. e.g. Dahlmann (1958), 346–7.

[110] See esp. *Epod.* 16. 66 *Vate me*; *Odes* 3. 14. 27–8 *non ego hoc ferrem calidus
iuventa | consule Planco.*

[111] For Augustus' *adventus* in 24 BC as the occasion of *Odes* 3. 14 see Nisbet (1983), 109.

In the only first-person reference in the poem (37–8 ' "longas o utinam, dux bone, ferias | praestes Hesperiae" dicimus', 'We say "O kindly leader, bring us the long, long-awaited festivities to Hesperia" '), the *nos* implied in *dicimus* is defined within the direct speech by *Hesperia* and the speaker is simply identified as representative of the *populus Romanus*. That is a very different thing from having Horace present an individualized version of himself as representative of the *populus Romanus*. It is, however, the opening stanza which most clearly insists on the representative nature of the speaker. There the speaker is expressing the feelings of sadness caused by the absence of Augustus. The emotion gains colour from the assertion that Augustus had promised an early return, and the solemnity of that promise is stressed by reference to the fact that it had been made *patrum sancto concilio*. The point, however is not really to offer a reprimand or rebuke to Augustus, much less to accuse him of having broken his word.[112] Rather the accusation here is intended to convey the emotional state of the speaker.[113] In such a context we expect the speaker to say something along the lines of 'I am very upset at your long absence, especially as you promised me a speedy return.'[114] In view of the ancient assumption that lyric poetry was normally intended to be performed by a chorus, the most natural inference to draw is that the speaker in this poem is a chorus which represents *senatus populusque Romanus*.

The speaker is calling upon the absent addressee to return. The poem is thus identified from the start as a *klētikon* and the conventions of this genre are evoked to provide one of the main contexts which will determine the relevant implications of the details of this utterance and their significance.[115] A Roman audience would have supplied the relevant framework almost subconsciously from its familiarity with literary examples and models, its rhetorical

---

[112] Contrast Radke (1964), 63; Syndikus (1973), 332.

[113] See e.g. Men. Rhet. 396. 3–32.

[114] Cf. Hor. *Ep.* 1. 7. 1–2 'quinque dies tibi pollicitus me rure futurum | Sextilem totum mendax desideror'; Ov. *Her.* 2. 1–2 and 23–4 'hospita, Demophoon, tua te Rhodopeia Phyllis | ultra promissum tempus abesse queror... at tu lentus abes; nec te iurata reducunt | numina, nec nostro motus amore redis.'

[115] For the *klētikon* see Giangrande (1971), 91–2; Cairns (1972), 114; Du Quesnay (1981), 90–7 with nn. 339–42.

education, and the experience of the ceremonial connected with the constant pattern of visits, arrivals, and departures which formed such an important part of the highly personalized socio-political life of antiquity. The modern reader can obtain a good idea of what those expectations might have been from a study of other examples of the genre and from texts such as Menander Rhetor's prescriptions for speeches of invitation (*klētikon*), welcome (*prosphōnētikon*), and arrival (*epibatērion*). It has long been recognized that the poem has certain hymnic features, and it may seem tempting to go further and classify the poem as a ὕμνος κλητικός (kletic hymn).[116] But, as we shall see, the basic pattern adhered to is that of the *klētikon* addressed to a ruler rather than to a god. The most important hymnic feature of the poem is that the speaker is not identified as part of an embassy but is represented as addressing an absent addressee from afar.[117] But it seems best to think of Horace as deliberately making use of the ambivalent and ambiguous area between two closely related genres in order to convey the ambivalent and ambiguous status of Augustus between the human and divine.

The primary concern of the speaker in these opening lines is to convince the addressee that he is missed and that he should return home. The sense of longing is well conveyed by the juxtaposition of the phrase *nimium diu* ('too long') with *maturum reditum* ('swift return'), which is given emphasis through alliteration and a note of urgency by being picked up by the imperative, *redi* ('return'). The request is grounded in the addressee's promise to the senate, which is given weight and solemnity by the intricate pattern of alliteration and assonance. The basic idea here is a commonplace of the *klētikon*, as we can see from Menander, who describes the city as 'having long desired to partake of your great qualities every day' (424. 6–8) and then urges the addressee: 'Hurry quickly with good omens in answer

---

[116] See Kiessling and Heinze (1914–30) *Odes* and *Epodes* volume (1), 413; Syndikus (1973), 331. Such a classification would have the advantage of clarifying the identity of the speaker, for hymns are normally thought of as being choric.

[117] Contrast Porphyrio on 4. 5. 1: 'populi ac senatus legationibus missis reditum eius precatum'; ps.-Acro on 4. 5. 1: 'de Augusto scribitur, qui in transmarinis provinciis diu residens senatus ac populi precibus legatione missa reditum suum promittens immorabatur'. The embassy they envisage derives from their recognition of the genre of the poem as a *klētikon* (cf. Men. Rhet. 424. 4–6) rather than displaced historical information (cf. Dio 54. 6. 2–3; 54. 10. 2).

to the city's summons, make haste' (425. 17–19). It is perhaps significant that Menander does not suggest that the speaker should recall the addressee's promise to return, even though such promises were a commonplace in the speeches of departure (the *syntaktikon*) and the wish for a swift return equally a commonplace of the send-off speech (the *propemptikon*).[118] Augustus may or may not have made such a promise on the occasion of his departure but Horace's decision to represent him as having done so is plausible and interesting,[119] especially in view of the elevated and honorific language used to describe the senate.[120]

At the time of his departure Augustus' relations with the senate were in fact under some strain.[121] The marriage legislation of 18 BC had provoked opposition, in spite of the fact that it was in these laws that the senators were first distinguished from equestrians in a move designed to enhance the dignity and authority of the senate. Similarly, the review of the membership of the senate was intended to reduce the numbers further towards the ancient 'ideal' of three hundred and so strengthen the dignity and authority of those that remained. Although in the end Augustus reduced it only to six hundred, this reform too had caused resentment, perhaps because there was such emphasis on removing those who were immoral and irresponsible as well as those insufficiently wealthy. Dio suggests that the invasion of Gaul by the Sugambri provided a welcome excuse for Augustus to leave Rome and allow time for the senate to come to terms with his reforms. Whatever the real reasons, morale among senators was low and there had been difficulties in recruiting new

[118] See Men. Rhet. 431.28 and 433.13 (*syntaktikon*), and cf. e.g. Livy 44. 22. 17 'sacrificio rite perpetrato protinus inde et consul et praetor Cn. Octavius in Macedoniam profecti sunt. traditum memoriae est maiore quam solita frequentia prosequentium consulem celebratum, ac prope certa spe ominatos esse homines, finem esse Macedonico bello maturumque reditum cum egregio triumpho consulis fore.'

[119] Suetonius at *Aug.* 92. 1 may be generalizing from a specific incident: 'si terra marive ingrediente se longinquam profectionem forte rorasset, [*sc.* id observabat] ut laetum maturique et prosperi reditus.'

[120] The phrase *patrum sancto concilio* is unique but an elevated variation on *sanctus senatus*, for which see Enn. *Ann.* 272 with Skutsch (1985), 455.

[121] See *RG* 8. 2; Suet. *Aug.* 35–7; Dio 54. 13–17. 3, 26.3–9, 35. 1 with Rich (1990) for references to some earlier discussions; Raaflaub and Samons (1990), 433–5; Chastagnol (1992), 31–56. On the senate under Augustus see Talbert (1984b); Brunt (1984).

senators during the period of Augustus' absence. It was a problem that was still very much alive at the time of his return in 13 BC, and one to which he then gave his urgent attention. Horace represents the relationship with great tact. He emphasizes precisely the view of the standing of the senate that Augustus' reforms were designed to safeguard and perpetuate. He also includes the senators implicitly in the feelings of longing for Augustus' return which would turn to joy when he did. In other words, Horace's poem works, like many of the celebrations devised for the *reditus*, to shape and orchestrate the feelings of both the senate and the people towards Augustus.

Although the addressee is not named until line 16, his identity is clear from the start. *Divis orte bonis* ('born of the good gods') is a poetic elaboration of the patronymic of Imperator Caesar Divi Filius Augustus.[122] The *divi boni* include Apollo, Jupiter, Venus, and Mars as well as the deified ancestors, Aeneas, Romulus, and Divus Iulius.[123] While it is the descent from Aeneas which is emphasized in 4. 6 and 4. 15, here it is Romulus and Divus Iulius: the line is framed by *divis* and *Romulae*.[124] The phrases *Divis orte* and *Romulae custos gentis* ('guardian of Romulus' people') pointedly allude to Ennius' description of Romulus as *patriae custos* and *sanguen dis oriundum* ('guardian of the fatherland' and '[carrier of a] blood-line sprung from the gods', *Annales* 107–8, Skutsch). The word *custos* was never a formal title but was used informally, especially of those who had secured the frontiers by military expeditions.[125] Its occurrence at *Odes* 4. 15. 17 (*custode rerum Caesare*, 'with Caesar as guardian of affairs') strongly suggests that it had especial currency at this time. It is therefore no surprise to find one of its rare semi-official uses in the *Feriale Cumanum* in connection with the *dedicatio* of the Ara Pacis: 'eo die

---

[122] This is standard Horatian usage: see *Sat.* 1. 5. 55; 1. 6. 10, 21; *Odes* 3. 6. 33; 4. 6. 31–2. See Brink (1982), 56: '*orior*, often in elevated style... indicates a person's provenance (as *diuis orte bonis*)'. Fraenkel (1957), 440 n. 2 is a very revealing piece of special pleading. See also Radke (1964), 59–60: Syndikus (1973), 332.

[123] At this time there is no distinction between *divus* and *deus*: see *Odes* 4. 6. 1–2, *Dive... Phoebe. Boni* is a standard epithet for *dei* (Appel 1909: 99; Fraenkel 1957: 440–1), perhaps with a view to the supposed etymology of both words: *quod beant, hoc est beatos faciunt* (Ulp. *dig.* 50. 16. 49); *deus dictus... quia omnia commoda hominibus dat* (Paul. Fest. 71). See Maltby (1991), 83, 185, 193.

[124] For *Romulae gentis* see *Carm. Saec.* 47.

[125] See Béranger (1953), 183–5; Syndikus (1973), 332–3; Woodman (1977), 136–7.

ara Pacis Aug. dedicata est, supplicatio Imperio Caesaris Augusti custodis imperi Romanorum ...' ('on that day the altar of Augustan Peace was dedicated, a thanksgiving [was offered] to the rule of Caesar Augustus, the guardian of the Romans' empire').[126] The adjective *bonis* is picked up and intensified by *optime* in the familiar encomiastic convention whereby descendants surpass the achievements of their ancestors.[127] The idea is well illustrated at Ovid, *Metamorphoses* 15. 50–1, where Divus Iulius, already transformed into a star, 'natique videns bene facta fatetur | esse suis maiora et vinci gaudet ab illo' ('seeing the good deeds of his son, he confesses they are greater than his own and rejoices in being surpassed by him'). But *optime*, in combination with *custos*, also points up Augustus' role as the supreme benefactor.[128]

This complex of connections is rich in contemporary significance. Augustus' use of the patronymic *Divi Filius* was not constant: it diminished in the late 20s but comes back dramatically in the following decade.[129] In 44 BC Octavian had set up in the Forum a *simulacrum* of Julius Caesar with a star on its head.[130] After Actium he had dedicated the temple of Divus Iulius on the site where a column inscribed PARENTI PATRIAE had previously stood. It contained a statue of Caesar similar to that erected in 44 BC.[131] A little later Augustus' *Autobiography* revealed that he saw the star not just as a sign of Caesar's apotheosis but of his own destiny.[132] In 25 BC Agrippa had wanted to place a statue of Augustus in his Pantheon. Augustus refused and a statue of Divus Iulius was installed instead, with statues of Augustus and Agrippa in the antechamber.[133] There was another statue of Divus Iulius in the temple of Romulus-Quirinus restored

[126] Degrassi (1963), 279; Radke (1964), 62. Cf. *ILS* 140. 7–8 'Augusti patris patriae pontiff. maxsumi custodis imperi Romani totiusque orbis terrarum praesidis.'
[127] See Norden (1927), 345; cf. Woodman (1977), 238–9.
[128] See Cic. *Dom.* 144 'propter beneficia populus Romanus [Iovem] optimum ... nominavit.' See also Woodman (1977), 245.
[129] See White (1988) and contrast Ramage (1985).
[130] Plin. *NH* 2. 93–4; Suet. *Caes.* 88; Dio 45. 7. 1.
[131] See White (1988), 336–8; Suet. *Caes.* 85; *ILS* 72.
[132] See Plin. *NH* 2. 94 'cometes ... admodum faustus Divo Augusto iudicatus ab ipso ... interiore gaudio sibi illum natum seque in eo nasci interpretatus est, et, si verum fatemur, salutare id terris fuit.'
[133] See Dio 53. 27. 2–3 with Rich (1990),163 for bibliography.

and dedicated by Augustus just before his departure for Gaul in 16 BC. A little earlier contemporary coins link the Ludi Saeculares and the refounding of the city with a comet which was identified with the *sidus Iulium*.[134] On one Augustus is depicted as placing the star on the head of a statue of Divus Iulius. On others there is a striking visual resemblance between the portraits of Augustus and Divus Iulius, as if to stress their filial relationship and to anticipate Augustus' own eventual apotheosis.[135] Augustus was always concerned to emulate Romulus.[136] Both the house of Augustus and the *casa Romuli* stood on the Palatine as a constant reminder of the link between them. An important illustration of an interest in Romulus contemporary with *Odes* 4. 5 is provided by his prominence on the Ara Pacis and by the rebuilding of the temple of Quirinus, who had long since been identified with the deified Romulus.[137] This was dedicated by Augustus on 29 June 16 BC, just before his departure for Gaul.[138] The temple had been built originally in 293 BC by L. Papirius Cursor, destroyed by fire in 49, and rebuilt by Julius Caesar in 45, when it was furnished with a statue of Julius Caesar inscribed with the words *Deo invicto*.[139] The pediment of the temple depicted Romulus sighting the twelve vultures, an *augustum augurium* for the founding of the city which had been repeated, it was said, on the occasion of Augustus taking the *auspicia* for his first consulship.[140] It was from this *augurium* that the honorific cognomen *Augustus* was derived, which he had chosen after Actium in preference to *Romulus*.[141]

It should also be remembered that the original builder of Quirinus' temple had set up in the precinct Rome's first sundial.[142] It is not known whether Augustus provided a new sundial when he rebuilt the

---

[134] See Weinstock (1971), 379; Sutherland (1984), Nos. 37, 38, 102, 337–40.

[135] See Pollini (1990), 352–3, who makes the unconvincing suggestion that this has to do with the fact that Augustus nearly died in 23 BC. It would be better to recall that Romulus was 54 at the time of his apotheosis (Plut. *Rom.* 29. 12; Dion. Hal. 2. 56. 7); Augustus technically became *senex* in 18 BC and would be 54 in 9 BC. See Trillmich (1988), 520–1 for a different view of these coins.

[136] See Binder (1971), 163–9; Porte (1981), 333–42; Evans (1992), 87–103, 112–18.

[137] See Binder (1971), 168.

[138] Ov. *Fasti* 6. 795–6; Dio 54. 19. 2; Degrassi (1963), 411–12, 475.

[139] See Weinstock (1971), 186–8.

[140] App 3. 94; Suet. *Aug.* 95; cf. Dio 46. 46. 3.

[141] See Bömer (1958), 68–70; Binder (1971), 272–4; Rich (1990), 148–9.

[142] Plin. *NH* 7. 213.

temple or, if he did, whether it was designed to draw attention to Romulus' horoscope.[143] This had been calculated by L. Firmianus Tarnutius, probably in the early 40s, at the request of Varro. Using the old variable or wandering Egyptian calendar, he fixed the date of Romulus' conception as 23 Choiac and of his birth as 24 Thoth, which, in terms of the Julian calendar, means that he was conceived on the summer solstice in 772 BC and born on the spring equinox. This would make his horoscope complement that of Augustus, who, as the Horologium advertised, was conceived on the winter solstice and born on the autumnal equinox.[144] In 26 BC Augustus replaced the traditional Egyptian calendar with the fixed Alexandrian calendar, in which the traditional names of the months were retained but 1 Thoth always fell on 29 August.[145] If subsequently Romulus' horoscope was interpreted, by accident or design, in terms of the new Alexandrian calendar, it would match that of Augustus: for in terms of the Alexandrian calendar 23 Choiac fell on the winter solstice and 24 Thoth on the autumnal equinox, and so both 'founders' were conceived under Capricorn and born under Libra.[146]

The second stanza reiterates the address, and the vocative *dux bone* picks up both *divis bonis* and *optime custos*, which eases the transition. The term *dux* is a standard way of referring to Augustus in poetry, but it especially suits the return of the *imperator rebus prospere gestis* ('commander with business well done').[147] It also suggests the popular nature of his support, as at *Res Gestae* 25. 2, 'iuravit in mea verba tota Italia sponte sua et me belli, quo vici ad Actium, ducem depoposcit' ('All Italy swore to me spontaneously and demanded me as leader of the war I won at Actium'). However, the epithet *bone* underlines Augustus' untiring service to the state

---

[143] See Plut. *Rom.* 12. For a good discussion see Brind'amour (1983), 240–7; Grafton and Swerdlow (1985), 463–4. For the traditional Egyptian calendar see Bickerman (1980), 40–3, 115–22.

[144] See Brind'amour (1983), 62–76.

[145] See Brind'amour (1983), 24–5.

[146] Bouché-Leclerq (1899) 369 with n. 1 interpreted the horoscope of Romulus in terms of the Alexandrian calendar, and is followed by Bowersock (1990), 387. The error is explained by Brind'amour (1983), 243 n. 8 and by Grafton and Swerdlow (1985), 460 n. 22.

[147] See Béranger (1953), 47–9; Nisbet and Hubbard (1970), 40; Hellegouarc'h (1972), 324–6.

and anticipates his role as a benefactor in a civil rather than a military capacity.[148] The simple possessive *tuae* picks up the notion contained in *custos* and suggests that the *patria* depends upon him in the same way as a family depends upon the *paterfamilias*.[149] Augustus refused the honour of the title *pater patriae* until 2 BC.[150] Nevertheless, he had accepted the *corona civica* and the honour of having libations poured to his *genius* as early as 29 BC.[151] It is only the formal acceptance of the title that is missing. Its unofficial use is clearly attested much earlier, not only in poetry but also on coins and inscriptions.[152]

The stanza conflates three standard encomiastic topoi:[153] the comparison of a return or arrival with the coming of spring after the cold of winter;[154] the appearance or gaze of the ruler; and the comparison or identification of the ruler with the sun.[155] The speaker explicitly 'recalls' the effect of Augustus' earlier returns in the perfect *adfulsit* ('shone') and implicitly compares their effect with the return of spring: *gratior it dies* ('the day goes more pleasing').[156] Horace is perhaps playing with the standard etymologies of *dies* and *sol*: *dies dictus quod divini sit operas* ('*dies* [day] is so called because it is the work of a god [i.e. of a *deus*]') and *sol . . . quod solus ita lucet, ut ex eo deo dies sit* ('sun because it alone shines just as "day" is from that god').[157] Augustus is a second sun, and his presence will bring a

---

[148] See Hellegouarc'h (1972), 485.

[149] Cf. Hor. *Ep.* 2. 1. 18 *tuus hic populus*; Wickert (1953), 2103–5; Radke (1964), 65.

[150] See *RG* 35; Suet. *Aug*, 58, where the wording of Valerius Messalla's proposal sounds like a prayer.

[151] Weinstock (1971), 203–4; Alföldi (1971), 67–79, 130–8; Fishwick (1987), 107–8.

[152] See Hor. *Odes* 1. 2. 45, 3. 24. 27; Sutherland (1984), 48 Nos. 96–101 SPQR PARENTI CONS(ERVATORI) SVO; *ILS* 96; *CIL* x. 823; cf. Ov. *Fasti* 2. 129–30; Dio 55. 10. 10.

[153] For *lucem redde* see Cic. *Dom.* 75; Curt. Ruf. 10. 9. 4; and cf. *lux adfulsit* at Livy 9. 10. 2: see Radke (1964), 63.

[154] See Aesch. *Ag.* 968–9 (the return of Agamemnon); Theoc. *Id.* 12. 3 (the return of a lover); *Pan. Lat.* 5 (8). 10. 4; 8 (5). 2. 2; 9 (4). 18. 4 Mynors; Nisbet (1969), 175; Pöschl (1963) 7–8. At Theoc. *Id.* 18. 26–7 in an encomiastic passage, the images of dawn after night and of spring after winter are also combined.

[155] See Doblhofer (1966), 86–91; Weinstock (1971), 375–84; Syndikus (1973), 333–4; Woodman (1977), 97–8; (1983), 121.

[156] For *gratus* of the return of spring see *Odes* 1. 4. 1 and, for the Gratiae and spring, Nisbet and Hubbard (1970), 62–3.

[157] See Maltby (1991), 187, 572.

second spring and lend an additional brightness to the day. The adverb *melius* picks up *bone* (5) and *optime* (1) and recalls the formulae of the prayer for the *salus rei publicae* and for the return of the Princeps. In the former the gods were asked 'ut populi Romani res meliores amplioresque facerent' (see above) and in the latter 'bonum eventum des, atque in eo statu, quo nunc est, aut eo meliori eum conserves eumque reducem incolumem victoremq(ue) primo quoq(ue) tempore in urbem Romam sistas' ('May you give a good outcome and may you preserve him in the state he is now in or better and may you set him with good return, safe, and victorious at the first chance back in the city of Rome').[158] Now the *salus* of the *res publica* is inseparable from the *incolumitas* of Augustus.

The image of the ruler as the sun is particularly associated with the *adventus* or *reditus*.[159] So Horace himself had said in *Odes* 4. 2. 46–8: '"O sol | pulcher! o laudande" canam recepto Caesare felix' ('"O beautiful sun! O you to be praised!" I will sing, happy since Caesar is back'). The conventional nature of the topic in this situation is illustrated by Menander Rhetor in his prescription for the speech of welcome (*epibatērion*):[160]

We have come to meet you, all of us, in whole families, children, old men, adults, priestly clans, associations of public men, the common people, greeting you with joy, all welcoming you with cries of praise, calling you our saviour and fortress, our bright star: the children call you their foster father and their fathers' saviour. If the cities could speak and take the form of women as in a play, they would have said 'O greatest of governors, O sweetest day, on which you came! Now the sun shines brighter, now we seem to behold a happy day dawn out of darkness. Soon we shall put up statues. Soon poets and writers and orators will sing your virtues and spread their fame throughout mankind. Let theatres be opened, let us hold festivals, let us avow our gratitude to the emperors and to the gods.'

(381. 7–23)

---

[158] See Val. Max. 4. 1. 10; *AFA* 107 Henzen.
[159] See Halfmann (1986), 58–9, 148–51 for its peculiar appropriateness to the *adventus*.
[160] Cf. Men. Rhet. 378. 10–13 ἀλλ᾽ ἥκεις ... λαμπρός, ὥσπερ ἡλίου φαιδρά τις ἀκτὶς ἄνωθεν ἡμῖν ὀφθεῖσα; 378. 21–3 ὥσπερ νυκτὸς καὶ ζόφου τὰ πάντα κατειληφότος αὐτὸς καθαπὲρ ἥλιος ὀφθεὶς πάντα ἀθρόως τὰ δυσχερῆ διέλυσας.

This last passage not only illustrates and explains what lies behind the second stanza of *Odes* 4. 5, but also evokes vividly the whole ceremonial of the *adventus* to which the original performance rather than the dramatic setting of *Odes* 4. 5 belongs. In the *klētikon* we would expect a stronger emphasis on the darkness and feeling of loss and less, other than in anticipation, of the joys which will attend the return.

While the conventional nature of the material softens the abruptness of the metaphor, the contemporary resonances deepen and enrich the passage. Augustus had long associated himself with Apollo, and identification of Apollo with the sun and of the sun with the ideal ruler were commonplace in Hellenistic literature.[161] Apollo had been prominent in the celebrations of the Ludi Saeculares in 17 BC and again in the following year with the celebration of the Ludi Quinquinnales on the fifteenth anniversary of Actium.[162] In both cases the games were celebrated by the Quindecemviri, to which priestly college Augustus belonged. But the relationship of Augustus to Apollo, ever since the building of his temple on the Palatine (28 BC), was even more special.[163] The *Carmen Saeculare* seems to identify Sol and Apollo (9–12), and it is to Sol that the obelisk of the Horologium will be dedicated.[164]

Horace exploits the conventions of the *prosphōnētikon* and *epibatērion* to make not only the transition from the darkness and longing of the first stanza to the brightness of return in the second, but also the subsequent transition to the comparison of the *patria* yearning for the return of Caesar to the mother waiting for the return of her son (9–16).[165] This can be seen as a refined variation on the idea

---

[161] For Apollo and Augustus, see Binder (1971), 252–5; Weinstock (1971), 12–15; Zanker (1988), 49–53, 67–8, 85–9; Rich (1990), 133. For the sun in Hellenistic kingship literature see Weinstock (1971), 381 with n. 7; Halfmann (1986), 149 with references in n. 564.

[162] For Apollo and the Ludi Quinquinnales in 16 BC see Sutherland (1984), 69 Nos. 365–6; Prop. 4. 6. See also *Odes* 4. 6.

[163] See Hor. *Carm. Saec.* 73–80.

[164] There is an anecdote associating Augustus with Sol which seems to belong to this period (Suet. *Aug.* 79. 1–2).

[165] At line 14 many editors print *dimovet*, but that suggests rather restive, darting glances in various directions: *demovet* seems to be exactly right. See *OLD* s.v. *demoveo* 1a; Radke (1964), 69–70.

of the πόλις represented as women, which is used repeatedly by Menander in his accounts of typical scenes of welcome.[166]

While the conventions of the genre serve to illuminate the run of thought, nothing can disguise the strong contrast between the elevated grandeur of the second stanza and the intimacy and warmth of feeling in the third and fourth. The image is almost certainly drawn from a lost Hellenistic classic, perhaps one describing the yearning of parted lovers and which served as a model for a splendid piece of post-Hellenistic grotesquerie in which Oppian describes the yearning of the sea bass for the goats who have left the shore and for Ovid's description of the abandoned Phyllis:[167] Horace focuses exclusively on the relationship of the mother and son, and transforms an erotic relationship into a dignified and moving familial one.[168] The plural *desideriis* is unique and striking, especially in conjunction with the collective singular *patria*: all the people are as one in their longing for the return of Augustus.[169] The love of a people for its ruler is conventionally expressed in erotic language, as can again be seen from Menander's prescription for the *klētikon*.[170]

You have captured our city with desire, O best of all governors, and this is the sign you have of her love, that she has sent again to summon you ... unable to endure a single day; like those who are struck by the arrows of the frenzied loves and cannot bear not to see their beloved, the whole city has poured out and come near to bursting in upon you.[171] (428. 19–26)

---

[166] See Men. Rhet. 381. 13–15, 417. 32–418. 3. Roma would be represented as just such a female figure on the Ara Pacis. See also Syndikus (1973), 335; Doblhofer (1981), 1978.

[167] See Opp. *Hal.* 4. 331–45 (which has both a mother and son and a wife and husband); Ov. *Her.* 2. 120–9; and cf. Hom. *Od.* 16. 17–19—see Radke (1964), 68. The combination of *Carpathium mare* and *Notus* at Prop. 2. 5. 11–12 and Ov. *Am.* 2. 8. 19–20, also suggests an allusion to an amatory context; but *Carpathium mare* at Prop. 3. 7. 12, where Paetus drowns with his mother's name on his lips, suggests other possibilities, although Putnam's suggestion of direct allusion (1986: 105–6) seems unlikely.

[168] Contrast Syndikus (1973), 335.

[169] Cf. Radke (1964), 65.

[170] Similarly in the *epibatērion* (384. 28–31) and in the *propemptikon* (395. 31–2).

[171] It belongs with the image of the ruler as the sun or a star: see Paul. Fest. 75 *desiderare ... a sideribus dici certum est* [so *desiderium quod sidus abest*, presumably]; Maltby (1991), 183. The conventionality of the language and of the thought here is also illustrated by Martial when he is urging Domitian to return: 7. 5. 1–3. 'si

The conventions serve only to throw into relief the restraint and dignity of Horace's simile. The mother's dependence on her son for support and succour is simply brought out by the juxtaposition of *mater* ∼ *iuvenem*, in such a way as to recall the standard etymology *iuvenis vocatus eo quod iuvare* [*potest*] ('a youth is called thus because he can help').[172] The sense of separation by time and immense distance is assisted by the rare geographical name *Carpathii* to denote the far eastern end of the Mediterranean, notorious for its dangers.[173] The son is prevented from sailing by the prevailing northerly winds and the *Notus* is seen as *invidus* because it refuses to blow and bring her son home quickly.[174] The mother's hurt and indignation are conveyed by the adjective *cunctantem* ('delaying'), while the longing of her son for his home is reflected in *dulci distinet a domo* ('keeps him from his sweet home'). In the next stanza her traditional piety and reliance on the gods to restore her son are brought out in *votis ominibusque et precibus vocat* ('she calls with vows, omens, and prayers'), a scene suitably set on the *litus*: 'quidam... litus ἀπὸ τῶν λιτῶν volunt esse, quia proficiscentes et revertentes solent ibi vota concipere' ('Some want "shore" to be from prayers, because those setting out and returning generally conceive their vows there').[175] The simile works through a series of parallels and contrasts. The *iuvenis*

desiderium, Caesar, populique patrumque | respicis et Latiae gaudia vera togae, | redde deum votis poscentibus.'

[172] See Maltby (1991), 320.

[173] Also at *Odes* 1. 35. 7. In view of the etymologies *aequor mare appellatum, quod aequatum cum commotum vento non est* (Varro, *LL* 7. 23) and *fluctus dicti quod flatibus fiant* (Isid. *Orig.* 13. 20. 2), there seems to be some point intended in the emphatic combination *Notus* and *flatu*, with the latter framing the line with *maris aequora*. The main effect seems to be to draw attention to the 'rejected' etymology of *litus*: *qua fluctus eluderet* (Cic. *Top.* 32; cf. *dictum litus quia fluctu eliditur, vel quod aqua adluitur*—see Maltby 1991: 14, 236, 344).

[174] The normal safe sailing period was reckoned to extend from 27 May to 14 Sep., and voyages were only made outside of that period with very good cause and only outside of the period 10 Mar. to 10 Nov. in emergencies: see Casson (1971), 270–3. The journey from Alexandria, which is probably what Horace has in mind, took at least a month, and ships on the spring run often arrived as late as the end of June or early July, i.e, about the same time as Augustus returned to Rome in 13 BC: see Casson (1971), 297–8.

[175] Prisc. *Gram.* 3. 493. 31: see Maltby (1991), 344. Cf. also Livy *Praef.* 13 *cum bonis... ominibus votisque et precationibus deorum dearumque*, which is obviously echoing a poetic model: see Radke (1964), 69.

is absent in the east, Augustus in Spain and Gaul. Yet it will readily be recalled that Augustus had himself been absent longer than a year in the east and from there had returned in triumph in all but name in 19 BC. That previous return was much in people's minds, as is clear from the parallelism between the Ara Fortunae Reducis and the Ara Pacis Augustae. Both were voted as substitutes for triumphal honours; both have separate festivals for their *constitutio* and *dedicatio*; both were situated where the returning armies of the future would re-enter the city: the Ara Fortunae Reducis marking the entrance from the south and east; the Ara Pacis Augustae the entrance from the west and north.[176] In recalling that earlier return, however obliquely, the simile enhances the claims of Augustus to be the greatest conqueror Rome had ever known and well on his way to completing Rome's historic mission.[177] This is also one of the images on the Ara Pacis itself, and the conquest of east and west is one theme of the entire Horologium complex, underlined by the connection between the obelisk, which commemorated the conquest of Alexandria, and the Ara Pacis, which commemorated the pacification of Gaul and Spain.

The simile recalls not just the earlier *reditus* of Augustus but also his departure in 16 BC, as depicted in *Odes* 4. 2 by Horace (42–3 *impetrato | fortis Augusti reditu*, 'granted the return of brave Augustus'). The coin legends recalling the official language of these *vota publica* and the inscription recording the celebration of the votive games have already been noted.[178] The evocation of such *vota publica* by the description of the mother's behaviour in the absence of her son is subtly picked up in the adjective *fidelibus*, which is a word used

[176] See Torelli (1982), 27–9.

[177] See Virg. *Aen.* 6. 851–3 'tu regere imperio populos, Romane, memento | (hae tibi erunt artes), pacique imponere morem, | parcere subiectis et debellare subiectos.'

[178] Such prayers follow a clear pattern, and those for Augustus probably closely resembled those for Trajan preserved in the *Acta fratrum Arvalium*: 'Iuppiter o(ptime) m(axime), te precamur quaesumus obtestamurque, uti tu imp(eratorem) Caesarem … ex is locis provincisq(ue), quas terris marique adierit, bene atque feliciter incolumem reducem victoremq(ue) facias earumq(ue) rerum ei, quas nunc agit agiturusve est, bonum eventum des, atque in eo statu, quo nunc est, aut eo meliori eum conserves eumque reducem incolumem victoremq(ue) primo quoq(ue) tempore in urbem Romam sistas; ast tu ea ita facsis, tum tibi nomine coll(egi) fratrum Arvalium bove aurato vovimus esse futurum' (p. 123 Henzen). See further Versnel (1980), 562–70; Scheid (1990), 294, 313–14, 372–80, 405–11.

especially of those who are dependent on the *fides* of some protector or guardian.[179]

The comparison of Caesar to the *iuvenis*, emphasized by the parallelism *ut mater iuvenem ~ sic... patria Caesarem* ('as a mother her son, so the fatherland Caesar'), is evocative. At the beginning of his career Octavian had been contemptuously styled *puer qui omnia nomini debet* ('a boy who owes everything to his name').[180] His supporters seem to have coined the designation *iuvenis* in retaliation. He is first so called at *Eclogue* 1. 42 by Tityrus, whose lands he has exempted from confiscation. The next occurrence is at *Georgics* 1. 500: 'Di |...hunc saltem everso iuvenem succurrere saeclo | ne prohibete' ('Gods, do not prohibit this youth at least from succoring this overturned era'). He has now become the universal benefactor, and the juxtaposition of *iuvenem* with *succurrere* makes plain the etymological significance: *iuvenes appellatos, eo quod rem publicam in re militari possent iuvare* ('youths [*iuvenes*] are so called because they can help [*iuvare*] the state in military affairs').[181] At about the same time Horace uses the same designation in *Satire* 2. 5. 62–4:

> tempore quo iuvenis Parthis horrendus, ab alto
> demissum genus Aenea, tellure marique
> magnus erit...

When the youth, fearsome to the Parthians, the race descended from high Aeneas, will be great on land and sea...

Revenge upon the Parthians (finally celebrated in 19 BC), the godsent saviour of the *saeculum*, and the Ludi Saeculares of 17 BC were closely intertwined concepts, and this perhaps makes less surprising the persistence of this way of referring to Augustus.[182] On the night after Augustus had departed for Gaul the temple of Iuventas burnt down.[183] Apart from the designation of Octavian/Augustus as

[179] See Hellegouarc'h (1972) 36–7.
[180] See M. Antonius (ap.) Cic. *Phil.* 13. 24 'O puer, qui omnia nomini debes'; Suet. *Aug.* 12. 1 'dicta factaque quorundam calumniatus, quasi alii se puerum...' At Cic. *Att.* 10. 12a. 4, 14. 17a. 2, 16. 14. 2 Octavian is referred to as *iuvenis*, although Cicero normally uses *adulescens*.
[181] Cens. 14. 2; see Maltby (1991), 320. Cf. Ov. *Fasti* 4. 675–6 'titulum imperii tum primum... Augusto iuveni prospera bella darent.'
[182] See Simon (1957), 61–4; Weinstock (1971), 196.
[183] Dio 54. 19. 7. The temple itself was rebuilt by Augustus (*RG* 19. 2).

iuvenis, the only known connection is the *supplicatio* offered to Iuventas on the anniversary of Augustus' assumption of the *toga virilis.*[184] It was the destruction of the temple of Iuventas that prompted the vows *pro salute et reditu.*

A sustained allusion to a famous passage of Ennius underlies the four opening stanzas. This is best considered along with the commentary and interpretation of Cicero, to whom its survival is owed (*De re publica* 1. 64):[185]

...iusto quidem rege cum est populus orbatus, 'pectora diu tenet desiderium', sicut ait Ennius, post optimi regis obitum:

> simul inter
> sese sic memorant: 'o Romule, Romule die,
> qualem te patriae custodem di genuerunt!
> o pater, o genitor, o sanguen dis oriundum!'

non eros nec dominos appellabant eos, quibus iuste paruerunt, denique ne reges quidem, sed patriae custodes, sed patres, sed deos; nec sine causa; quid enim adiungunt?

> tu produxisti nos intra luminis oras.

vitam, honorem, decus sibi datum esse iustitia regis existimabant, mansisset eadem voluntas in eorum posteris, si regum similitudo permansisset, sed vides unius iniustitia concidisse genus illud totum rei publicae.

Indeed, when the people was deprived of a just king, 'longing holds their hearts for a long time', as Ennius says, after the death of an excellent king:

Thus they say in unison among themselves: 'O Romulus, divine Romulus, what a guardian of the fatherland the gods bore in you! O father, o progenitor, o blood risen from the gods!'

They did not call those they justly obeyed masters, nor even kings, but guardians of the fatherland, fathers, gods; and not without reason. For what do they add?

> You brought us into the shores of light.

They thought life, honor, glory had been given them by the king's justice—the same good will would have remained among their descendents if the

[184] Jointly with Spes: see Degrassi (1963), 523; Fears (1981a), 862 n. 146.

[185] See Skutsch (1985), 255–60, who argues that *diu* and *post optimi regis obitum* both belong to Cicero, not Ennius. If that is correct, then Cicero must be allowing his language to be coloured by the wording of the original context, for both *diu* and *optimi* are picked up by Horace.

nature of the kings had remained the same, but you see, through the injustice of one, that whole type of state collapsed.

Cicero is clearly tailoring the poet to his own argument, but it is still significant that he sets such emphasis on the *iustitia* of Romulus. This was the supreme virtue of kings and the most essential to the achievement of immortality.[186] Perhaps Ennius, like Ovid, had depicted Romulus as dispensing justice immediately before his disappearance and apotheosis.[187] The first passage quoted by Cicero describes the reactions of the *populus* to the loss of their king, and their words are addressed to him in his absence. The second was presumably part of a contrast between the brightness of their lives while he was with them and the darkness of the despair in which they now find themselves. It appears that at this point there occurred a comparison of their *desiderium* with that of a child deprived of its parent, as is suggested by Cicero's *orbatus* and Livy's version (1. 16. 2): 'Romana pubes sedato tandem pavore... tamen velut orbitatis metu icta maestum aliquamdiu silentium obtinuit' ('When their fear was finally calmed, the Roman youth, as if struck with fear of orphanhood, keep a sad silence for a while').[188] Horace's substitution of a mother and her son for the children and parents brilliantly conveys not just the helplessness and dependence of the *patria* deprived of Augustus but also his love and respect for the SPQR. The allusion to Ennius seems in fact to underpin the whole poem, for Ennius apparently went on to tell of the apotheosis of Romulus and the cult instituted for him by the people.[189] Horace goes one better and tells how the people treat Augustus as a god even while alive. In both cases the concept of *iustitia*

[186] Cf. Cic. *De rep.* 6. 16; Hor. *Odes* 3. 3; and see Weinstock (1971), 243–8; Binder (1971), 92–5; Millar (1977), 3–5; Cairns (1989), 19, 64.

[187] Ov. *Fasti* 2. 492 'forte tuis illic, Romule, iura dabas'. In Livy he is addressing the troops.

[188] Other parallels with Livy may also reflect a common source in Ennius: for *desiderium* cf. 1. 16. 5, 'sollicita civitate desiderio'; 1. 16. 8 'desiderium Romuli apud plebem exercitumque facta fide immortalitatis lenitum sit'; for *preces* cf. 1. 16. 6 'petens precibus'.

[189] Whether or not he identified him with Quirinus: see Skutsch (1985), 245–9 (against an early identification with Quirinus) and 260–3 (on the apotheosis); Weinstock (1971), 176–7 (for an early identification with Quirinus); see further Evans (1992), 103–6.

as the fundamental virtue of the ideal ruler provides the explanation and justification of their behaviour, as Cicero explains.

It is the *iustitia* of Augustus which provides the transition to the next section (4. 5. 17–24).[190] These stanzas present a highly stylized and encomiastic description of Italy.[191] The image of peaceful prosperity derives ultimately from Homer and, particularly, from Hesiod's account of the prosperous πόλις which thrives under a just ruler:[192] the *iustitia* of the good leader secures the blessings of the gods and brings victory in war and prosperity in peace. The imagery employed is conventional and stylized, but, precisely because of this, it is rich in associations.[193] It is a standard part of the *klētikon* to proceed from the proem to the description of the place to which the addressee is being summoned and to give an account of it in terms which make it attractive to the addressee.[194] Menander, however, also recognizes a standard procedure in which the speaker 'handles the encomium of the city and of the governor as a unity' (429. 28–30). Similarly, the speaker in *Odes* 4. 5 presents his praises of Italy not only to persuade the addressee to return but also as further implicit praise of the addressee and as further explanation—*etenim* (17) picks up on *enim* (6)—of the request to the absent Augustus to return and restore light to his people. The speaker wants him back both because his presence bathes the world in sunshine and because all the attractions that Italy has to offer flow from him. Italy is what it now is because it stands under the protection of Augustus. The keynote is struck by the opening *tutus*, which picks up both *optime Romulae custos gentis* ('best guardian of Romulus' race', 1–2) and *dux bone*

[190] I would print Faber's *prata* in line 17 rather than the manuscripts' *rura*. The latter gives either an unwanted emphasis on work (Varro, *LL* 5. 40 'quod in agris quotquot annis rursum facienda eadem, ut rursum capias fructus, appellata rura') or a poor joke (*rura... rura = rursum*). *Prata* better conveys that the *bos* wanders at ease after its work is completed: Colum. 2. 16. 2 'prata dicta ab eo, quod protinus esset paratum nec magnum laborem desideraret'; Maltby (1991), 494. See Syndikus (1973), 337–8; and, for the problem, Nisbet (1989), 93 and contrast Fraenkel (1957), 443 n. 5.

[191] For the division into the blessings of the gods secured by the *iustitia* of Augustus and the effects of his lawmaking cf. Men. Rhet. 361. 17–25.

[192] See Hes. *WD* 225–37; Hom. *Od.* 19. 109–14; Theoc. *Id.* 17. 77 ff.; Cic. *De rep.* 2. 26. 1; Syndikus (1973), 337; Woodman (1983b), 255.

[193] See Fuchs (1926), 182–205.

[194] Men. Rhet. 426. 7–14; 428. 7–11; 429.

('good leader', 5).[195] The normal order for dealing with the achievements of the addressee is 'deeds in war', then 'deeds in peace', if he is
distinguished in war.[196] By reversing the standard order, Horace's
emphasis precisely reflects the decision to 'accept' the honour of an
altar dedicated to the Augustan Pax to be erected on the Field of Mars
rather than any more obviously triumphal monument.[197]

As has often been noted, the image of peaceful prosperity and
abundance in *Odes* 4. 5. 17–20 finds a striking visual counterpart on
the Ara Pacis Augustae.[198] It should be recalled that during the 20s
there had been a series of acute food shortages which had led at times
to rioting. Augustus himself took control of the supply of grain from
22 BC and distributed massive handouts of grain from his own
granaries in 18 BC.[199] This is why, on both the Ara Pacis Augustae
and in this poem, Augustus and the peace that he has secured by his
victories are presented as guarantees of future prosperity and abundance. The phrase *pacatum . . . per mare* ('over the secured sea') has
its counterpart in the *Res Gestae* at 25.1 *mare pacavi a praedonibus* ('I
made the sea secure from pirates'). There the reference is to the
victory over Sextus Pompeius in 36 BC, more than twenty years
earlier. In the period 41–36 BC the blockade of Italy by Sextus
Pompeius had caused especially acute food shortages.[200] But this
earlier victory is also recalled on a series of coins belonging to the
years 15–11 BC which bear the head of Diana.[201] Recollection of
Augustus' own earlier victories seems primarily intended at this
time to offset the redefinition of his role and the new victories of
Drusus and Tiberius under his *auspicia.*[202] But recollection of the
defeat of Sextus also serves to recall the food shortages associated
with civil war and Augustus' part in bringing them to an end.

[195] Cf. Hor. *Odes* 4. 14. 43–4, 'o tutela praesens | Italiae dominaeque Romae'; *Ep.* 2.
1. 2–3 'res Italas armis tuteris, moribus ornes legibus emendes'. See further Béranger
(1953), 204–6, 257–60, 266–9; Woodman (1977), 141–2; Brink (1982), 36.

[196] Men. Rhet. 372. 25–8.

[197] Cf. Putnam (1986), 114.

[198] See Benario (1960); Syndikus (1973), 340–1; more recently De Grummond
(1990), who identifies the figure as Pax; and Spaeth (1994), 91, who argues that it is,
at least primarily, Demeter/Ceres.

[199] See Dio 54. 1. 1–4; *RG* 5, 18; Garnsey (1988), 227–40; Rich (1990), 172.

[200] See Dio 48. 18. 1, 48. 31; App. *BC* 5. 67–8; Garnsey (1988), 202.

[201] See Sutherland (1984), 53 Nos. 172–3, 175, 181–3; Kraft (1978), 321–8.

[202] See Kraft (1978), 323–4; Trillmich (1988), 522.

The preceding lines are framed by *tutus* and *Faustitas*, both suggestive of the protection afforded by Augustus through his success as *dux*. Faustitas is a novelty, apparently a poetic synonym for Felicitas or Fausta Felicitas. These latter two were both goddesses who received sacrifice, the former on 1 July (perhaps the anniversary of the dedication of her temple in 44 BC by Julius Caesar); the latter, if different, on 9 October in conjunction with the Genius Populi Romani and Venus Victrix.[203] Felicitas is an essential quality of the successful military leader and closely associated with both the triumph and the *adventus*.[204] It is therefore perhaps more relevant to recall that there was a *supplicatio* to Felicitas Imperii on the anniversary of Augustus' *dies imperii* (16 April) and a sacrifice to Felicitas in the Campus Martius on Augustus' birthday.[205] Callimachus had prayed to Ceres to 'nourish peace' (Hymn 6. 137 φέρβε . . . εἰράναν). Horace stands the idea on its head: Faustitas or Felicitas stands by metonomy for Pax and borrows the conventional epithet of Ceres, *alma*: for *est a gerendis frugibus Ceres* ('Ceres is from bearing fruits').[206] Ceres in turn nourishes the *rura*, which stands by metonomy for *fruges*. The idea of security guaranteed by arms is even more clear in the next line, with *pacatum . . . per mare*. Nothing can better illustrate the general sense than the *omina fausta* of the Alexandrian *nautae* in Suetonius (*Augustus* 98. 2, quoted above).[207]

The final line of this stanza (20 *culpari metuit fides*, 'trust fears blame') effects a transition to a description of another aspect of Augustus' *iustitia*, as is clear from Menander (375. 24–6): 'Under justice you will speak of his legislative activity, saying that he makes

---

[203] See Degrassi (1963), 475, 518. For Felicitas see Weinstock (1971), 84, 113–18, 127. Felicitas Caesaris provided a model for the Augustan Fortuna Redux in 19 BC: see Weinstock (1971) 126–7. 9 Oct. was also the annual festival for the birthday of the temple of Apollo on the Palatine.

[204] See Versnel (1970), 356–71.

[205] Degrassi (1963), 442, 512. The underlying idea is similar to that expressed at Ov. *Fasti* 1. 701–4, 4. 407–8.

[206] Cic. *ND* 2. 67; see Maltby (1991), 122. For *alma Ceres* see Lucil. 200 Marx; Virg. *Georg.* 1. 7. However, one etymology derived *pax a pascendo*: Maltby (1991), 458; cf. Tib. 1. 10. 67 *Pax alma*.

[207] See Syndikus (1973), 339–40, Cf. Men. Rhet. 377. 13–14 γεωργεῖται μετ' εἰρήνης ἡ γῆ, πλεῖται ἡ θάλασσα ἀκινδύνως; Ehrenberg and Jones 98a εἰρηνεύουσι μὲν γὰρ γῆ καὶ θάλαττα, πόλεις δὲ ἀνθοῦσιν εὐνομίαι ὁμονοίᾳ τε καὶ εὐετηρίᾳ.

just laws, that he strikes out unjust laws, and himself proposes just ones.' The allusion to the civil wars in the reference to Sextus Pompeius is followed by an account of the beneficial effects his legislative programme has had in restoring the fabric of society. The sequence of thought is illuminated by Cicero, *Pro Marcello* 23: 'Omnia sunt excitanda tibi, C. Caesar, uni quae iacere sentis belli ipsius impetu, quod necesse fuit, perculsa atque prostrata: constituenda iudicia, revocanda fides, comprimendae libidines, propaganda suboles, omnia quae dilapsa iam diffluxerunt severis legibus vincienda sunt' ('All that you perceive lying shaken and prostrate from the shock of war itself, which was necessary, C. Caesar, these things you alone must raise up: the law courts must be reestablished, trust recalled, license suppressed, children borne, all that dissolved in collapse must be bound by strict laws'). What Cicero sees as the essential task facing Caesar now that the civil war is over, the speaker in *Odes* 4. 5 represents as having been achieved by Augustus. The sense of *culpari metuit fides* becomes clear only at the end of the following stanza when *culpari* is picked up by anaphora in *culpam poena premit comes* ('punishment follows on the heels of wrong doing, an inseparable companion', 24). *Fides* is now afraid to be found guilty because punishment will follow as it properly should: *poena ... quod post peccatum sequitur* ('punishment because it follows after a sin').[208] The Romans have, so to speak, learnt the lesson from the Scyths and Getae that Horace had urged upon them in *Odes* 3. 24. 21–4. That they have done so is because Augustus, when requested by the SPQR on his return from the east in 19 BC to become *curator legum et morum* ('carekeeper of laws and morals'), had accepted the challenge though not the title.[209] The *leges Iuliae de adulteriis coercendis* and *de maritandis ordinibus* ('Julian laws for suppressing adultery' and 'about the marriage of the orders') were the result.[210] Like the recovery of the standards from the Parthians and the celebration of the Ludi Saeculares, the moral legislation is part of

---

[208] Varro, *LL* 5. 177; Maltby (1991), 481. For *fides* see Hellegouarc'h (1972), 23–35.
[209] Cf. Suet. *Iul.* 41–2. See Syndikus (1973), 338. For Augustus and the *cura legum et morum* see *RG* 6; cf. Dio 54, 10. 5–7, 16 with Rich (1990), 187.
[210] There is a huge bibliography on this topic: see Rich (1990), 192 and add Treggiari (1991), 60–80, 277–90; Mette-Dittmann (1991). The most useful for the present purposes are Galinsky (1981) and des Bouvrie (1984).

Caesar's legacy of unfinished business to which Augustus gave increasing attention. In the *Carmen Saeculare*, after the laws had been
brought in, the chorus was able to request Diana, as goddess of
childbirth, to favour the *patrum . . . decreta* ('decrees of the senators',
17–18) and to ask the gods (47–8) 'Romulae genti date remque
prolemque | et decus omne' ('give to Romulus' people prosperity
and offspring and every blessing'). They then proclaim (57–60) the
return of the gods (Fides, Pax, Honos, Pudor, and Virtus, all perso-
nifications of traditional Roman virtues), which is associated with
the idea of peace and plenty, just as it is in *Odes* 4. 5 with the presence
of Ceres, Faustitas/Felicitas, and Fides. The temple of Honos and
Virtus had received attention when the Ara Fortunae Reducis was
erected in its precinct in 19 BC, and Dio, in the same sentence as he
records the Ludi Saeculares (54. 18. 2), records that Augustus moved
the date of their festival.[211] The altar to Pax Augusta was 'constituted'
in 13 BC. Perhaps the temples or the cult of Fides and Pudicitia were
also given attention around this time.[212]

In the *Carmen Saeculare* Horace had carefully attributed the
severae leges to the senate (17–18). In *Odes* 4. 5 they redound to the
credit of Augustus. But there is no inconsistency: the laws were
approved by the senate and carried through the assemblies by Augustus using his *tribunicia potestas*.[213] The senate had wanted to
honour him after his return in 19 BC by calling them *leges Augustae*
and by taking an oath that they would obey them (Dio 54. 10. 6– 7).
Augustus declined both honours, but they still bore the name *leges
Iuliae*. The chorus in 4. 5, representing the SPQR, treats the passage
of these laws as illustrating his *iustitia* or the closely related virtue:
moderatio/ σωφροσύνη.[214] Once again, Horace is using a stock theme,
as Menander's prescription suggests: 'For temperance (σωφροσύνη) is
very closely related to justice. So what will you say there? That
because of the ruler marriages are chaste, fathers have legitimate
offspring' (376. 2–8).

---

[211] Rich (1990), 195 for details and bibliography.
[212] Prop. 4. 4 (Tarpeia) is suggestive.
[213] See *RG* 6. 2 and Rich (1990), 192.
[214] For *moderatio*/ σωφροσύνη as one of the virtues of Romulus see Dion. Hal. 2.
18. 1–2.

And again the theme has special contemporary significance. There were not only the *lex Iulia de maritandis ordinandis* and the *lex Iulia de adulteriis coercendis* but also *leges Iuliae de sumptu* and *de ambitu* ('Julian laws about luxury' and 'about bribery'). These measures went hand in hand with the review of the senate in which moral criteria also played a significant part. There was considerable resistance, and, as already noted, Dio actually suggests that the unpopularity of these measures had been the real reason for Augustus' going to Gaul in 16 BC.[215] This was a matter to which Augustus had to give his attention once the elaborate and extended celebrations of his return were over.[216] It is of importance, therefore, to see that Horace has here allowed no hint of such dissension to emerge. On the contrary, he represents the laws as having already achieved their intended effect.

In *Odes* 3. 6. 17–20 Horace had offered a diagnosis of Rome's recent and present ills:[217]

> fecunda culpae saecula nuptias
> primum inquinavere et genus et domos:
>   hoc fonte derivata clades
>   in patriam populumque fluxit.

Generations fertile in sin first defiled marriage and the family and the home: from this source sprang the disaster which has flooded our fatherland and its people.

He then presents two vividly contrasting pictures: first, the modern wife who has been dreaming of *incestos amores* ('unchaste love', 23) since childhood and now takes as lovers, *non sine conscio... marito* ('not without her husband's knowledge', 29–30), *iuniores... adulteros* ('more youthful adulterous lovers', 29), with no regard to their social status or her own dignity; then the young men of old who, toughened by work on the farm and schooled by a *mater severa* (39–40), defeated Rome's greatest enemies. The poem ends with a grimly pessimistic prognosis (45–8). The implication is clear: unless the Romans return to the moral standards of their ancestors, they are

[215] Dio 54. 19. 2 with Rich (1990), 196.
[216] Dio 54. 26. 3–9.
[217] Syndikus (1973), 338.

finished. They will be unable to sustain their position as rulers of the largest empire ever created; they will be unable to withstand their enemies; they will lose the prosperity that is the concomitant of peace. It is precisely the ills diagnosed by Horace in *Odes* 3.6 that the *leges Iuliae* were designed to deal with.

There was a widespread view in antiquity that marriage and the family provide the essential foundations of the state. It is found in philosophers, poets, and rhetoricians.[218] Whatever threatens the foundations threatens the very existence of the state. Conversely, the stability of the family and the production of children guarantee the prosperity of the state and its capacity to defend itself, and, above all, secure its future. It is no coincidence that this legislation on these matters was introduced in the year preceding the Ludi Saeculares, which mark the end of one age and the beginning of the next, a time very much concerned with looking to a new future and the next generation.

Horace's reference to these laws in *Odes* 4.5 is precise, tactful, and subtly persuasive. The emphasis is upon the *lex Iulia de adulteriis coercendis.* The law dealt with *stuprum* in a way which was scarcely to be distinguished from *adulterium.* It may also have dealt with *incestum.*[219] It is tempting to think that Horace might have wanted *edomuit* understood as meaning 'has driven out of the home': for *domare* was derived from *domus: hoc est sub domo et potestate mea facio* ('that is I put it under my house and purview').[220] Horace's wording may also reflect the language of the *lex,* if one may judge by the definitions of the ancient etymologists: *adulter... eo quod alterius torum polluat; quia alterius torum commaculavit, adulterii nomen accepit* ('adulterer: because he polluted the bed of another; because he has befouled another's bed, he received the name adulterer').[221] Certainly the hendiadys *lex et mos* seems designed to recall the senate's request to Augustus to become *curator legum et morum.*[222]

---

[218] See Woodman (1983b), 281–2; Treggiari (1991), 205–27; Cic. *De off.* 1. 54; Calvus fr. 6 Courtney; Cat. 61. 61–75; Men. Rhet. 401. 23–36, 411. 14–18; ps.-Dionysius 262–4 Russell-Wilson; Aphthonius 13A. For the 'marriage legislation' of Romulus see Dion. Hal. 2. 4.

[219] See Mette-Dittmann (1991), 40–9; Treggiari (1991), 278, 281.

[220] Maltby (1991), 195.

[221] Maltby (1991), 9–10.

[222] See Brink (1982), 37–8; Rich (1990), 187.

The reference to punishment evokes the series of punishments prescribed by the law, including the apparent innovation of the right of
the woman's father to execute the adulterer summarily as long as he
also killed his daughter.[223] The words *laudantur simili prole puerperae*
('mothers in childbirth are praised for their children's resemblance to
their fathers') brings out the reasons that stood behind the attack
upon adultery: the protection of marriage, the creation of legitimate
children.[224] There is a striking parallel in the speech attributed to
Augustus by Dio when he is addressing those who have complied
with this legislation:

I praise you all the more because you have accepted your obligations and are
helping to replenish your native land.... Is it not a joy to acknowledge a
child who possesses the qualities of both parents, to tend and educate a
being who is both the physical and the spiritual image of yourself, so that, as
it grows up, another self is created?... If you are to rule others and the rest of
the world is to obey you, there should be a flourishing race of ours; such a
race as will in time of peace till the soil, sail the seas, practise the arts, and
pursue handicrafts, and in time of war protect what we hold with an ardour
which is all the greater because of the ties of blood, and which will bring
forth others to take the place of those who fall. (56. 2–4)

Augustus may have spoken similarly when introducing his legislation
in 18 BC.

The choral speaker passes from the achievements of Augustus in
peace, which illustrate his *iustitia*, to his achievements in war (25–8).
Here again it is Menander who provides useful guidance to the
sequence of thought:

You will speak of the prosperity and good fortune of the cities: the markets
are full of goods, the cities full of feasts and festivals, the earth is tilled in
peace, the sea is sailed without danger, piety towards god is increased,
honours are given to all in due fashion. 'We fear neither barbarians nor
enemies, the ruler's arms are a safer fortress for us than our cities' walls.'
(377. 10–17)

---

[223] Treggiari (1991), 264–77, 282–5, 290.

[224] The wording goes back to Hes. *WD* 235: if men break their oaths and act
unjustly their wives will bear monstrous children. In Theoc. *Id.* 17. 44 and Cat. 61.
221–5 the idea that children resemble their fathers is a guarantee of the wife's chastity.
See Fraenkel (1957), 444; Syndikus (1973), 338. For Horace the restoration of *fides*
within marriage is coupled with a return of *fides* generally.

But here again the stanza is charged with contemporary significance. In 55 BC the Parthians had captured legionary standards from Crassus. These were restored when Augustus returned in 19 BC and a long-standing humiliation for Rome was at last avenged. It was a success for negotiation and diplomacy rather than for arms, but Augustus had been offered a triumph which he declined and the Parthians are represented in the *Res Gestae* as posing no further threat to Rome.[225] Augustus also mentions the Scythians among those who *nostram amicitiam appetiverunt per legatos* ('sought our friendship through legates'), and that must have happened not long after his return in 19 BC, as it is also celebrated in the *Carmen Saeculare*.[226] They are mentioned together here partly to make the learned point that the Parthi *Scythorum exules fuere... Scythico sermone exules 'parthi' dicuntur* ('were the Scythians' exiles... in Scythian, exiles are called parthians'), and so not, as others held, *Parthi dicti eo, quod virtute praestent nec habeant pares* ('Parthians are called thus because they excel in virtue and do not have peers').[227] It was the invasion of Gaul by the German Sugambri which had caused Augustus to leave Rome, and Germania receives the more elaborate treatment. As an ancient etymologist explains, the name *Germania* conjures up 'terra dives virum ac populis numerosis et immanibus unde et propter fecunditatem gignendorum populorum Germania dicta est' ('a land rich in men and of peoples numerous and huge, from which and from its fecundity in raising peoples it is called Germany').[228] Horace is deliberately using language suggestive of the Earth-born Giants who had opposed the gods, a conventional image for the forces of barbarism and chaos ranged against those of order and civilization.[229] Their teeming fecundity underlines the significance of the legislation dealt with in the previous stanza, one

[225] See Syndikus (1973), 339; *RG* 29. 2 'Parthos trium exercitum Romanorum spolia et signa reddere mihi supplicesque amicitiam populi Romani petere coegi.' Cf. 32. 1, 33.

[226] See *RG* 31. 2; Hor. *Carm. Saec.* 55, *iam Scythae responsa petunt.*

[227] See Maltby (1991), 453.

[228] See Maltby (1991), 257, and 228 *fecunda a fetu dicta, quasi fetunda.*

[229] See esp. *Odes* 3. 4. 42–80. The Raeti and Vindelici might also have been thought of as a Germanic people: see Oros. 6. 21. 12. For their barbarity see Dio 54. 22. 1–2 and see *RG* 26. 2 with Brunt and Moore (1967), 81.

purpose of which was to ensure that Rome had the manpower to withstand its enemies.

The stanza ends with the reference to the ending of the threat of war in Spain after some two centuries.[230] The main period of Augustan conquest fell in 26–25 BC, but resistance had continued and war flared up in both 22 and 19 BC.[231] Augustus spent most of 14 BC in Spain completing the pacification of the province and establishing colonies. The ferocity and the stubborn resistance of the Cantabri are now seen as a thing of the past. The reference to Spain fixes the dramatic date of the poem to late 14 or early 13 BC: the threat of war is over and Augustus can now return.

This sense of freedom from the threat of war depends upon the safety of Caesar. The inseparability of the *salus* or *incolumitas* of the *res publica* and Augustus was proclaimed in a senatorial decree that lay behind a coin issued in 16 BC bearing the inscription *Senatus consulto ob rempublicam cum salute imperatoris Caesaris Augusti conservatam* (see above).[232] Similar language no doubt echoed through the prayers to the gods which accompanied the various votive offerings, as may be inferred from a later prayer of the Fratres Arvales *pro salute imperatoris... ex cuius incolumitate omnium salus constat* ('For the safety of the emperor... from whose well-being depends the safety of all').[233]

The final section of the poem turns from the absent addressee to the welcome that is even now being prepared for his return (29–40).[234] Here again Horace's poem follows the traditional pattern of the *klētikon*, as is clear from Menander:[235]

[230] The Augustan view is reflected in Vell. Pat. 2. 90, esp. 4 'has igitur provincias tam diffusas, tam frequentes, tam feras ad eam pacem... perduxit Caesar Augustus ut, quae maximis bellis numquam vacaverant, eae... postea etiam latrociniis vacarent.'

[231] See Dio 53. 25. 2–7, 29. 1–2; 54. 5. 1–3, 11. 2–5, 20. 3, 23. 7, 25. 1; Flor. 2. 33. 46–60; Oros. 6. 21. 1–11; Woodman (1983b), 264–7; Rich (1990), 160.

[232] See Sutherland (1984), 68 Nos. 356–7; Weinstock (1971), 171–2; but it seems to me that the surrender of the Sugambri rather than recovery from an otherwise unattested illness is the more likely occasion.

[233] See *AFA* 110 Henzen. Cf. Cic. *Pro Marc.* 22 'nam quis est... qui non intellegat tua salute contineri suam et ex unius tua vita pendere omnium', 32 'nisi te, C. Caesar, salvo... salvi esse non possumus.' See Alföldi (1970), 86–7 n. 4; Syndikus (1973), 338–9.

[234] At 4. 5. 31 Shackleton Bailey (1985), 158 proposes *tecta* for *vina*, but see Syndikus (1973), 342.

[235] Contrast Syndikus (1973), 341, 343, who sees Horace increasingly losing sight of the situation depicted in the opening stanza.

Add to the epilogue: 'The city already stands before the gates, with whole families, meeting you, greeting you, praying to the gods to see you soon. Do not disappoint her hopes, nor change her expectations into distress. As she used to welcome Apollo...so she is waiting for you; poets are ready with works of the Muses fashioned for the occasion, prose writers too: all are ready to hymn and praise you.'[236] (427. 17–27)

But the passage of Ennius dealing with the disappearance and apotheosis of Romulus is also still in play. Livy, following Ennius, tells how the people recovered from their despair and then prayed to the deified Romulus: 'deinde a paucis initio facto deum deo natum, regem parentemque urbis Romanae salvere universi Romulum iubent; pacem precibus exposcunt, uti volens propitius suam semper sospitet progeniem' ('Then from a beginning made by a few all bid them to salute Romulus as a god born from a god, king, and parent of the city of Rome; they request peace from him in prayer, that willing and propitious he guarantee forever the safety of his offspring', 1. 16. 2–3). In *Odes* 4. 5 the movement from *desiderium* for the absent benefactor and ruler to honouring him as a god runs parallel to Ennius' account, and the context evoked by the allusion to Ennius in the opening stanzas underpins the coherence of the poem.

The closing sequence begins with the image of the *civis Romanus* cultivating his land in the manner of the idealized youth of the past.[237] At the end of the day he returns from cultivating his vineyard to enjoy the fruits of his labours. Both his *securitas* and the *fecunditas* of his land derive from Augustus, and so he invites him as a *deus* to join his feast. Through this image the choral speaker in effect proclaims his representative role: everyone feels the joy that characterizes a speech of welcome and calls upon the addressee to be present as a god, in recognition of the benefits he has conferred upon them all.[238]

The phrase *condit quisque diem* is striking and alludes to Virgil, *Eclogues* 9. 46–52:[239]

---

[236] Cf. Men. Rhet. 377. 21–30; 381. 19–23; 417. 32–418. 3. See Price (1980), 29–30 (hymnodes in the cult at Pergamum), 32 (ritual of the *adventus*).

[237] See esp. *Odes* 3. 6. 33–44.

[238] For joy as the distinguishing characteristic of the *epibatērion* see Men. Rhet. 382. 1–6; cf. 378. 3; 381. 10, 26–7.

[239] So ps.-Acro; see Fraenkel (1957), 445 n. 3; rightly emphasized by Putnam (1986), 110–11.

LYCIDAS

'Daphni, quid antiquos signorum suspicis ortus?
ecce Dionaei processit Caesaris astrum,
astrum quo segetes gauderent frugibus et quo
duceret apricis in collibus uva colorem.
insere, Daphni, piros: carpent tua poma nepotes.'

MOERIS

Omnia fert aetas, animum quoque, saepe ego longos
cantando puerum memini me condere soles.

Lycidas: 'Daphnis, why do you look up at the ancient risings of the constel-
lations? Behold, here advances Caesar's star, Dione's descendant, a star by
which the crops may rejoice in their fruits and the grape draw its color on
the sunny hills. Graft pears, Daphnis: your grandchildren will pluck your
fruit.' Moeris: 'Time bears all away, including the mind. I recall that I often
put the long days to bed with song when I was but a boy.'

Eclogue 9 is set against the background of the eviction of Italian
farmers to provide land for the settlement of veterans discharged
after Philippi in 41–40 BC. Lycidas is recalling a song Moeris had sung
some years before that had hymned the new god, Divus Iulius, as a
source of fertility, prosperity, and security. The eclogue depicts the
bitter disappointment of those hopes in the ensuing chaos of civil
war. The general sense of the allusion is clear enough: Augustus has
brought an end to civil war and its concomitant upheavals, and *certa
cuique rerum suarum possessio* ('certain possession by each of his own
property') counted among the blessings he had conferred.[240] But the
emphasis upon the security of ownership conveyed by the phrase
collibus in suis ('on his own hills') has a more specific contemporary
reference.[241]

In his account of Augustus' speech to the senate delivered on his
return, Dio reports:[242]

He enumerated his achievements and prescribed the years which citizens
should serve in the army and the money which they should receive on
discharge in place of the land which they were constantly demanding.... The
immediate reaction of the soldiers to the announcement was neither delight

---

[240] Vell. Pat. 2. 89. 4; Hor. *Odes* 4. 15. 17–20. See Nicolet (1984), 111–12.
[241] Cf. Hor. *Epod.* 2. 3 'ut prisca gens mortalium, | paterna rura bobus exercet suis.'
[242] See *RG* 16; Suet. *Aug.* 49. 2; Brunt (1971), 332–42; Kepple (1983), 82–6, 208–9.

nor anger since they had gained some but not all of what they had hoped for, but the rest of the population welcomed the prospect of no longer having their property taken from them. (54. 25. 5–6)

The problem of finding a suitable way of rewarding those who had served in the armies without evicting existing owners or tenants had long eluded a solution. Augustus had dealt with it after Actium by paying compensation for the lands he had taken over in Italy. In 14 BC he did the same for lands in the provinces. On his return he introduced this new scheme, whereby the soldiers would receive cash grants rather than land on discharge. The importance of the problem and the significance of its solution are confirmed by the space allocated to it in the *Res Gestae,* where the details are accompanied by the proud claim: 'id primus et solus omnium, qui deduxerunt colonias militum in Italia aut in provinciis, ad memoriam aetatis meae feci' ('According to the memory of my era, I did this first and alone of all who established colonies of soldiers in Italy or the provinces', 16. 1). By evoking Virgil's celebrated literary account of the earlier sufferings caused by the settlement of veterans, Horace underlines the significance of this new proposal, of which his audience can have become aware only days if not hours before they heard his poem. Horace must have been aware of the proposal considerably in advance of those outside the most intimate circle of Augustus' friends.

In a kletic hymn articulated by the characteristic anaphora of *te... te... te... tuum,* the farmer calls upon Augustus as a *deus* to attend his meal. *Odes* 3. 14 provides a parallel and an instructive contrast.[243] There the individualized speaker ends his welcome by giving instructions for a private party which underlines and guarantees the sincerity of his feelings of joy at the return of Augustus. In *Odes* 4. 5 the chorus portrays each and every one of the citizens that it represents preparing his own private meal and his own spontaneous ritual expression of gratitude for the benefits conferred by Augustus' leadership.[244] This is a private cult and a spontaneous act of gratitude to a benefactor for the benefits enjoyed as a result of Augustus' rule.[245] It is an

---

[243] Syndikus (1973), 343–4 notes the parallel but does not note the crucial difference in conception.

[244] Plin. *NH* 2. 18 *deus est mortali iuvare mortalem.*

[245] See Habicht (1972), 42–3, 45; Fishwick (1991), 436–7.

action characteristic of the people Horace is describing: it was the ordinary people who had worshipped the Gracchi as gods after their death; hailed C. Marius as a new founder of Rome and made offerings of food and libations of wine to him; and honoured M. Marius Gratidianus, the praetor of 85 BC, with supplications of incense and wine.[246] But the citizen farmer is also shown universally (*quisque*) complying happily with the honour voted by the senate to Augustus on his return after Actium, which Dio describes as follows:[247] 'The priests and priestesses were instructed, when they offered up prayers for the senate and Roman people, to pray for him likewise, and both at public and at private banquets everyone was to pour a libation to him' (51. 19. 7).

At mealtimes small statues of the Lares were placed on the table and with them a statue of Augustus, usually holding a cornucopia.[248] The libation, the *grati pignus honoris*, was accompanied by a prayer which is described by Ovid:[249]

> iamque, ubi suadebit placidos nox umida somnos,
>   larga precaturi sumite vina manu,
> et 'bene vos, bene te, patriae pater, optime Caesar'
>   dicite; suffuso sint bona verba mero.
>
> (*Fasti* 2. 635–8)

And now when the dewy night urges restful sleep, take up generously filled cups of wine in your hands to pray and say 'bless you all, bless you, father of the fatherland, most excellent Caesar'; let the words of blessing accompany the pouring of the unmixed wine.

In *Odes* 4. 5 the farmer then honours him with a libation and sets his *numen* in the company of the Lares.[250] It is generally assumed that

[246] Plut. *Gracch.* 39. 2–3; *Mar.* 27. 9; Val. Max. 8. 15. 7; Cic. *De off.* 3. 20. 80; Sen. *De ira* 3. 18. 1; Alföldi (1971), 134–5; Fishwick (1987), 53–4.

[247] See Fishwick (1991), 375–6 n. 2 for discussion and bibliography.

[248] See, most recently, Fishwick (1991), 376, 383 with nn. 36–7 for bibliography; pl. LXXV(b).

[249] There is a similar account in Petronius: 'consurreximus altius et "Augusto, patri patriae, feliciter" diximus.... inter haec tres pueri candidas succincti tunicas intra-verunt, quorum duo Lares bullatos super mensam posuerunt, unus pateram vini circumferens "dii propitii" clamabat' (60. 7–8). See Alföldi (1971), 134 n. 91.

[250] The order of events seems to have been dislocated to convey a sense of excite-ment: presumably the statues of the Lares and of the *numen Augusti* were brought out from the *lararium* before the invocation and certainly before the libation.

in such cultic acts the statue normally represented the Genius
Augusti, the *deus cuius in tutela ut quisque natus est vivit* ('god
under whose tutelage each lives as he was born'),[251] and that it was
to the *genius* rather than the living Augustus that the libation was
made. Neither Dio nor Ovid bothers to make the theologically
correct distinction between Augustus and his *genius*, and Horace
specifies the *numen Augusti*.

The word *numen* is notoriously difficult to define.[252] Ancient
definitions equate it with *potestas* or *imperium*. It is perhaps best
seen as being the quintessential property of a god, that through
which he manifests his power or efficacy.[253] The farmer treats Augustus like a god because of what he has done and especially because
of the benefits he has conferred.[254] He 'recognizes' that the *felicitas
saeculi* depends upon Augustus. He also 'knows' that it is beyond
the power of any mere man to bring about such a state of affairs.
He therefore attributes to him superhuman or divine power. The
cult-act of prayer and libation is the only proper way to express due
gratitude to so beneficent a divine power.[255]

The farmer sets the *numen* of Augustus among the statues of his
Lares, and the speaker compares the way in which the Greeks recognized the divine power of their benefactors, Castor and Hercules.[256]
Yet the Lares were themselves believed to be *animae... hominum
redactae in numerum deorum* ('souls of people adlected to the ranks
of the gods').[257] Moreover, the *populus Romanus* had worshipped the
living Marius in their homes along with their household gods and
had set up statues of Marius Gratidianus alongside those of the Lares
Compitales and supplicated them with incense and wine. The reference to Greece therefore serves primarily to legitimize the action of
the citizen farmer by providing it with ancient and respectable
precedent.[258] Both the Dioscuri and Hercules had been used to

[251] Cens. 3. 1. See Niebling (1956), 329–31; Fishwick (1991), 382–3 with nn. 32–4
for bibliography.

[252] See Fishwick (1991), 375–87.

[253] See Pötscher (1978), 358, 391–2; Fishwick (1991), 383.

[254] See Fishwick (1987), 26, 184.

[255] Cf. *Epist.* 2. 1. 15–17.

[256] See Radke (1964), 73: for *adhibet deum* cf. Virg. *Aen.* 5. 62–3; for the whole
scene cf. Stat. *Silv.* 4. 6. 32–9.

[257] Paul. 121M. (108L.); Fraenkel (1957), 447; Weinstock (1971), 292.

[258] See Doblhofer (1966), 125; Brink (1982), 39.

establish precedent for the deification of Alexander, whose achievements and honours were consciously emulated not just by Augustus
but also by Pompey, Caesar, and Antony.[259] But both the Dioscuri
and Hercules were important gods for the Romans as well. As long
ago as 484 BC the Romans had provided Castor with a temple and
cult in recognition of the divine aid given at the battle of Lake
Regillus.[260] The temple stood in the Forum Romanum close by the
temple of Divus Iulius, dedicated in 29 BC, and the Arch of Augustus
which commemorated the *signa a Parthis recepta* ('standards taken
back from the Parthians') in 19 BC and bridged the space between
them.[261]

The name of *Magnus Hercules* seems at first to point to Hercules
Magnus Custos, especially in view of the designation of Augustus as
Romulae custos gentis (4. 5. 1–2).[262] But the primary reference must
be to Hercules Victor or Invictus, the exemplary conqueror, whose
victories rid the world of barbarism and chaos, the embodiment of
virtus and prototypical *triumphator* whose reward for the benefits he
bestowed upon mankind was divinity. It was Hercules Invictus who
had provided the model for Alexander Magnus, Pompeius Magnus,
and Octavian, who in the years immediately after Actium himself
receives the title *Magnus* or *Maximus*.[263] When Augustus returned in
29 BC, the timing of his triple triumph was made to coincide with the
sacrifice to Hercules Invictus at the Ara Maxima in the Forum
Boarium: it was even contrived that a Potitus Valerius should perform the sacrifice on the arrival of Augustus on behalf of the
SPQR.[264] The aetiology of this altar became one of the major

[259] See Bellinger (1957); Kienast (1969).

[260] Livy 2. 20. 12–13, 42. 5; Dion. Hal. 6. 13.

[261] See Zanker (1972), 12–13, 18–19.

[262] So Putnam (1986), 112.

[263] See A. R. Anderson (1928); Fears (1981b) 819–22; and, for further bibliography, Brink (1982) 45. For Alexander and Pompeius Magnus see Spranger (1958),
36–44; for Hercules Magnus Custos see Spranger (1958), 33. For *Caesar maximus* see
Virg. *Georg.* 2. 170; for *magnus* see Virg. *Georg.* 4. 560; Hor. *Sat.* 2. 5. 63; *Odes* 1. 12,
51; Prop. 2. 1. 26, 2. 7. 5, 2. 31. 2; Spranger (1958), 45. In the event he took the
cognomen Augustus: see Erkell (1952), 13–15. On *magnus* see also Mette (1961b),
and, for its use in acclamations, Peterson (1926), 196–210.

[264] See Dio 51. 21. 2–3; Syme (1979), 260–70; (1989), 228–9. The significance of
the name goes unremarked by Dio, but see Livy 1. 7. 12–14; Virg. *Aen.* 8. 269. On
Hercules and Augustus see Binder (1971), 141–9, 258–9.

myths of Augustan Rome. Hercules had been returning from Spain when he destroyed the monstrous Cacus and established the Ara Maxima. One of his rewards was to be included in the hymn of the Salian priests, another of the honours voted to Augustus after Actium.[265] The association with Augustus was brought to the fore again when Augustus returned from Spain in 24 BC: 'Herculis ritu . . . Caesar Hispana repetit penatis | victor ab ora' ('Like Hercules, Caesar seeks his household gods again, victorious from Spanish shores', *Odes* 3. 14. 1–4).[266] Hercules also appears on the coinage of 19 BC which celebrates the return of the standards;[267] and at the Ludi Saeculares Hercules Victor was among the gods addressed in Augustus' prayer.[268] The Ara Maxima perhaps served as a precedent for both the Ara Fortunae Reducis and the Ara Pacis Augustae, which were both voted as monuments designed to commemorate victories. The relationship of Hercules Victor or Invictus to Hercules Magnus Custos is unclear.[269] But in view of the fact that the temple of the latter was built or restored by Sulla, and given its position in the Circus Flaminius, it may be assumed that he was also closely connected with the triumph and so with the *adventus*.[270] One of the calendars even records a sacrifice to both Castor and Pollux and to Hercules Magnus Custos on 13 August, the anniversary of the first day of Augustus' triple triumph.[271] In *Odes* 4. 5 Augustus is being urged to return from Spain, and the comparison with Hercules in this context must recall the association of Hercules with all his earlier returns.

[265] For Augustus see *RG* 10. 1; Dio 51. 20. 1; for Hercules see Virg. *Aen.* 8. 280–305. See further Binder (1971), 192–4.

[266] For the interpretation of 3. 14. 1–4 see Nisbet (1983), 106–7. For Hercules-Augustus cf. *Odes* 1. 12. 25; 2. 12. 6–12; 3. 3. 9–16.

[267] Sutherland (1984), 64 No 314.

[268] See Moretti (1984), 370, 375–7.

[269] Hercules is *maximus ultor* at Virg. *Aen.* 8. 201 with obvious reference to the Ara Maxima; Horace prays that Hercules *custos mihi maximus adsis* (*Sat.* 2. 6. 15), in what sounds like a playful allusion to the title Magnus Custos.

[270] See Richardson (1992), 83, 186.

[271] The *Fasti Vallenses*, which Degrassi (1963), 403–4 thinks are just confused, as Ovid gives the date of the festival of Hercules Magnus Custos as 4 June (*Fasti* 6. 209–12). It may also be relevant that Augustus' stepfather rebuilt the temple of Hercules Musarum and dedicated it in 29 BC (Ov. *Fasti* 6. 797–812; Suet. *Aug.* 29. 5).

In the final stanza the chorus identifies with the *populus* that it represents and utters its own prayer.[272] The phrase *dux bone* reiterates *dux bone* in line 5 and signals the closure of the poem.[273] The preceding comparison of Augustus with Castor and Hercules, both of whom have strong associations with victory, brings out the military connotations of the word *dux* (*dux dictus eo quod sit ductor exercitus* 'leader called from his leading the army'), while *bonus* is used, as often in prayers, to encourage a favourable response and anticipates Augustus' resumption of his role as *dux togatus, custos gentis*, the *de facto pater patriae*.[274]

The emphatic positioning of *longas*, which is emotionally intensified by the following *o utinam* ('would that'), seems to be intended primarily to convey the sense of 'long awaited' or 'long deferred' and so to pick up on the sense of longing expressed at the beginning of the poem (2 *abes iam nimium diu*, 'you have now been gone too long').[275] But the adjective may also be taken to convey a wish for many more victories in the future, as a variation on the encomiastic commonplace of wishing for a long life for the *laudandus*.[276] The emphasis falls on the wish for Augustus' return, for it is by returning that he will provide *feriae* ('festivities').[277] The emotional intensity of the prayer partly accounts for the use of the poetic *Hesperia*.[278] But it is striking that Hesperia can be used to denote both Spain, where Augustus is lingering, and Italy, to which the chorus yearns for him

[272] Both *o utinam* and *praestes* belong to the language of prayer: Appel (1909), 136–7.

[273] Syndikus (1973), 342–3.

[274] For *dux* see Maltby (1991), 198; for *dux armatus* contrasted with *dux togatus* see Cic. *Marc.* 24; for *bonus* see Appel (1909), 99; Hellegouarc'h (1972), 485.

[275] For this sense of *longus* see *OLD* s.v. 14. This seems more likely than stressing that the *feriae* themselves should be long, even though the length of the *supplicatio* was a measure of the honour being voted: Augustus records 890 days of *supplicatio* on 55 occasions: *RG* 4. 2.

[276] So ps.-Acro on 4. 5. 37: 'aut propter continuationem victoriarum longas optavit ferias aut ominando vitam prolixam.' For the 'long may you live' topos see Doblhofer (1966), 53–4; Nisbet and Hubbard (1970), 37; Woodman (1977), 281–2.

[277] See Dyson (1990), and contrast Radke (1964), 74; Syndikus (1973), 342 with n. 77. It is worth emphasizing that at the time of writing this poem Horace is aware that there will be no triumph: contrast 4. 2. 41–60. *Feriae* were voted *senatus consulto* for the *constitutio* of the Ara Pacis.

[278] Enn. *Ann.* 20 Skutsch 'est locus Hesperiam quam mortales perhibebant'; Virg. *Aen.* 1. 530, 3. 163 with Skutsch (1985), 178–9.

to return. Horace is perhaps making use of a dispute over the true significance of the name to make a point. *Hesperia* could be explained as derived from *Vesperus*, the *sidus Veneris*,[279] and Venus is not only *Aeneadum genetrix* but also and in particular the divine ancestor of the *gens Iulia*. If this is what Horace is intending to recall then the point is that Italy, not Spain, is home.

The daily reiteration of the prayer, at sunrise and at sunset, parallels the farmers' earlier libation and prayer to the *numen Augusti*. That such prayers were made to the *genius Augusti* is attested by Ovid both for the evening and for the morning.[280] Given the immediately preceding comparison with Hercules, it is natural that the chorus should model its cult-act on that associated with Hercules, to whom sacrifice was also made both in the morning and in the evening.[281] The humorously contrasting adjectives *uvidi* and *sicci* neatly suggest the joy of the worshippers. The worshippers are *sicci* when they make the morning prayers, as soon as they wake at the break of day. It was normal for the Lar or the Genius of the *paterfamilias* to receive the first libation, then the person who had made the libation could drink and only after that the other members of the *familia*.[282] Now Augustus as the ultimate benefactor of each individual and his household takes precedence and is counted among the household gods. The evening prayers were made *secunda mensa*, after the first and main course, during which wine had already been drunk to accompany the food, had been cleared.[283] The prayer was accompanied by a libation of *vina pura*, which was then shared by the worshippers.

---

[279] Plin. *NH* 2. 36; Maltby (1991), 640.

[280] See Ov. *Fasti* 2. 635; *Ex P.* 3. 1. 159–66; 4. 9. 105–6, 111–12.

[281] Servius ad *Aen.* 8. 269: '[Hercules] cum ergo de suo armento ad sua sacrificia boves dedisset, inventi sunt duo senes . . . quibus qualiter se coli vellet ostendit, scilicet ut mane et vespere ei sacrificaretur.' In the cult of Dea Dia the Fratres Arvales greeted her *primo mane* and invited her to attend *secunda mensa* in the evening: see Scheid (1990), 478, 487, 504, 509–10, 517–18, 527, 541, 550, 635, 640.

[282] For the Lar see Hor. *Sat.* 2. 5. 14 'ante Larem gustet venerabilior Lare dives'; and for the Genius Cens. 2. 3 'illud etiam . . . observandum quod genio factum neminem oportet ante gustare quam eum qui fecerit.'

[283] Ps.-Acro on 4. 5. 33: 'antiquorum consuetudo talis fuit, ut sublata prima mensa poneretur secunda atque in ea positis pomis infusoque vino libaretur diis.'

The poem ends with the image of the rising (implicit in *mane*)²⁸⁴ and setting of the sun. This picks up the earlier sun imagery and serves to remind us that Augustus' own return will be like that of the sun, and that he too must return from the west. But the image of the rising and setting sun also serves to complement the earlier allusions to the conquest of east and west, and so reminds us that

> ... Latinum nomen et Italae
> crevere vires famaque et imperi
> porrecta maiestas ad ortus
> solis ab Hesperio cubili.
> (*Odes* 4. 15. 13–16)

The name of Latium and the power of Italy has grown and the fame and majesty of the empire have been extended to the rising of the sun from its bed in the West.

The emphasis on the divinity of Augustus at the end of the poem should not come as a surprise. The poem started by invoking his divine ancestry and then moved on through the evocation of Ennius' account of the death and apotheosis of Romulus. Then the emphasis fell on the achievements of Augustus, in peace and in war, especially those illustrating his *iustitia*. Finally comes the recognition of his divinity as Augustus is shown to have fulfilled the hopes that people had once had of the new god Divus Iulius. What he has achieved and the effects of his achievements can only be attributed to a divine power. So in the absence of the *praesens deus* the farmer summons to the feast his *numen*.

This private and domestic cult is not identical with the cult of the Genius Augusti and the Lares Compitales, which is a public cult introduced in Italy from about 12 BC and in the city of Rome in 7 BC, with the organization of the *vici*.²⁸⁵ Nor is it the same as the public cult of the Numen Augusti which was established by Tiberius in honour of the living Augustus in AD 6.²⁸⁶ Yet neither can it be

²⁸⁴ Varro, *LL* 6. 4 'diei principium mane, quod tum manat dies ab oriente.'
²⁸⁵ Contrast Syndikus (1973), 342 n. 76; see Niebling (1956), 329–31; Liebeschuetz (1979), 69–70; Dio 55. 8. 6–7 with Rich (1990), 226–7, with further bibliography.
²⁸⁶ See *Fast. Praen.*: 'Pontifices augures xv viri sacris faciundis vii viri epulonum victumas immolant numini Augusti ad aram quam dedicavit Ti. Caes'; Degrassi (1963), 401; Fishwick (1991), 378.

considered in isolation from these later developments. For it can hardly be a coincidence that, so shortly before the introduction of these public cults, the *populus* is suddenly and prominently represented as honouring the *numen/genius* of Augustus as if he were their *paterfamilias*. The decade in which *Odes* 4 was being written saw an increasing emphasis on the divinity of Augustus. Outside of Italy, the worship of the living Augustus was established at Tarraco, probably in the 20s, and at Lyons in 12 BC.[287] In Rome there was the renewed emphasis on Augustus' relationship with Divus Iulius, which is clearly designed to suggest his own divinity and eventual apotheosis. The introduction of Pax Augusta at Rome marks a significant increased emphasis on the ambiguous position occupied by Augustus between the human and the divine. But Augustus' special status found its most powerful expression in the Horologium complex which proclaimed him as both conqueror and bringer of peace, and as a new Romulus whose apotheosis had been earned by these achievements. The planning of this monument must have gone on through much of this decade and started well before his return. There are many themes in common between it and *Odes* 4 in general and 4. 5 in particular. Given Horace's position as *in numero amicorum Caesaris* ('counted among Caesar's friends'), it seems more likely that this is a result of Horace being a party to the thinking and planning that went into it than of mere chance. *Odes* 4. 5 helps to define and to promote this new image of Augustus and his unique position in the state.

6. CONCLUSION

Odes 4. 5 belongs to the genre *klētikon*. The opening stanzas (1–16) constitute the prologue, in which the speaker issues the invitation and expresses a sense of longing for the return of the addressee. The central stanzas (17–28) provide an encomiastic description of the place to which he is being invited. But since the addressee is the *custos*

[287] For the altar at Tarraco see Fishwick (1987), 172–9; for that at Lyons see Fishwick (1987), 97–9.

gentis and *dux bonus*, and since the place to which he is being invited
is what it is because of what he is and what he has achieved, these
central stanzas also constitute praise of the addressee, ordered un-
typically and therefore emphatically as 'deeds in peace' (17–24) and
'deeds in war' (21–4). Here, as is conventional in the *klētikon*, praise
of the addressee is used to provide an explanation or justification
(17 *etenim*) of the speaker's request for him to return, of the affectionate longing, and of gratitude for the benefits he has conferred
(7 *gratior it dies*). The final section (29–40) describes the welcome
that is already being prepared throughout Italy by the *populus Romanus*, who express their gratitude to their *dux bonus* by treating him as
a god in recognition of his godlike power and the godlike benefits
which he has conferred upon them.

In terms of its genre the poem has two interesting features. First,
there is no account of the journey to be undertaken by the addressee,
and that is a noticeable omission. Consideration of the likely date of
composition for the poem and of the date of 'publication' both
suggest that the poem was composed before the return of Augustus
in July 13 BC but always intended for publication and performance
on his return. The omission of the journey topos would be natural in
those circumstances. If the poem was always intended to be performed after Augustus' return, that would also explain the emphasis
on the joy that is felt at his presence rather than the sadness and
longing that are felt in his absence. Second, the speaker is not
portrayed, as is normal in the *klētikon*, as an ambassador who has
been sent on behalf of the SPQR to urge Augustus to return. The
request is made to the addressee in his absence and from afar. In
other words, the speaker, like the citizen farmer at his meal,
summons the addressee as one would a god. This would be quite
normal in a kletic hymn, and Horace has borrowed this feature from
that closely related genre in order to convey the ambiguous status of
his addressee between man and god or, rather, as both man and god.
The poem has other hymnic features which serve the same purpose:
for example, the opening participle (*divis orte*), the introduction of
the justifications for the imperatives by *enim* (6) and *etenim* (17), the
intricate patterns of assonance and alliteration, and the anaphora
of *te* ~ *tuum* (32–4). In a hymn the speaker is normally a chorus.
That this is also the case in this poem is confirmed by the plurals

(38–9 *dicimus*), the role of the speaker as representative of the SPQR, and, given ancient assumptions that lyric was normally performed by a chorus, the lack of any counter-indication.

The poem derives its coherence and the logic of its argument from the familiar pattern of the *klētikon*. It is also underpinned by a sustained allusion to a famous passage of Ennius which related the death or disappearance of Romulus, the sense of sadness and loss that his people experienced when deprived of their *pater patriae*, their praises of the just king they had lost, and their subsequent recognition of him as a *deus* and their decision to institute a formal cult. The allusion constitutes an invitation to compare and contrast the situations of Augustus and Romulus. The inference which we are being invited to make is clarified by the complementary references to Castor (35) and Hercules (36), and to Divus Iulius (1). These past benefactors, who have been equalled or surpassed by Augustus, were only recognized as gods after their death or apotheosis. Augustus, by contrast, is worshipped while he is still alive. The message implied in *Odes* 4. 5 is the same as that stated explicitly in the near-contemporary *Epistles* 2. 1. 5–15: earlier benefactors receive worship and recognition as gods only after their deaths, while Augustus' divinity is fully recognized during his lifetime.

Into the framework provided by this sustained allusion to Ennius Horace works several other allusions. Perhaps in place of a simile in Ennius comparing the grief of the Roman people at the death of Romulus to the grief of children deprived of a father, Horace has substituted the long simile (9–16) comparing the yearning of the *patria* for the absent Augustus to the yearning of a (presumably) widowed mother for the return of her only son, on whom her welfare totally depends. The exact source of this allusion is not known but it seems to have come from a lost Hellenistic classic. It appears that Ennius placed considerable emphasis on the *iustitia* of Romulus in his account of the apotheosis and of what was subsequently said in praise of him. Horace has complemented the allusion to Ennius by working in a sustained allusion (17–24) to Hesiod's classic account of the peaceful prosperity enjoyed by the πόλις which is ruled by just men, in order to praise Augustus for his *iustitia* and to paint an alluring picture of Italy, transformed by its just ruler into a land that enjoys prosperity, security, and good order. Finally, at the end of the

poem, there is an allusion to Virgil's *Eclogues* (1 and 9). Through a
striking phrase (29 *condit…diem*, 'puts away the day') Horace
evokes the scene in *Eclogue* 9 where the hopes that peaceful prosperity and security would be guaranteed by the new god, Divus Iulius,
shatter on the brutal realities of the confiscations of land required to
settle the veterans of Philippi. At that time Octavian could only act as
benefactor to a single individual, as he did to Tityrus in *Eclogue* 1 by
exempting his land from confiscation, and Tityrus had expressed his
gratitude by instituting for his saviour a private cult. Now Augustus
has guaranteed the *securitas* of all and guarantees everyone possession of his land, secure from the threat of external enemies and from
civil war. Now everyone responds, not just one individual, by recognizing the *numen* of Augustus and worshipping him, spontaneously
and privately, as a god.

The dignified simplicity of *Odes* 4. 5 belies the richness of its
literary techniques, the complexity of its *arte allusiva*, and the doc-
trina displayed in the learned play with ancient etymologies (analysed above). Yet to view the poem only in terms of its literary and
rhetorical background is to miss much of its essential character. This
is an occasional poem, written to be performed, it is argued, by a
chorus as part of the celebrations, whether private or public or
indeed both, for the return of Augustus on 4 July 13 bc. Features of
the poem that may seem at first glance no more than literary commonplaces take on new significance when seen in this context. The
abruptness of the solar imagery (5–8) will have been less obtrusive in
the context of an *adventus*, and less startling to an audience familiar
with the statue of Augustus *habitu et statu Apollinis* ('in the garb and
guise of Apollo', Suetonius, *Augustus* 29. 3) in the portico of the
temple of Apollo on the Palatine, on the roof of which there was a
statue of Sol, to whom in due course the obelisk that formed the
gnomon of the Horologium would be dedicated in commemoration
of the victories won at Actium and Alexandria with the assistance of
Apollo. The implicit comparison with Divus Iulius will have seemed
less oblique at a time when efforts were being made to stress Augustus' status as *Divi filius* and to advertise his claim to have already
merited his own apotheosis by his achievements at home and abroad.
The comparison with Romulus that permeates the poem will have
been more apparent given its topicality: it had been strongly

promoted by the imagery on the pediment of the temple of Quirinus rebuilt and dedicated by Augustus just before his departure in 16 BC, and would play a prominent part on the Ara Pacis and in the symbolic messages to be communicated by the Horologium. Even the apparently standard comparison with Hercules gains an emotional charge from the strong associations of Hercules with Augustus' previous triumphal or quasi-triumphal *reditus*, and more specifically from the fact that Hercules' arrival at the site of Rome from Spain was commemorated by the Ara Maxima and the return of Augustus from Spain in 13 BC was marked by the *constitutio* of the Ara Pacis Augustae.

But it is not only contemporary art and architecture which point up the topicality of the poem. Its central theme is the idea that the *salus* of all is bound up in the *salus* of the person of Augustus. This theme echoed through the language of the senatorial decrees concerned with the return, as we know from contemporary coin legends and inscriptions, and through the prayers of the various priesthoods as they offered thanks for his safe return. The day of his return also saw the recognition of a new divinity, Pax Augusta, who manifested herself exclusively in and through the deeds of Augustus. What people were saying on this day about their new divinity or in what terms they anticipated the benefits expected to flow from the institution of the new cult can only be guessed or inferred from the imagery on the Ara itself or from what is now known of the messages to be conveyed by the Horologium complex as a whole. Horace exploits to the full the context in which the poem will be performed. The *adventus* was a time of carnivalesque festivity, with crowds of people thronging the streets. Baths and barbers were made available free of charge. The atmosphere of joyful excitement was punctuated by periods of solemn and dignified civic ceremonial and by inspiring and awesome religious acts of ritual prayer accompanied by music, libations, and blood-sacrifice. Horace can rely on the mood of such an occasion. With everything focused on Augustus, the poet can rely on the audience to pick up any allusion. He can afford to understate because in such an emotionally charged atmosphere he can, with the slightest hint, set off a train of reverberating associations. He also knows that the audience will want to be part of it all and will be glad to be 'reminded' of their sense of yearning and loss during Augustus' absence.

He can afford to catch the mood of the moment and represent Augustus' relationship with the senate as Augustus 'wanted' it to be rather than reflect the stresses and strains that were the underlying reality of the time. He can even turn to a brilliantly imaginative use Augustus' proposals to end the system of giving land to veterans on discharge by recalling the havoc and dislocation previously caused by this system as it had been memorably depicted in Virgil's *Eclogues*, and by using the implied contrast between the conditions in the years immediately following the death of Julius Caesar and the present to exemplify the benefits conferred by Augustus, the ending of civil war and the favour of Pax Augusta.

If the significance of the allusion to the *Eclogues* has been correctly understood, it has an important consequence: it shows that Horace was well informed of what was being planned for the return of Augustus and that he knew of these specific proposals before they were revealed in the senate. Given what is now known about the elaborate planning and construction of the Horologium and the skilful political manoeuvring that went into securing the proposal of the Ara Pacis Augustae as the honour to mark Augustus' return, it is time to give more credence than has recently been fashionable to the idea that Augustus' image was constructed and promoted by his friends only after concerted effort and careful thought and preparation. The image of Augustus presented in *Odes* 4 is fully in line with that presented in other media. At the beginning of the decade Augustus' constitutional position had been finally defined and stabilized; there was only the office of Pontifex Maximus to add. Constitutionally he was *primus inter pares* ('first among equals'), superior to others in *auctoritas* rather than in *potestas* ('formal magisterial power'). This formulation (*Res Gestae* 34. 3) underestimates the effect of the combination of offices and powers that he held, but also explains why in the next decade Augustus is marked off from other men by the accumulation of quasi-divine honours and by the promotion of his claims to divinity rather than by a further increase in constitutional powers. *Odes* 4. 5 makes its contribution to building up this image of Augustus, and that is what makes it a perfectly conceived and perfectly executed *donum adventicium pro reditu Imperatoris Caesaris Divi filii Augusti* ('Welcome home present for Imperator Caesar Augustus, son of the Divine').

15

A Parade of Lyric Predecessors:
Horace C. 1.12–18

Michèle Lowrie

The sequences that are generally accepted in Horace's *Odes* show both formal linkage and a shared subject or purpose. Metrical patterning has been a favored clue to a deeper connection between groups of poems. The Parade Odes opening the first collection of *Odes* are characterized by metrical diversity; an alternation of Sapphics and Alcaics joins the first eleven poems of book two into a significant whole; the Roman Odes at the beginning of book three comprise the largest group to share a single meter, Alcaics.[1] In each group an identifiable metrical pattern signals a common purpose, whether based on similarity or the principle of *uariatio*. I would like to propose a sequence that has gone unnoticed presumably because the formal feature linking it is not metrical. In *C.* 1.12–18 Horace alludes successively to a number of important Greek lyric predecessors and the combined weight of these allusions establishes a poetic program, an internal connection revealing a purpose outside shared subject matter. This sequence follows on the Parade Odes and extends their program. Horace's roll-call of *lyrici uates* ('lyric bards') defines the tradition he reinvents with *Odes* 1–3; in inscribing himself into this tradition, he asserts both his similarity to and difference from his predecessors.

---

[1] Parade Odes: Santirocco (1986), 42; Porter (1987), 15; also see discussion below, n. 5. Book two: Port (1926), 299–300; Ludwig (1957); Eisenberger (1980); Santirocco (1986), 85; Porter (1987), 12, 109. Roman Odes: Witke (1983); Santirocco (1986), 110–12, with bibliography 203, n. 7; Porter (1987), 13, 152.

The two most recent treatments of arrangement in the *Odes* have
reopened the question of where the Parade Odes end and, since my
proposed sequence follows on the recognized parade, the articulation
of the two will be at issue. M. Santirocco favors a narrow definition:
in a group defined by metrical diversity, the first repetition of a meter
(Sapphics) at *C.* 1.10 signals closure.[2] D. Porter views the repetition
of Sapphics in *C.* 1.10 and again in *C.* 1.12, with a new meter in
between, as a flourish bringing the sequence to an end; responsion to
C. 1.2 accounts for *C.* 1.12's climactic position.[3] Santirocco does
grant that Horace blurred the edges of the sequence: the issues of
the parade continue beyond its formal end, with *C.* 1.12 providing a
second closure to the group.[4] The two views differ more in emphasis
than radically disagree.[5] Since the parade of lyric predecessors begins
with *C.* 1.12 and is defined according to a formal principle different
from the metrical parade, I suggest that the poems between the two
sequences allow the first formal principle, metrical variety, to fade
while preserving an essential connection. In the first sequence we find
a series of different lyric meters, shortly thereafter we find a series of
different lyric predecessors; the common denominator is lyric and
the lyric tradition. This second sequence continues the lyric parade
on the programmatic level while shifting the formal terms in such a
way that formalists and essentialists should both be satisfied.

[2] Santirocco (1986), 42.
[3] Porter (1987), 15.
[4] Porter (1987), 58–77; Santirocco (1987), 42–3. Since these two books were
written without knowledge of each other, my juxtaposition of their views is strictly
for the sake of the argument.
[5] von Christ (1868), 36, n. 12, called attention to the principle of metrical variety
in the first nine odes. Kiessling (1881) argued that the Sapphics in *C.* 1.10 are a
variant on the usual meter and that the sequence extends until the first real repetition
in *C.* 1.12. Although Seidensticker (1976) argues for a more narrowly formal definition, Kiessling (1881) added a thematic element to the discussion by suggesting that
the ring formed by *C.* 1.12 and *C.* 1.2 in subject matter as well as meter continues the
sequence. While Porter (1987) emphasizes content over form and Santirocco (1986)
the opposite, they each recognize a link between *C.* 1.2, 1.10, and 1.12 in both theme
and form—all in Sapphics and distributing the terms Augustus and Mercury between
them. Another recent work on arrangement in the *Odes*, Dettmer (1983) has other
interests and does not really add to the debate about the Parade Odes. The actual term
'parade' appears as a metaphor later than the idea of a metrically determined
sequence, apparently for the first time in Teuffel (1920), 55. Since the word does
not appear in earlier editions, it seems to have been added by W. Kroll or F. Skutsch,
who reworked this edition: see Edmunds (1992), 43, n. 5.

By and large the allusions in the seven odes from *C.* 1.12 through *C.* 1.18 are to passages that were not only famous in antiquity, but could and still can be seen as representative of their authors. In each ode a single lyric poet predominates; in *C.* 1.16 and 1.17 an additional non-lyric poet is set against the lyric. In order, Horace alludes to Pindar in *C.* 1.12, Sappho in *C.* 1.13, Alcaeus in *C.* 1.14, Bacchylides in *C.* 1.15, Stesichorus and Archilochus in *C.* 1.16, Anacreon and Homer in *C.* 1.17, Alcaeus again in *C.* 1.18. Archilochus and Homer contribute to Horace's lyric definition by the contrast first with iambic poetry, stylistically lower than lyric, secondly with epic, stylistically higher. The repetition of Alcaeus, analogous to the repetition of the Sapphics in the metrical parade, signals closure.

Some of these allusions are more secure than others, but all have been proposed independently from my thesis and hold their own in commentaries.[6] I mean 'allusion' in its broadest sense: Horace can evoke a predecessor with a verbal reminiscence, or simply point to the predecessor by a topos originating with him or her, or mention the poet so to speak by name (e.g., *fide Teia*, 'lyre from Teos,' i.e., Anacreon, *C.* 1.17.18). For the sake of the argument, I assume that lack of absolute security in several cases is the fault of the Greek lyric transmission rather than due to fantasy on the part of ancient (or modern) commentators.

Another caveat: the proposed sequence is a surface feature linking these poems in a static arrangement. Allusion to a Greek lyric predecessor in this parade is the formal equivalent of the metrical variety in the Parade Odes; I will return to the dynamic readings of these poems by Santirocco and Porter, and while this sequence does not by and large conflict with either of their views, I would not be disturbed if the static arrangement turned out to have slightly different boundaries from the groupings we perceive on reading the poems in order. As a surface feature the sequence of allusions should not affect the interpretation of the individual odes as wholes, even if participation in the sequence may highlight a given ode's programmatic function or endow it with a previously unrecognized programmatic role (*C.* 1.15). I do not mean to suggest new interpretations of

---

[6] e.g., Nisbet and Hubbard (1970). I take their views to establish the *communis opinio* unless otherwise stated.

these seven poems except to the extent that linking them sheds new light on the group.

C. 1.12 opens with a motto from Pindar: *quem uirum aut heroa lyra uel acri | tibia sumis celebrare, Clio? | quem deum?* ('What man or hero do you undertake to celebrate, Clio, on the lyre or keen reed? What god?' 1–3).[7] Horace virtually translates Pindar's τίνα θεόν, τίν᾽ ἥρωα, τίνα δ᾽ ἄνδρα κελαδήσομεν;... ('What god, what hero, what man shall I celebrate?' *O.* 2.2), with the exception of a complete transposition of the order of god, hero and man.[8] Pindar answers the question in the same order over the next three lines: Zeus, Heracles, and Theron.[9] Horace takes the rest of the poem to answer and his answer is chiastic. A variety of gods (with Jupiter preeminent) and heroes (starting with Hercules) culminates in the man *par excellence*: Caesar Augustus. Horace begins and ends with the man—a mark of the distance between his Roman reinvention and the archaic hymnic form, which, if it focuses on Theron, at least begins with the god. The poem's ending further distances Horace from Pindar: the first and last terms of the tricolon meet in the melding of a conditional epinician to Augustus with a hymn to Jupiter. Man and god are no longer distinct.

In the first two lines of this poem Horace joins the lyre, the emblem of monody, with the tibia, that of choral lyric. Sapphics ground the poem in the monodic tradition and the allusion to Pindar in the choral. The evocation of the two branches of lyric functions as a complementary or merism which stands for the genre as a whole.[10] This conjunction of the tibia with the lyre recalls their joint appearance at the end of *C.* 1.1 (*si neque tibias | Euterpe cohibet nec Polyhymnia | Lesboum refugit tendere barbiton,* 'if neither Euterpe inhibit the reeds nor Polyhymnia shrink from

[7] Nisbet and Hubbard (1970), 143. On the 'motto', see Fraenkel (1957), 159, n. 2: 'This sort of limited adoption will often be found when a classicistic school of poetry insists on its connexion with some admired forerunners.'

[8] Kiessling and Heinze (1917), *ad loc.*; Oksala (1973), 92, also notes the chiastic answer.

[9] See the proposed scheme by Gildersleeve (1890), *ad loc.*

[10] I take it for granted that Horace distinguished between these branches whether or not they were separated by the Greeks: Davies (1988). For the importance of the complementary, or 'dichotomized whole' as a rhetorical device in Horace, see Davis (1991), *passim.*

stringing the bass lyre', 32–4), the first poem not only of the collection but of the metrical parade. *C.* 1.12, first in this second parade, recalls the programmatic fusion of monody and choral lyric in *C.* 1.1. Horace's *Odes* are monodic in form, but sometimes rise to choral heights. The two instruments are conjoined again in the opening of *C.* 3.4 (*tibia . . . seu fidibus citharaue Phoebi*, 'on the reed or strings or cithara of Phoebus', 1–4), where Horace alerts us to the sublimity to follow.

Just as Pindar is the key predecessor to a combined hymn to Jupiter and epinician to the head of state, Sappho is the key predecessor to a love poem. The nature of the allusion, however, is different. Instead of a motto we find rather the descendant of an 'illustrious prototype.'[11] The physical manifestations of violent emotion in *C.* 1.13 along with the triangular relationship of the poet, a female erotic object as the addressee (Lydia) and a male third person (Telephus) recall Sappho 31. The extent to which Horace evokes Sappho herself, as opposed to the tradition of imitation of this poem, is a question which will recur for the role of Alcaeus in the next poem.[12] I assume that when a tradition of imitation intercedes between a famous passage and a later imitation, the history of the topos does not dilute the force of the association with the original author. Clearly it is a question of degrees. In this case, as for Alcaeus in the next poem, the originals were not only famous in themselves, but much more famous than the interceding imitations. The situation would be different if the earliest version were already a topos and did not stand out with the vividness of Sappho's catalogue of symptoms. If anything, a strong history of imitation burnished the reputation of the original.

Additional evidence for Horace's dependence on Sappho is the triangular relationship between the characters in both poems. A difference, however, obtains in the nature of the two triangles. If

---

[11] Nisbet and Hubbard (1970), 169; 'una libera ripresa', Cavallini (1978–9), 377. Commager (1962), 152 thinks that the primary impetus for Horatian imitation was Catullus' translation of Sappho in poem 51; maybe, but one would then expect more specifically Catullan traces in the poem.

[12] Smyth (1963), 234 lists as imitations or descendants Phaedra's love illness in Eur. *Hipp.*, Plato *Phdr.* 251a, Ap. Rhod. *Argon.* 3.962 ff., Theoc. 2.106 ff., Lucr. 3.152, Valerius Aedituus in Gellius 19.9 = Courtney frg. 1.

we accept Marcovich's arguments that Sappho 31 does not represent a love-triangle but that the dispassionate man in the poem is a foil for the poet's own passion, Horace's love-triangle still bears a greater resemblance to Sappho than to the intervening imitations in the presence of three characters, whatever their roles.[13] Horace playfully misreads Sappho 31 as a poem about jealousy—anticipating, or even eliciting one strand of modern interpretation.[14] The reduction of noble feeling to the crass jealousy of a rival is in line with the overall tone of self-mockery that colors the poet's description of his emotion.[15] Horace's ironic treatment of himself sets him apart from Sappho; his refusal to present passion 'straight' posits a difference between his lyric and hers.[16] Not of course that Sappho's poem lacks irony and a sense of play, but her passion in itself does not lack dignity.[17]

It is remarkable that Horace shuns the vocabulary of Catullus' translation of Sappho in poem 51; if Horace's self-differentiation from Sappho exposes his poetic debt, his neglect of Catullus here

[13] Marcovich (1972). In none of the imitations cited by Smyth (1963), 234 are the symptoms motivated by the presence of a rival, or even of a third person. These imitations strengthen Marcovich's argument that the symptoms in Sappho 31 are those of love, not of jealousy. See also Race (1983), 92–101, with other relevant bibliography 94, nn. 8 and 9.

[14] e.g., Page (1955), 19–33, especially 28; Devereux (1970). Race (1983), 93, n. 4 suggests that the jealousy interpretation may derive from Hellenistic and Latin love elegy but does not name *C.* 1.13 in particular.

[15] West (1967), 65–71; Nisbet and Hubbard (1970), 170 note the colloquialisms; Santirocco (1986), 45. Keyser (1989) traces medical and philosophical language in the poem. These distancing clinical terms contribute to the poet's light-hearted treatment of his emotion.

[16] I do not mean that Horace trivializes or disparages Sappho either in general or here. Her taking second place to Alcaeus and Horace's ambivalence to passion can both be overstated as a negative reaction to her. See La Penna (1972) on the comparison of Sappho to Alcaeus in *C.* 2.13. Horace appears to leave Sappho behind in *Epist.* 1.19.23–33 (passage cited below) where she falls between Archilochus and Alcaeus. The dependence of both Lesbians on Archilochus is a parallel proving Horace's originality in the *Epodes*, Fraenkel (1957), 339–50; see Woodman (1983a). Once the Lesbians have been named, Alcaeus provides the transition to the assertion of originality in the *Odes* (*hunc*, 'this one', 32) but the greater emphasis on Alcaeus, Horace's single most important lyric model, by no means precludes a positive attitude toward Sappho. Why mention her if unimportant?

[17] See Race (1983), 95 on Sappho's play.

vaunts his originality on his home turf.[18] In addition to self-mockery, a second characteristically Horatian gesture establishes a difference between his love poetry and that of his predecessors and elegiac contemporaries. The closing emphasis on mature love (*felices ter et amplius | quos irrupta tenet copula...*, 'three times and more fortunate are those an unbroken bond holds', 17–18), particularly after the outburst, lends an aura of sophistication to the erotic persona in the *Odes* and distinguishes him from the complaining lover typical of elegy. Horace assimilates Sappho to elegy when he characterizes her as *querentem* ('complaining', *C.* 2.13.24) and while the lyric lover of the *Odes* may complain, as here (*uae*, 'woe', 3), he does so tongue in cheek. Even Horace's 'maturity' turns out to be ironic, since its function as a seductive ploy compromises its authority.[19]

The ship imagery of *C.* 1.14 evokes Alcaeus. The derivation of the imagery is separate from its allegorical import, although the issues are closely tied in the scholarship.[20] For my purposes it is sufficient

---

[18] Syndikus (1972), 156 stresses the greater freedom of Horace's poem than Catullus' from its Greek predecessor but does not then consider Horace's relation to his Latin predecessor, which is complex. Horace makes programmatic gestures of excluding Catullus as a predecessor: e.g., not using the Phalaecean hendecasyllable signals a distance from Catullus and from Hellenistic epigram, even though both clearly not only influenced the *Odes* but are objects of allusion. Lee (1975) sees Catullan influence in *C.* 1.13 (and *C.* 1.25, also addressed to Lydia) as well as allusion to Catullus 51 elsewhere: '... [Horace's] Lydia is cast as Catullus' Lesbia (the desire for her causing jealousy and extreme physical sensations in the hapless poet, her last days spent *leuis, in angiportu...*)' (36); *C.* 1.22.24 *dulce loquentem* alludes to Catullus 51.5 *dulce ridentem*, adding by the way ἆδυ φωνείσας from Sappho 31.3–4, omitted by Catullus (38). What I find interesting is that this latter type of allusive cleverness is displaced onto a poem other than Horace's imitation of Sappho, where we might expect it. See Santirocco (1986), 20 on the relation of Catullus and Horace (bibliography at n. 19).

[19] Davis (1991), 39 (maturity in Horatian erotic lyric), 58 (*querela* as a catch phrase for elegy), 85 (the reduction of Sappho), with n. 8 (on *queror*), 39–71 (Horace's complex relation to elegy and the elegiac stance). Segal (1973) pursues the dialectical relationship between the irony and the seriousness of the final lines of the poem in the 'pull between the poet as a troubled participant and the poet as wise, aloof spectator' (45). The difference between Horace and Sappho could be that for the latter, irony lies in the gap between the participant and the spectator, for the former, both positions are already in themselves rhetorically constructed and ironized.

[20] For the standard version of the ship of state interpretation, deriving from Quintilian, see Fraenkel (1957), 154–8; Nisbet and Hubbard (1970), 179–82; Syndikus (1972), 162–70. Against this view, see Anderson, (1966); Seel (1970); Zumwalt (1977–8); Woodman (1980); Davis (1989). Anderson shows that *C.* 1.14 is inconsistent with the conventions of the ship of state; Seel objects that Asclepiadeans,

that the poem look to Alcaeus no matter what the ship stands for. Allegorical interpretations of Alcaeus' several ship poems are found in Heraclitus and the scholiasts, and the favored interpretations are the ship of state or political party and the ship as woman.[21] I think that, given the remarks in Heraclitus and the Alcaeus commentaries, we can assume that Alcaeus was known for ship allegories, regardless of whether the commentators interpreted the tenor correctly or even whether their identification of these poems as allegories was in itself correct.[22] There are two aspects to this observation. The first is the particular association of Alcaeus with ship imagery over and above the sizeable tradition of such imagery.[23] Horace certainly associated Alcaeus with ships (*C.* 1.32.8, 2.13.27, both passages cited below). Secondly, a striking aspect shared by the Alcaeus fragments—as far as we can tell—and Horace's ship poem is their openness to allegorical interpretation: that is, unlike the ship metaphors cited by Anderson and Woodman, there is no internal revelation of their tenor.[24] It is in fact the referential indeterminacy of Horace's poem that links it specifically to Alcaeus' ship poems and distances it from the erotic

especially the third, point to a private meaning; Zumwalt argues for a ship of erotic poetry; Woodman traces the imagery within the ship-of-love conventions; Davis alters the ship of erotic poetry to a self-referential ship of Horace's own poetry. Woodman is the only one to deny the particular influence of Alcaeus. Jocelyn (1982) offers a critique of the ship/woman allegory on the grounds that the topos is not flattering to the woman. Santirocco (1986), 46–9 takes further Commager's remark (1962), 169 that nothing in the poem tells us what the ship represents, and suggests that the allegory is open.

[21] Page (1955), 179–97. Woodman (1980), 62 points out that whether or not one agrees with Page that the fragmentary commentary of *POxy.* 21.105 has Alcaeus 73 as its subject, the commentary indicates that 'Alcaeus was thought in antiquity to have exploited the identification of women with ships'.

[22] Davis (1989), 344 calls attention to Pasquali's remark (1920), 21 that Horace would have been likely to use a commentary in reading Alcaeus and that such a commentary would have been likely of the Hellenistic, allegorizing variety; see also Fraenkel (1957), 156, n. 4.

[23] Woodman (1980), 62, n. 14; 64 with n. 26 emphasizes the tradition of ship imagery and denies a peculiar role to Alcaeus within that tradition.

[24] Anderson (1966), 93–4 cites Theognis 457–60 and Cat. 64.97–8, both of which are formally similes. Woodman (1980), 62–3 quotes three epigrams, *Anth. Pal.* 5.44, 161, 204, that use the ship-woman metaphor, but each epigram contains the name of at least one woman and Woodman rightly speaks of metaphor in these cases, not allegory.

ship epigrams of the tradition closer to Horace. Furthermore, the ship poems of Alcaeus were presumably much more famous than the intervening epigrams.

Short of positing an entirely self-referential 'ship of allegory', I would accept Zumwalt's suggestion that Horace misleads his readers into initially assuming a political allegory and then, by using imagery consistent with an erotic allegory, calls into question the appropriateness of 'serious', i.e., political poetry within lyric.[25] It is the openness of the allegory that allows for such a shift in meaning.

Under this interpretation the juxtaposition of the ship/war side of Alcaeus with his love poetry in another Horatian poem has significance for *C.* 1.14:[26]

> Lesbio primum modulate ciui,
> qui ferox bello, tamen inter arma
> siue iactatam religarat udo
>   litore nauim,
> Liberum et Musas Veneremque et illi
> semper haerentem puerum canebat
> et Lycum nigris oculis nigroque
>   crine decorum.   *C.* 1.32.5–12

[Bass lyre], first played by the Lesbian citizen, who, fierce in war, nevertheless whether he was in arms or had tied his tossed ship on the wet shore, always sang of Bacchus, and the Muses, and Venus, and that boy always clinging to her, and Lycus, beautiful with his black eyes, black hair.

In this passage a 'serious Alcaeus' is followed by a 'sympotic/erotic Alcaeus', a movement analogous to the internal progression in *C.* 1.14 from a political allegory to metapoetics. The juxtaposition of Sappho and Alcaeus in *C.* 2.13 likewise contrasts the erotic with the serious, but here each poet stands for one term, as in the juxtaposition of

On the openness of *C.* 1.14, see Santirocco (1986), 48. R. G. M. Nisbet in the opening lecture of the annual meeting of the Classical Association in Durham, England, April 1993, attacked those who would see Horace's allegory as open. He believes that an allegory must have a single, determinate meaning and that the ship of state remains the most likely.

[25] Zumwalt (1977–8), 254; Davis (1989), 332, 344 sees this shift as an implicit subversion of the political reading and of the critical clichés that produced such a reading of Alcaeus, and indeed of Horace himself.

[26] Zumwalt (1977–8), 254.

the Sapphic *C.* 1.13 with the Alcaic and—at least at first reading—
political *C.* 1.14:[27] in *C.* 1.13 the poet complains about a female love-
interest; *C.* 1.14 treats the travails of a ship:

> Aeoliis fidibus querentem
> Sappho puellis de popularibus,
> et te sonantem plenius aureo,
>   Alcaee, plectro dura nauis,
>   dura fugae mala, dura belli!   *C.* 2.13.24–8

Sappho complaining about the girls of the people on the Aeolian strings, and
you, Alcaeus, sounding the hardships of sea-faring, the evil hardships of
exile, of war, more fulsome on your golden plectrum.

Each of these passages reveals something about our sequence. *C.* 2.13
polarizes the Lesbian poets in a complementary: erotic and serious
topics cover the range of monody and this range is likewise suggested
by *C.* 1.13 and 1.14 taken together. A similar complementary obtains
in the portrait of Alcaeus on his own, both in *C.* 1.32 and within the
dynamic internal to *C.* 1.14.[28]

Porphyrio informs us that *C.* 1.15's model was a dithyramb by
Bacchylides: 'with this ode, he imitates Bacchylides. For as the one
has Cassandra predict the future of the Trojan war, so this one has
Proteus'.[29] This uniquely narrative Horatian ode makes a ring with
C. 1.12, the choral poets encircling the Aeolic, and rather than representing the most characteristic side of Bacchylides *qua* poet, the poem
embodies the aspect of choral lyric that went unrepresented in *C.* 1.12,

---

[27] Horace often links individual predecessors with a conspicuous aspect of their
tradition in such a way as to simplify both the tradition and the predecessor's role
within it. Archilochus is synonymous with iambic poetry, which itself is simplified
and means invective (*numeros animosque secutus* | *Archilochi, Epist.* 1.19.24–5; *Archi-
lochum proprio rabies armauit iambo, Ars P.* 79) Pindar stands for loftly lyric (*C.* 4.2;
in *C.* 4.9.6, he follows immediately after Homer; *Pindarici fontis qui non expalluit
haustus, Epist.* 1.3.10), Sappho is strictly a love poet (*Aeoliis fidibus querentem* |
Sappho puellis de popularibus, C. 2.13.24–5; *spirat adhuc amor* | *uiuuntque commissi
calores* | *Aeoliae fidibus puellae, C.* 4.9.10–12). On Horace's simplification of prede-
cessors as paradigms, see Davis (1991), 85, 139–40.

[28] On the contrast between Horace's simplification of Alcaeus as representative of
high monody and the fuller view expressed in *C.* 1.32, as well as on complementaries,
see Davis (1991), 85–6, 139–40.

[29] Nisbet and Hubbard (1970), 188–9.

namely mythological narrative.[30] *C.* 1.15 is emblematic for many Horatian narratives within his discourse-centered lyric: a brief narrative introduction yields to a speech by a character so that discourse reasserts its control.[31] Dithyramb was generally associated with narrative in antiquity, and Horace certainly associates dithyramb with the high style of choral lyric (*C.* 4.2.10).[32]

Within the four poems of the sequence we have looked at so far, two salient aspects of choral lyric, praise of men and of gods on the one hand and mythological narrative on the other, enclose Horace's complementary for monody. Various elements in these poems (hymnic form, epinician to Augustus, mythological narrative, allegory) are fully integrated only later in the Roman Odes. The juxtaposition of choral with monodic lyricists here is paradigmatic for the mixture of public and personal throughout Horatian lyric. It is the isolation and definition of different lyric elements within these individual poems that constitutes their programmatic burden.

The operative lyric predecessor in *C.* 1.16 is Stesichorus. Porphyrio and Ps.-Acro recognize the Stesichorean background of *recantare* ('recant') in line 27, which calques *palinodein* ('sing back'),[33] and it has been suggested that the first line of the poem *O matre pulchra filia*

---

[30] Cairns (1971b), 447–8 calls attention to the syntactical structure of the opening of Simonides 13D = *PMG* 38 (543) as a parallel for the syntax of the first strophe of *C.* 1.15. He concludes that this form represents a distinct category of poem characteristic of early Greek lyric and that Porphyrio was probably right to look back to Greek lyric as a model for this ode and almost certainly right about Bacchylides. If Horace was imitating the subject matter of an ode by Bacchylides and the syntax of one by Simonides—if Cairns's pattern should be less common than he supposes—the joining of these poets reinforces the importance not of a single lyric predecessor, but of the branch of the genre.

[31] Compare *Epodes* 13, *C.* 1.7, 3.3, 3.5, 3.11, 3.27, 4.4. *C.* 3.3 is unusual in ending with authorial comment, *C.* 3.5 in that narrative ends the poem. Who speaks the final stanza in *C.* 4.4 is disputed. For speeches in the *Odes* see Helm (1935).

[32] Harvey (1955), 173. A. Hardie's (1977) suggestion that dithyramb lies behind *nunc est bibendum* supports the high-style associations of the genre.

[33] Ps.-Acro: *imitatus [est] Stesichorum poetam Siculum, qui uituperationem Helenae scribens caecatus est, at postea responso Apollinis laudem eius scripsit et oculorum adspectum recepit. cuius rei et in Epodon libro poeta meminit* (17.42): *infamis Helenae Castor offensus uice | fraterque magni Castoris uicti prece | adempta uati reddidere lumina. Porphyrio: hac ode* παλινῳδίαν *repromittit ei in quam probrosum carmen scripserat Tyndaridae cuidam, amicae suae, id est recantaturus ea quae dixerat dicitque se iracundia motum haec scripsisse.*

pulchrior ('O girl more beautiful than your beautiful mother') has the form of a 'typical Horatian motto'[34] and also the form of taking something back.[35] Neither of the first lines of Stesichorus' palinodes to Helen nor the line from the Cologne Archilochus, which has also been suggested as the source for the motto, is close enough in my view to Horace's line to be the actual source.[36] Nevertheless even without an identifiable motto this poem strongly evokes not just one but two archaic predecessors. Archilochus underlies the *iambi* from which the poet now distances himself (3; 24). The palinode is generic and Horace's recantation has everything to do with lyric definition.[37] Horace makes a point of disavowing the iambic, Archilochean poetry of the *Epodes* in the service of generic definition in the *Odes*. In *Epistles* 1.19 meter and the proper names of his generic predecessors (my emphasis below) identify Horace's shift from iambic poetry to lyric.

> Parios ego primus *iambos*
> ostendi Latio, *numeros* animosque secutus
> *Archilochi*, non res et agentia uerba Lycamben.
> ac ne me foliis ideo breuioribus ornes
> quod timui mutare modos et carminis artem,
> temperat *Archilochi* Musam *pede* mascula *Sappho*,
> temperat *Alcaeus*, sed rebus et ordine dispar,
> nec socerum quaerit quem uersibus oblinat atris,
> nec sponsae laqueum famoso carmine nectit.
> hunc ego, non alio dictum prius ore, Latinus
> uulgaui fidicen.   *Epistles* 1.19.23–33

---

[34] Nisbet and Hubbard (1970), *ad loc.* refer to Ritter (1856–7), *ad loc.*, who thinks that the words of Horace's first line were *ad exemplum Stesichori expressa*. Also Hendrickson (1931), 4, 6.

[35] Syndikus (1971), 181. See Cairns (1978).

[36] For the Stesichorus, see Nisbet and Hubbard (1970), 202; for Archilochus, see Davis (1991), 76, n. 78. Marcovich (1975), 8 *ad* line 7 gives the first line of *C.* 1.16 as a parallel for addressing a daughter in a way that pays a compliment to her mother (which of course reverts back to the daughter), but does not suggest that Horace's line was modeled on Archilochus.

[37] The lyric program in this poem in combination with the next was suggested by Hendrickson (1931) and taken up more recently by Syndikus (1972), 180–7, Santirocco (1986), 51, and Davis (1991), 74–7. Kiessling and Heinze (1917), 103 had already suggested the generic relevance of the lyric distance from epodic anger in *C.* 1.16.

I first showed Parian iambs to Latium, following the meters and spirit of Archilochus, but not the subject and the words harassing Lycambes. And lest you adorn me with lesser leaves because I feared to change the modes and art of the song, manly Sappho tempers her Muse with Archilochus' meter, as does Alcaeus, but different in subject and arrangement, nor does either seek to smear their father-in-law with dark verses nor to knot a noose for their betrothed with a damning poem. I made him accessible—he had not been sung previously by any other mouth—I, a Latin lyrist.

The emphasis on meter and generic forebears accords with the opening programmatic sequences in the *Odes:* a parade of meters and a parade of predecessors. In *C.* 1.16 Horace embraces lyric over the iambics of the *Epodes* not only by his rhetoric of recantation, which in itself alludes to Stesichorus, but by the generic application of the technique: affirmation of Stesichorus goes hand in hand with disavowal of Archilochus, the preeminent Greek predecessor of the *Epodes. C.* 1.17 has a number of features that link it to *C.* 1.16: they are both in Alcaics; Tyndaris, the addressee, continues the covert references to Helen;[38] and this poem also engages in generic definition by setting two poets against each other. In each case lyric scores a rhetorical point over a rival genre. Here the genre is epic and Anacreon is instrumental to converting Homer into lyric. Tyndaris' transformation from the epic Helen of Troy to a Greek slave girl is one sign of lyric's ascendancy over epic, but it is the song that she will sing that is most telling for the genre:[39]

> fide Teia
> dices laborantis in uno
> Penelopen uitreamque Circen.   *C.* 1.17.18–20

You will tell, on Anacreon's lyre, of Penelope and glassy Circe competing over the same man.

The plot of the *Odyssey* is reduced to a love-triangle that reflects—genders reversed—the love-triangle in the poem between Tyndaris, the poet, and Cyrus. That Tyndaris is to sing this song on the lyre of Anacreon follows the pattern where one of the canonic lyric poets has served as the locus for establishing Horace's own lyric task.

---

[38] Hendrickson (1931), 7.
[39] Santirocco (1986), 52 and Davis (1991), 203.

The sequence closes with a repetition. A secure motto from Alcaeus opens *C.* 1.18: *nullam, Vare, sacra uite prius seueris arborem*
('don't sow, Varus, any tree before the sacred vine'); μηδ᾽ ἓν ἄλλο
φυτεύσῃς πρότερον δένδριον ἀμπέλω, ('don't plant any other shrub
before the vine'), Alcaeus 342 LP.[40] Closure is signaled by returning
to a poet who has already figured in the sequence, and by the return
to the pattern of the first four poems that announce their allegiance
in the first strophe. If the opening of *C.* 1.16 is in fact a motto of
Stesichorus, it conforms to the pattern of the preceding four poems
(it certainly announces its relation to Archilochus with *iambis* in the
third line); without a Stesichorean motto, it falls more in line with
C. 1.17, where the model poet appears closer to the end.

Why do I not include *C.* 1.19 in the sequence? It opens with a
reminiscence of Philodemus, if not a motto in the strict sense: *mater
saeua Cupidinum* ('cruel mother of Desires'); Κύπρι Πόθων μῆτερ
ἀελλοπόδων, ('Cypris, mother of swift-footed Desires'), *AP* 10.21.2.[41]
The phrase, however, seems to be conventional and Horace's poem
does not bear an additional mark of similarity to the epigram, as we
saw in the case of possible conventions in *C.* 1.13 and 1.14.[42] *C.* 1.19
brings us halfway through the first book of *Odes* and closes the door
on the opening parades; *C.* 1.20 provides a new start with the address
to Maecenas. As we saw in the Parade Odes, however, it is characteristic of Horace to blur the boundaries of sequences. Here the blurring
consists first of a convention in the place of a more firm allusion, and
secondly, even with a secure reference, Philodemus would mark a
category shift. Instead of an archaic lyric predecessor, we find a
contemporary epigrammatist. While Horace clearly owes as much,
if not more, to Hellenistic epigram as to archaic lyric, the epigram-
matists function differently from the archaic predecessors as norma-
tive figures. Horace brings the canonical lyric poets to the fore as

---

[40] Nisbet and Hubbard (1970), 228. My arguments from here to the end of the
paper owe much to A. J. Woodman, who suggests an analogy between the metrical
ring composition in the Parade Odes and the allusive one here (see below, 46).

[41] Richmond (1970), 202. He defines a motto as a first line that alludes to another
first line, although he is not bothered by τίνα θεόν... of Pindar *O.* 2 being a second
line.

[42] Nisbet and Hubbard (1970), *ad loc.* also cite Pindar fr. 122.4 ματέρ᾽ ἐρώτων,
Bacch. 9.73, Orph. *Hymn.* 55.8, Babrius 32.2.

influences by naming them; the proper names of the Hellenistic poets go unmentioned in the *Odes* and the contemporary poets who are mentioned are Latin poets (Vergil, Varius, Albius—whether or not identical with Tibullus—, Pollio, Valgius, Iullus Antonius).

It does not appear coincidental that the catalogue of poets listed by Horace in the fourth book of *Odes* corresponds closely to the catalogue established in this second parade:

> non, si priores Maeonius tenet
> sedes Homerus, Pindaricae latent
>   Ceaeque et Alcaei minaces
>   Stesichorique graues Camenae;
>
> nec, si quid olim lusit Anacreon,
> deleuit aetas; spirat adhuc amor
>   uiuuntque commissi calores
>   Aeoliae fidibus puellae.   *C. 4.9.5–12*

If Maeonian Homer holds first place, Pindar's Muses do not on that account lie hidden, or Simonides', or Alcaeus' threatening or Stesichorus' serious Muses; nor if Anacreon once fooled around, has age destroyed it; the love still breathes and the passions still live, entrusted to the lyre of the Aeolian girl.

There are two differences between the poets listed here and those of *C.* 1.12–18. Archilochus has been left out—appropriately since only positive models occur here; Bacchylides has been replaced by Simonides, in line with my suggestion that it is not the individual poet at issue in *C.* 1.15 but rather some representative of choral lyric.[43] One choral poet substitutes for another, but the subject matter of *C.* 1.15 returns under the guise of a narration of the Trojan War, starting in line 13. The two versions yield a number of resemblances: the opening focuses on adultery; a periphrasis denotes Paris and mention is made of his hair; the proper names Helene, Teucer, Sthenelus are shared; focus falls briefly on one hero after another within the narration, which is compressed. Homer is included, as he and the elevated subject matter reflect well not only on Lollius, but on

---

[43] See above, n. 30. Fraenkel (1957), 424 suggests that Ceos denotes both Simonides and Bacchylides. The functional interchangeability of these two poets may be facilitated by their belonging not only to the same genre, but to the same family.

the poet. If Horace can openly assert Homer's preeminence here, it is because he has already incorporated him within his lyric earlier. The catalogue in itself establishes the tradition to which Horace belongs, but by looking back to the second parade in his first collection of *Odes* he reminds his audience of his credentials as a *uates sacer* ('holy bard', 28).[44]

The sequence of meters in these seven poems offers tangential support to their constitution as a group. *C.* 1.12 in Sapphics is followed by three poems in differing kinds of Asclepiadeans, in order fourth, third, second. *C.* 1.16 and 1.17 in Alcaics bring us back to *C.* 1.12 with a complementary Lesbian meter. The fifth Asclepiadean in *C.* 1.18 recalls the same meter—the only instances in *Odes* 1–3—in the most recent purely sympotic poem, *C.* 1.11, which articulates this sequence with the Parade Odes.[45] *C.* 1.11 falls between the first repetition of a meter (Sapphics) in *C.* 1.10, the signal of a turn away from the pattern of metrical variety, and the return of Sapphics in *C.* 1.12, which signals some kind of continuation and is the first poem in the next sequence. It is hardly fortuitous that the poem that provides the hinge between the two parades is *C.* 1.11, the '*carpe diem*' poem that defines so much of Horatian ideology. I would suggest that while no neat pattern connects these sequences, they are somewhat interwoven. Porphyrio calls *C.* 1.10 a

---

[44] Syndikus (1973), 379 remarks that these six names stand for the entire canon of Greek lyric poets—a type of synecdoche. It is noteworthy that Horace's shorter canon corresponds to Dionysius of Halicarnassus' shorter canon (*de imitatione* 421 ff.) at least of the serious poets. Horace separates the two lighter erotic poets Anacreon and Sappho from the stanza containing Pindar, Simonides, Alcaeus, and Stesichorus. These last four are the lyric poets Dionysius recommends for imitation, as does Quintilian (10.1.61 ff.) who is dependent on Dionysius. See Cousin (1967), 552–4; (1979), *ad loc.* The order of the poets seems to be according to stylistic height, not according to chronological order, *pace* Cousin in the commentary. Wilamowitz (1900), 6 characteristically posits a common Hellenistic source for Dionysius and Quintilian. Was Horace reading Dionysius (or the common source), or does this narrower selection from among the nine lyrists represent a second canon? For the canon, see Färber (1936), 25–6.

[45] Seidensticker (1976), 34 calls attention to the tendency of the sequences opening each of the books of the *Odes* to form rings. His criteria are thematic and I am generally sceptical about schemes determined by simplified reductions of poems' subject matter (spring, sympotic, erotic). If the proposed sequence forms a ring, it is not thematic but metrical: 5 Asclep. / Lesbian / Asclep. / Asclep. / Asclep. / Lesbian / Lesbian / 5 Asclep.

'hymn to Mercury by Alcaeus, the lyric poet'. Alcaeus' hymn to Hermes was also in Sapphics and told of the theft of Apollo's cattle and possibly quiver, although the extant first stanza does not have a motto's verbal similarity to Horace.[46] If *C.* 1.10–12 winds down the metrical parade, the Alcaic allusion in *C.* 1.10 prepares for the next sequence.

Alcaeus' influence in *C.* 1.10 raises some inevitable questions: But doesn't Horace use mottoes and allusions in the Parade Odes? What about the Alcaic mottoes in *C.* 1.4 and 1.9 in particular?[47] How do the allusions here differ from those in the first sequence, or indeed from anywhere else? The answer lies not in the exclusivity of allusions to these poems, any more than that of the meters to the Parade Odes. All odes have meter and it is a rare Horatian ode, if any, that does not allude to someone. What differentiates any sequence from its surroundings is the establishment of a pattern, whether metrical, or, as I suggest here, allusive. In this section of the *Odes,* the allusions to lyric predecessors come together to a highly dense degree and the systematic covering of monodic and choral lyrists argues for a certain unity. Neither the Parade Odes, taken jointly, nor this sequence is set apart as sharply as the Roman Odes, where the change of meter and radical switch in subject matter of *C.* 3.7 leave no doubt that the collection is moving on.[48] Nor does either sequence display the same degree of internal unity as the Roman Odes, understood as consistency of subject matter and educational purpose. The bond has to do rather with Horace's program and his definition of his own lyric, as he does elsewhere, through meter and tradition.

The parade of predecessors as I define it is compatible with the most recent treatments of arrangement in *Odes* 1.[49] My suggestion of an interwoven transition between the two parades accords with

[46] Nisbet and Hubbard (1970), 125–6; Richmond (1970), 202.

[47] Richmond (1970), 200–1.

[48] Even in this instance Horace blurs the boundaries of his sequences to some extent. Santirocco (1986), 125 remarks that despite *C.* 3.7's function as a formal break, it can be seen as offering a specific case of the danger of sexual degeneracy, an issue in the preceding poem, *C.* 3.6.17–32.

[49] Dettmer's (1983) preoccupation with ring composition on a large scale makes her study idiosyncratic. Her closest grouping to those of Santirocco (1986) and Porter (1987) is *C.* 1.15–19, which ostensibly forms a ring with *C.* 3.12–16 (128, 171–3). I find her criteria for such a correspondence too schematic.

Santirocco's view that the poems in the aftermath of the Parade Odes continue with some of the same themes. At *C.* 1.13 he leaves off tracing this aftermath with the observation that connections with the Parade Odes could be made indefinitely, given that the initial group introduces the major concerns of the first collection of *Odes*. He then pursues a dynamic progression between poems until we reach the midpoint of the book: *C.* 1.15 follows on another ship poem; the change from *tristia* to *mitia* in *C.* 1.16 paves the way for the contrast of Cyrus with the poet in *C.* 1.17; Cyrus' violence likewise prepares for the insistence on moderate drinking in *C.* 1.18. With *C.* 1.20 and the three poems that follow he sees a new beginning and something of a recapitulation of *C.* 1.1–1.4.[50] The end of the parade of predecessors at *C.* 1.18 with something of a blurring at *C.* 1.19 coincides with a new start in *C.* 1.20. My views in no way contradict his and add only a static link to dynamic development.

I am less convinced by Porter's more mechanistic arrangement of *C.* 1.13–1.19 (the first and last poems of this group have to do with passion, as does the central poem *C.* 1.16; *C.* 1.14 and 15 form a pair of ship poems that balances another pair in *C.* 1.17 and 18, both about wine's inspiration of peace as well as of violence), but the parade of predecessors is if anything more of a piece with this scheme than with Santirocco's.[51] Since Porter continues the Parade Odes to *C.* 1.12, it would be easy to make *C.* 1.12 a hinge connecting the first group with the second, which Porter likewise brings to the midpoint of the book. Although Porter's interest in 'the inefficacy of human agency' in *C.* 1.13–19 gives me pause,[52] the rough correspondence of a group of poems following the Parade Odes and ending with the midpoint of the book in Porter, Santirocco, and also my own scheme bolsters my confidence in such a group, particularly since we each use different criteria for its isolation.[53]

Evoking predecessors, whether overtly or by allusion, is a favorite Horatian method for establishing his literary filiation. The chiastic

---

[50] Santirocco (1986), 42–57.　　[51] Porter (1987), 20–1.
[52] Porter (1987), 77.
[53] My own view of this group has expanded organically from my first observation of the chiastic order of choral and Lesbian poets in *C.* 1.12–15, to include *C.* 1.16, then *C.* 1.17, and most recently *C.* 1.18 with a definite halt at *C.* 1.19. I did not look for the midpoint of the book and then find continuity.

pattern of choral and Lesbian poets in *C.* 1.12–15 expands on the compressed statement of *C.* 1.1.32–4: *si neque tibias | Euterpe cohibet nec Polyhymnia | Lesboum refugit tendere barbiton* ('if neither Euterpe inhibit the reeds nor Polyhymnia shrink from stringing the bass lyre'). What makes this sequence stand out is the technique, consistent from poem to poem, of alluding to one lyric poet after another— a formal pattern that in itself creates a message beyond the subjects of individual poems or even of these poems taken together. In his parade of lyric predecessors Horace's juxtaposition of erotic, sympotic, and political poetry conveys for a second time the point made in the metrical parade: that his lyric subsumes all aspects, high and low, of the genre he reinvented.[54]

[54] The idea behind this article originated in R. J. Tarrant's seminar on Horace's *Odes* at Harvard, spring 1988, and was inspired by reading Santirocco (1986). It was given as a paper at the spring meeting of the Classical Association of the Atlantic States, 1992. I offer thanks to Matthew Santirocco in person for his support and encouragement, as to A. J. Woodman, whose prompt and painstaking criticism challenged and helped me enormously. I am also grateful for the suggestions made by Martha A. Davis and by the anonymous readers.

16

Horace, a Greek Lyrist without Music

Luigi Rossi

1. THE PREMISS

That Horace is a Greek lyric poet is almost obvious—a fact needing qualification only in that the Roman component is strong in him as well. Besides the plainly Roman compositions, we have learned for a long time now[1] that in odes beginning with an open declaration of debt toward Greek models, the declaration is merely an initial 'motto' that gives way to an inspiration and themes which are utterly autonomous. Furthermore, to say Horace is the *greatest* Greek lyrist of his time and beyond, seems a paradox—one, however, I feel able to support: he was without competitors, Greek or Latin, for centuries in the grand metrical programme realized in his lyrical *corpus*.[2] His pride, expressed many times throughout his works, is fully justified. Despite lasting exegetical questions, *Epist.* 1. 19. 21–34 is noteworthy: in it we find the strongest expression of self-awareness: *libera per vacuum posui vestigia princeps, | non aliena meo pressi pede, qui sibi fidet | dux reget examen* ('I first placed free footsteps on empty ground, I pressed with my foot ground belonging to no other; he who trusts himself will rule the swarm as leader', 21–3).

---

[1] Pasquali (1920). La Penna (1964), xii f.: 'The concept belongs to Norden, but we owe to Pasquali the importance the concept took on in the interpretation of Horace's lyric poetry.' See most recently Cavarzere (1996).

[2] For an up-to-date panorama of Horace's lyrical system, see Rosellini (1997) (with bibliography). The bibliography in Kissel (1981) is also useful, for both metre and music.

But to be a real Greek lyric poet Horace lacked music in the sense of *organic and constant* musical performance. Since music was an essential component of the Greek poetic event and not merely ornamental, its absence weighs heavy in determining precisely the status of Horatian lyric (§2). In the following, I wish to discredit the idea of a musical Horace, however meritorious the supporters of that hypothesis have been or are.[3]

A few authoritative voices, past and present, have come down for the absence of music,[4] but the topic is still controversial. I will attempt to assemble some old ideas, my own and others'.[5] Taking their cue and perhaps adding some new associations, I will present *all together* what seems to me proof of my argument. It may be useful to clarify from the start one fundamental point to avoid misunderstanding:[6] to deny music as a *founding* component in the composition of the *Odes* does not signify denying either that musical practices existed at Rome or that Horace himself *occasionally* performed or had performed his four books of *Odes* with musical accompaniment.

2. GREECE AND ROME: LYRIC POETRY AND LITERARY COMMUNICATION

It would seem a peculiar contradiction were Horace's poetry to lack an essential component of Greek lyric—constant musical accompaniment—when Horace is a poet who wanted and indeed appears to be Greek from many angles. For the Greeks, music was closely linked

---

[3] Bonavia-Hunt (1969) wants to reconstruct the image of a cithara-playing Horace, which seems rather ingenuous. Wille (1967) (on Horace at 234–81) is, on the other hand, a bountiful collection of material on music in Rome, which remains extremely useful though many of the testimonies collected there can be used precisely as arguments for the contrary view. Recently von Albrecht (1993) supports the musical view (though with caution: 99 f.). A brief history of the matter in Milanese (1997), 921 f.

[4] Heinze (1918) remains fundamental, in particular regarding the testimonies of the ancient grammarians, as we will see (§6); more recently Pöhlmann (1965).

[5] I have tried as far as possible to do justice to anyone who in some isolated piece of argumentation has preceded me in this line of thought.

[6] It seems there is precisely this sort of misunderstanding in von Albrecht (1993) (see n. 3 supra), however praiseworthy his prudence.

to the rhythmical score, though this is just about as much information as remains about the interweaving of rhythm and melody in Greek lyric. However, once the absence of music in Horace is ascertained, this will no longer be a true contradiction. Indeed, the conditions of literary communication had already changed in Greek circles since the fourth and third century BCE and transformed as a cultural phenomenon from oral/aural transmission to book publication. The growing and intensified circulation of books led to corresponding mutations in the composition of literary works, signally in lyric poetry.[7] It would have then been a case of *adapting* the Greek models to a radically different system of communication, and it is interesting to ask whether Horace was fully aware of this adaptation or not. I will suggest that he was.

Now, to return to our initial question, did Horace compose his *Odes* for musical performance? Among the answers, negative or affirmative, some have sought a sort of compromise: some odes were intended to be sung, others not. But this is merely a solution for convenience's sake that may express a truth, but does not reach the heart of the problem. This problem, as stated above (§1) and which we will see better below, consists in answering the question whether the *Odes*, *all* the *Odes*, were originally intended for particular occasions where they were to be performed to music, or whether they were composed simply to be read. Reading aloud was indeed the norm in those days and would still be for a long time to come.[8] Certainly the *Carmen Saeculare* was destined for musical performance. We have epigraphic evidence[9] it was sung in 17 BCE by a chorus of boys and girls; it was composed in public honour of Augustus for the *ludi saeculares* he himself had restored.

---

[7] I have examined the impact of changing conditions of communication within a broader account of Greek literature in Rossi (1995).

[8] Gavrilov (1997, with Burnyeat's 1997 additions), in the wake of a famous article by Knox (1968), is an up-to-date review of the sources for the extent of silent reading as a practice. Whether one agrees or not with their interpretation of the sources, it is clear that the base level of the literary reception of texts was reached by reading aloud—this is well attested. Oral reception was independent of silent reading, which itself depended on the availability of books (constantly increasing over the centuries).

[9] *CIL* 6. 32323, especially II 3, 20 ff., 147 ff.

The *Odes*, in four books, appear to be edited by the author himself,[10] with great care and attention given to the order of the poems—with care therefore far beyond the particular occasions for which the *Odes* were created. An examination of the 'occasionality' of Horace's lyric production would sin in illicitly searching for similarity between or merely analogy with the editorial conditions of archaic and late-archaic Greek monody. For the Greeks, the publication of particular odes was subordinate to the specific occasional events that transpired mostly in the symposium.[11] The Alexandrian philologists were the first to think of assembling these poetic *corpora* and ordering them into books. But the order within these books was far from that planned and desired by the author himself. It was rather the merely external order of an editor prompted by a variety of criteria of convenience (occasion, metre, topic, etc., with many compromises). The author's own edition became common from Callimachus onwards, that is, in Hellenistic times (from the third century BCE onwards), a time when the musical performance of poetry was already signally long a usage of the past.[12]

Moreover, it has been rightly claimed[13] for some time that Horace could not find a place *institutionally* designated for singing poetry at Rome. Furthermore, the poetic *liber* was intended to offer compositions arranged in an order designed by the author, since they were part of an organic whole. The order was therefore *tied to the page*, so to speak, where the position of each ode had a precise compositional function within the whole. These are obvious considerations, but they should not be forgotten when we face the problem at hand: were Horace's *Odes* intended to be sung or not?

---

[10] In fact, there are two authorial editions: Books I–III, published in 23 BCE, Book IV in 13 BCE or soon after. We need hardly recall here the now abundant bibliography on Callimachus as his own editor. On the authorial epigram editions in the Hellenistic world, see Argentieri (1998).

[11] Sappho's case is obviously unique, but her poems were nevertheless always intended for group celebration.

[12] Despite Cameron's (1995) recent attempt to prove the contrary, especially 71–103 (Chapter 3, *The Symposium*).

[13] Birt (1925), 158, and Klingner (1930), 76, from the days when no one spoke of Greek banquets (both are honestly quoted, but not, I think, contradicted by Wille 1967: 248 n. 388).

The considerations made above seem to me to weigh strongly in favour of denying decisively *original* musical performance for the *Odes*. The considerations are made on the basis of a comparison of the various conditions of literary communication in Greece from the seventh to the fourth centuries and those in Roman culture. For the latter, the book definitely prevails and more particularly the poetic *liber*, ordered and edited by the author himself.

It is not pertinent to look for analogies with the medieval and modern eras, for which Gunther Wille[14] deserves great credit for gathering a rich documentation: that many of Horace's *Odes* were set to music in the Middle Ages, the Renaissance, the seventeenth, eighteenth, and nineteenth centuries until our own time, proves nothing. Whoever sought texts to put to music for various diverse occasions, the *Odes* offered a verbal basis of high quality. But, these were all re-uses unrelated to the initial reasons and original criteria for their composition. Goethe, Heine, Mörike—to mention but a few names from the high season of German Romanticism—*wrote* their poems with great internal musicality in both word and stanza. Musicians like Schubert, Schumann, Brahms, and Wolf exploited these *after the fact* as texts for music. They made their own compositions in their own way, independent and new with respect to the bare poetic text.

As for occasions for real musical performance, I repeat that at Rome, the most important and practically only occasion for *organic* and *systematic* performance of monody was missing, namely the symposium.[15] In Greece, the symposium was a real political institution that enabled the participants of a well-individuated political group to gather together. On the occasion of drinking together, a number of ritualized aspects were planned, such as singing poetry to musical accompaniment (by a string instrument, a lyre or *barbiton*, and a wind instrument, the *aulos*). The presence of music is attested by our sources, which often mention it, but we have testimony from the Greek poems themselves. They make continual allusion to this

---

[14] See Wille (1967), 253 ff., 260 ff., and Draheim-Wille (1985) for an anthology and Draheim (1981) for an overview of modern music using various ancient authors.

[15] For the symposium, I suggest beginning with the contributions collected in Vetta (1983), Murray (1990), and Murray and Tecuşan (1995).

theme when, as often, the poems sing of the progress of the actual symposium and music's presence in it: we therefore speak of metasympotic poetry. At Rome, there was no institution resembling a symposium in the least. Similar entertainments took place, but they certainly were not institutionalized as in Greece. They were consequently not at the origin of a literature specifically designed for them. Indeed we should not look for a parallel to the Greek symposium in the simple Roman *cena*.[16] As for the *carmina convivialia* ('convivial songs'), besides the controversy over their nature, they belong to a period which for Rome is even pre-archaic.[17] Horace's ideal of the symposium is what he describes at the end of Book 1 (*Odes* 1. 38):

> Persicos odi, puer, apparatus,
> displicent nexae philyra coronae,
> mitte sectari, rosa quo locorum
>   sera moretur.
> Simplici myrto nihil adlabores   5
> sedulus, curo: neque te ministrum
> dedecet myrtus neque me sub arta
>   uite bibentem.

I disdain, boy, finery from Persia. Garlands woven with string displease. Leave off pursuing where the late rose lingers. Labour to add nothing to the single myrtle—busily—this I desire. The myrtle fails to suit neither you tending nor me drinking under the close vine.

The ideal expressed in this brief ode is a symposium whose only overt touch of ceremony is the myrtle crowning master and servant. Nothing could be farther from the formality of the socially selective Greek symposium. Now, this ode is the last of Book 1 and, as Eduard Fraenkel pointed out,[18] it is not only the last of the book, but the arrangement of *Odes* 1. 37 before it sets it further in relief: *nunc est*

---

[16] Aulus Gellius 19.9 reports on a *cena* attended by the orator Antonius Julianus, at which Greek verse was sung, together with some Latin epigrams. For testimony from Martial, Petronius, etc., see the rich documentation in Wille (1967, in the index under *Tafelmusik*).

[17] On the *carmina convivialia* and the history of the question, see Zorzetti (1990); on Horatian conviviality, Landolfi (1990); on sociological aspects of Roman conviviality, D'Arms (1990).

[18] Fraenkel (1957), 297–9.

bibendum ('now is the time to drink', *Odes* 1. 37. 1) *explicitly* calques (through the *incipit*) a famous sympotic poem by Alcaeus with strong political import. Horace offers a victory cry for the success of his own side. *Odes* 1. 38 by contrast declares for the simple life and poetics expressed elsewhere in Horace,[19] but here serves as a poetic programme given its highlighted position at the book's conclusion. Two symposia come face to face on the page by authorial intention: one is Roman-Alcaic and finishes with the very Roman *superbo* | ... *triumpho* (31 f.); the other is Roman-Horatian and, in addition, a pastoral symposium (while the Greek symposium was a city institution).[20]

To conclude: the culture of Horace's times lacked the institutions to support, in both place and function, the musical performance of his poetry. Editorial arrangement clearly reveals the bookish nature of his *Odes*.

3. MUSICAL ANTIQUITIES IN HORACE

These initial considerations about the relation between poetry and music aim to bring out, as I have said, the differences in the general conditions of literary communication (mere reading in contrast to music) and in social-political institutions (absence of the symposium).

Let us turn now to what has seemed to many the most important piece of evidence for the musical performance of the *Odes*,[21] namely the presence, in Horace, as in the Greek poets, of the thematics of musical practices (both terminology and instruments) within the *Odes* themselves. For indeed the symposium, the *komos* ('drunken procession'), and other typically Greek institutions are very much

[19] Fraenkel (1957), 297–9.
[20] Let us recall how *Theocritus* 3 transfers the *komos*, a city institution, to a pastoral setting through literary virtuosity.
[21] Doblhofer (1992), 79, is a good synthesis of the four groups of testimony on which Wille (1967) and Bonavia-Hunt (1969) ground their faith in the musical destiny of the poems: the *Carmen Saeculare* (see below), reference to music, the claims of the late grammarians (epecially Marius Victorinus, on whom see Pöhlmann 1965), the medieval codices with their neums (*supra* §2)

present in his poetry along with their music. Often Horace speaks in the first person as a musician. But too rarely has it been considered that these elements do not necessarily reflect a real Roman situation but are owed solely to the imitation of Greek models. Alcaeus, Sappho, Anacreon, Pindar—to name Horace's main predecessors— are steeped in ancient musical practices which were referentially linked to live musical performance only at their (Greek) origin. For Horace, we may speak of an *imitative* representation of reality mediated through a very literate intertextual relation.[22] If I succeed, through other paths, as I am trying here, in proving that the *Odes* were not intended for musical performance, their rich musical thematics will have the status of the mimesis of a musical event. By *mimesis*, I understand here a method whereby a real situation is described as a point of reference, which is absent, however, from the pragmatic context of an event. The reality is therefore merely literary:[23] mimesis in this sense means 'representation' in that a real situation is depicted rather than enacted. It is by now a solidly established principle that the more detailed a description, the more it signals the absence of the situation described, whether on stage as in the false *deixis*[24] of a dramatic text or as a point of reference in a non-theatrical text.[25] What is present in a real, i.e. pragmatic context, need not be mentioned.[26] It is precisely the emphasis put on mentioning a detail (which would play no role had it been real) that creates the suspicion—sometimes the certainty—of the presence of literary mimesis.

I would not grant much importance, in one or the other sense, to the fact that sometimes Horace speaks explicitly of literature and of

---

[22] For sound thoughts on the *mimetic* symposium in Horace, see Nisbet-Hubbard (1970), xv f. The whole section (xi ff.), 'The Odes and their Literary Form', is important on genre and the poets Horace takes as models.

[23] Albert (1988) offers a useful overview, in which Horace has a place, but not for music. A forerunner of these ideas about mimesis is Weber (1917): the richer an epigram's, such as a funerary epigram, description of its natural setting (tree, fountain etc.), the more likely it is to be literary.

[24] I refer here to the internal stage directions of dramatic texts.

[25] For example, in the mimetic Hymns of Callimachus (2, 5, 6).

[26] We should remember that, in the symposium, the meta-sympotic theme is but *one* possible theme.

364   *Luigi Rossi*

chartae ('papers')[27] given that, in both Greek and Latin, the lexicon of 'singing' is often confused with that of 'speaking' or 'reading'.

I will not go over Horace's musical terminology in detail.[28] I will merely give some examples, chosen among those focused on by music-minded interpreters. We should not rely on the knowledge of music transmitted through literature, as in *bibam | sonante mixtum tibiis carmen lyra | hac Dorium, illis barbarum* ('I will drink, with the lyre sounding a song mixed with the reed, the one Dorian, the other barbarian', *Epodes* 9. 4–6).[29] It is common practice in Roman literature, extensive in Horace, to describe musical phenomena following the details of Greek practice and Greek theory, especially when these are transmitted by literary texts. In the passage quoted above, two musical instruments are contrasted one with the other: the *tibia* corresponds to the Greek *aulos*, the most common of wind instruments, and the lyre stands for any string instrument (in Horace, *lyra, cithrara, fides, testudo*, and *barbiton* are used interchangeably). The *tibia*, a wind instrument, is designated above as the appropriate instrument to accompany a 'barbarian song'; elsewhere it is given the qualification *Berecynthia* from the mountain in Phrygia, sacred to Cybele (*Odes* 1. 18. 13 f. [*cornu*], 3. 19. 18, 4. 1. 22). It is ecstatic and orgiastic. The string instrument is instead appropriate for accompanying a 'Dorian song' according to Greek musical tradition, which attributed the qualities of seriousness, courage, greatness of soul, etc. to Doric harmony.[30] Here, the contrast is between the Roman world, which takes its inspiration from the musical ethos of Greek 'seriousness' (Dorian), and the barbaric world with its orgiastic music, represented by Cleopatra and those Romans Horace rejects

[27] In an honest examination, Wille (1967) does so, 237 nn. 284, 285, 286 (only to rightly exclude its importance): *Epist.* 1. 19. 35 f.; ibid. 41 f.; *Odes* 4. 8. 20 ff. and 4. 9. 30 f.

[28] If one wanted to analyse Horace's musical lexicon more closely, particularly in the *Odes*, I refer again to Wille (1967) and more recently to Milanese (1997, with bibliography).

[29] If we are tempted to read this as a meta-sympotic poem, let us remember it is an epode; on the difference propounded by Horace himself between epode and ode, see below (§6, middle).

[30] For the Greek musical ethos, see Abert (1899) (especially 74 ff., 80 ff.); Anderson (1966).

for siding against Rome (*Epodes* 9. 11–16). Other qualities of the same string instrument confirm the 'Doric' touch of our passage: *fidibus ... severis* ('harsh strings', *AP* 216); *decus Phoebi ... testudo* ('the tortoise, Phoebus' honour', *Odes* 1. 32. 13–14); *seu fidibus citharave Phoebi* ('whether on the lyre or cithara of Phoebus', *Odes* 3. 4. 4); etc. All this material seems taken not only from Greek poetry, but almost directly from Greek theories of musical ethos of which so many traces remain. While we may appreciate the efforts of those who have claimed an autonomous musical life at Rome[31] (a fact which should, however, be conscribed within limits), is it not then remarkable that Horace so ostentatiously proclaims his loyal adherence to Greek tradition in the majority of cases where he speaks of music? His music is, so to speak, literary. The more Greek his lexis and musical culture are, the more suspect is their eventual worth as references to actual Roman reality.[32]

Supporters of musical accompaniment have found comfort in Horace's use of musical terminology when laying out his grand programme. We find it for example when he presents himself as *Romanae fidicen lyrae* ('string-player of the Roman lyre', *Odes* 4. 3. 23), namely the heir of the Greek lyrists; at *Epist.* 1. 3. 12f., etc. One thinks especially of *princeps Aeolium carmen ad Italos* | *deduxisse modos* ('I first brought Aeolian song to Italian measures', *Odes* 3. 30. 13–14): this ode begins *exegi monumentum aere perennius* ('I have built a monument more lasting than bronze'), and in it he shows himself more Roman than ever. Even if, an (absurd) hypothesis, an archaic Greek poet had collected his own occasional poems, I could not imagine him making such a programmatic declaration. For Horace tears the poem away from any ephemeral occasion and projects it into the perennial existence of an object identified with

---

[31] See in particular Wille (1967).

[32] The same goes for poems such as the ode to Phyllis (*minuentur atrae carmine curae*, *Odes* 4. 11. 35 f.), where the idea of music and song as consolation for woe goes back to the Greek tradition of musical ethos. Both *Odes* 4. 11 and 3. 28 (to Lyde) take the form of invitations (*Einladungsgedicht*, von Albrecht 1993: 95 and n. 60) to Roman *cenae* that are not even masked as symposia. The injunction expressed in the programme is to sing at dinner (*Odes* 3. 28. 9 f., 11 f., 16; 4. 11. 34–6). It is not so much a question of affirming or denying that singing took place at Roman dinners (for the affirmative, see von Albrecht 1993: 97), but to clarify whether it was expected that the Horatian poem before us would be sung.

his own poetic *corpus*, with his book entrusted to the written page.[33]

Fraenkel comes out definitely against any correspondence to a musical reality. He considers all the situations where Horace speaks of *cithara, barbiton, lyra* as simply mimetic.[34] Horace rather refers to himself as a performer: 'to play a string instrument' or 'sing' were already exhausted metaphors for 'being a lyric poet' or being a poet *tout court*.

A good example of mimesis is *Odes* 4. 2 (*Pindarum quisquis*). As is well known, the ode is a response to the invitation by Iullus Antonius to Horace to celebrate the return of Augustus, who had left Rome in 16 BCE for serious military reasons to return only in 13. Horace turns the invitation around to Iullus himself (*concines maiore poeta plectro* | *Caesarem*, 'a poet of a greater plectrum, you will sing of Caesar', *Odes* 4. 2. 33–4), leaving himself but a minor role in the celebration (*ego apis Matinae* | *more modoque*, 'I, in the way and manner of a Matine bee', 27–8; *tum meae, si quid loquar audiendum,* | *vocis accedet bona pars*, 'Then a good part of my voice will be added, if I should say something worth hearing', 45–6) with all the appropriate musical 'stage-directions': *concines... plectro* ('you will sing with the plectrum', 33); *concines laetosque dies et urbis* | *publicum ludum* ('you will sing of happy days and the public festivity of the city', 41–2); then the first person continues from the passage cited above: *et 'o sol* | *pulcher, o laudande' canam* ('and I will sing, "O beauteous sun, O praiseworthy"', 46–7); then *teque, dum procedis, 'io triumphe'* | *non semel dicemus 'io triumphe'* | *civitas omnis* ('and you, while you process, will say 'Hail triumph', we will say not once 'Hail triumph', we the whole state', 49–51). What reveals to us the mimesis is the textual indication, in direct discourse, to sing:[35] we will see how similar our position on *Odes* 4. 6 (in §5) will be.

---

[33] Still lacking is a comprehensive study of the desire in antiquity to disseminate one's works through the axes of time and space: here Horace positions himself proudly on the axis of time. For the temporal immortality of both work and author from Homer to Pindar, see Goldhill (1991), especially 69–166.

[34] Fraenkel (1957), 403 ff.

[35] This is a 'declared mimesis' (in itself a form of injunction); as for the 'non-declared' ones, I see the same relation as between simile and metaphor.

Musical antiquities, to conclude, appear to be present only in Horace's *text* and not in the reality referred to. Their referential function is realized through an intertextual relation with Greek models: it would not be fitting to talk, in Horace's case, of a meta-symposium, nor of meta-music. Let us convince ourselves that Horace, in all of these cases, is telling an innocent literary 'lie'—innocent because it is due to his love for his models, who, by contrast, were telling the truth. In the ample space of the metaphor created by intertextuality, a risk of error lies in the lack of orientation, in not being aware of the code.

4. THE PROOF OF A HORATIAN METRICAL INNOVATION

I will not insist on refuting further those who believe they hear Horace sing or having his *Odes* sung on the basis of musical terminology found in the poems. I acknowledge there is a great danger, too great for others and perhaps even for me, of violating texts through one's own prejudice in one way or the other. I rest content that I have brought out the ambivalence of this view (§3) and with what I have said, in the negative, about the lack of a sociological place (and thus of an occasion) for song and about the existence of a book culture (§2).

I would like now to produce a proof, which seems to me compelling, of the absence of authorial music in Horace's *Odes*. I ground this proof on an internal, and more precisely a metrical, analysis of his poems. I consider this analysis precious indeed for our assessment of his sensitivity and self-awareness, and consequently of his intentions. I am pleased to find this idea anticipated by Heinze, who, however, did not draw out all its implications.[36]

With but few exceptions, Horace notoriously normalizes the caesura at the fifth element of all his Sapphic and Alcaic hendecasyllables:

---

[36] Heinze (1918), 68 (II, 3): he starts off, rightly so, from the 'trauma' of the *Carmen Saeculare* (see below).

the Sapphic hendecasyllable: - ⌣ - - - // ...

the Alcaic hendecasyllable: x - ⌣ - - // ...

There is reason to believe he knew very well the Greeks did not do this, that is, they were very free with word endings in these lines. He thus introduced a refinement, a 'normalization', which he must have recognized as his own: it is not in Catullus.[37] Moreover, in isolating the central choriamb with a word ending in his greater Asclepiadeans and in separating the two choriambs in his minor Asclepiadeans, he carried out another innovation he also knew was his alone. This innovation was all the more evident because it created a refined rhythmical monotony:

> *Odes* 1. 11. 1–3 *tu ne quaesieris,* | *scire nefas,* | *quem mihi quem tibi*
> *Finem di dederint,* | *Leuconoe,* | *nec Babylonios*
> *Temptaris numeros.* | ...
> *Odes* 1. 1. 1 <u>*Maecenas atavis*</u> | *edite regibus* | ...[38]

He was playing at virtuosity and firmly intended to do so. We must be grateful to him for normalizing word endings, because he has thereby given us a precious implicit indication of how his sensitivity to the great lyric poetry of Greece had changed. The Greek lyric lines did not have intermediate caesurae; it was not appropriate to speak of *métrique verbale*, simply because it was the music, the melodic phrasing that gave structure to the line and not the words.[39] The hexameter and other recitative lines did have caesurae, however, since they had a reduced degree of music (such as the *parakatalogé*) or no music at all (as in the iambic trimeter of theatre). Therefore they needed *métrique verbale* to structure the rhythmical discourse through speech. Who would think of introducing caesurae into the

---

[37] This obviously does not mean that Catullus' poetry was necessarily set to music from the start.

[38] See below for a systematic discussion of these two types of lines.

[39] The relevance of *métrique verbale* only for recitative and not for Greek lyric is an old idea of mine, Rossi (1966), especially 195–204. In 1965, my internal evidence was the comparison of the recited hexameter with the pseudo-hexameters (actually dactylo-epitrite) of Pindar (*Nem.* 9, stanza 1); see Rossi (1966), 273 n. 11, 310 f. In 1971, Dietmar Korzeniewski told me in Köln he had heard this idea in Rupprecht's classes in Munich. When I was writing that article, I had not realized the extent of Heinze's intuition (see Heinze 1918, n. 36 above). What is more, Seel-Pöhlmann (1959) had noted that in Horace lyric lines were treated as recitative.

lyric line, if not one who, like Horace, no longer used music? To my mind, this is very strong evidence that Horace's *Odes* were composed to be read, whether aloud or in silence.[40] Reading valorizes all the more the virtuosity of the caesurae (however monotonous).[41] Horace introduced to lyric a typical method of recitative: he could do so in a culture that no longer distinguished between verse originally intended for song and verse that was only recited.[42] But was he capable of making such a distinction? He composed both literary poetry and, luckily for us, the *Carmen Saeculare*: can we perceive a behavioural difference within his literary production?

Indeed, the manifest proof that Horace's method of *métrique verbale* was the fruit of a fully conscious sensitivity can be found by an internal examination of the *Carmen Saeculare*, composed in Sapphic stanzas, over against the rest of his lyric production. I set out here a chart of the number of lines with the number of violations of the caesura after the fifth element, respecting the chronological sequence of his poems' publication:

Books I–III (23 BCE): 447 Sapphic hendecasyllables; 7 violations (1.57%).[43]

Carmen Saeculare (17 BCE): 57 Sapphic hendecasyllables; 19 violations (33.34%).[44]

[40] On kinds of reading, see n. 8 above.

[41] This monotony, which strikes us as somewhat laboured, seems a rhythmic surplus and is not rhythmically Greek, even if we think of lyric lines converted to recitative. Suffice it to think of the mobility of the caesurae in dactylic hexameter or iambic trimeter. It seems like something the ancient literary critics would have called κακόζηλον. Obviously, for Horace, rhythmical monotony was supposed to highlight his virtuosity in normalizing the pace; for its sake, rhythmical variety is sacrificed. This seems to me the only explanation for such rigour. This was a Roman tendency in real recitative verse: the Latin hexameter prefers greatly the third-foot strong caesura.

[42] In Rossi (1966), I was implicitly considering this fact as a sign of an unconscious change of sensitivity on Horace's part: but now I am utterly convinced that Horace realized perfectly well the significance, value, and function of his metrical experimentation (more below).

[43] In *Odes* I–III: 1. 10. 1, 10. 6 (-*que*), 10. 18 (-*que*), 12. 1, 25. 11, 30. 1; 2. 6. 11. The number of violations would further decrease were we to consider as justified, as some do, virtual word endings before -*que*. However, I prefer, for the sake of prudence, to include the cases in -*que* as well as cases of full word endings together with cases of word composition. No change of criterion can affect the result of the statistics presented here.

[44] In the *Carm. Saec.*: 1 (-*que*), 14, 15, 18, 19 (-*que*), 35, 39, 43, 51, 53 (-*que*), 54 (-*que*), 55, 58, 59 (-*que*), 61, 62 (-*que*), 70, 73, 74 (-*que*).

Luigi Rossi

Book IV (after 13 BCE): 106 Sapphic hendecasyllables; 22 violations (20.96%).[45]

Let us try to interpret these statistics. First, the dates of publication of the *Odes*: Books I–III in 23 BCE, the *Carmen Saeculare* in 17, Book IV after 13. The very small quantity of violations of normalized caesurae in Books I–III (1.57%) marks a fully conscious intention. After it, comes the *Carmen Saeculare*, which, with its sudden increase of violations (33.34%), shows clearly that less attention is paid to the phenomenon. This can only be explained by the poem's composition for musical performance. Here I see Horace's sensitivity to the *métrique verbale* of recitative, which I can only explain by a strong intention (a real *Kunstwollen*) to normalize. He abandons this intention once it becomes clear that a structure with caesurae (*métrique verbale*) would no longer have an effect in musical performance, which was in this case choral. If in 17 BCE, Horace who already had a long career as a lyrist behind him, went against a self-imposed norm he had loyally respected, he obviously did so because he was aware his celebrative poem was to be set to music. This was new, since the rest of his poetic production was meant solely for recitation.

How can we account then for the persistence of violations, though to a lesser extent (20.96%), in the three Sapphic odes of Book IV (2, 6, 11)? Should we think all of Book IV was meant to be set to music? No, and this for a precise reason. All the other kinds of lines Horace had submitted to the process of normalization of the caesura, throughout the whole *corpus*,[46] behave in exactly the same way in Books I–III as in Book IV, that is, they strictly respect the self-imposed rule. Here is the chart:

Alcaic hendecasyllable: 634 occurrences, 106 in Book IV; 3 violations (0.47%).[47]

Minor Asclepiadean: 507 occurrences, 129 in Book IV; 1 violation (0.78%).[48]

---

[45] In *Odes* IV: 2. 7 (-*que*), 2. 9, 2. 13 (-*que*), 2. 17, 2. 23, 2. 33, 2. 38, 2. 41 (-*que*), 2. 47, 2. 49, 2. 50, 6. 10, 6. 13, 6. 27, 6. 30 (-*que*), 6. 33, 6. 35, 11. 23, 11. 27, 11. 29, 11. 30, 11. 34.

[46] I neglect the single occurrence of major Sapphic (*Odes* 3. 8).

[47] *Odes* 1. 16. 21, 1. 37. 5 (*de-promere*), 4. 14. 17.

[48] *Odes* 2. 12. 25 (*de-torquet*); I exclude 4. 8. 17, normally excluded by many because of the violation of the *lex Meinekiana*.

Greater Asclepiadean: 32 occurrences, 8 in Book IV: 1 violation (3.13%).[49]

To distort these statistics the least, it would be better to avoid fractions and then add together the occurrences of the three types of verse (1173) and the violations (5): the result is 0.42% of all violations.

We can then ask ourselves why only the three Sapphic odes of Book IV have so many hendecasyllables with violations (22 out of 105: 20.96%), with a percentage that is so close to the Sapphic *Carmen Saeculare* (19 out of 57: 33.34%).[50] The most obvious explanation, perhaps the right one, seems to be that, after the experiment of composing the *Carmen Saeculare* according to a looser norm, Horace then continued composing Sapphic odes with 'poetic licence' for reading, though he continued to treat other lines with his usual scrupulousness.

5. MORE ON MUSICAL MIMESIS

But there is noteworthy additional evidence which turns out to be another case of mimesis.[51] A certain importance has been given by music-minded interpreters to *Odes* 4. 6, one of the three poems in Sapphics in Book IV.[52] In it, Horace teaches a chorus of boys and girls to sing his words (31–44):

> Virginum primae puerique claris
>   patribus orti,
> Deliae tutela deae, fugacis
> lyncas et ceruos cohibentis arcu,
> Lesbium seruate pedem meique   35
>   pollicis ictum,
> rite Latonae puerum canentes,
> rite crescentem face Noctilucam,
> prosperam frugum celeremque pronos
>   volvere mensis.   40

[49] *Odes* 1. 18. 16 (*per-lucidior*); I exclude *Odes* 1. 18. 5, which can be explained by the orthotonic accent on *aut*.
[50] Faced with the brute uniformity of all the other statistics, I do not honestly feel that the difference between 33.34% and 20.96% is of any significance.
[51] On the mimesis in *Odes* 4. 2, see above §3, end.
[52] It contains 6 violations out of 33 hendecasyllables (18.18%, very close to the 20.96% of Book IV): 10, 13, 27, 30 (*-que*), 33, 35.

Nupta iam dices: 'Ego dis amicum,
saeculo festas referente luces,
reddidi carmen docilis modorum
vatis Horati.'

First of maidens and boys of renowned parents, whom the Delian goddess
protects, she who restrains with her bow lynxes and deer in flight, keep the
Lesbian metre and the beat of my thumb, ritually sing the son of Latona,
ritually sing that Noctiluca, whose torch waxes, is propitious for crops and
quick to turn the months headlong. Soon you'll be married and say:
'I performed a song dear to the gods, when the century brought back festive
days. I learned the modes of Horace, the bard.'

This poem is very interesting because it seems as though we were
attending a rehearsal: but this is one of many cases where the musical
rehearsal is clearly *mimed*, as indeed Porphyrio notes with great
perspicacity in the scholium to *Odes* 4. 6. 35 ff.,[53] where, comment-
ing on *meique pollicis ictum* (35–6),[54] he candidly says:

Id est: modulationem lyrici carminis, et suaviter hoc dicitur, quasi ipsam
lyram percutiat.[55]

That is: the modulation of a lyric song, and this is said neatly, as though he
were striking the lyre itself.

We should note how Horace insists, with the anaphora, on *rite*
(37, 38), which means 'according to the norm, the rite' and is
obviously related to music.[56] But everything here is prescriptive
and therefore musically mimetic. The most eloquent indication is
the poem's introduction, here too in direct discourse (41–4; as at
Odes 4. 2, *supra* §3, end): the poet turns to his chorus, as the
chorodidaskalos teaching it, suggesting which words to sing. The
poet, once again, reveals the mimesis.

Now, to what musical performance was Horace referring in *Odes*
4. 6? As if by coincidence, he is referring precisely to the performance
of the *Carmen Saeculare*. He means to recall the *Carmen* with this

---

[53] It is not methodologically reliable to rely on the statements of (late or very late)
scholiasts to support modern arguments: however Porphyrio is relevant in so far as he
opposes the scholastic practice of considering the poems musical!

[54] I leave aside here the controversy over the problem of *ictus*.

[55] As always, honestly reported by Wille (1967), 239 n. 97.

[56] *Rite* at *Carm. Saec.* 13 refers to something quite other than music.

ode, which is obviously not itself sung. The *Carmen Saeculare* (17 BCE) was signally positioned outside *Odes* IV (published after 13 BCE) and it is meaningful that such an important occasion for Augustan politics be present in the *corpus* as a purely literary 'doublet'. Similarly, in *Odes* 4. 2, also a musical mimesis, another great Augustan celebration is evoked, though it was not actually carried out (§3, end). If it had been, it may very well have been the case that a poem that was really sung would have been coupled with the *Carmen Saeculare* in the editorial transmission.

Besides, as an additional proof that the *Carmen Saeculare* was really sung, are there any traces in it of musical mimesis? No: all that concerns the musical performance are the last two lines: *doctus et Phoebi chorus et Dianae | dicere laudes* ('a chorus taught to speak the praises of Phoebus and Diana', 75–6). But here the performance is *acted* and not imitated, in the form of a final invocation. Any element of stage direction in this ode (e.g. 5–8, 21–4) is nothing more than the enunciation of the norms imposed by tradition for the renewal, planned by Augustus, of the *ludi saeculares* ('Century games'), of which we get a sort of *aition*. We should note the semantic correspondence of *docilis* (*Odes* 4. 6. 43), where the chorus sings within the imitative scenic action staged by Horace, with *doctus* (*Carm. Saec.* 75), where the chorus sings in the first person.

In other words, *Odes* 4. 6 is famously the literary counterpart of and closely related to the *Carmen Saeculare*, the poem really composed to be sung. Musical annotations are present in the literary poem, precisely because the absence of music created the conditions for the music to be simply imitated. It is therefore highly significant that such musical annotation is lacking in the *Carmen Saeculare*, precisely because this poem *really* was set to music.

6. HORACE, A LATIN POET WITH AN (ALMOST) GREEK EAR

These, to my mind, propitious *tests* establish Horace as a very sensitive connoisseur of both Greek poetry and the reasons for its varied configurations according to its own compositional laws. One of the

great merits of Heinze[57] was to have denied, against Christ and Kiessling, that Horace was following, in his versification, abstruse metrical
theories circulating in his time. Rather, he affirmed that Horace's
school was the Greek poets themselves. He practised what he preached:
vos exemplaria Graeca | nocturna versate manu, versate diurna
('Thumb the Greek examples, thumb them night and day', *AP* 268–9).

There is a *cahier de doléances* ('list of grievances') registering a few
unique cases of Horace's incomprehension of Greek metrical technique,[58] with which I personally agree. But I am happy to have found,
some years ago,[59] further proof to Heinze's claim that, in his treatment of asynarteta, Horace directly follows the technique of his
model Archilochus: he read Archilochus, not the theories of the
grammarians. Here I let Heinze speak for himself;[60] he defends
with vivacity Horace's 'competence':

The hypothesis ventured by Christ-Kiessling presents a poet who, on deciding to compose some odes, consults a recent handbook of prosody built on
an abstruse theory and imitates with painful diligence (*mit peinlicher Befl-
iessenheit*) syllable by syllable what the handbook presents as the 'correct'
Aeolian metre. He even goes beyond what was required in the handbook
(*über das dort Verlangte hinausgeht*) and, happy to have understood the
origin of the lines from the union of two *cola*, wanted to hammer them
(*einhämmern*) into his readers' ears by letting word endings come at the end
of each *colon*. I would rather like to honour the poet (*den Dichter zu Ehren
bringen*) who heard Lesbian verse with the ears of his times and whose
technique arose from developments in Hellenistico-Roman metrics.[61]

From another piece of evidence music-minded interpreters have
advanced in favour of the *Odes'* composition for performance,

---

[57] Heinze (1918).

[58] The discussion about Horace's incomprehension of certain metres will never
end: Pindar (*Odes* 4. 2. 11 f.), Anacreon (*Epod.* 14. 9–12), and even Plautus (*AP* 268–
74). Horace is at his lowest in his incoherent treatment of the passage from the third
to the fourth colon of the Sapphic stanza (sometimes at the line end, sometimes with
synaphea). I confess that, in comparison with his merits and his competence, I am at
a loss to explain these facts.

[59] See Rossi (1978), especially 37 f., on the free treatment of the pause between the
two *cola* of the asynarteta.

[60] Heinze (1918), 31 f. (Chapter 1, 6).

[61] The last words are the formulation, here synthetic, of the fact that Heinze
(1918), *passim* saw in Horatian technique, which was so rigorous, the terminus of a
tendency traceable among the Hellenistic poets.

I glean a further strong indication of Horace's sensitivity and, to my mind, even of Horace's historical awareness. The evidence is the well-known *lex Meinekiana*,[62] according to which Horace seems to generalize the four-line stanza, even in stichic or distich verse.[63] He obviously considered paradigmatic the Aeolian stanza, which he heard (though wrongly[64]) as four lines long. From the work of Otto Jahn to the recent and exhaustive study of Bohnenkamp,[65] many have thought the *lex* a lyrico-musical expedient. For lyric, I agree, for it is one of the normalizations Horace imposed on himself with great virtuosity even regarding the stanza. But I cannot make the further jump from the lyric to the musical aspect, which is an utterly arbitrary shift.[66] To me it appears on the contrary that here also his great sense of system is evident. The epodic distichs he couples in the *Odes* according to the *lex Meinekiana*,[67] he treats correctly in *Epodes* as distich stanzas, without producing a systematically even number of distichs: out of the 16 'epodic' *Epodes* (the 17th is in stichic iambic trimeter) only seven (4, 6, 7, 10, 11, 14, 15) have a number of lines divisible by four, a result which therefore appears to be by chance.[68] The definitive confirmation is found in the direct comparison of *Epodes* 12 with *Odes* 1. 7 and 28 (hexameter + Alcmanian): the two

[62] Formulated by August Meineke in his second edition of Horace, Berlin 1854, xliii f., (but already applied in his first); Bohnenkamp (1972), p. 4 n. 14.

[63] With the only exception of *Odes* 4.8, which has received emendation.

[64] Wrongly because Aeolian stanzas are formed of *three* lines (the third and the fourth *cola* make up one single line): he was used to Alexandrian editorial practice, which wrote the verse out over four lines.

[65] Jahn (1867); Bohnenkamp (1972). I recall here that Otto Jahn was an archaeologist, a philologist, and a musicologist. His agreement with the musical interpretation is thus justifiable on the basis of his culture and in itself interesting.

[66] Also von Albrecht (1993), 81, 99.

[67] For testimony on Greek epodic stanzas, I refer to Rossi (1978), table I: *Odes* 4. 7 (stanza I, hexameter + hemiepes), 1. 7, 28 (stanza II, hexameter + alcmanian), 1. 4 (stanza XV, alcmanian and ithyphallic [with a simple caesura] + cataleptic iambic trimetre); for the others, I refer to Klingner's *systemata carminum*: *Odes* 1. 3, 13, 19, 36; 3. 9, 15, 19, 24, 25, 28; 4. 1, 3 (*systema* IV, glyconic + asclepiadean minor); 1. 8 (*systema* VII, aristophanic + greater Sapphic); 2, 18 (syst. XII, Hipponactean + catalectic trochaic dimeter). It is possible (though not probable) that a number of the forms of the stanzas not attested in Greek are not Greek, but prudence is required, since new material may still be found. The prevailing opinion is that this would be Alexandrian poetry.

[68] From Bohnenkamp (1972), 9 and n. 43, I learn that G. Jachmann, *Philologus* 90 (1935) 350 n. 27, already used Horace's different treatment of epodic forms as a confirmation of the validity of the *lex Meinekiana*.

odes respect the *lex Meinekiana* but *not* the epode! For that is how the
Greeks handled epodes—especially Horace's beloved Archilochus.[69]

Horace's behaviour is correct conservatism in the *Epodes* and
legitimate innovation in the epodic forms taken up in the *Odes*.
His freedom consists, in this case, in admitting to lyric (namely
melic in the Greek sense) stanzas that in Greek belonged to a different
poetic genre (traditionally related to elegy) and in adapting them to
his fourfold conception of the stanza, but *only* for the *Odes*. He knew
full well what he was doing.

Now, from the third century BCE on, who practised Greek lyric
versification in the Mediterranean basin? By lyric, I mean something
beyond the simple elegiac distich, which had become almost the only
lyric form in use. Let us recall *per vacuum* ('on empty ground', 1. 19.
21) quoted at the beginning (§1). Much is lost from the Hellenistic
world, but there are no traces of polymetric verse beyond the little
found in Book XIII of the *Anthology*. If we look for Horace's Greek
colleagues, our list is rather dismal: Callimachus has the sober variety
of his *Iambs*, Sotades his bizarre *Sotadeans*, Cercidas his prudent
dactylo-epitrite, the *Hymn to Rome* by Melinno is in five Sapphic
stanzas (perhaps from the beginning of the first century BCE). Between the Archaic Latin poets and Martial, we have only the genial
cantica by Plautus, the sober variety of the neoterics and Catullus. In
no one do we find such metrical variety and so very many strophic
systems. Horace may serve as a template for what is not attested but
perhaps existed also in Greek, as if he were a sort of museum of
metres. This is why he was perfectly right to be proud of the renewal
of Greek poetry he effected. And he had no followers.[70] I allow myself
now to formulate without hesitation the paradox presented at the
beginning: Horace was the only Greek lyric poet of great import not
only in his day, but also for the past few centuries of Alexandrian and
Roman literature. For the Roman world, this is not surprising; it
should not be either for the Greek, for the loss of a tie between poetry
and music was a sufficient deterrent from complex poetic forms that

---

[69] Whom Horace followed also for the internal construction of the asynarteta: see
above and n. 59.

[70] If he had followers, they were only partial and late: Rosellini (1997), 917 (a taste
for polymetric verses can be found in Ausonius and Prudentius, to a more limited
extent in Paulinus of Nola).

had been created to serve that connection. This situation, far from diminishing it, increases the audacity of Horace's grand programme.

7. CONCLUSIONS

I hope I have at least corroborated the claim that Horace's *Odes* were not sung, but meant to be read in recitation. The testimony of the *Carmen Saeculare* proves only that *one* ode was sung by two choruses for one *single* ritual occasion. Explicit evidence for the use of song—i.e. monody—does not exist for *carmina* ('songs') in general as a literary genre. And, if we find *external* testimony of the occasional performance of one or another poem (§2), we may calmly believe it: it would be absurd to deny the possibility that *sometimes* poems were also sung, probably in para-sympotic social gatherings. It would be a typical case of an exception which confirms the rule and would only anticipate Horace's musical destiny in the Middle Ages and beyond (§2).

The result of this investigation is not only a more precise idea about the production of Horatian lyric: it was not set to music but rather meant to be recited and read. It has also resulted, as we have seen, in a greater recognition of Horace's awareness of the change in conditions of literary communication from that of his Greek models. We may recognize his awareness through his actual behaviour. He advanced some innovations (the regularization of word endings) where he felt it was fitting for a lyric no longer structured on the musical phrase but on speech (*métrique verbale*). But in exceptional circumstances such as the *Carmen Saeculare*, where musical performance structured the poem, he abandoned that innovation. His choice of verse technique derives from his vivid awareness of actual performance. The internal testimony of the *Carmen Saeculare* and comparison with the patent mimesis of *Odes* 4. 6 offer confirmation of what prudent scholars could deem until recently a simple argument from silence, namely that this choral poem was the *only* poem composed with musical performance in view.[71]

[71] For this work, I am greatly indebted to friends from the Roman Seminar. A special thanks goes to Lucio Ceccarelli.

17

The Word Order of Horace's *Odes*

R. G. M. Nisbet

Summary. The intricate word order of Horace's *Odes* is brought about by the repeated separation of adjectives from their nouns. Sometimes adjectives and nouns are interlaced in a pattern attested in Hellenistic poets and developed by their Roman imitators. As a result the force of the adjective comes over more sharply, and the structure of the sentence is more tightly integrated. The word order of the *Odes* conveys subtle shades of meaning, especially when a word's place in the line is also considered: possessive adjectives and personal pronouns sometimes have more emphasis than is recognized. A few points are added about Horace's colometry: his Graecizing use of participial and similar clauses to extend a period, his partiality for prosaic ablative absolutes even at the end of a sentence, his transposition of words to a colon where they do not properly belong. But even his abnormalities follow a system, and though the mosaic is so artificial, he follows his own rules rigorously without showing any constraint.

> Quis multa gracilis te puer in rosa
> perfusus liquidis urget odoribus
>   grato, Pyrrha, sub antro?
>   cui flavam religas comam,
> simplex munditiis? heu quotiens fidem   5
> mutatosque deos flebit, et aspera
>   nigris aequora ventis
>   emirabitur insolens,
> qui nunc te fruitur credulus aurea,

qui semper vacuam, semper amabilem   10
    sperat, nescius aurae
      fallacis. miseri quibus
    intemptata nites. me tabula sacer
    votiva paries indicat uvida
      suspendisse potenti   15
        vestimenta maris deo.   (Horace, *Odes* 1.5)

What thin boy drenched with liquid scents presses you, Pyrrha, amid much rose under a welcome cave? For whom do you tie back auburn hair with artless neatness? Ah how often will he weep for faith and fortune changed, and marvel unaccustomed at calm seas rough with dark winds, who now has the use of you, credulous, as made of gold, who hopes you always available, always lovable, unaware of the deceitful breeze. Unhappy those for whom you glisten unexplored! Me the sacred wall with votive tablet declares to have hung up damp clothes for the divinity who rules the sea.

The familiarity of this poem disguises its oddity. The vocabulary is normal enough, sometimes even a little prosaic (*gracilis, emirabitur, vacuam* in a semi-legal sense, *vestimenta*); the constructions are straightforward; there is ambiguity indeed in the words that refer both to the girl and the sea, but none of the off-centre use of language that makes Virgil so elusive. Yet though the components are simple, the composition is intricate: we can say with more reason than Lucilius ever could 'quam lepide lexis compostae ut tesserulae omnes | arte pavimento atque emblemate vermiculato' ('how neatly his phrases are put together, all like pieces of mosaic skilfully arranged, on a paved floor with involuted inlay', 84–5 M). A scrutiny of Horace's word order may explain something about the character of his lyrics; it also reveals shades of emphasis that have received regular attention only in H. D. Naylor's neglected commentary (1922). As situations recur, any study must deal with the *Odes* as a whole, but I shall revert from time to time to the ode to Pyrrha; when the composition of the individual poems is so carefully integrated, it is desirable as often as possible to look at the total context.

The distinctive word order of the *Odes* depends above all on the placing of adjectives, which Horace, like the other Roman poets of his time, uses far more freely than prose writers. Though his lines tend to be short, he averages about an attribute a line ('attributes' include not just adjectives but participles); and as a rule the nouns with attributes considerably outnumber those without. Of course particular circumstances may distort the statistics: when a noun has a dependent genitive, it is less likely to have an attribute as well; and when three parallel nouns are joined by connectives, one at most is likely to have an attribute (as at 2.4.21 'bracchia et voltum teretisque suras'). When an ode is elaborate and picturesque, the incidence goes up (with 22 attributes in the 16 lines of the ode to Pyrrha), but it declines in an austere poem like 4.7 ('diffugere nives') or a boring poem like 4.8 ('donarem pateras'). All in all, Horace uses far more attributes than Greek poets even of the Hellenistic age, and it is not till we come to Nonnus that we find a comparable profusion (Wifstrand 1933: 80).

A poet's adjectives, for the most part, are not simply objective (as in *ius civile*); so, though various factors may operate, they are usually placed before their nouns (Marouzeau 1922; Hofmann and Szantyr 1965: 406–7; Adams 1976: 89). What is more, 40 per cent of Horace's adjectives are separated from their nouns (Stevens 1953: 202); in the ode to Pyrrha this is always the case except for 12 *fallacis*, and even that is in a different line from 11 *aurae*. Hyperbaton was a familiar feature of literary prose that becomes more abundant in the imperial period (Hofmann and Szantyr 1965: 690–1; Adams 1971); but the Roman poets of the first century BC use it much more freely than contemporary prose writers. To some extent they are following the patterns of their Hellenistic predecessors (Van Sickle 1968), but they go much further. Part of the reason lies in their greater number of adjectives: that helps to explain why the *Aeneid* has less hyperbaton than the *Eclogues* or for that matter than Lucan (Caspari 1908: 80–93). Other factors were the avoidance of homoeoteleuton (for which see now Shackleton Bailey 1994) and the attraction of rhyme; for Greek poets were less averse to homoeoteleuton and less attracted by rhyme.

Horace in the *Odes* often interlaces adjectives and nouns in a double hyperbaton: thus in the poem to Pyrrha we find 1 'quis multa gracilis te puer in rosa', 6 f. 'aspera | nigris aequora ventis', 9 'qui nunc te fruitur credulus aurea', 13 f. 'tabula sacer | votiva paries indicat'. Various sorts of interlacing are attested in Plato (Denniston 1952: 54–5) and in late Greek prose, but Latin prose is much more restrained. Norden collected some examples in the notable third appendix to his commentary on *Aeneid* VI (1957: 393–6), and others have been added (Goodyear on Tac. *Ann.* 1.10.1, Woodman [1977] on Vell. 2.100.1, Winterbottom 1977a and 1977b); but prose parallels to the verse pattern are rare in the central period, at least when special cases are excluded (as when one of the attributes is a genuine participle). There is a striking early instance at *Rhet. Her.* 4.63 'aut (ut) aliquod fragile falsae choragium gloriae conparetur', 'or that some flimsy props of his bogus celebrity shall be made ready'; but as that comes from a quotation it may be the rendering of a Greek orator. At Cic. *Phil.* 2.66 we find 'maximus vini numerus fuit, permagnum optimi pondus argenti'; but here *permagnum* picks up *maximus*, and *optimi pondus argenti* can be regarded as a single unit (cf. Caes. *Gall.* 5.40.6 'multae praeustae sudes, magnus muralium pilorum numerus'). There is a more unusual instance at Plin. *N.H.* 10.3 'caeruleam roseis caudam pinnis distinguentibus', 'with rose-colored feathers picking out the blue tail'; but here the metrical *caeruleam roseis* may suggest the imitation of a poet or at least the manner of poetry.

For though so rare in classical Latin prose, this sort of interlacing is superabundant in the Roman poets of the first century BC and later. Norden attributed their predilection to the influence of rhetorical prose (cf. *Rhet. Her.* cited above); but in that case it is strange that the arrangement is not significantly attested in Cicero's speeches or the declamations in the elder Seneca (though note *Suas.* 3.1 'miseri cremata agricolae lugent semina'). It is better to look for poetical origins for a poetical phenomenon (Boldt 1884: 90–6; Caspari 1908: 86–90). The interlacing of adjectives is attested in Greek poetry as early as Theognis 250 ἀγλαὰ Μουσάων δῶρα ἰοστεφάνων ('the glorious gifts of the violet-crowned Muses'), and Pindar provides lyric examples, but they usually lack the symmetry characteristic of Roman poetry. Such symmetry appears occasionally in Hellenistic poetry (e.g. Call. *H.* 4.14 Ἰκαρίου πολλὴν ἀπομάσσεται ὕδατος ἄχνην, 'wipes off much spue from the Icarian water', 6.9), and particularly in pentameters (ibid. 5.12 πάντα χαλινοφάγων ἀφρὸν ἀπὸ στομάτων, 'all the foam from the mouths that champed the bit', 5.34); but among extant poets it is not common till Nonnus (Wifstrand 1933: 139–40), who is likely to have been influenced by Hellenistic rather than Roman prototypes. On the other hand interlacing appears abundantly in Catullus 62–8 (so also Cinna, *FLP* fr. 11), occasionally in Lucretius, more often in an innovating earlier poet, namely Cicero (Pearce 1966: 164–6 and 299–301). As both hexameters and pentameters naturally fall into two sections, this favoured a balanced distribution of adjectives and nouns (Patzer 1955: 87–9; Conrad 1965); and as Latin hexameters usually have their main caesura after the first syllable of the third foot (rather than after the trochee as in Greek), this made it easier to deploy adjectives before this caesura. As the interlaced pattern was already established in Horace's day, and was used by him both in the iambics and hexameters of the *Epodes* (2.15, 43, 47; 16.7, 33, 55), it is not surprising that he extended it to lyrics.

What then is the function of hyperbaton in the *Odes*? It is often pointed out that it adds 'emphasis' to the adjective (cf. Marouzeau 1922: 112–18; Fraenkel 1928: 162–8), but some qualifications are desirable (Stevens 1953; Dover 1960: 32–4). In the first place 'emphasis' in this context need not imply a raising or other modification of the voice: that might be superfluous in a language with a more flexible word order than English. In a complex sentence other factors may play a part, for instance rhythm in a prose writer (Quint. 8.6.62–7), metre in a poet. Sometimes there is a wish not so much to add emphasis to the adjective as to stow away less important words between the adjective and the noun. Hyperbaton also helps to bind the sentence into an integrated unit; this aspect is particularly important for Horace.

It should also be recognized that the Roman poets developed their own conventions about word order and took a delight in their own symmetrical patterns. Sometimes an adjective is brought forward not because its semantic significance is great by prosaic standards but to set it against some parallel or contrasting expression: for one of many instances see 1.3.10 f. 'qui fragilem truci | commisit pelago ratem', where by a typical chiasmus the fragility of the boat is set against the savagery of the sea. Even when there is no parallelism or antithesis a poet may highlight an adjective in a way that would seem excessive in prose: to cite again the ode to Pyrrha, 2 'liquidis . . . odoribus' underlines the paradox that smells can be liquid, 4 'flavam . . . comam' plays on the name 'Pyrrha', which suggests auburn hair, 14 ff. 'uvida . . . vestimenta' underlines in a vivid way that Horace has suffered shipwreck himself. Even adjectives that are described as 'conventional' may have more life in them than emerges from the English translations: thus at 1.38.1 'Persicos odi puer apparatus' the adjective evokes a picture and expresses an emotion. So instead of denying any emphasis to such adjectives in Horace, we can sometimes say that he gives his adjectives more prominence than would be natural in prose.

We may go further. When an adjective is detached from its noun, 'the temporary isolation of each word makes its own peculiar imagery the more vivid' (T. F. Higham, cited by Leishman 1956: 85). The ear is kept waiting for the corresponding noun, which often rhymes; this is a persistent feature of classical Roman poetry, notably in the 'golden lines' of Catullus and the pentameters of Ovid. Sometimes the noun may surprise the reader; thus at 1.5.6 f. 'aspera | nigris aequora ventis' it is a paradox that flat *aequora* should be rough, and *ventis* is also more arresting than the expected word for water. But it is the hardest thing for moderns to take the words in the order that they come: Milton is thought to force the English language when he translates 1.5.9 'qui nunc te fruitur credulus aurea' by 'Who now enjoys thee credulous all gold', but he is representing precisely what he found in the Latin.

The complexity of the *Odes* is not uniform throughout but is influenced by the context. Erotic and sympotic odes may be particularly intricate to suit the sensuous subject-matter; see the first line and last stanza of the ode to Pyrrha (1.5), the last stanza of the ode to Thaliarchus (1.9.21 ff.) 'nunc et latentis proditor intimo | gratus puellae risus ab angulo' (with triple interlacing), the closing couplet of the ode to Quinctius (2.11.23 f.) 'maturet incomptum Lacaenae | more comae religata nodum' (where the intricacy of the word order makes a piquant contrast with the simplicity of the girl's hair). On the other hand the great political poems are often written more directly, in what Horace would have called a more 'masculine' style (cf. *Serm.* 1.10.16, 91; Pers. 6.4); there is nothing involuted about the end of the ode to Lollius (4.9.45 ff.): 'non possidentem multa vocaveris | recte beatum; rectius occupat | nomen beati qui deorum | muneribus sapienter uti, | duramque callet pauperiem pati, | peiusque leto flagitium timet…'. Metre also plays a part: Sapphics give relatively little scope for complexity, and the *Carmen Saeculare*, which was meant to be sung, has a notably simple texture.

The word order of classical poetry is sometimes said to correspond to the situation described (Wilkinson 1963: 65–6); thus at 1.5.1 'quis multa gracilis te puer in rosa' the girl and the boy are in the middle of the line surrounded by *multa rosa*, and in 3 'grato, Pyrrha, sub antro' *Pyrrha* is indeed enclosed by *grato antro*. This aspect of Horace's hyperbata is subsidiary at most, for it affects a very small proportion of the material; see for instance 1.3.21 ff. 'nequiquam deus abscidit | prudens Oceano dissociabili | terras', where the artificial placing of *terras* suits a special explanation (I owe this suggestion to Dr S. J. Harrison), 4.3.14 f. 'dignatur suboles inter amabilis | vatum ponere me choros'. By a more general phenomenon a vocative is enclosed by words appropriate to the person addressed: thus at 1.5.3 (cited above) the cave is welcome to Pyrrha, at 1.17.10 'utcumque dulci, Tyndari, fistula' Tyndaris may enjoy the pipe because she is herself a musician (Fraenkel 1957: 206), at 2.1.14 'et consulenti Pollio curiae' the republican Pollio is associated with the senate-house (it is pointless to add that he is inside it), at 3.29.3 'cum flore, Maecenas, rosarum', the roses suit the notorious sybarite.

It has been calculated that in 85 per cent of the hyperbata in the *Odes* there is an interval of only one or two words (Stevens 1953: 202); just as in hexameters and pentameters, the incidence of two-word intervals is greater than in prose. Longer hyperbata in prose tend to be reserved for special cases, as with interrogatives, or adjectives of size or quantity, or where there is a particular degree of emphasis or floridity (Adams 1971: 13). In poetry longer hyperbata are used more freely: see for instance 1.17.1 f. 'velox amoenum saepe Lucretilem | mutat Lycaeo Faunus', where the postponement of the subject makes us wonder who is bounding in, while the chiastic order sets *Lucretilem* against *Lycaeo*. In other places a special point may be recognized, or missed: thus at 1.4.7 f. 'alterno terram quatiunt pede, dum gravis Cyclopum | Volcanus ardens visit officinas' *gravis* underlines a contrast with the nimble feet of the Graces. At 2.14.5 ff. 'non si trecenis, quotquot eunt dies, | amice, places inlacrimabilem | Plutona tauris ...' the hyperbole justifies the unusual emphasis on *trecenis* (though numerals are sometimes separated even in comedy and prose). At 3.10.19 f. 'non hoc semper erit liminis aut aquae | caelestis patiens latus' the emphatic *hoc* suggests 'whatever other people might put up with'. Occasionally a long hyperbaton recalls

the grand style of Pindar: see 3.4.9 ff. 'me fabulosae Vulture in Apulo |
nutricis extra limina †Pulliae | ludo fatigatumque somno | fronde
nova puerum palumbes | texere', 4.4.7 ff. 'vernique iam nimbis remo-
tis | insolitos docuere nisus | venti paventem'.

One type of hyperbaton is too common to be noticed: when a
genitive depends on a noun that is qualified by an adjective, it is
usually sandwiched between them. When this word order is upset,
the effect is often to emphasize the genitive; Horace is particularly
precise in his regard for such nuances (Naylor 1922: xxiii and xxvi).
See 1.10.6 'Mercuri, facunde nepos Atlantis': the balancing proper
names frame the line (cf. 1.19.1 'mater saeva Cupidinum'). 1.13.1 ff.
'cum tu, Lydia, Telephi | cervicem roseam, cerea Telephi | laudas
bracchia...': in this position the first *Telephi* underlines Lydia's
infatuation. 2.1.17 'iam nunc minaci murmure cornuum': *cornuum*
balances *litui* in the next line. 2.1.23 f. 'et cuncta terrarum subacta |
praeter atrocem animum Catonis': the proper name marks the cli-
max. 3.5.53 f. 'quam si clientum longa negotia | diiudicata lite relin-
queret': *clientum* emphasizes the mundane business that usually
concerned Regulus. 3.28.1 f. 'quid festo potius die | Neptuni faciam?':
Naylor explains 'What better can I do on a *feast-day*, and that the
feast-day of Neptune?' 4.7.19 f. 'cuncta manus avidas fugient heredis,
amico | quae dederis animo': the alien heir is contrasted with Tor-
quatus' own dear heart (with appropriate stress on *amico*). The same
principle operates with the ablative at 3.4.37 ff. 'vos Caesarem altum,
militia simul | fessas cohortes abdidit oppidis, | finire quaerentem
labores | Pierio recreatis antro': here *militia* is not sandwiched be-
tween *fessas* and *cohortes*, but stressed to produce a balance with
labores and a contrast with *Pierio*.

Little need be said about the position of genitives where no
adjective is present. Here classical Latin uses both possible orders,
with a tendency for the earlier position to add emphasis (Adams
1976: 73–82). Horace sometimes highlights such genitives in the
same way that he highlights adjectives: see for instance 1.2.9 f. 'pis-
cium et summa genus haesit ulmo | nota quae sedes fuerat columbis'
(where by a characteristic chiasmus the fish are contrasted with the
birds). There is an illuminating case at 1.1.6 'terrarum dominos
evehit ad deos'; as Naylor points out, the emphasis on *terrarum*

confirms that the first two words refer to the victors rather than the gods.

In classical Latin, adjectives derived from proper names regularly follow their noun, as *forum Romanum, horti Sallustiani*. In the *Odes* these adjectives often come first, sometimes with hyperbaton: thus in the opening poem we find 10 'Libycis...areis', 12 'Attalicis condicionibus', 15 'Icariis fluctibus', 28 'Marsus aper'. Horace prefers the livelier order because he tends to treat such adjectives as ornamental and emotive rather than factually descriptive (Marouzeau 1922: 28–32). On the other hand when an adjective describes a particular place, he often gives it its standard position immediately after the noun: cf. 1.2.14 'litore Etrusco', 1.3.6 'finibus Atticis', 1.11.5 f. 'mare | Tyrrhenum', 1.31.14 'aequor Atlanticum', 3.4.15 'saltusque Bantinos', 3.7.26 'gramine Martio'. Sometimes he reverses this tendency for particular reasons: cf. 1.1.13 f. 'ut trabe Cypria | Myrtoum pavidus nauta secet mare' (another chiasmus), 3.5.56 'aut Lacedaemonium Tarentum' (at the end of the Regulus Ode *Lacedaemonium* is evocative rather than merely factual), 3.14.3 f. 'Caesar Hispana repetit Penatis | victor ab ora' (*Hispana* underlines the analogy with Hercules). Of course other exceptions to the general tendency can be noted: thus the adjective is ornamental at 1.31.6 'non aurum aut ebur Indicum', 2.13.8 'venena Colcha', 2.18.3 'trabes Hymettiae' and particular at 2.1.16 'Delmatico...triumpho' (yet emphasis is appropriate), 3.12.7 'Tiberinis...undis'. When people are given a geographical epithet this often comes immediately before the name (1.15.22 'Pylium Nestora', 2.5.20 'Cnidiusve Gyges'); but this order is attested in Ciceronian prose (*Amic.* 88 'a Tarentino Archyta' with Seyffert and Müller's [1876] note).

I turn now to possessive adjectives, where Latin normally puts the possessive after the noun (*pater meus*); when this order is reversed the effect is to emphasize the possessive, especially when the two words are separated by hyperbaton (Marouzeau 1922: 137–44). There are many instances in Horace of this kind of point, though the nuance is sometimes ignored. See 1.13.3 f. 'vae meum | fervens difficili bile tumet iecur' (a contrast with 1 'tu, Lydia'), 1.15.7 f. 'coniurata tuas rumpere nuptias | et regnum Priami vetus' (Paris is set against Priam, as Naylor says), 1.22.9 f. 'namque me silva lupus in Sabina | dum meam canto Lalagen...' (*meam* is not predicative, as

Naylor suggests, but 'my very own Lalage', picking up the emphatic
me), 1.26.9 f. 'nil sine te mei | possunt honores' (*mei* is set against *te*
as at 4.9.30), 2.6.6 'sit meae sedes utinam senectae' ('I' and 'you' are
often contrasted in the ode to Septimius, as in the following ode to
Pompeius), 2.8.21 'te suis matres metuunt iuvencis' (underlining the
possessiveness of the mothers), 3.29.54 f. 'et mea | virtute me involvo'
(a man's own *virtus* is contrasted with external possessions), 4.1.33 f.
'sed cur heu, Ligurine, cur | manat rara meas lacrima per genas?'
(correcting 29 '*me* nec femina nec puer'), 4.6.35 f. 'Lesbium servate
pedem meique | pollicis ictum' (Horace's thumb balances Sappho's
metre), 4.10.2 'insperata tuae cum veniet poena superbiae' (the
penalty is least expected by Ligurinus). There is a more difficult
case at 3.4.69 f. 'testis mearum centi-manus Gyges | sententiarum',
where the emphasis on the trisyllabic *mearum* has seemed excessive
to some editors; but the transmitted text is protected by Pindar, fr.
169.3 f., where after saying that the violent are punished he adds
τεκμαίρομαι | ἔργοισιν Ἡρακλέος ('I infer from the deeds of Hera-
cles'). Perhaps Horace is saying with the self-assertion of a *vates*
'That's what *I* think, and Gyges proves it.'

Possessive adjectives that follow their nouns and are separated by
hyperbaton sometimes have more emphasis than is realized, particularly when they occur at the end of a line; in the same way at the end
of an elegiac pentameter the characteristic *meo, tuo*, etc. often have
point. The situation is fairly clear at 1.16.15 f. 'desectam et insani
leonis | vim stomacho adposuisse *nostro*' (where the emphatic *nostro*
is contrasted with *leonis*), 2.1.34 ff. 'quod mare Dauniae | non deco-
loravere caedes? | quae caret ora cruore *nostro*? (where *nostro* balances
Dauniae). Sometimes there is a contrast between the first and second
personal pronouns: 2.13.10 f. 'agro qui statuit *meo* | te, triste lignum',
2.17.1 'cur *me* querelis exanimas *tuis*?' (followed by 2 ff. 'nec dis
amicum est nec *mihi te* prius | obire, Maecenas, *mearum* | grande
decus columenque rerum. | a, *te meae* si partem animae rapit, |
maturior vis, quid moror alteram?', 3.13.13 ff. 'fies nobilium *tu*
quoque fontium, | *me* dicente cavis impositam ilicem | saxis, unde
loquaces | lymphae desiliunt *tuae*' (*tuae*, the last word of the poem,
continues the 'Du-Stil' of this hymnal address, and is also contrasted
with *me* at the beginning of line 14). In view of Horace's liking for
point, I also see emphasis in passages where some would deny it: 1.3.8

'et serves animae dimidium *meae*' ('I have entrusted *you*, the ship, with half of *my* life'), 1.7.20 f. 'seu densa tenebit | Tiburis umbra *tui*' (Plancus came from Tibur), 3.4.65 'vis consili expers mole ruit *sua*' ('collapses from its own bulk'), 3.19.28 '*me* lentus Glycerae torret amor *meae*'. There is a puzzle at 2.7.18 ff. 'longaque fessum militia latus | depone sub lauru mea, nec | parce cadis tibi destinatis'; here *mea* seems to make a contrast with *tibi*, for though it follows immediately on *lauru* it comes at the end of its clause and at a very unusual position in the line.

After possessive adjectives I come to personal pronouns, where the distinction is familiar between emphatic *me*, the equivalent of Greek ἐμέ and weak *me*, the equivalent of enclitic με; on the same principle Milton spelt 'mee' when the pronoun was emphatic and 'me' when it was weak. In his famous article Wackernagel (1892) discussed the tendency of weak pronouns to occupy the second place in the colon, but the case should not be overstated; J. N. Adams (1994) has shown that a weak pronoun sometimes nestles in the lee of a significant word, what he calls the 'focused host', even when this is not the first word in the colon. In the more informal registers the pronoun may come even at the end of the colon; thus Adams (1994: 108) cites Varro, *Rust.* 1.2.2 'nos uti expectaremus se, reliquit qui rogaret', 1.2.7 'simul aspicit me . . .'. When we turn to Horace as to the other Roman poets, it is not always obvious whether a pronoun is weak or emphatic; but I believe that we should be readier to recognize emphasis than editors sometimes are, particularly when the pronoun comes at the end of the line.

Thus at 3.9.1 'donec gratus eram tibi', I regard *tibi* as emphatic: the amoebaean ode to Lydia repeatedly underlines personal pronouns. 3.13.6 f. 'nam gelidos inficiet tibi | rubro sanguine rivos'; an emphatic *tibi* suits the hymnal aspect of the ode to Bandusia (cf. 9 f. 'te . . . tu'). 3.16.33 ff. 'quamquam nec Calabrae mella ferunt apes, | nec Laestrygonia Bacchus in amphora | languescit mihi, nec pinguia Gallicis | crescunt vellera pascuis'; here weak *mihi* at the very end of the second colon seems too inert for the *Odes* (contrast Varro cited above), and I should rather place it in the emphatic position at the beginning of the following colon (positing an influence by the ἀπὸ κοινοῦ principle on its two predecessors); for the same emphasis cf. line 27 'occultare *meis* dicerer horreis' and in a similar context 2.18.1 f. 'non ebur

neque aureum | *mea* renidet in domo lacunar', probably also 2.18.7 f.
'nec Laconicas *mihi* | trahunt honestae purpuras clientae'. 3.29.1
'Tyrrhena regum progenies, tibi...'; the pronoun is emphatic after
the long vocative, which forms an independent colon (cf. 4 'pressa
tuis balanus capillis'). 4.3.13 ff. 'Romae principis urbium | dignatur
suboles inter amabilis | vatum ponere me choros'; here *ponere* does
not seem significant enough to act as 'focused host', so I regard *me* as
emphatic, balancing *vatum*. Contrast 4.15.1 f. 'Phoebus volentem
proelia me loqui | victas et urbis increpuit lyra'; here Naylor again
regards the delayed pronoun as emphatic, but this time *proelia* is
important enough to be regarded as the 'focused host'.

When *mihi, tibi, sibi* come after the main caesura in a Sapphic
hendecasyllable, they may be either weak or emphatic according to
circumstances. For weak instances (following a 'focused host') see
2.2.13 'crescit indulgens sibi dirus hydrops', 2.4.1 'ne sit ancillae tibi
amor pudori', 3.11.38 f. 'surge, ne longus tibi somnus unde | non
times detur', 3.14.13 f. 'hic dies vere mihi festus atras | exiget curas',
3.27.45 f. 'si quis infamem mihi nunc iuvencum | dedat iratae'. But at
other times I regard the pronoun as emphatic, sometimes against the
general opinion. See 1.20.5 ff. 'ut paterni | fluminis ripae simul et
iocosa | redderet laudes tibi Vaticani | montis imago' (the emphatic
pronoun is natural in a panegyric, as also above at 2 ff. 'Graeca quod
ego ipse testa | conditum levi, datus in theatro | cum *tibi* plausus'),
2.6.13 f. 'ille terrarum mihi praeter omnis | angulus ridet' (cf. 6 'sit
meae sedes utinam senectae'), 2.8.17 'adde quod pubes tibi crescit
omnis' (cf. 21 *'te* suis matres metuunt iuvencis'), 3.8.19 'Medus
infestus sibi luctuosis | dissidet armis' (*sibi* is to be taken with
luctuosis, but not with *infestus* or *dissidet*), 3.11.15 f. 'cessit immanis
tibi blandienti | ianitor aulae' (following the hymnal *tu potes* at the
beginning of the stanza), 3.18.14 'spargit agrestis tibi silva frondes'
(again hymnal, like 10 above 'cum *tibi* Nonae redeunt Decembres'),
4.11.17 f. 'iure sollemnis mihi sanctiorque | paene natali proprio'
(*mihi* like *proprio* underlines Horace's respect for Maecenas'
birthday).

When the pronoun follows the central diaeresis in the Asclepiad
line, I suggest that it is usually emphatic and perhaps always so. At
1.15.23 ff. 'urgent impavidi te Salaminius | Teucer, te Sthenelus sciens
| pugnae' the first *te* is emphatic (as the second clearly is) to underline

the concentration of the Greeks on Paris. At 1.23.1 'vitas inuleo me similis, Chloe' it is generally assumed that *me* is weak, stowed away as it is between *inuleo* and *similis*, but the meaning is perhaps rather 'you avoid *me*' or even 'do you avoid *me*?'; in the last stanza (1.23.9 f.) Horace proceeds 'atqui non ego te tigris ut aspera | Gaetulusve leo frangere persequor' ('after all, *I'm* not pursuing you like a tiger...'). At 4.1.7 f. Horace says to Venus 'abi | quo blandae iuvenum te revocant preces'; here *te* may be the emphatic pronoun familiar from hymns. The case is clearer at 4.13.9 ff. 'importunus enim transvolat aridas | quercus, et refugit te quia luridi | dentes, te quia rugae | turpant et capitis nives'; here the position of 11 *te* at the beginning of its clause shows that 10 *te* in the middle of the Asclepiad line is also emphatic. There is a more problematic instance at 1.19.1 f. 'mater saeva Cupidinum | Thebanaeque iubet me Semelae puer | et lasciva Licentia | finitis animum reddere amoribus'; here most readers will regard *me* as weak (as at 5 'urit me Glycerae nitor'), but at 9 'in me tota ruens Venus' *me* is undoubtedly emphatic. To return to the ode to Pyrrha, a similar situation arises in the first line (1.5.1) 'quis multa gracilis te puer in rosa...'; here *te* seems usually to be regarded as weak, but perhaps the meaning is 'What mere boy presses a voluptuous person like *you*?' (with a contrast first between *multa* and *gracilis* and then between *te* and *puer*).

When the pronoun is first word in the line it cannot be enclitic, any more than με can begin a line of Greek verse. Consider the ode to Postumus, 2.14.21 ff. 'linquenda tellus et domus et placens | uxor, neque harum quas colis arborum | te praeter invisas cupressos | ulla brevem dominum sequetur'; here *te* must be emphatic, perhaps balancing *uxor*, which also derives point from its place in the line. 4.1.38 ff. 'iam volucrem sequor | te per gramina Martii | Campi, te per aquas, dure, volubilis'; the position of *te* at the beginning of one line and another clause underlines Horace's obsession. 4.5.31 f. 'hinc ad vina redit laetus et alteris | te mensis adhibet deum'; here *te*, in spite of its position between *alteris* and *mensis*, has the emphasis common in panegyrics as in prayers (note also the following line 'te multa prece, te prosequitur mero'). There is a striking instance at 1.8.1 ff., where the commentaries offer no comment: 'Lydia, dic per omnis | te deos oro, Sybarin cur properes amando | perdere'. If this had been prose we should all have assumed that *te* was weak, hidden away between *omnis* and *deos*; but that leaves us with weak *te* at the beginning of the line, where μϵ would be intolerable in Greek. It seems that *te* is more insistent than is sometimes realized; *te oro* is a common word order.

It is already clear that metre has an effect on Horace's word order, not because it imposes abnormalities (as is too often implied), but because certain positions in the line tend to suit particular elements. The word at the beginning of a self-contained line often agrees with the word at the end; this can sometimes produce an epigrammatic effect, as at 2.16.30 'longa Tithonum minuit senectus'. Such lines are attested in Greek and are familiar in Latin from the time of Cicero and Catullus (Norden 1957: 391; Conrad 1965: 225–9; Pearce 1966: 162–6; Van Sickle 1968: 500); they are notably common in the *Odes*, where it has been calculated that 247 lines (one in fourteen) are thus bound into a single colon (Stevens 1953: 203). The word before the caesura often agrees with the word at the end of the line, and the word after the caesura often agrees with the word at the beginning (cf. 3.3.5 'dux inquieti turbidus Hadriae'); for other standard distributions see Drexler (1967: 126–34). A word in one line is sometimes picked up by a corresponding word at the same place in a following line (for such 'vertical responsion' cf. Boldt 1884: 82–3; Stevens 1953: 203–4; Conrad 1965: 252–3). See for example 1.1.9 f. 'illum si *proprio* condidit *horreo* | quidquid de *Libycis* verritur *areis*', and for longer intervals 2.14.5 ff., 4.4.7 ff.; for a less obvious instance one may cite the balancing adjectives at 1.22.5 ff. 'sive per Syrtis iter *aestuosas*, | sive facturus per *inhospitalem* | Caucasum, vel quae loca *fabulosus* | lambit Hydaspes'.

The last word in the line may or may not be significant. One in three of the hyperbata in the *Odes* crosses verse boundaries (Stevens 1953: 203), compared with one in seven in the *Aeneid*; when an adjective in such circumstances comes at the end of the line, its position may reinforce the emphasis imposed by the hyperbaton itself (as at 2.10.6 ff. 'tutus caret *obsoleti* | sordibus tecti, caret *invidenda* | sobrius aula'). On the other hand the last word may be a mere connective like *et* or *neque*; for an extreme instance of the former cf. 2.6.1 ff. 'Septimi, Gadis aditure mecum et | Cantabrum indoctum iuga ferre nostra et | barbaras Syrtes', where the repeated enjambment may be meant to suggest persistent scurrying. For other weak line-

endings cf. such passages as 1.5.12 f. 'miseri quibus | intemptata nites'
(so 4.4.18), 3.7.14 f. 'nimis | casto Bellerophontae'.

    When the first word in the line is followed by a pause (not always
marked by punctuation in modern texts), it often has particular
significance (just as in hexameters); thus we find in the ode to Pyrrha
1.5.10 ff. 'qui semper vacuam, semper amabilem | sperat, nescius
aurae | fallacis', where *sperat* and *fallacis* are given an extra edge by
their position. The slight emphasis may easily be missed: cf. 1.9.17 f.
'donec virenti canities abest | morosa', 2.2.19 ff. 'populumque falsis |
dedocet uti | vocibus' ('empty words', as Naylor suggests), 2.11.21 f.
'quis devium scortum eliciet domo | Lyden?' (the climax, with
devium scortum in apposition, cf. 3.7.4 f.), 2.16.9 ff. 'non enim
gazae neque consularis | summovet lictor miseros tumultus | mentis'
(the tumult of the mind is contrasted with the tumult of the streets,
and *mentis* derives emphasis from its place in the line as well as its
place outside *miseros tumultus*; cf. 2.13.7 f. 'nocturno cruore | hospi-
tis'), 2.16.21 f. 'scandit aeratas vitiosa navis | cura' (the climax comes
at the end of the clause and the beginning of the line), 3.2.5 f.
'vitamque sub divo et trepidis agat | in rebus' ('in action', as Naylor
says), 3.10.16 f. 'supplicibus tuis | parcas' (the key word of the sup-
plication), 3.17.6 f. 'qui Formiarum moenia dicitur | princeps . . .' (the
founder was particularly important, cf. 1.3.12 '*primus*' in the same
position). When a first word followed by a pause seems over-empha-
sized, it may prove to be contrasted with another word in the context:
see 1.3.21 ff. 'nequiquam deus abscidit | prudens Oceano dissociabili |
terras, si tamen impiae | non tangenda rates transiliunt *vada*', 2.1.1 ff.
'motum ex Metello consule civicum | . . . (7) *tractas*, et *incedis* per
ignes' (handling is balanced by walking), 2.3.9 ff. 'quo pinus ingens
albaque populus | umbram hospitalem consociare amant | *ramis*?
quid obliquo laborat | lympha fugax trepidare *rivo*?' (the pause after
ramis need not be strong, a fact obscured by the modern question-
mark), 3.10.5 ff. 'audis quo strepitu ianua, quo nemus | inter pulchra
satum tecta remugiat | *ventis*, et positas ut glaciet *nives* | puro numine
Iuppiter?', 4.1.38 ff. 'iam volucrem sequor | te per gramina Martii |
Campi, te per *aquas*, dure, volubilis'. But not every word in this
prominent position has point; see for instance 2.9.1 ff. 'at non ter
aevo functus amabilem | ploravit omnis Antilochum senex | annos,
nec . . .' (where Naylor notes the oddity), 2.10.13 ff. 'sperat infestis,

metuit secundis | alteram sortem bene praeparatum | pectus', 4.13.9 f. 'importunus enim transvolat aridas | quercus' (for further material see Drexler 1967: 128).

Sometimes a different effect may be recognized. Consider 1.11.7 f. 'dum loquimur, fugerit invida | aetas: carpe diem, quam minimum credula postero': not only does the emphatic *aetas* balance *diem*, but the enjambment seems to underline the speed of time (note also 5 f. 'mare | Tyrrhenum'). There are a number of similar enjambments in the poem to the ship (1.14), perhaps suggesting that things are out of control: see 2 f. 'fortiter occupa | portum', 6 ff. 'ac sine funibus | vix durare carinae | possint imperiosius | aequor', perhaps 14 f. 'nil pictis timidus navita puppibus | fidit' (though there the contrast between *pictis* and *fidit* may be more significant). In 3.19 (on the celebration for Murena) the combination of enjambments and short sentences may suit a party that is livening up: see 10 f. 'da, puer, auguris | Murenae' (with emphasis on the proper name), 14 f. 'ternos ter cyathos attonitus petet | vates', 21 f. 'parcentis ego dexteras | odi: sparge rosas'.

Sometimes the enjambment is so strange that the text has been doubted. Such a case arises at 2.18.29 ff. 'nulla certior tamen | rapacis Orci fine destinata | aula divitem manet | erum. quid ultra tendis?'; here the position of *erum* before the pause seems intolerable, and I have proposed joining the word to the following sentence ('why do you strain proprietorship farther?'). Or consider 3.6.9 ff. 'iam bis Monaeses et Pacori manus | non auspicatos contudit impetus | nostros, et adiecisse praedam | torquibus exiguis renidet'. Here *nostros* before the pause seems too emphatic, seeing that *impetus* is already qualified by *non auspicatos*; Bentley (1711) proposed *nostrorum* with *impetus*, Shackleton Bailey (1985) with *praedam* or alternatively *nostratem*, I have tried *praeclaram*, which if it was corrupted to *praedam* would have caused rewriting. Some editors have felt difficulty at 4.11.4 f. 'est hederae vis | multa, qua crines religata fulges': *multa* seems very emphatic in its isolated position at the beginning of the stanza. But here the adjective may be pointed, balancing 2 '*plenus* Albani cadus'; for other instances of an isolated *multus* at the beginning of a line cf. 2.16.17 f. 'quid *brevi* fortes iaculamur aevo | *multa*' (a contrast), 3.17.10, 4.9.26.

This leads to the controversy about 3.6.25 ff. 'motus doceri gaudet Ionicos | matura virgo et fingitur artibus | *iam nunc* et incestos amores | de tenero meditatur ungui'. Here editors disagree about whether to take *iam nunc* with the preceding or the following clause; this is linked to the problem about *de tenero ungui*, which is explained as either 'from earliest infancy' or 'with every fibre of her being'. I take it that the former is correct; this alone suits *meditatur* ('practises' or 'rehearses'), which itself balances *doceri* and *fingitur*. If that is so, *iam nunc* must be taken with *fingitur artibus* and followed by a comma; now each clause includes an indication of time (*matura, iam nunc*, and finally the hyperbole of *de tenero ungui*). This is not the only place where Horace emphasizes an adverb by placing it at the beginning of a line and end of a colon: see 1.34.5 ff. 'namque Diespiter | igni corusco nubila dividens | plerumque...', 2.9.4 'usque', 2.20.9 ff. 'iam iam residunt *cruribus* asperae | pelles, et album mutor in alitem | *superne*...'. But though an adverb may come at the end of a colon, it is less natural at the end of a sentence; here the movement of formal Latin differs from Greek.

This leads one to ask what part of speech most often ends a sentence in the *Odes*. In prose of the first century BC there is still a considerable tendency to end with the verb: thus in a sample of Caesar 84 per cent of verbs come at the end of the main clause, and though the proportion declines in the imperial period, even in a sample of Seneca the figure is 58 per cent (Linde 1923: 154–5). In Horace, on the other hand, the last word is most often a noun, and a verb ends only a quarter of the sentences (Stevens 1953: 202). This is partly a consequence of the greater use of adjectives than in prose and the higher incidence of hyperbaton; by an increasingly common word order a verb is often interposed between the adjective and noun (Adams 1971). In rhetorical Latin there is some reluctance to let an isolated noun dangle at the end; but when the noun is supported by an adjective and the verb interposed, the sentence is clearly incomplete till the noun falls into place.

Horace sometimes places an adjective at the end of a sentence, usually with hyperbaton; this reversal of the normal tendency gives it particular point (see also above on possessives). Such adjectives may be contrasted with earlier words, sometimes with chiasmus: see 2.1.5 ff. '*nondum expiatis* uncta cruoribus, | *periculosae* plenum opus aleae | tractas, et incedis per ignes | suppositos cineri *doloso*', 2.8.15 f. 'semper *ardentis* acuens sagittas cote *cruenta*', 3.3.72 '*magna* modis tenuare *parvis*', 3.6.35 f. '*ingentem* cecidit | Antiochum Hannibalemque *dirum*', 3.15.6 'et stellis *nebulam* spargere *candidis*'. Or the adjective may be important even where there is no antithesis: cf. 1.9.24 'aut digito male pertinaci' (where the last word has the force of *resistenti*), 2.3.15 f. 'dum res et aetas et sororum | fila trium patiuntur atra' (but there may be a contrast with 14 *rosae*), 3.2.31 f. 'raro antecedentem scelestum | deseruit pede Poena claudo', 3.6.7 f. 'di multa neglecti dederunt | Hesperiae mala luctuosae', 3.24.44 'virtutisque viam deserit arduae'. There is an unusual case at 4.4.3 f. 'expertus fidelem | Iuppiter in Ganymede flavo', where an ornamental adjective with no particular emphasis immediately follows its noun at the end of the sentence and the stanza. Here the word order seems to give a conventionally 'poetical' effect, like the relaxed closure of Catullus 64 'nec se contingi patiuntur lumine claro' or the mock-neoteric cadence of Juvenal's ninth satire, 'quae Siculos cantus effugit remige surdo'.

In considering word order, questions about colometry are sometimes relevant, though in the case of poets they seldom attract attention (Quint. 11.3.36–8, Serv. *Aen.* 1.1, Norden 1957: 376–90). A descriptive clause may be separated from the vocative to which it belongs (as sometimes in Pindar); cf. 3.29.1 ff. 'Tyrrhena regum progenies, . . . | . . . 3 Maecenas', and in a hymnal context 3.21.1 ff. 'o nata mecum consule Manlio, | . . . 4 pia testa'. There is a controversial passage at 1.12.19 ff. 'proximos illi tamen occupabit | Pallas honores. | proeliis audax, neque te silebo | Liber'; here in another hymnal context I am now inclined to take 'proeliis audax' not with *Pallas* but with *Liber* (note the weapons associated with Diana and Phoebus later in the same stanza). A different question arises at 3.14.1 ff. 'Herculis ritu, modo dictus, o plebs, | morte venalem petiisse laurum, | Caesar Hispana repetit Penatis | victor ab ora'. Against the commentators I take *Herculis ritu* not with *petiisse* but with *repetit*; Augustus was recently thought to have sought the bay-wreath at the cost of his life, but the resemblance to Hercules lies not in this but in his triumphant return from Spain. A short clause like *Herculis ritu* can be an independent colon, and need not cohere closely with what immediately follows.

Horace sometimes develops a sentence by means of a participial clause, in a manner more characteristic of Greek than of standard Latin; or sometimes the appended clause depends on an adjective where Greek would have supplied the participle of the verb 'to be'. Thus in the ode to Pyrrha we find 2 'perfusus liquidis...odoribus' (too compressed for Cicero), 5 'simplex munditiis', 10 f. 'nescius aurae | fallacis' (appendages more characteristic of Tacitus than of republican Latin). I add a selection of many other instances; just as in prose, editors do not always use punctuation to indicate colometry, preferring to follow irrelevant modern conventions. 1.29.7 ff. 'puer quis ex aula capillis | ad cyathum statuetur unctis, | doctus sagittas tendere Sericas | arcu paterno?' 1.33.14 ff. 'grata detinuit compede Myrtale, | libertina fretis acrior Hadriae, | curvantis Calabros sinus' (where many wrongly punctuate after *libertina* rather than *Myrtale*). 1.36.18 ff. 'nec Damalis novo | divelletur adultero, | lascivis hederis ambitiosior' (a comparative may link an independent colon as at 1.18.16 'arcanique Fides prodiga, perlucidior vitro', 2.14.28). 1.37.25 ff. 'ausa et iacentem visere regiam | vultu sereno, fortis et asperas | tractare serpentis, ut atrum | corpore combiberet venenum, | deliberata morte ferocior, | saevis Liburnis scilicet invidens | privata deduci superbo, | non humilis mulier, triumpho' (the accumulation of appositions is remarkable even for Horace). 3.6.31 f. 'seu navis Hispanae magister, | dedecorum pretiosus emptor' (here the sentence is developed by a noun in apposition). 4.9.49 ff. 'duramque callet pauperiem pati, | peiusque leto flagitium timet, | non ille pro caris amicis, | aut patria timidus perire'. 4.14.17 ff. 'spectandus in certamine Martio, | devota morti pectora liberae | quantis fatigaret ruinis, | indomitas prope qualis undas | exercet Auster, Pleiadum choro | scindente nubes, impiger hostium | vexare turmas, et trementem | mittere equum medios per ignis' (another triumphant period).

Horace in the *Odes* shows a partiality for ablative absolutes that is unusual in a poet: the construction helps his desire for brevity, and if it suggests the language of historians and official discourse, that gives no cause for surprise. Sometimes he separates his ablative with the subject of the sentence or other elements (Naylor 1922: 23); cf. 1.10.14 'Ilio dives Priamus relicto', 2.7.27 f. 'recepto | dulce mihi furere est amico', or with an interlaced word order 1.16.27 f. 'fias recantatis amica | opprobriis', 3.16.39 f. 'contracto melius parva cupidine | vectigalia porrigam'. In these places the components are short enough to be accommodated in a single colon; so there is no more difficulty in splitting the ablative than there would be with an ablative of quality. Such hyperbaton is rare in early Latin (cf. Plaut. *Stich.* 602 f. 'non me quidem | faciet auctore', with emphasis on *me*), and though Cicero has no difficulty about interposing a connective or an adverb, he does not normally do so with more significant elements (*Sest.* 11 'quibus hic litteris lectis' is an exception, but *hic* slips in very easily). On the other hand the subject is freely interposed in Caesar and particularly Livy (Hofmann and Szantyr 1965: 402). Here again we find that Horace's practice has more affinities with historiography than with oratory or poetry.

Horace's ablative absolute often comes after the main verb, sometimes at the very end of the sentence, even when it describes an antecedent action. See for instance 2.7.9 f. 'tecum Philippos et celerem fugam | sensi, relicta non bene parmula . . .', 3.1.33 f. 'contracta pisces aequora sentiunt, | iactis in altum molibus', 3.3.17 f. 'gratum elocuta consiliantibus | Iunone divis', 3.3.52, 3.3.65 f., 3.5.2 ff. 'praesens divus habebitur | Augustus, adiectis Britannis | imperio gravibusque Persis' (such 'officialese' suits the Roman Odes), 3.5.12 'incolumi Iove et urbe Roma', 3.6.27 f. 'cui donet impermissa raptim | gaudia luminibus remotis' (an austere description of an erotic situation), 3.14.14 ff. 'ego nec tumultum | nec mori per vim metuam, tenente | Caesare terras', 4.5.27 'incolumi Caesare'. Such postponement of the ablative absolute is found occasionally in early Latin (Plaut. *Amph.* 998 'vobis inspectantibus') and Cicero's letters (*Q.F.* 1.4.2 'infidelibus amicis, plurimis invidis'), but is untypical of his speeches, where he is working towards a climax. On the other hand the ablative absolute often follows the main statement both in Livy and Tacitus, though even in the historians it is relatively rare at the very end of the sentence.

I turn now to places where by a procedure common in Greek and Latin poetry the elements of two cola are intertwined. For a simple instance see once again the ode to Pyrrha, 1.5.1 f. 'quis multa gracilis te puer in rosa | perfusus liquidis urget odoribus?'; here the main verb is included within the participial clause, as at 1.21.13 ff. 'hic bellum lacrimosum, hic miseram famem | . . . vestra motus aget prece'. For a somewhat different trajection see 3.27.18 f. 'ego quid sit ater |

Hadriae novi sinus', where *novi* is inserted in the indirect question
that depends on it; cf. Soph. *O.T.* 1251 χὤπως μὲν ἐκ τῶνδ' οὐκέτ'
οἶδ' ἀπόλλυται ('and how after this she perishes I no longer know'),
Theoc. 16.16 f. πόθεν οἴσεται ἀθρεῖ | ἄργυρον ('looks from where he
will win money', Boldt (1884: 130–59). There is a more unusual case
at 1.22.17 f. 'pone me pigris ubi nulla campis | arbor aestiva recreatur
aura'; here the effect is to throw greater emphasis on *nulla*. See also
3.14.21 f. 'dic et argutae properet Neaerae | murreum nodo cohibere
crinem'; far from being hidden away, *properet* is emphasized by its
unusual position and underlines the poet's impatience. At first sight
we assume that *properet* means 'hurry to come' (cf. 2.11.23 *maturet*),
so the infinitive *cohibere* comes as a surprise; there is something to
be said for Muretus' *cohibente*, which gives a more straightforward
word order.

   I come now to other sorts of dislocation, beginning with the
ἀπὸ κοινοῦ construction, where an element common to two parallel
clauses is postponed till the second clause (Leo 1896); the figure is
common in Greek and Latin poetry, and though it may have originated as a metrical convenience, Horace must have felt it as an elegant
poeticism that served the interests of balance and economy. To turn
first to the ode to Pyrrha, we find 'heu quotiens fidem | mutatosque
deos flebit' (1.5.5 f.); here some editors interpret *fidem* as *perfidiam*,
but it suits Horace better to understand *fidem mutatam*. For other
examples of the construction see for instance 2.7.23 ff. 'quis udo |
deproperare apio coronas | curatve myrto?', 3.1.12 'moribus hic
meliorque fama', 3.4.19 'lauroque conlataque myrto', 3.11.6 'divitum
mensis et amica templis', perhaps 4.2.41 f. 'concines laetosque dies et
urbis | publicum ludum' (where Naylor explains the unexpected
prominence of *urbis* by taking it with *dies* as well as with *ludum*).
For an unusual repetition of the figure see the last three stanzas of the
Alcaic ode to Bacchus, 2.19.23 f. 'leonis | unguibus horribilisque
mala' (where *horribilisque* is Bochart's plausible conjecture for *horri-
bilique*), 28 'pacis eras mediusque belli', 32 'ore pedes tetigitque crura'.
Perhaps Horace is using a construction that he regarded as typical of
Greek hymns; in similar contexts note 1.30.5 f. (to Venus) 'fervidus
tecum puer et solutis | Gratiae zonis properentque Nymphae', 3.21.18
(the parodic hymn to the wine-jar) 'viresque et addis cornua
pauperi'.

For a common kind of ἀπὸ κοινοῦ construction cf. 3.25.2 'quae nemora aut quos agor in specus'; here by a figure common in Greek and Latin poetry a preposition is attached to the second of two nouns to which it applies. For more complex cases see 1.27.11 f. 'quo beatus | vulnere, qua pereat sagitta', where by a familiar elegance the common elements (*beatus* and *pereat*) are distributed between the two clauses; so also 2.8.3 f. 'dente si *nigro* fieres vel *uno* | turpior ungui', 2.15.18 ff. 'oppida *publico* | *sumptu iubentes* et deorum | templa *novo decorare saxo*'. There is a controversial passage at 3.12.8 f. 'eques ipso melior Bellerophonte neque pugno | neque segni pede victus', where some take *segni* with *pugno* as well as with *pede*; I have suggested elsewhere (1995: 263–4, 434) that the adjective conceals a proper name, say *Cycni*, that again has to be taken with both ablatives.

I turn now to a few places where there is a more unusual dislocation. Consider 1.23.11 f. 'tandem desine matrem | tempestiva sequi viro', where *tempestiva viro* is interrupted by the intrusive *sequi*. The metre is not a significant factor (for Horace could have written *tempestiva viro sequi*); in fact the artificial hyperbaton emphasizes *viro* and sets it against *matrem*. A similar case may be suspected at the end of the ode to Pyrrha, 1.5.14 ff. 'uvida suspendisse potenti | vestimenta maris deo'; normally *maris* would come immediately after *potenti*, on which it depends, but its dislocation gives it unusual emphasis. This might support the idea that there is a pun on Neptune who rules the sea and Venus who rules the male (Quinn 1963: 194 n. 2); it is desirable that the ambiguity of the ode should be sustained to the end, and Horace makes a similar pun at *Serm.* 2.8.14 f. 'procedit fuscus Hydaspes | Caecuba vina ferens, Alcon Chium maris expers'.

There is a stranger instance of a displaced genitive at 1.35.5 ff. (the ode to Fortune): 'te pauper ambit sollicita prece | ruris colonus, te dominam aequoris | quicumque Bithyna lacessit | Carpathium pelagus carina'. Here *ruris* must be taken not with *colonus*, where it is otiose, but with *dominam*, where it is needed to balance *aequoris*. The emphasis on *pauper* might suggest a contrast with the merchant, but it is particularly difficult to give *ruris* the necessary emphasis when it interrupts the sequence of *pauper* and *colonus*. For these reasons I have sometimes been tempted to read 'te ruris ambit sollicita prece | pauper colonus, te dominam aequoris...'. The long hyperbaton would put great weight on *ruris*, which combines with *aequoris* to show the extent of Fortune's power (a kind of polar expression common in hymns); any contrast between the poor man and the rich man is much less significant in this context.

In discussing this last passage Housman said that 'every Roman child felt in the marrow of his bones that *ruris* depended on *dominam*' (Diggle and Goodyear 1972: ii. 581). That is an implausible assertion, even allowing for characteristic hyperbole: not just in this exceptional case but in general the word order of the *Odes* must have seemed strange to the uninitiated, and it is not surprising that the first reactions were disappointing (*Epist.* 1.19.35 ff.). It is often remarked that in late antiquity the literary language was very different from spoken Latin, but the same was true to some extent of the Augustan poets, especially of one so original as Horace in the *Odes*. The formal organization of their verse is indeed remarkable, but it is unprofitable to look for explanations in the national character. Roman poetry was not an indigenous growth, and when it peaked it was very dependent on Hellenistic models, where the divorce from living Greek was greater than in the classical period.

All the same, Horace achieves such regularity in his self-imposed rules that they begin to seem inevitable. Far from cramping his style, they are an inseparable part of it. He achieves his effects not by flowery colouring but by balance and antithesis, precision and intensity, concentration and cohesion. The words interact as in a miniature physical system, the adjectives may seem conventional but their placing makes them tell, the interlocking produced by the hyperbata helps to bolt the monument together. Nothing could be more unlike the triteness and triviality of the usual English translations.

18

Horace Talks Rough and Dirty: No Comment (*Epodes* 8 & 12)[1]

John Henderson

This essay debates whether abusive insult be given a history. If this question is brought to classical Antiquity, to Rome, then Horace's book of *Epodes* is the crucial test-case. Scholarly strategies for moderating the force of the insult in its scandalous pair of women-baiting poems are reviewed, and a strong reading of *Epode* 12 as erotic play with verbal violence is outlined, against the simpler abusive scenario of *Epode* 8, in accordance with the contemporary critical model of writer-reader relations as 'staining': the bind of reading into social discourse.

THE FRAGILITY OF INSULTS

Abusive insult survives from Roman culture in well defined, all too well-defined, pockets. True, accidental survival hands us robust performances that were never designed for *reading*—Pompeian and

[1] This paper was given at the Warburg Institute on 29 November 1997 for the colloquium on 'Insults and Abusive Language: Historical Perspectives' organized by Peter Burke, David Chambers, and Will Ryan. Fully detailed commentary on both poems under consideration here is now set out in Watson (2003): 40–3, 287–309 on *Epode* 8; 382–416 on *Epode* 12. The health warning for the present essay promises (40 n.240) 'a characteristically impenetrable piece, featuring a gratuitous techno-paegnic vagina' ('a'? 'gratuitous'? 'vagina'? Beats me.).

other graffiti, for instance, that went (as they were meant to go) unremarked in the authorized culture that was deliberately delivered to posterity. But besides this jetsam, both primary and secondary Roman texts themselves present, identify and construe a welter of material which ancient historians can re-read, hard, until cultural locations for *conuicium* can be recognized and construed, ranging from stylized, ritualized, routinized 'vocal mobbing', through to casually improvised occasions for 'expressive versions of flyting'. Overviews have been organized, analysis progressed.[2]

One general feature of this terrain is a given: when it comes to classical texts that host or feature this aeschrology, we can be sure that across the millennia between their writing and our reading, they have been filtered, weeded, and censored through successive revisionary interventions, with their various criteria, imperatives, and hang-ups. Thus expurgation, sanitization, and defusion strongly intervene to shape the transmission, forever threatening the lifeline of infamy. We know too that this constitutive aspect of tradition was in on the act right from the very start of Latin Literature; it was already theorized by Greek critics, philosophers, writers, and was one of the basic assumptions built into the cultural production and consumption of writing, along with the panoply of terms and manoeuvres for its abjection, erasure, and pulping. Romans could not pre-date this industry of monitoring by the agents of decorum; they were latecomers to license.

The *opprobria* (insults) of *Latinitas*, then, fly under customized flags. There are the mannered topics of invective in court; there is a slot for the mandatory rudeness of the matey lyrics associated with sympotic bonhomie; in another package, find the stylized comic theatre and mime neatly tagged as popular festival, carnival license, and official arena for *parrhesia*, or 'paraded freedom of speech' (in Latin, *libertas*). As a particular badge of Romanness, however derivable, plottable, theorizable and therefore ratified by Hellenism it might be (and was), the naming of names in *ad hominem* mockery of important citizens before their assembled community was adopted as the specific of Lucilian *satura*; and, ever after, it was thematized as the generic limit to the production of contemporary

---

[2] See esp. Richlin (1992), esp. 109–14; Opelt (1965), Koster (1980), Graf (1997).

satire, which must wear on the sleeve its own caution. This was Latin Literature's insult to, and abuse of, the epic hexameter, and Romans could wear Satire as their *getting real* badge (true-to-life = slumming it; = gutter-sniping).[3]

When the Late Republic set about generating upbeat subjectivities for the élite male as a central project for 'poetry', particularly in the trajectories of the first person in Elegy, free spirits such as Catullus and friends could find precedents and springboards in Hellenistic institutions such as Epigram, which allowed virtually any mix or slice of content, provided that no attempt be made to elaborate the product beyond a single breath, and off into the realm of *argument*. Their *scurrilitas* (laddishness) courted oblivion, trading authority and prestige for urbanity in a haze of nonchalance: only Catullus is extant—in a single MS, saved by a fellow gentleman of Verona proud of his town.[4] Martial would later become the classic instance, the instant classic, and the classic *of* the instant, of this epigrammatist's self-marginalization: Martial's swarming minimalia are predicated on variety as the pledge of inconsequentiality, and transgress more by their performance of self-cancellation than by either their (in)famous motley of ultra abasement before the Lord God Almighty Caesar (Domitian), or by their Sadean *inguinity*—the ingenious performance of language as body-stain in every crevice; artifice through every combination of orifice. In short, the axiom of Epigram is the paraded refusal to recognize the importance of *anything*, for the moment.[5]

So a comprehensive account of Roman abusive insult would need to take in many a location on the cultural scene; and, as I have indicated, all this *is* more or less securely mappable. Yet in scarcely any area is there the possibility of a genuine narrative of change, of diachrony. No, Roman vituperation has range, but hardly a *history*. Accordingly, this essay will instead focus on a star item that would necessarily headline in any *grand récit* of aeschrology in the western tradition, precisely so as to trouble any such project, and contend that 'history' would only

---

[3] On the macho gendering of the genre of Roman satire, see Henderson (1987) and (1989) = (1999), 93–113, 173–201.

[4] For exemplary exploration, cf. Fitzgerald (1995), esp. 59–86, 'Obscenity Figures'.

[5] See now Fitzgerald (2006), esp. Chapter 1, 'Martial and the World of the Epigram'.

represent one variety of critical feint to detoxify abuse.⁶ Working back
from the instance, I shall take the risk of denouncing subsumption within
'a historical perspective' as *prophylaxis*, as a deliciously academic man-
oeuvre to disarm the insult. Rubbing noses in an *undeniable* scandal from
(literary) history is, in any case, the necessary antidote to scholarly
understanding. As plenty of contemporary criticism has demonstrated,
the insistence of the instance always embarrasses un(der-)problematized
deployment of general concepts and categories. 'The Insult' (there's no
such thing; what makes us think we know what we're talking about; who
are you to compare my insult with yours; don't pretend you can speak
for your history, your language, your people, let alone mine; XXXX!; and
so on) surely calls for insulting treatment. Abuse *must* have it coming.

THE *EPODES* LIMP THROUGH

Iambic lyric was the one department of ancient sympotica where
unruly transgression of politeness was *constitutive*. And this is where
abusive insult infiltrates the literary canon by right. Roman readers
could make the acquaintance of pre-classical Greek poems from beastly
Archilochos and from the specially foul and *déclassé* Hipponax, could
read them with Hellenistic commentaries and could try out revivals of
the genre, especially in Callimachus' book of *Iamboi*. Miserable scraps
of this tradition survived Antiquity, either in short quotes hygienized
by citation or on tattered papyri rescued from Egyptian cartonnage and
rubbish-dumps. In Latin, however, we do have one complete collection
of iambics. This is Horace's book of seventeen *Epodes*.⁷

The instant canonization of Horace, always just one step behind his
comrade Virgil, secures this book for eternity (like the *Eclogues*); these
poets became standard-bearers of Roman culture for the rest of Roman
time, paradigmatically enlivening the mutation of Roman order from

  ⁶ 'The outstanding examples of invective against old women in Latin are, surpris-
ingly, by Horace—*Epodes* 8 and 12. The two poems are not only the longest and most
personal attacks on old women, they are also even more than usually savage.... *Epode*
12 outdoes *Epode* 8.' (Richlin 1992: 109, 111).
  ⁷ See Barchiesi (2001) for Horace as literary profiler of *iambos*. For a fresh reading
of the *Epodes* as a patterned book, see Lyne (2005).

the chaos and socio-political obscenity of triumviral proscription and
civil war into the ideology of consensual compromise which inaugurated the autocracy of the Caesars as quasi-perpetual Presidential Leadership. The transformation of the boy Octavian into the first Emperor
Augustus provided the foundation myth for all the monsters, usurpers
and strong men that followed. These poets were instantly and indelibly
installed at the core of the imperial curriculum and book-culture for
the Latin-speaking West. It is extremely probable that the juvenilia of
neither Virgil nor Horace would have been prized and conserved had
their authors not gone on to lift their sights progressively toward
producing their Augustan chefs d'oeuvre, as the model writers at court.

Now the *Epodes* embody textually the officially and unanimously
recognized watershed moment of paradigm-shift, the battle of Actium and its triumph (31 and 29 BCE); the same critical moment that
Virgil articulated as the *Georgics* (where his earlier *Eclogues*, like
Horace's first production, *Satires* I, operate in the menacing uncer-
tainties of the world cracking apart, between Octavian and Antony,
and then who knew what waited in the wings). As such, the *Epodes* are
virtually 'undeniable' as a key component in the narrative of legitimation for the autocracy. As their author had made clear in his first
publication, they were written by a convert to Octavian's ascendancy,
a former rebel who had as an undergraduate fought against the united
Caesarian forces for the tyrannicides, but lived on to join the new
faction as it made up an acceptable and winsome face for itself, and
othered Antony as Cleopatra's eunuch and minion princeling. The
Epodes were hard to obliviate, or disavow, for all that they incarnate
juvenile excess and reflect forward regrettably on their eventually
laureate poet.[8] These are prize insults that Classics must swallow.

HITTING THE SACK WITH HORACE

We shall be getting to grips with the eighth and twelfth *Epodes*, where
the iambic staining of writer, victim, and reader performs abusive
erotics. After brusquely indicating how scholarship formerly negotiated

---

[8] For the *Epodes*' 'Historical background', see Watson (2003), 1–4.

these challenges to decency, I shall notice the strategies adopted in current Latin criticism; finally I shall poke round these texts to question what histories they may belong to—in the perspectives of erotics, gender, subjectivity. To make sure of implicating us all in the *contrectatio* programmed into these stunts, let me forewarn you: try not to denounce the tastelessness of 8; and don't look a gift-horse in the mouth of 12.[9]

These iambics are as finished, controlled, and crafted a coup of verse-composition as you could wish; but they are energized, worded, and voiced as raw as the crudest bawdy from any mouth almighty: I therefore defam(iliariz)e Horace with abusive translation. This will be an insult, for a start, to Translation, but Horace is just asking for it here, out loud:

[1] *EPODE* 8

rogare longo putidam te saeculo | uiris quid eneruet meas
cum sit tibi dens ater et rugis uetus | frontem senectus exaret
hietque turpis inter aridas natis | podex uelut crudae bouis?
sed incitat me pectus et mammae putres | equina quales ubera
uenterque mollis et femur tumentibus | exile suris additum.   10
esto beata, funus atque imagines | ducant triumphales tuum
nec sit marita quae rotundioribus | onusta bacis ambulet.
quid quod libelli Stoici inter sericos | iacere puluillos amant?
illiterati num minus nerui rigent | minusue languet fascinum,
quod ut superbo prouoces ab inguine | ore allaborandum est tibi.   20

[2] *EPODE* 12

quid tibi uis, mulier, nigris dignissima barris? | munera quid mihi
  quidue tabellas
mittis nec firmo iuueni neque naris obesae? | namque sagacius
  unus odoror,

---

[9] 'The word "contrectation"... usefully combines all those activities whereby the male and female attempt to *approach* each other sexually, whether by sight, smell, touch, or any other sense' (Legman 1972: I. 245).

polypus an grauis hirsutis cubet hircus in alis, | quam canis acer
    ubi lateat sus.   6
qui sudor uietis et quam malus undique membris | crescit odor,
    cum pene soluto
indomitam properat rabiem sedare; neque illi | iam manet umida
    creta colorque   10
stercore fucatus crocodili, iamque subando | tenta cubilia tectaque
    rumpit.
uel mea cum saeuis agitat fastidia uerbis: | 'Inachia langues
    minus ac me;
Inachiam ter nocte potes, mihi semper ad unum | mollis opus.
    pereat male, quae te   16
Lesbia quaerenti taurum monstrauit inertem, | cum mihi Cous
    adesset Amyntas,
cuius in indomito constantior inguine neruus | quam noua
    collibus arbor inhaeret.   20
muricibus Tyriis iteratae uellera lanae | cui properabantur? tibi nempe,
    ne foret aequalis inter conuiua, magis quem | diligeret mulier sua
    quam te.
o ego non felix, quam tu fugis ut pauet acris | agna lupos
    capreaeque leones.'.   26

[1] *EPODE* 8

    1   Ask YA have to ask uh Get lucky n in death   11
      long lifetime stink a she parade conquistadors
    whats zapping heman me   prize body guard all yours
3 you u huh toothsome black   an a missus nowhere   13
  an bygone years gone down   with still mo orotund
  plough creases cross frown   load a pearls about town
   5 & opened wide horrid   are there hardcover Thoughts   15
in among some dried bums   in among some satin
  farthole flop like cow's run   loveprops to lie back in?
   7   it gets me on you bet   dont suppose lack a school   17
  the breast an udder sags   stiffens up hemen less
  mare-ish sorta horse dug   or droops the less er sex
    9 & a womans belly   to coax it up from swank   19
  an the thigh plus bulbous a scrotal area
  calves sums up twigginess? mouthwwork wwanted from YA.

[2] *EPODE* 12

1 Whaddya at, SHE, take a
whole herd of trunks to tar ya,
what's my freebies, why the fax
3 coming when this boy's not steel,

　　　his snout aint blocked?
cos I'm the one can smell real sharp
5　any squid growth holed up
armchair goat in pits of hair—
beat keen hound to under cover pig
7 The sweat every shrivelled bit
of body that foul all over
rising smell, while shot prick
9　calms her fit of wild

　　rush, & now no way HER
　　foundation loses gloss
11　croc-shit factor make-up,
　　& now the sow on heat
strains a bed n busts a ceiling,
13 or while this savage gets me sick with abuse:

'Flop with Inez, worse wid me
Inez O.K. three times a night,　15
I every time get the one
go outa softy. Curse the one
picked YOU,
Madonna, a motor was needed
& you outa gas,　17
when I had Ashley de la Couche
on wild him stands firmer
rod in crotch.　19
than new tree rooting in the hills
Purple for a prince, double-fast
fur soaked again—.　21
whose express delivery? Rushed just
for you
so none in your bunch
can go party & get more.　23
real lurve outa his SHE than YOU.
Ah I'm so outa luck, you run away
like panic at wild
wolves, she-lamb, deer n lions'

WE'RE ALL IN THIS TOGETHER

To let this sink in, I now take another gentle swipe at what scholars of abusive insult have been getting up to, or at least at some likely versions of that—as if no one has thought of it.

In most senses of 'history', a history of insults in ancient culture would be uncomfortably like a history of the unconscious. Nice to refer to (but preferably from a different discipline). In a straightforward way, a chronotopically organized narrative would insult 'The Insult' (like The Proverb, The Joke, The Gesture) by displacing the effectual narratives that are the condition of its possibility. Namely the histories of the processes of intervention, of interference with the traces of insult: the reception history of successively compounded censorship, and the diligent militance of repression and distantiation.

Take any model for dealing with The Insult by appeal to 'authority', postulating and operating a hierarchic relation of extrinsic ordering: imagine *telling* abuse to fit into a story of ours. This fits into the familiar pattern of condescension to lowlife as comedy and comedy as lowlife which traditionally dominated criticism. This is the strategy which governed approaches to Insult, too, unchallenged before the relatively recent incursion of the model of 'staining', of participation in social discourse, blew it away, by opening scholarly analysis to communality: 'Horace's poems are not detached representations of society but *consequential acts within society*'.[10]

For the *Epodes*, this shift can be given an effective date *post quem* of *circa* 1982:

Needless to say, the unpleasant epodes...were omitted by the Victorian commentaries; and as these admirable scholars have not yet been superseded it still has to be pointed out that Horace was not invariably polite.[11]

Before the 1980s, that is, historical perspectives on the *Epodes* as insult would necessarily take the form of imperious modes of containment: 'No comment'. The *Epodes* were hidden away in editions, as in MSS, tucked away after four books of *Odes* and the *Carmen Saeculare*, out of the sequence of composition which otherwise reigns as the cardinal principle of such series as *Oxford Classical Texts* and the *Teubner* library. They were kept off-limits, out of public examinations and missing from such canons as Oxbridge B.A. syllabuses. Bowdlerized and euphemizing translations were all that there were. One way or another, the grossest abuses were simply suppressed: indicatively, the *woman*-baiting poems 8 and 12 (and only these poems) altogether disappeared from virtually all editions which carried commentary.

More subtly, this material was studied as *instances of* insult. Scholarship could reputably do its linguistic and lexicographical duty, identify which subject is which-verbing-what to whom, so long as the vernacular could be decently avoided.[12] And as respite from sweeping them under a carpet of *Quellenforschung*, criticism could

---

[10] Oliensis (1998), 2–3 (q.v.); cf. Miller (1997). This principle was most clearly formulated for the *Epodes* by Oliensis (1991), 107–38, at 126: 'The author of the *Epodes* is no more omnipotent than his various personae; Horace is not a detached analyst of current events but a compromised participant' (Repeated, but with 'an enmeshed participant' at (1998), 77). It remains to enfold reader-Horaces (see Oliensis 1991: n. 33 = (1998), 77 n. 36). [Oliensis (1991) is Ch. 9 in this volume.]

[11] Rudd (1982), 372.

[12] Indispensable: Grassmann (1966), esp. 70–90 on *Epode* 12.

objectify the poems, too. Self-referentiality as the pledge of literariness could evince the 'anti-Muse' of Iambic, analogizing the female figures in 8 and 12 as the mock-inverted poetics of this urbane genre: these literary tropes *complete* the classical canon, and bear with them the legitimation of traditionality (Hellenism as sanction).[13] Other, less theory-laden (= more positivistic) readings sieve *Epodes* 8 and 12 for thematic threads, then defuse them as ancillary to the referentiality that stakes out the collection as a whole: the mock-referential status of these unnamed SHEs ('probably the same woman', 'probably the same as Canidia'...) subordinates them to the rank of atmospheric colouring, emblematic coding, backdrop to the world stage bestridden by Maecenas, by Caesar, and Actium. Strong 'historical' (even ideological) reading works away from these vignettes of 'Hag §1' and 'Hag §2',[14] to concentrate on the grand masculinism of feud, vendetta, aggressive militarism, the cosmogonic triumph and victory.[15]

But The Insult *scorns* referentiality.[16] Its *point* is performativity. (Monstrous) Categorization of these poems as 'Vetula-Skoptik' (crone-baiting) can only be an insult to The Insult: there are *no* 'Hags' here, in either poem. Far from it: these are *bad-mouthed* females, women treated to bad-mouthing, and made to bad-mouth. Yet virtually everything in print on *Epodes* 8 and 12 falls at this first fence round abuse.[17]

---

[13] Esp. Clayman (1975), esp. 60, Gowers (1993), 288–9.

[14] Perpetuated in the spanking new commentaries of Mankin (1995), 153, 'the hag', 205, 'a hag', and of Watson (2003)—despite 288, '(allegedly) ageing females'— ibid. 'the *vetula*', etc., 382, 'an old woman...the *vetula*', etc.

[15] Esp. Fitzgerald (1988), 189–90. [Ch. 8 in this volume.]

[16] The first false step, away from the insult and the insulting, goes like this: '[*Epode* 8] begins *mediis rebus*, and it is left to the reader to infer the circumstances of this miniature drama. Apparently H. is intimately closeted with a woman: 5–10 suggest that he is looking at her naked body, 15–16 that the scene takes place in her private quarters...' (Watson 2003: 287; so 291, '...the devastating realism', etc.).

[17] Typical: 'The issue is this: how on earth has Horace become embroiled erotically with a hag of almost unparalleled repulsiveness?' (Watson 1995: 191). Distantiation from the reader is salient here: 'Of course the *vetula* is made to appear every bit as ridiculous as Horace—with her unseasonable and insatiate sexuality, her insensitivity to her raddled exterior, and her absurd and mealy-mouthedness at 12. 13 ff. Such even-handedness in dispensing mockery...' (196). On classical impotence in Antiquity: McMahon (1998), esp. 32–3 on *Epodes* 8 and 12. On the crone at Rome, cf. Rosivach (1994), Myers (1996), 1–21.

For all that, we are in fact being treated to a dousing in the *gendering of Lifetime*, which traditionally confines female existence to the sex-market of male selection ('Totty, and non-totty', as the (self-?)satirizing lads would sum up women in the emblematic 90s sit-com *Men Behaving Badly*). Sure, for whatever it's worth, the unnamed *male* in our poems is in some senses Horace, the poet (for example) of the book, and Maecenas' sidekick; but for all that, these SHEs get no names (once they are no husband's wife, no son's mother or father's daughter, any name would scarcely function as a status-marker within civic discourse—Inachia, or Lesbia, *uel sim.*). But none of this can securely other any of the *dramatis personae from the reader*. Rather, both poems body forth provocation in the form of pollution of writer/reader relations. I submit that there is now no escaping this.

STOP IT, HE LIKES IT (EPODE 8)

First things first, the badmouthing of 8's 'genital kiss' forces readers to perform in the theatre of Roman masculinities. Reading is folded here into the erotics of phallocracy, as we get to play (our own) victim when *malediction*, verbal abuse, collapses to *male diction*, the utterance of sexual abuse. For when poetry plays oral rape, so directly, *in second person 'exchange'*, make no mistake about it, we are handed parts in a scene that violates standards of public hygiene. This will have been abusive *profanation*.

Hence the 90s debate has been—was—whether the Roman insult of irrumation, forced fellatio, mixes in fear with the hatred, betraying or parading the denial of phallic autonomy implicit in the degradation of demonized woman. Is the axiom here impotence defensively exorcized as disgust displaced onto HER? Is the glimpse of HIS vulnerability the acceptable price of the demonstration that the writing male always retains control of representation of the written female? Or is the floppy male's powerlessness-in-power an exposé of the problematic impossibility of a fully vindicated masculinity, proof against sentiment, ironclad in the unfailing mechanics of

HIS potency? Maleness sets so high a threshold for inclusion that inadequacy is, not the exception, but the norm—is *that* it? Did Romen make very sure that *none* of them can qualify *securely* as Men? If anyone did count as a man among men, what kind of *amor* ('love, lust, desire, . . . ?'—ask Aeneas) could they ever risk letting within their defences?

All (as promised) *in the worst possible taste*, unforgivably ROUGH *Epode* 8 stages personal politics such that the utterance compromises each of us as participants—*as Horaces*. Through every reading of this mouthful of invective, potent myths of sexual rapacity operate dynamically: and, one way or another, we are left with a very particular taste in the mouth.[18]

DON'T STOP, HE LIKES HER LIKE THAT (EPODE 12)

If that was rough trade, impure and simple, now for ROUGH-AND-DIRTY, rather more of a complex, and a collaborative pastime. In *Epode* 12, we act out play between second and third person insult, and savour lengthy ventriloquist mockery of the SHE: does this decisively shift the dynamics around?[19] Here the repulsion is positioned *within* a liaison, for this woman knows her man—he has been HERS. Inadequately, SHE is made to say. Made to say this *to* him, for us to hear. So he's her butt—he's our butt *and* HERS? And, no doubt, since no one stays clean when abuse hits the fan, both of them are ridiculed, ineluctably. This, then, is (it must be) a skit. In which he is playing, at playing the victim.[20] These misfits, notice, aren't even iambics, but dactylic verses (the Alcmanian: 'ironically . . . the metre closest to elegy'[21]) trapped in a wilting book that prematurely waved

---

[18] An infamous 80s essay on just *Epode* 8, Henderson (1987), 'Suck it and see', made an unwelcome come-back (with make-over) in Henderson (1999), 93–113: consult, for the full Monty.

[19] For the shift from the second person addresses of vv. 1–3 to the third person at v. 13, cf. Carrubba (1969), 49–51.

[20] This is the laddish line taken by Watson (1995), esp. 202: He 'succeeds chiefly in repeating and indeed bolstering the case he sets out to overturn' (Oliensis 1998: 74 n. 26).

[21] Heyworth (1993) 89, q.v.

iambic couplets goodbye a couple of pieces back, and now goes off half-cocked.[22] The HE is taking another transgressive role, as he pleases, to show that in erotics men can take any mask, they can sing HIMs to pleasure themselves.[23]

To date, *Epode* 12 has scarcely been read any more intimately than this. I must then sketch out a line you could hate yourself liking, and then point out what may be happening to The Insult in *this* abuse of insult. As we remarked, this poem too no longer awaits our bidding. Horace again confronts us with ourselves, affronts all reading. No, there is no staining without being stained, and certainly not here. That was just the old self-protection agency putting the poem where it belongs, telling it where to go. Not an option for us.

To get involved, feel what happens if you underscore that the phrase *mea . . . agitat fastidia*, 'gets me sick', v. 13, at the hinge of the poem, is irremediably caught straddling the two senses '*attacks* my scorn for her' and '*provokes* my scorn for her'. Now match the parallel *cum*-clauses of vv. 8 f., '*while* shot prick calms her fit of wild rush', and v. 13, 'or *while* this savage gets me sick with abuse' (*cum pene soluto | indomitam properat rabiem sedare ~ uel mea cum saeuis agitat fastidia uerbis*): and you will find her *sexual* rush and her *verbal* rush inter-implicated between our othering of her and our impersonation of her.[24] Her body and her speech are super-imposed, in ours. We speak her savage insults, at our own peril.

Next reflect on the presents and the messages she sends, vv. 2 f., *munera . . . tabellas*, 'freebies . . . fax'. These are pictured again in their caricatures at v. 21, *uellera*, 'Purple for a prince, double-fast fur soaked again', and at vv. 13–26, in . . . her whole speech. For purple dye *stinks*, as Martial's epigram on Philaenis immortalizes (9. 62):[25]

[22] Cf. Oliensis (1998), 93.

[23] 'In the social situation of love-making, the male retains control by his right to choose how he will perceive the female.' (Richlin 1984: 75).

[24] Add that 'The . . . word order . . . may suggest that H.'s *fastidia* are also *saeua*, and, on another level, that the woman's words are in a sense his own (*mea*), since she is a character in his poem' (Mankin 1995: 210, *ad loc.*).

[25] The *dibaphos* was a specially conspicuous item of waste (Pliny, *Natural History* 9. 63), so a lavish token of unconditional lurve. . . . For '(Fear of) The Female Genitals' and Freudian 'velvet and fur': Legman (1972), I. 383. For olfactory tolerance and repression in modern texts, cf. Rindisbacher (1992), esp. 27–142, 'The German realist project of deodorization'.

She wears purple-dyed robes night and day—why?
delectatur odore non colore:
She's turned on by the stench, not the blench.

So the love-gift SHE furiously works to deliver, in order that he can
be beau of the ball, is retaliation in kind for everything in HIS volley
of olfactory abuse in vv. 3–11: the underarm and all-over body
odours of sex as sweat, scent and stink, re-doubled in the caked-on
crocodile dung for face-paint.[26] That twice-dyed fleece rushed over
to HIM, SHE says, and tells us that she wants more than one shot of
love, his usual ration (vv. 15–16):[27] we can't miss it, surely, when we
say she's being 'impossible'—in a *rush* again, and needs someone
who can stay with her, ride out HER *wildness*:

properabantur, v. 22, '*rushed* just for you' ∼ *properat*, v. 8, 'calms her
fit of wild *rush*';[28]

indomito, v. 19, 'on *wild* him . . . rod in crotch' ∼ *indomitam*, v. 9, 'her
fit of *wild* rush'.

And so it is that getting to grips with the responsion between the two
halves of the poem is the fate of the reader, as our paper-lovers couple
textually, the only way they can. In our performance of their abusive
insults, we get them, and we get it, together. In a lather of make-up on
the run and streaming pores, courtesy of our bodily inter-locking of
their mutual aggression. For this is what our voicing of HIM and HER
comes to, in the end: the exchange in which they share *sexual response*.[29]
Now just as *agitare*, v. 13, is commonly used of sexually pulsating
bodies (wiggling, waggling, wanking . . .), so *munera*, v. 2 ('gifts'), in

[26] The exotic foundation lightened skin tone: Hendry (1995), 583–8, esp. 584 and
n. 3.
[27] From time out of mind, females gave men cloth, as seduction, in entrapment:
Scheid and Svenbro (1996), esp. 70–1.
[28] '*Propero* seems to have been idiomatic in much the same sense as Eng. *come*'
(Adams 1982: 144): hence the propriety of the Latin Joy-King's name *Propertius*.
[29] Just as the cue for HER tirade, *cum saeuis agitat fastidia uerbis*, v. 13, 'while this
savage gets me sick with abuse', succinctly defines iambic modality, so *semper ad
unum | mollis opus*, vv. 15 f., 'every time . . . the one go outa softy', boasts of the
integrity of each composition (*opus*) and its consistency with the ensemble of the
poet's book (*opus*), in its self-glorified phallocratic power to unman all—including
itself, himself.

erotica signify sexual 'services' rendered, so 'freebies'.[30] And what we are reading is a 'message', *tabellas*, v. 2, so 'fax'. A message that writes in a return-message from the other. HE is making HER talk as rough as he wants, maybe as rough as he does, about how rough he treats her, making him loathe her/let her down, by giving him all a real man could ever want, except that she ruins it by saying so, this 'impossible' woman, this 'nympho', and thus matches him *all the way*.[31] Yes, on his account, she must be his rough trade; and he, hers (the pronouns tango through the lingo: *minus ac me* |... *te* |... *mihi* ... *tibi* ..., *te* |... *ego* ... *quam tu* ..., vv. 14–25).

True, several third persons in this poem do surround the duet—a menagerie of metaphors, and a human zoo. As if the performance is for the implied audience of *aequalis inter conuiua*, v. 23, 'none *in your bunch* can go party', to chortle over: that sex-machine Inachia, the cursed Lesbia, the trainee toy-boy Amyntas from Cos.[32] But the sympotic listener is compromised, all the same, by the erotic exchange *about* erotic exchange: can any of them boast that *their* SHE loves them more, or less, than this?—No way! (vv. 23 f.) She's quite a catch, this too much of a Good Thing, this Sure Thing? So hasn't this H[orac]E got it made (with HER[ace])?

Always, the poem brags, brags of her insults, even as his insults include them as his brag: he's here to wag his multi-performance (with Inachia) in *our* faces, to tell us this is how (much) SHE wants him, she goads-and-spurs him to it.[33] Surely these are *lovers*, not a

---

[30] '*Agito* had various sexual uses.... it could be used of the motions of the passive partner in intercourse ...; and for the meaning "masturbate"...'; '*Munus* could be used of the services of either partner' (Adams 1982: 144, 164).

[31] Female sexual desire insulted as her 'impossible' lack of a male to mate: Purdie (1993), 134–7.

[32] These names crackle with kudos and infamy: *Inachia* is myth's tragic princess Io, named for her father: she resounds with keen grief (*acer*, ἄχος: Paschalis (1997), 251; *Lesbia*: spells the charged erotics of Sappho and Catullus, and λεσβιάζω—'virtually the *vox propria* for fellatio' (Henderson 1975: 183); *Amyntas* was the name of many a wielder of Hellenistic power, and via classical pastoral poetry has come to code gay attraction, = '(Keep your filthy) Han(d)s Off' (from ἀμύνω): Clausen (1994), 108 on 3. 66, cf. Gide (1988), with Kandiyoti (1997), 239–40; *Cos* was a respectable Greek isle, home of poets and physicians, until Latin made it reverberate with *coitus*, cf. material in Mankin (1985), 211 on *Epode* 12. 18.

[33] Watson (1995), 193 rightly concludes: 'For her, man exists only in so far as he has the capacity to service her sexual needs'. But he elides the status of HER speech as the creation of HIS fantasy, malice, turn-on: 'a complaint which is really a back-handed compliment' (Oliensis 1991: 124 = 1998: 75).

smart-talking young poet with 'The Hag'. And these lovers talk DIRTIER than we are prepared to admit we could. They talk sex, ROUGH-AND-DIRTY. They verbalize sex as insult.

Is this, then (it is), the closest we are likely to get to pillow-talk in Latin? Is this, at any rate, how the lads improvised slagging off women, for each other's benefit? Look at what SHE needs from a man, begging for it—what HE needs her to want: if she was after a 'bull' and turned down a 'tree rooting in the hills' (vv. 17, 19 f.), and she's worth a pack of 'wolves', a pride of 'lions', scaring the boys into a bunch of 'she-lamb' and 'does' (vv. 25 f.), then she takes a lot of living up to.

Now the question Horace set himself at the outset was, in fact, *quid tibi uis, mulier*, v. 1, 'Whaddya at, SHE?' (= 'What does a woman want?'; = 'What does woman mean?'). And his answer was cued at once, in *nigris dignissima barris*, v. 1, 'take a whole herd of trunks to tar ya'. For this creature incarnates the 'blackness' of malice, *iambic* malice,[34] and 'merits' a virtuoso *Epode* of the 'choicest' abuse. Fit for her, a whole herd of 'well-endowed' elephants.[35] Waving their 'trunks' in tribute to her, and ready to *trumpet* phallic menace at her body and soul (*barris*, v. 1, the onomatopoeic name).[36] So this challenge to scream pure HATE is set too high for any mere male to live up to; and at the same time the insults he hands her to roar at him are, he told us from the start, a work of adoration, the loving craft of abuse. The scream of pure HEAT, body heat, sex, rough-and-dirty. Don't we even know that?

EFFACING, DEFACING, AND FACING UP

For the *Epodes*, at any rate, the history of any critique but evasion of reading ('no comment') has now had a very shallow time-depth—

[34] Cf. the 'black tooth' of *Epodes* 6. 15 and 8. 3, Dickie (1981), 205 n. 37.

[35] Oliensis (1991), 124; for nose=proboscis=trunk=penis=dangling projection, cf. Garber (1997), 32, Legman I. 57 and 200–3 (The elephant's 'cryptorchidism is a well-kept secret', ibid. 201).

[36] *nec firmo iuueni neque naris obesae*, v. 3, 'this boy's not steel, his snout ain't blocked', at once trumps the leering innuendo, as the male protests he's no bull elephant, and doesn't pack a 'trunk'.

about the [fifteen?] year span that ancient Rome gave any grown female before she was on the discard pile (and ripe for *Vetula-Skoptik*).[37] Classical scholarship is no isolated case where academic strategies have sought to abjure the insult *in* insult, displacing insults on paper with papers on insult so as to occlude the performativity which abusive language generates within the specifics of its discursive context. But now there is nothing to protect us from The Insult, and this (per)verse is out to make Whoraces of us all—whether ROUGH, or ROUGH-AND-DIRTY, well worth insulting:

Two Trappist monks sitting in separate cubicles have been busy copying old manuscripts for years, without ever speaking. Late one afternoon, during a thunderstorm, one whispers to the other, 'Let's talk'. The other whispers back, 'Well, all right. What shall we talk about?'. 'Let's say dirty words.' 'I don't know about that. You say one first.' 'Hair under your arms. There! Now you say one.' 'I can't', says the other; 'I'm cccccccooooommmmmiiiiinng!'[38]

---

[37] This claim, like this sentence to be sure, is forever dating just the way that *The Spider and the Fly* made Mick Jagger say 'my, my', and throwaway the immortal line 'coming flirty [*really* 'common, dirty'] | she looked about thirty' into the makeshifty 'nifty, shifty | she looked about fifty' (1966 <–> 1994).

[38] Legman (1978), 781.

19

Rituals in Ink: Horace on the Greek Lyric Tradition

Alessandro Barchiesi

If I were to suggest a simple explanation of why the problems of genre in Augustan poetry differ from those typical of Greek poetry, I would point to three main areas where I find a Roman peculiarity, at least in terms of intensity and investment. In so doing, I am not claiming that Hellenistic poetry did not have similar concerns, only that the following features became dominant in the Roman tradition:

1. *Thematization and dramatization:* The 'folding' of genre, by which I mean that genre as a theme becomes the productive, and at the same time, a problematic condition of those same texts. One might even speak of the 'theatralization of genre': in linguistic jargon, it is now more mentioned than simply used.
2. *A sense of rift and loss:* That is, a sense of breaking away from 'moments of truth', and from origins. The idea of genre oscillates

I thank Depew and Obbink for being inspiring critics as well as smooth organizers, and Carolyn Dewald and Kathryn Morgan for their generous contributions to the discussion in Washington. Part of this material has been discussed with the participants at seminars organized by Kirk Freudenburg at Ohio State University and by Karl Galinsky at the University of Texas. I thank both of them, and also Stephen White (University of Texas).

Before completing this manuscript, I was able to see some recent or forthcoming work (Feeney 1998; Oliensis 1998), and I thank the authors. I have, however, not seen other important recent (M. Lowrie, *Horace's Narrative Odes.* Oxford 1997) or forthcoming work (Rutherford [2001]). [On the Carmen Saeculare see also my paper in Woodman and Feeney (2002), 107–23.]

between the actual internalized matrix of the new work and a regressive vision of genre as it used to be, or should be.

3. *Politicization:* Generic divisions and oppositions take on specific political and social values, for example, discussions of epic versus elegy in Roman poetry imply discussions of 'what to do with the Principate in literature'; the limits of the bucolic genre involve the limits between private and political; small forms versus large forms; popular versus elitist ethos, and so on.

I cannot formulate these sketchy theses without the embarrassing feeling that I should immediately qualify and revise them. Their general thrust is reminiscent of the generalizations about Hellenistic poetry that provoked Dover to show that all its 'new' features were in fact pre-Hellenistic. In the same way, it could be shown that Greek poetry already employs each of these three points. More particularly, item (2) is dangerous if it leads to acritical assumptions about the guilt of being a latecomer; in fact, I would not claim that the only response to the rift idea is nostalgia and exclusion. Of course, Roman poets are able to foster a feeling of distance in order to create specific poetic and social effects, and not just naively to admit secondarity. However, I would like to retain my illusion that all three items together provide a reasonable description of how poetic genres work in the milieu of Augustan Rome. Moreover, the importance of item (3) seems to me to be unparalleled in Hellenistic poetry.[1]

I will refer to these three provisional generalizations in what follows. I have two specific aims in discussing the lyric Horace: the role of performance as a central issue in item (2); and the centrality of authors—that is, of impersonating authors—for the dynamics of this particular genre. The colloquium has confirmed my suspicion that performance and authorial voice would be central topics in its proceedings, and I hope that Horace can bring some contribution to this discussion. More than this, my own discussion is aligned with a working definition of genre sketched by Dirk Obbink in his introductory remarks at the colloquium. I rephrase: let us imagine genre as *a conceptual, orienting device that suggests to an audience the sort of*

---

[1] I deliberately avoid the issue of 'generic impurity', on which see Hinds (2000); Barchiesi (2001c).

receptional conditions in which a given fictive discourse might have been delivered or produced. My discussion begins from this point and will progressively address the three preliminary generalizations.

THE PROBLEM OF PERSONAE

The lyric genre exists for Horace in close symbiosis with images of authorship. Thus the title of this conference seems very fitting for an author who defines his production as a response to a canon of nine great authors (the *lyrici vates* of 1.1.35)[2] and then singles out two of them, who will even guarantee metrical form. From this moment on, 'Aeolian' and 'Lesbian' will be generic markers for the Roman poet and will imply two individuals: Alcaeus and Sappho. It is not easy in such a context to disentangle formal patterns of continuity from the problem of subjectivity and authority.

In Greece, the tradition of lyric was constituted through repetition, reenactment, and reperformance. Its survival was tied to symposia: in the frame of the symposion, performing Sappho and Anacreon means 'becoming' the authorial voice of Sappho and Anacreon.[3] It is no surprise that the first word of the first poem of the 'Anacreontea' is 'Anacreon', but of course impersonation can become a foil for diversification. Thus Catullus, in poem 51, launches his appropriation of Sapphic lyric by almost, but not quite, becoming Sappho. This is also how the shield episode at 2.7.10 works: the poet has been reformed into a 'shield-loser' by the choice of singing 2.7 in a sympotic frame ('welcome home, let's drink and remember and forget'). Thus he not just imitates, but becomes Archilochus, Alcaeus, and Anacreon. The rare (in the *Odes*) diminutive *parmula* perhaps indicates that the poet cannot shoulder a full regular shield, an *aspis*. Therefore, this episode can exist only in a poem like 2.7, and not in an epistle, or in satire. Horace incorporates similarity and distance: he will come out alive as a poet, but after Philippi he will not be a poet-soldier (contrast the *bioi*

---

[2] Feeney (1993), 41–2. [Ch. 11 in this volume.]
[3] See, e.g., Nagy (1990) and (1996), 54–5.

of Archilochus and Alcaeus, who are portrayed as having taken on a new shield to keep on fighting).[4]

Horace accepts the challenge set by the nexus of lyric tradition and impersonation. Lyric texts have an influence that induces role-playing, not just aesthetic pleasure: the roles of authors can be accepted, or, on the other hand, redefined. At moments the poet can get intoxicated like Anacreon, can be proud like Pindar, negotiate patronage like Simonides, and then step back and assert control.[5] Even gender problems will arise in this arena: feminization is an inherent danger or temptation in Sapphic influence, and Horace responds to the danger with the construction of a masculine artist in a woman's body: *mascula Sappho* (*Ep.* 1.19.28). In other words, within the general view that imitation is what creates literature, lyric posits a special problem: more than other genres, it implies the imitation of individuals, not just texts.

This approach to Horatian lyric in terms of impersonation leads directly into my first generalization, the folding of genre, or the thematization of genre, as productive of new texts. Horace raises the construction and assertion of a lyric personality to the status of a significant recurring theme in his collection, and the problem of how to establish a personal voice that confronts the canonical voices of the Greek masters becomes not only a prerequisite but also a part of his poetic representation. Time-honoured clichés can be reappraised in this context: Horace saying 'Come to me Venus, leave your favourite places in Cyprus' is clearly reenacting a plurality of traditional lyric voices—Alcman, Sappho, and Pindar—and yet making no explicit change to the tradition. Yet by the very fact of being uttered in Roman lyric verse, the invocation acquires a new status: this time Venus has a longer way to go, and by attending to this prayer, she will bear witness to a successful translation across a wide gulf of culture, time, and idiom. With this approach, Horace develops a paradox that was already inherent in the tradition of lyric reperformance: by invoking Aphrodite with the words of, say, Alcman or Pindar, the

---

[4] This is clear from Archilochus; about Alcaeus, I would guess that the point of the situation is that the Athenians have *dedicated* the spoils of Alcaeus, thus showing that he is a famous enemy (so Lapini (1996), 88 n. 26).

[5] Of course, this means that the lyric tradition consists not only of texts but also of imagined authorial voices and *bioi,* as well as posthumous revisions of *bioi.*

speaker is both impersonating the author and distancing himself from the *origo* of the enunciation. The distance of place and time from that *origo* is compressed into the gaps created in the utterance by the deictic markers 'come here, leave your favourite Cyprus', but the paradox is now intensified and becomes something of a shock to the system. Now 'here' corresponds, unpredictably, to the Tiber and to Rome. The emphasis on displacement so typical of poems for the gods now also involves displacement from Greece to Italy, and it involves, moreover, the making of a literary transference. This transference occurs as a 'live' event, created by the individual poem.

This point about the function of authorial personae brings me to a second problem: performance versus textuality.

THE CRISIS OF PERFORMANCE

If I begin this section by saying that Greek lyric is composed to be performed and that Horatian lyric is written for publication,[6] I will commit myself to a dualistic image of the lyric tradition. Since, however, I am interested in the interplay of performance and textuality in the Horatian oeuvre, I will attempt to be more nuanced. For my present purposes, it will not do simply to say that Horace, operating in a different historical context, supplants a performance culture with a new model of bookish lyric.

Horatian lyric confronts us with two different perspectives: (1) lyric as the product of a transformation of performances into texts, and (2) lyric as streamlined by its intention to re-create or to project performance. The first perspective involves the dynamics of the tradition, from Greece to Roman reception; the second concerns Horace's rewriting of the genre. The process of change 'from performance to text' writes traces into Greek texts that in turn become models for Horace. The process of re-creation then begins from these

---

[6] Don Fowler rightly stressed in the discussion that recitation is not to be imagined as a mediation between book and performance. Whatever the true importance of recitation in a literary society, Horace fights constantly to reduce its authority; satires and epistles are faithful allies of Horatian lyric in creating a gap between the poet's voice and the recitation arena, the rat maze of the *literati*.

very traces and works toward a poetics of 'live' performance.[7] This reconstructed idea of performance, in turn, is inseparable from its opposite, pure textuality. There are two contrasting dynamics at work in this poetics: on the one hand, the permanent fascination of a song-and-performance culture, on the other, the influence of books of poetry as made or remade by the Alexandrians. In both, Horace mixes continuity and discontinuity. I will begin with the second point, which is perhaps the simpler: the use of the book as a model for lyric 'performance'. That Horace acknowledges the book as a basic format of lyric has been thoroughly studied, but Krevans[8] is right to point out that Horace presupposes, yet also resists, the transformation that such an assumption entails. His collection of *carmina* suggests a collective reading but also encourages a reading of every single poem as an autonomous utterance. It is significant that most books of Greek lyric are already a similar mix of autonomy and planning. Individual songs take on a new meaning from the

---

[7] (a) Performative into textual: 4.8.20–2, 'for if no texts celebrate your worthy deeds, you reap no recompense', alludes to Pind. *Nem.* 4.5–6: 'praise, the companion of the lyre. For the word lasts longer than any deed'; but compare the Pindaric scholia *ad loc.* (10a): 'the word lasts longer than any deed, and by word he means "song."' In fact, every utterance *or written text* is more durable than actions. Clearly, actions pass away; *texts* are transmitted endlessly', rendering Pindaric 'lyre' and 'spoken word' through the scholiastic γραφόμενα. Lyric tradition 'glides' from spoken to written signs. Horace's next poem (4.9) glosses the evolution by juxtaposing lines 30–1, 'I will not, oh Lollius, pass you over in silence, unadorned in my texts' (the only other example of poetry as text in the lyric Horace), with the Pindaric representation of lines 1–4, 'Do not believe that they will die, those words which I am speaking, to be accompanied on the strings of the lyre.'

(b) Books regenerating performances: the practice in Horatian first lines (mottoes) of alluding to Greek first lines implies textuality: classical poems were catalogued and quoted by ancient critics by their first lines, but the setting of every Horatian song also performs a kind of 'live' improvisation that swerves from the model. One feels the textuality of Greek models' being reshaped in performance. According to Aristoxenos (fr. 71 a-b Wehrli), Alcaeus and Sappho were using *their own books of poetry* as a 'confidante' for their private passions; this for Horace becomes 'still breathes the love of the Aeolian girl, still lives her passion, confided to the lyre' (4.9.10–12). Sappho 'entrusts' her flames *to her musical instrument*: I suspect a pun on *fidis*, 'lyre', versus *fidus*, 'confidante'. Contrast also the Alexandrian epigram (Poseidippos, in Athen. 13.69) where the 'white speaking *pages* of Sappho's lovely *song* remain and will remain'.

In other words, Horace can travel the whole way between performance and writing, and back again.

[8] Forthcoming.

Alexandrian arrangement, but they also resist the same restructura-
tion. A complex two-way traffic is involved in this process: philologists
select poems because of their programmatic potential, and poems
receive a new programmatic potential through their positioning in a
book.

It is not difficult to conjecture why the poem known for more than
twenty centuries as 'Sappho One' has been selected to introduce the
Complete Works of Sappho, but of course it is also true that '*Poikilo-
thron' athanat' Aphrodita*' is invested with a new meaning[9] precisely
as a result of its inclusion as a first poem in a standard collection.
This is a different situation from the one familiar to Roman elegiac
and epigrammatic authors, who are looking back to Greek collections, which were planned and composed from the start to be read in
book format. Our evidence on lyric books is of course very scanty,
but in the hope to recover fragments of textuality in the Horatian
reception of canonical lyric, some conjectures can be attempted.

FIRST POEMS IN BOOKS

Of course, the evidence we have is very fragmentary, but it could be
interesting to start from what is known about first poems in Hellenistic collections and to look for traces of those poems in the Horatian
collection. I am thinking, for example, of Horace 1.1. An initial
priamel is, of course, a widespread feature of poetic beginnings, but
if we take the initial priamel of 1.1 and focus on its first element,
which is, of all things,[10] Olympic games and their glory, and if we
combine this reference with the first line's laudatory flavour[11]—

---

[9] Similarly, Hunter (1996), 153 connects the initial position of the *partheneia* in
Alcman's Alexandrian edition with their influence on Theocritus 18 (he allows me to
report that he withdraws the point about the Louvre *partheneion* being the first poem,
compare *POxy* 2389); his whole approach to Alexandrian intertextuality is important
to scholars of Roman poetry.

[10] See West (1995), 6 on chariot races at Olympia as a pointer to Pindar.

[11] Compare, e.g., the Pindaric incipit of Callimachus's 'Victoria Berenices', *SH* 254.
2–3: '. . . oh lady, holy blood of our majesties, the brother and sister, my victory song
for your horses', linking games, victory, praise poetry, and kings.

Maecenas atavis edite regibus—why should we not assume that
Horace is referring here to Pindar?

It is not self-evident why 'Olympian One' is 'Olympian One', but it
may be that the poem merited its first place in book one of the four
books of *epinikia* because it begins with a priamel, the purpose of which
is to put the Olympic games first, and then recounts the origins of these
games.[12] Poem one in book one by the first of lyric poets: this initial
allusion would be consonant with Horatian strategies of reduction and
self-protection, because after gesturing towards Pindar—the king of
the lyric canon for the king of patrons, Maecenas—the collection falls
back to Lesbian models, and it distances Pindar as a model too ambitious to handle. The end of 3.30 saturates the paradigm: the poem is the
boldest Pindaric reworking in the *tribiblos,* and the final crown of
Delphic laurel[13] links the success of the lyric poet with the Pythian
games—an allusion precisely to the book of *Pythionikai* that inspired
the text's initial movement (*exegi monumentum*). At 3.30.15–16, *lauro
cinge volens | Melpomene comam* (with Delphic laurel, oh Melpomene,
graciously wreathe my hair) may be intended to recall, with the final
position of 'hair' and the loaded image of crowning, the close of the
Alexandrian book-roll of *Olympian Odes.* Pindar *Ol.* 14.35, 'has
wreathed his hair with the radiant wings of victory'.[14]

By the end of 1.1, Horace has shifted from a Pindaric gesture to an
appropriation of Aeolic poetry. This gambit creates expectations about
the role of Alcaeus in 1.2, the first (Aeolic) poem inside the collection
after the preface offered by 1.1. Poem 1.2, then, is an experimental one
for a lyric bard: Horace laments a crisis in Roman society and religion,
then mentions the failure of choral prayers, and finally examines
alternative invocations to saviour gods. The two prominent gods in

---

[12] This motivation is actually provided by the Pindaric scholia *ad loc.* See also
Willcock (1995), 4. The poem is certainly not representative in terms of agonistic
occasion, since it is about a horse, and not a chariot race.

Note also the effect of having *ariston* as a first word in the book: this implies a
certain reading of Pindar but is also a choice bound to affect successive readings of
Pindar: labels of excellence will often function as a synecdoche for praise poetry.

[13] I owe this parallel to Oliensis (1998), 104 n. 3.

[14] In the context, Horace might have seen the muse Thalia, line 21, as the active
force. For the ideology of 'wings of victory', compare *palma . . . evehit* at 1.1.5–6
(compare 4.2.17–18; Pind. *I.* 2.28–9), in the 'Olympic Games' opening of the whole
collection.

the list, Apollo and Hermes, are known to be the dedicatees of the two
first poems in the first book of Alcaeus's collected songs (= frr. 307, 308
Voigt).[15] Perhaps Horace is practising to become a new Alcaeus after
all. Later in the first book (1.10.9 ff.) he will imitate extensively
Alcaeus's 'Hymn to Hermes',[16] but in the meantime, he recalls Alcaeus
One, although κατ᾽ ἀντίφρασιν. Alcaeus One is a successful invocation
to Apollo and incorporates the joy of the epiphany of Apollo to answer,
whereas Horace simply canvasses hope in his coming (*tandem venias
precamur | nube candentis umeros amictus | augur Apollo,* 'Oh come at
last, we pray, in a cloud come, prophetic Apollo, your radiant shoulders
veiled', 1.2.30–2). The demoralization created by the portentous flood-
ing of the Tiber (13–20) perhaps reverses the miraculous and joyous
'rising in flood' of the river Cephisus, which forms the climax of the
extant summary (307c V),[17] when Apollo comes for good to the land of
divination and paians.

A clearer example of Horace's Aeolic modelling is suggested by the
first poem in the second collection, 4.1. It has already struck others that
the initial address here to Venus, complete with military metaphors and
the theme of *rursus* ('once again,' δηῦτε, a password of lyric ideology),[18]
requires the intertext of Sappho One. The model is first subverted
(Horace tries to avoid, not to provoke, the epiphany), then delayed
(Horace substitutes another person as a candidate for Venusian intervention; the goddess never appears or speaks), and finally confirmed
(by a surprise ending: Horace cannot get rid of Ligurinus and of erotic
poetry after all). Of course, book IV as a whole is anticipated in this
tormented and problematic revision of earlier erotic poetry. But my
point is that the influence of Sappho here is not just the influence of a
poetic voice; it is the influence of a specific poem, empowered by its

[15] On what is known of ancient editions of the poet, see Porro (1994), 139–41,
with bibliography.

[16] In the meantime, the god himself performs an act of imitation (1.2.42 *imitaris*).

[17] The paraphrasis of the song to Apollo by Himerius suggests that Alcaeus was
singing the successful invocation of Apollo by the Delphians, the radiant epiphany of
the god on his arrival, the miraculous flowing of Castalia and the rising in flood of the
Cephisus, when it reacted to the epiphany. Presumably, the poem was regarded as a
powerful example of what poetry for the gods can perform—praising Apollo, retell-
ing the successful choral invocation of the Delphians, and implicating the power of
Alcaeus's own poetry. Horace thus places an experimental 'crisis poem' as the
frontispiece of his lyric career and uses Alcaeus's beginning as a contrasting foil.

[18] Mace (1993), 335–64.

textual dislocation. The text is now inseparable from its bookish label. 'Sappho One' has become a source of programmatic effects: the ease of personal communication between poetess and goddess, the summing-up intonation of the dialogue ('again...once more...what do you want from me this time'), the programmatic value of the text's military metaphors (σύμμαχος, 'ally', line 28)—all of this influences Horace through the positioning of this text as a programmatic poem, a frontispiece of classical love poetry. The poet oscillates between Sapphic impersonation and a sense of absence and surrogate: the unbelievably long sentence that begins by addressing the epiphanic goddess of Sappho One and that therefore suggests a live dialogue, ends up unpredictably, at lines 19–20, by addressing a *statue* of Venus—that is by definition a Roman replica, a cold *Ersatz* poised between presence and absence, a copy instead of a model.[19]

I would suggest, then, that this process I have been describing can be viewed from three angles: (1) the Hellenistic critics arrange the lyric texts in groups, books, and series of books with an eye on the potential of individual pieces for generic recognizability, artistic design, programmatic emphasis, authorial characterization, and more; (2) this very process of positioning and assembling *creates and teaches* new effects of artistic design;[20] (3) Horace reacts to this dynamic and perceives the whole tradition both as a final artefact (the 'Works of the Canonical Lyric Authors') and as a memory of lost voices, songs, and occasions.[21]

[19] In the discussion, Fantuzzi nicely pointed out that the other major influence on the 'amour, encore' dynamics of 4.1 is (compare Mace 1993 for Anacreon's fondness for the motif) Anacreon. Thus when 4.1 sabotages its Sapphic model and delays the final onrush of love, the Anacreontic voice keeps whispering that yes, love and middle age can be reconciled in the poetics of love lyric, although Sapphic inspiration might be difficult for the aging author of book IV.

[20] See my principle (1) above. L. E. Rossi (in conversation) has influenced my vision of the process with his usual clarity of thought.

Every edition of course had its own problems and priorities. From the remains, at least one general pattern is visible: some major collections had a song 'for the gods' as a first poem: compare Pindar's 'Hymn to Zeus'; Alcaeus for Apollo (307 V.); Sappho for Aphrodite; Anacreon for Artemis (348 Page, 1 Gentili).

[21] Another interesting approach to lyric textuality would be comparing Horace with ancient commentaries, e.g., to Alcaeus. I provided one specific example in the oral version of this paper, discussing the ship poems of Alcaeus, their exegesis, and their influence on Horace. On the importance of commentaries for the study of ancient genres, see Sluiter (2000).

Alessandro Barchiesi

The study of how performance poetry trespasses into the poetic book has an interesting flip side: the study of how the Horatian collection projects and suggests performance. In the next section, I will examine the occasional nature of Horatian lyric. In general, it is important to note that Horace suggests performance both as a background and as a future expectation. His four-book opus ends by looking forward, self-reflexively, to reperformance (4.15.32 *canemus*); the poet's afterlife is imagined as an occasion for listening to dead Aeolic poets performing in the Underworld.[22]

OCCASION AND TIME

The semiotics of Horatian odes has been described by Heinze as a three-tiered fiction: 'It is a fiction that the poet is facing an addressee. It is a fiction . . . that the poet wants to influence his addressee.'[23] It is a fiction that the listener is able to reconstruct from the song the situation in which the song originates.'[24] But of course Heinze thought that the three fictions were highly motivated and productive, and not just frivolous play. In a more general way, Reitzenstein had already crossed the gap between books and aural communication thirty years earlier:[25] 'We know that the Alexandrian poet was

---

[22] The irony of 2.13.25–32 is that, as part of an audience, Horace might like Sappho and Alcaeus less than he expected as a reader; in this (so to speak) 'live' version, Sappho is at her most passionate and 'Lesbian' ('lamenting about the girls of her island'); Alcaeus is powerful, but his success has dangerous hints of late-Republican demagogy ('but the mob, packed shoulder to shoulder, would rather hear with avid ears tales of battle and banished tyrants'). In a sense, the Underworld perpetuates the Greek poets as 'alien' masters, while Horace transforms their model and attunes them to modern Rome, e.g., producing a less 'effeminate' Sappho and a less aggressive Alcaeus (note the harsh, not very Horatian, triplication of *dura* in lines 26–7, *dura navis | dura fugae mala, dura belli* (the bad times of seafaring, the bad times of exile, the bad times of war), suggesting that Alcaeus's poetic success depends on a tough and manly persona).

[23] This must be an especially powerful fiction, since it is the source of many important currents in recent Horatian criticism, such as the focus on addressees in Nisbet and Hubbard (1970) and (1978), the more sociological approach of Citroni (1995) [see Ch. 5 in this volume], and the postmodernist rhetorical approach of Davis (1991).

[24] Heinze (1960b), 188 [Ch. 1 in this volume.].   [25] Reitzenstein (1963), 1.

working for a bookish circulation, just like the modern poet; yet we should not forget that the poet always counterfeits a performance, and his work becomes alive for us only insofar as we imagine it as performed.' There are, of course, other ways of complicating the picture. A constructive discussion should take into account the more recent problems generated by the (post-Heinzian) evolution in the study of Greek lyric and its poetics. A few *aporiai* should be mentioned here, because they have a bearing on our approaches to Horatian lyric:

1. *Is genre shaped by performance, or by its loss?* If one can assume that the original performance and its social context made genre superfluous, then genre, as Nagy has suggested, is a postmortem of performance. This is, however, a valid point, as many have seen, but only, as Nagy himself has clearly explained in a recent paper, if we are contrasting original performance with late textual circulation. What if we focus instead on the idea of reperformance?[26]

We should beware that the idea of performance in itself can easily become metaphysical and thus static, if we forget to keep an eye on social change. For our generation, television 'performances' are a simple test case. In the early days of this technology in Italy, in the 1950s, there were individual events of 'television' to be contemplated in religious silence and dark living rooms; nowadays a TV set is more like a radio, always on, while the family negotiates its daily life under varying conditions of attention, competing with other sources of light and interest. Yet from a distance, one is not prepared to admit that TV performances have changed over the lifespan of one generation, especially since some of its genres have achieved a considerable stability over time.

2. *'Spontaneity' and 'directness' are limited as concepts in interpreting archaic lyric.* We cannot take early lyric poetics for granted when confronting Horace. Precisely because the interpretation of Greek lyric has always been controversial, we need to clarify how selective our own approach is and how different interpretive communities will have reacted differently to this issue.[27]

[26] Nagy (1990), 362; Feeney (1993), 56; Citroni (1995), 276 (and in performances subsequent to the 'first', the original situation had to be reconstructed at best on the basis of signs present in the text).

[27] Feeney (1993), 56.

3. *How did the written, bookish Alexandrian text encourage the remake of a performative culture?* It would still have been possible in Classical times to view the unfolding of the collection as a new kind of performance and to equate occasion with the position of a text in a book, playing on similarities and differences in these two sets of contexts.[28] On the other hand, as we will see, the textual transmission of choral lyric, for example, encourages reflections on its original context, in spite of the complete loss, over time, of music and dance.

4. *Does Horace exploit 'edges' and clashes between different aspects of the lyric genre to generate meaning, for example, 'solo' lyric versus 'choral' lyric?*[29]

This is but a list of open-ended questions. They can, however, help us to return now to Heinze and to his conception of the threefold fictionality of Horatian poetics. From a historicist point of view, as Mario Citroni has argued in a number of papers,[30] it is not really helpful in understanding how literary communication works to see the fictional role of addressee as what really counts, since such a role can be saturated by anyone or anything, including Marcus Vipsanius Agrippa, a stock character, a personal friend of the poet, a slave, a lyre, or a ship. From a more formalist point of view, Heinze presupposes that the original context of performance is artificial but necessary to Horatian lyric, whereas it is natural and self-evident in early Greek poetry. Now, in the performative context of this volume, I could refer to Depew's cogent argument that the development of hymn is a process whereby deictic markers function as signs both of presence and of absence, and of a continuum in which the markers glide progressively into a conventional and a connotative function.[31]

Let me make a similar, brief argument about one sympotic poem, Anacreon, fragment 7 G:

The month of Poseidon has come, clouds are heavy with water, savage storms are rumbling heavily.

---

[28] Hinds (1996), 253 offers a dense formulation; see also Krevans (forthcoming).

[29] Bearing in mind that this polarity can be partly a Hellenistic, partly a modern, construct. Horace's perception of choral versus monodic would repay further discussion. Lowrie (1995), 36 reads 1.12.1–2 as an evocation of 'the two branches of lyric' through the use of lyre and *tibia* [Ch. 15 in this volume.].

[30] Collected in Citroni (1995).   [31] [Depew (2000)].

I do not have much to say about the first performance of this poem, but it is my impression that, unless it was regularly reperformed at the winter solstice, the reception of the text would have been shaped by the aesthetic pleasure created by a gap between its *origo* and the present occasion: even without any written circulation, the meaning of the poem would be re-created by unmooring its enunciation from its original context. If we take one more step, we can visualize a poet creating a song about a given calendrical occasion ('The day of Neptune has come, let's celebrate'), while he foregrounds the future of the same poem as the loss of its compositional 'occasion'. A radical opposition between writing and orality, and between Roman and Greek, is of very little heuristic utility here.[32]

What is left to say in favour of Heinze's generalization? At least in one sense, I still like his extreme formalism; it is a merit of Citroni to have shown that attempts at compromise that followed Heinze's *pronunciamiento* were much worse than his original approach.[33] *Extreme* formalism is always a helpful approach because it helps to generalize (an indispensable function of criticism), and it is easily deconstructed when it becomes a nuisance.

In fact, Heinze's position can be recuperated through the idea of thematization, my principle (1) at the beginning of the chapter, or the folding of genre. Consider all the themes and situations that we all spontaneously associate with Horace: a sacrifice, a birthday,[34] a drinking party, the homecoming of a friend, vintage wine, and so on. Not all of these are characteristic of Greek lyric models, for example birthdays or sacrifice; however, some, like symposia, are indeed typical. But what this material has in common is the idea of its occurrence in a particular moment of time. Consider sacrifice: once the blade strikes, there is no turning back—and more animals are sacrificed in Horace's *oeuvre* than in the text of any other ancient poet I can think of.

In other words, Horace begins from a reception of Greek lyric where the quest for original occasion is a dominant feature, and then he folds

[32] Dupont (1994) is, *malgré soi*, a *reductio ad absurdum* of this whole approach, when she tries, simplistically, to identify Greek culture with orality and Roman culture with books.

[33] e.g., Klingner's (1965) Hegelian reading of lyric form as a mechanism which needs a *Du* to express an *Ich*.

[34] On the cultural poetics of birthdays and the Julian calendar, see Feeney (1993), 58–9.

the occasion into a thematic 'inside' of his poetry. The folding intern-
alizes a feature that had been visible on the surface. Then the thematic
dominance of occasionality evolves into the practice of reading Horace:
every reading is a reperformance, and the position of the text in a book
is a surrogate occasion. Feasts for the gods, so often mentioned or
implied in individual poems, are a case in point: although they represent unique events, they can and should be regularly reperformed, as
the individual poems do in fact anticipate their own performance.

With profound insight, Horace first promotes the use of occasion
as a marker of lyric to a generic convention, and then he shifts it from
a convention to a theme. Being in time, the times of life, the passing
of time, the unique nature of moments, and the caducity of moments
will become, as the collection unfolds, the main preoccupations of
the poet.[35] The convention that enables the poem to participate in
the lyric tradition is now part of an existential problem. Conversely,
the repetition of themes like caducity and the moments of private life
recuperates performance at the level of readerly reception.

Clearly, from this angle, the importance of individual addressees is
lessened, hence the justified protest of critics preoccupied with social
context. But the reception of Greek lyric is an anticipation of the kind
of relationship that Horace is projecting: his lyric forestalls the
process by which important people of the past become dependent
on literature for their long-distance public image. This is, after all,
what time had done to Polycrates in Ibycus and to Hieron in Pindar.

PUBLIC POETRY: THE MOMENT OF TRUTH

My final discussion, which is about choral voices, develops an idea
that has appeared throughout this paper: the impulse to a new poetics
of performance comes to Horace through Alexandrian books. Here
we notice an intriguing difference in textual transmission. As a reader
of Sappho and Alcaeus, Horace would probably have encountered
poems catalogued according to their incipit. His own practice was

---

[35] Contrast temporality in elegy (often used as a foil in Horace, e.g., Davis (1991),
39–70), where love tends to be an absolute 'here and now'.

similar. Horace favours initial mottoes, and his own incipits are flags for their poems; he would certainly have preferred his last lyric poem to be quoted as 'Phoebus volentem proelia me loqui' than as '4.15'.

As a reader of Pindar and Simonides, however, Horace could not fail to notice that epinician songs were grouped by Alexandrian editors according to their destination—whether by athletic speciality or by games ('For Boxers' or 'Nemean')—whereas paians were regularly prefaced by a heading mentioning not just the location of the first performance but also the names of the performers or *committenti*.

In other words, the editorial praxis of the Alexandrians would have encouraged readers to think that some categories of poems comprise not only poems but also records of long-lost communal occasions. (I deliberately skirt the difficult question of how the early Greeks themselves would have differentiated the so-called monodic from the so-called choral.)

Now the books of Horatian *Odes are* structured around a progression from address to individuals to more communal situations. As we have seen, the mention of Olympic games in *Carm.* 1.1 evokes Pindar, the king of poets, for Maecenas, the king of patrons, but the whole model of praise poetry will be reformulated in this text. This new lyric poet is (Callimachus-wise) separated and insulated from his audience through the same devices that had once worked to integrate the proud Pindaric bard into occasion and community:

> The ivy crowns which reward the brows of the learned
> link me with the gods above, and the cool groves
> where agile nymphs dance with Satyrs
> distinguish me from the crowd...   (1.1.29–32)

Now crowns and dancers enact separation from, not integration into, society; reeds and barbitons are used to create a music that will be inscribed into a canon of published masterpieces (*inseres*) but that will never be brought to the ears of a public. As we saw, Sappho and Alcaeus still sing to a full house, but it is the simulacrum of an audience. Yet as Horace's collection unfolds, references to choral utterances and performances increase; as is well-known, the shift is connected to a growing presence of Augustus and of praise poetry in the poetics of Horace. This evolution provides another example of my principle (3), the politicization of genre. The four books of odes end with a promise of a collective song accompanied by *tibiae*, a self-definition that could have been used by Pindar and that is mirrored in the collective celebration for Venus in 4.1.23–4 (those who believe that the end of 4.15 basically means 'we shall rehearse Vergil's epic verse' should think harder about the mixture—*remixto*—here of *carmen* and Lydian flute).[36]

Yet a sense of fracture is still present here: Horace reports as a collective utterance the basic (trochaic) slogan *o sol pulcher, o laudande* (Oh glorious sun, oh worthy to be praised, 4.2.46–7), along with the prefascist *longas, utinam, dux bone ferias | praestes Hesperiae* (Bring, oh good prince, long holidays to Italy, 4.5.37–8). He begins another poem as a master of ceremonies for the epinician homecoming of Augustus, but at mid-poem he shifts to a monodic request for wine and wreaths and a dinner for two (3.14). Only at 4.6 does he tell us that he has become a choral poet. The 'occasion' has finally come true! This extraordinary moment deserves to be the focus of my final section, and I now turn to the *Carmen Saeculare* and to 4.6, and in particular to how these two poems are both united and separated.

Of course, 4.6 is a very self-conscious poem. The only lyric poem in which Horace names himself, 4.6 ends by reporting as a future event the voice of a *choreut* looking back to her participation in the *Carmen Saeculare* (hereafter *CS*).[37] Horace is a *poeta* by the gift of Apollo, says the central section of 4.6; he is now a *vates*, a seer, because he has been a *chorodidaskalos*, a chorus-master, says the final section of the same poem. The way in which Horace comes to this revelation is extraordinary: the first section of 4.6 invokes Apollo as a saviour of the Trojan origin of Rome: no Apollo, no Trojan Rome.

[36] See, for instance, Pind. *Ol.* 5.42; *Pae.* 9.36–7 (references to the *Paians* are from Bona 1988 throughout my paper).

[37] The link between the two poems goes beyond explicit intertextuality: the choral singer will remember her *chorodidaskalos* as a married woman, and Apollo, the divine hinge connecting 4.6 to the *CS*, is a protector of transitions to marriage. On the theme of marriage and addresses to young people in Callimachus *Hymn* II, see Calame (1993), 50. The indecision between private negotiation with the god and triangulation with a chorus of young people (being trained by the poetic voice and by the musical authority of the god) is important in the *Hymn to Apollo* and is clearly an influence on the connection between 4.6 and the *CS*.

That is, by analogy, we can infer also this: no Caesar, no Horace. What I find striking here is that the Greek destruction of Troy has annihilated not just a town but also a town of music and dance (4.6.13–16): the strong Graecism *choreis*[38] suggests that a possible legacy of choral celebrations existed and was almost wiped out, until, in the last part of 4.6, we discover that choral song has resurfaced in Rome as a celebration of survival and resilience—the *Carmen Saeculare:* from a treacherous festival for Pallas (*male feriatos*) to a beneficent Apolline celebration.

My main point, however, is that the first part of 4.6 features an imitation of one of the most celebrated Pindaric paians, *Paian* VI. This is one of the most extensive imitations of Pindar in Horace, and it is uncommon to find traces of Pindar's religious poetry in Augustan Rome. Of course, the survival of poems in book form was not problematic in this period, and paianic performances still occurred, even though the genre was neither vital nor prestigious, in the first century BCE.[39] Moreover, Pindar's religious poetry was widely read, as Oxyrhynchus has shown, alongside the four books of epinicians, which we continue to this day to associate with the very name 'Pindar'.

It gives me pause, however, to consider that paianic poetry is found specifically in a poem that is both for Apollo and for the *CS* and that is about Horace as a *poeta* and as a *vates*. As we have just seen, the poem has a problematic link with choral song: 4.6 authenticates the *CS* as the work of Horace—the poet who has no name in the text of the *CS,* although his name is now part of a *monumentum,* the official inscription of which is 'carmen composuit Q. Horatius Flaccus'. In addition, 4.6 authenticates the *CS* as choral poetry, but it does not authenticate 4.6 as choral poetry. Indeed, the move of introducing a personal utterance by a speaker who is looking back to a different occasion would be hard to account for in the tradition of choral poetry. Suffice it to say that 4.6 and the *CS* are companion pieces but also that their link is a source both of difference and of generic contrast.

This is where Horace's reference to Pindar's sixth *Paian* becomes important: the *CS* takes from *Paian* VI a very important formulation

---

[38] An insidious, loaded word in Roman culture, compare Verg. *Aen.* 9.615.

[39] As Rutherford's [2001] book will, I hope, confirm. (*non vidi*). Rutherford (1995) argues that the genre was declining, or perceived as old-fashioned, as early as the fourth century BCE.

of its occasional nature: *tempore sacro* (in this holy time) at line 4 mirrors ἐν ζαθέῳ με δέξαι χρόνῳ at *Paian* 6.5 and has a parallel function in the song's rhetoric of establishing occasion and function. More generally, if I may be slightly dogmatic, the *CS* is a paian. This simple truth has long been occluded by different scholarly agendas. Pasquali, who took the issue of Greek models seriously, was happy with a vague nod towards epinician poetry.[40] But the discussion has been mesmerized by the spectacular opposition of Mommsen and Fraenkel, still a very instructive *querelle*.[41] In short, Mommsen did not like the *carmen* and interpreted it as part of a complex programme of ritual and celebration. Fraenkel did like the *carmen* because it was totally independent from an occasion. For Mommsen, Horace was a great poet—for a Roman—but Mommsen knew that the *carmen* could have been better, and he even suggested how to make it better according to Romantic taste. For Fraenkel, the *CS* is a masterpiece because Horace was providentially free from external pressures: it is vintage lyric in an uncommon setting. In other words, this text is good if it is just poetry; it is bad if it is public poetry. There is thus an unspoken assumption shared by both Mommsen and Fraenkel: Greek lyric is good because it is rooted in its sunlit and merry communal setting; Roman lyric is good only when it is not dependent on artificial, boring ceremonies. Let me try to fit these two giants into a suitably old-fashioned structural grid:

	Public Orientation	Literary Merit
Mommsen	strong	weak
Fraenkel	weak	strong

A way out of this impasse is indicated by Feeney in his recent book (1998) on religion and Roman poetry. Feeney takes the *Ludi* as a whole and considers them a worthy object of study in terms of a semiotics of culture. As a result, the *CS* becomes a text that interacts with a broader complex of signs. Following Feeney's example, I reiterate my suggestion that the *CS* is a paian. It is relatively simple

---

40 Pasquali (1964) 736 n.1; contrast 752–5.
41 Mommsen (1905) 351–9; Fraenkel (1957) 364–82.

to demonstrate why this is so. The standard definition of the genre in antiquity—a song to Apollo and Artemis, on behalf of a community, either to cure a state of crisis and/or to celebrate their help—is relevant to the whole structure of the *CS*. Its simple initial invocation to Apollo and Diana matches the incipits, which were recognized as typical in Alexandrian editions (*colendi semper et culti*, 'always to be worshipped, always worshipped', 1–2, spans both Greek poetry and Roman cult). The subdivision into two choral groups, male and female, is not characteristic of paians,[42] but once you accept a basic similarity, other contacts spring to mind. *Tempore sacro*, as we have seen, matches Pindar's ἐν ζαθέῳ χρόνῳ: now, *for once in a lifetime*, the time is right for a communal song. This interpretation thus provides an example of my principle (2), a sense of rift. Pindar's definition of the paianic genre, 'the *seasonal* songs of Paian in honour of the children of gold-distaffed Leto' (fr. 128c, 1–2 S.-M.), foregrounds the regular and frequent use of poetry in celebrations. We may contrast this with the uniqueness of song for the Roman *Ludi*.

Horace plays with the similarity and the difference between Apollo and Sol, with puzzling effects. A famous Pindaric paian (IX), however, had already shown the same kind of cultural syllepsis: the poem starts with a bold address to the sunbeam, after the crisis initiated by a solar eclipse, and then moves on to a ritual invocation to Phoibos. There is a clear but unspoken link between the two sections, since in Pindar's time, Helios and Apollo are even closer to each other than their Roman counterparts will be. The solar atmosphere of the third Horatian stanza is in implicit contrast to the hidden 'half' of the official ritual, the nighttime sacrifice,[43] but paians are by definition tied to daytime celebrations of a luminous god, Phoibos; the reference to a Greek poetic genre supports the asymmetric position of the Horatian song in the celebration.[44]

---

[42] Kappel (1992), 81.

[43] This duality is implicitly mapped by Horace onto the sun/moon polarity of Apollo and Diana.

[44] Of course, solar imagery has a strong Augustan implication (compare Barton (1995), 45 on the horoscope, *Horologium Augusti*, and links between the prince and Helios). My intention, however, is precisely to show that issues of literary influence and Augustan ideology should be taken in conjunction.

The *CS*, however, commemorates only briefly, on the nocturnal and chthonic side of the feast, a sacrifice that few, if any, Roman magistrates had ever held before: for Eileithuia and the Moirai. Yet Pindar had explained how these divinities fit into the birth of Apollo and Artemis: 'they were born into the shining daylight, like a body of sunshine' with the support of Eileithuia and Lachesis (*Paian* XII 14–17): *lucidum caeli decus.*

When all is said and done, the poem is still an outrageous innovation: it is ironic to recall that the Sibyl had requested—in Greek!—*Latinoi paianes* to be sung, as though doing this were as simple and easy as immolating some more sheep. The paianic tradition, however, had its share of experiments and literary self-consciousness. I am impressed by the reading of the fourth-century poet Philodamos of Scarpheia recently offered by Lutz Käppel, who argues that this paian thematizes its own generic dynamics. Thus, a main theme of this late paian is how to cope with the tradition and yet to be a paian for Dionysos, and not for Apollo. (This theme exemplifies my first principle, the folding of genre.) And of course, Horace is writing in Sapphics, an important choice, and an author's signature—the only one possible in this context, connecting as it does the *CS* with poems such as 4.6. The choice is also a self-conscious literary statement: Horace is using here the metre that he himself had domesticated and reformed.[45] The choral Sapphics of the *CS* imply a dynamic transference from poets like Alcaeus and the *mascula Sappho.*

Again, generic reform here has a political implication: the issue of Hellenization is not just a matter of poetics, it is also a central theme of the *Ludi* (my principle (3), politicization). Augustus is testing the limits of Hellenization in Roman culture, and the *Ludi* are a revolutionary step forward in the process of Roman Hellenization, after a whole history of power struggle and aristocratic competition. One of the main innovations of the festival is, of course, the centrality of Apollo and Diana,[46]

---

[45] Whatever reading we adopt for the many problems of Hor. *Ep.* 1.19.19–33, the idea there of bringing Greek poems to Rome is connected to the continuity of the metre, but also to the revision and reform of metrical conventions.

[46] Initial invocation of Apollo and Diana is enough to spell out 'Paian'; even Socrates, we are told, composed a paian, and the incipit is enough to identify it: 'Hail, Apollo the Delian! Hail, Artemis, you noble pair of youths!' (Diog. Laert. 2.42). As a former Alcaic poet, Horace might also have thought of the formal invocation to Apollo placed by the Alexandrians as an incipit to Alcaeus's collected poems (fr. 307 Voigt).

set, as it is, against the traditional Capitoline gods: the generic choice of a Latin paian is not just a poetic experiment but also a response to the whole dynamics of religious politics. The main paradox of the *CS* as a text of Roman literature, then, is that one cannot have a genre 'just once', while the main challenge of the *Ludi* as a programmatic ritual is that they are 'once in a lifetime' (*quos aetas aspicit una semel*, 'to be seen just once in a generation', is Ovid's Latin for *Saeculares*, *Trist.* 2.26). The relationship between text and genre—where the text re-creates for just one time its generic matrix—is parallel to the relationship between ritual and religious tradition—where the ritual has to happen just once, thus enhancing uniqueness rather than routine and repetition. Like it or not, there is some interaction of text and occasion here: interaction between performance and society is not the privilege of Greek literature, except that Horace makes capital out of his *exclusion* from the felicitous routine of Greek paians and regular festivals.[47] In other words, the points I have been listing in order to argue that the *CS* is generically recognizable as paianic performance are also functional links with the Augustan programme of the festival. The more we move toward formal issues of genre and literary programme, the closer we are to cultural and social context: this context is not simply mirrored by the text; the text enacts and problematizes its social and ritual setting.

This politics of genre brings me back to the tantalizing interplay between the *CS* and 4.6, as well as to the role and authority of the author in Horatian lyric. I will also recall at this point my three principles: folding, rift, and politicization. As I suggested earlier, the influence of Pindar's *Paean* VI acts as a link, but also as a telling difference. Horace's allusions to this model have a negative implication as well. In fifth-century BCE Greece, the paian was a tradition of

---

[47] But if the prayer is successful—and how can we separate its success from the effect of the poetic performance itself?—the continuity of the Roman nation will bring back, in 110 years, not just another festival, but *song* and another festival: *certus undenos deciens per annos | orbis ut cantus referatque ludos | ter die claro totiensque grata | nocte frequentes* (so that a precise cycle, in 110 years, will bring back songs and the Games, celebrated by the people in three luminous days and three amiable nights) (*CS* 21–4). The position of *cantus* suggests the importance of this unique performance for keeping alive a slender tradition of communal lyric at Rome (see my comments on 4.6, above). The *CS* depends, with the *ludi*, on Greek Sibylline poetry (*Sibyllini monuere versus*, 'the Sibylline verses warned us', 5), but the next celebration will have to look back to Horace's song—and text—as its forerunner.

communal song that famously combined authorial voice and choral utterance. Reading *Paian* VI means accepting a flexible compromise[48] between the chorus and the authority of the author: the self-representation of *aoidimos Pieridon prophatan* is a teasing example of this process. (Even Lefkowitz has accepted that the voice of the *Paians* represents the chorus in performance, but can we resist thinking of the author when reading the sentence 'prophet of the Muses, famous in / for songs' halfway into the *Complete Works of Pindar*? Imagine you are a Roman reading *Paian* VII b: the idea of a public performance by a chorus uttering a sentence like 'I am riding my chariot outside Homer's beaten track' would be enough to show that, as Horace famously put it, it is suicide to imitate Pindar.) Whatever 'prophet of the Muses' ultimately means, Horace had moved from similar expressions to become, in the Roman odes, a *Musarum sacerdos* addressing the community of Roman youths. Ironically, to become the author of the *CS*, he has to renounce this legacy. The voice of the *CS* is self-consciously more exclusively choral than the Pindaric original. But no Roman choral poet could have spoken with the complex voice of *Paian* VIIb, which is the closest extant model of Callimachus's *Aitia* prologue. By bringing back choral lyric in such a different setting, Horace is testing the limits[49] of a poet's authority in Augustan Rome.

[48] In fact, contemporary discussions show how difficult it is to separate the two voices: D'Alessio (1994); Lefkowitz (1995), for example.

[49] But see above, n. 45.

Bibliography

Abbreviations

AFA Henzen	W. Henzen (1874), *Acta Fratrum Arvalium quae supersunt. Restituit et illustravit Guil. Henzen. Accedunt fragmenta fastorum in luco Arvalium effossa* (Berlin).
ANRW	H. Temporini (ed.) (1972–), *Aufstieg und Niedergang der römischen Welt: Geschichte und Kultur Roms im Spiegel der neueren Forschung* (Berlin and New York).
BRUGNOLI and STOK	G. Brugnoli and F. Stok (eds.) (1997), *Vitae Vergilianae Antiquae* (Rome).
CHCL	see Kenney and Clausen (1982) below.
CIL	*Corpus Inscriptionum Latinarum* (Berlin, 1863–).
COURTNEY	E. Courtney (ed.) (1993), *The Fragmentary Latin Poets* (Oxford).
DAVIES	M. Davies (ed.) (1991), *Poetae Melici Graeci* (Oxford; post Page).
EHRENBERG and JONES	V. Ehrenberg and A. H. M. Jones (eds.) (1976), *Documents illustrating the reigns of Augustus and Tiberius* (Oxford, 2nd edn.).
ENCOR	F. della Corte and S. Mariotti (eds.), *Orazio, Enciclopedia Oraziana* (Rome, 1996 (vol. 1), 1998 (vol. 2)).
HARDIE	C. Hardie (ed.) (1966), *Vitae Vergilianae antiquae* (Oxford).
HENZEN	W. Henzen (ed.) (1874), *Acta Fratrum Arvalium quae supersunt* (Berlin).
ILS	H. Dessau (1892–1916), *Inscriptiones latinae selectae* (Berlin, 2nd edn. 1954–55).
KLINGNER	F. Klingner (ed.) (1959), *Horatius: Opera* (Leipzig).
MARX	F. Marx (ed.) (1904 and 1905), *C. Lucilii Carminum Reliquiae*, 2 vols. (Leipzig).
MOREL	W. Morel (1975), *Fragmenta Poetarum Latinorum* (Stuttgart).

MYNORS   R. A. B. Mynors (ed.) (1964), *XII Panegyrici Latini* (Oxford).

PAGE or *PMG*   D. L. Page (1962), *Poetae Melici Graeci* (Oxford).

PIGHI   G. Pighi (1965), *De ludis saecularibus*, 2nd edn. (Amsterdam).

RE   A. Pauly, G. Wissowa, and W. Kroll (eds.) (1894–1972), *Real-Encyclopädie der classischen Alterumswissenschaft*. Neue Bearbeitung unter Mitwirkung zahlreicher Fachgenossen herausgegeben von Georg Wissowa (Stuttgart).

RIPOSATI   B. Riposati (ed.) (1939), *M. Terenti Varronis De Vita Populi Romani*, Pubblicazioni dell'università cattolica del S. Cuore (Milan).

RUSSELL-WILSON   D. A. Russell and N. G. Wilson (eds.) (1981) *Menander Rhetor* (Oxford).

SKUTSCH   O. Skutsch (ed.) (1985), *The Annals of Quintus Ennius* (Oxford).

VOIGT   E. M. Voigt (ed.) (1971), *Sappho et Alcaeus* (Amsterdam).

WEST   M. L. West (ed.) (1971 and 1972) *Iambi et Elegi Graeci*, 2 vols. (Oxford).

ABERT, H. (1899), *Die Lehre vom Ethos in der griechischen Musik* (Leipzig).

ABLEITINGER, D., and GUGEL, H. (eds.) (1970), *Festschrift Karl Vretska* (Heidelberg).

ACOSTA-HUGHES, B. (2003), 'Aesthetics and Recall: Callimachus Frs. 226–9 Pf. Reconsidered', *CQ* 53: 478–89.

ADAMS, J. N. (1971), 'A Type of Hyperbaton in Latin Prose', *PCPhS* 17: 1–16.

—— (1976), 'A Typological Approach to Latin Word-Order', *Indogermanische Forschungen*, 81: 70–99.

—— (1982), *The Latin Sexual Vocabulary* (London).

—— (1994), 'Wackernagel's Law and the Position of the Unstressed Personal Pronouns in Classical Latin', *TPhS* 92: 103–78.

AHERN, C. F. (1991), 'Horace's rewriting of Homer in *Carmen* 1.6', *CP* 86: 301–14.

AHL, F. (1985), *Metaformations* (Ithaca).

ALBERT, H. (1988), *Das mimetische Gedicht in der Antike: Geschichte und Typologie von den Anfängen bis in die augusteische Zeit* (Frankfurt am Main).

ALFÖLDI, A. (1970), *Die monarische Repräsentation im römischen Kaiserreiche* (Darmstadt).

—— (1971), *Der Vater des Vaterlands im römischen Kaiserreiche* (Darmstadt).

ALLEN, A. W. (1962), 'Sunt qui Propertium malint', in Sullivan (1962: 107–48).

ALTHEIM, F. (1931), *Terra Mater* (Giessen).

—— (1953–6), *Römische Religionsgeschichte*, 3 vols. (Baden-Baden; 1st edn. 3 vols., 1931–3).

ANCONA, R. (1994) *Time and the Erotic in Horace's Odes* (Durham, NC).

ANDERSON, A. R. (1928), 'Herakles and his Successors', *HSCP* 39: 422–36.

ANDERSON, W. D. (1966), *Ethos and Education in Greek Music* (Cambridge, Mass.).

ANDERSON, W. S. (1966), 'Horace *Carm.* 1.14: What Kind of Ship?', *CP* 61: 84–98.

—— (1972), 'The Form, Purpose, and Position of Horace's *Satire* I, 8', *AJP* 93: 4–13. = *Essays on Roman Satire* (Princeton, 1982), 74–83.

ANDRÉ, J. (1949), *La Vie et l'oeuvre d'Asinius Pollion* (Paris).

APPEL, G. (1909), *De Romanorum Precationibus* (Giessen).

ARANS, O. (1988), *Iambe and Baubo: A Study in Ritual Laughter* (Urbana; Diss.).

ARGENTARI, L. (1998), 'Epigramma e libro: Morfologia delle raccolte epigrammatiche premeleagree', *ZPE* 121: 1–20.

AUDOLLENT, A. (ed.) (1904), *Defixionum tabellae* (Frankfurt am Main).

AXELSON, B. (1945), *Unpoetische Wörter* (Lund).

BABCOCK, C. L. (1966), '*Si Certus Intrarit Dolor*: A Reconsideration of Horace's Fifteenth Epode', *AJP* 87: 400–19.

—— (1974), '*Omne militabitur bellum*: The Language of Commitment in *Epode* 1', *CJ* 70.1: 14–31.

BAIN, D. (1986), ' "Waiting for Varus?" (Horace, *Epodes*, 5, 49–72)', *Latomus*, 45: 125–31.

BARCHIESI, A. (2001a), 'Horace and *Iambos*: The Poet as Literary Historian', in Cavarzere, Aloni, and Barchiesi (2001: 141–64).

—— (2001b), *Speaking Volumes* (London).

—— (2001c), 'The Crossing', in Harrison (2001: 142–63).

—— (2002), 'The Uniqueness of the *Carmen saeculare* and its Tradition', in Woodman and Feeney (2002: 107–23, 229–35).

BARINA, A. (1980), *La sirena nella mitologia* (Padua).

BARNES, T. D. (1974), 'The Victories of Augustus', *JRS* 64: 21–6.

BARTON, C. A. (2001), *Roman Honor: The Fire in the Bones* (Berkeley).

BARTON, T. (1995), 'Augustus and Capricorn: Astrological Polyvalency and Imperial Rhetoric', *JHS* 85: 33–51.

BARWICK, K. (1933), 'Das Kultlied des Livius Andronicus', *Philologus*, 88: 203–21.

—— (1959), *Martial und die zeitgenössische Rhetorik* (Berlin).

BASTA DONZELLI, G. (1984), 'Arsinoe simile ad Elena (Theocritus Id. 15,110)', *Hermes* 112: 306–16.

BASTO, R. (1982), 'Horace's *Propempticon* to Vergil', *Vergilius*, 28: 30–43.

BAYER, K. (ed.) (1977), *Vergil-Viten* (Munich).

BEARD, M. and NORTH, J. A. (eds.) (1990), *Pagan Priests* (London).

BECKER, C. (1959), review of Fraenkel (1957), *Gnomon*, 31: 592–612.

—— (1963), *Das Spätwerk des Horaz* (Göttingen).

BELLINGER, A. R. (1957), 'The Immortality of Alexander and Augustus', *YCS* 15: 103–12.

BENARIO, J. M. (1960), 'Book 4 of Horace's *Odes*: Augustan Propaganda', *TAPA* 91: 339–52.

BENJAMIN, W. (1968), 'The Work of Art in the Age of Mechanical Reproduction', in *Illuminations*, ed. H. Arendt (London), 219–53.

BENTLEY, R. (ed.) (1711), *Q. Horatius Flaccus* (Cambridge).

BÉRANGER, J. (1953), *Recherches sur l'aspect idéologique du principat* (Basle).

BERGSON, L. (1970), 'Zu Horaz, Carm. IV. 5', *RM* 113: 358–63.

BERVE, H. (1967), *Die Tyrannis bei den Griechen* (Munich).

BIBAUW, J. (ed.) (1969), *Hommages à Marcel Renard*, 3 vols. (Latomus 101; Brussels).

BICKERMAN, E. J. (1980), *Chronology of the Ancient World*, rev. edn. (London).

BILLOWS, R. (1993), 'The Religious Procession of the *Ara Pacis Augustae*: Augustus' *Supplicatio* in 13 BC', *JRA* 6: 80–92.

BINDER, G. (1971), *Aeneas und Augustus: Interpretation zum 8. Buch der Aeneis* (Meisenheim).

—— (ed.) (1988), *Saeculum Augustum* (Darmstadt).

BING, P. (1988), *The Well-Read Muse: Present and Past in Callimachus and the Hellenistic Poets* (Diss. Göttingen).

BIRT, T. (1925), *Horaz' Lieder: Studien zur Kritik und Auslegung* (Leipzig).

BLISS, F. R. (1960), 'The Plancus Ode', *TAPA* 91: 30–46.

BO, D. (1960), *De Horati poetico eloquio, Indices nominum propriorum, metricarum rerum prosodiacarum grammaticarumque* (Turin).

BÖCKEL, O. (1913), *Psychologie der Volksdichtung* (2nd edn., Leipzig and Berlin).

BOLDT, H. (1884), *De liberiore linguae Graecae et Latinae collocatione verborum* (Göttingen).

BOLL, F. (1917), 'Sternenfreundschaft', *Sokrates: Zeitschrift für Gymnasialwesen* 4: 1–10 = F. Boll (1950), *Kleine Schriften zur Sternkunde des Altertums* (Leipzig: 115–24) = Oppermann (1972: 1–13).

BÖMER, F. (ed.) (1958), *P. Ovidius Naso: Die Fasten*, 2 vols. (Heidelberg).

BONA, G. (1988), *Pindaro: I Peani* (Cuneo).

BONAVIA-HUNT, N. (1969), *Horace the Minstrel* (Kineton).

BOUCHÉ-LECLERQ, A. (1899), *L'Astrologie grecque* (Paris).

Boucher, J-P. (1965), *Études sur Properce: Problèmes d'inspiration et d'art* (Paris).

Bowditch, P. L. (2001), *Horace and the Gift Economy of Patronage* (Berkeley).

Bowerstock, G. W. (1990), 'The Pontificate of Augustus', in Raaflaub and Toher (1990: 380–94).

Bowie, E. L. (1986), 'Early Greek Elegy, Symposium and Public Festival', *JHS* 106: 13–35.

—— (1993), 'Lies, Fiction and Slander in Early Greek Poetry', in Gill and Wiseman (1993: 1–37).

Bradshaw, A. (1970), 'Some Stylistic Oddities in Horace, Odes III 8', *Philologus*, 114: 145–50.

—— (1989), 'Horace in Sabinis', in Deroux (1989: 160–86).

Bradshaw, A. T. v. S. (1970), 'Horace, *Odes* 4.1', *CQ* ns 20: 142–53.

Brakman, C. (1921), 'Horatiana', *Mnem.* ns 49: 209–22.

Bramble, J. C. (1974), *Persius and the Programmatic Satire* (Cambridge).

Bremer, J. M. (1990), 'Pindar's Paradoxical ἐγώ and a Recent Controversy about the Performance of his Epinikia', in Slings (1990: 41–58).

—— and Handley, E. W. (eds.) (1993), *Aristophane: sept exposés suivis de discussions* (Entretiens Hardt 38; Vandoeuvres and Genève).

—— van Erp Taalman Kip, A. M., and Slings, S. R. (eds.) (1987), *Some Recently Found Greek Poems* (Leiden).

Bremmer, J. N. and Roodenburg, H. (eds.) (1997), *A Cultural History of Humour: From Antiquity to the Present Day* (Cambridge).

Bright, D. F. (1978), *Haec Mihi Fingebam: Tibullus in His World* (Cincinnati Classical Studies ns 3; Leiden).

Brind'amour, P. (1983), *Le Calendrier romain* (Ottawa).

Brink, C. O. (1971), *Horace on Poetry II: The 'Ars Poetica'* (Cambridge).

—— (1982a), *Horace on Poetry III:* Epistles *Book II: The Letters to Augustus and Florus* (Cambridge).

—— (1982b), 'Horatian Notes III', *PCPS* ns 28: 30–56.

Broccia, G. (1982–3), 'Modelli omerici e archilochei negli Epodi di Orazio', *Quaderni AICC Foggia*, 2–3: 75–91.

Brown, C. G. (1988), 'Hipponax and Iambe', *Hermes*, 116: 478–81.

Brown, E. (1963), *Numeri Vergiliani* (Collection Latomus 63; Brussels).

Brunt, P. A. (1965), '*Amicitia* in the Late Roman Republic', *PCPS* 11: 1–20.

—— (1971), *Italian Manpower 225 B.C.–A.D. 14* (Oxford).

—— (1984), 'The Role of the Senate in the Augustan Regime', *CQ* 34: 423–44.

—— (1988), *The Fall of the Roman Republic* (Oxford).

—— and Moore, J. M. (1967), *Res Gestae Divi Augusti* (Oxford).

Buchheit, V. (1962), *Studien zum Corpus Priapeorum* (Zetemata 28; Munich).

BUCHHOLZ, K. (1912), *De Horatio hymnographo* (Diss. Königsberg).

BUCHNER, E. (1982), *Die Sonnenuhr des Augustus* (Mainz).

—— (1988), 'Horologium Solarium Augusti', in Heilmeyer (1988: 240–5).

BÜCHNER, K. (1962a), *Studien zur römischen Literatur III, Horaz* (Wiesbaden).

—— (1962b), 'Der Superlativ bei Horaz', in Büchner (1962a: 23–37).

—— (1970a), 'Die Epoden des Horaz', in Büchner (1970b: 50–96).

—— (1970b), *Werkanalysen* (Studien zur Römischen Literatur 8; Wiesbaden).

BURCK, E. (1964), *Interpretationen* (Gymnasium Beiheft 4; Heidelberg).

—— (1966), 'Drei Begrüssungsgedichte des Horaz (2, 7; 1, 36; 3, 14)', in *Vom Menschenbild in der römischen Literatur* (Heidelberg), 153–74.

BURNETT, A. P. (1983), *Three Archaic Poets: Archilochus, Alcaeus, Sappho* (London).

—— (1989), 'Performing Pindar's Odes', *CP* 84: 283–93.

BUSHALA, E. W. (1968), 'Laboriosus Ulixes', *CJ* 64: 7–10.

BUTTREY, T. V. (1972), 'Halved Coins, the Augustan Reform, and Horace, *Odes* I.3', *AJA* 76: 31–48.

CAIRNS, F. (1969), 'Catullus I', *Mnemosyne*, 22: 153–8.

—— (1971a), 'Horace *Odes* 1. 2', *CP* 84: 283–93.

—— (1971b), 'Five "Religious" Odes of Horace', *AJP* 92: 433–52.

—— (1972), *Generic Composition in Greek and Roman Poetry* (Edinburgh).

—— (ed.) (1977), *Papers of the Liverpool Latin Seminar 1976* (Liverpool).

—— (1978), 'The Genre Palinode and Three Horatian Examples: *Epode*, 17; *Odes,* I, 16; *Odes,* I, 34', *AC* 47: 546–52.

—— (1984), 'Propertius and the Battle of Actium (4. 6)', in Woodman and West (1984: 129–68, 229–36).

—— (1989), *Virgil's Augustan Epic* (Cambridge).

—— (1992), 'Theocritus *Idyll* 26', *PCPS* 38: 1–38.

CALAME, C. (1993), 'Legendary Narration and Poetic Procedure in Callimachus' Hymn to Apollo', in Harder, Regtuit, and Wakker (1993: 37–55).

CAMERON, A. (1994), *Callimachus and His Critics* (Princeton).

CAMPBELL, D. A. (1983), *The Golden Lyre: The Themes of the Greek Lyric Poets* (London).

CANCIK, J. (1996) 'Carmen und sacrificium. Das Saecularlied des Horaz in den Saecularakten des Jahres 17 v. Chr.', in R. Faber and B. Seidensticker (eds.), *Worte, Bilder, Töne, Studien zur Antike und Antikerezeption* (Würzburg: 99–113).

CAPASSO, M. (ed.) (1992), *Papiri letterari greci e latini* (Lecce).

CARDAUNS, B. (1976), *M. Terentius Varro:* Antiquitates rerum divinarum, 2 vols. (Mainz).

Carey, C. (1989), 'The Performance of the Victory Ode', *AJP* 110: 545–65.
—— (1991), 'The Victory Ode in Performance: The Case for the Chorus', *CP* 86: 192–200.
Carlsson, G. (1944), 'Zu einigen Oden des Horaz', *Eranos*, 42: 1–23.
Carratello, U. (1979), *Livio Andronico* (Rome).
Carrubba, R. (1969), *The Epodes of Horace: A Study in Poetic Arrangement* (The Hague).
Caspari, F. (1908), *De ratione quae inter Vergilium et Lucanum intercedat quaestiones selectae* (Diss. Leipzig).
Casson, L. (1971), *Ships and Seamanship in the Ancient World* (Princeton).
Cavallini, E. (1978–9), 'Saffo e Alceo in Orazio', *MCr* 13–14: 377–80.
Cavarzere, A. (1992), *Orazio: Il libro degli Epodi* (Venice).
—— Aloni, A., and Barchiesi, A. (eds.) (2001), *Iambic Ideas: Essays on a Poetic Tradition from Archaic Greece to the Late Roman Empire* (Lanham).
Chastagnol, A. (1992), *Le Sénat romain à l'époque impériale* (Paris).
Christ, K. (1977), 'Zur Augusteischen Germanienpolitik', *Chiron*, 7: 149–205.
Cichorius, C. (1922), *Römische Studien* (Leipzig).
Citroni, M. (1995), *Poesia e lettori in Roma antica* (Rome and Bari).
—— (2000), 'The Memory of Philippi in Horace and the Interpretation of Epistle 1. 20. 23', *CJ* 96: 27–56.
Clausen, W. (1964), 'Callimachus and Roman Poetry', *GRBS* 5: 181–96.
—— (ed.) (1994), *Virgil*, Eclogues (Oxford).
Clauss, J. J. (1988), 'Vergil and the Euphrates', *AJP* 109: 309–20.
Clayman, D. L. (1975), 'Horace's *Epodes* VIII and XII: More than Clever Obscenity?', *CW* 69: 55–61.
—— (1980), *Callimachus' Iambi* (Mnemosyne Supplement 59; Leiden).
Collinge, N. E. (1961), *The Structure of Horace's Odes* (London).
Commager, S. (1957), 'The Function of Wine in Horace's Odes', *TAPA* 88: 68–80. [Chapter 2 in this volume]
—— (1962), *The Odes of Horace: A Critical Study* (New Haven and London).
—— (1980), 'Some Horatian Vagaries', *SO* 55: 59–70.
Conrad, C. (1965), 'Word Order in Latin Epic from Ennius to Virgil', *HSCPh* 69: 194–258.
Costa, C. D. N. (ed.) (1973), *Horace* (London).
Cousin, J. (1967), *Études sur Quintilien* (Amsterdam).
—— (1979), *Quintilien, Institution Oratoire* 6 (Paris).
Curtius, E. R. (1954), *Europäische Literatur und lateinisches Mittelalter* (Bern).
Dahlmann, H. (1958), 'Die letze Ode des Horaz', *Gymnasium*, 65: 340–55.
D'Alessio, G. B. (1994), 'First-Person Problems in Pindar', *BICS* 41: 117–39.
Dalzell, A. (1956), 'Maecenas and the Poets', *Phoenix*, 10: 151–62.

D'Arms, J. (1990), 'The Roman Convivium and the Idea of Equality', in Murray (1990), 308–20.

Davies, M. (1988), 'Monody, Choral Lyric and the Tyranny of the Hand-Book', *CQ* ns 38: 52–64.

Davis, G. (1975), 'The Persona of Licymnia: A Revaluation of Horace, *carm.* 2, 12', *Philologus*, 119: 70–83.

—— (1989), '*Ingenii cumba*? Literary *aporia* and the rhetoric of Horace's *O navis referent* (C. 1.14)', *RhM* 132: 331–45.

—— (1991), *Polyhymnia: The Rhetoric of Horatian Lyric Discourse* (Berkeley).

Degani, E. (1993), 'Aristofane e la tradizione dell'invettiva personale in Grecia', in Bremer and Handley (1993: 1–49).

Degrassi, A. (1963), *Fasti Anni Numani et Iuliani* [*Inscriptiones Italiae 13.2*] (Rome).

De Grummond, N. T. (1990), '*Pax Augusta* and the *Horae* on the *Ara Pacis Augustae*', *AJA* 94: 663–77.

Delatte, L. (1942), *Les Traités de la royauté d'Ecphante, Diotegène et Sthenidas* (Liège).

Den Boer, W. (ed.) (1973), *La Culte des souvrains dans l'empire romain* (Entretiens Hardt 19; Geneva).

Dennison, W. (1904), 'The Movements of the Chorus Chanting the Carmen Saeculare of Horace', in Sanders (1904: 49–66).

Denniston, J. D. (1952), *Greek Prose Style* (Oxford).

Depew, M. (2000), 'Enacted and Represented Dedications: Genre and Greek Hymn', in Depew and Obbink (2000: 59–79, 254–63).

—— and Obbink, D. (2000), *Matrices of Genre: Authors, Canons, and Society* (Cambridge, Mass.).

Deroux, C. (ed.) (1980 and 1989), *Studies in Latin Literature and Roman History* 2 and 5 (Collection Latomus 168 and 206; Brussels).

Des Bouvrie, S. (1984), 'Augustus' Legislation on Morals: Which Morals and What Aims?', *SO* 59: 93–113.

Detienne, M. (1977), *The Gardens of Adonis*, tr. J. Lloyd (London).

Dettmer, H. (1983), *Horace: A Study in Structure* (Hildesheim).

Deubner, L. (1933), 'Ein Punkt: Zum Aufbau des Carmen Saeculare', *Philologus*, 88: 469–73.

Devereux, G. (1970), 'The Nature of Sappho's Seizure in fr. 31 LP as Evidence of Her Inversion', *CQ* ns 20: 17–31.

Dickie, M. W. (1981), 'The Disavowal of *Invidia* in Roman Iamb and Satire', *Papers of the Liverpool Latin Seminar*, 3: 183–208.

Dicks, D. R. (1963), 'Astrology and Astronomy in Horace', *Hermes*, 91: 60–73.

Diels, H. (1890), *Sibyllinische Blätter* (Berlin).

Diggle, J. and Goodyear, F. R. D. (eds.) (1972), *The Classical Papers of A. E. Housman* (Cambridge).

—— Hall, J. B., and Jocelyn, H. D. (1989), *Studies in Latin Literature and its Tradition in Honour of C. O. Brink* (Cambridge).

Doblhofer, E. (1966), *Die Augustuspanegyrik des Horaz in formalhistorischer Sicht* (Heidelberg).

—— (1981), 'Horaz und Augustus', *ANRW* II. 31. 3. 1922–86.

—— (1992), *Horaz in der Forschung nach 1957* (Darmstadt).

Dover, K. J. (1968), *Greek Word Order* (Darmstadt; corrected reprint of 1960 edn.).

Downing, E. (1990), 'Apate, Agon, and Literary Self-Reflexivity in Euripides' Helen', in Griffith and Mastronarde (1990: 1–16).

Draheim, J. (1981), *Vertonungen antiker Texte vom Barock bis zur Gegenwart* (Amsterdam).

—— and Wille, G. (1985), *Horaz-Vertonungen vom Mittelalter bis zum Neuzeit* (Amsterdam).

Dunn, F. (1997), 'Ends and Means in Euripides' *Heracles*', in Dunn, Fowler, and Roberts (1997), 83–111.

—— Fowler, D. P., and Roberts, D. (1997), *Classical Closure: Reading the End in Greek and Latin Literature* (Princeton).

Dupont, F. (1994), *L'Invention de la littérature* (Paris).

Dupont-Roc, R. and Le Boulluec, A. (1976), 'Le Charme du récit (Odyssée IV 1–305)', in *Ecriture et théories poétiques: Lectures d'Homère, Eschyle, Platon, Aristote* (Paris).

Dyson, M. (1990), 'Horace *Carmina* 4. 5. 36–37', *CP* 85: 126–9.

Edmunds, L. (1992), *From a Sabine Jar: Reading Horace, Odes 1.9* (Chapel Hill).

—— (2001), *Intertextuality and the Reading of Roman Poetry* (Baltimore).

Ehrenberg, V. and Jones, A. H. M. (1976), *Documents Illustrating the Reigns of Augustus and Tiberius*, 2nd edn. (Oxford).

Eisenberger, H. (1980), 'Bilden die Horazischen Oden 2.1–12 einen Zyklus?', *Gymnasium*, 87: 262–74.

Eitrem, S. (1924), 'Die rituelle diabolé', *SO* 2: 43–61.

—— (1933), 'Sophron und Theokrit', *SO* 12: 10–38.

Elder, J. P. (1952), 'Horace, *C.* I.3', *AJP* 73: 140–58.

—— (1953), 'Horace *carmen* 1. 7', *CPh* 48: 1–8.

—— (1966), 'Catullus I, His Poetic Creed, and Nepos', *HSCP* 71: 143–9.

Erkell, H. (1952), *Augustus, Felicitas, Fortuna: Lateinische Wortstudien* (Göteborg).

Ermatinger, E. (1921), *Das dichterische Kunstwerk* (Leipzig and Berlin).

ESSER, D. (1976) *Untersuchungen zu den Odenschlüssen bei Horaz* (Beiträge zur klassischen Philologie 77; Meisenheim am Glan).

ESTEVE-FORRIOL, J. (1962), *Die Trauer- und Trostgedichte in der römischen Literatur* (Diss. Munich).

EVANS, J. D. (1992), *The Art of Persuasion* (Ann Arbor).

EVJEN, H. D. (ed.) (1984), *Mnemai: Classical Studies in Memory of K. K. Hulley* (Chico, Calif.).

FARAONE, C. (1992), 'Aristophanes, Amphiaraus fr. 29 (Kassel-Austin): Oracular Response or Erotic Incantation?', *CQ* 42: 320–7.

—— and OBBINK, D. (eds.) (1991), *Magika Hiera: Ancient Greek Magic and Religion* (New York and Oxford).

FÄRBER, H. (1936), *Die Lyrik in der Kunsttheorie der Antike* (Munich).

FARRELL, J. (2005), 'Eduard Fraenkel on Horace and Servius, or, Texts, Contexts, and the Field of "Latin Studies"', *TAPA* 135: 91–103.

FEARS, J. R. (1981a), 'The Cult of Virtues and Roman Imperial Ideology', *ANRW* II.17.2: 827–948.

—— (1981b), 'The Theology of Victory at Rome: Approaches and Problems', *ANRW* II.17.2: 736–826.

FEDELI, P. (1979), 'Il V epodo e i Giambi d'Orazio come espressione d'arte alessandrina', *MPhL* 3: 67–138.

—— (1983), *Catullus's Carmen 61* (Amsterdam).

FEENEY, D. C. (1991), *The Gods in Epic* (Oxford).

—— (1992), 'Si licet et fas est: Ovid's *Fasti* and the Problem of Free Speech under the Principate', in Powell (1992: 1–25).

—— (1993), 'Horace and the Greek Lyric Poets', in Rudd (1993: 41–63). [Ch. 11 in this volume].

—— (1998), *Literature and Religion at Rome: Culture, Contexts, and Beliefs* (Cambridge).

FERRI, R. (1993), *Il dispiacere di un epicureo* (Pisa).

FINE LICHT, K. DE (ed.) (1983), *Città e architettura nella Roma imperiale* (*Analecta Romana Istituti Danici* 1983 Suppl. 10; Odense).

FISHWICK, D. (1987–2005), *The Imperial Cult in the Latin West*, 3 volumes with up to 4 parts (Leiden).

FITZGERALD, W. (1988), 'Power and Impotence in Horace's Epodes', *Ramus*, 17: 176–91. [Chapter 8 in this volume].

—— (1995), *Catullan Provocations: Lyric Poetry and the Drama of Position* (Berkeley).

—— (2006), *Martial: The Epigrammatic World* (Cambridge).

FLORES, E. (1973), *Letteratura latina e società* (Naples).

FOUCAULT, M. (1985), *The Use of Pleasure*, tr. R. Hurley (New York).

FOWLER, D. P. (1989a), review of R. F. Thomas, *Virgil: Georgics* (Cambridge, 1988), *G&R* 36: 235–6.

—— (1989b), 'Lucretius and Politics', in Griffin and Barnes (1989: 120–50).

—— (2007), 'Laocoon's Point of View', in Heyworth, Fowler, and Harrison (2007: 1–17).

FRAENKEL, E. (1928), *Iktus und Akzent im lateinischen Sprechvers* (Berlin).

—— (1950), *Aeschylus, Agamemnon*, 3 vols., multiple editions with multiple dates (Oxford).

—— (1956), 'Catulls Trostgedicht fur Calvus', *WS* 69: 278–88 = *Kleine Beiträge zur klassischen Philologie* II (Rome, 1964), 103–13.

—— (1957), *Horace* (Oxford).

—— (ed.) (1960), *Friedrich Leo, Ausgewählte kleine Schriften*, 2 vols. (Rome).

—— (1961), 'Die klassische Dichtung der Römer', in Jaeger (1961: 47–73).

FRANK, T. (1921), 'The *Carmen Saeculare* of Horace', *AJP* 42.4: 324–9.

—— (1925), 'On Augustus' References to Horace', *CP* 20: 26–30.

FRASER JENKINS, A. D. (1970), 'Cosimo de' Medici's Patronage of Architecture and the Theory of Magnificence', *Journal of the Warburg and Courtauld Institutes*, 33: 162–70.

FREUDENBURG, K. (1993), *The Walking Muse: Horace on the Theory of Satire* (Princeton).

FREYBURGER, G. (1978), 'La Supplication d'action de grâces', *ANRW* II.16.2: 1418–39.

FRIEDRICH, G. (1894), *Q. Horatius Flaccus* (Leipzig).

FUCHS, H. (1926), *Augustin und der antike Freidensgedanke* (Berlin).

GABBA, J. (1956), *Appiano e la storia delle guerre civili* (Florence).

GAGÉ, J. (1934), *Recherches sur les jeux séculaires* (Paris).

—— (1955), *Apollon romain* (Paris).

—— (1972), 'Beobachtungen zum Carmen saeculare des Horaz', in Opperman (1972: 14–36; first publ. as 'Observations sur le Carmen Saeculare d'Horace', *REL* 9 [1931] 290–308).

GALINSKY, G. K. (1967), 'Sol and the Carmen saeculare', *Latomus*, 26: 619–633.

—— (1981), 'Augustus' Legislation on Morals and Marriage', *Philologus*, 125: 126–44.

GARBER, M. (1997), 'Out of Joint', in Hillman and Mazzio (1997: 23–51).

GARNSEY, P. (1988), *Famine and Food Supply in the Roman World* (Cambridge).

GAVRILOV, A. K. (1997), 'Techniques of Reading in Classical Antiquity', *CQ* 47: 56–73.

GENETTE, G. (1992), *The Architext: An Introduction*, tr. J. E. Lewin (Berkeley and Los Angeles).

GENTILI, B. (1988), *Poetry and its Public in Ancient Greece: From Homer to the Fifth Century*, tr. A. T. Cole (Baltimore).

GIANGRANDE, G. (1968), 'Sympotic Literature and Epigram', in Raubitschek, Gentili, and Giangrande (1968: 93–177).

GIDE, A. (1988), *Amyntas*, tr. R. Howard (New York).

GIGANTE, M. (1993), 'Lettura di Orazio, Carm. I 24. Requiem per Quintilio', in R. Uglione (ed.), *Atti del convegno nazionale di studi su Orazio* (Torino, aprile 1992), (Turin: 149–77).

GILDERSLEEVE, B. (1890), *Pindar, Olympian and Pythian Odes* (New York).

GILL, C. and WISEMAN T. P. (eds.) (1993), *Lies and Fiction in the Ancient World* (Exeter).

GOLD, B. (ed.) (1982), *Literary and Artistic Patronage in Ancient Rome* (Austin).

GOLDHILL, S. (1991), *The Poet's Voice* (Cambridge).

GONIS, N. *et al.* (2005), *The Oxyrhynchus Papyri*, vol. LXIX (London).

GOODYEAR, F. R. D. (ed.) (1972), *The Annals of Tacitus, I: Annals 1.1–54* (Cambridge Classical Texts and Commentaries 15; Cambridge).

GORDON, M. (1934), 'The Family of Vergil', *JRS* 24: 1–12.

GOWERS, E. (1993), *The Loaded Table: Representations of Food in Roman Literature* (Oxford).

GRAF, F. (1997), 'Cicero, Plautus and Roman Laughter', in Bremmer and Roodenburg (1997: 29–39).

GRAFTON, A. T. and SWERDLOW, N. M. (1985), 'Technical Chronology and Astrological History in Varro, Censorinus and Others', *CQ* 35: 454–65.

GRASSMANN, V. (1966), *Die erotischen Epoden des Horaz* (Zetemata 39; Munich).

GREEN, L. (1990), 'Galvano Fiamma, Azzone Visconti and the Revival of the Classical Theory of Magnificence', *Journal of the Warburg and Courtauld Institutes*, 53: 98–113.

GRIFFIN, J. (1976), 'Augustan Poetry and the Life of Luxury', *JRS* 66: 87–105.

—— (1980), review of Nisbet and Hubbard (1970), *JRS* 70: 182–5.

—— (1984), 'Augustus and the Poets: "Caesar qui cogere posset"', in Millar and Segal (1984: 189–218).

—— (1985), *Latin Poets and Roman Life* (London).

GRIFFIN, M. T. and BARNES, J. (eds.) (1989), *Philosophia Togata* (Oxford).

GRIFFITH, M. and MASTRONARDE, D. J. (eds.) (1990), *Cabinet of the Muses: Essays in Honor of T. G. Rosenmeyer* (Atlanta).

GRUBER, J. (1978), *Kommentar zu Boethius de consolatione philosophiae*, multiple editions with multiple dates (Berlin and New York).

GUTHRIE, W. K. C. (1950), *The Greeks and Their Gods* (London).

HABICHT, C. (1973), 'Die Augusteische Zeit und das erste Jahrhundert nach Christi Geburt', in den Boer (1973: 41–8).

HABINEK, T. (1986), 'The Marriageability of Maximus: Horace *Ode* 4.1.13–20', *AJP* 107: 407–16.

—— (2005), *The World of Roman Song: From Ritualized Speech to Social Order* (Baltimore).

—— and SCHIESARO, A. (eds.) (1997), *The Roman Cultural Revolution* (Cambridge and New York).

HAHN, E. A. (1939), '*Epodes* 5 and 17, *Carmina* 1.16 and 1.17', *TAPA* 70: 213–30.

HALFMANN, H. (1986), *Itinera Principum* (Stuttgart).

HALLETT, J. (1981), '*Pepedi / Diffissa Nate Ficus*: Priapic Revenge in Horace, *Satires* I.8', *RhM* 124: 341–47.

HARDER, M. A., REGTUIT, R. F., and WAKKER, G. C. (eds.) (1993), *Callimachus* (Groningen).

HARDIE, A. (1977), 'Horace Odes 1,37 and Pindar Dithyramb 2', in Cairns (1977: 113–40).

HARRISON, S. J. (1989), 'Two Notes on Horace, *Epodes* (10, 16)', *CQ* 39: 271–4.

—— (ed.) (1995), *Homage to Horace: A Bimillenary Celebration* (Oxford).

—— (ed.) (2001), *Texts, Ideas, and the Classics: Scholarship, Theory, and Classical Literature* (Oxford).

—— (ed.) (2007), *The Cambridge Companion to Horace* (Cambridge).

HARVEY, A. E. (1955), 'The Classification of Greek Lyric Poetry', *CQ* NS 5: 157–75.

HEATH, M. (1988), 'Receiving the κῶμος: The Context and Performance of Epinician', *AJP* 109: 190–5.

—— and LEFKOWITZ, M. (1991), 'Epinician Performance', *CP* 86: 173–91.

HEILMEYER, W.-D. (ed.) (1988), *Kaiser Augustus und die verlorene Republik* (Berlin).

HEINZE, R. (1918), 'Die lyrischen Verse Des Horaz', *Ber. Sächs. Akad. d. Wiss.*, Philol.-hist. Kl. 70.4 = Heinze (1960a), 227–94; cited from Heinze (1960a).

—— *Vom Geist des Römertums*, ed. E. Burck, 3rd edn. (Stuttgart; repr. Darmstadt 1970).

—— (1960b), 'Die horazische Ode', in Heinze (1960a: 172–89; originally published 1923) [chapter 1 in this volume].

HELD, D. T. D. (1993), '*Megalopsuchia* in Nicomachean Ethics iv', *AncPhil* 13: 95–110.

HELLEGOUARC'H, J. (1972), *Le Vocabulaire latin des relations et des partis politiques sous la République* (Paris).

HELM, R. (1935), 'Reden in den Oden des Horaz', *Philologus*, 90: 353–71.

—— (ed.) (1956), *Die Chronik des Hieronymus* (Berlin).

HENDERSON, JEFFREY (1975), *The Maculate Muse: Obscene Language in Attic Comedy* (New Haven).

HENDERSON, JOHN (1987), 'Suck It and See (Horace, *Epode* 8)', in Whitby, Hardie, and Whitby (1987), 105–18 = Henderson (1999), 93–113.

—— (1989), 'Satire Writes Woman: *Gendersong*', *PCPhS* 35: 50–80 = Henderson (1999): 173–201.

—— (1999), *Writing Down Rome: Satire, Comedy, and other Offences in Latin Poetry* (Oxford).

HENDRICKSON, G. L. (1931), 'The First Publication of Horace's *Odes*', *CP* 26: 1–10.

HENDRY, M. (1995), 'Rouge and Crocodile Dung: Notes on Ovid, *Ars* 3.199–200 and 269–70', *CQ* 45: 583–8.

HERRNSTEIN SMITH, B. (1968), *Poetic Closure: A Study of How Poems End* (Chicago).

HERTZ, N. (1983), 'Medusa's Head: Male Hysteria under Political Pressure', *Representations*, 4: 27–54. = *The End of the Line* (New York, 1985), 161–92.

HEYWORTH, S. J. (1993), 'Horace's *Ibis*: On the Titles, Unity, and Contents of the *Epodes*', *Papers of the Leeds International Latin Seminar*, 7: 85–96.

—— (2007), *Classical Constructions: Papers in Memory of Don Fowler, Classicist and Epicurean* (Oxford).

HIERCHE, H. (1974), *Les Epodes d'Horace* (Latomus 136; Brussels).

HIGHBARGER, E. L. (1935), 'The Pindaric Style of Horace', *TAPA* 66: 222–35.

HILLMAN, D. and MAZZIO, C. (eds.) (1997), *The Body in Parts: Fantasies of Corporeality in Early Modern Europe* (New York).

HINDS, S. (1987), 'The Poetess and the Reader', *Hermathena*, 143: 29–46.

—— (1996), 'Books, Poetic', in *The Oxford Classical Dictionary*, 3rd edn., S. Hornblower and A. Spawforth (eds.), 252–3 (Oxford).

—— (2000), 'Essential Epic: Genre and Gender from Macer to Statius', in Depew and Obbink (2000: 221–44, 302–4).

HIRSCHBERG, L. (1915), 'Carl Loewe und das klassische Altertum', *NJbb* 36: 190–212.

HITLER, A. (1937), *My Struggle* (London).

HOFMANN, J. B. and SZANTYR, A. (1965), *Lateinische Syntax und Stilistik* (Handbuch der Altertumswissenschaft ii.2.2; Munich).

HORNSTEIN, F. (1957), 'Vergilius ΠΑΡΘΕΝΙΑΣ', *WS* 70: 148–52.

HORSFALL, N. M. (1981), 'Poet and Patron', *Publ. of the Macquarle Ancient History Association*, 3: 1–24.

HOUSMAN, A. E. (1907), 'Luciliana', *CQ* 1: 51–74, 148–59 = Diggle and Goodyear (1972: ii. 662–97).

HOWALD, E. (1948), *Das Wesen der lateinischen Dichtung* (Zurich).

HUBBARD, M. (1973), 'The *Odes*', in Costa (1973: 1–28).

HUBER, G. (1970), *Die Wortwiederholung in den Oden des Horaz* (Diss. Zürich).

HUNTER, R. (1996), *Theocritus and the Archaeology of Greek Poetry* (Cambridge).

INGALLINA, S. S. (1974), *Orazio e la magia* (Palermo).

IRIGARAY, L. (1985), *This Sex Which Is Not One*, tr. C. Porter (Ithaca).

JACKSON KNIGHT, W. F. (1945), *Roman Vergil* (London).

JACOBY, F. (1950), *Die Fragmente der griechischen Historiker*, III B (Leiden).

JAEGER, W. (1943), *Paideia* 2 (New York).

——(1961), *Das Problem des Klassischen und die Antike* (Darmstadt).

JAHN, O. (1867), 'Wie wurden die Oden des Horaz vorgetragen?', *Hermes* 2: 418–33.

JAKOBSON, R. (1968), *Closing Statement: Linguistics and Poetics*, in Sebeok (1968: 350–77).

——and LÉVI-STRAUSS, C. (1962), '"Les Chats" de Charles Baudelaire', *L'Homme, Revue française d'anthropologie* 2.1: 5–21.

JENKYNS, R. (1982), *Three Classical Poets: Sappho, Catullus, and Juvenal* (London).

JOCELYN, H. J. (1982), 'Boats, Women, and Horace *Odes* 1.14', *CP* 77: 330–5.

JOHNSON, T. (2004), *A Symposion of Praise: Horace Returns to Lyric in Odes IV* (Madison).

JOHNSON, W. R. (1982), *The Idea of Lyric: Lyric Modes in Ancient and Modern Poetry* (Berkeley and Los Angeles).

JOLIVET, V. (1989), 'Les Cendres d'Auguste: Note sur la topographie monumentale du Champ de Mars septentrionale', *Archeologia laziale*, 9: 90–6.

KAHN, H. A. (1967), 'Horace's Ode to Virgil on the Death of Quintilius: 1, 24', *Latomus*, 26: 107–17.

KANDIYOTI, D. (1997), 'Roland Barthes Abroad', in Rabaté (1997: 228–42).

KÄPPEL, L. (1992), *Paian: Studien zur Geschichte einer Gattung* (*Untersuchungen zur antiken Literatur und Geschichte*, vol. 37: Berlin).

KENNEDY, D. (1992), '"Augustan" and "Anti-Augustan": Reflections on Terms of Reference', in A. Powell (ed.) *Roman Poetry and Propaganda in the Age of Augustus* (London: 26–58).

KENNEY, E. J. (1982), 'Books and Readers in the Roman World', in Kenney and Clausen (1982: 3–32).

——and CLAUSEN, W. V. (eds.) (1982), *The Cambridge History of Classical Literature*, ii (Cambridge).

KEPPIE, L. J. F. (1983), *Colonization and Veteran Settlement in Italy 47–14 BC* (London).

KEINAST, D. (1969), 'Augustus und Alexander', *Gymnasium*, 76: 430–56.

——(1982), *Augustus: Prinzeps und Monarch* (Darmstadt).

KEYSER, P. (1989), 'Horace *Odes* 1.13.3–8, 14–16, Humoural and Aetherial Love', *Philologus*, 133: 75–81.

KIBEDI VARGA, A. (1970), *Rhétorique et litérature: Études de structures classiques* (Paris).

KIESSLING, A. (1876), *De Horatianorum carminum inscriptionibus commentatiuncula* (Greifswald).

——(1881), 'Horatius I: Zur Chronologie und Anordnung der Oden', *Philologische Untersuchungen*, 2: 48–75.

——(1884), Q. *Horatius Flaccus, Oden und Epoden*, multiple editions with multiple dates (Berlin).

——and HEINZE, R. (1957–8), Q. *Horatius Flaccus*, 3 vols., multiple editions with multiple dates (Berlin).

KING, H. (1986), 'Tithonus and the Tettix', *Arethusa*, 19: 15–35.

KISSEL, W. (1981), 'Horaz 1936–1975: Eine Gesamtbibliographie', *ANRW* II 31. 3: 1403–1558.

KLEVE, K. and LONGO AURICCHIO, F. (1992), 'Honey from the Garden', in Capasso (1992: 213–26).

KLINGER, F. (ed.) (1959), Q. *Horati Flacci, Opera*, 3rd edn. (Leipzig).

KLINGNER, F. (1930), 'Horazische und moderne Lyrik', *Die Antike*, 6: 65–84.

——(1965), *Römische Geisteswelt* (Munich).

KNOX, B. (1968), 'Silent Reading in Antiquity', *GRBS* 9: 421–35.

KONSTAN, D. (ed.) (1995), *Horace: 2000 Years*, special volume of *Arethusa* 28.

KOSTER, S. (1980), *Die Invektive in der greichichen und römischen Literatur* (Meisenheim-am-Glan).

KOTANSKY, R. (1991), 'Incantations and Prayers for Salvation on Inscribed Greek Amulets', in C. Faraone and D. Obbink (1991: 107–37).

KRAFT, K. (1967), 'Der Sinn des Mausoleums des Augustus', *Historia*, 16: 189–206.

——(1978), *Gessammelte Aufsätze zur antiken Geldgeschichte und Numismatik*, i (Darmstadt).

KRANZ, W. (1967a), *Studien zur antiken Literatur und ihrem Fortwirken* (Heidelberg).

——(1967b), 'Sphragis. Ichform und Namensiegel als Eingangs- und Schlussmotiv antiker Dichtung', in Kranz (1967a), 27–78 (= *RhM* 104 [1961]: 3–46, 97–124).

KRASSER, H. (1995), *Horazische Denkfiguren: Theophilie und Theophanie als Medium der poetischen Selbstdarstellung des Odendichters* (Hypomnemata 106: Göttingen).

KREVANS, N. (forthcoming), *The Poet as Editor* (Princeton).

KROLL, W. (1924), *Studien zum Verständnis der römischen Literatur* (Stuttgart; repr. Darmstadt 1973).

Kühn, A. (1877), *De Q. Horatii carmine saeculari* (Diss. Breslau).

Kühn, J.-H. (1961), 'Die Prooimion-Elegie des zweiten Properz-Buches', *Hermes* 89: 84–105.

Kumaniecki, K. F. (1935), 'Die epodis quibisdam Horationis', in *Commentationes Horatianae* (Cracovia), 139–57.

Lämmert, E. (1970), *Bauformen des Erzählens* (Stuttgart).

Landmann, M. (1961), 'Die Aufteilung der Chöre im Carmen saeculare', in Radke (1961: 173–9).

Landolfi, L. (1990), *Banchetto e società romana archaica* (Rome).

La Penna, A. (1963), *Orazio e l'ideologia del principato* (Turin).

—— (ed.) (1964), re-edition with introduction to Pasquali (1920).

—— (1968), *Orazio e la morale mondana europea*, introduction to La Penna and Cetrangolo (1968).

—— (1972), 'Sunt qui Sappho malint: Note sulla σύγκρισις di Saffo e Alceo nell'antichità', *Maia*, 24: 208–15.

—— and Cetrangolo, E. (ed.) (1968), *Orazio, Le Opere. Antologia* (Florence), multiple editions with multiple dates.

Landolfi, L. (1990), *Banchetto e società romana archaica* (Rome).

Lapini, W. (1996), *Il POxy: 664 di Eraclide Pontico e la cronologia dei Cipselidi* (Florence).

Latte, K. (1960), *Römische Religionsgeschichte* (Munich).

Lausberg, H. (1960), *Handbuch der literarischen Rhetorik* (Munich).

Lee, M. O. (1969), *Word, Sound and Image in the Odes of Horace* (Ann Arbor).

—— (1975), 'Catullus in the Odes of Horace', *Ramus*, 4: 33–48.

Leeman, A. D. (1971), 'Complexiteit en intentie in Vergilius' eerste ecloga', *Lampas* 4: 210–24.

Lefèvre, E. (ed.) (1975), *Monumentum Chiloniense: Studien zur augusteischen Zeit* (Amsterdam).

—— (1990), 'Die römische Literatur zwischen Mündlichkeit und Schriftlichkeit', in G. Vogt-Spira (ed.) *Strukturen der Mündlichkeit in der römischen Literatur, ScriptOralia* 19. Tübingen (1990): 9–15.

—— (1993), 'Waren horazische Gedichte zum "öffentlichen" Vortrag bestimmt?', in G. Vogt-Spira (ed.), *Beiträge zur mündlichen Kultur der Römer, ScriptOralia* 47. Tübingen (1993): 143–57.

Lefkowitz, M. (1988), 'Who Sang Pindar's Victory Odes?', *AJP* 109: 1–11.

—— (1995), 'The First Person in Pindar Reconsidered—Again', *BICS* 42: 139–50.

Legman, G. (1972), *Rationale of the Dirty Joke: An Analysis of Sexual Humour*, First Series, i–ii (London).

—— (1978), *Rationale of the Dirty Joke. An Analysis of Sexual Humour*, Second Series (London).

LEISHMAN, J. B. (1956), *Translating Horace* (Oxford).

LEO, F. (1896), 'Analecta Plautina de figuris sermonis I' (Göttingen) = Fraenkel (1960: 1.71–122).

——(1900), 'De Horatio et Archilocho' (Göttingen) = Fraenkel (1960: 2.139–57).

LEVINE, P. (1969), 'Catullus c. 1: A Prayerful Dedication', *CSCA* 2: 209–16.

LEWY, H. (1929), *Sobria Ebrietas: Untersuchungen zur Geschichte der antiken Mystik* (Giessen).

LIEBESCHUETZ, J. H. W. G. (1979), *Continuity and Change in Roman Religion* (Oxford).

LILJA, S. (1976), *Dogs in Ancient Greek Poetry* (Commentationes Humanarum Litterarum 56; Helsinki).

LINDE, P. (1923), 'Die Stellung des Verbs in der lateinischen Prosa', *Glotta*, 12: 153–78.

LINDO, L. I. (1969), 'Horace's Seventeenth Epode', *CPh* 64: 176–7.

LISSARRAGUE, F. (1987), *Un flot d'images: une esthétique du banquet grec* (Paris).

LOWRIE, M. (1991), review of Davis (1991) in *Bryn Mawr Classical Review* 2.7: 417–22.

——(1992), review of Edmunds (1992) in *Bryn Mawr Classical Review* 3.4: 260–5.

——(1995), 'A Parade of Lyric Predecessors: Horace *C.* 1.12–18', *Phoenix* 49: 33–48. [Chapter 15 in this volume].

——(1997a), *Horace's Narrative Odes* (Oxford).

——(1997b), review of Ancona (1994) in *CR* 47: 205–6.

——(1997c), review of Ancona (1994), Harrison (1995), Krasser (1995), Lyne (1995), and David West (1995) in *CJ* 92: 295–301.

——(1999), review of Ludwig (1993) in *CR* 49: 386–8.

——(2000), review of Oliensis (1998) in *CR* 50: 49–50.

——(2002), review of Bowditch (2001) in *AJP* 123: 305–8.

——(2003), review of Putnam (2000) in *CW* 96.2: 226–7.

——(2005a), review of Nisbet and Rudd (2004) in *New England Classical Journal* 32.4: 329–39.

——(2005b), review of Watson (2003) in *CR* 55: 628–30.

——(2009), *Writing, Performance, and Authority in the Age of Augustus* (Oxford).

LUCK, G. (1976), 'An Interpretation of Horace's Eleventh Epode', *ICS* 1: 122–6.

——(1985), *Arcana Mundi* (Baltimore and London).

LUDWIG, W. (1957), 'Zu Horaz, *C.* 2,1–12', *Hermes*, 85: 336–45.

——(ed.) (1993), *Horace: l'oeuvre et les imitations* (Entretiens Hardt 39; Vandoeuvres).

Luppe, W. (1993), 'Zum neuesten Stesichoros, POxy 3876 fr. 35', *ZPE* 95: 53–8.

Lyne, R. O. A. M. (1995), *Horace, Behind the Public Poetry* (New Haven).

—— (2005), 'Structure and Allusion in Horace's Book of *Epodes*', *JRS* 95: 1–19.

MacCormack, S. G. (1972), 'Change and Continuity in Late Antiquity: The Ceremony of Adventus', *Historia*, 21: 721–52.

—— (1981), *Art and Ceremony in Late Antiquity* (Berkeley).

McDermott, E. A. (1981), 'Greek and Roman Elements in Horace's Lyric Program', *ANRW* 2.31.3: 1640–72.

—— (1982), 'Horace, Maecenas and Odes 2, 17', *Hermes* 110: 211–28.

Mace, S. (1993), 'Amour, Encore! The Development of *deute* in Archaic Lyric', *GRBS* 34: 335–64.

MacKay, L. A. (1942), 'Notes on Horace', *CP* 37: 79–80.

McKinlay, A. P. (1946), 'The Wine Element in Horace', *CJ* 42: 161–8, 229–36.

Macleod, C. (1979), 'Horace and the Sibyl (*Epode* 16.2)', *CQ* 29: 220–1. = *Collected Essays* (Oxford, 1983), 218–19.

McMahon, J. M. (1998), Paralysin caue: *Impotence, Perception, and Text in the* Satyrica *of Petronius* (Mnemosyne Supplement 176; Leiden).

Maltby, R. (1991), *A Lexicon of Ancient Latin Etymologies* (Leeds).

Mankin, D. P. (1985), *The Epodes of Horace and Archilochean Iambus*: *A Preliminary Study* (Charlottesville, Diss.).

—— (ed.) (1995), *Horace,* Epodes (Cambridge).

Manning, C. E. (1970), 'Canidia in the *Epodes* of Horace', *Mnemosyne*, 23: 393–401.

Marcovich, M. (1972), 'Sappho fr. 31: Anxiety Attack or Love Declaration?', *CQ* ns 22: 19–32.

Marouzeau, J. (1922), *L'Ordre des mots dans la phrase latine, I: Les groupes nominaux* (Paris).

Martindale, C. A. (1992), *Redeeming the Text: Latin Poetry and the Hermeneutics of Reception* (Cambridge).

—— (1993), 'Introduction', in Martindale and Hopkins (1993: 1–26).

—— and Hopkins, D. (eds.) (1993), *Horace Made New* (Cambridge).

Masters, J. (1992), *Poetry and Civil War in Lucan's* Bellum Civile (Cambridge).

Mattingly, H. B. (1957), 'The Date of Livius Andronicus', *CQ* ns 7: 159–63.

Maurach, G. (1970), *Der Bau von Senecas Epistulae Morales* (Heidelberg).

Meister, K. (1952), 'Horazens Willkommengruss an einen Spätheimkehrer (*c.* 2, 7)', in Ἑρμηνεία, *Festschrift für Otto Regenbogen* (Heidelberg), 127–34.

Mendell, C. W. (1950), 'Horace, Odes II, 18', *YCS* 11: 281–92.

—— (1975), 'A New Poem of Archilochus: *P. Colon.* inv. 7511', *GRBS* 16: 5–14.

Menozzi, E. (1905), 'La composizione strofica del Carmen Saeculare', *SIFC* 13: 67–73.

METTE, H. J. (1961a), '*Genus tenue* und *mensa tenuis* bei Horaz', *MH* 18: 136–9. = Mette (1988: 188–91). [Ch. 3 in this volume]

—— (1961b), 'Der "große Mensch"', *Hermes*, 89: 332–44.

—— (1988), *Kleine Schriften* (Frankfurt).

METTE-DITTMANN, A. (1991), *Die Ehegesetze des Augustus* (Historia Einzelschriften 67; Stuttgart).

MILANESE, G. (1997), 'Musica', in EncOr II: 921–4.

MILLAR, F. (1964), *A Study of Cassius Dio* (Oxford).

—— (1977), *The Emperor in the Roman World* (London).

—— and SEGAL, E. (eds.) (1984), *Caesar Augustus: Seven Aspects* (Oxford).

MILLER, W. I. (1997), *The Anatomy of Disgust* (Harvard).

MINADEO, R. (1982), *The Golden Plectrum* (Amsterdam).

MOLES, J. L. (1987), 'Politics, Philosophy, and Friendship in Horace Odes 2, 7', *QUCC* 54: 59–72.

MOMMSEN, T. (1905), *Reden und Aufsätze* (Berlin) (orig. publ. 1891; multiple editions with multiple dates).

—— (1905–13), *Gesammelte Schriften*, 8 vols. (Berlin).

—— (1913), 'Commentaria ludorum saecularium quintorum a. u. c. DCCXXXVII', *Epigraphische und numismatische Schriften*, vol. 1 (Berlin: 567–622).

MOORE, C. H. (1902), *Horace: The* Odes, Epodes, *and* Carmen Saeculare (New York).

MØRLAND, H. (1966), 'Wortbrechungen und Hypermetra in den Oden des Horaz', *SO* 41: 108–14.

MÖRLAND, H. (1965), 'Zu Horaz, *carm.* II 17', *SO* 40: 75–80.

MORRIS, B. R. and WILLIAMS, R. D. (1963), 'The Identity of Licymnia: Horace, *Odes* II 12', *PhQ* 42: 145–50.

MUELLER, L. (ed.) (1900), *Q. Horatius Flaccus, Oden und Epoden* (St Petersburg and Leipzig).

MURRAY, O. (1968), review of F. Dvornik, *Early Christian and Byzantine Political Philosophy*, in *JTS* 19: 673–8.

—— (1985), 'Symposium and Genre in the Poetry of Horace', *JRS* 75: 39–50. = Rudd (1993: 89–105).

—— (ed.) (1990), *Sympotica: A Symposium on the Symposium* (Oxford).

—— and TEÇUSAN, M. (eds.) (1995), *In uino ueritas* (Oxford).

MUTSCHLER, F.-H. (1978), 'Kaufmannsliebe: Eine Interpretation der Horazode "Quid fles Asterie" (*C.* 3.7)', *SO* 53: 111–31.

MYERS, K. S. (1996), 'The Poet and the Procuress: The *Lena* in Latin Love Elegy', *JRS* 86: 1–21.

NAGY, G. (1976), 'Iambos: Typologies of Invective and Praise', *Arethusa* 9: 191–205.

—— (1979), *The Best of the Achaeans* (Baltimore).

—— (1990), *Pindar's Homer: The Lyric Possession of an Epic Past* (Baltimore).

—— (1996), *Poetry as Performance: Homer and Beyond* (Cambridge).

NAYLOR, H. D. (1922), *Horace, Odes and Epodes: A Study in Poetic Word-Order* (Cambridge).

NEDERGAARD, E. (1988), 'Zur Problematik der Augustusbögen auf dem Forum Romanum', in Heilmeyer (1988: 224–39).

NEWMAN, J. K. (1967a), *The Concept of Vates in Augustan Poetry* (Brussels).

—— (1967b), *Augustus and the New Poetry* (Brussels).

NICOLET, C. (1966), *L'Ordre équestre a l'époque républicain* 1 (Paris).

—— (1976), 'Le Cens sénatorial sous la République et sous Auguste', *JRS* 66: 20–38.

—— (1984), 'Augustus, Government and the Propertied Classes', in Millar and Segal (1984: 89–128).

NIEBLING, G. (1956), '*Laribus Augustis Magistri Primi*: Der Beginn des Compitalkultes der Lares und des Genius Augusti', *Historia*, 5: 303–31.

NISBET, R. G. M. (1962), 'Romanae fidicen lyrae: The Odes of Horace', in Sullivan (1962: 181–218).

—— (1969), review of Doblhofer (1966), in *CR* 19: 173–5.

—— (1983), 'Some Problems of Text and Interpretation in Horace *Odes* 3. 14 (Herculis ritu)', *PLLS* 4: 105–19.

—— (1984), 'Horace's Epodes and History', in Woodman and West (1984: 1–18).

—— (1987), 'Pyrrha among Roses: Real Life and Poetic Imagination in Augustan Rome', review of Griffin (1985), *JRS* 77: 184–90.

—— (1989), 'Footnotes on Horace', in Diggle, Hall, and Jocelyn (1989: 87–96).

—— (1995), *Collected Papers on Latin Literature*, ed. S. J. Harrison (Oxford).

—— and HUBBARD, M. (1970), *A Commentary* on *Horace:* Odes *Book I* (Oxford).

—— and—— (1978), *A Commentary on Horace:* Odes *Book II* (Oxford).

—— and RUDD, N. (2004), *A Commentary on Horace:* Odes, *Book III* (Oxford).

NORDEN, E. (1903), *P. Vergilius Maro: Aeneis Buch VI*, 2nd edn. (Stuttgart). multiple editions with multiple dates.

—— (1913), *Agnostos Theos* (Leipzig).

NUMBERGER, K. (1972), *Horaz lyrische Gedichte: Kommentar für Lehrer der Gymnasien und für Studierende* (Münster).

OBBATIUS, T. (1848), *Horace, Carmina* (Jena).

OBBINK, D. (2005), 'POxy 4708. Archilochus. Elegies', in Gonis: 18–42.

O'HIGGINS, D. (1988), 'Lucan as *vates*', *CA* 7: 208–26.

OKSALA, T. (1973), *Religion und Mythologie bei Horaz, eine literarhistorische Untersuchung* (Helsinki).

OLIENSIS, E. (1991), 'Canidia, Canicula, and the Decorum of Horace's *Epodes*', *Arethusa*, 24: 107–38. [Chapter 9 in this volume]

—— (1998), *Horace and the Rhetoric of Authority* (Cambridge).

OLIVIER, F. (1963a), *Essais dans le domaine du monde gréco-romain antique et dans celui du Nouveau Testament* (Genève).

—— (1963b), 'Les *Epodes* d'Horace', in Olivier (1963a: 45–126).

ONIANS, R. B. (1951), *The Origins of European Thought* (Cambridge).

OPELT, I. (1965), *Die lateinischen Schimpfwörter und verwandte sprachliche Erscheinungen: Eine Typologie* (Heidelberg).

OPPERMAN, H. (1972), *Wege zu Horaz* (Darmstadt).

OTIS, B., 'Horace and the Elegists', *TAPA* 76: 177–90.

OTTERLO, W. A. A. VAN (1944), *Untersuchungen über Begriff, Anwendung und Entstehung der griechischen Ringkomposition* (Mededel. Der Ned. Akad. V. Wet. afd. Lett. N. R. d. 7, no. 3; Amsterdam).

PAGE, D. (1955), *Sappho and Alcaeus: An Introduction to the Study of Ancient Lesbian Poetry* (Oxford).

—— (1962), *Poetae Melici Graeci* (Oxford).

PAGE, T. E. (1895), *Q. Horatii Flacci Carminum Libri IV* (London).

PASCAL, C. B. (1969), 'Horatian chiaroscuro', in Bibauw (1969: 622–33).

PASCHALIS, M. (1997), *Virgil's Aeneid. Semantic Relations and Proper Names* (Oxford).

PASCHOUD, F. (1971), *Zosimus: Histoire nouvelle. Tome I, Livres I et II* (Paris).

PASQUALI, G. (1920), *Orazio lirico* (Florence; repr. 1964; 2nd edn., rev. A. La Penna, 1966).

PATZER, H. (1955), 'Zum Sprachstil des neoterischen Hexameters', *MH* 12: 77–97.

PATTERSON, J. R. (1992), 'The City of Rome: From Republic to Empire', *JRS* 82: 186–215.

PEARCE, T. E. V. (1966), 'The Enclosing Word Order in the Latin Hexameter', *CQ* NS 16: 140–71; 298–320.

—— (1970), 'Notes on Cicero *In Pisonem*', *CQ* NS 20: 311–21.

PECK, J. and NISETICH, F. (trans.) (1995), *Euripides: Orestes* (New York and Oxford).

PELLIZER, E. (1981), 'Per una morfologia della poesia giambica arcaica', in *I canoni letterari. Storia e dinamica* (Trieste).

PETERSON, E. (1926), *Εἷς θεός: Epigraphische formgeschichtliche und religionsgeschichtliche Untersuchungen* (Göttingen).

—— (1930), 'Die Einholung Des Kyrios', *Zeitschrift für systematische Theologie*, 7: 682–702.

PETROPOULOS, J. C B. (1993), 'Sappho the Sorceress—Another Look at fr. 1 (LP)', *ZPE* 97: 43–56.

PFEIFFER, R. (1943), 'A Fragment of Parthenios' Arete', *CQ* 37: 23–32. = *Ausgewählte Schriften* (Munich, 1960), 133–47.

—— (1968), *History of Classical Scholarship: From the Beginnings to the End of the Hellenistic Age* (Oxford).

PIGHI, G. (1965), *De ludis saecularibus*, 2nd edn. (Amsterdam).

PÖHLMANN, E. (1965), 'Marius Victorinus zum Odengesang bei Horaz', *Philologus* 109: 134–40 = *Beiträge zur antiken und neueren Musikgeschichte* (Frankfurt, 1988), 135–43.

POISS, TH. (1992), 'Plenum opus aleae: Zum Verhältnis von Dichtung und Geschichte in Horaz carm. 2.1', *Wiener Studien* 105: 129–53.

POLLINI, J. (1990), 'Man or God: Divine Assimilation and Imitation in the Late Republic and Early Principate', in Raaflaub and Toher (1990: 334–57).

PORRO, A. (1994), *Vetera Alcaica* (Milan).

PORT, W. (1926), 'Die Anordnung in den Gedichtbüchern der augusteischen Zeit', *Philologus*, 81: 299–300.

PORTE, D. (1981), 'Romulus-Quirinus, prince et dieu, dieu des princes', *ANRW* II. 17.1: 5. 300–42.

PORTER, D. (1987), *Horace's Poetic Journey* (Princeton).

PÖSCHL, V. (1956a), *Horaz und die Politik* (SHAW 4; Heidelberg; 2nd edn. 1963).

—— (1956b), 'Horaz', in J. Bayet (ed.), *L'Influence grecque sur la poésie latine de Catulle à Ovide* (Entretiens Hardt 2; Vandoeuvres and Genève), 93–130.

—— (1959), 'Ovid und Horaz', *RCCM* 1: 15–25.

—— (1970), *Horazische Lyrik, Interpretationen* (Heidelberg).

POSNER, R. (1969), 'Strukturalismus in der Gedichtinterpretation, Textdeskription und Rezeptionsanalyse am Beispiel von Baudelaires "Les Chats"', *Sprache im Technishchen Zeitalter* 29: 27–58.

PÖTSCHER, W. (1978), '"Numen" und '"Numen Augusti"', *ANRW* II. 16. 1: 355–92.

POWELL, A. (ed.) (1992), *Roman Poetry and Propaganda in the Age of Augustus* (London).

PRICE, S. R. F. (1980), 'Between Man and God: Sacrifice in the Roman Imperial Cult', *JRS* 70: 28–43.

PUCCI, J. (1991), 'The Dilemma of Writing: Augustine *Confessions* 4. 6 and Horace *Odes* 1.3', *Arethusa*, 24: 257–81.

PURDIE, S. (1993), *Comedy: The Mastery of Discourse* (Hemel Hempstead).

PUTNAM, M. C. J. (1969), 'Horace *C.* 1.20', *CJ* 64: 153–7.

—— (1970), 'Horace *Carm.* 1.5: Love and Death', *CP* 65: 251–4. = *Essays on Latin Lyric, Elegy, and Epic* (Princeton, 1982), 95–8.

—— (1972), 'Horace and Tibullus', *CPh* 67: 81–8.

PUTNAM, M. C. J. (1986), *Artifices of Eternity: A Commentary on Horace's Fourth Book of* Odes (Ithaca, NY).

—— (2000), *Horace's Carmen Saeculare: Ritual Magic and the Poet's Art* (New Haven).

QUESTA, C. (1984), *Numeri innumeri* (Rome).

QUINN, K. (1959), *The Catullan Revolution* (Melbourne).

—— (1963), *Latin Explorations* (London).

RAAFLAUB, K. A. and SAMONS, L. J. II (1990), 'Opposition to Augustus', in Raaflaub and Toher (1990: 417–54).

—— and TOHER, M. (eds.) (1990), *Between Republic and Empire* (Berkeley).

RABATÉ, J.-M. (ed.) (1997), *Writing the Image after Roland Barthes* (Philadelphia).

RACE, W. H. (1978), 'Odes 1.20: An Horatian Recusatio', *CSCA* 11: 179–96.

—— (1983), ' "That Man" in Sappho fr. 31 L-P', *CA* 2: 92–101.

RADKE, G. (1959), 'Vergil's Cumaeum Carmen', *Gymnasium*, 66: 217–46.

—— (ed.) (1961), *Gedenkschrift für Georg Rohde* (Tübingen).

—— (1964), 'Dux bonus (Horat. C. 4. 5)', in Burck (1964: 57–76).

—— (1978), 'Aspetti religiosi ed elementi politici nel Carmen saeculare', *RCCM* 20: 1093–1116.

—— (1979), *Die Götter Altitaliens*, 2nd edn. (Münster).

RAKOB, F. (1987), 'Die Urbanisierung des nördlichen Marsfeldes', in *L'Urbs: espace urbain et histore* (CEFR 98; Rome), 687–711.

RAMAGE, E. S. (1985), 'Augustus' Treatment of Julius Caesar', *Historia*, 34: 223–45.

RAUBITSCHEK, A. E., GENTILI, B., and GIANGRANDE, G. (1968), *L'Épigramme grecque* (Entretiens Hardt 14; Geneva).

RECKFORD, K. J. (1959), 'Horace and Maecenas', *TAPA* 90: 195–208.

—— (1969), *Horace* (New York).

REDSLOB, E. (1912), *Kritische Bemerkungen zu Horaz* (Weimar).

REINHOLD, M. (1988), *From Republic to Principate: An Historical Commentary on Cassius Dio's Roman History, Books 49–52 (36–29 B.C.)* (Atlanta).

REITZENSTEIN, E. (1931), *Festschrift Richard Reitzenstein* (Leipzig and Berlin).

REITZENSTEIN, R. (1908), 'Horaz und die hellenistische Lyrik', *Neue Jahrb.* 21: 81–102 (= Reitzenstein 1963: 1–22).

—— (1913), 'Horaz Ode I 32', *RhM* 68: 251–6.

—— (1963), *Aufsätze zu Horaz* (Darmstadt).

RICH, J. W. (1990), *Cassius Dio: The Augustan Settlement* (Warminster).

RICHARDSON, L. (1992), *A New Topographical Dictionary of Ancient Rome* (Baltimore).

RICHARDSON, N. J. (1985), 'Pindar and Later Literary Criticism in Antiquity', *PLLS* 5: 383–401.

RICHLIN A. (1983), *The Garden of Priapus. Sexuality and Aggression in Roman Humor* (New Haven; rev. edn. 1992).

——(1984), 'Invective Against Women in Roman Satire', *Arethusa*, 17: 67–80.

RICHMOND, J. A. (1970), 'Horace's "Mottoes" and Catullus 51', *RhM* 113: 197–204.

RINDISBACHER, H. J. (1992), *The Smell of Books: A Cultural-Historical Study of Olfactory Perception in Literature* (Ann Arbor).

RITTER, F. (1856–7), *Q. Horatius Flaccus* 1 (Leipzig).

ROHDE, E. (1893–4), *Psiche* (Rome and Bari; repr. 1989).

ROMANO, E. (1991), *Orazio Flacco, Le Opere,* 1.2 (Rome).

ROSE, C. B. (1990), ' "Princes" and Barbarians on the Ara Pacis', *AJA* 94: 453–67.

ROSELLINI, M. (1997), 'Metri lirici', in EncOr II: 912–19.

ROSEN, R. (1988), 'A Poetic Initiation Scene in Hipponax?', *AJPh* 109: 174–9.

ROSENSTEIN, N. S. (1990), *Imperatores Victi* (Berkeley).

ROSIVACH, V. (1994), '*Anus*: Some Older Women in Latin Literature', *CW* 88: 107–17.

RÖSLER, W. (1980), *Dichter und Gruppe* (Munich).

ROSS, D. O. (1975), *Backgrounds to Augustan Poetry: Gallus, Elegy and Rome* (Cambridge).

ROSSI, L. E. (1966), 'La metrica come disciplina filologica', *RFIC* 94: 185–207.

——(1978), 'Teoria e storia degli asinarteti dagli arcaici alessandrini: Sull'autenticità del nuovo Archiloco', in *Problemi de metrica classica*, Univ. di Genova, Fac. di Lettere, 1st. di Filol. Class. e Medioev.: 29–48.

——(1995), *Letteratura greca*, with R. Nicolai, L. M. Segoloni, E. Tagliaferro, and C. Tartaglini (Florence).

——(1996), 'Estensione e valore del colon nell'esametro omerico', in M. Fantuzzi and R. Pretagostini (eds.), *Struttura e storia dell'esametro Greco* II (Rome): 271–320 (from *StudUrb* 39 [1965] 239–73, revised with a postscript 1995).

ROWE, C. J. (1987), 'Platonic Irony', *Noua Tellus*, 5: 83–101.

RUSSELL, D. A. and WINTERBOTTOM, M. (1972), *Ancient Literary Criticism: The Principal Texts in New Translations* (Oxford).

RUDD, N. (1966), *The Satires of Horace* (Berkeley).

——(1982), 'Horace', in Kenney and Clausen (1982: 370–404).

——(ed.) (1989), *Horace: Epistles Book II and Epistle to the Pisones* (Cambridge).

——(ed.) (1993), *Horace 2000: A Celebration* (London).

RUTHERFORD, I. (1995), 'Apollo's Other Genre: Proclus on "Nomos" and his Source', *CP* 90: 354–61.

——(2001), *Pindar's Paeans: A Reading of the Fragments with a Survey of the Genre* (Oxford).

SALLER, R. P. (1982), *Personal Patronage under the Early Empire* (Cambridge).

—— (1989), 'Patronage and Friendship in Early Imperial Rome', in Wallace-Hadrill (1989a: 49–62).

SALLMANN, K. (1987), 'Lyrischer Krieg: Die Verschiebung der Genera in der Pollio-Ode 2, 1 des Horaz', in *Filologia e forme letterarie: Studi offerti a F. Della Corte*, 3, (Urbino: 69–87).

SANDERS, H. A. (ed.) (1904), *Roman Historical Sources and Institutions* (New York).

SANTIROCCO, M. S. (1980a), 'Horace's *Odes* and the Ancient Poetry Book', *Arethusa*, 13.1: 43–57.

—— (1980b), 'Strategy and Structure in Horace, *C.* 2.12', in Deroux (1980: 223–36).

—— (1982), 'Poet and Patron in Ancient Rome', *Book Forum*, 6.1: 56–62.

—— (1984), 'The Poetics of Closure', *Ramus*, 13: 74–91.

—— (1985), 'The Two Voices of Horace: *Odes* 3. 1–15', in Winkes (1985: 9–28).

—— (1986), *Unity and Design in Horace's Odes* (Chapel Hill).

—— (ed.) (1994), *Recovering Horace*, special volume *Classical World* 87.

—— (1995), 'Horace and Augustan Ideology', *Arethusa* 28: 225–43.

SCHADEWALDT, W. (1928), *Der Aufbau des Pindarischen Epinikion* (Schriften der Königsberger Gelehrten Ges., G. Kl. V 3; 1928).

SCHANZ, M. and HOSIUS, C. (1911–59), *Geschichte der römischen literatur*, 4 vols. (Munich), multiple editions with multiple dates.

SCHEID, J. (1990), *Romulus et ses frères arvales* (Rome).

—— and SVENBRO, J. (1996), *The Craft of Zeus: Myths of Weaving and Fabric* (Harvard).

SCHETTER, W. (1971), 'Zum Aufblau des Mevius-Jambus des Horaz (Epode 10)', *Philologus* 115: 249–55.

SCHIESARO, A. (1997), 'The Boundaries of Knowledge in Vergil's *Georgics*', in Habinek and Schiesaro (1997: 63–89).

SCHMIDT, E. A. (1977), 'Amica vis pastoribus: Der Jambiker Horaz in seinem Epodenbuch', *Gymnasium* 84: 401–23.

SCHMIDT, P. L. (1968), *Julius Obsequens und das Problem der Livius-Epitome* (Akademie der Wissenchaften, Geistes- und Sozialwissenschaftliche Klasse 5; Mainz).

—— (1984), 'Structure and sources of Horace, *Ode*, 1.12', in Evjen (1984: 139–49).

SCHNEGG-KÖHLER, B. (2002), *Die augusteischen Säkularspiele* (Archiv für Religionsgeschichte 4; Munich).

SCHORK, R. J. (1971), '*Aemulos Reges*: Allusion and Theme in Horace 3.16', *TAPA* 102: 515–39.

SCHRIJVERS, P. H. (1970), *Horror ac Divina voluptas: Études sur la poétique et la poésie de Lucrèce* (Amsterdam).

—— (1973), 'Interpreteren van een horatiaanse ode, I. 10', *Lampas* 6. 2: 126–52.

SCHUBERTH, D. (1968), *Kaiserliche Liturgie* (Göttingen).

SCHÜTZ, M. (1990), 'Zur Sonnenuhr des Augustus auf dem Marsfeld', *Gymnasium* 97: 432–57.

SEBEOK, TH. A. (ed.) (1968), *Style and Language* (Cambridge, Mass.).

SEDGWICK, A. D. (1947), *Horace* (Cambridge).

SEEL, O. (1980), 'Zur Ode 1,14 des Horaz, Zweifel an einer communis opinio', in Ableitinger and Gugel (1970: 204–49).

—— and PÖHLMANN, E. (1959), 'Quantität und Wortakzent im horazischen Sappiker', *Philologus* 103: 237–80.

SEGAL, C. (1973), 'Felices ter et amplius, Horace, Odes, I 13', *Latomus* 32: 39–46.

SEIDENSTICKER, B. (1976), 'Zu Horaz, *C.* 1.1–9', *Gymnasium* 83: 26–34.

SETAIOLI, A. (1981), 'Gli "Epodi" di Orazio nella critica dal 1937 al 1972 (con un appendice fino al 1978)', *ANRW* II.31.3: 1674–1788.

SETTIS, S. (1988), 'Die Ara Pacis', in Heilmeyer (1988: 400–26).

SEYFFERT, M. and MÜLLER, C. F. W. (1876), *M. Tullii Ciceronis Laelius: de amicitia dialogus* (Leipzig; repr. 1965, Hildesheim).

SHACKLETON BAILEY, D. R. (1982), *Profile of Horace* (London).

—— (1985), *Horatius: Opera* (Stuttgart).

—— (1994), *Homoeoteleuton in Latin Dactylic Verse* (Stuttgart and Leipzig).

SHARROCK, A. (1994), 'Ovid and the Politics of Reading', *MD* 33: 97–122.

SHEY, H. J. (1971), 'The Poet's Progress: Horace, Odes I,1', *Arethusa*, 4: 185–96.

SHOREY, P. (1898), *Horace: Odes and Epodes* (Boston).

SIEBOURG, M. (1910), *Horaz und die Rhetorik* (Neue Jahrb f.d. Klass. Alt. 23; 1910).

SILK, E. T. (1952), 'Notes on Cicero and the Odes of Horace', *YClS* 13: 193–212.

—— (1956), 'A Fresh Approach to Horace, II.20', *AJP* 77: 255–63.

—— (1969), 'Bacchus and the Horatian *Recusatio*', *YClS* 21: 195–212.

SIMON, E. (1957), 'Zur Augustusstatue von Prima Porta', *MDAI(R)* 64: 46–68.

SINGLETON, D. (1972), 'A Note on Catullus' First Poem', *CP* 67: 192–6.

SISTI, F. (1967), 'L'Ode a Policrate: Un caso di recusatio in Ibico', *QUCC* 4: 59–79.

SKUTCH, O. (1985), *The Annales of Quintus Ennius* (Oxford).

—— (1987), 'Helen, Her Name and Nature', *JHS* 107: 188–93.

SLINGS, S. R. (ed.) (1990), *The Poet's 'I' in Archaic Greek Lyric* (Amsterdam).

SLUITER, I. (2000), 'The Dialectics of Genre: Some Aspects of Secondary Literature and Genre in Antiquity', in Depew and Obbink (2000: 183–203, 294–307).

SMITH, C. L. (1903), *The* Odes *and* Epodes *of Horace* (Boston).

SMITH, P. L. (1968), 'Poetic Tensions in the Horatian Recusatio', *AJP* 89: 56–65.

SMYTH, H. W. (1963), *Greek Melic Poets* (New York).

SOLMSEN, F. (1932), 'Die Dichteridee des Horaz und ihre Probleme', *Zeitschrift für Ästhetik und allgemeine Kunstwissenschaft*, 26: 149–63.

SPAETH, B. S. (1994), 'The Goddess Ceres in the Ara Pacis Augustae and the Carthage Relief', *AJA* 98: 65–100.

SPERDUTI, A. (1950), 'The Divine Nature of Poetry in Antiquity', *TAPA* 81: 209–40.

SPINA, L. (1993), 'Orazio nell'Ade', *Lexis* 11: 163–88.

SPRANGER, P. R. (1958), 'Der Große: Untersuchungen zur Entstehung des historischen Beinamens in der Antike', *Saeculum*, 9: 22–58.

STEVENS, E. B. (1953), 'Uses of hyperbaton in Latin poetry', *ClW* 46: 200–5.

STEVENSON, T. R. (1992), 'The Ideal Benefactor and the Father Analogy in Greek and Roman Thought', *CQ* NS 42: 421–36.

STEWART, J. A. (1892), *Notes on the* Nicomachean Ethics *of Aristotle* (Oxford).

STROUX, J. (1935), 'Valerius Flaccus und Horaz', *Philologus*, 90: 305–30.

SULLIVAN, J. P. (ed.) (1962), *Critical Essays on Roman Literature* (London).

SUTHERLAND, C. H. V. (1984), *The Roman Imperial Coinage, i: 31 BC–AD 69* (London).

SYME, R. (1933), 'Notes on Some Legions under Augustus', *JRS* 23: 14–33.

—— (1939), *The Roman Revolution* (Oxford).

—— (1978), *History in Ovid* (Oxford).

—— (1979), *Roman Papers*, vol. 1 (Oxford).

—— (1986), *The Augustan Aristocracy* (Oxford).

—— (1989), 'Janus and Parthia in Horace', in Diggle, Hall, and Jocelyn (1989: 113–24).

SYNDIKUS, H. P. (1972 and 1973), *Die Lyrik des Horaz,* 2 vols. (Darmstadt).

TALBERT, R. J. A. (1984a), *The Senate of Imperial Rome* (Princeton).

—— (1984b), 'Augustus and the Senate', *G&R* 31: 55–63.

TAYLOR, L. R. (1925), 'Horace's Equestrian Career', *AJP* 46: 161–70.

—— (1968), 'Republican and Augustan Writers Enrolled in the Equestrian Census', *TAPA* 99: 469–86.

TEUFFEL, W. S. (1920), *Geschichte der römischen Literatur*[7] 2 (Leipzig).

THESLEFF, H. (1961), *An Introduction to the Pythagorean Writings of the Hellenistic Period* (Abo).

—— (1965), *The Pythagorean Texts of the Hellenistic Period* (Abo).

THOMAS, R. F. (ed.) (1988), *Virgil: Georgics* I (Cambridge).

—— and SCODEL, R. (1984), 'Vergil and the Euphrates', *AJP* 105: 339.

TIMPE, D. (1975), 'Zur Geschichte der Rheingrenze zwischen Caesar und Drusus', in Lefèvre (1975: 124–47).

TORELLI, M. (1982), *Typology and Structure of Roman Historical Reliefs* (Ann Arbor).

TREGGIARI, S. (1991), *Roman Marriage* (Oxford).

TRILLMICH, W. (1988), 'Munzpropaganda', in Heilmeyer (1988: 474–528).

TROXLER-KELLER, I. (1964), *Die Dichterlandschaft des Horaz* (Heidelberg).

USSANI, V. (1900), *Le liriche di Orazio* I (Torino).

VAHLEN, J. (1911 and 1923), *Gesammelte philologische Schriften*, 2 vols. (Leipzig and Berlin; reprinted 1970 Hildesheim and New York).

VAIO, J. (1966), 'The Unity and Historical Occasion of Horace *carm*. 1. 7', *CPh* 61: 168–75.

VAN SICKLE, J. B. (1968), 'About Form and Feeling in Catullus 65', *TAPA* 99: 487–508.

VERMEULE, E. (1979), *Aspects of Death in Early Greek Art and Poetry* (Berkeley).

VERSNEL, H. S. (1970), *Triumphus* (Leiden).

——(1980), 'Destruction, *Devotio* and Despair in a Situation of Anomy: The Mourning for Germanicus in Triple Perspective', in *Perennitas: Studi in onore di Angelo Brelich* (Rome), 541–618.

VETTA, M. (ed.) (1983), *Poesia e simposio nella Grecia antica* (Rome and Bari).

VEYNE, P. (1990), *Bread and Circuses*, tr. B. Pearce (London).

VILLENEUVE, F. (1927–34), *Horace* (Paris).

VON ALBRECHT, M. (1988), 'Properz als augusteischer Dichter', in Binder (1988: 360–77) = (1982), 'Properz als augusteischer Dichter', *WS* 16: 220–36.

——(1993), 'Musik und Dichtung bei Horaz', in *Atti del Convegno di Venosa (8–15 novembre 1992)* (Venosa), 75–100.

VON CHRIST, W. (1868), 'Über die Verskunst des Horaz im Lichte der alten Überlieferung', *SBMünch* 1: 1–44.

VON HESBERG, H. (1988), 'Das Mausoleum des Augustus', in Heilmeyer (1988: 245–51).

VON KROYMANN, J. (ed.) (1961), *Eranion: Festschrift für Hildebrecht Hommel* (Tübingen).

WACKERNAGEL, J. (1892), 'Über ein Gesetz der indogermanischen Wortstellung', *Indogermanische Forschungen*, 1: 333–436 = Wackernagel (1955: i. 1–104).

——(1955), *Kleine Schriften*, 2 vols. (Göttingen).

WALLACE-HADRILL, A. (1981), 'The Emperor and his Virtues', *Historia*, 30: 298–323.

——(1982), '*Civilis Princeps*: Between Citizen and King', *JRS* 72: 32–48.

——(1986), 'Image and Authority in the Coinage of Augustus', *JRS* 76: 66–87.

Wallace-Hadrill, A. (1987), 'Time for Augustus: Ovid, Augustus, and the *Fasti*', in Whitby, Hardie, and Whitby (1987: 221–30).

—— (ed.) (1989a), *Patronage in Ancient Society* (London).

—— (1989b), 'Rome's Cultural Revolution' [Review of Zanker (1988) and Heilmeyer (1988)], *JRS* 79: 157–64.

Watkins, O. D. (1985), 'Horace, Odes 2.10 and Licinius Murena', *Historia* 34: 125–7.

Watson, L. C. (1987), '*Epode* 9, or The Art of Falsehood', in Whitby, Hardie, and Whitby (1987: 119–29).

—— (1995), 'Horace's *Epodes*: The Impotence of *Iambos*?', in Harrison (1995: 188–202).

—— (2003), *A Commentary on Horace's* Epodes (Oxford).

Waszink, J. H. (1959), 'Zur Odendichtung des Horaz', *Gymnasium*, 66: 193–204.

Weber, L. (1917), 'Steinepigramm und Buchepigramm', *Hermes* 52: 536–57.

Wehrli, F. (1944), 'Horaz und Kallimachos', *MH* 1: 69–76.

Weinstock, S. (1936), 'Diehl und Gagé zu den lud. saec.', *Gnomon*, 12: 657–63.

—— (1960), 'Pax and the Ara Pacis', *JRS* 50: 44–58.

—— (1971), *Divus Julius* (Oxford).

Welin, E. (1939), 'Die beiden Festtage der Ara Pacis Augustae', in *Dragma M. P. Nilsson Dedicatum* (Lund), 500–13.

Wellek, R. and Warren, A. (1956), *Theory of Literature* (New York).

Werner, R. M. (1890), *Lyrik und Lyriker* (Hamburg and Leipzig).

West, D. (1967), *Reading Horace* (Edinburgh).

—— (1991), 'Cur me querelis (Horace, Odes 2.17)', *AJP* 112: 45–52.

—— (1995), *Horace: Odes Book I* (Oxford).

West, M. L. (1974), *Studies in Greek Elegy and Iambus* (Berlin and New York).

Whitby, M., Hardie, P., and Whitby, M. (eds.) (1987), *Homo Viator: Classical Essays for John Bramble* (Bristol).

White, P. (1978), '*Amicitia* and the Profession of Poetry in Early Imperial Rome', *JRS* 68: 74–92.

—— (1988), 'Julius Caesar in Augustan Rome', *Phoenix*, 42: 334–56.

—— (1993), *Promised Verse: Poets in the Society of Augustan Rome* (Cambridge, Mass.).

Wickert, L. (1953), 'Princeps', *RE* xxii. 1998–2296.

Wifstrand, A. (1933), *Von Kallimachos zu Nonnos* (Lund).

Wilamowitz, U. von (1900), *Die Textgeschichte der Griechischen Lyriker* (Berlin).

—— (1913), *Sappho und Simonides* (Berlin).

—— (1921), *Griechische Verskunst* (Berlin).

—— (1959), *Euripides, Heracles*, 3 vols., multiple editions with multiple dates (Darmstadt and Berlin).

WILI, W. (1948), *Horaz und die augusteische Kultur* (Basel and Stuttgart; 2nd edn., 1965).

WILKINSON, L. P. (1945), *Horace and His Lyric Poetry* (Cambridge, repr. 1946; 2nd edn., 1951).

—— (1963), *Golden Latin Artistry* (Cambridge).

WILL, E. L. (1982), 'Ambiguity in Horace Odes 1.4', *CPh* 77: 240–5.

WILLCOCK, M. M. (1995), *Pindar: Victory Odes* (Cambridge).

WILLE, G. (1961), 'Singen und Sagen in der Dichtung des Horaz', in von Kroymann (1961: 169–84).

—— (1967), *Musica Romana* (Amsterdam).

—— (1977), *Einführung in das römische Musikleben* (Darmstadt).

WILLIAMS, G. W. (1962), 'Poetry in the Moral Climate of Augustan Rome', *JRS* 52: 28–46.

—— (1968), *Tradition and Originality in Roman Poetry* (Oxford).

—— (1969), *The Third Book of Horace's* Odes (Oxford).

—— (1972), *Horace* (Greece & Rome New Surveys in the Classics 6; Oxford).

WILSON, A. M. (1985), 'The Prologue to Manilius 1', *PLLS* 5: 283–98.

WIMMEL, W. (1954), 'Eine Besonderheit der Reihung in augusteïschen Gedichten', *Hermes* 82: 199–230.

—— (1960), *Kallimachos in Rom* (Hermes Einzelschriften 16; Wiesbaden).

WINKES, R. (ed.) (1985), *The Age of Augustus* (Providence and Louvain-la-neuve).

WINKLER, J. J. (1990), *The Constraints of Desire* (New York).

—— (1991), 'The Constraints of Eros', in Faraone and Obbink (1991: 214–43).

WINTERBOTTOM, M. (1977a), 'A Celtic Hyperbaton?', *The Bulletin of the Board of Celtic Studies*, 27: 207–12.

—— (1977b), 'Aldhelm's Prose Style and its Origins', *Anglo-Saxon England*, 6: 50–1.

WISEMAN, T. P. (1979), *Clio's Cosmetics: Three Studies in Greco-Roman Literature* (Leicester).

—— (1985), *Catullus and His World* (Cambridge).

—— (1989), 'Roman Legend and Oral Tradition', *JRS* 79: 129–37.

WISSOWA, G. (1904), *Gesammelte Abhandlungen* (Munich). (orig. publ. 1894).

—— (1912), *Religion und Kultus der Römer*, 2nd edn. (Munich).

WITKE, C. (1983), *Horace's Roman Odes: A Critical Examination* (Mnemosyne Suppl. 77; Leiden).

WOODBURY, L. (1985), 'Ibycus and Polycrates', *Phoenix* 39: 193–220.

WOODMAN, A. J. (1974), '*Exegi monumentum*: Horace, *Odes* 3.30', in Woodman and West (1974: 115–28).

WOODMAN, A. J. (1977), *Velleius Paterculus: The Tiberian Narrative* (*2. 94–131*) (Cambridge).

—— (1980), 'The Craft of Horace in *Odes* 1.14', *CP* 75: 60–7.

—— (1983a), 'Horace, *Epistles* 1,19,23–40', *MusHelv* 40: 75–81.

—— (1983b), *Velleius Paterculus: The Caesarian and Augustan Narrative* (*2. 41–93*) (Cambridge).

—— (1984), 'Horace's First Roman Ode', in Woodman and West (1984: 183–214).

—— and FEENEY, D. (eds.) (2002), *Traditions and Contexts in the Poetry of Horace* (Cambridge).

—— and POWELL, J. G. F. (eds.) (1992), *Author and Audience in Latin Literature* (Cambridge).

—— and WEST, D. (eds.) (1974), *Quality and Pleasure in Latin Poetry* (Cambridge).

—— and —— (eds.) (1984), *Poetry and Politics in the Age of Augustus* (Cambridge).

ZANKER, P. (1972), *Forum Romanum* (Tübingen).

—— (1983), 'Der Apollontempel auf dem Palatin: Ausstattung und politische Sinnbezüge nach der Schlacht von Actium', in Fine Licht (1983: 21–40).

—— (1988), *The Power of Images in the Age of Augustus*, tr. A. Shapiro (Michigan).

ZETZEL, J. E. G. (1982), 'The Poetics of Patronage in the Late First Century BC', in Gold (1982: 87–102).

—— (1983), 'Re-Creating the Canon: Augustan Poetry and the Alexandrian Past', *Critical Inquiry*, 10: 83–105.

ZORZETTI, N. (1990), 'The *Carmina Convivalia*', in Murray (1990: 289–307).

ZUMWALT, N. K. (1977–78), 'Horace's *Navis* of Love Poetry (*C.* 1.14)', *CW* 71: 249–54.